Introduction to Management Practice

Ronald S. Burke
Instructor
Lord Fairfax Community College

Lester R. Bittel
Professor, School of Business
James Madison University

Gregg Division
McGraw-Hill Book Company

New York   Atlanta   Dallas   St. Louis   San Francisco   Auckland
Bogotá   Guatemala   Hamburg   Johannesburg   Lisbon   London
Madrid   Mexico   Montreal   New Delhi   Panama   Paris
San Juan   São Paulo   Singapore   Sydney   Tokyo   Toronto

Sponsoring Editor: Lawrence H. Wexler
Editing Supervisor: Gary Schwartz
Production Supervisor: Frank Bellantoni
Design Supervisor: Howard Brotman

Interior Designer: Sharkey Design
Cover Photographer: Karen Leeds
Technical Studio: Burmar Technical Corp.
Illustrator: Jack Weaver

Library of Congress Cataloging in Publication Data

Burke, Ronald S.
 Introduction to management practice.

 Includes index.
 1. Management.   I.   Bittel, Lester R., joint
author.   II.   Title.
HD31.B7699   658   80-19088

ISBN 0-07-009042-4

INTRODUCTION TO MANAGEMENT PRACTICE

1234567890 DODO 876543210

Contents

Introduction to Management Practice was conceived and developed especially for today's job-conscious college students. The text presents an easy-to-follow introduction to management concepts, theory, and practice. It has a uniquely practical orientation, focusing on what managers do, how they do it, and what factors determine whether or not they will be successful. *Introduction to Management Practice* provides more opportunities—at least twice the number as in other texts—for active student involvement in applying theory to practice. The text orients young men and women to the various career opportunities available to them in management today. The style of writing is deliberately lively and readable to engage student interest and sustain a steady, but quick pace of comprehension. *Introduction to Management Practice* is a sound program of instruction for the beginning course in management.

A COMPREHENSIVE AND CONTEMPORARY OVERVIEW OF MANAGEMENT

Study the table of contents. Glance at a chapter. Review the index. The text clearly provides a balanced, but comprehensive overview of the various approaches to management—process, human relations, quantitative, and contingency—as well as management information systems. It also provides substantitive treatment of contemporary trends, issues, and practices in management—Management by Objectives (MBO), the impact of government regulation and social responsibility, zero-based budgeting, and queuing theory, to name only a few.

A TWO-PHASE FORMAT LINKING THEORY TO PRACTICE

Each chapter follows a fully integrated two-phase learning format: a *resource unit*, survey by nature, reduces management concepts and theory to the essentials; an *application unit*, immediately following, allows students to convert theory into practice. The true foundation of this instructional system, the student involvement material in the application unit, is especially rich and varied. It provides numerous opportunities for students to sense, feel, and to a degree, experience what it is like to be a manager. Through the activities and exercises in a chapter's "Problems and Projects" and "Cases for Analysis and Discussion," students can carry out management tasks, solve related problems, make management decisions, and evaluate decisions made by others. Students also can experience different managerial roles in a variety of businesses, as well as in government and nonprofit organizations. In this way, management theory is linked directly with management practice, helping to bring the reality of the business world closer to the classroom.

STUDY AIDS TO ENHANCE
STUDENT COMPREHENSION
Each chapter includes numerous aids to structure student study and assure greater student comprehension.

- **OBJECTIVES** Performance goals introduce the resource unit of each chapter. These goals are especially detailed and specific, giving direction to the whole learning process.
- **CHAPTER SECTION HEADINGS AND SUBHEADINGS** Headings are usually expressed as full statements, enabling students to preview a chapter and grasp its key highlights in only a few minutes.
- **CHAPTER OPENING ILLUSTRATIONS, TABLES, AND GRAPHS** Visual aids provide graphic reinforcement of important points.
- **MANAGERS IN ACTION** These highlighted features show one example of what managers actually do in carrying out the ideas presented in the chapter. In some chapters (17 to 23), they take the form of want ads, enabling students to see the qualities and skills that are required for filling managerial positions in various types of organizations.
- **SUMMARY** A restatement of the chapter's major points is keyed to each section of the resource unit.
- **REVIEW AND DISCUSSION QUESTIONS** This section completes the resource portion of a chapter and provides students with an opportunity to check their comprehension and prepare themselves for discussion of pertinent topics in class.
- **THE APPLICATION UNIT** "Problems and Projects" and "Cases for Analysis and Discussion" reinforce student comprehension at the level of practical application and analysis.

A GENUINE CAREER
ORIENTATION
Chapters 17 to 23 are devoted to an examination of the functions and responsibilities of managers at all levels and in various fields, but most particularly in finance and accounting, marketing, production, and personnel administration. These are the career specialties that students are most likely to pursue. A uniquely well-rounded picture of these management specialties is provided by the examination of managerial functions not only in business but also in government and nonprofit organizations. Students will find this section especially useful and meaningful in selecting their next college course in management. It will also help students choose the management specialty they wish to pursue, while providing a firm base for their ultimate entry into the job market. The appendix, "Pursuing a Management Career," should also make a positive contribution toward this goal.

A TOTALLY INTEGRATED TEACHING-LEARNING SYSTEM

Introduction to Management Practice is designed as a total instructional system for the introductory course in management. Although the text is the centerpiece, the system includes other important elements:

- **SELF-STUDY GUIDE**   This guide gives students the option of learning at their own pace. The guide includes objectives, an outline of key concepts, suggested further readings, a vocabulary development exercise, self-check objective questions, and answer keys for self-check questions.

- **COMPUTER-BASED SIMULATIONS IN MANAGEMENT**   Two simulations enable students to experience and compare typical planning, budgeting, and decision-making situations at the upper and middle levels of management are also included as part of the instructor's set of materials. The programs for the simulations are written in BASIC (Beginner's All-Purpose Symbolic Instruction Code) and can be used on a variety of computers with only minor modification. An Administrator's Guide to the computer programs offering easy-to-follow instructions on how to implement and use the simulations to maximum benefit, as well as reproducible student materials, are provided free to adopters of the *Introduction to Management Practice* program.

- **COURSE MANAGEMENT GUIDE AND KEY**   This manual provides the instructor in management with learning objectives, an audiovisual guide, lesson plan outlines for each chapter, discussion stimulators, answers to all questions, problems, and cases in the text, transparency masters, and reproducible tests for each text part and for mid-term and final examinations. These elements work jointly with the text to make delivery of management instruction more reality-based, more manageable, and in the end, we believe, more effective.

RONALD S. BURKE
LESTER R. BITTEL

Organizations Need Management

The Function and Environment of Management

1

After completing Chapter 1, you will be able to do the following:

- Justify the need for management.
- Describe the vital requirements of an organization.
- Decide whether or not a given group of people and resources make up an organization.
- Define management and managers.
- Distinguish between managerial and nonmanagerial activities.
- Recognize the extent of management specialization in a given organization.
- Explain two important differences between business and government or nonprofit organizations that affect the outlook and activities of their managers.
- Give examples of management approaches that preceded the industrial revolution.

On Salisbury Plain, some 80 miles southwest of London, stands Stonehenge. It is a monumental earth and stone circle built in stages between 2600 and 1400 B.C. The religious and astronomical significance of Stonehenge to its builders is still uncertain today. One thing is clear, though. Its construction was an incredible accomplishment for the relatively crude technology of the day. To build Stonehenge, granite-like stones of up to 50 tons in weight and 22 feet in length were shaped by hand and set upright in the earth. Other hand-shaped stones weighing 7 tons or more were raised 15 to 20 feet above the ground and placed on top of these upright pillars. Before construction, many of the mammoth stones had to be transported by land and water from as far as 150 miles away.

How could such a project have been completed without cranes, power hammers, railroads, dynamite, and other tools of present-day stone construction? The answer is simple. The construction of Stonehenge was accomplished through planning, organization, and management. These are the same basic requirements for accomplishing important and complex goals today.

As a manager, you may never have to oversee a project quite like Stonehenge. But in every business enterprise, in every governmental agency, and in every other organization, managers are confronted with the continuing task of finding ways to match people and resources to achieve complex and difficult goals.

MANAGEMENT SETS GOALS AND HELPS PEOPLE ACCOMPLISH THEM

Why do we have managers in the first place? Just as one person working alone could not have built Stonehenge, most important goals in business and government today cannot be achieved without groups of men and women working together. For groups of people to work together effectively, many things are necessary.

- The overall *goals* of the group must be decided on and defined in a practical, achievable form.
- Specific *subgoals* must be identified to make it possible to fulfill the overall goals.
- Work must be divided into smaller units so that each person and small group has specific jobs to do.
- Work methods for performing the jobs must be set.
- People doing individual jobs must receive instructions on methods and must be supervised to make sure the work is being done adequately.
- The actual performance of the work must continually be checked against the goals and subgoals of the group to make sure progress is being made as planned.
- It is especially important that all of the people in the group be inspired and motivated to contribute their best efforts to reach the goals of the whole group.
- All of the above requirements, and many other related ones, are provided by managers.

MANAGERS WORK FOR AND WITHIN ORGANIZATIONS

Where do managers perform the functions outlined above? Managers work within organizations. A baseball team, for example, is an organization. So is the United States government with over three million employees. A small-town amateur theater group is an organization in exactly the same sense that U.S. Steel, Ford Motor Company, IBM, and other industrial giants are organizations. An immense organization like the United States government is actually composed of hundreds and thousands of smaller organizations. For example, there is the Labor Department, the Bureau of the Census, the Antitrust Division of the Department of Justice, the stock and shipping department of the National Audiovisual Center of the General Services Administration, and so on.

What do these groups have in common? They consist of people who work together in some way. The people have certain relationships, resources, and methods of doing things. The work and the methods are applied to accomplish some purpose. An *organization*, then, may be defined as a group of people sharing relationships who use technology to achieve goals. Every element of this definition is important to understanding the role of management. Figure 1-1 is a schematic representation of the manager's role in an organization.

People Sharing Relationships

One could choose 11 people at random from among the spectators at a football game, but these people would not constitute an organization.

Figure 1-1. What Managers Do.

MANAGERS HELP PEOPLE WHO SHARE A COMMON RELATIONSHIP IN AN ORGANIZATION TO CARRY OUT TECHNOLOGICAL PROCESSES IN THE PURSUIT OF COMMON GOALS.

GOALS

The actions of one fan normally will have little effect on other fans. There are no hierarchies, no established and continuing relationships, and no assigned roles existing among the people in this randomly selected body.

Contrast this with the 11 members of a football team. The players have very distinct relationships and are highly organized. On each play, every player has a definite role and knows what to do and who to work with in fulfilling the role. Each player watches for certain actions of teammates and opponents in deciding what to do next. The main work of many players is to help teammates carry out their assignments. One team member blocks for the runner carrying the ball; another protects the passer from the defensive rush; the quarterback has special responsibilities for deciding which play to run and for starting each play. This is an organization.

Establishing and maintaining this kind of interrelationship among people, and allowing and helping people to exercise relationships and perform their roles, is a prime function of management.

Technology   An organization must have technology to function. *Technology* is the collection of processes and methods a society uses to provide its material needs and to operate its governments, businesses, and other organizations. It is the knowledge of how to do practical things. Even the methods used by the football team are technology by this definition. Other instances of technology are the countless ways of doing work in business and government. These methods allow us to make steel and computers, tricycles and space rockets, to produce and distribute food, to travel around the country and the world, to keep track of billions of monetary transactions, and to communicate vast amounts of information among individuals and organizations.

Every organization shares in the technology of the overall society and each organization uses technology that is specific to its own activities and aims. A TV repair shop uses telephone service, electricity, trucks and roads, bookkeeping methods, advertising facilities, banks, and other services of the community. In addition, its managers must devise or adopt troubleshooting and repair techniques, procedures for ordering and storing electronic parts, customer relations practices, and all of the other methods needed specifically for the operation of that particular business.

Goals   Virtually all organizations have basic overall goals. A business may be set up to make a living for its owner; a government agency may be created to regulate the operation of retail pharmacies; a nonprofit organization may be established to educate the public about mental health issues. Overall goals, however, are neither clear enough nor detailed enough to guide the day-to-day operating decisions of an organization.

Specific, achievable goals are essential for the efficient operation of an organization. Setting these goals is a major responsibility of management. For example, the advertising department of a medium-sized manufacturing company may exist for the general purpose of publicizing the firm's products to its industrial customers. This general purpose can only be met, however, if the advertising managers are able to establish a series of specific goals on which they can take action. They must decide to place so many ads of a certain type in specific media. They must aim for a certain financial return on their advertising expenditures. They must find some way to measure whether the results are being met. They must have goals for how much and what kind of work each employee will do, for scores of different kinds of costs, for employee training and promotion, and for developing methods to reach new markets. All of these goals must be coordinated. Each should reinforce the others, and all should function together to satisfy the basic purpose of the advertising organization.

MANAGEMENT IS A
DECISION-MAKING PROCESS
A manager's work within an organization is controlled by what is needed for the organization to succeed. *Management* is the process of setting organization goals, deciding what actions and resources must contribute to meeting goals, and then coordinating, guiding, and encouraging the cooperative work of other people to meet the goals.

Management is the function that maintains the organization, coordinates its parts, and helps its members work together to accomplish an overall purpose. It is the main factor that enables organizations to get more work done than its individual members could accomplish working alone.

Managerial Versus
Nonmanagerial Work
In general, work that directly produces goods or services for distribution outside the organization is nonmanagerial. People who put their hands in the work are said to perform the "do" function of an organization. Operating a punch press, painting billboards, answering customer inquiries, processing unemployment insurance claims, removing a gall

bladder, operating a cyclotron for nuclear energy research, or playing the violin in an orchestra are all essentially nonmanagerial work.

Managerial work involves *creating the conditions* for best doing non-managerial, productive work. Although some aspects of management, such as setting goals and planning strategies, must be performed even in a one-person shop, management concentrates largely on the productive work of other people. A case worker for a social service agency is doing nonmana-gerial work when counseling a client. As soon as the case worker supervises others in their work, plans the future work load for others in the organization, or assigns cases to others, he or she is doing managerial work. If the head of an advertising department writes advertisements to appear in magazines, that is nonmanagerial work. If he or she sets the goals for an ad campaign; plans specific actions to meet the goals; divides up the design, writing, and placement work among other specialists; supervises their work and monitors the results; then he or she is doing managerial work. Figure 1-2 illustrates the distinction between managerial and nonmanagerial work.

Many jobs consist partly of managerial work and partly of nonmanagerial work. A construction plumber working on new houses, for instance, would usually spend 80 to 85 percent of his or her time in direct work installing water and waste facilities. The remainder of the time might be devoted to managerial work such as directing a helper or planning work methods. Many other jobs consist almost entirely of managerial work. This is espe-cially true in larger organizations.

MANAGERS HAVE DIFFERENT RESPONSIBILITIES

The nature of specific managerial jobs varies widely. Each will be affected by the size and purposes of the organization and the manager's particular role within it. These factors will control the specific duties and responsibilities of each manager.

Sarah Barnes owns and runs a dress shop. She has two full-time employ-ees. In a good year, Sarah makes $16,000 for her work. In a bad year, she

MANAGERIAL WORK	NONMANAGERIAL WORK
■ Deciding	■ Building
■ Directing	■ Doing
■ Organizing	■ Fixing
■ Planning	■ Making

Figure 1-2. Some Differences Between Mana-gerial and Nonmanagerial Work.

Managers in Action

As a senior product manager for Kool-Aid at General Foods, Lois Juliber had the responsibility for supervising two people while assuring an effective sales and promotion program for her product. In 1978, when she was promoted by General Foods to product group manager for marketing all of the company's children's cereals, it was "scary," Juliber recalls. "At first, it almost seemed like an empire. The people were new to me, and so was the business. I was also afraid of the 'woman' issue (the product managers who report to her are men), but that turned out to be a non-issue."

In her new job, Juliber got the responsibility for marketing four brands, which had sales estimated at some $115 million. To get the job done, she leaves her New York apartment at 6:30 each morning to get to her office by 7:00. Generally, she goes home twelve hours later. Two nights a week she does "heavy work" at her apartment, and she usually works on Sunday nights as well. She likes her work so much, however, that she was genuinely surprised when an interviewer added up her work week hours and found they totaled seventy.

Source: Wyndham Robertson, "Women M.B.A.'s, Harvard '73—How They're Doing," *Fortune*, August 28, 1978, pp. 50–60.

makes much less. Harry Gray is president of United Technologies Corporation in Hartford, Connecticut. He is responsible for the productive output of 197,000 employees. In 1980 Gray earned more than $650,000.

Both Sarah Barnes and Harry Gray are managers, but the way they spend their workdays is quite different. Differences in daily routines are found among all managers, in spite of many similarities in their basic responsibilities. The two main reasons for this variability are that organizations differ and that the divisions of responsibilities within organizations vary.

Organizations Are Specialized

Although organizations range from a group of children meeting in a treehouse to the United Nations, certain types are of particular interest to students of management. The main kinds of organizations that employ professional managers are businesses, governments, and nonprofit associations.

Businesses make a product or provide a service for sale to customers. *Government* organizations provide the public with police and military protection, public schools and colleges, and other services. *Nonprofit groups* operate churches, charities, hospitals, and thousands of other service-oriented organizations.

Under each of these general types of organizations there are countless, varied organizations which present their managers with different goals, different sources of operating funds, and different ways of judging success.

Responsibilities Are Divided

A further source of variability among management jobs is division of responsibilities within organizations. As responsibilities are divided, managerial work becomes more specialized. This specialization is a particular application of the *division of labor*.

It has long been observed that complex tasks can be completed faster and with less total labor if the overall activity is divided into separate steps with a different worker assigned to each step. When each worker specializes, performing only one step, more products can be produced than when each worker performs all of the different steps.

The most famous example of the division of labor is the economist Adam Smith's observations of pin makers in an eighteenth-century English factory, as presented in his 1776 book *Wealth of Nations.*

> "One man draws out the wire, another straightens it, a third cuts it, a fourth points it, a fifth grinds it at the top for receiving the head; to make the head requires two or three distinct operations; to put it on is a peculiar business, to whiten the pins is another; it is even a trade by itself to put them into the paper; and the important business of making a pin is, in this manner, divided into about eighteen distinct operations."

The division of labor is an important tool used by managers to improve the efficiency of direct production work. More important, though, management work itself is also divided into specialties. Even in relatively small organizations, *specialization* divides the overall management job into parts. A manager or group of managers is given prime responsibility for each part. Handling these subdivisions of management requires special skills in addition to general management ability.

MANAGERS IN BUSINESS ORGANIZATIONS AIM AT PROFITS

For decades serious study of managers concentrated on big business management, because that is where the money and glamour were. The domineering executive sitting in a fortieth-floor office suite was a modern American hero. Emphasis on big business in the study of management has lessened somewhat in recent years. Small- and medium-sized businesses have become much more conscious of the value of informed professional management. Government service has emerged as an important and influential management field. Even the management of private nonprofit organizations offers attractive career opportunities. Whether small, medium, or large, private business still remains a major focus both in the study of management and as a source of management jobs.

Business converts resources into goods and services to satisfy the needs and wants of people. Business is performed with the intention of making a profit for its owners. The resources used by business mainly consist of: materials derived from the earth, such as minerals, timber, and agricultural products; labor; capital (production facilities and machinery); and technological know-how. Business managers must find ways to use these resources to create end products that will be of value because people want them. Managers must use resources in such a way that the product created is worth more than the total cost of making it. This excess of value of end products over production costs is the source of business profit.

For example, consumers might be willing to pay $75 for a well-made wooden chair. The goal of the managers of a furniture manufacturer would be to make the chair for less than this amount, considering all the costs for use of design, equipment, wood, glue, fasteners, stain and finish, skilled and unskilled workers, packing, shipping, and selling.

Certain similar goals are shared by nonbusiness organizations, but these do not stem from the need to create a profit. Examples of goals that contribute to profit making include the following.

- Obtaining needed materials at the lowest possible cost consistent with desired quality.
- Finding out what kinds of goods and services buyers want and are willing to pay for.
- Finding ways to reduce the costs associated with producing goods and services without reducing product quality and attractiveness to buyers.
- Exposing the product to as many potential buyers as possible without using up all of the profits in the selling effort.

Areas of Management Responsibility

Most companies have established separate management responsibilities which cover:

- Production and operations.
- Marketing, distribution, and sales.
- Finance and accounting.
- Personnel and labor relations.
- Executive-level general management.

A particular business organization may not have a separate manager to handle each of these areas. A small company may assign more than one type of responsibility to a single manager; in effect, the manager can wear many hats. On the other hand, a huge multinational corporation will often have hundreds of managers working on different aspects of a single management specialty.

PRODUCTION AND OPERATIONS   The process of converting resources to saleable products is called *production* in a company that makes physical goods and *operations* in one that provides services. *Production management* oversees all of the activities needed to manufacture a company's products. It determines how much of each product to make in a given period, it sets schedules, improves work methods, and controls quality. The concerns of *operations control* are similar except that the activities combine to produce services, such as dry cleaning clothes or insuring automobiles against losses from damage, rather than making physical products.

MARKETING, DISTRIBUTION, AND SALES   Since business creates goods and services for sale to buyers, it is logical to have a management specialty concerned with relations with customers. *Marketing management* controls the parts of an organization which promote the sale of products through advertising, personal selling, or other means and those which physically move goods to buyers. Marketing people may also be charged with providing information about buyers' wants and needs and with helping to develop new saleable products.

FINANCE AND ACCOUNTING   The resources that directly produce goods and services are usually nonmonetary: machines, raw materials, and labor. In practice, however, these resources can only be obtained with money. *Financial management* is concerned with accounting for and controlling the sources and uses of the funds a company employs in its operations. It attempts to provide needed money in the most economical way from borrowing, owners' investments, or sales. Then it tries to regulate the use of this money to produce the greatest profit.

PERSONNEL AND LABOR RELATIONS   All managers deal with employees. The importance of employees is so great that most medium- and large-scale organizations maintain a *personnel management* specialty which concentrates on employee and labor relations. Personnel managers provide guidance to other managers in matters that affect staffing, internal organization, safety, employee training, development, promotions and successions, and compensation levels. Some personnel managers also specialize in negotiating and administering contracts with labor unions.

EXECUTIVE-LEVEL GENERAL MANAGEMENT   In organizations where specialists handle separate components of a total job, someone must be responsible for the smooth operation and progress of the entire effort. That is the job of *general management* at the executive level of the organization. General managers are especially concerned with tying together the work of management specialists. General managers also plot the long-range course of the entire organization and originate and approve changes that affect the basic makeup of the company. Although business managers at any level must be conscious of profits and losses, the final responsibility for profitability falls on the executive-level general manager.

Small Business Management

Businesses of any size, from the butcher shop to General Motors, are concerned with production and operations, marketing, finance, personnel, and general management. Small business, though, has enough special features that it deserves separate attention in the study of business management. Starting and operating a small business present unique challenges and opportunities. The challenges center on increased risk and personal responsibility. The opportunities derive from the chance to benefit fully from one's own skill and hard work.

The risk of failure is high for a small business. In an organization with the size and resources of, say, IBM, Exxon, or General Foods, it would take severe mismanagement to run the company out of business in a year or two. This is not true in a small business. For the corner drugstore or the local building-supply house, relatively small miscalculations or changes in customer buying habits can spell disaster.

Another distinction of small-business management is its relative lack of specialization. The smaller the business, the greater the likelihood that all management responsibility must be shouldered by one person. In local businesses with only a few employees, the manager (often the owner) must directly control production or operations, marketing, finance, and personnel while still trying to plan and work for the future growth and prosperity of the business as a whole. On top of this, the small-business manager often is only a part-time manager, devoting the rest of his or her time to direct production or service work.

MANAGERS IN GOVERNMENT AND NONPROFIT ORGANIZATIONS AIM AT SERVICE TO SOCIETY

The basic purpose of *government* is to ensure social order. This is accomplished through the government's authority to (1) pass laws that are enforced by an internal police force and (2) protect society from outside attack by maintaining armed forces. In practice, every modern government (and nearly every government throughout history) has elaborated considerably on this simple formula.

Government Services

In the United States, government also protects the rights of individuals, their freedoms of speech, religion, assembly, the right to own property, and numerous others. The federal government supports a huge defense organization to protect the country from foreign attack. In addition to these basic activities, the government is involved in some way in nearly every aspect of our society. Government provides most education in the United States; the poor receive government support through welfare and other payments; government regulates and influences the economy and private business practices, and it strictly controls activities affecting health and safety. These and other activities of government require large groups of employees providing services, groups which need managers.

SIMILARITIES OF GOVERNMENT AND BUSINESS MANAGEMENT Much of what government managers do is quite similar to what business managers do. Both decide on how resources will be used and then direct and coordinate the uses. Both function largely by coordinating and guiding the work of other people.

DIFFERENCES BETWEEN GOVERNMENT AND BUSINESS MANAGEMENT Businesses receive funds from investment by owners, from loans, and from revenue created by selling their goods and services. Governments also receive funds from borrowing and, to a limited extent, from selling goods and services, as when a city government sells electricity to private consumers. The main source of income for governments, however, is tax money paid by citizens and organizations. As a general rule, taxes must be paid whether taxpayers wish to or not. It is not possible, for instance, for a resident to tell the local government, "I don't want police protection any more. I'll stop paying taxes for that service and you cancel my protection." We are, by and large, required to consume the services of government.

Business and government also differ in the overall goals of their activities; that is, in their basic reasons for operating. No matter how much social benefit a business may provide, the fundamental goal of the business almost always is to make a profit. The success of business management ultimately can be judged by profitability. Government does not have this goal. Its main concern is performing activities and achieving results as dictated by law. The measure of management success in government is whether these results are attained in an efficient and economical manner. Profit is not a consideration.

These differences have a practical effect on how decisions on similar problems might be managed differently in government than in business. For example, consider the following problems.

- Planning where the money will come from to meet the payroll.
- Deciding whether to expand the computer department and put it under the control of a new manager.
- Evaluating whether the purchasing department is really contributing effectively to the organization.

Decisions for government managers will differ somewhat from those of business managers because of the differences in funding and overall objectives of each. The kinds of problems are similar: financing operations, finding and working with good personnel, initiating and controlling operations, and dealing with consumers of products or services, but ways of dealing with them will often vary.

Nonprofit Organizations Differences in managerial approach are also found between businesses and private nonprofit organizations. A nonprofit research organization, for instance, is concerned with bookkeeping, work assignments, planning, purchasing, facilities maintenance, and other details of operation common in a business or government agency. However, specific management orientation will depend on the particular sources of income available. Income may derive from government grants, from contracts with hospitals or universities, or from donations from charitable foundations. The concern with income source and with the overall objectives set up when the organization was formed will shape a specific managerial approach.

Management specialization occurs in nonprofit organizations as it does in business. The specialties are similar, but they are tailored to the needs of the specific organization. A government agency, for instance, does not normally have a sales manager.

MANAGEMENT HAS REFLECTED SOCIETY THROUGHOUT HISTORY

Management has been the subject of systematic study and definition only in recent decades. Nevertheless, organizations have functioned and managers have managed for thousands of years, since hunters first banded together to improve their odds against their elusive prey. The organizations of the past were often cruel and inefficient by today's standards, but they kept society running. A brief look at management practice of the past is enlightening, not as a guide to how to manage, but as a demonstration of a fundamental fact: management is one expression of the moral, social, and political values and beliefs of a people; as beliefs and expectations change, the definition of "good" management also changes.

Management and Its Environment

From earliest times, management decisions and actions have been controlled by forces outside the organization. Population, climate, raw materials, states of war, and outbreaks of disease have always shaped the destinies of businesses and governments, just as they do now. Managers have always functioned within interacting influences of government, social belief, and technological capability.

Governments have always limited management's freedom. Some three thousand years ago the code of Hammurabi set strict rules for business proprietors and managers in Babylon. The code even established minimum wages for certain kinds of employment. From that beginning, governments continued to protect society from certain kinds of business management actions. In the Middle Ages, for instance, a merchant named William de Schachtelweghe was branded with a hot iron and exiled for seven years for falsifying a government seal to make his stock of dress-goods appear of a higher quality than it was. In the fourteenth century, managers faced regulations of prices, competition, advertising, and even product designs and production methods, as set by the quasi-governmental Hanseatic League.

One of the most striking examples of the influence of social belief on management practice is the change in methods of disciplining and motivating employees. Through much of history, the whip was one of management's tools. Physical force and punishment of slaves as well as free workers was still common in many places well into the nineteenth century. Supervision today rarely involves anything approaching physical discipline. Motivation, not discipline, is the main concern. The change has been brought about mainly by shifts in social beliefs about right and wrong ways of treating people.

Technology has obviously affected the way managers work and what they are able to accomplish. The emergence of written language made it possible to keep records of complicated inventories and trade activities. This brought about larger businesses, making more difficult demands on managers. Larger and faster ships and improved navigation expanded trade, requiring even better management. While the industrial revolution vastly increased productive capacity it also brought awesome problems of scheduling and coordination. Management has had to respond every time with improved understanding and skill to meet these technological challenges.

Management Techniques

It has been true throughout history that an increase in the size and complexity of organizations has brought new techniques for their management. Thousands of years ago in Babylon, trade had already grown to a scale demanding careful inventory control. Colored tags on grain jars were used to indicate when the grain had been received and how long it had been in inventory. Similar systems are in use today.

The chain of command, an effective way of maintaining administrative control of large groups of people, was developed early in history. It was surely used in the construction of the pyramids and was highly developed in the Roman army and civilian government.

Division of labor was a key technological force in building the pyramids. Tens or hundreds of thousands of workers had to be assigned to varied jobs. Managers had to plan, schedule, and coordinate the efforts of all these workers to produce the final result. Large-scale production using a division of labor was carried on in the Roman Empire. One wealthy baker, M. Virgilius Eurysaces, immortalized his production management skills on his mortuary monument, which still stands in Rome. The monument shows Eurysaces' bakers at work, some grinding grain, others kneading dough and doing other distinct jobs.

Later, in the days of the Dutch East India Company, the wealthy Bicher family of Holland used geographical specialization of management to control their business empire. One son managed the Russian fur monopoly; another operated the family businesses in the Americas; another controlled the Baltic regions.

Another element in the formal structure of organizations that has been used for centuries is the staff principle used in the management of the Roman Catholic Church. Ultimate responsibility for directing, making decisions, and supervising lay with one who might be called a line manager; an abbot of a monastery, for instance. The line manager, however, was encouraged, and sometimes required, to consult experienced elders or specialists before making decisions. This practice is similar to the modern use of staff specialists—lawyers, accountants, psychologists, and others—to aid line managers who retain authority.

The Lessons of History   To a modern manager, the point of historical examples of management practices is twofold:

1. History shows clearly that management is a human activity enclosed by the ethical, social, economic, and political beliefs and conditions of the whole society. This is as true now as it was when the pyramids were being built. What a manager wishes to do and is able to do is largely controlled by forces outside the manager's organization.

2. As these outside conditions change, management practices must change with them. To the chief of a crew moving stones for a pyramid, it was natural and socially acceptable to use physical force. Today, to walk onto the shop floor with a whip would probably cause a riot. One of the prime concerns of managers today is to adapt management techniques to changing requirements and expectations of workers, customers or clients, government agencies, competitors, and of society as a whole.

Other traditional management principles and practices continue in use because they still help managers to accomplish goals. Even some of the most ancient practices, such as chain of command and division of responsibility, are still used. The formal study of management today, discussed in the next chapter, incorporates the successes of the past into systematic approaches to better management.

SUMMARY

1. Managers carry out their work within organizations. An organization is a group of interrelated people who use technology to achieve goals.

2. Management is a process that decides on the specific goals of an organization and directs the efforts of other people to accomplish actions needed to meet the goals.

3. Managers in all kinds of organizations have some responsibilities and concerns in common. However, specific management jobs differ in many ways because (a) specific organizations make particular demands of managers and (b) management responsibility is divided into specialized functions within organizations.

4. The three most general types of organizations that use professional managers are businesses, governments, and nonprofit organizations.

5. Business enterprise converts resources into valuable goods and services for private profit. Business management responsibilities are usually divided into (a) production and operations; (b) marketing, distribution, and sales; (c) finance and accounting; (d) personnel and labor relations; and (e) executive-level general management.

6. Management in government is influenced by its sources of funds, mainly compulsory taxes, and by its overall goal to efficiently carry out activities determined by law.

7. The history of management from earliest times demonstrates two important facts: (a) Management is a human activity; what managers wish to do and are able to do is strongly influenced by social, political, and economic forces, and (b) the conditions that shape management are continually changing, and management attitudes and practices must change with them.

REVIEW AND DISCUSSION QUESTIONS

1. Why are managers necessary?

2. Give an example of one group of people and resources that does not constitute an organization and of another group that does make up an organization. Why is the one group an organization and the other not?

3. "An important difference between ancient organizations and our organizations today is that we have technology and they did not." Is this statement true? Support your answer.

4. What is management? How can you tell whether a particular activity is an example of management or is not?

5. What are two main factors that cause managers' activities and approaches to be different in different jobs?

6. Describe some important differences between business and government that might affect managers' approaches and responsibilities.

7. Specialization of management in a business organization usually creates at least five distinct areas of management responsibility. Briefly describe the five.

8. Discuss the statement, "Throughout history, management and organizational skills have contributed more to major accomplishments than technical or scientific knowledge." Use examples from the text and from your own knowledge to support, refute, or qualify the statement.

Problems and Projects

1. Make a list of all the organizations you belong to. Include your school, your job, clubs, religious organizations, civic organizations, or others. Briefly show how each fits the complete definition of an organization, stressing relationships, technology, and goals. Discuss the results in class.

2. On a separate sheet of paper, write the letters *a* to *t* corresponding to the following list of activities. Beside each letter, write the letter *M* if the activity is a managerial task or the letter *N* if it is a nonmanagerial task.

   a. Deciding to hire six temporary employees for the holiday sales season.
   b. Receiving inventory stock and allocating it among proper storage categories in the warehouse.
   c. Calling likely donors to solicit contributions to a nonprofit charitable organization.
   d. Scheduling the market research department to complete interviewing by a certain date and to begin analyses on the next day.
   e. Promoting the manager of the data processing department to assistant vice president, equal in status to the manager's former boss, the company controller.
   f. Determining that one of the new contract writers has consistently been missing his deadlines.
   g. Deciding to create product diversity by buying or merging with a medium-sized food processing company by 1985.
   h. Deciding to reduce voltage in a circuit to prevent overheating.
   i. Abolishing the order checking department and giving its work to the packers.
   j. Determining through diagnostic tests that a carburetor is malfunctioning and needs to be rebuilt or replaced.
   k. Assigning a mechanic to service the next car on the schedule.
   l. Filming an auto accident for the news.
   m. Measuring the height of grain in a field treated with an experimental fertilizer.
   n. Inspecting a restaurant to find whether it complies with state health laws.
   o. Deciding to allocate 14 percent of the year's budget to advertising and promotion.
   p. Sending a unit manager to a corporate training program in preparation for a future promotion.
   q. Operating a turret lathe.

r. Writing a computer program to summarize sales revenue created by each company product.

s. Deciding to use 42 percent of profits to repay borrowed funds and reduce indebtedness.

t. Reducing the price of an obsolescent typewriter in an effort to increase sales.

3. On a sheet of paper, write the letters *a* to *l* corresponding to the following elements from job descriptions.

a. Evaluate likely sales volumes for new products early in their development period.

b. Maintain adequate cash reserves to meet current operating expenses.

c. Ensure that adequate communication and coordination exist among company divisions.

d. Assess management training needs and provide instructional programs to meet the needs.

e. Schedule the use of facilities in all manufacturing departments.

f. Plan the orderly growth of the corporation to maintain a competitive position in the future.

g. Assure the availability of investments and borrowed funds for scheduled expansions.

h. Evaluate the training, experience, and aptitudes of applicants for employment.

i. Plan advertising activities, including general media selection, for a two-year period beginning each July.

j. Make daily assignments of technicians to handle current customer repair calls.

k. Carry out contract negotiations with pipefitters, stationary-boiler mechanics, and other unionized employees.

l. Oversee scheduling of freight shipments of all goods leaving the warehouse for movement to customers.

Now, beside each letter, write the number of the following management specialty that best matches each job description element.

(1) Production and operations.

(2) Marketing, distribution, and sales.

(3) Finance.

(4) Personnel and labor relations.

(5) General management.

4. *Performance Situation—The Cost of Management:* The assembly department at Thompson Toy Company puts together toy trucks, cars, and other vehicles from plastic and metal parts bought from outside suppliers or manufactured by other departments in the factory. Thompson is an old company with a rather paternalistic attitude toward its employees. Worker turnover has been low; 7 of the 13 assemblers have been with Thompson for over ten years. Wages are not high, but are competitive with those paid for similar

work elsewhere in the area. Specifically, one assembler who was hired recently receives $3.80 an hour; three of the others receive $4.25 an hour; eight get $4.65 an hour; and the last, who also serves as unit chief, gets $5.05 an hour. All work 40 hours a week. In a 6-week manufacturing run of a medium-priced toy truck early in 1979, the department turned out 93,600 units.

Thompson's market share is beginning to expand because of an aggressive sales program, and the company's managers have started to worry about productivity. They realized that the assembly department had been operating without management. The assemblers came in, went to work on the materials delivered to them, and went home at the end of the day. The managers decided, without further investigation, that there was surely room for improvement. Morton Jackson, a management trainee with a little experience, was free to take a new assignment. He was made manager of the assembly department in 19X2 and added to the department payroll.

Jackson did his job well, it seemed. Although the morale of the workers suffered temporarily, production soon increased. Jackson streamlined assembly procedures, cut out waste time and motions, and improved the flow of materials within the department. A 6-week production run of the same truck in 19X2 produced 102,262 units, a 9 percent increase over the 19X1 run without raising the wages of the assemblers.

Jackson was paid a salary of $13,000 a year. With fringe benefits and some overhead items, his work cost the company a total of $19,500 a year. Even with this cost, Jackson's superiors thought that creating the job for him as assembly manager had brought a real improvement to company efficiency.

A. What was the total cost an hour for assembly labor?
B. What was the total cost of assembly labor for a 6-week truck-production run?
C. What was the average assembly labor cost for each unit in the 1979 run?
D. If Jackson's salary and fringe were based on a 52-week year, what did the company have to pay for six weeks of his work?
E. If assembly labor was paid the same in 19X2 as in 19X1, what were total assembly labor costs, including the costs of Jackson's management, for the 6-week truck run in 19X2?
F. What was the average assembly labor cost for each unit in the 19X2 run?
G. Basing your answer only on the information given above, was it a good idea to add a manager to the assembly department?

5. *Performance Situation—Differences in Organizational Objectives:* Three managers are studying three similar proposals.

■ Manager 1 is the managing editor of a medium-sized publishing company, a business corporation. A staff editor has proposed publishing a booklet on the dangers of cigarette smoking along with suggestions on how to stop smoking. The booklet would be sold to individuals for $2.95 and at bulk rates to doctors, hospitals, and other organizations.

■ Manager 2 is the assistant director of the state health department, a government agency. A statistician in the department has determined that diseases related to cigarette smoking are approaching the epidemic level in the state. The department medical staff has worked out a proposal to prepare a booklet on the dangers of cigarette smoking including suggestions on how to stop. The booklet would be given away to individuals, doctors, hospitals, and anyone else who wanted it. It would be paid for from the regular department budget.

■ Manager 3 is the executive director of Breath of Life, Inc., a private nonprofit corporation. The organization uses money from private donors and from foundation grants to publicize issues relating cigarette smoking and health. A new booklet on smoking and how to stop has just been proposed by the organization's publicity consultant.

What is there about each of these three organizations that might affect each manager's decisions on whether to publish the booklet? On what basis might each decide?

6. A group is being formed to put on a variety show to raise money for the fiftieth anniversary of the founding of Platte Valley College. The group has to start from the beginning because no organization exists. Everything from finding a director to cleaning the hall after the performance has yet to be arranged. You are selected by acclamation to manage the project. On a separate sheet of paper, make a list of some of the *managerial* things you would want to accomplish in the first two or three weeks.

Cases for Analysis and Discussion

CASE 1: TOMORROW, WE'VE GOT TO GET ORGANIZED

"How was I supposed to know you expected me to do it?!" John was upset again, for the third time in the last 45 minutes. In fact, all of the Lost Souls were upset. Their music wasn't the problem. When the band was playing, everything went fine. But that was the only time it did.

John had just learned of the latest in a long series of blunders. The band had missed a good chance of getting steady work at a local club because no one had sent in an audition tape. Now the club had hired another group. John thought Jill and Tommy were going to handle the booking, because they had formed the band. Jill and Tommy thought John was going to send the tape, because he had made the original arrangements to have it recorded.

The band members had learned earlier that their publicity photo had not gotten to the newspaper in time for a Saturday advertisement. Once, several months ago, they had even accepted jobs at two different places on the same night; Maury had heard of an opening caused by another band cancelling out, and he said, "Sure, we'll be there." He didn't know that Jill had already arranged to play at a campus party that night.

A. Do these people constitute an organization? Consider all parts of the definition.
B. What is the trouble here? What can the Lost Souls do about it?
C. If the band were to use management specialization, how might responsibilities be divided?
D. Can these kinds of problems ever occur in large organizations? In government agencies?

CASE 2: HELP!

Morris Banks, the Fairlane town administrator, had good news and bad news. The good news was that Fairlane had just received $600,000 from the federal government to rehabilitate some of the substandard houses on the west side of town. The bad news was that Morris was already working 12-hour days and still falling far behind. He dreamed the other night that he was walking on a slippery river bed with water up to his chin. With all the complicated administration needed for the new government grant, Morris was afraid he was going to go under.

In the 11 years Morris had worked for Fairlane, the population had grown from 2,800 to nearly 4,000. The town budget had increased from $800,000 to over $2 million. Yet, the only office employees that had been added were one extra clerk, a secretary in the engineer's office, and a second full-time bookkeeper. Elected town officials were proud of their tight budget, and regularly turned down requests for more administrative assistance.

But help was essential. Morris was handling the entire management of the town government, finance, personnel, and all the rest. He decided to sit down and prepare one more request for reorganization and management assistance.

A. What should Morris Banks say in his request?
B. What kind of reorganization might he propose? Remember that the new grant must be dealt with and that it will involve complex financial, personnel, and legal requirements as well as actual construction work on the housing.
C. Is it right for the elected officials of the town to keep management costs to a minimum? What might convince them to go along with the proposal for management help, considering the town government's sources of funds and overall goals?
D. In general, is management worth what it costs?

CASE 3: BLEEDING HEARTS DESTROY THE FACTORY SYSTEM

When people in early nineteenth-century England began to argue against the near enslavement of thousands of children in manufacturers' factories, managers began to worry.

Many thought, "The factory system of production cannot exist without child labor. Our labor costs would be exorbitant. We'd be driven out of business. Besides, many of our child workers are orphans and have no other place to go."

Beginning in 1800, Robert Owen, a pioneer British social reformer, experimented with limiting child labor in the New Lanark cotton mills in Scotland. When he took over management of the mills, 500 of his 2,000 employees were children. He began reforms which in his day were viewed by many to be dangerously radical. He employed no one younger than 10 years old, sending the younger children to school instead. The children aged 10 and older who did work in the factory were treated relatively leniently: their work day was only 10¾ hours long, and they were no longer physically beaten.

Owen's experiment, along with other humanistic changes he made, created a very successful factory. Yet, it remained unthinkable to many in business that industrial production could continue without the labor of children. The change came anyway, no matter what factory owners thought. The opposition of society to child labor in factories grew so great that many companies voluntarily stopped employing the very young. Finally, child labor was prohibited outright by the government, not only in Britain but in nearly every country.

The factories are still running, bigger than ever.

A. What does this instance demonstrate about the relationship between managers and the general society?
B. Are any changes in social beliefs occurring today that might affect managers in a way similar to this?
C. Are social changes possible that would bring about the end of the factory system of production?

The Study of Management

After completing Chapter 2, you will be able to do the following:

- Compare the methods and aims of the classical, human relations, and quantitative schools of management.
- Give at least one example of the approach typical of classical or scientific management, either in the area of production efficiency or in that of motivating workers.
- Describe an important contribution of Henri Fayol to the definition of management.

- Describe the distinguishing characteristic of the human relations movement.
- Give an example of a problem particularly suitable for solution by quantitative management.
- Sort given management activities into five defined functions.
- Outline a current approach to management based on a synthesis of past emphases in the study of management.

At one time, the bicycle was an important form of transportation in the United States. Delivery men carried light packages, messages, and telegrams by bicycle; men and women commuted to and from work by bicycle; some doctors even made house calls by bicycle. The widespread use of the bicycle created a substantial industry—the making of bicycles and the component parts that went into them.

One businessman, S. E. Thompson, owned a factory that manufactured ball bearings for bicycles. Thompson one day realized that he had a problem: It took 120 women working full-time—10½ hours per day—to inspect the bearings and pick out the defective ones. Inspection costs were beginning to be significant. Thompson did not take his employees to task for not working faster, but neither did he just accept the high inspection costs. Instead, he approached the problem scientifically.

After analyzing the problem, Thompson realized that the job of inspection required a number of skills. Inspectors needed perseverance, of course, to pay close attention to ball bearings for 10½ hours a day. In addition, inspectors needed sharp visual perception and fast physical response time to spot and remove defective bearings. Thompson tested his employees for reaction time, and he laid off the slower workers. He was able to reduce his staff of inspectors from 120 to 35, while maintaining the same output as before, increasing accuracy by 67 percent, reducing work hours, and doubling the wages of the remaining workers.[1]

The important point is that Thompson approached his problem scientifically, or systematically, using a formal study of the job requirements and of the workers. This approach is typical of the management style that developed early in the industrial era. During the nineteenth and early twentieth centuries, as industry grew larger, the importance and difficulty of planning and management grew immensely. In both business and government, the

[1]Frederick Winslow Taylor, *The Principles of Scientific Management*, Harper and Row, New York, 1911, pp. 86–97.

response of managers was to begin to study the tasks of improving skills and developing new techniques.

This emphasis on the formal study of management problems and techniques continues today. The earliest school of modern management, associated with the nineteenth and early twentieth centuries, is called *classical management.* A later body of management theory, dating from the 1930s, is referred to as the *human relations* movement. In the 1950s wide acceptance was found for a number of contributions to management that may be loosely grouped together as the *quantitative and systems approach.*

Management thought today, to an important extent, is concerned with integrating these three streams of management theory and increasing the usefulness of management study. In case after case, it is clear that the manager in a tough spot can find practical help only by combining the kinds of actions proposed by these and other schools.

The formal study of management is also now more than ever conscious of influences outside the individual organization. Business practices are increasingly being shaped by government regulation. Government administration requires an unprecedented awareness of complex social, governmental, and political interactions. Both public and private enterprises have come face to face with a more aggressive populace. The social responsibility of organizations is rapidly gaining importance as a factor in management decision making. All these issues call for, and are receiving, careful study and attention by managers.

CLASSICAL MANAGEMENT LAID THE FOUNDATIONS

The concerns and conclusions of classical management thought in the nineteenth and early twentieth centuries were really quite diverse and did not form a unified body of thought. Certain themes were prominent, however. Many early writers on management were filled with scientific zeal. They believed that scientific investigation of the work place would immensely improve management practices. Classical management theorists placed great emphasis on methods of paying workers to increase their productivity. Overall, most prominent figures of this period tried to develop general principles of management that could be applied systematically in every organization and situation to improve management success.

Taylor and Scientific Management

The work of Frederick Winslow Taylor is an excellent example of the early application of scientific investigation to improving work methods. Taylor, in fact, was the originator of a school of thought called *scientific management,* which applied scientific analysis to help solve management problems. Taylor began work as an apprentice machinist and pattern maker in 1874. By 1884, he had received a degree in mechanical engineering and

Managers in Action

Speaking of the study of management, Michel C. Bergerac, chairman of Revlon, Inc., commented: "The American educational system has devised the very difficult trick of graduating the most ill-educated people at the highest cost." His suggestion for improvement? Restore a balance between theory and practice. And most college schools of business administration are doing just that.

At the Wharton School of the University of Pennsylvania, Dean Donald C. Carroll stresses business experience for his faculty. "We feel it is OK for our teachers to get a little cutting oil under their fingernails," he says. Yet, Wharton still assigns a 45-person staff to conduct "pure" research into what makes some managers better than others. Dean J. D. Steele of the Graduate School of Business Administration at the University of Southern California says the needed balance between theory and practice calls for walking a fine line between "esoteric meaninglessness on the one hand and vocationalism on the other."

One popular way to keep the study of management practical at colleges has been the use of advisory committees made up of successful, practicing managers and business people. Columbia University's Graduate School of Business has a series of such committees in areas such as marketing and accounting. Corporate executives meet periodically with faculty members to brainstorm about current issues and major trends in the future. Professors at the University of Pittsburgh's Graduate School of Business invite executives from firms like Rockwell International Corporation to discuss matters ranging from the impact of cancellations of defense contracts to minority business development. Faculty and students in such schools benefit from the practical interpretations of classroom theory about management.

"History is important," says Peter C. Krist, senior vice president at Mobil Oil Corporation, "but students spend all their time reading cases instead of the *Wall Street Journal*." An editorial in *Consultant News* also worries about managerial study that has become too "scholarly" and that behavioral sciences are overemphasized at the expense of line managerial experience. The answer, most authorities say, lies in placing the essential managerial theory into a practical business (or operational) context.

Source: "The Swing to Practicality in the B-schools," *Business Week*, July 23, 1979, p. 190.

was working as chief engineer for the Midvale Steel Company. He later worked briefly as the general manager of a paper mill in Maine and in 1893 began his own business as a consulting engineer. Some of his most famous work related to job design and factory management at the Bethlehem Company, beginning in 1898.

MEASUREMENT OF WORK TIME AND EFFORT   Taylor was a pioneer in the experimental study of work methods and the careful measurement of performance. His study of shoveling iron ore and rice coal demonstrates his general approach.

In Taylor's time much of the raw material used in the manufacture of steel was still moved by hand, specifically by shoveling. Two materials in particular interested Taylor: iron ore, which is quite heavy, and rice coal, which is relatively light. The standard practice at the time was to require each worker to bring his own shovel. Since each man used the same shovel all the time, each was throwing very heavy shovelfuls of iron ore but light shovelfuls of coal. Through analysis and experimentation, Taylor determined that 21 pounds was the optimum weight for one shovelful. He began the practice of providing company-owned shovels in two different sizes: a small shovel that held 21 pounds of iron ore and a large one that held 21 pounds of rice coal.

The results of the change were gratifying to Taylor. The size of the work force was reduced from 600 to 140. The average man could now shovel 59 tons of material in a day instead of the 16 tons moved with the old shovels. With increased productivity, the company was willing to raise wages (up to $1.88 per day).

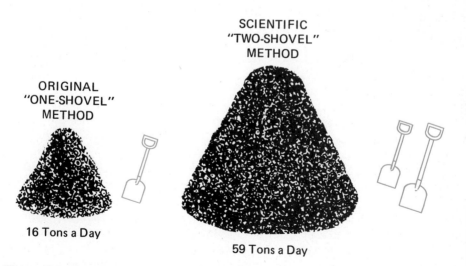

ORIGINAL
"ONE-SHOVEL"
METHOD

16 Tons a Day

SCIENTIFIC
"TWO-SHOVEL"
METHOD

59 Tons a Day

Figure 2-1. Taylor's Study of the Impact of Shovel Size on Handling Coal and Iron Ore.

This experiment and the resulting changes in procedure are typical of the general approach of scientific management. The shoveling study used exact measurement and analysis; it concentrated on objective physical behavior on the shop floor; and it was undertaken with the express intent of making changes in work procedures to increase productivity. This kind of study was the forerunner of present-day time-and-motion studies. It is part of the foundation of modern industrial engineering.

A SCIENTIFIC PHILOSOPHY OF MANAGEMENT   Eventually, Taylor developed a philosophy of management that was meant to extend beyond narrow studies of work methods in the industrial shop. In 1911, in his *Principles of Scientific Management,* and in later speeches and publications, Taylor laid out four duties that he saw for managers. He said management had the responsibility to:

1. Develop a science to replace the old rule-of-thumb knowledge of the worker.
2. Scientifically select workers best suited to specific jobs and then guide their development through good job instruction, training, and other means.
3. Inspire and cooperate with workers to ensure that the scientifically developed work methods are diligently applied on the job.
4. Divide the work between workers and managers, with the managers becoming more directly involved in deciding the details of how the work will be done.

Monetary Incentives   Taylor was also involved in one of the most frequently discussed management issues of the day: What kind of pay plan gives workers the incentive to put forth their best efforts on the job?

DIFFERENTIAL PIECE RATE   Taylor's idea was to set up a "differential" piece rate. Each job would be subjected to study and analysis to determine how much output was a fair day's work. A worker who produced below this amount in a day would be paid a certain rate for each piece produced. A worker who exceeded the standard output would be paid a *higher* rate for all pieces produced.

As an example, take the job of attaching screwdriver blades to wooden handles. Assume that the job consisted of the following steps: (1) picking up the two halves of the handle and assembling them with the blade by inserting two rivets, (2) placing the assembly in a machine that expands the rivets, and (3) pressing a foot pedal to activate the machine. The piece is then removed and passed on to another work station where smoothing and finishing are performed. Taylor would study the job to find out exactly what motions the worker would have to make, and he would measure how much time each assembly *should* take. If he found that, working at a steady but unhurried pace, a worker could assemble 3,000 screwdrivers in a 10-hour day, that amount would constitute the standard. A worker who produced fewer than 3,000 screwdrivers might receive $0.035 per 100 pieces; one who produced 3,000 or more might receive $0.063 per 100. Thus, an assembler whose output was 2,850 screwdrivers in a day (below standard) would get $1 for the day's work. Another worker who produced 3,025 screwdrivers would receive $1.91 for the day. Taylor thus used piecework rates as an incentive for workers to achieve a predetermined production rate.

DEPARTMENTAL GAIN-SHARING   Henry R. Towne, president of Yale & Towne Manufacturing Company for nearly half a century, also contributed to this early debate on incentives in employee compensation. Towne was a progressive manager in his day and advocated that managers share their experiences to mutually improve methods. This sharing of knowledge among managers helped establish management as a profession. Towne presented his pay plan, called *gain sharing*, in 1889. Under the plan, he proposed establishing production standards for each department. Whenever the department exceeded the standards through extra efforts, a gain in revenue or a reduction in production costs should occur. This gain was to be shared equally between owners and managers on the one hand and workers in the excelling departments on the other. Departments that did not exceed standards would not share in the gain.

PERSONAL-STANDARD PLAN   Frederick Halsey in 1891 put forth a different idea on the same subject. Halsey's goal was to reward individual workers for improved productivity. He began with a minimum wage to be paid to everyone. He then proposed paying an additional premium to every worker who exceeded his or her own average past performance. Thus Halsey's plan provided a monetary incentive to each worker not to meet an absolute standard, but simply to produce more than that worker had in the past. Halsey believed that this was a reasonable goal and that his plan would provide true incentive, be more fair to workers, and be more acceptable to owners than piecework rates or profit sharing.

Other Scientific Managers

Many other early management theorists and practitioners made important contributions to the foundations of management thought. Four who were particularly associated with scientific management were Morris L. Cooke, Henry L. Gantt, Frank B. Gilbreth, and Lillian M. Gilbreth. Especially during the first two decades of this century, their work greatly extended the influence of scientific management.

PUBLIC ADMINISTRATION   Morris L. Cooke was an early proponent of time-and-motion study and other scientific management practices applied to nonindustrial work. He was a pioneer in the development of sound administrative practices in municipal government. Working especially in the Philadelphia city government, he was able to streamline operations, reduce costs, and improve personnel policies and procedures.

PRODUCTION SCHEDULING   Henry L. Gantt is best remembered for his work with production scheduling. He originated a number of methods of scheduling the use of machines and workers to avoid wasted time and to balance production output. Many of these methods are still in use today. Gantt shared Taylor's belief that management has the duty to select, train, and develop workers carefully, and he proposed separate personnel departments to carry out these efforts.

PRECISE MEASUREMENTS   Lillian and Frank Gilbreth, developed time-and-motion study to a high level. They used photographs and motion pictures, combined with precise time measures, to analyze in detail the movements made by workers and the time required for each movement. They then selected the best set of movements to perform a given job in the least amount of total time.

Fayol and the Study of General Management

Scientific management, with its emphasis on time-and-motion study and precise physical measurement, led its practitioners to concentrate on workers on the shop floor. The study of general management, especially as applied to higher levels in the organization, did not receive significant attention until Henri Fayol filled the gap.

Fayol was the manager of a successful mining enterprise in France from 1888 until 1918. He believed that management practices could be improved through study and training and that a general theory of administration could be worked out to guide practical decisions. His 1916 publication, *Administration Industrielle et Générale*, contains a basic statement of an important part of management theory widely accepted even today.

FUNCTIONS (OR PROCESS) OF MANAGEMENT   Fayol divided the activities of organizations into six general types:

1. Technical (production).
2. Commercial (buying, selling, and trading).
3. Financial (finding capital and allocating it for effective use).
4. Security (protecting facilities, goods, and people).
5. Accounting (inventory, costs, and statistics).
6. Administration (planning, organization, command, coordination, and control).

Fayol believed that the first five of these concerns were better understood and handled than the sixth, administration. His analysis of administration, or general management, broke down the overall management job into a number of *functions*: planning, organizing, commanding, and so forth. The functions, sometimes called the "process of management," describe what it is that a manager really contributes to the running of an organization. This breakdown by function is among the basic concepts of management theory, and is one of Fayol's major contributions.

PRINCIPLES OF MANAGEMENT   Fayol proposed 14 principles of sound management, intended as practical and flexible guides to managing successfully. He recognized that administration is concerned largely with dealing with people in various contexts, and his principles reflect this concern more thoroughly than did the precepts of scientific management.

In his principles, Fayol discusses such issues as the division of work, discipline, equity, initiative, and the sources and uses of authority and responsibility. He strongly advocates unity of command, under which each employee is directly responsible to one and only one immediate superior. He explores the issue of centralization versus decentralization, and concludes that the characteristics of the particular organization determine the degree of centralization to strive for. He further touches on many other concerns that remain central to management and organization today.

HUMAN RELATIONS ARE A CONCERN OF MANAGEMENT
It is clear that much of classical management thought included basic assumptions that were not entirely adequate. Many early analyses of work methods seem to have viewed workers more as machines in the industrial process than as human beings. The repeated proposals for incentive pay plans clearly were based on the assumption that employee motivation could be increased by wages alone. The concentration of management efforts on the shop floor showed little understanding of the social interactions of which an organization is composed.

In what was probably the most important step toward broadening the view of early management theory, in 1924 a group of Harvard social scientists began studies of social conditions and productivity at Western Electric's Hawthorne Works in Illinois.

The Hawthorne Experiments
The Western Electric Company, in collaboration with the National Research Center, set out to determine the relationship between the intensity of interior lighting and the efficiency of workers. They selected two groups of workers, and varied the amount of light for one group while keeping the light constant for the other. They expected that the output of the first work group would vary with the changing light conditions, while the output of the second group would remain fairly constant.

They did not get the expected results. The output of the first group increased no matter what light level was provided. Even when lighting was reduced enough to make it difficult to see well, production rates went up.

The output of the group with constant lighting also went up, just as much as for the first group. Clearly, something other than the amount of light was affecting production levels.

After years of further study, researchers believed they had found a number of factors that clearly affected production. A company report from 1931 sums up: "Upon analysis, only one thing seemed to show a continuous relationship with this improved output. This was the mental attitude of the operators."[2] After over twenty thousand interviews with employees and extended close observation of numerous work groups, the researchers also felt that they had some ideas about what affected this all-important mental attitude.

One conclusion was that output was improved by the experimental situation itself; namely, (1) the observers' presence, (2) the workers' knowledge that they were being studied, and (3) the novelty of the experimental manipulations. The observation that any kind of attention or variety for workers, especially experimental work changes, will produce a temporary improvement in production has ever since been called the *Hawthorne Effect*.

A more important conclusion was that output was affected by the social organization and psychological setting in which the work was performed. Of special value to management was the realization that it could partially control these factors to improve output. The researchers observed, for instance, that:

- Some groups of workers purposely restricted output for various reasons.
- Groups of workers often exerted more control over the behavior of individuals than did the formal rules of management.
- The human content of supervision was at least as important to job satisfaction as wages and other monetary incentives.
- Human relations issues were often more important in controlling productivity and satisfaction than wages and physical factors such as lighting.

The Human Relations Movement

The discovery by the Harvard researchers of the extreme importance of psychological and social factors in the work place was an important step forward in the growth of management. It created an interest in the contributions of workers' beliefs, expectations, social groups, and other personal factors relating to work success. From the 1930s through the 1950s, many theorists and some managers paid considerable attention to the personal interests and problems of employees. This attention was paralleled in part by the growth of employee activism, especially as demonstrated in organized labor unions. Through the unions, workers became more able to

[2]George C. Homans, "The Western Electric Researches," in Michael T. Matteson and John M. Ivancevich (eds.), *Management Classics*, Goodyear, Santa Monica, Calif., 1977, pp. 50–57.

demand attention to their needs. The resulting consideration of these needs when making management decisions came to be called the *human relations movement*.

In some cases, attention to human relations factors got out of hand; some managers complained that they were being asked to act more as psychiatrists for their workers than as supervisors or managers. In general, though, the human relations movement was a positive force. It brought attention to some of the genuine effects of psychological and social features of the work world. Much of the modern interest in communication, social group effects, motivation, and leadership in organizations and management groups grew from this early focus on human relations.

THE QUANTITATIVE AND SYSTEMS APPROACHES HAVE BROADENED MANAGEMENT

Along with the extreme demands made on industry and government because of World War II, came rapid advances in the technical and theoretical tools available to managers. From its beginnings in the nineteenth century, scientific management had focused on practical problems of running factories and other production facilities. But problems involving complex scheduling tasks were beyond the abilities of scientific management techniques. Such tasks involved hundreds of different machine and human operations, the purchase and movement of many different materials, and the coordination of subassemblies in different plants and even in different countries. The question of how to manage projects that *had* to be completed in time went unanswered. What could managers do when faced with erratic machine breakdowns, an uncertain labor supply, and the possibility that materials would be unobtainable? At the same time, managers needed new ways to assure that the end products of a production process including thousands of separate steps would be of high quality.

Quantitative Management

Beginning in the 1940s, these complex technical problems were tackled by a new kind of manager. The outstanding characteristics of the new approach were that (1) it analyzed a large number of interacting features of a problem rather than focusing on a single part in isolation, and (2) it used sophisticated mathematical methods. This kind of approach is called the *quantitative* school of management. Its methods, which were used to improve performance in organizations, are often referred to as *operations research* (OR). Many quantitative techniques that were developed for fairly narrow application in OR have spread to general use today in all kinds of management. Mathematical descriptions of the behavior of such general entities as entire industries and national economies are now in fairly common use.

Systems Theory Related to the development of quantitative methods was the growing influence of systems theory on management thought. Since the 1960s, the analysis of organizations as *systems* has been among the most powerful unifying concepts in management.

A system may be loosely defined as a group of parts that are organized so that the individual parts affect and are affected by the behavior of the other parts. A clock, for instance, is a system. It functions only because each of its parts is arranged so that it moves other parts in a prescribed way. The human body is an extremely complex system. Hard exercise, for example, causes chemical changes in glands and other parts of the body. These changes in turn cause other reactions in the liver, pancreas, and elsewhere. These reactions in their turn bring about yet other changes. The interactions become almost indescribably complex. Eventually, they may even directly control the stimulus that started the reactions in the first place; that is, hard exercise, if continued long enough, will eventually bring about enough physical changes to create exhaustion and force the person to stop the exercise.

A system need not operate for an identifiable purpose. The weather surrounding the earth is a complex physical system involving the interactions in the atmosphere of the sun's heat, the rotation of the earth, the absorption and reflection of heat and light by the earth's surface, evaporation, and other forces. It is clearly a system, but its "purpose" would be hard to define.

In the study of management, however, a system is normally assumed to have a purpose; it is organized with the intention of accomplishing something. To managers, most systems of interest include:

- Groups of men and women.
- Machines and equipment.
- Materials.
- Methods and means of communication.
- Money.
- Other resources or facilities organized to achieve some purpose.

Figure 2-2 shows the relations of these elements. Looked at in this way, the similarity of a system to the general definition of an organization becomes clear.

The systems concept has had great theoretical importance to management and widespread practical applications for solving real management problems. It has provided a basis for looking at things in a way that can bring more success in planning, organizing, decision making, and problem solving. Today's managers are clearly aware that changes in a single component of a system may very well affect the operation of the entire system, for better or worse. This knowledge can help managers judge the most likely causes of problems and, at the same time, the most probable consequences of their decisions.

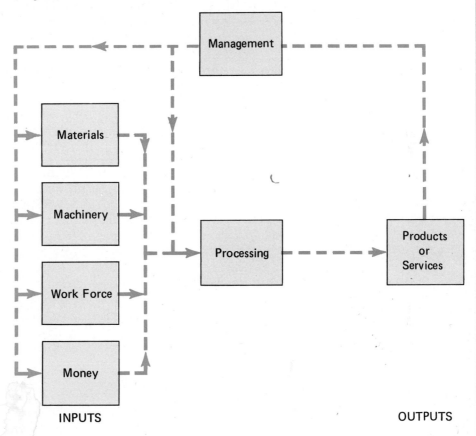

Figure 2-2. A Management Control System. *Management monitors and controls in a systematic way the acquisition, integration, and use of resources (inputs) and their processing in order to produce goods and services (outputs).*

TODAY'S CONTINGENCY MANAGEMENT USES NEARLY ALL THAT HAS GONE BEFORE

The main characteristics of the classical, human relations, and quantitative developments in management thought (see Figure 2-3 on page 38) form the basis for a variety of approaches and techniques available to managers today. As new ways of thinking about management come along, they usually add to the older bases, rather than taking their place.

Management Based Upon the Situation

The typical view of the "right" way to manage today is not as simple as the principles of Taylor and Fayol. Every management action is seen as operating in a complex organizational situation. Even a decision on

Figure 2-3. Principal Features of Different
Approaches to Management.

CLASSICAL (SCIENTIFIC)	HUMAN RELATIONS	QUANTITATIVE
■ Measurement of time and effort.	■ Emphasis upon human concerns.	■ Use of mathematics and statistics.
■ Scientific principles.	■ Awareness of group influence.	■ Search for system relationships.
■ Monetary incentives.	■ Complexity of human motives.	■ Interdependencies of different technologies and disciplines.

how to run the plant cafeteria is affected by scores of variables: work schedules, labor union relations, and even popular beliefs about nutrition. The cafeteria operations in turn exert some influence, however small, on nearly every other feature of the organization, including employee morale, operating costs, facilities utilization, and production scheduling. Since every management function and action will be controlled by the interaction of many diverse elements of the particular situation in the real organization, no single approach is best for every problem. A time-and-motion study might be the answer in one case. A supportive, democratic discussion of a problem might be best in another case. Management action is contingent on the features and relationships of a particular situation. For this reason, management based on the situation is often called *contingency management*, or situational management.

The rest of this book examines what today's managers do and the ways they look at their organizations. It should be clear throughout that managers need a *range* of activities, skills, and attitudes to successfully guide the operations of an organization. To succeed in production, finance, or marketing, for example, demands more than just a sound knowledge of manufacturing, money and banking, or advertising. It demands management ability, the knowledge and skill to:

■ Carry on the management process.
■ Understand organizations.
■ Use technical management tools.
■ Handle relations with the environment outside the organization.

These components of the management job are described briefly below, and each is discussed in detail in the following chapters.

The Management Process

The view, pioneered by Fayol, that management is a process in which certain functions must be performed persists today because of its utility in helping managers grasp some of their fundamental responsibilities. Specific management functions have been defined differently at different times and have been placed in different orders of relative importance. Most would agree, however, that no matter what a manager's philosophy, he or she must get these five jobs done:

1. *Planning.* Setting goals and devising specific activities, procedures, and schedules for meeting the goals.
2. *Controlling.* Finding out what is really being accomplished in the organization, and solving problems and revising plans when goals are not being met.
3. *Organizing.* Establishing the formal relationships among people and facilities in the company or agency, which will partly determine how these resources interact in pursuing goals.
4. *Staffing.* Finding and training the right person for the right job in the organization.
5. *Directing.* Using leadership, motivation, communications, and other skills to ensure that people in the organization know what their work is, and do it.

These management functions interact in many complex ways when they are applied. Planning and controlling are central. They provide a chosen direction to the organization and provide for continual adjustments to operations to see that the direction is followed. They steer the organization. The other three functions put the organization to work. They decide what specific tasks are to be completed by individual people; they find these people and give them the skills to work; and they issue the orders and provide the motivation to get the people in the organization to give their best efforts. See Figure 2-4 on page 40.

The management process is the core of the management job. Chapters 3 through 10 discuss its component functions and their interactions. But knowledge of the management process alone does not make a complete manager. Further skills and responsibilities are essential.

Understanding and Functioning in the Organization

One positive result of the human relations school of management was the growing realization that organizations, especially in their human aspects, are not as simple as they were once thought to be. It is now apparent that even the clearest and most reasonable directives of management may not bring the desired results. Subtle but very potent human forces exert their influences. Group beliefs, personal values, or social conflicts, for example, can in some cases exert stronger controls over behavior than all the rational planning and organizing done by managers.

Managers today accept the importance of human forces. They try to understand these forces and use them to the benefit of the organization and its members. For example, since nearly all work takes place in social

Figure 2-4. Relationship of Functions in the Management Process.

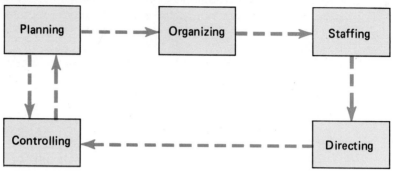

groups, knowledge of how groups influence individual behavior and how individuals affect groups will help managers increase the effectiveness of their actions. These and other related interactions have been called *organizational behavior.*

Technical
Management Tools

Quantitative methods—those using numbers, statistics, and mathematical analysis—have gained an unprecedented importance in management. Much of the raw information managers work with is expressed in numbers: income, costs, production quantities, quality control measures, and inventories, for example. One of the first jobs of management is to establish a system for collecting, analyzing, and summarizing this information, and getting it to the people who need it. This task has been eased somewhat by computers, which are becoming increasingly common even among relatively small organizations.

Modern management also benefits from the increased availability of mathematical approaches to a range of difficult tasks. Production planning, complex scheduling problems, resource allocation, and many other management concerns can often be handled best by using the relatively sophisticated tools of operations research. Increasingly, numerical methods are also being applied to general management problems: forecasting and planning, cost analysis, and controlling operations, for instance.

The Environment
of the Organization

No organization is an island. Every business, government, and private, nonprofit group is affected by complex forces from the society as a whole. Organizations have always been concerned with the outside world because that is where the money comes from. But in recent decades managers have, sometimes unwillingly, shown a far greater concern for the society outside the organization than had been typical before. This has been brought about by increasingly aggressive government regulatory activity and by the growing belief among consumers that all organizations must act with greater social responsibility.

Businesses have been forced to pay more attention to government because government is paying more attention to business. Government directly regulates competitive practices, safety and health conditions, environmental effects of products and facilities, labor relations, and many other aspects of business operations. Even the decisions made by managers in government offices are strongly influenced by the actions and requirements of other branches and levels of government.

All modern organizations have been faced with increasingly active representation of the interests of consumers in general, minorities, and other groups. This has created a greater public awareness of the power of businesses, government, and other organizations to affect the well-being of everyone. This greater awareness has led to a more thorough consideration by managers of the social and environmental effects of their decisions and actions. Today's managers, in addition to improving their knowledge of government and social forces, are developing formal management techniques for handling relations with the public.

SUMMARY

1. Three main schools of thought have provided a theoretical basis for management practice: (a) classical management, including scientific management; (b) the human relations movement; and (c) the quantitative and systems approaches.

2. Scientific, or systematic, management applied concrete measurements and analysis to solve certain management problems. Scientific managers proposed a number of incentive pay plans, new work methods, and other measures to increase productivity and efficiency.

3. Henri Fayol, a pioneer in the formal study of general management, defined management as a process of performing certain functions unique to management: planning, organization, command, coordination, and control. He also proposed 14 principles of management, many of which are still recognized as sound.

4. The Hawthorne experiments pointed up the important influences of social and psychological effects on work effectiveness. These and similar studies, combined with other factors such as the growing strength of labor unions, produced a rapid increase in management's concern for the desires and expectations of humans in organizations. This growth of concern has been called the human relations movement.

5. Quantitative management tools are especially useful in controlling undertakings that involve many variables interacting in complex ways. Systems theory has provided a rational basis for understanding such interactions and for identifying the true causes of problems and the most likely consequences of decisions.

6. Events and processes in an organization take place in a complex situation with interacting elements. Management actions must be contingent on (dependent upon) the specific situation, and managers must employ a wide range of tools and approaches in accordance with the variety of situations.

7. The current study of management focuses on (a) carrying out the management process through planning, controlling, organizing, staffing, and directing; (b) the understanding and functioning of organizations; (c) using technical management tools; and (d) handling relations with the environment outside the organization.

REVIEW AND DISCUSSION QUESTIONS

1. Why was scientific management called "scientific"? How was Taylor's shoveling experiment typical of its methods?

2. What were Taylor's four principles of scientific management? Do any managers today do what the principles call for? For example?

3. What assumption did scientific management wage-incentive plans appear to hold in common? Is there any evidence in the chapter that this assumption is faulty?

4. What was one important difference between Fayol and the scientific managers? How did Fayol define management?

5. What were some of the failings of scientific management that contributed to the rapid development of other approaches?

6. Why are the Hawthorne experiments seen as one foundation of the human relations approach? What did the experimental results show to support an increased concern with human relations?

7. What are two main characteristics of modern quantitative management techniques? What were some of the problems that led to the development of these methods?

8. Give an example of a system. What makes it a system? Why has this concept become so influential in management and in other fields?

9. Why does the text say that "managers today use nearly all that has gone before?" How are modern management approaches related to the three earlier management schools of thought presented?

Problems and Projects

1. On a separate sheet of paper, write the letters *a* through *g*, corresponding to the names of important figures in the classical management period. After each letter, write the number of each contribution with which the person is identified.

   a. Frederick Winslow Taylor
   b. Henry R. Towne
   c. Frederick Halsey
   d. Morris L. Cooke
   e. Henry L. Gantt
   f. Frank and Lillian Gilbreth
   g. Henri Fayol

   (1) Developed methods for detailed time-and-motion study.
   (2) Proposed a gain-sharing plan under which departments that increased productivity would share in the gains from the increase.
   (3) The major originator of scientific management.
   (4) Applied many of the precepts of scientific management to municipal government administration.
   (5) Influential in the development of the separate personnel department to select and train employees.
   (6) Developed the techniques of using exact measurement and scientific analysis to improve work methods in the steel industry.
   (7) Noted for establishing methods for scheduling production facilities for efficient use.
   (8) Proposed a pay plan for rewarding individuals who exceeded their average prior output.
   (9) Defined management as a process through which certain functions are performed.
   (10) Was influential in getting managers to share their experiences and knowledge, as is typical of a profession.
   (11) Was among the first to apply formal study and analysis to general management.

2. Henri Fayol divided the activities within an organization into the six categories listed below. He believed that a manager could be concerned with any or all of these activities, but that all managers must handle administration, no matter what their other duties. On a separate sheet of paper, write

the letters of the categories. Next to each, write the numbers of each activity that belongs in that category.

   a. Technical
   b. Commercial
   c. Financial
   d. Security
   e. Accounting
   f. Administration

(1) Buying 100,000 tons of iron ore for steel making.
(2) Establishing who will supervise whom in the organization.
(3) Requiring visitors to the plant to wear hardhats.
(4) Laying out a plan for expanding the agency to enforce new legislation.
(5) Contacting current investors to inform them of a new stock issue.
(6) Operating an arc welder to assemble tractor frames.
(7) Performing a statistical analysis of cash flow.
(8) Allocating funds to departments within a government agency.
(9) Writing news releases for a nonprofit labor organization.
(10) Checking operating records to see whether goals have been met.
(11) Protecting a manufacturing plant from damage by vandals.
(12) Dividing the marketing department into four separate departments: advertising, product development, sales, and distribution.
(13) Buying a stock of men's ties for the spring season.
(14) Recording the exact amount of each sale and the items sold.
(15) Selling the remaining stock of obsolete electric skillets in bulk to a discount chain store.

3. A roller assembly consisting of two rollers and a spacer held on a spindle by two clips is being put together by hand. The assemblies are produced in great quantities. The manufacturer, filled with zeal for the new scientific management, decides to apply a little analysis to the assembly procedure.

Workers take parts from trays in front of them and assemble them in a jig. The procedure takes eight steps, as shown in Figure 2-5.

Step 1: Pick up clip; place in jig.
Step 2: Pick up spindle; force through clip into jig.
Step 3: Pick up roller; place on spindle.
Step 4: Pick up spacer; place on spindle.
Step 5: Pick up roller; place on spindle.
Step 6: Pick up clip; position loosely near top of spindle.
Step 7: Pick up hammer and clip-setting sleeve; place sleeve over spindle; tap with hammer to set clip.
Step 8: Remove assembly from jig; place in output box.

Serving as this manufacturer's scientific manager, work out the best way for this job to be done. Try to achieve the fewest and shortest motions. Where should the parts and tools be placed? Draw a diagram to show the best

Figure 2-5.

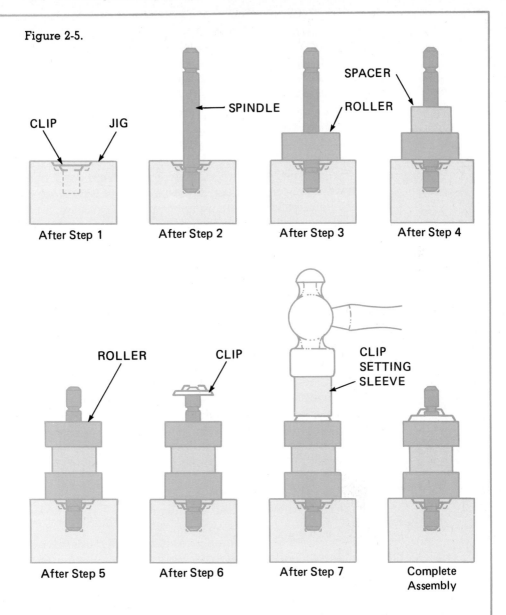

After Step 1

After Step 2

After Step 3

After Step 4

After Step 5

After Step 6

After Step 7

Complete Assembly

placement for a left-handed person; for a right-handed person. Give exact instructions to a new employee on how to do the job. Suggest any other changes (a different kind of jig or clip sleeve, for instance) you think management should make.

4. *Performance Situation—A Systems Approach:* Terry Webb got her degree in public administration in the early 1970s, and she is a firm believer in the systems approach to management. Asked by her superiors in the employment security division of a state government in the Southwest to describe a system, she chooses the division's small printing department as an example.

"There are many different kinds of systems. One kind that managers are especially interested in describes the situation in which some kind of processing is applied to one or more inputs to create a desired output. Look at the printing department. You walk up to their front desk with a single copy of a report and instructions on what to do with it. A day or two later you go back and get 1,000 copies of the report. That wouldn't be possible if the department weren't a system.

"John is the head of the department. He runs the offset press and the platemaker, schedules the work, gives work assignments to Lisa and Don, and deals with suppliers and with you other people in the agency who are his 'customers.' Lisa operates the cold type machine and the photocopier and types clean originals when they're needed. Don keeps all the records, tells John when supplies like paper and ink are needed, operates the offset press, does regular machine maintenance and lets John know when outside repair work or replacement is needed."

A. Show why this department is a system. How does it fit the definition?

B. Draw a diagram of the system. Show all of the inputs on the left, the people and machines that process them in the center, and the outputs on the right. Include all of the inputs and outputs that you think apply, not just the ones mentioned in the description. In the processing section of the diagram, show the relationships among the people and machines.

C. List some specific things in the inputs, in the functioning of the processor, or in the outputs that would affect the operation of this system for better or worse. Examples would be: that the printing paper received is a half-inch too long in one direction; that John has a fight with Don; or that some printed reports are found by the user to be too faint to read easily. Which items on your list can managers control? How might they go about controlling them?

5. Douglas M. McGregor, an eminent teacher and consultant in management and psychology, described some common beliefs among managers about employees:

"The average man is by nature indolent—he works as little as possible.

"He lacks ambition, dislikes responsibility, prefers to be led.

"He is inherently self-centered, indifferent to organizational needs.

"He is by nature resistant to change.

"He is gullible, not very bright, the ready dupe of the charlatan and the demagogue."[3]

[3]Douglas M. McGregor, "The Human Side of Enterprise," in Michael T. Matteson & John M. Ivancevich (eds.), *Management Classics*, Goodyear, Santa Monica, Calif., 1977, pp. 41–49.

Survey the class or other classes to determine the extent to which these beliefs are held. Place the statements to the left on a sheet of paper. To the right, make a scale as shown below.

Disagree Strongly	Disagree Somewhat	Undecided	Agree Somewhat	Agree Strongly
1	2	3	4	5

Ask each student to express an opinion on each statement. If he or she agrees strongly with a statement, score a 5; if he or she disagrees somewhat, score a 2, and so forth. Add up all scores for each statement separately, and divide by the number of people interviewed; this will give an average measure of agreement with each statement.

Based on the results of the survey, which approach to management discussed in the chapter would the group interviewed feel most comfortable with? Why? Does this mean it is generally the best approach?

6. *Performance Situation—The Busiest Day:* Thomas Muñoz looked forward to the day. The week before last was almost entirely lost to making the annual budget, showing how much would be spent in the coming year for each of the activities of his department. Last week was mainly used up by the public hearings on the water-resource development project and by the two-day workshop on improving communications in government agencies. This week, he would get back to the normal daily routine and get his desk cleared off.

Muñoz is assistant director of public information for a city in the Midwest. The basic purpose of his department is to present the activities of the city government—in a favorable light, if possible—to residents of the city and surrounding areas. Muñoz is also especially responsible for finding out what citizens think and want done about projects the city is involved with.

Muñoz always begins his day with brief conferences with each of the five people he supervises. The meetings are a little more extended today because he has been out of the office most of the time for nearly two weeks. He finds that all the work of his subordinates is on schedule and is presenting no serious problems, with one notable exception. The mayor's office last month directed Muñoz's department to put on a real selling effort for the school bond referendum coming up in November. The mayor wants a full-fledged publicity campaign. After giving a few general guidelines, Muñoz had turned the job over to Martin Allman, the department publicity specialist. Now it turns out that Allman has produced some good news releases and has boxes full of background and research material, but he has made almost no progress toward a planned, coordinated campaign.

Muñoz decides to get involved himself, since the bond issue is of such great political importance. The first job, he thought, is to get some kind of scheduling set up for all of the activities to be included in the campaign. This scheduling can be very complex when dealing with a large number of press conferences, radio and TV stations, newspapers, speeches, and other means of public access. Every presentation takes a different length of time to prepare, and many of them need special materials or skills, such as films, slides, or other art work.

Muñoz decides to set up the effort as a special project with himself as project manager. He is able to temporarily borrow a specialist from the city's small operations research department to use a mathematical scheduling method to work out the best arrangement and sequence for all the tasks. He makes Allman assistant project manager, assigns a clerk full-time and a graphics specialist part-time to the project.

One of the real problems, Muñoz thought, would be to get the best work from Allman. Whether or not Muñoz was project manager, Allman was still going to have to carry most of the weight; time limitations demanded it. Muñoz sat down with Allman, and together they worked out the specific goals of the campaign. They negotiated the exact responsibilities Allman would have and how it would be determined whether the responsibilities were being met. Muñoz felt that if Allman played an active role in setting up the goals and actively proposed some of the ways his own success could be measured, he would be more strongly motivated to make his best effort.

Show how Muñoz's job demonstrates the modern contingency approach to management described at the end of Chapter 2. Write a description showing how Muñoz's specific activities fit into the categories of management concern given in the chapter.

Cases for Analysis and Discussion

CASE 1: PESSIMISTIC REVERY

Many jobs in industry are not much fun. Mule spinning, named after the spinning machine called a "mule," was an old way of spinning yarn that created jobs that could hardly be less suited to human beings. The work was tedious and fast paced. It required walking up and down a long corridor in the spinning room, tying knots when yarn came free and performing other trivial but necessary jobs to keep the machines producing. Worse, the layout of the machines and the pace of the work completely isolated each worker, making it impossible to talk or have any other human contact.

It is not surprising that one textile mill in Philadelphia found that personnel turnover in the mule spinning department was as high as 250 percent each year, while it was only 5 to 6 percent in the rest of the company.

The managers tried a scientific management approach. They tried to make the workers more efficient, more productive. But production did not improve; turnover did not go down.

As a last resort, they called in a sociologist who had considerable interest in industry, Elton Mayo. Mayo, along with a nurse whom he used as an interviewer and as what would today be called a "counselor," talked at length to the workers in the mule spinning department. Mayo concluded that there were two main causes of the problems: physical fatigue and a personal factor he called "pessimistic revery." This revery consists of the irrational, melancholy thoughts and the low self-esteem which assail people who work in isolation at tedious jobs. He prescribed rest periods, and suggested installing beds in the factory to encourage complete relaxation. He believed this would overcome the fatigue and dispel the cumulative effects of the dissatisfaction and monotony that accompanied the mule spinning work.

Mayo was right about something. Productivity jumped dramatically and turnover nearly disappeared, especially after the workers themselves were given complete control over the timing of the rest periods.[4]

A. What might be a more thorough explanation of the results than "recovery from pessimistic revery"? In light of the Hawthorne experiments, what else might have caused the increased productivity and reduced turnover?

B. Was there a social group in the mule spinning department before Mayo's work? During it? After it?

C. How is this experience in the textile industry related to the human relations movement?

D. Could this problem and these results occur in a nonindustrial setting?

CASE 2: WHAT'S WRONG WITH THE PACKERS?

Bert Johnson was at it again. He had an orderly mind, orderly appearance, an orderly desk, and he wanted an orderly packing department, or else!

"The only thing wrong with the packers is that nobody down there knows what they're doing. The only way we're ever going to solve the problems is to get an expert to look at every possible step, work out the best way to wrap and pack, and make sure every packer does it exactly that way and no other way."

Johnson did have some reason for concern. Even casual observation showed that productivity was not what it should have been. Material was

[4]George Elton Mayo, "The First Inquiry," in Harwood F. Merrill (ed.), *Classics in Management*, American Management Association, New York, 1960, pp. 407–416.

being wasted and occasionally orders were mysteriously delayed for days, and even for two or three weeks in some cases. The worst problem, though, was breakage, both during packing and then during shipment because the packing had been faulty. Repeated meetings with Jerry Gwain, the department supervisor, had brought no improvement.

Johnson's partner, Frank Ellis, knew about the problems. He did not agree with Johnson's diagnosis and prescription, though.

"Bert, the real problem with the packers is morale. Most of them are experts; they know how to pack. But they won't do the best job because Jerry rides them all of the time so they don't even concentrate on the work. What they need is *more* freedom to decide how to do their job, not less. We ought to set up some kind of system where the packers can work out their own goals and methods and take responsibility for the results—and take some pride in their work."

A. Who do you think is right in this situation?

B. Is it possible to make a compromise between Johnson's and Ellis's views, to get the best from both?

C. Could an authoritarian supervisor like Jerry cause delays and breakage?

D. What schools of management thought do you think would appeal to Johnson? To Ellis?

CASE 3:
WHAT INCENTIVE
DO WE HAVE?   Jane Landrum was talking to her salespeople:

"Ladies and gentlemen, I want to thank all of you for the efforts you have put out during the last year, and for your loyalty to the company. I assure you it's a pleasure to work with each of you.

"I'm sure you all know that the economy is in bad shape and sales are harder to get. We expect some decline when times are like this. But, the sales loss we are experiencing is more than the company can stand for very long.

"So, we're going to try something different. You have all been getting straight salaries. We are changing now to a salary-plus-commission pay plan. In the future, you will each receive a 9 percent commission on your gross sales. Your salaries will be adjusted downward so that your total income for next year will be the same as for this year if you sell the same amount. But if, for example, your sales this year were $150,000, you can earn an extra $4,000 next year if you sell 30 percent more. If you increase your sales by 50 percent, you can earn $6,750 more."

A. If you were one of Jane's salespeople, what would you think of this change?

B. What will happen when the economy gets better? Will the plan be a good idea?

C. How is this pay plan related to the incentive wage plans of the scientific managers? How is it different?

CASE 4: THE UNPREDICTABLE MANAGER

Harry Martello was again mystifying some of his colleagues in the claims division. He had just brought in every single worker in the building engineering and maintenance crew and read the riot act to them. There had been a lot of horseplay in the heating plant room and someone had finally gotten hurt. The injured man was getting better now, but it could have been serious.

Contrasted with this, when Juliet Majeski, supervisor of the record clerks, had complained that the clerks were not working hard enough, Harry brought in a psychological consultant to talk to them and find out what the problem was.

The contract administrators and auditors in the funds management department were organized like a committee, almost a community of equals. The claims administration department, on the other hand, had a quite clear chain of command, and Harry was always upset if someone ignored the proper channels without a very good reason.

Harry used a sophisticated mathematical model run at the computer center for claims-volume forecasting. When it came to making changes in the division to anticipate the effects of government reorganization following the last election, Harry said his instincts from 13 years of government service were the only tools he needed.

A. Is Harry Martello erratic, or do you think he knows what he is doing?

B. What are some of the factors that might control the specific approach he would take to a situation or problem?

C. If you wanted to label Harry, what kind of management would you say he probably uses?

Managers Plan and Control

2

The Planning Process

3

After completing Chapter 3, you will be able to do the following:

- Define planning and controlling and describe the relationship between them.
- Identify the steps in the planning process and describe how the process is used to create plans in a real situation.
- Propose subsidiary objectives to support an overall goal, given adequate information about an organization.

- Determine the types of subplans needed to create a comprehensive plan for a given organization.
- Name seven types of plans and briefly describe the kind of information each contains.
- Assign an appropriate time span to specific types of plans.

"We, the people of the United States, in order to form a more perfect union, establish justice, insure domestic tranquility, provide for the common defense, promote the general welfare, and secure the blessings of liberty to ourselves and our posterity, do ordain and establish this Constitution for the United States of America."

The purpose of your organization may not be as clearly and elegantly stated as this extract from the preamble to the Constitution. Nevertheless, your organization will have a purpose. Your success will be judged by how well you guide operations to fulfill that purpose.

The basic tools for guiding organizations to achieve their purpose are planning and controlling. These processes are linked together inseparably. Managers plan future activities to anticipate opportunities and problems and to make sure resources are available when needed. They then continually check what is actually taking place in the organization to make sure it agrees with their plans. That is the only certain way to insure that progress toward meeting goals takes place in an orderly way.

You may ask, Can the future really be anticipated? The answer is yes, but only up to a point. If you ran a company that manufactured an eyewash, for example, you probably would not have met your production and sales goals in 1977: an essential ingredient, boric acid, was then in short supply. In theory, it would have been possible to foresee the chain of events that caused the shortage. The Arab oil embargo of 1973–1974 caused the costs of fuel oil and other heating sources to soar. The high heating costs, combined with promised tax incentives, created a strong interest in insulation for buildings. Boric acid is used as a fire retardant in many insulating materials. Thus, the demand for insulation caused the shortage of boric acid.

It is always difficult and often impossible to predict this kind of occurrence in advance. Much about the future environment, however, is routine and fairly predictable, especially for the coming year or so. A manager who fails to anticipate and plan, and then stay on top of events as they unfold to see that plans are carried out, will not be a successful manager for long. A successful manager combines instinct, orderly thought, experience and research to make sound, practical plans. This kind of manager is well on the way to making his or her organization fulfill its purpose, now and in the future.

MANAGERS PLAN AND CONTROL TO KEEP ON COURSE

Suppose you were visiting an unfamiliar city and wanted to eat at a restaurant in the suburbs. If so, you would have to follow a process similar to that used by managers in planning and controlling. You would first choose a specific restaurant, based, for example, on your taste in food and decor and on how much you can afford to spend. You might then consult a map to find the location of the restaurant and to pick the best route for driving to it. While driving in your car on the way, you will check route signs and street names to find whether you are still on the right track, to see where to turn, and to determine how far you still have to go. If this checking shows that you have gotten off the route, you will have to check the map again, ask directions, or do something else to get going the right way again. If you pick a good restaurant to begin with, choose an adequate route to get there, and check carefully to stay on the route, you should achieve your goal of having a good meal.

The same kind of thing is true of managing. When managers set practical goals, devise adequate activities and methods for reaching the goals, and make sure they stay on the planned path—or get back on when things go wrong—their organizations are likely to fulfill their purposes.

Planning and controlling work together to choose goals, find ways to reach them, and make sure the ways are put into action. *Planning* is the process of selecting and defining specific objectives and of devising concrete courses of action to achieve the objectives. *Controlling* is the process of continually (1) measuring actual activities and results and (2) comparing them with plans to judge whether adequate progress is being made and to take corrective action when needed. Controlling can take place only after planned actions have been put into operation. Thus, to be effective, good controlling depends on good plans. Planning, in turn, depends on good controls. This is so because past results and experiences provide some of the best information on which to base future plans.

MANAGERS PLAN BY CHOOSING FROM AMONG POSSIBLE FUTURE ACTIONS

If a tornado is about to strike your home, you do not have time to do much planning. For most of us most of the time, though, the future is filled with uncountably numerous possibilities.

One prime purpose of planning is to sort out these possibilities, grasp the desirable ones, and fend off the undesirable ones. Planning, then, helps us as managers to *choose* from many alternate strategies.

At other times, managers may wish to accomplish something for which no good strategies are immediately obvious. Therefore, another purpose of planning is to *develop* possibilities where none appear to exist. Planning, then, also helps managers to find ways to meet goals.

A Written Purpose   Developing and choosing among possible future actions within businesses, government agencies, or other formal groups is guided by two main forces: (1) the purpose of the organization, and (2) its beliefs about the future. An organization will not exist without some general purpose. A supermarket chain, for example, might fundamentally exist to create profits for investors. A nonprofit group, such as an alumni association, might exist to raise funds for scholarships to a private college. Whatever else managers do, they must make sure their planning is guided by their organization's purpose. As a practical matter, it is very useful to clearly define the overall purpose of your organization in writing. This statement of purpose can then be used to evaluate the suitability of the specific objectives you are trying to reach.

Planning Premises   Planning tries to control the future. This cannot be done without some idea of what the future may bring in the outside environment and in the organization. Planners make efforts to improve their knowlege of likely future conditions. They use formal forecasting methods; they study causes of economic, political, and social changes; they collect the opinions, beliefs, and goals of other people. The resulting beliefs about what the future will be like are called *premises*. These are assumptions about future economic conditions, taxes, legal requirements, consumer desires, resource availability, and scores of other factors that will control what can be done and what will be best to do. The value of plans is dependent on the accuracy and completeness of the premises on which they are based. This means that a manager should keep as fully informed as possible about developments in business, trade, government, politics, and society. Such awareness requires the use of formal forecasting methods when appropriate. Above all, managers must read widely, listen to others, and make conscious efforts to remain well informed. Forecasting and premising are discussed in more detail in Chapter 4.

The Planning Process   The statement of organization purpose together with the planning premises control the planning process. These two factors influence what managers want to do and what they are able to do. With these factors as background, trained managers carry out an orderly planning procedure aimed at providing specific answers to specific questions. The steps of the procedure are:

- Setting objectives.
- Discovering alternate ways to reach objectives.
- Evaluating the alternatives.
- Making decisions.

STEP 1. SETTING OBJECTIVES   The first planning step is to decide what the organization should try to accomplish. The clear and specific aims set forth in plans are called *objectives*. Objectives are needed for the organization as a whole and for each of its divisions and departments. Objectives may also be set for different functions of the organization or its divisions: objectives for financial performance, for personnel development, for facilities maintenance and improvement, and others.

The essential reason for setting objectives is to create a set of interrelated goals that, if accomplished, will allow the organization to fulfill its purpose.

STEP 2. DISCOVERING ALTERNATE WAYS TO REACH OBJECTIVES   If the manager of a social service agency sets an objective of processing 12 percent more cases in the coming year, one way to do it is obvious: hire another caseworker. There may be better, cheaper ways, however. The planning process should include a search for such other, less obvious ways to reach goals. It might be possible, for instance, to eliminate processing steps for certain kinds of cases so they take less time.

This second planning step also requires a quick rejection of certain alternatives that are clearly impossible or impractical. In some cases, there are so many possible ways to tackle a problem that most of the possibilities cannot be closely considered. If so, the manager must, using experience and a clear understanding of objectives and premises, pick those few alternatives that are the most likely to succeed.

STEP 3. EVALUATING THE ALTERNATIVES   At this point, the manager has a list of possible actions that, if carried out, would accomplish a given objective. He or she must ask, How good is each of the possibilities? What will each cost? Will they interfere with other activities and goals? Are the possible actions so expensive or difficult that the objective itself should be changed or dropped?

This is the planning step where a manager confronts reality, sometimes painfully. A proposed advertising program might increase sales by 20 percent, but be so expensive that proposed salary increases would have to be postponed. A new research laboratory would attract a better college faculty, but the legislature may not come up with the funding. Closing the Brook Street welfare office would save $250,000, but the public might think the agency was abandoning the people who need services the most?

STEP 4. MAKING DECISIONS   Decision making is easy to describe, but hard to do. After evaluating alternative courses of action, a manager will know a lot about the advantages and disadvantages of each. None will be ideal; sometimes none will seem even tolerable. But the manager must choose one or more plans to put into action. Plans can always be changed, of course, but the choice of a course of action is a genuine commitment that, for example, the money really will be spent, the division closed, or the new product designed.

Managers in Action

Life Office Management Association (LOMA), a trade organization of insurance companies, holds 124 business and educational meetings at various locations each year. Sara Elliot, meetings administrator for LOMA, makes these meetings less costly and more productive by careful advance planning. To do so, Elliot sends planning forms to member companies in areas where seminars are scheduled. Each company is asked to detail its meeting rooms and capacities, travel time from airport to office, and restaurants and hotels nearby. The object is to see if space in member company offices could be used rather than paying for public accommodations.

"I send a cover letter," says Elliot, "explaining that the cost of meeting space is going up, fees will be higher for attendees, and therefore we were looking for ways to hold in-house meetings. There are advantages to using member company space," says Elliot. "The member company where the meeting is held will usually take care of lodging arrangements, audiovisual equipment, chalk and blackboard, and other requirements."

If she decides that it is best to hold a meeting in a public facility, Elliot looks for negotiating points. "If I know that another hotel in the city will give me free meeting space (in return for luncheon guarantees) but I'd rather be in one particular hotel, that is good bargaining power. . . . By negotiating this way in one city, we got five meeting rooms and three discussion parlors at a rate of $25 per room rather than $50."

Source: Muriel Adams, "LOMA Dodges Room Rentals in Booking 124 Small Meetings," *Meeting News*, February 1978, pp. 1–18.

The Complexity of
Planning
The process just described typically produces one planned course of action to achieve one objective. This is just a beginning. Even small organizations have many different objectives at different levels. Each should be supported by a plan.

Planning is complex, but to plan is less complex, and less costly, than not to plan. Orderly, routine planning is far simpler than trying to approach every decision from scratch when it arises. A situation that is dealt with only when forced will be a problem; the same situation dealt with in advance will be an opportunity.

MANAGERS SET OBJECTIVES TO MEET THE NEEDS OF THEIR ORGANIZATIONS
Ask businessmen or businesswomen why they are in business, and chances are good that they will say "to make a profit." Yet, industries with billions of dollars worth of capital invested in facilities and operations return only 2 or 3 percent profit on investments. The capital would earn more profit if kept in savings accounts! This does not mean that profit is an unimportant goal, or objective, of businesses. It does show, however, that most business organizations have a wide range of goals beyond that of making a profit. Moreover, a business serves a purpose even when it does not make the most profitable use of resources. Similarly, government agencies and nonprofit enterprises have a wide range of organization goals. It is important that these multiple aims be recognized and defined when managers plan to meet overall organization objectives.

Overall Objectives
An organization is inseparably related to the lives of its members. An organization's objectives are set by the people who are its members, the employees, participants, and especially the managers. These people choose goals based at least partly on their personal view of what is important, and they modify these goals to try to provide what is needed to make the overall organization strong, healthy, and long lasting. Thus, a particular manager might have a strong desire for prestige in the community. This desire might be incorporated in organization goals and be expressed through a company's charitable work and its luxurious offices. Another manager may have a goal of personal power, and may seek this goal by hiring more people than needed in his or her department. When such personal values and desires conflict with the needs of the organization—when they are so expensive that they threaten its soundness, for instance—their expression in organization goals must be suppressed. Otherwise, the organizational goals will suffer. There are exceptions to this, however, such as ethical values, which will be discussed later.

When establishing an organization's objectives, it is essential to keep in mind the organization's function. Whether it is set up to make money, to administer laws, or for any other reason, an organization performs some kind of processing to create goods and services for people outside the organization. As a practical matter, this processing must be a prime consideration in setting overall goals whether for a business, a government agency, or a nonprofit enterprise. How these overall objectives are developed is discussed below.

BUSINESS ORGANIZATION OBJECTIVES   Businesses produce things of value, of utility, for sale to others. After paying for production and operation costs, good management strives to create a surplus, a profit. Providing quality goods or services that are saleable at a price that will make a profit is an important objective for nearly every business. Overall business objectives go beyond this, however. They often include:

- Creating high quality products for their own sake.
- Operating in a socially responsible way.
- Gaining prestige, respect, and a good company reputation.
- Providing benefits, development and training, and safe and satisfying work conditions for employees.
- Allowing the organization to grow in size and influence.

These are objectives at the highest level, expressed in abstract language. It is better, however, when objectives are expressed in measurable, or at least specific, terms. The top manager of a small manufacturing firm might state overall objectives like this:

"Next year I want to continue to produce kitchen cabinets and to begin making a small line of hardwood bookcases. In spite of the costs of the expansion, I want to keep profits at 6 percent of sales without changing present designs or quality of workmanship. I will involve other managers and employees in decisions about the new products and about other matters and will try to keep employees' compensation about the same as other companies in the area."

NONBUSINESS ORGANIZATION OBJECTIVES   Formal organizations that are not profit-seeking businesses, such as government agencies or colleges and universities, also try to create a surplus, but not in the form of profits. Good management in these organizations creates a bonus of added services from the fixed amount of resources available. On a fixed budget of $1 million, one poorly run state agency might serve 50,000 people. A similar agency with good management in another state might serve 75,000 people as well or better on the same budget. The difference is the surplus created by the good managers.

In addition to their primary objective of carrying out operations in the most cost-effective way, nonbusiness organizations are also concerned with community service and prestige, employee welfare, and social responsibility. In their overall objectives, they typically include statements on these topics.

Subsidiary Objectives   So, if your organization wants to help its employees, do the world some good in the form of products or services, and make money at the same time, how do you do it?

The answer is to create a network of supporting objectives that will, within the limits of available resources, allow the overall objectives to be satisfied. Figure 3-1 shows some interrelationships among objectives at different levels in a manufacturing company. Among the overall goals are (1) creating customer satisfaction by providing high quality products, (2) making a profit of 6 percent of sales, and (3) growing in size. These objectives can be achieved only if other defined goals are reached. Product quality will be improved through finding and using better materials. Reducing waste in production will help pay for the more expensive materials and will contribute to profits. Improving productivity will contribute to profits and will make it possible to increase output to satisfy a larger market share. Advertising the new higher quality of products should win a larger market share, contribute to growth, increase company prestige, improve competitive ability, and help meet a number of other objectives.

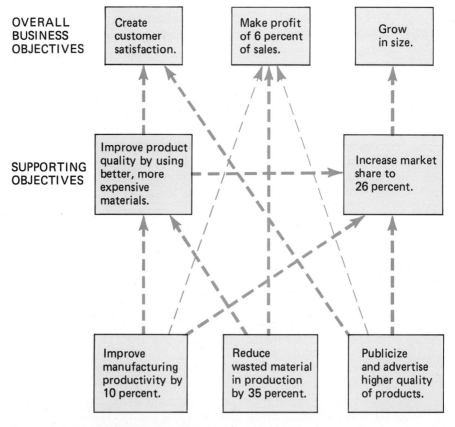

Figure 3-1. Partial Network of Objectives.

The supporting objectives often become the main goals of subdivisions of the overall organization. For the company portrayed in Figure 3-1, the production department, for example, would include among its objectives "to improve productivity by 10 percent and reduce waste by 35 percent." A purchasing department objective might be to locate and obtain certain quantities of new materials with defined high-quality characteristics. Lower-level objectives then would be constructed to lead to meeting the department objectives.

It is often a good idea to begin company planning by thinking of higher-level supporting objectives independently of the specific department that might carry out the work to meet them. This encourages setting goals that meet real organization needs. It avoids the tendency to continue to do what has always been done in the past. The overall objectives can then be modified when necessary when they are included in specific operating plans of divisions or departments.

How to Set Objectives

Setting objectives is the real "make or break" phase of planning. Managers must make objectives ambitious enough that they will push the organization to strive for improvement and success. At the same time, objectives should be practical so that managers and their subordinates will really use them as concrete, attainable goals. With good objectives, hard work and creativity make the planning program and the organization work. A few specific guidelines help in setting objectives.

1. *Write them down.* Objectives should be made explicit in writing. This helps to ensure that they have been clearly thought out. Things sometimes look different in black and white. Written objectives are then available for frequent reference and are more easily communicated to everyone who is expected to help achieve them.

2. *Make them concrete.* If you have a goal like "manage the department better," it will be impossible to tell whether you have achieved the goal or not. Objectives should be measurable when possible, such as: "Increase output by 1,500 units in the first six months." However, being "number happy" will not solve every problem. Many goals are best defined qualitatively. Measurable statistics on employee turnover and absenteeism, for example, will tell you a lot about the job satisfaction and morale of employees, but honest opinions in open communication may tell you more.

3. *Start at the top and work down.* Set high-level objectives first. Then work out each set of lower-level goals to contribute to meeting the goals above it. Clarify overall objectives first; judge other objectives in relation to these. It is impossible to set goals for the shipping department without knowing the production and sales goals. It is impossible to know production and sales goals without knowing the financial and market-share goals. Nor can a manager set financial and market-share goals without knowing overall goals.

4. *Encourage participation of others in the organization.* "These are your goals. Meet them!" This method of setting objectives in isolation and then imposing them on the organization is outmoded. Opinions and information from those above and below you in the organization should influence the objectives you set. Those above you will have access to the "big picture." Their guidance will help keep your objectives tuned to overall goals. The people who work for you will often have ideas and knowledge that will be useful in setting objectives, especially in making them practical. Also, it has been shown time and again that people work harder to meet goals which they have played a part in shaping. People who have been involved from the beginning also find more satisfaction and reward when goals are met.

5. *Double check for coordination and conflicts.* More often than most managers would like to admit, totally conflicting goals are adopted simultaneously. Suppose, for example, you want to expand your organization by 20 percent and at the same time pay back 80 percent of its outstanding debt. These goals may be incompatible. Avoiding this problem is the main purpose of a final check of objectives. It helps you to see if plans provide a mutually supporting network of goals that, if accomplished, will allow overall objectives to be met.

6. *Imagine the objectives in action.* One of the best ways to check whether objectives are coordinated is to start with the lowest-level goals and mentally picture what will happen if the goals are met. Then move up through the levels of goals. Bring together all of the objectives for all departments, on a large chart if possible. Imagine the organization actually operating to meet all objectives simultaneously. Does the finance department have a goal that will support the changes in the operations department? Are the salespeople working toward goals that will support the general marketing objectives?

This process of running through a proposed group of actions to check on their results and interactions is called *simulation*. The simulation can be a very sophisticated mathematical process when the actions and goals are defined numerically. In most cases, however, simply sitting down and running through the network of objectives mentally will be very useful. It often reveals holes and conflicts that can be resolved before the objectives are adopted.

ORGANIZATIONS NEED A HIERARCHY OF PLANS

Since objectives exist in a hierarchy in which lower-level goals are set to serve higher ones, it is natural that plans will take this same form. A *comprehensive plan* is one in which this hierarchy is established. It shows specific activities that will be carried out to achieve subgoals and indicates how these will contribute to meeting the overall goals and purpose. In comprehensive planning, all important aspects of an organization are planned.

A comprehensive plan can be arranged in any way that is convenient for a particular manager or organization. A small local government agency with only five or six employees might have a plan of only a few pages. It would show overall objectives and give subgoals for each functional area of the agency. The subgoals would show the specific actions to be carried out in each area. The comprehensive plan of a giant corporation will often be thousands of pages long. In essence, however, it is simply an orderly compilation of subplans for many product lines, divisions, subsidiary companies, and departments. Such a plan is the work of many people and represents in itself a major activity of the company. Table 3-1 illustrates one subplan in a comprehensive plan.

From Abstract to Specific

When specific activities are planned to meet objectives, the plans must be clearly tied to the departments and even to the people in the organization. When objectives were first being set, for instance, "production" may have been viewed as an abstract process in which a certain quantity of products mysteriously appeared. Now it is time to look at every department and work unit and make sure each is settled on its goals and methods.

"Inside" as Well as "Outside"

Plans concentrate on what the organization and its subdivisions must accomplish. They stress, for example, a certain quality of service to a given number of clients, or manufacturing and selling a certain number of products. These are plans directed toward "outside" considerations. Plans also must include provision for maintaining and improving the organization itself. These might be called "inside" plans. The manager of the distribution department for a wholesaler, for instance, will judge her success primarily by the timeliness and cost effectiveness of getting goods shipped to customers. But she also needs plans and goals for a number of activities that do not relate directly to getting goods shipped; for example, training and promoting employees or changing the internal organization of the department. These internally oriented activities are important and should be explicitly included in the plans.

Types of Plans

Whatever level of planning a manager decides is right for the organization, plans should cover certain essential points. Overall goals should be clearly stated. The specific functions of marketing or client relations, production or operations, finance, and personnel usually should be treated separately. Separate consideration should also be given the facilities and equipment an organization uses and the activities needed to develop new products, services, or processes. Typically, all of the kinds of the following plans warrant consideration.

TABLE 3-1. EXAMPLE OF COMPANY OBJECTIVES AND SUPPORTING PLANS FOR INTRODUCING A NEW SHADE OF LIPSTICK.

OBJECTIVE	PLANS
Introduce a new shade of lipstick and have it displayed for sale on counters of 10,000 drug and variety stores in the 12 Southeastern states by the end of 12 months.	1. Earmark $100,000 for developing, producing, advertising, and distributing this new shade. (Finance department.) 2. Develop new shade by end of 3 months. (Research and Development department.) 3. Field test new shade in three consumer test markets by the end of 5 months. (Market Research department.) 4. Secure approval by Food and Drug Administration by end of 6 months. (Legal department.) 5. Design new package by end of 6 months. (Design department.) 6. Review progress toward objectives at end of 6 months and take whatever corrective steps that are necessary. (General manager.) 7. Purchase new production and packaging materials by end of 7 months. (Purchasing department.) 8. Begin production of new shade by end of 8 months. (Production department.) 9. Prepare advertising and promotion campaign for TV and consumer magazines by end of 9 months. (Advertising department.) 10. Have salespeople call on distributors to secure initial orders by end of 10 months. (Sales department.) 11. Ship 40,000 cases of new shade to distributor warehouses by end of 11 months. (Shipping department.) 12. Release advertising campaign to consumer magazines at end of 11 months. (Advertising department.) 13. Release advertising campaign to TV at end of 12 months. (Advertising department.) 14. Check to see that new lipstick is in fact on counters of 10,000 drug and variety stores in 12 Southeastern states. (Spot check by Market Research department.) Take corrective action if necessary. (General manager.) 15. Develop plans for next 12 months for setting new objectives and plans for the new lipstick shade. (General manager, with contributions from Finance, Research and Development, Market Research, Legal, Purchasing, Production, Sales, Advertising, Shipping, and Quality Control departments.)

OVERALL PLAN The overall plan controls the kinds of goods or services an organization provides. It specifies profitability or effectiveness goals and cost and income targets. It describes activities meant to improve the relationship between the organization and the public, whether customers and clients or society as a whole.

PRODUCTION OR OPERATIONS PLAN   This plan describes how facilities will be used to produce the organization's output. It covers such items as purchasing, materials movement, production scheduling, and productivity. This plan usually contains information on production costs and worker utilization, even though related figures often appear in separate financial and personnel plans. Production and operations planning should cover goals and methods for quality control. Sometimes these are made into a separate plan if appropriate to the specific organization.

MARKETING PLAN   For a business, the marketing plan includes the goals and activities associated with pricing, advertising, selling, and distributing its goods and services. Often, separate plans for each of these areas will be combined to form the marketing plan. Agencies and other nonprofit organizations engage in similar contact with clients or other members of the public, and they need similar plans. Marketing plans cover the gathering and analysis of market research and statistics, selling goals and activities, market expansion efforts, order entry and shipping methods, and related activities.

FINANCE PLAN   The purpose of the finance plan is to control the sources and uses of money. It covers borrowing, investment, donations, income from sales, government funding, and all other money the organization will use. It includes goals and methods for using the money to finance operations, expansion, or other activities. It specifies recording (accounting) and auditing plans. A separate plan, called a *cash-flow plan*, is often worked out to make sure that cash will be available to meet bills as they come due. This plan expresses objectives in terms of the dates when certain amounts of money should be received. It projects expenditures for the same periods to make sure the organization does not end up having bills due and nothing to pay them with.

PERSONNEL PLAN   Each department plan may include information on employees needed, training, promotions, and other personnel matters. In addition to this, an overall organization personnel plan will help coordinate employment practices and integrate the development and use of human resources. This plan includes goals for meeting future personnel needs, for developing, training, and promoting current employees, for recruiting and selection, and for the general improvement and development of the internal structure of the organization.

PRODUCT AND PROCESS DEVELOPMENT PLAN   Developing new products is usually a joint effort of marketing, production, and other departments. It is so important to the strength of the whole organization, however, that a separate plan is often made. Product development calls upon resources from everywhere in the organization. Separate product and process (production) planning imposes order on the many efforts, people, and departments that contribute to this essential organizational concern.

FACILITIES PLAN   Each department will often include in its own plan sections on facilities and equipment. An overall facilities plan coordinates and integrates these. Because they are so expensive, physical facilities, machinery, and equipment often set major limits to growth for an organization. Careful planning of future needs and uses is especially important where expenditures are very large, such as in manufacturing plants and office buildings.

PLANS DIFFER IN THE LENGTH OF TIME THEY COVER

If an individual wants to play a little golf or basketball, he or she might plan to do it tomorrow. If the same person wants to plan a career as a stockbroker and then run for the U.S. Senate, he or she will have to plan ahead over a period of decades. The same distinction applies to planning in organizations.

Many important objectives must be planned far into the future. This is especially true of overall objectives and the highest-level goals that support them: the kinds of products or services to offer, the market share for each product, acquisitions of other companies or combinations of agencies, major expansions, or major changes in profitability or financial structure.

Sometimes lower-level activities and objectives also need long-range planning. Many organizations have learned this when installing computer systems. Usually, computers are first used to perform routine accounting jobs, to improve order entry procedures, or for similar "simple" applications. In almost every case, though, it turns out that the conversion from manual to automatic processing takes longer than expected. It often would be better to view such changes in procedures as long-term programs to begin with. That way, their use could be planned over a period of several years. Many operating activities, manufacturing processes, and service procedures fall into the same category.

A Hierarchy in Time

Since high-level objectives tend to be long-term objectives, plans also form a hierarchy in time. Short-range plans and goals are designed to help meet long-term objectives, such as company growth, just as low-level goals and plans support high-level objectives. This has implications for the best way to plan. If a manager starts out by making a lot of short-range changes in the organization, the changes may not work together to reach long-term goals. It is better for the manager to begin by asking, "Where do we want the organization to be in five years?" Then he or she can work backwards in time to help decide on the short-term actions and goals that will put the organization there.

LONG-TERM PLANS   What time periods do managers use? High-level objectives usually are covered in considerable detail in a one-year plan and more generally in a three-to-five year plan. Some organizations use even longer periods. The main focus of these long-term plans is on overall goals such as products or services to be offered, relations with the public and with society as a whole, profitability or efficiency, and company growth.

SHORT-TERM PLANS   Operating plans for subdivisions of an organization, especially on the department level, usually concentrate on a one-year planning period. The goals and planned activities for a department, for instance, usually are set for the coming year. Expenditures, production and sales, quotas, and other targets may then be broken down into three-month quarters or into monthly figures to aid in control. Even on the department level, though, long-term plans should be developed for facilities development, procedures improvement, finance, and other specific areas where they are seen to be needed. It is often misleading to force management activities into a one-year planning period.

DAY-TO-DAY PLANS   Smaller work units may make plans that cover only a few weeks or even a few days. At the level of the shop floor or operations, highly specific daily, weekly, or monthly goals may be set as the work progresses. This requires flexibility, too, so that supervisors may react quickly to changing conditions: new orders, out-of-stock materials, and so forth. It takes constant vigilance and checking, though, to make sure these short-term plans made on the spot are coordinated so as to contribute to formal longer-term plans.

Planning and Managerial Levels

Differences in the time spans of plans affect how far into the future individual managers must look. A first-line supervisor will concentrate on the near term, a few days or weeks in the future. Middle managers are more concerned with a period three months to a year in the future. Top-level managers usually devote most of their planning time to one to five years in the future. See Figure 3-2. Also, as a manager moves up in the organization, he or she normally will devote a greater proportion of the workday to planning.

Uncertainty and the Future

As plans deal with goals further and further in the future, uncertainty increases. In spite of forecasting methods, orderly procedures, and a constantly practical orientation, no one really knows whether production will be 60 percent higher in four years as called for in the plans. Any number of important factors are unpredictable; for example, consumer tastes, government action, interest rates, economic growth, or material and labor supplies. One thing is sure, though: managers are better prepared for the future with planning than without it.

Figure 3-2. Relative Concern for Plan Duration at Three Levels of Management.

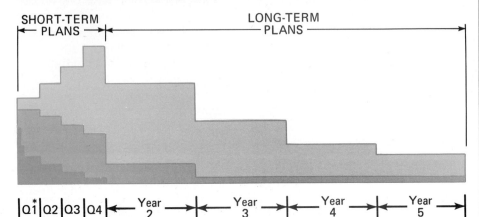

SHORT-TERM PLANS

LONG-TERM PLANS

|Q1*|Q2|Q3|Q4|←— Year 2 —→|←— Year 3 —→|←— Year 4 —→|←— Year 5 —→|

*Q stands for Quarter.

■ First-level supervision
■ Middle management
□ Top-level management

SUMMARY

1. Planning and controlling work together to set objectives, to devise specific activities and methods that will lead to meeting the objectives, and to continually check that actual operations are following planned courses.

2. Plans are guided by the purpose of the organization and by a group of beliefs or assumptions about what future conditions will be. These beliefs are called premises. An organization's purpose should be clearly defined and written down. Premises should be based on the widest information and knowledge possible.

3. Planning is an orderly process of setting objectives, discovering alternate means for reaching the objectives, evaluating the alternatives, and making decisions.

4. Organization objectives exist in a hierarchy. An integrated network of lower-level objectives support the highest-level overall objectives. These objectives should be written and concrete; they should be developed with the cooperation of others; they should be coordinated so they are mutually reinforcing.

5. A group of subplans is needed to support the hierarchy of objectives; the coordinated subplans make up a comprehensive plan. Specific goals and activities are needed in production or operations, marketing, finance, personnel, and in other major areas, depending on the specific organization.

6. High-level plans designed to reach overall objectives are usually long-term, covering a period of up to five years. Plans on the department level usually concentrate on the following year. Some plans for individual work groups may extend for only a few weeks or even a few days.

REVIEW AND DISCUSSION QUESTIONS

1. What is the relationship between planning and controlling? Can either be eliminated?

2. What are two main factors that influence the specific plans an organization makes? What are the practical implications of these for managers?

3. Briefly describe the steps of an orderly planning procedure.

4. Why should managers plan in the first place, if the organization is running well?

5. How might a nonprofit, private college define its overall goals?

6. What is wrong with an objective like "manage the department better"? How could it be improved?

7. When setting objectives, why start at the top and work down?

8. Why is it a good idea to invite the participation of others in the organization when setting objectives?

9. What is comprehensive planning? What are its advantages? Can you think of any disadvantages it might have?

10. Why do plans differ in the length of time they cover? How is this related to levels in an organization?

Problems and Projects

1. The following list contains some of the objectives set by a medium-sized business organization. Arrange them into a hierarchy by placing each in one of three categories: low level objectives, medium level objectives, or high level (overall) objectives. Do these objectives form a network? Do lower-level objectives support higher-level ones? What are some objectives you might want to add if you managed this company?

    a. Diversify product line to overcome cyclical changes in sales volume.

    b. Manufacture 5,000 transformers in next six weeks.

    c. Develop alternative suppliers of transformer cases to increase competition among suppliers.

    d. Make a profit of 4 percent of sales.

e. Increase market share from 9 percent to 15 percent.
f. Increase productivity in the plant by 5 percent.
g. Expand existing plant by adding one line (increasing capacity by 20 percent).
h. Ship all orders from stock within 72 hours of receipt of order.
i. Reduce average inventory on hand by 10 percent.
j. Increase by 10 percent the sale of transformers for use as components by other manufacturers.
k. Maintain current rate of sales to end users such as local power companies.
l. Reduce total worker hours required for unloading and receiving supplies and components to 10,800 hours per year from the current 11,200 hours in spite of the expansion.
m. Reduce machine downtime rate by 3 percent.
n. Finish the paper work on the new government order before Christmas holiday.
o. Expose 2,000 new potential industrial customers to advertising.

2. A middle-level administrator for a state division of trade and commerce set up a list of objectives for her department. After trying them for a year, though, she found that they really did not help much in guiding her decision making and other management responsibilities. It also became obvious that her subordinates were completely ignoring the objectives while doing things the way they always had. These are some of the objectives:

- Handle licensing of businesses and corporations better and faster.
- Prepare more effective displays for trade shows and business association meetings.
- Do a better job of presenting the advantages of the state to companies considering locating here.
- Gather more accurate statistical information and present it in a more useful way.
- Improve management of the department.

Why did these objectives not work better? Rewrite them so they would be more likely to succeed. You may want to divide some into more than one objective.

3. *Performance Situation—The Hot Stove Market:* Suddenly, when the fuel shortage struck, everyone wanted wood-burning stoves to heat with. Simon Vintnor thought he was ready. He had been in the hardware business for 9 years, had a good supplier, and had given the opportunity a lot of thought. Vintnor made careful annual plans. For the coming year he projected that sales, not counting wood stoves, would bring in $180,000. Total costs, including the cost of goods sold during the year, payroll, rent, and everything else, were expected to be $165,000. The profit of $15,000 would be about average, although not quite as good as last year.

Vintnor hopes to add to these profits by meeting the sharp demand for wood stoves. He sets his profit goal for the year at $20,000. The stoves are a good item for a hardware store, anyway, because they are priced more like furniture than like the typical hardware item: the average stove costs Vintnor $100 and sells at retail for $180. Each of the three models sells about equally well.

Question: Assuming that selling the stoves does not increase other costs such as payroll or rent, how many stoves would Simon have to sell to meet his profit goal of producing a $5,000 profit from store sales?

Vintnor knows that he will not sell many stoves without advertising. He sets two general goals: advertise enough to sell enough stoves to meet his profit goal, and design the ads to establish his store as a well-known source of wood stoves. Using knowledge of his market, information from the stove manufacturer, and his general experience, Simon makes this table:

ADVERTISING EXPENSE	EXPECTED NUMBER OF UNITS SOLD
a. $ 0.00	15
b. 1200.00	40
c. 2800.00	85
d. 3800.00	110
e. 6000.00	125

A. Vintnor's profit on sales for items other than stoves is 8 percent (15,000 ÷ 180,000 = .083 = 8%). What will his profit percentage be if he chooses alternative *d* in the table above? What if he chooses alternative *e?* Don't forget that advertising cost is an expense.

B. What should Vintnor set as his sales objective for wood stoves?

C. How can Vintnor tell if his advertising objectives are being achieved?

4. *Performance Situation—Funding for Learning Disabilities:* There was never enough money at Learning Disabilities, Inc. Linnitz could not get the new equipment when he needed it. Samuelson is working even longer hours than usual because she needs another assistant. Hunt passed up the conference in Frankfurt to save the money to pay for more data processing. As executive director of LD, Inc., Kate Schulz spent a lot of her time just making sure the organization had enough money and other resources to keep on operating at its present level.

Not that money was her only concern. LD, Inc. is a nonprofit corporation, and Kate and the rest of the staff had an underlying dedication to something beyond the balance sheet. They considered their work on learning disabilities to be a high calling, and Kate stretched their resources to the absolute limit to get as much results for the dollar as possible. The work of collecting research studies on learning disabilities and communicating them to agencies that provide practical therapy and rehabilitation was fairly routine. Years of trimming costs and improving methods had made that activity about as efficient and inexpensive as possible. Much the same was true of the work to provide technical assistance to agencies looking for funding, although there were occasionally some nasty surprises like crisis workloads to meet deadlines.

Performing research was the big item that kept Kate scrambling to get as much money as possible for the corporation. She and her colleagues worked continually to get more donations, grants, and contracts to finance their expanding research program. They dreamed of growing to a really substantial size in order to be able to support the expensive equipment and ambitious programs their work needed to succeed.

And they were making progress. The aggressive program to make the public aware of LD, Inc., was paying off. The good administrative record of the corporation was earning the respect both of the general public and the agencies the corporation dealt with. Kate's thorough efforts to improve the professional skills of the staff, to tighten up operating procedures, and to sharpen her own and others' management skills were bringing in more money and making better use of it.

Describe the purpose of this organization as if you were going to use the statement as a basis for planning. Write four to six overall objectives for LD, Inc. Make them as specific as possible.

5. The study of business and management is increasingly popular at campuses everywhere. This has created a bind at many schools. Many more students want to take introductory management courses, but the department budgets for teaching these courses have not increased proportionately. In some cases, budgets have even been reduced. An administrator at one such school was planning for the next two years. He set down three alternative actions:

   a. Add no new general management courses; restrict enrollments to present levels.
   b. Increase the teaching load of instructors by requiring each to take on two more general management classes.
   c. Eliminate specialized small-enrollment advanced classes and transfer these instructors to general management classes.

Evaluate these alternatives as if you have to make the decision. What are some advantages and disadvantages of each? What would you decide to do? Are there better alternatives?

6. Write down your immediate career goals for the next five years. State the objectives specifically so you would be able to tell if they were being achieved or not. Describe at least three alternative courses of action that will lead to achieving your objectives. Evaluate the alternatives and choose one. What basis did you use for the evaluation? Are the objectives important enough to you and is the evaluation of alternatives convincing enough that you feel committed to the chosen course of action?

Cases for Analysis and Discussion

CASE 1: WHERE DO WE GO FROM HERE?

The three art students thought that their T-shirts with the Rosetta stone, a sixteenth-century Durer engraving of a rhinoceros, and other esoteric graphics looked pretty good. They had sound design, visual sophistication, and a large dose of snob appeal. Others agreed, notably such stores as Saks Fifth Avenue, Lord & Taylor, and Henri Bendel. The shirts were a hit; they sold quickly to affluent, sophisticated buyers.

The Williams College students, Blair Brewster, Susan Lyons, and Phillip Eagleburger, together with their professor, Thomas Krens, and some other interested people struggled to form a company after their initial success. As usual, money for growth was hard to find. Production problems cropped up. Management experience was lacking. But they succeeded, propelled by strong consumer demand for the highbrow design of their T-shirts. Their company, Alliance Editions, Inc., had 1976 sales of $42,000. 1977 sales were expected to be twelve times that, at $500,000. In 1977, though, Alan Ulick, director of fashion merchandising at Lord & Taylor, said of T-shirts, "It's last year's look." Nevertheless, Alliance Editions, Inc., did not lack creativity. Its principals came up with some 300 different designs in two years. However, more than creativity would be needed if their sole product died as a fast-selling item.[1]

A. What kind of planning is Alliance in need of? When should the planning ideally have been started?
B. What do you think the overall objectives of this company might be?
C. What course do you think Alliance should follow? What should its long-range plans be? What can it do to meet its objectives?

CASE 2: OFF WE GO, INTO THE WILD BLUE YONDER

Allen never thought he was the greatest management talent in the country, or even in Mantua, Wisconsin, population 28,900. But things had gone quite well ever since his father had left him as majority owner and president of Northcentral Wholesale. Allen had studied management and used a lot of the formal methods he had learned. He planned; he kept good

[1] Based on "Genesis of a Firm: Three Art Students in a Seminar Project," *Wall Street Journal*, December 19, 1977.

books; he put a lot of his own time into handling the really large retail accounts because they were what kept the company going.

But the other owners of Northcentral were not happy. They complained that profits were not what they had been when Allen's father had run the company. They thought the new offices were too fancy. They thought meat and potatoes were good enough for entertaining clients, while Allen preferred champagne and caviar. And they nearly went through the roof when they saw this item in the plans for the coming year:

"Objective: Reduce travel costs for personally servicing major clients throughout the Midwest.

"Means: Purchase company airplane for use of president, sales manager, and other sales personnel as available. Specifications and costs are attached."

A. Why is Allen making plans that displease the other owners of Northcentral?

B. Who is right here, Allen or the other owners? How would you be able to tell?

C. Is there anything Allen could do as part of the planning process to make the other owners less unhappy?

CASE 3: I'LL PLAN IT, YOU DO IT

Margaret Pittman included this introduction in the work unit plans she gave to each of her subordinate supervisors:

I have prepared the following plans for your work unit for the coming year. As you know, our agency is in a transition period; in the future we will have far greater responsibilities than in the past. For this reason, it is more important than ever that you read these plans and give every effort during the year to meet the goals I have set. I have determined the specific objectives you are to meet and the methods you are to use. This has been done only after careful study of our operations, of forecasts of workloads, of changes in other agencies that will affect you, and of many other factors. These goals are essential to the efficiency of our organization. I hope you will view them that way and do your best to meet them.

Margaret felt some kind of pep talk was needed because most of the work units had not really done a good job of following plans in the past. Everyone had worked hard, but they hadn't followed planned priorities. They had worked on the wrong projects. They had even seemed to go out of their way to miss deadlines and to otherwise interfere with meeting the objectives set for them.

A. Why might Margaret's employees be acting this way?
B. Do you think her introduction will work? How will the supervisors and workers respond?
C. What should Margaret do to get better cooperation in meeting planned objectives?

CASE 4: TAKE CARE OF TOMORROW, AND TODAY WILL TAKE CARE OF ITSELF

"Bob, I'm afraid we've got another problem. You know we were running a little late on that order for Lake Equipment? Well, we're going to be even later. We didn't get our order for flanges in on time and we're going to run out of parts early next week."

Elliot's interruption was a jolt to Bob, even though he should have been used to it by now. The bad news had a particularly sour taste because Bob had just been feeling especially satisfied with himself. As the top manager in his young company, Bob believed in devoting much of his time to long-range planning. He was congratulating himself on finishing an unusually thorough five-year forecast and plan. Everything for 1985 was there in clear, orderly sections: products, customer demand, sales strategy, financial sources and uses, quality control, plant expansion, and all the rest. Bob had even worked with the economics department at a nearby university to get special projections of economic factors important to his industry.

But Elliot's news about the Lake Equipment order added to a suspicion that had been gnawing at Bob: maybe things weren't going so well. Running out of parts might be just a routine mistake, but there had been a lot of routine mistakes recently. The gearbox cases for the government had been shipped out before anyone realized that they didn't meet specifications. In June, the controller saw that cash was so short that they couldn't even meet the payroll; they had to go out and get a short-term loan to pay employees.

Bob was beginning to think, "Maybe this planning isn't a very practical approach after all."

A. Is Bob right? Is long-term planning an impractical approach in the real world?
B. What do you think Bob's trouble is? Is he correct in believing that top-level managers concentrate on long-term planning?
C. If Bob becomes convinced that he has to make some changes, what should he do?
D. Is Bob's company likely to meet its long-term objectives if things continue as they are now? Why or why not?

Forecasting and Premising

LONG RANGE CHART
19X3
19X2   19X
19X1

BUDGET

4

After completing Chapter 4, you will be able to do the following:

- Describe the purpose of planning premises, and identify the kind of forecast needed to establish a specific premise.
- Estimate the extent to which a given premise is internal or external, controllable or uncontrollable, measurable or not measurable.
- Describe four areas of an organization's environment for which premises may be needed, and give examples of premises for each area.
- Identify some sources of data

and of forecasts for external premises, and provide some examples of the use of specific external forecasting in management planning.
- Name and describe some general types of internal premises used in planning, and utilize internal forecasts to establish premises and plans.
- Propose specific internal forecasts that will be useful for decision making in a given organization.

Would you have thought of inventing an appliance to grill a single sandwich, or to deep-fry one serving of french fries, or to slow-cook just enough stew for one person? Would you have developed soup-for-one as Campbell Soup Company did, or started packaging casseroles in single servings as Green Giant Company has? If in your planning you had studied forecasts of household sizes in the United States, the answer is yes, you very well might have.

Looking at figures available to everyone from the federal government, you would find that the average household size in 1900 was 5.8 persons. Since then, family size has continuously and drastically shrunk. By 1976, there were fewer than three people in the average household. When you think of how many households there are with husbands, wives, and children living together, that must mean that there are a lot of people living alone.

There are. Almost sixteen million people in the United States live by themselves. In 1977 they accounted for 21 percent of all households, up from 17 percent only seven years earlier. For a number of years, most signs have pointed to a continuing trend toward more people living alone. The divorce rate continues to climb; people are marrying later or not at all; older people prefer to, or are forced to, have their own place rather than live with their children. And there are more old people because people are living longer. All of these people living alone create demands for specialized products. Manufacturers with foresight seek to tap this demand.

It takes many months, if not years, to develop and manufacture a gadget to grill a sandwich. How did the appliance makers know enough to start development in time to have the product on the market just when single-person households were becoming significant? They knew because they made plans based on forecasts of future conditions.

PREMISES FORM THE BASIS FOR MANAGERIAL PLANNING

When managers plan, they follow this train of thought: "We believe A, B, and C will be true during the next year and, therefore, we will do X, Y, and Z." The A, B, and C in this statement are *planning premises*. These are beliefs, or assumptions, about future conditions that have been developed or adopted specifically for use as a sound basis for planning. An example of a premise is, "We will assume that short-term interest rates on loans to small businesses will average 14 percent during the next year." Based on this premise, a small business might plan to borrow as little money as possible.

Premises are derived from forecasts. A *forecast* is a prediction about some future event or condition. A forecast becomes a premise only when it is accepted by management as an expectation upon which active plans will be based.

Premises vary in a number of ways. For plans made by organizations, managers distinguish between premises dealing with conditions outside the organization, such as the economic situation, and premises about conditions inside the organization, such as production costs. "The gross national product will increase by 6.5 percent in 1981," is an *external premise*. "Machine number six will be worn out by 1982," is an *internal premise*.

Premises also differ in the degree to which managers can control them. Individual managers have no real control over most external conditions such as gross national product, population levels, income levels, or competitors' actions. Some external factors, however, are partly controllable. Public opinion, for example, often can be swayed through advertising and publicity. Government actions can sometimes be influenced by lobbying and information campaigns.

Premises about internal conditions are usually more controllable. A manager who predicts a 20 percent increase in the number of employees can make the prediction come true simply by hiring 20 more people for every 100 on the payroll now. Many internal factors are not this controllable, of course. A prediction of sales revenues is usually viewed as an internal premise, but if customers will not buy, there often is little that managers can do about it.

Premises also vary considerably in how concrete they are and how well they can be measured. Some premises are very concrete: "One out of every five American families will buy a new or used car next year"; "The average employment rate for the year will be 6.4 percent." Others are necessarily far less tangible: "Selling price will have far more influence on buying decisions than in recent years." "Untested food additives will be less acceptable to the public." In general, premises, like objectives, should be made as measurable as possible. But important factors should never be ignored just because specific numbers cannot be attached to them.

GOOD PLANS REFLECT THE CONDITIONS EXPECTED IN THE OUTSIDE WORLD

External premises define what managers think the world outside of the organization will be like during the time covered by its plans. As with the weather, everybody talks about the environment, the social, political, and economic forces that surround their organization, but no one can do much about it. Nevertheless, it is essential that we try to anticipate changes in the environment, even if we cannot control them.

Common Types of External Premises

A manager who tries to anticipate everything in the environment that could possibly have a favorable or adverse effect on company operations will soon have to give up in dismay. The unexpected death of the leader of a foreign country can disrupt the economy in that country, causing a shortage of raw materials. A storm can damage facilities. An unusually cool summer can change retail buying habits on the local level. Fortunately, forecasting external influences can be useful even if every base is not covered. Managers usually look for changes and form premises in four major areas: government action, economic conditions, social changes, and technological developments.

GOVERNMENT ACTION Most decisions that managers make today are influenced by some kind of government regulation or influence. Government rules directly affect nearly every issue with which managers are concerned: pricing, personnel practices, hiring, advertising, competitive practices, mergers and acquisitions, labor policy, packaging, shipping, labeling, materials used, customer relations, and safety. Government policies toward money supply, imports and exports, domestic trade, and many other factors are basic to determining the economic conditions an organization must face.

Governments work slowly. The manager who looks for it will find advance warning of government actions, such as in proposed laws, changes in policy, court cases, and legal interpretations. Even without change, existing laws and policies in effect create planning premises as do new laws and shifts in policy.

THE ECONOMY The economy can be defined in many ways. For planning premises, it is convenient to view it as a gigantic mass of financial transactions among governments, businesses, nonprofit organizations, and individuals. Everyone is continually buying from and selling to everyone else. Businesses buy materials, equipment, and supplies from other companies and pay employees for their work. The employees, in turn, buy the goods and services that yet other businesses provide. The government buys goods and services from businesses, pays its own employees, and distributes social security, welfare, and other payments. Businesses and individuals, in turn, make tax payments to governments in return for the services the governments provide.

This vast complex of interactions undergoes rapid fluctuations while also undergoing long-term changes. This is described as "the state of the economy." It reflects and controls prices, interest rates, material and labor supply, energy availability, market demand, and scores of other important variables that affect organizational plans.

Many economic influences are hard to understand and use in planning. Their interpretation often requires the help of a person with an education in economics. Every manager who plans, though, should take into account certain key economic factors, especially business cycles, inflation, money supply, and interest rates. Other more specific factors such as projected labor and materials costs and the availability of investment capital are also vital. An example of the use of this kind of economic information is given later in the chapter.

SOCIAL CHANGES   Historical research helps to identify past changes in beliefs, morals, interests, and desires. Understanding these changes while they are taking place, or particularly *before* they take place, is a far harder task. Yet, a good manager must try.

The effects of the beliefs and attitudes that surround an organization are subtle. They are often hard to recognize, but may spell the difference between success and failure. Social factors strongly affect markets. Fashions change; customer tastes and desires change. These changes can cause products and services to become obsolete very rapidly; the hula hoop and the Nehru jacket are notable examples. Social changes can also create markets overnight, as happened recently with CB radios and skateboards.

Society at large effects management practices by enforcing its ethical beliefs. Vigorous movements to protect the interests of consumers and to save the environment, for example, have forced important changes upon organizations of all kinds. Product standards, employment opportunities for minorities, and fair treatment of competitors are other examples.

Expectations of workers have risen markedly as a result of social forces. Increasingly, employees ask for job satisfaction and personal fulfillment at work in addition to good wages. Managers consider such expectations in their plans.

TECHNOLOGICAL FORECASTS   As the pace of technical discovery has quickened, managers, scientists, and scholars have begun to predict its future course. Such predictions are called *technological forecasting*. The

Managers in Action

When virtually 100 percent of all wired American homes have an electric refrigerator, how much further can a company's appliance business grow? That is the kind of question posed by General Electric Company's top executives to its managers of strategic planning. These managers, together with their staffs of economists and market researchers, had to come up with reliable forecasts about the future. Based on their estimates in 1976, GE's top management would decide how much to invest in tooling and equipment and in building and manufacturing and marketing staffs.

Here's what the planners forecast. Of the 78 million refrigerators in use in 1976, many are over ten years old; accordingly, the replacement market ought to total 6 million units a year. There were some 350 million large appliance units of all kinds; the expectation was that 55 percent of all future sales will represent replacements. This is mainly because the replacement cycle will shrink from 10–12 years to nearer 5 because of new technology and the demand for more energy efficient models.

The planners also expected the "saturation" usage levels of many appliances to rise due to a forecast increase of women in the work force from 47 percent in 1976 to 55 percent in 1990. This would raise the potential for sales of dishwashers, clothes dryers, microwave ovens, and trash compactors. And the planners also pointed to growth of international markets for appliances at double the U.S. rate.

An important contributing factor in the appliance market was the forecast for continuing growth in real disposable personal incomes. It was roughly $12,300 per household in 1976 and forecast to rise to $14,000 in 1982.

Source: "Unfinished Business in the Home," *General Electric Investor*, Winter 1977, pp. 15–19.

goal is to determine when particular technical developments, inventions, and scientific discoveries will be made and what their effect will be on human life and society. Forecasting methods include projections of past trends, surveys of current research, and the informed opinion of experts.

Technological forecasting is not idle dreaming; it can be of practical value. It can reveal new processes, materials, and products that should be planned for now, even though they may not be available for a number of years. It may give clues to the kinds of developments that may be expected from competitors. It may reveal the likelihood of new consumer needs or new markets. Even if the technical developments discovered do not directly relate to a particular organization, related needs may arise. In the past, for example, the railroads brought prosperity to many companies by providing efficient transportation or by creating a demand for the equipment needed to build and operate the railroads. The automobile spawned huge industries in tires and accessories, oil refining, accident insurance, road building, and auto servicing. It also fostered the mobility that brought about the tremendous surge of suburban shopping and housing.

Table 4-1 provides a checklist of areas external to an organization for which planning premises may be needed. Any given item may not be important for a particular company, department, or agency. Each, however, has a potential influence and should be considered when planning. It pays for a manager to develop a list like this of the specific premises that are influential in his or her organization. Through the years, experience will show what factors are truly vital and which are not. Prudent managers will check their lists every planning period to be sure they are not ignoring any relevant factors in the plans they make.

Information For External Premising

Good premises require that managers be well informed. Much of what is discussed in newspapers, on radio and TV, in movies, books, magazines, and in conversations bears some relationship to environmental influences. Trade, industry, and professional organizations provide members with relevant data and interpretations concerning government, economic, and technical developments. Governments, especially the federal government of the United States, are important information sources about their own actions and about changes and trends in economic, social, and technical areas. The U.S. Department of Commerce is an invaluable source of market data; the *Federal Register* publishes detailed information on regulations, legislation, and pending federal actions. Many states provide similar services.

Other government publications and the general business press give periodical statistical reports on hundreds of measures and indicators of current and projected business and financial conditions. The *Business Conditions Digest*, published by the Bureau of Economic Analysis of the U.S. Department of Commerce, gives detailed information on cyclical indicators, employment, production, capital investment, prices, money and credit, and other topics, both in tabular and graphic form. The *Federal Reserve Bulletin* publishes extensive statistical data with an emphasis on financial activities and conditions. Table 4-2 shows a typical format. Changes and trends in this data are easier to estimate from a graphic plot of the tabular data, such as the one shown in Figure 4-1, based on part of the information given in Table 4-1.

Nearly every publication specializing in business and finance provides digests and summaries of important economic indicators. A partial example from *Business Week* is given in Table 4-3.

TABLE 4-1. CHECKLIST OF FACTORS IN THE EXTERNAL ENVIRONMENT FOR WHICH PLANNING PREMISES MAY BE NEEDED.

I. Government Actions
  A. Direct Regulation
    1. Advertising and publicity
    2. Personnel practices, hiring, promotions, equal rights and labor regulations
    3. Antitrust, competitive practices, mergers, and acquisitions
    4. Solicitation of investment, stock and bond sales
    5. Pricing
    6. Packaging, labeling, and shipping
    7. Employee safety
    8. Product safety
    9. Accounting, reporting, and taxation
    10. Customer relations, truth of claims
  B. Indirect Influence
    1. Government budgets, procurement practices, purchasing, and employment
    2. Employment subsidies and policies
    3. Monetary policy influencing money supply and interest rates
    4. Import-export aids, tariffs, quotas, and controls
    5. Taxation policies and practices
    6. Subsidies in agriculture and other areas
    7. Other direct economic influence programs, antiinflation "jawboning", and so forth

II. The Economy
  A. Business Cycles
    1. Inventories
    2. Capital spending
    3. Employment and unemployment
    4. New business formations
  B. Consumer Demand
    1. Real income
    2. Savings
    3. Credit load and availability
    4. Inflation and prices
    5. Spending patterns based on economic factors
    6. Poverty
  C. Nonfinancial Resources
    1. Labor supply and cost, productivity, strikes and work stoppages
    2. Materials supply, shortages, and cost
    3. Energy supplies and cost
    4. Facility and equipment availability and cost
  D. Financial Resources
    1. Credit availability
    2. Interest rates
    3. Investment patterns
    4. Securities volumes and prices
  E. Foreign Competitive and Supply Patterns

III. Social Influences
  A. Population Factors
    1. Population size
    2. Growth rate
    3. Composition by sex, age, education, vocation, place of residence, and so forth
  B. Market Factors
    1. Tastes, fashions, and fads
    2. Spending patterns based on interests, leisure activities, attitudes, and beliefs
  C. Active Social Pressure
    1. Consumerism
    2. Environmental protection and improvement
  D. Work Force Influences
    1. Worker expectations, the work ethic
    2. New entrants to work force; women, youth, minorities, and handicapped workers
    3. Educational preparation
  E. Ethical Influences
    1. Management practices
    2. Organizational functions in community

IV. Technological Developments
  A. Products
  B. Processes
  C. Materials and Energy Sources
  D. Demands
    1. Consumer or client
    2. Industrial
    3. Government

TABLE 4-2. TYPICAL TABLE OF DATA ON BUSINESS AND FINANCIAL CONDITIONS PUBLISHED MONTHLY IN THE *FEDERAL RESERVE BULLETIN*: EXPENDITURES ON NEW PLANT AND EQUIPMENT.											
INDUSTRY	1977	1978	1978				1979			
			Q1*	Q2	Q3	Q4	Q1	Q2	Q3	Q4[2]
1 All industries	135.72	153.60	144.25	150.76	155.41	163.96	165.94	173.48	175.29	179.56
Manufacturing										
2 Durable goods industries	27.75	31.59	28.72	31.40	32.25	33.99	34.00	36.86	38.03	40.38
3 Nondurable goods industries	32.33	35.86	32.86	35.80	35.50	39.26	37.56	39.56	40.27	41.58
Nonmanufacturing										
4 Mining	4.49	4.81	4.45	4.81	4.99	4.98	5.46	5.31	5.30	5.58
Transportation										
5 Railroad	2.82	3.33	3.35	3.09	3.38	3.49	4.02	3.66	4.13	3.92
6 Air	1.63	2.34	2.67	2.08	2.20	2.39	3.35	3.26	2.92	3.15
7 Other	2.55	2.42	2.44	2.23	2.47	2.55	2.71	2.79	3.24	3.08
Public utilities										
8 Electric	21.57	24.71	23.15	23.83	24.92	26.95	27.70	28.06	28.52	27.46
9 Gas and other . .	4.21	4.72	4.78	4.62	4.70	4.78	4.66	5.18	4.74	5.33
10 Communication . . .	15.43	18.15	17.07	18.18	18.90	18.46	18.75	20.29	} 48.13	49.08
11 Commercial and other[1]	22.95	25.67	24.76	24.71	26.09	27.12	27.73	28.51		

*Q1 means first quarter, Q2 second quarter, and so on.
1. Includes trade, service, construction, finance, and insurance.
2. Anticipated by business.

NOTE. Estimates for corporate and noncorporate business, excluding agriculture; real estate operators; medical, legal, educational, and cultural service; and nonprofit organizations.

Source: *Survey of Current Business* (U.S. Dept. of Commerce).

Local and state chambers of commerce and the U.S. Chamber of Commerce are useful sources, especially of local data. Specific newsletters zero in on a variety of fields. Economic forecasts are available from many universities, from the National Planning Association, and from government sources such as the President's Council of Economic Advisors. Information on technological forecasting and the forecasts themselves are available at large libraries. Reports from the Hudson Institute, the Rand Corporation, and other "think tanks" cover an enormous range of topics.

Also available is a tremendous amount of raw statistical data, which is useful when managers wish to make their own forecasts. Again, the federal government and state and local governments are prime sources. A good starting place is with two publications of the Bureau of the Census of the U.S. Department of Commerce: *Directory of Federal Statistics for States* and *Directory of Non-Federal Statistics for States and Local Areas*. These two

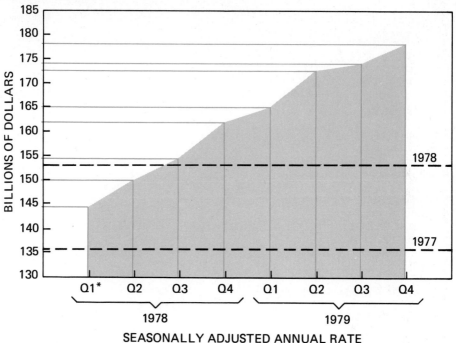

Figure 4-1. Graphic Presentation of Business Expenditures on New Plant and Equipment for All Industries.

*Q stands for Quarter.

Source: *Federal Reserve Bulletin,* vol. 66, no. 1, January 1980, p. A38.

guides lead to much of the statistical data published by the federal and state governments. In the second directory, for instance, you can learn that among dozens of statistical summaries of the California state government, information as detailed as wages and hours in laundries and cleaning services is available. The two directories cover sources of data on such diverse subjects as population, health and vital statistics, education, income and earnings, labor and employment, vocational rehabilitation, welfare services, public grants and services, construction, commerce and trade, and banking and finance.

Informed managers use the library, take advantage of the skills of the librarians, and ask others in their field where they get their information. They contact associations related to their industry. Anyone can call the federal information telephone number listed in the local telephone book or in the directory of a large city nearby. Staying on top of the information needed for developing thorough and reliable premises is the manager's responsibility.

TABLE 4-3. EXAMPLE OF ECONOMIC INDICATORS IN BUSINESS PUBLICATIONS: PRODUCTION INDICATORS FROM *BUSINESS WEEK.*

FIGURES OF THE WEEK		LATEST WEEK		PREVIOUS WEEK	MONTH AGO	YEAR AGO	1967 AVERAGE
Production Indicators							
Raw steel/Amer. Iron & Steel Inst., thous. of net tons ..	Dec. 8	2,290		2,270#	2,385	2,705	2,440
Automobiles/*Ward's Automotive Reports*	Dec. 8	147,959		145,872r#	180,629	193,728	142,438
Trucks/*Ward's Automotive Reports*	Dec. 8	47,640	I	43,863r#	43,363	85,811	30,490
Electric power/Edison Elec. Inst., millions of killowatt-hours	Dec. 8	44,843	N D E	43,360#	41,910	44,086	23,169
Crude-oil refinery runs/Amer. Pet. Inst., daily av., thous. of bbl.	Dec. 8	14,667	X	15,071#	14,366	15,716	9,815
Bituminous coal/Energy Dept., thous. of net tons.......	Dec. 1	15,235#		14,000	16,670	16,270	10,627
Paperboard/Amer. Paper Inst., thous. of tons	Dec. 1	620.4#	W E	615.5	640.8	584.0	438.8
Paper/Amer. Paper Inst., thous. of tons................	Dec. 1	591.0#	E K	600.0r	605.0	537.0	402.8
Lumber/WWPA, SFPA, 225 mills, millions of ft.	Dec. 1	206.5#		101.2	220.4	238.6	186.4
Rail freight traffic/Assn. of Amer. RRs, billions of ton-miles	Dec. 1	17.8#		15.2	18.3	18.8	13.8

Source: *Business Week*, December 24, 1979, p. 2.

SELECTED EXTERNAL FORECASTS IMPROVE PLANNING PREMISES

Many external premises can be based on specific numerical data or on mathematical forecasts. Many trends that affect plans show up in basic figures on population, income, economic activity, finance, and employment.

How Forecasts are Made

A forecast was defined at the beginning of this chapter as any prediction about some future event or condition. This covers a lot of territory. Managers often limit the definition to include only estimates of future conditions that are based on some systematic study and understanding of past and current conditions. Specifically, many have come to believe that the best forecasts are based on the statistical analysis of numerical measurements. Others, however, still stress the prime value of the judgment of an experienced and informed manager. The most common view today probably is that both statistics and judgment are needed.

The easiest way to "make" a forecast is to buy or borrow forecasts made by others in areas critical to the organization. General and specific economic forecasts are regularly made by a number of universities, especially the University of Maryland, University of Pennsylvania, and U.C.L.A. Government agencies publish completed forecasts; some of the best known are developed by the staff of the President's Council of Economic Advisors. Private companies also make forecasts for publication or sale.

Many managers, though, will wish to make and use their own forecasts in areas of specific interest, and certainly will want to have some understanding of the process by which forecasts are made by others. Modern statistical forecasting is a complex and sophisticated discipline; mastery requires lengthy and detailed study. An exposure to some essentials, though, is helpful in understanding the forecasts used for establishing external premises—and for projecting internal conditions, discussed later.

HISTORICAL PATTERNS   A common way of making forecasts is to analyze past measurements of some important condition or performance, and to project the past behavior into the future, assuming that the trends and cycles found up to this point will continue. A furniture wholesaler, for example, might find that company income this past year was closely related to the number of new people entered on the tax rolls in the region. Forecasting the size of this tax-paying population is thus useful in planning. The simplest way to make this forecast is to look at changes in the annual population size and, if a consistent increase or decrease is found, to project that change into the future. If the number of taxpayers has increased about 3 percent a year and is currently 100,000, for instance, the forecasters would project the number to be 103,000 next year, 106,090 the following year, and so on.

However, such consistent changes are seldom found in the real world. Hidden patterns often underlie figures on total population, sales volume, the unemployment rate, consumers' income levels, and other measures of interest. The furniture wholesaler's sales volume, for example, could be expected to reflect a number of factors, seasonal changes, cyclical changes, trends, and random variations.

Many measures show a fairly consistent seasonal variation: snow tires sell very well in the fall months and far less well in the spring and summer. Cyclical variations are similar to seasonal ones, except that they do not follow consistent time patterns. The economy as a whole goes through cycles of more rapid growth alternating with recession and lessened growth. Projecting these cycles from past data is difficult, but still has been done with some success. Trends are overriding increases or decreases in the measure being studied. For the managers of the furniture company to estimate their sales in five years, they will project the underlying trend in sales volume. Mathematical techniques are available for removing seasonal, cyclical, and random components from historical data to reveal trends that may have been obscured by them.

This careful analysis of historical records to project past changes into the future is often called *trend analysis*. It has been a useful forecasting method, especially as applied to relatively short periods of time. One problem with trend analysis, though, is that it does not take into account the causes of the changes that are found. Even a long-standing trend may suddenly change if the factors underlying it also change.

CAUSE-AND-EFFECT FORECASTS   Other forecasting methods try to overcome this problem, often by seeking the actual causes of the external and internal changes that are important to a company's plans. Continuing the example of the furniture company, total sales will almost certainly be found to increase when the number of new houses being built increases. The growth of housing *causes* an increase in furniture sales because the house buyers need furniture for their new homes. Carrying the process one step further, forecasters will seek the causes of changes in the number of new houses being built. The mortgage interest rate, the number of new employers in the region, the unemployment rate, income levels, and many other factors will influence the housing market. It is always possible, of course, to extend the chain further and look for the causes of changes in the interest rates, income levels, and so on.

Forecasting conditions according to their causes and then carefully monitoring changes in these causes promises to be a powerful management tool for the future. Modern mathematical techniques and electronic computers have made it possible to study the relations among thousands of economic, social, and political variables and to begin to judge the cause-and-effect relations that exist. This method of accounting for a large number of interacting variables in the economy in order to predict changes that are useful for planning is called *econometrics* or econometric modeling.

ECONOMIC INDICATORS   Some economic measures have been found to have a consistent enough relationship with the overall state of the economy that they have come to be accepted, almost by tradition, as useful in forecasting and in understanding the current economy. These important measures, such as the size of business inventories, the size of the money supply, and the rate of consumer deposits in savings accounts, are called *economic indicators*. Three types are commonly recognized:

1. *Leading indicators* occur in advance of general changes in economic activity. A buildup in the size of inventories of manufactured goods is often seen as a leading indicator of economic retrenchment, since it shows that production is exceeding demand. Leading indicators are the most useful economic indicators for forecasting, since they are the only ones that precede future changes in conditions.
2. Some measures, called *current indicators*, are seen to reflect the state

of the economy as it is now. The unemployment rate is usually taken as a current indicator.

3. Other measures, the *lagging indicators*, indicate what the economy has recently been through. Capital spending by businesses is an often-used lagging indicator. Its rise and fall tend to be late. When business conditions improve, the expected rise in capital spending is delayed; when economic conditions sour, capital spending tends to stay high longer than it might be expected to.

These indicators, together with whatever other forecasts can be obtained, are important in shaping premises in plans. The next section gives some examples of how premises and forecasts are used, but some general rules are applicable to all their uses:

1. The manager must decide what premises and forecasts will really be practical in shaping plans. Thousands of facts might be interesting; the effective manager will select and concentrate only on the ones that will contribute to practical decision making.
2. Managers watch the selected indicators over a period of years. Experience with the actions and effects of statistical indicators will show what to expect from them. Continual changing from one forecast to another is not as wise as following familiar ones regularly.
3. Managers read, study, and analyze to learn what the true relations are between their organizations and the indicators. If the average age of the population is related to sales volume, for instance, managers will try to find out why that is so. It may be only a coincidence.

How Forecast Data Aid Plans

Some examples will show ways in which statistical data can be used in planning. These are examples only. Based on the kind of premises needed, managers must find their own data sources and interpret the information to answer questions important to their specific organizations.

INCOME TRENDS   Managers of companies that make and sell nonessential consumer goods—jewelry, for instance—keep a careful watch on trends in personal incomes. They are especially interested in income left over after necessities like food, clothing, and shelter are paid for. Income levels, however, are reported in a number of ways. *Real income* is a useful one. It shows the true buying power of individuals or families, how much goods and services they can buy with their income at today's prices. It eliminates the influences of inflation and takes into account taxes, social security deductions, and other such charges that are taken out of gross pay to produce take-home pay.

Consumers buy more if real income increases, less if it decreases. Many organizations watch this indicator carefully, looking at past changes and current levels while trying to project them into the future. They may use a mathematical technique. Or they may look at a graph of past income levels and estimate whether a downtrend is occurring. An up trend, for instance, might cause managers to plan for increasing sales volume. Sometimes specific occurrences may be expected to change real income. If Congress lowers taxes, for example, real income may jump when the tax cut becomes effective, because more would be left over after taxes.

Discretionary income is a measure that is especially useful to a dealer in luxury goods. Discretionary income is a direct measure of how much money is left to spend after buying all of the necessities of living; it is money which can be used at the discretion of the earner.

ECONOMIC CYCLES   Business cycles are of interest to nearly every organization, even ones that do not engage in business. Economists have long observed that periods of high market demand and high employment tend to alternate with periods of lesser demand and growing unemployment. These alternating periods are called *business cycles*. When the economy takes a downturn, sales are off and production is off. This causes unemployment as businesses retrench. Welfare and public employment services always have heavier demands when unemployment is high. Government revenues slump when business is bad, because a major part of government income is based on business profits. Also, unemployed people do not pay taxes.

Businesses obviously are interested in business cycles because they help to tell whether markets are shrinking or growing. Control of inventory and costs based on watching trends in the general economy can make a big difference in profits.

POPULATION TRENDS   Population figures are of primary importance to many kinds of planning. Furthermore, population forecasts are fairly reliable. Even such characteristics as proportions of males and females, age and race distributions, and urban-rural residence distributions can be determined with fair accuracy. Such characteristics play a role in market demand for many goods and services. Baby food is hard to sell in a retirement community, for instance.

A school district administrator can get a pretty good idea of how many children will enter kindergarten next year if she can find out how many five-year-olds there are this year. She will also have to consider data on mortality, on how many families, on the average, move into and out of her district, and on other refinements. Nevertheless, this examination of population statistics alone will give her a pretty good estimate of how many children will start school next year.

Consider a company that sells school supplies in the mountain states. See Table 4-4. In this region, there are only 85 percent as many preschool children (younger than age five) as there are children between five and nine years old. Since school children are the consumers of school supplies, this company's potential market seems to be shrinking. The company will have to look at other trends, of course—birth rates and movements of families, for

TABLE 4-4. POPULATIONS IN TWO AGE GROUPINGS FOR EIGHT MOUNTAIN STATES.			
STATE	UNDER 5 YEARS	5 YEARS TO 9 YEARS	YOUNGER GROUP AS PERCENT OF OLDER GROUP
Arizona	158,675	185,514	0.86
Colorado	186,368	224,171	0.83
Idaho	63,840	72,961	0.87
Montana	57,054	72,258	0.79
Nevada	43,844	50,652	0.87
New Mexico	96,659	119,216	0.81
Utah	111,798	117,179	0.95
Wyoming	28,372	33,857	0.84
Total	746,610	875,808	0.85

Source: Derived from *Statistical Abstract of the United States*, 1976.

example. But if it appears that school enrollments are going down and will stay down, the managers must draw up new plans. They might decide to diversify into a different market, for instance, or to fight harder for a larger share of their shrinking market.

FACTORS EXPECTED INSIDE AN ORGANIZATION SHAPE ITS PLANS

Many of the factors that control the nuts-and-bolts of planning are internal to the organization. A company's resources and ways of doing things exert major influences. Sales, revenues, costs, the money available for equipment and materials, the capabilities of employees, organization policies, and processing methods play a forceful role in determining not only what managers will want to do but what they will be able to do. Thus, the forecasts and premises of internal factors are among the most important planning tools a manager has. They also serve as guidelines while carrying out the total management job in regular operations.

Old Plans Affect New Plans

Plans build upon one another from year to year. This year's plan is based on last year's plan and includes parts of it. Policies and procedures, once tested, may endure for decades. Experience gained in carrying out past plans points the direction for making new plans. As a new planning cycle begins, this becomes the time to reevaluate long-standing policies and procedures. Managers must make sure these are still doing their job, and they must revise or reject them if they are not.

Existing policies serve as premises for plans. They set limits to the variability with which future situations will be handled. Suppose that a business has a policy that "no product will be priced to yield a gross profit of less than 20 percent." That is a statement of what the business expects the future to be like. It is a planning premise, and it must be considered when making plans.

In general, a *policy* is a guideline for how decisions will be made in a particular area. Policies help ensure that all of the managers in an organization will decide issues in ways that are consistent with objectives. Policies permit, and often encourage or require, discretion on the part of the decision maker. If you were a manager with the authority to set prices under the policy mentioned above, it would be up to you to use skill and information to decide what the prices will be. But you had better be sure that whatever price you set, it will bring in at least a 20 percent gross profit.

Policies are thus a major way of keeping the organization moving toward goals. They are a result of planning, and they are the premises upon which further plans are based. They are plans, and they form guidelines for other plans. The same is true of procedures.

Procedures are orderly statements of the methods that will be used to accomplish the work of the organization. Procedures specify exactly how to do things, usually leaving little room for individual decision making. Even small organizations have large numbers of procedures. Typically, procedures anticipate and answer questions like these: How is an order written? Who can write checks, and how are they recorded? What information must be gathered on new clients? What analytical tests will be used to judge product quality?

Procedures obviously define some of the specific courses of action to be followed to meet planned objectives. Often they also form planning premises because they specify the way things will be in the future.

MANAGERS MAKE SPECIFIC INTERNAL FORECASTS WHEN PLANNING
Policies and procedures form a general background for planning. More specific and detailed forecasts of many changeable internal elements, however, are also needed. In particular, most managers need forecasts of sales or service demand, operating expenses, and capital investment.

Sales or Service-Demand Forecasts
Sales forecasts are usually the most important internal forecasts made by a business. Almost all essential internal planning premises are related closely to sales: production levels, revenue available to finance operations, personnel needs, and materials needs.

Nonbusiness organizations have slightly different forecasting needs. For them, the projection of service demands for a future period is similar to a sales forecast. A social service or welfare agency, for instance, must have a good idea of how many clients it will be called upon to serve. This forecast provides the basis for operations planning, the nonbusiness equivalent of production planning.

For nonbusiness organizations, a forecast of product demand gives little or no information about income, since its revenues are not generated by the sale of products. Thus, other projections are needed. For agencies of a state government, for example, income will usually be set by the state legislature, often after a period of negotiation. In this case, exact income will be known in advance. Projecting income for the state itself is harder, since tax revenues depend on many variables. Complex forecasting schemes are used for this purpose. Variables may include estimates of property values, business and personal income figures, and population projections. Nonprofit organizations typically combine certain methods used for sales forecasting with other methods used by government agencies to get an idea of expected revenue from contributions, grants, and contracts.

BUSINESS SALES FORECASTS   Three methods for making sales forecasts are most common: informed opinions, customer surveys and statistical analysis.

1. *Informed opinions.* A manager who deals with customers, sales promotion, advertising, production, and purchasing has a pretty good idea of what is going on in the marketplace. His or her firsthand knowledge can generate useful sales forecasts if it is systematically applied. Salespeople, too, have been shown to have considerable skill in predicting sales levels in their region or product line. These relatively informal prediction methods work best, however, when the salespeople and managers are asked to approach the problem in an orderly way. When possible, they should give reasons to support their predictions. Sales forecasts provided by salespeople and managers may then be mathematically averaged in some way. One technique works this way: Of the sales estimate classified as "sure," 90 percent is accepted; of that classified "good chance," 30 percent is accepted; and of that classified "outside chance," only 10 percent is accepted. In many instances, the forecasts may simply be reviewed by top executives and incorporated into their guesses about future sales.

2. *Customer surveys.* These simply ask present customers how much they plan to buy in an upcoming period. For some companies, especially ones that handle relatively few large orders rather than many small orders, these surveys provide useful information. The common failing of these surveys, though, is that customers often do not plan far ahead enough to know how much they expect to buy.

3. *Statistical forecasts.* These are made in a manner similar to formal forecasts of external factors. They look at past or present results and try to project these into the future. Many companies use statistical forecasts of a very crude sort: "Sales have increased pretty consistently at 4 percent per year; we'll plan on that to continue again this year." When sales fluctuate considerably, up one year and down the next, more sophisticated mathematical approaches are available. Cause-and-effect forecasting and numerous variations and combinations of economic indicators may also be useful in forecasting internal conditions.

NONBUSINESS FORECASTS   Organizations such as government agencies and nonprofit service groups such as the Red Cross also need to know how much their services will be demanded in a coming period. Managers for these nonbusiness organizations use much the same techniques as do business managers. A consensus of informed persons, predictions, consumer surveys, and statistical forecasts can all provide useful information. Studies of population growth and composition, income, unemployment, and other factors yield quite accurate predictions of client demands from social service agencies, for example.

Nonbusiness organizations have a particular problem when they try to forecast their expected income. Managers in this nonprofit sector must keep alert to the status of appropriations and possible new sources of funds. Governments, especially at the federal level, rely on complex statistical approaches to predict tax revenues.

Internal Forecasts Other Than Sales

While sales and income forecasts form the backbone of most internal premising, other forecasts also contribute to the planning program.

Costs of personnel, materials, equipment, supplies, and facilities continually change, usually by increasing. These price changes are usually external to the organization, but they are included in a key internal forecast: the budget. In its simplest form a *budget* is a forecast of the costs of everything that will have to be bought during a planning period. This is a vital internal forecast because it places limits on production, operation, or expansion plans. A budget is also both an actual plan and a vital control tool, as will be discussed in later chapters.

Most organizations also make forecasts of capital outlays. *Capital expenses* are those incurred in building or buying facilities such as factories, office buildings, and long-lasting equipment or machinery. Facilities wear out, and they must be replaced. Expansions usually require capital expenditures. These forecasts are made more difficult by the need to predict future construction costs or price levels for the desired facilities. A hospital, for example, might cost $10 million to build today; price inflation might be forecast to raise that figure to $14 million in three years.

SUMMARY

1. Planning premises are statements of the conditions managers think will exist during the life of a plan. They define the resources, demands, limitations, and opportunities that will influence the operation of an organization in the future.

2. The future environment of an organization can be predicted by assessing changes in government actions and policies, economic conditions, social beliefs and patterns, and technological capabilities. The best way to spot trends in these areas is to strive to remain well-informed and to use formal forecasts prepared by governments and research organizations.

3. After clearly defining the kinds of premises needed for the plans of their specific organizations, managers often can prepare numerical forecasts upon which to base external premises. The forecasts can be formed from analyses of population size and composition, income, business cycles, or other types of data.

4. Internal premises are partly shaped by existing plans, policies, and procedures. These control some of the important internal conditions that will exist in the future.

5. Internal premises also are based on numerical forecasts of important factors such as sales, costs, and capital expenses. For businesses, sales forecasts guide both income expectations and production levels. Nonbusiness organizations usually must project service demand and income separately.

REVIEW AND DISCUSSION QUESTIONS

1. How do premises differ from forecasts?

2. Why are some premises said to be controllable?

3. Give some examples of ways in which government action can shape the future operations, and thus plans, of organizations.

4. Think of an organization with which you have been associated. Name a technological advance that you predict might affect its future performance.

5. A manufacturer of baby food wants to know whether to expand its product line in the next five years. What are some specific numerical external forecasts its managers might look for?

6. Why would a government agency or a welfare agency be interested in projecting business cycles?

7. How do policies and procedures relate to planning premises?

8. How does a policy differ from a procedure?

9. What are three general methods for making sales forecasts?

10. Why are nonbusiness organizations unable to rely on a single service-demand forecast similar to a sales forecast used by business?

Problems and Projects

1. The following is a selection from a list of premises made by a building supply manufacturing company. On a sheet of paper, write the letters *a* through *t*, corresponding to the premises, and mark each as follows:

I if the premise is *internal*; *E* if it is *external*.

C if the premise is mainly *controllable*; *U* if it is mainly *uncontrollable*.

M if the premise is mainly *measurable*; *N* if it is mainly *nonmeasurable*.

Each item will thus be given three letters. For example, a premise that is internal, controllable, and measurable should be marked I, C, M.

a. Average mortgage interest rates nationwide will be 11 percent.

b. No new types of products will be marketed during the year.

c. The average price of the raw material we buy will increase by 11 cents per pound.

d. The federal government will set new safety standards by May 15.

e. Our main customers have cut their inventories below normal levels and plan to rebuild stock during the year.

f. The local labor supply will increase by 10 percent because another manufacturer has stopped operations.

g. The population between the ages of 30 and 50 in our sales area will increase by 3.5 percent.

h. Up to $1.2 million will be allocated for capital expenditures during the year.

i. New management personnel will be developed from among existing employees to the greatest extent possible, rather than being hired from outside.

j. Capital spending by industrial companies nationwide will be 8 percent higher than last year.

k. The real gross national product will grow by 5.5 percent.

l. The federal government will not impose an import quota on any of our products or make changes in related tariffs.

m. Sales for the year will total $66.5 million.

n. The county government will reassess all property during the year.

o. Smaller families, high utility costs, and other factors will cause buyers to become more interested in small houses.

p. Workers will demand more direct job satisfaction rather than emphasizing only wages.

q. Our current advertising procedures will continue unchanged.

r. As in the past, at least 80 percent of our assets must be paid for with equity financing.

s. There will be more social acceptance of unconventional housing.

t. Federal tax reform will probably increase corporate taxes by an unknown amount.

2. The country's second largest manufacturer of electric water heaters is engaged in making a one-year plan and a five-year plan. Some hypothetical planning premises are shown here. For each premise, devise at least three specific actions the company might plan to take.

Premise 1: Market demand will shift significantly toward solar water heaters, especially in the far Southeast, the Southwest, and part of the mountain states. Total sales of electric water heaters by all manufacturers will increase at an annual rate of 3 percent rather than the 5 to 7 percent rate of recent years.

Premise 2: Average costs of electricity will increase by 10 percent during the next year.

Premise 3: Consumption of hot water in the average home will continue to increase in spite of increased energy costs and scattered water conservation efforts.

Premise 4: The federal government is considering setting water heater design standards within the next two years. None of our current models meets the standards that have been proposed for discussion.

Premise 5: Future production of solar water heaters, if undertaken, will require substantial investment in production facilities. Our indebtedness is already considerable. Profits have been quite good and are projected to remain high at least for the next two years.

3. *Performance Situation—Forecasting the Trends:* Rockton is a small Midwestern city. A government agency operates there to provide social and nutritional services to anyone aged 65 years or older. The agency has a very limited budget and its managers try to make the most of what they do have. In planning how to allocate their strained resources, they make a careful estimate of how many people will be eligible for agency services in the coming year. The managers are now making this estimate for 1980, and will be using this table for their projections:

	1970	1971	1972	1973	1974	1975	1976	1977	1978	1979
Total population	22,500	22,950	23,409	23,877	24,354	24,842	25,339	25,846	26,363	26,890
Population over age 64	1,125	1,262	1,405	1,552	1,705	1,863	2,027	2,198	2,373	2,554

These are actual population figures for the past ten years, and the managers believe they are accurate. (In fact, the figures have been made up to show consistent trends. Genuine figures are rarely so consistent.)

Answer the following questions on a separate sheet of paper.

A. The total population has increased by a fixed percentage each year. What is the percentage?

B. Has the population of people over the age of 64 increased at the same rate as the general population? Why?

C. For each year, what percent (expressed to three decimal points) of the total population is over the age of 64?

D. Assuming the trends for total population growth and for *percent of total population that is over age 64* continue through 1980, what will be the 1980 total population? The 1980 population over age 64?

E. How confident can the managers be that their 1980 projections are accurate, using this method of forecasting; very confident, somewhat confident, or not confident at all?

F. Could these trends be expected to continue for a long time into the future? Why?

4. *Performance Situation—Where the Taxes Come From:* Arco is like many other small towns: its citizens want more services but they don't want to pay more taxes. The town's planning is made even more difficult because revenues vary a good deal from year to year and are sometimes hard to predict. Arco's revenues derive from six main sources: real estate and personal property taxes, revenue-sharing funds from the U.S. government, sales tax revenues returned in part from the state government, state school funds, water and sewer hook-up and use charges, and business licenses and franchise fees.

Real estate and personal property taxes are the single largest revenue source; they are based on the value of all privately owned property in town as determined by annual assessments. Business licenses and franchise fees are a relatively minor item based on the number and size of businesses operating in town. Water and sewer revenue depends on the amount of building in town and on the actual amount of water used by patrons during the year. Revenue sharing and the money returned by the state government depend on the revenues and legislative decision of those governments. Sales tax income is directly proportional to the amount of local retail sales.

Prepare six questions that a manager for this town would want answered by external premises in the town's plans for the coming year. The premises should combine to help the manager estimate total revenues for the year.

5. You have just joined the planning department of a Northwestern manufacturer of machinery and tools used by producers of lumber. Your company makes bark strippers, log transport equipment, and multi-blade saws. Part of your responsibilities will be to assist in forecasting the performance of these products in the market. Top managers are also considering the introduction of new products, such as industrial planers, veneering machines, laminating equipment, and others.

Your first assignment is to compile as complete a list as possible of sources of information related to the company's field. Your boss wants the names of periodicals, data digests, and trade organizations that relate directly to the lumber and plywood production industries and to the manufacture of tools, machinery, and equipment used by those industries.

Using your school's library, and with the assistance of the librarians, compile such a list on a separate sheet.

6. Students are the "customers" of a school or college, buying the "product," which is education. This puts schools in the position of trying to estimate the sales for each of their products, the individual classes, so they can plan to meet specific demands. Conduct a survey of classmates and other students, asking them to name the courses they plan to take next quarter or semester. Use the actual list of course offerings, if one is available, or get a copy of last year's list if the new one has not been prepared yet. Total the choices of each course to get an estimate of enrollment for each. Discuss the results in class.

A. What type of sales forecasting is this survey?
B. How accurate a method of forecasting is this?
C. What would affect its accuracy?
D. How willing would you be to use this forecast alone to set demand premises in your plans?

Cases for Analysis and Discussion

CASE 1: LOOK WHAT YOUR FORECASTS MADE ME DO

"Ben, I've had enough of your forecasts to last me a thousand years! Look at the people on the shop floor. Are they making three-wall flanges? Were they last week? Were they last *month*? No; they're making two-wall flanges. Look at these orders. Are the buyers clamoring for two-wall flanges? Are they? You bet they're not; they want three-wall flanges and we haven't got them!"

Ben had a scholarly bent and was usually deferential to his superiors to a fault. This time, though, he'd heard enough. "If you had the sense to use the forecasts the way they're meant to be used, we wouldn't be in this mess. The buyers said they were going to want two-walls. I'm not Zeus sitting on a mountain reading minds. The buyers were wrong. If you had made production plans more flexible and had reacted faster when you saw what was happening, you could be shipping those orders, not shouting at me."

A. Whose side are you on in this confrontation? Why?

B. How can this occurrence be used to improve future forecasting and planning?

C. Who is responsible for the difficulties the company is in?

D. Should this company give up forecasting?

CASE 2: THE MISSING FACTOR

"So we know the store's in a good location. There must be something wrong with the management in the new store. I think it's time to tell them they'd better get their sales up or expect to be replaced." Frazer's face was growing hard as he stopped speaking.

The executive committee at Frazer Foods was perplexed and even a little angry over the very poor showing of their latest addition, a brand new retail store in a fairly affluent neighborhood of a New England city. Jacob Frazer had a new marketing idea and had made a small fortune from it. His company ran retail stores that sold nothing but convenience foods: open a can, unwrap a package, boil a bag. There was not a fresh tomato or a piece of perishable beef to be seen anywhere in one of their outlets.

Experience had shown that one of the best forecasters of sales was the number of single-person households in the neighborhood of a store. Their line was, after all, especially heavy on single-serving portions and on microwave cookery items. Now, though, their new store was in an area with a very high proportion of single-person homes—over 38 percent. But from the beginning sales had been poor, and Frazer wanted action.

Martin, the new accountant, suddenly spoke up with an idea that had struck him. "How old are the people in that neighborhood?" he asked.

A. Why does Martin want to know the age of the people around the store?

B. What might this case show about the use of numerical forecasts?

C. What can a manager do to avoid the situation Frazer is faced with?

CASE 3: THEY CAN'T BOTH BE RIGHT

Joe Benton was hoping the slight omission in his report would not be noticed. But it was.

"What happened to the salespeople's estimates? I don't see them," said his boss, the sales manager for the furniture factory.

Joe cleared his throat, a little uneasy about his ability to explain his decision to leave them out. "They were so far off base that I thought they would be more confusing than enlightening, so I left them out. I have them with me, though."

"What do you mean 'off base'? Off base from what?" his boss asked.

"From the sales projections made mathematically from the previous years."

"So how are you so sure the salespeople are wrong and not you? Let's see the reports."

Something was indeed off base. The forecasts Joe had made using trend analysis and projections showed that total sales would increase by over 10 percent for the coming year. The consensus of the salespeople was that sales wouldn't increase at all, and actually might show a slight decline.

The boss spoke again after looking over the estimates. "Joe, you made a serious mistake by leaving these out. We'd better look into this a little deeper."

A. How would you go about looking deeper into it?

B. Do you agree that it was a mistake to leave out the estimates of the salespeople? Why?

C. What new information might Joe and his boss try to get to improve their confidence in premises based on their sales forecasts?

CASE 4: THE BORING NUMBERS

"You know, Larry, these statistical abstracts may not be as uninteresting as I thought they were," said Ellen.

Ellen Baker had been going over the columns of figures for the last quarter hour, making occasional notes and computations on her calculator. The figures were summaries of real incomes, price indexes, savings account deposits, extent of personal indebtedness, and other measures of personal financial position. Ellen was the executive director of a private agency to provide social services to older people. The main emphasis of the agency had always been nursing and nutrition aids. But now Ellen had an idea.

"These numbers remind me of an article I read a couple of weeks ago. It was about how many people didn't know how to handle their money well enough to get by, even when they theoretically had enough income to live on easily.

"I've been looking here, and there are two things that really stand out. People are borrowing tremendous amounts of money compared with a couple of years ago. At the same time, deposits in savings accounts are going down. If that's true of the whole population, I wonder if it isn't especially true of our people. And I wonder if it doesn't mean they're going to be in financial trouble in another year or so when payback time comes and savings are low and inflation has made their income worth less than ever.

"Do you think we could do something about that? A training course in financial management? Maybe even some emergency money?"

A. Is this an example of forecasting?

B. What kind of premises is Ellen setting up?

C. Shouldn't this kind of analysis be confined to the formal planning process?

Planning and Decision Making

MONTHLY PLAN

TIME PERIOD	EVENT	PRODUCTION
JULY 5-10	A	PLACE ORDER
JULY 14	B	COMPLETE MOUNTING SLAB
JULY 23	C	COMPLETE ELECTRIC
		INSTALLATION
JULY 30	D	COMPLETE WATER COOLING AND
		WASTE LINES

5

After completing Chapter 5, you will be able to do the following:

- Analyze the links between planning and the other management functions in a specified organization.
- Propose methods for specifying, given desired actions in measurable terms.
- Evaluate the likely degree of uncertainty of planning premises, given a knowledge of the evidence on which they are based.
- Make use of conscious estimates of risk and probability in making decisions.
- Assess the suitability of several formal methods for use in specific planning and decision-making applications.
- Apply simple guidelines for effective planning in a real-life situation.
- Weigh the limitations and costs of a planning program against its current and potential benefits.

"What do you want to do tonight?" "I don't know. What do you want to do?" "I don't know." This exchange is repeated everyday in countless living rooms, school hallways, factories, and offices. In the casual planning of two friends looking for a way to kill some time, a failure to come up with a good answer may have no more serious effects than missing a good movie or spending a few hours in boredom. The friends may simply end up doing nothing. An organization that is trying to accomplish something, however, cannot simply do nothing; to do nothing is to fail.

PLANNING MUST PRODUCE ACTIONS
Future action is the essence of planning. Good plans represent potential events and they produce actions. The quality of plans can best be judged by the extent to which they yield actions that lead to desired goals.

Planning's Dependence on Other Management Functions
A manager who is ready to plan has already considered all of the desirable and reasonable goals of the organization. The manager has put together the best possible estimates of the forces that will influence operations in the future. Now the manager must face the real issue: "What will we do?" Plans must be practical and active. They must be prepared in a way that will facilitate the teamwork that is basic to an organization's function.

Organizations can accomplish tasks because they make it possible for people to pool their strengths and abilities. This simple principle guides all phases of planning, but it is especially important in the development and adoption of specific courses of action. The actions chosen must be the ones that will best use and coordinate the people and facilities of the organization.

As each plan is adopted, the planner must judge whether the other management functions can easily be applied to carry it out. Is the planned course of action expressed in a way that it will be controllable over a period of time? Will it be easy to integrate with existing reporting and accounting procedures? Is it set up so that small adjustments can be made as it is operating, or will the slightest deviation require a major overhaul? Can the plan be carried out within the existing organization structure? If people and positions and authority relationships must be shuffled, will this throw the whole group out of balance? Will it thus interfere with other goals? Who is going to carry out the actions? Will they be able to? How much training will they need? If additional people are needed, will they be available? Do the company managers have the abilities—and the willingness—to oversee and encourage the proposed actions adequately?

Before adopting a planned action, you must consider each of the management functions needed to carry it out. If there are unresolved questions of control or staffing or organizing, the plan is immediately suspect, no matter how desirable it might be from other points of view.

Need for Measurable Objectives

The stage when the actions to be taken are about to be adopted is another good opportunity to check the plans for measurability. The fundamental requirement of measurability is that an independent observer should be able to judge reliably whether the plans are being carried out and goals are being met. Anyone can tell if the goal "20 units a day" is being met. On the other hand, great disagreement might result if the goal were expressed as "adequate production quantities." There can be no question as to whether reports are being received "by noon on the Friday of each week." But who could consistently judge success if the reports were called for "on a timely basis?" Anyone with a calculator can tell if the requirement that "80 percent of clients will be placed in employment" is met. But "achieve a high level of employment" can mean something different to everyone who reads it.

PLANNING IS DECISION MAKING

Many of the earlier steps of the planning process are investigative. They aim at discovering, understanding, estimating, establishing, and using contacts with other people and organizations. The final steps of the process are evaluative and active. Managers must finally decide exactly what to do and how to do it.

Their investigations, forecasts, and premises will have set a framework for action. Problems will be apparent: profits may be less than desired; contacts with customers and clients may be slow and inaccurate; quality may be slipping; prices may be rising too fast. The problems may be hints of opportunities: consumer tastes may be changing; new materials may have become available; competitors' decisions may have made them weak in certain market segments. Plans *make decisions* about how to solve the problems and take advantage of the opportunities. The process of deciding deserves every manager's attention.

The Goal and Setting of Decision Making

Decision making is a process of resolving, under conditions of uncertainty, to take described and defined actions with the hope and expectation of achieving goals. It is the moment of saying, "All right, here's what we'll do."

The uncertainty that surrounds decision making is the real core of the process. If there were no uncertainty, often no real decision would have to be made. When the exact consequences of courses of action are known, the best course often becomes obvious. It is the uncertainty that makes decision making so difficult. Hard work and painstaking investigation can do a pretty good job of bringing the facts about a situation to light. The true decision maker, though, must rise above simple hard work. It takes creativity to discover the "what ifs" about alternative actions, and it takes courage to make a commitment to one action while facing an unknown future.

The practical goal of decision making, then, is usually to estimate outcomes that appear to have the best chance of success. The best managers seem able to combine intuition and rational judgment for the job. Intuition based on past experience helps managers judge just how reliable estimates are likely to be. As an extreme example, if a particular plan demands a sales increase of 50 percent to succeed, long experience with the customers in the market can help in judging how likely such a large increase is. Rational judgment, the systematic approach, uses a step-by-step effort to pin down important factors, numerically if possible, and to draw logical conclusions. The systematic approach alone is fairly easy to apply to a question such as when to replace a production machine. So many facts are known—current maintenance costs, typical life span, cost of current downtime, and cost of a replacement machine—that the systematic approach may be sufficient by itself. But most practical situations demand the effective use of both intuition and systematic decision making.

Levels of Decisions

Systematic decision making can be improved by recognizing the existence of levels of decisions. For example, a company once was wrestling with the tough problem of whether to expand its regional sales effort to a national area. The managers were juggling complex cost estimates together with highly speculative sales estimates for the unknown territory outside their current sales area.

One manager realized that this was not dealing with the company's basic concern. The organization's number of salespeople, support staff, and managers had already been growing faster than revenues. What the company really needed was to produce more revenue without increasing sales and marketing staff. With this realization, things started to fall into place. Efforts were aimed at producing more revenue with the current sales force.

The managers looked carefully at alternatives such as using motivational programs, adding a new product targeted to current customers, and raising prices on the current product. The first decision was to add a new product that could be sold by current salespeople to current customers. The managers then looked at alternative products. From many possibilities, they decided on a final list of five good prospects; that was the second-level decision. On the third level, they examined alternative ways to obtain the product: they could manufacture it; they could wholesale it for another manufacturer; they could buy out a current manufacturer of the product. They investigated these alternatives and chose to obtain an exclusive license to distribute one of their prospective products made by another manufacturer. And it worked. Their sales force was able to sell the two products together and produce higher income for nearly the same cost as selling only the former product.

The Evaluation Process

Clearly, the skill and care used in evaluating alternatives contribute greatly to the effectiveness of decision making. Numerous approaches are useful in this evaluation. Some common techniques are described in the following section of this chapter, "Formal Methods Help in Planning and Decision Making." Some of the more common numerical methods that are applicable to many decisions are covered in Chapter 25. These methods can contribute to making a good estimation of the costs and outcomes of alternatives. Two other approaches need specific mention, both of which can improve decision making: looking for bad consequences, and experimentation.

IDENTIFYING UNDESIRED CONSEQUENCES   The purpose of systematic decision making is not to cause undue caution; a decision maker must be bold enough to accept risk. But even the most courageous manager must try to anticipate and avoid unacceptable outcomes. For this reason, including a specific step for trying to identify adverse results can improve decision making. Some creative thought is called for. Managers seek effects on the organization, on products, on costs, and on relations with customers, the government, and society. Sometimes focusing consciously on these matters reveals important, but not obvious, effects that are so unacceptable that an otherwise attractive course of action should be rejected.

EXPERIMENTATION   When possible, it is a good idea to try out major decisions on a small scale before applying them across the board. The best known example of this is probably test marketing. Introducing a new product and package nationwide can be tremendously expensive. Many companies try out the new product in small test markets before undertaking national sales. Risky products that sell poorly in test markets are often dropped, saving the larger advertising, promotion, and selling costs.

The same approach will often work for other decisions. New work methods can be tried out by only a small portion of the work force. New materials can be used experimentally. A new advertising approach can be used in a small geographical area. One advantage to experimentation is that confidence in good decisions is increased when a try out has been successful; everyone involved feels better about the decision and will accept it more enthusiastically.

Risk, Probability Estimates, and Decisions

No amount of care will eliminate risk from decisions. The information that convinces you to take a certain course of action is *probably* wrong to an extent. The action you choose may not have the effect you intend and expect. It *probably* will have a somewhat different effect, from insignificantly different to radically and disastrously counter to your expectations.

Risk is a fact of life and cannot be avoided. But careful thought and study help a manager to make reasonable and promising decisions in an atmosphere of risk. Making estimates of the probabilities associated with alternative courses of action is a good starting point. The goal of using probability estimates in decision making is to increase the application of reason rather than emotions or hunches.

In a systematic planning program, the situation typically arises in which several attractive alternative actions exist, any of which could be undertaken. The alternatives usually will have different costs, different values of benefits, and different likelihoods of success. The manager's task is to choose the best one to pursue.

CONVERTING PROBABILITIES TO DECISIONS   The use of probability estimates requires four steps:

1. *Assignment of a numerical value to the benefit.* This may be a monetary profit for a business ($100,000 this year) or some other measure for a nonprofit organization (70 of 100 welfare clients properly sheltered and fed).

2. *An estimate of the probability of successfully achieving each alternative.* *Probability* is the relative possibility that a particular condition or event will occur. It is expressed by the proportion of times an event will occur out of all the possibilities that it will occur. If the event in question is getting "heads" when tossing a coin, there are only two realistic alternatives: heads or tails. Each is equally likely to happen with a fair coin, so that in very many tosses, 50 of every 100 would be heads, on the average. The probability is 0.50. Some real alternatives, such as introducing a hot new product, may be very desirable to a company

but rather unlikely to be achieved. Others less spectacular may be more likely to succeed. Numerical probabilities range from 0 for an event that is certain *not to* occur to 1 for an event that is certain *to* occur. An alternative that is rather likely to succeed thus might get a probability estimate of 0.80; one that is a real long-shot might have an estimated probability of 0.10.

3. *Weighting of the benefit by multiplying it by the probability of its being achieved.* Weighting the benefits reflects their relative risks. Risky undertakings receive a lower weight. The company seeking a $100,000 profit from a venture whose probability estimate was 0.80 would equate that alternative to a weighted benefit of $80,000. If the company had a long-shot alternative of making $500,000 profit from a venture with a probability only of 0.10, this would equate to a weighted benefit of $50,000.

4. *Selection of the alternative that produces the highest weighted benefit.* The manager of the business in the example would select the $100,000 profit alternative because its weighted benefit, taking into account the risks involved, is higher.

EVALUATING ALTERNATE COURSES OF ACTION   Many decisions can be improved with this technique. A suburban retail jewelry store, for example, might be faced with three alternative approaches for the coming year. The owner is fairly sure of making a $30,000 profit just by replenishing the present stock. He has recently looked at an attractive line of expensive, and high-profit jewelry, but has some doubts whether the line can be sold to the store's market. Several customers also have inquired about buying diamonds solely for investment purposes. This manager could make probability estimates like those in Table 5-1.

STRENGTHS AND WEAKNESSES OF THIS APPROACH   *The conditional value* is the expected benefit or return if successful. The *expected value* is the benefit weighted by the probability of its being achieved. In this example, strategy A is the adoption of the high-priced, high-profit jewelry, B is the continuation of present stock, and C is the continuation of present stock with the addition of diamonds selected for investment purposes. Alternative C is quite attractive; the most attractive, since it projects the largest return. A closer look shows that it could have a probability of success as low as 0.45

TABLE 5-1. USE OF PROBABILITY ESTIMATES IN EVALUATING ALTERNATIVE ACTIONS.

STRATEGY	CONDITIONAL VALUE	PROBABILITY OF SUCCESS	EXPECTED VALUE
A	$185,000	0.10	$18,500
B	30,000	0.75	22,500
C	50,000	0.65	32,500

and still match the expected value of the next best strategy (0.45 × $50,000 = $22,500).

Assigning good probability estimates is obviously not always easy. In some cases, the probabilities can be assigned objectively, based on hard evidence. This is true, for instance, for organizations with years of experience with market research or production analysis. For example, an expert market research department may be able to use customer surveys that allow a confident prediction that a certain new product has an 0.80 probability of selling a million units in the coming year if priced at $10.

In many other cases, however, probabilities cannot be set in this way and must be arrived at subjectively. A manager uses experience and general knowledge of factors influencing the issue to make "an educated guess" of the likelihood of success of the alternatives. Still, even when using this subjective approach where the probabilities chosen may be unreliable, the method has the advantage of forcing decision makers to focus on the real issue: Will the proposed actions work?

FORMAL METHODS HELP IN PLANNING AND DECISION MAKING

Thought and analysis will not solve every problem. But most planning and management problems are more likely to be solved in a satisfactory way when they are considered systematically. Formal methods of planning and decision making encourage this approach. Among the great variety of such techniques available, some basic methods include: (1) cost-benefit analysis, (2) cash-flow analysis, (3) budgeting, (4) planning with charts, and (5) scheduling and coordinating with PERT and CPM.

Cost-Benefit Analysis

A constant question arises in planning: Will the results be worth the cost? If I hire ten new workers, will they produce enough to pay their wages and leave a profit? If I buy the new machinery, will it pay for itself? If I do everything needed to increase production by 50 percent, will that produce more profits or less? Cost and benefit analysis and cash-flow analysis contribute to answering questions of this sort.

Table 5-2 shows the kind of information collected for an analysis of costs and benefits. In this case, the benefits are monetary profits, but a similar technique can be applied to other types of benefits if a numerical value can be set for them.

The figures in Table 5-2 represent a manufactured product that sells for $250 a unit. It could be a new stereo speaker system, a kitchen food processor or a small engine for garden tractors. Costs of producing the units are divided into two components, fixed costs and variable costs. *Fixed costs* are those that must be paid no matter what the level of production. These are expenses such as rent, insurance, and investment costs in the factory and equipment. These costs stay about the same even when production levels

TABLE 5-2. PRODUCTION LEVELS, COSTS, AND PROFITS.						
	UNITS PRODUCED					
	0	500	1000	1500	2000	2500
Fixed Cost	$125,000	$125,000	$125,000	$125,000	$125,000	$125,000
Variable Cost/ Unit	100	100	100	100	150	200
Variable Cost	0	50,000	100,000	150,000	300,000	500,000
Total Costs	125,000	175,000	225,000	275,000	425,000	625,000
Revenue/Unit	250	250	250	250	250	250
Total Revenue	0	125,000	250,000	375,000	500,000	625,000
Profits or Loss	−125,000	−50,000	25,000	100,000	75,000	0

change significantly. *Variable costs* are directly incurred from production, and they increase or decrease as output increases or decreases. Raw materials, power to operate machinery, and wages of workers who directly produce goods are examples of variable costs.

In the table, fixed costs—the costs of simply staying in business even if nothing is produced—are $125,000. Variable costs normally are $100 a unit. If over 1,999 units are produced, however, the capacity of the factory is strained: machinery needs more maintenance; many new, untrained workers must be hired, and they are slow producers; and overtime must be paid to the experienced workers. These and other factors make variable costs jump to $150 per unit for 2,000 to 2,499 units, and to $200 a unit for 2,500 units or more.

Profit (or loss) represents the net difference between the total costs and the total revenue from sale of the predicted number of units. Cost and benefit analysis in any organization simply compares the costs of doing something with the benefits expected (revenue, income, or values).

Table 5-2 illustrates some important conclusions that can be drawn from this kind of simple analysis. If production is zero, profits obviously are unobtainable because there is no revenue. Even if 500 units are produced and sold, the company suffers a loss because there is not enough income to cover fixed costs. Only at a point between 500 and 1,000 units does revenue increase to a high enough level to cover both fixed costs and the variable costs associated with producing the output. The exact break-even figure is 833 units; this can be calculated by an arithmetic method described in the Problems and Projects following this chapter.

The *break-even point* is the production and sales level at which income exactly matches total costs, fixed and variable, for making the amount of goods sold. If forecasts and research show that this company cannot sell significantly more than 833 units at $250 each, the business should not be undertaken because it will be impossible to make a profit.

Table 5-2 also illustrates what can happen when production is pushed very high and facilities and personnel are strained. Revenues continue to increase, but often variable costs for each unit produced also go up, causing profits to drop. At 2,000 units, profits have fallen back to zero. This kind of information is essential to planning. If sales are expected to increase significantly in this company, managers must arrange for a permanently enlarged facility and work force, and for training and other activities that will reduce variable costs and protect profits. (Figure 5-1, shown on page 114, portrays the data in Table 5-2 graphically.)

Some production level between 1,500 units and 2,000 units will be most profitable for the manufacturer described in the table. The exact figure cannot be calculated from the information given because it will depend on the exact sources of increased variable costs per unit. Managers must analyze their production procedures carefully to find out what production level requires overtime, what level overtaxes machinery, and so forth, to determine this point of maximum profits.

Cash-Flow Analysis   A popular way to estimate the potential financial success of a proposed course of action is cash-flow analysis. It charts the actual cash outlays likely to be required and then estimates the return expected from these expenditures over a period of time.

The method requires managers to make estimates of all future cash expenditures, for both operating costs and capital investments, and estimates of all future revenues. The projected expenditures are added together, and the total is subtracted from total revenues. If the result is negative, expenses have exceeded revenues and a negative cash flow is said to exist. A positive cash flow shows that revenues were or are expected to be greater than expenses. In new undertakings, expansions, or start-ups, the cash flow is negative in the beginning. The managers hope, of course, that this will turn positive after a period of time; the shorter, the better.

Table 5-3, on page 115, shows a version of this kind of analysis. It shows the projected cash flow for the first five years of a new business, a relatively labor-intensive, small manufacturing company. The cash outflow is large in the first year. Much of the equipment must be paid for in full. Rent, design costs, legal fees, and many personnel costs must be paid even before any revenue has been generated. In the second and third years, production increases through the addition of personnel. Cash is still being devoted to paying off equipment. In the third year, revenues exceed outflow for the first time. However, the cumulative cash flow—the difference between total cash paid out and total cash received from the beginning of operations—is still strongly negative. In fact, if conditions continue as they are it would take eight more years beyond Year 5 to totally recover the cash invested in this business. A manager looking at this projection might observe, "We'll be in the black by Year 3, but it'll be Year 13 before we earn back our cash investment."

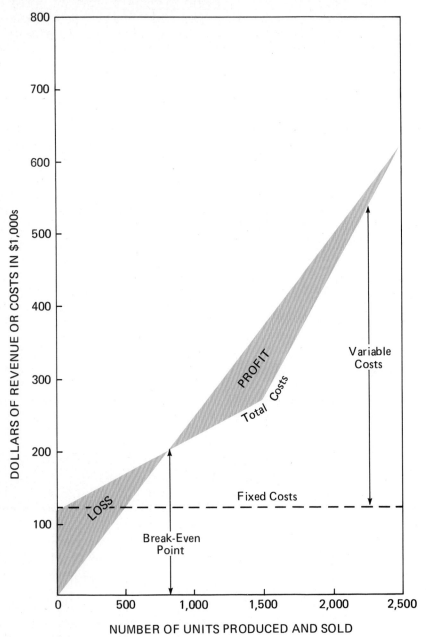

Figure 5-1. Graphic Representation of Cost-Benefit Analysis and Break-Even Point.

Note that cash-flow analysis is not a direct measure of profitability. Accounting practices normally spread out the initial investment costs over a number of years, even if they were actually paid in full at the beginning. This and other factors affect the strict profitability of an undertaking. Note also that Table 5-3 takes no account of inflation. Costs for rent and utilities, for example, would be very unlikely to remain constant over a five-year period. This and other factors can be included in the cash-flow analysis to create a more accurate model of the flows of funds into and out of an organization.

Budgeting Budgets have already been mentioned as a form of forecast. Budgets are also plans. When they are thoughtfully prepared, they form the most substantial bridge between the planning program and the other management functions. Many planning programs succeed or fail according to how well the budgeting process is carried out.

A *budget* is a type of plan that describes how the resources of an organization will be used—what portion of total resources will be devoted to each unit and activity. The resources allocated in budgets are usually expressed by their monetary cost, but may also be shown as time, materials, personnel, or any other measurable quantity.

TYPES OF BUDGETS An organization may have few or many budgets. Usually the overall, or master, budget will show the general sources of income for a planning period and will divide the revenue up among operating units. These very general budget categories are then broken down into specific division or department budgets that give details of how the money will be spent: so much for wages, so much for supplies, so much for maintenance, and so forth. Budgets are thus like other plans in that they vary from one level of the organization to another.

Budgets also vary in the length of time they cover. Some may cover only a month; others may outline expenditures over a period of up to five years or more.

TABLE 5-3. CASH-FLOW ANALYSIS.					
	YEAR 1	YEAR 2	YEAR 3	YEAR 4	YEAR 5
Rent and Utilities	$ 10,800	$ 10,800	$ 10,800	$ 10,800	$ 10,800
Personnel	44,000	62,000	102,000	102,000	102,000
Equipment	220,000	30,000	30,000	1,000	1,000
Materials	21,000	48,000	61,000	62,000	62,000
Miscellaneous	14,000	11,000	6,000	6,000	6,000
Total Outflow	$309,800	$161,800	$209,800	$181,800	$181,800
Revenue	80,300	109,500	210,000	210,000	210,000
Net Annual Cash Flow	−229,500	−52,300	+200	+28,200	+28,200
Cumulative Cash Flow	−229,500	−281,800	−281,600	−253,400	−225,200

Many different kinds of budgets can be created to meet the particular needs of a given organization. Seven of the most common are noted below. Each of these budget types may vary in its level and duration.

1. *Income and expense budgets* show sources and amounts of income and how the income will be spent, divided among categories of costs.
2. *Sales budgets*, or quotas, show how many units of output are projected to be sold during the budget period. These are often broken down by territory and even by individual salesperson.
3. *Production budgets*, or quotas, show how many units of output must be produced by specific dates to meet the goals for the planning period.
4. *Materials budgets* detail the starting materials and their costs that will contribute to the output called for in the production budget.
5. *Personnel budgets* detail the number and type of workers and managers who will be needed to produce the output described in the production budget. Personnel costs often are broken down by categories of output.
6. *Cash budgets* project the receipt and use of cash to make sure adequate funds will be available when bills come due.
7. *Capital expenditure budgets* allocate funds, usually on a longer-term basis, to meet planned needs for major improvements in facilities and equipment or to expand operations or undertake new lines of business.

To be effective, budgets must be taken seriously. They will be taken seriously only if it is obvious that care and study were devoted to their preparation. Budgets set a more or less flexible upper limit to expenditures that managers will be allowed to make. The limits will not work unless detailed cost estimates, pricing forecasts, and production and sales estimates or service estimates underlie them.

Charts for Planning   Planning on the action level requires detailed decisions about: (1) the order of steps that should be carried out, (2) how long each step will take, and (3) how different phases of an entire action or program must fit together. For tasks ranging from running a one-day sales meeting to a three-year launching of a new government agency, planning charts can help answer these questions.

A device as simple as the *bar chart* shown in Figure 5-2 is useful in working out realistic material, personnel, and production budgets. The figure shows simplified steps for making and shipping a run of a custom metal casting. Such a chart indicates when each department is busy or is free for assignment to other jobs. It is also useful for controlling each job after the plans are put into operation, because progress of the work can easily be

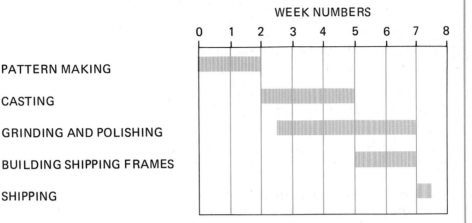

Figure 5-2. Bar Chart for Planning Production Activities.

checked against the chart. The bar chart (also known as a Gantt chart, after its inventor) is by far the most commonly used production planning and control device.

A *milestone chart,* as in Figure 5-3, has a similar use. Such charts are quite common in contract work where a unique product, such as a research report, is being produced. Milestone charts are especially useful in planning any activity that can be broken down into separate phases. The activity planned in Figure 5-3 is the preparation of a print advertisement to appear

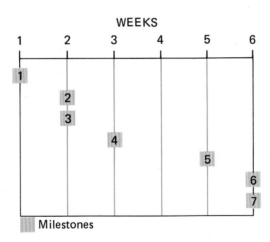

Figure 5-3. Milestone Chart for Planning a Newspaper Ad.

1. *Complete data gathering from client.*
2. *Approve placement plans and schedule.*
3. *Present sample copy and art.*
4. *Approve final copy and art content.*

5. *Prepare finished art and complete typesetting.*
6. *Give final approval.*
7. *Deliver to scheduled newspaper media.*

in local newspapers and magazines. The milestone chart, as with the bar chart, can be adapted to somewhat more complex situations. Its characteristic is that it monitors a number of activities that must be carried on at one time, with progress in one activity depending on a certain level of progress in the other activities.

PERT and CPM   A further extension of the milestone approach has been developed which is useful for extremely complex planning and scheduling applications. The method is called *Project Evaluation and Review Technique* (PERT). PERT is commonly used for such construction projects as dams, bridges, office buildings, and highways, or for massive, one-of-a-kind projects such as putting a man on the moon. Most managers may never be called on to work out the details of PERT because it is most appropriate to nonrecurring planning tasks. PERT is at its most useful only when scores or hundreds of separate activities must be coordinated. The method is referred to so often, however, that a basic familiarity will be useful.

PERT is a graphic and mathematical method of coordinating activities that must work together to achieve a goal. It takes into account (1) estimates of the time required to complete each subactivity, and (2) the ways activities are related, specifically whether certain activities must be completed before others can begin.

PERT creates networks like the greatly simplified one shown in Figure 5-4. The chart shows activities and events and the way they are related. An *event* is similar to a milestone; it is the beginning or end point of some phase of the overall project. Events are usually shown as circles on PERT charts. An *activity* is the actual work or process needed to accomplish subgoals. If an event is "finish blueprints for steel frame," the associated activity is the real work of drawing the blueprints. Activities are represented by arrows.

In a PERT chart, when an event precedes another event and is connected to it with an arrow, the preceding event must be accomplished before the activity associated with the later event can be begun. Figure 5-4 shows the steps needed to install a large piece of industrial machinery. Events B, C, and D must be accomplished before F can be begun because the slab, wiring, and water pipes are all needed for hooking up the cooling pumps. Similarly, the rigging (I) cannot be finished nor the crane set up (J) until the base assembly is completed (G). The chart also shows what activities can be carried on simultaneously. Pouring the slab, installing the electric service, and pipefitting are examples.

Planners must estimate how long each separate step of the project will take. (In actual practice, they make three different estimates: an optimistic, a probable, and a pessimistic.) These estimates are placed over the arrow for each activity. In the figure, pouring the slab is expected to take six days; setting up the crane will take two days.

One of the great advantages of PERT is that it forces managers to plan, sort everything out before any work is actually begun. To make the chart or do

Figure 5-4. PERT Chart for Installing an Industrial Machine. *Numbers above activities indicate days required to complete. The events are:*

A. *Place order.*
B. *Complete pouring of mounting slab.*
C. *Complete electrical installation.*
D. *Complete installation of water cooling and waste lines.*
E. *Receive machine.*
F. *Begin installing cooling pipes.*
G. *Complete base assembly.*

H. *Complete and test cooling system.*
I. *Complete installation of rigging.*
J. *Complete installation of temporary crane.*
K. *Begin moving machine to mounts.*
L. *Complete tie-down of base assembly.*
M. *Complete mounting.*

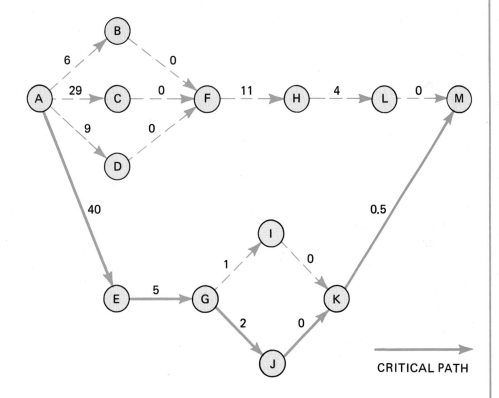

CRITICAL PATH

any of the associated mathematical estimating, planners have to be clear on what comes when, what depends on what, and on how long individual steps are likely to take. The method has a further advantage in showing how long a total project will take when only estimates of the time needed for individual parts are available.

A path through the PERT network is any series of connected events. A–D–F–H–L–M in the figure is a path. A–D–E–G–I–L–M is not a path because the events are not connected. The *critical path* is the path through the network that takes the *longest* to complete. It is called critical because it is the one that sets the limit on the time required to finish the whole project. In the figure, A–E–G–J–K–M is the critical path. It is 47.5 days long, the time expected to be needed to complete the entire installation. Planning and control techniques that concentrate on this path are often called *Critical Path Methods (CPM).*

Assume, for instance, that 47.5 days is too long for the installation because the manufacturer desperately needs the machine in 42 days. Thus, 5.5 days must be shaved from the critical path. The only likely candidate is the activity from A to E: shipment. Can the shipping dates be shortened from 40 to 34.5 days? If so, the original critical path is thus reduced to 42 days. Then the path A–C–F–H–L–M becomes critical. It is now the longest, 44 days. It is also over the goal of 42 days; two days must be saved somehow.

This kind of analysis also shows where changes would be *less* useful. For example, to pour the slab in four days rather than six days would have no effect on total project time.

HOW TO MAKE PLANS MORE EFFECTIVE

After setting up clear, realistic objectives, getting good forecasts and premises, and making sound decisions in advance, the manager's final goal when planning will be plans that work in the organization. To achieve this goal, the manager must look beyond the plans themselves and pay attention to integrating the planning process with everything else that goes on in the organization. A few key concerns are especially important to the planning process.

Participation

For plans to work, they must be understood and must be taken seriously by the people who will play a part in carrying them out. Encouraging participation will contribute to both these needs. People support plans more enthusiastically when they have helped make the plans. Both formal and informal efforts will help. Informally, it is wise to make it known that suggestions and opinions are welcome from everyone who will be affected by the plans. Ask subordinates and colleagues for their ideas on objectives, courses of action, and likely future conditions.

Formal means for involving others in planning should center on routine and continuous distribution of authority for planning:

- *Do not* create a plan and simply impose it on those you supervise.
- *Do* delegate authority for planning at each level below you.
- *Concentrate* your own energies on coordinating these plans and on the objectives, premises, and actions suitable to your own level.

Managers may make their own budgets and be required to defend them. They may negotiate objectives with their superiors, making all parties accountable for reaching the goals. Planning committees may provide a formal means for developing goals, premises, and actions. The key is to both (1) *invite* participation and (2) set up reports, meetings, or channels that *require* participation.

Communication   When plans are being made and when they are being carried out, managers must make sure that everyone affected understands what to do and why they are supposed to do it. Participation in the formation of plans will accomplish this to a considerable extent. Further efforts will be needed, though, to make sure everyone has specific and clear information about the organization's goals, premises, and plans:

1. Set up routine procedures to educate managers and workers about how their work contributes to higher-level activities.
2. Create channels to ensure that plans are communicated horizontally from one department or unit to others on the same level.
3. Do not assume that others understand. If you wonder why Marion is not doing what the plans call for, ask her; maybe she thinks she is. If you are puzzled by Tom's lack of interest in his job, discuss it with him; maybe he doesn't understand how his job contributes to organizational goals.

Timing and Coordination   The formal system of participation and communication must take account of another prime need: coordination. For a major goal to be reached, many other goals and activities in the hierarchy below it must work together in harmony. The manager's job is to make sure that subsidiary plans are consistent and to ensure that the plans at his or her own level do not conflict with other plans at that level.

1. Make a conscious check as you plan to be sure that different parts are coordinated.
2. Be very specific about objectives and about the people, facilities, and money that will be used and when they will be used.
3. Find out about other objectives and uses of resources elsewhere in the organization that might interfere.
4. Try to resolve conflicts *in advance* before they become operating problems.

Review of Plans   Plans that are used every day as hard, practical management tools will get continuous review as a matter of course. Outcomes will diverge from forecasts; planned actions will be adjusted to the developing situation; goals will shift to meet changing conditions.

In spite of this continuing review, it is wise to build into the planning cycle a specific period for a comprehensive review. Normally this will be during the making of the annual plan, but it may be less often or more often. The purpose of the review is twofold:

1. Look at every aspect of plans to see whether revisions are needed. Many parts of plans are carried over from year to year. It is easy to ignore long-standing policies and procedures and assume they are optimum because "that's the way it has always been done." Look at them periodically to see if they could be improved.
2. Judge how well the planning process is working. Are you and others really communicating? Do you need more or different forecasts? Are the reports and information you require from others adequate to the job? Are your objectives stagnant or unrealistic? Do you need more scheduled planning meetings? Do you need fewer?

Managers in Action

Texas Instruments Company, of Dallas, Texas, has scored a number of startling firsts: the first commercial pocket radio (1954), the first silicon transistor (1954), the first integrated electronic circuit (1958), the "calculator-on-a-chip" (1971), and the first $20 electronic watch in 1975. Its success is largely due to a sophisticated planning system.

"We've exposed the system to others," says Robert Pearson, TI's controller, "and they have been aghast at the intensity of detail."

Where do ideas come from at TI? Typically, the company scouts a market, figures what the next breakthrough has to be, then puts as many researchers, engineers, and managers on the project as required.

One observer remarks, "Goals are what drive TI." In a major strategy session held every March, product and division managers get up on stage, make sales and profit projections, and commit themselves to the projections in front of their peers. They constantly are reminded of these goals every month by computerized reports that show how each product line is doing.

TI's targeting process actually starts at the top with the board of directors, which every 12 years or so fixes a long run target. In 1974, for example, when the company was doing little more than $1 billion a year, the board set a sales target of $10 billion by 1990.

Source: Bradley Graham, "Calculating Success At Texas Instruments," *Washington Post*, August 27, 1978, p. K–1.

EVEN GOOD PLANNING HAS LIMITATIONS

Planning cannot solve all problems, no matter how skillfully and carefully it is done. In fact, planning can create some knotty problems of its own. The great advantage of planning is that it provides a systematic approach to the future. Managers must remain cautious, however.

Forecasts and Premises

Forecasts of all kinds are subject to error. Some are better than others, but all leave a good deal of room for doubt. No manager *knows* what the future will bring. The potential failure of forecasts does not doom the planning effort unless managers forget to take it into account. It is safer to assume that forecasts and premises will be wrong to some extent. That way it is possible to build in flexibility and alternate actions to be brought into effect when those nasty surprises do occur.

Conflicts in Planning

Planning recognizes, and in many cases increases, the extent to which different units of the organization interlock. Despite their best efforts, planners often are unable to make the best plans for one part of the organization without harming another part. Planning will usually be unable to resolve all conflicts in uses of resources, in objectives, or in management freedom and initiative.

Another type of conflict is common. Planning is an active, aggressive approach to managing the future, and this aggressiveness implies changes that may cause employee and manager resistance, frustration, and confusion. This conflict between the desire for security and the demands of aggressive plans can be very serious. The two are irreconcilable in some situations, and technically good plans simply cannot be adopted, much less carried through to completion.

Rapid Changes

Unexpected shifts in economic conditions, in personnel performance, in financial backing, in production rates, in sales, and in countless other areas are almost sure to occur at one time or another. Such rapid changes usually can be managed successfully only if the proper control and flexibility are maintained. In addition, the likelihood of rapid change sets a limit on the reliability of plans. In spite of technological forecasting, the rapid pace of technical development has made planning difficult for some organizations. Many developments are achieved far later than anticipated; others emerge unexpectedly, with few people prepared for them.

Costs and Personnel

One major obstacle to running a comprehensive planning program is the cost, time, and personnel needed to carry it out. An *undue* emphasis on planning may consume more resources than the productive work of the organization.

Planning is time consuming. Further, much planning work cannot be delegated; it must be done by the people who have major responsibility for running the organization. But it is impossible for those managers to devote more than a portion of their time to planning.

Planning is also expensive. Data gathering, report writing, cross-checking, and coordinating can become a burden, especially for smaller organizations.

Obviously, planning can become a resource allocation problem. Planning *should* be limited in a rational organization. As with any other decision, resources and their costs should be devoted to planning only to the extent that the resulting plans create a balance of benefits, in reduced costs, increased revenue, or better service.

SUMMARY

1. Planning is valuable only when it produces concrete actions that lead to meeting goals. The quality of plans can be judged by the extent to which they serve as practical guides to carrying out the other management functions during operations.

2. Planning is decision making. It relies on uncertain information to decide how things will be done in the future. As in all decision making, risk is involved. The risk can be managed and the chances of success increased if the probabilities of events are estimated and used to guide action.

3. Planning and decision making can often be improved through the use of formal methods such as cost-benefit analysis, cash-flow analysis, budgeting, charting, and PERT. Managers should recognize the kinds of applications for which these techniques are suitable.

4. Plans and planning must be integrated with the whole organization. Formal and informal participation of and communication with those affected by plans contributes to this. Plans are more effective if they are carefully coordinated and periodically reviewed thoroughly.

5. Even thorough and careful planning will be limited in effectiveness by unreliable forecasts, unresolvable conflicts, a rapidly changing environment, and high costs in time and money.

REVIEW AND DISCUSSION QUESTIONS

1. What is the final test of the value and quality of plans?
2. How can plans be made that will form an active basis for the other management functions?
3. Why are probability estimates useful in decision making?
4. Discuss the statement, "Managers are fooling themselves when they use probability estimates in decision making, because the true probabilities can never be determined."
5. Why would the break-even point be of interest to a manager?
6. How can budgets be made so they will be taken seriously and truly guide operations?

7. What is the critical path, and how is it useful to planners using PERT?
8. What are some of the advantages of encouraging wide participation in planning?
9. What are some of the main limitations on the effectiveness of planning?

Problems and Projects

1. On a sheet of paper write the numbers 1 through 10 corresponding to the 10 planning and decision situations listed below. Each of these situations can be aided by *one or more* formal methods. Assign the method or methods that would be suitable for each by placing the letter of the method next to the number of the situation. The methods are:

   a. Assignment of probability estimates to alternatives.
   b. Calculation of break-even point.
   c. Cash-flow analysis.
   d. Bar chart.
   e. PERT analysis.

The situations are:

(1) Determining whether it would be profitable to open and operate a gas station.
(2) Deciding on the size of a new factory to produce milk cartons.
(3) Choosing among three alternative marketing plans for introducing an important new product.
(4) Planning the construction of a computer-controlled subway system, requiring 2,800 separate design, construction, and test activities.
(5) Planning the filling of an order for a custom-made kitchen cabinet and counter top.
(6) Finding how long it will take to earn back the investment in a dress shop.
(7) Choosing among five proposed plans to use federal training funds to get jobs for welfare recipients.
(8) Setting minimum production levels for the coming year.
(9) Planning a simple research project to get a rough idea of market size for a new kind of peanut butter.
(10) Deciding which of four different-sized and different-priced dry cleaning shops to buy.

2. *Performance Situation—The Government Contracts:* Metrox, Inc., is a nonprofit corporation that does research and development work for the U.S.

Department of Agriculture and other farm-related organizations. Even though the corporation is nonprofit, Alice Clare, its manager, must run it just as if it were a business. The corporation provides services in return for grant and contract moneys. It must bid competitively against other such organizations and against colleges and universities for each project it undertakes. Preparing such proposals and bids is a very expensive proposition because some of the actual development work must often be done in advance, at Metrox's own risk, to show managers whether the project can be done at all and, if so, how much it will cost.

Alice is a methodical manager, and she uses probability estimates for decision making. Faced with a choice now, she is using her experience with government agencies plus hours of background work to judge some future possibilities. Three contracts are up for proposals.

Contract A would provide revenue of $150,000; the proposal and bid would cost $25,000 to prepare. Contract B would bring in $1,050,000 at a cost of $190,000. Contract C would produce $710,500 at a cost of $86,000. Alice believes that the probabilities of success, that is, of getting the contracts after putting out the money for the proposals, are: 0.90 for Contract A, 0.45 for Contract B, and 0.65 for Contract C. She begins this chart:

CONTRACT	COST TO OBTAIN	SIZE OF CONTRACT	CONDITIONAL VALUE	PROBABLITY OF SUCCESS	EXPECTED VALUE
A	$ 25,000	$ 150,000	_____	0.90	_____
B	190,000	1,050,000	_____	0.45	_____
C	86,000	710,500	_____	0.65	_____

On a separate sheet of paper, copy and then complete the chart and decide what Alice should do.

3. The break-even point is useful in many kinds of decisions because it shows a relationship among fixed and variable costs, production, and sales. It can be estimated from a chart similar to the one in Table 5-2 or can be determined from a graph. When the variable cost per unit remains constant regardless of the number of units produced, the break-even point can also be calculated from the formula:

$$\text{Break-even point} = \frac{\text{Total fixed cost}}{\text{Sales price per unit} - \text{Variable cost per unit}}$$

Thus, for a shop with fixed costs of $180,000 per year, making copper kettles that sell for $60 at a variable cost of $26 per unit, the break-even point would be 5,294 kettles per year:

$$\frac{180,000}{60 - 26} = 5,294$$

What is the break-even point for a firm that manufactures pencils if total fixed costs are $2,890,000, variable costs per gross (12 dozen) are $5.90, and a gross sells for $12.80? Assuming that fixed and variable costs remain as given here, how much profit or loss would the company have if forecasts showed that it could sell 350,000 gross? How much if 500,000 gross?

4. *Performance Situation—Asparagus Profits Not Overnight:* Marty has always liked to grow things. After years of dissatisfaction working in a bank, he has finally gotten the nerve and saved the money to start a part-time operation growing asparagus for the commercial market. Marty hopes to expand and go full-time if it works out well. He has made a cash flow projection to see roughly how much money he needs and how long it will take to get his investment back.

Once it is planted, asparagus will keep on producing for up to 20 years. Planting is expensive, though, especially since Marty has decided to plant one-year old roots rather than seed, so as to reap his first crop a year earlier. For $1,500 per year, Marty has leased a small, flat field with the proper soil and drainage. He plans to plant 86,000 roots which he can buy at 6 cents each. Some will die after planting, and in the second year he plans to replant 10 percent of them at the same cost. The first planting will cost $3,180 in labor, and labor costs for replanting the second year will be 10 percent of that. In the first year, he will have a one-time cost of $960 for preparing the ground for planting. He does not expect to have to plant after the second year.

Regular annual expenses, in addition to the rent payment, work out to $395 for fertilizer and sprays, $530 for cultivation, and $425 for machine use.

Harvesting will cost nothing in the first year because there will be no crop. Since the second year's crop is expected to be only 25 percent of full production, harvesting costs will be 25 percent of the full production rate. In the third and following years, harvesting will cost $4,240 annually.

Marty projects revenues to be $13,760 per year after full production is reached in the third year and beyond. He bases this estimate on selling 34,400 pounds per year at an average price of 40 cents per pound. Revenue for the second year will be 25 percent of that, and for the first year it will be zero.

On a separate sheet of paper, copy the form shown at the top of page 128. On the copy, make a cash-flow analysis of this business like the one shown in Table 5-3. Extend the projection for five years.

A. How much money should Marty plan to use to set up this operation?
B. How long will it take him to earn back his investment?
C. Does this seem like a sound business, assuming that the information he gathered is fairly accurate?

5. A club you belong to has been asked by a local civic group to write a plan for a project they are undertaking: turning a vacant lot owned by the town into a neighborhood park. The group wants club members to talk to people

CASH-FLOW ANALYSIS FOR ASPARAGUS VENTURE					
	YEAR 1	YEAR 2	YEAR 3	YEAR 4	YEAR 5
Plants	_____	_____	_____	_____	_____
Land Preparation	_____	_____	_____	_____	_____
Planting	_____	_____	_____	_____	_____
Fertilizers and Sprays	_____	_____	_____	_____	_____
Cultivation	_____	_____	_____	_____	_____
Harvesting	_____	_____	_____	_____	_____
Machine Use	_____	_____	_____	_____	_____
Land Rental	_____	_____	_____	_____	_____
Total Outflow	_____	_____	_____	_____	_____
Revenue	_____	_____	_____	_____	_____
Net Annual Cash Flow	_____	_____	_____	_____	_____
Cumulative Cash Flow	_____	_____	_____	_____	_____

in the neighborhood to find out how many would use the park and what facilities they would like. The club then wants to seek funds from contributions from individuals, businesses, and local governments to cover the costs of facilities. They then plan to find and direct volunteers from the club and from the neighborhood to clean up the lot, install the playground equipment and other facilities, and do the landscaping.

Prepare a milestone chart for this project. Decide the best ways to progress from the empty-lot stage to the finished park. Divide the project into discrete phases or steps and establish milestones for each. Estimate the time needed for each activity and step, and arrange the milestones accordingly on a chart. Do not forget that some steps can be carried on at the same time, in parallel, while others cannot begin until some previous step is completed.

6. As an individual project (or in conjunction with others in your class) locate a manager who uses a budget in day-to-day operations. Interview the manager on the preparation and function of the budget. Concentrate on the budget as a forecast, as a planning tool, and as a plan, but do not avoid discussion of its use as an aid in control.

Find out how the budget was arrived at. Did the manager who is using the budget take part in writing it? What kind of budget is it? How accurate is it proving to be as a forecast (of expenses, production, or whatever its subject is)? What kind of study went into determining the entries? For cost budgets, how strictly is the manager required to stick to the figures? Discuss the results of the interviews in class.

Cases for Analysis and Discussion

CASE 1: THE BEST OF PLANS

"Why does the old man make us read these plan summaries anyway? What do I care what the finance department or the people in purchasing are going to do next year? I'm not going to read them now. I'll get to it later. Much later!"

But Carl, the sales manager for Ajax Hand Tools, never did get to it. The summaries ended up in the file, unopened.

Seven months later, Carl stood behind his desk waving a stack of pink copies of orders, his face red with anger. "What do you mean, you can't ship them as specified? This whole sales push is based on getting them there in a hurry." He riffled through the orders. "Look! These are big orders. Our sales-people *promised* they'd get there in a hurry."

The shipping manager didn't seem to think that was his problem. "Carl, we can't ship air parcel post. It's too expensive. We don't even have the heavy-duty mailing equipment anymore. We got rid of it. Since last month, the only thing we use the mail for is letters. We did it to cut costs. It was all planned out months ago; I'm surprised you didn't hear about it."

"Well, why didn't you hear about our sales campaign?" Carl asked, "Don't they have memos down in the catacombs, or do the rats carry them off?"

A. Could this kind of situation arise in a real company?
B. What caused the trouble? What kind of failure caused the problem?
C. Can you suggest ways to keep this kind of incident from happening in the future?

CASE 2: THE CHANGED MANAGER

From the very beginning, twelve years ago, when she had been an assistant caseworker, Barbara had been innovative, cooperative, and a very hard worker. She moved up rapidly in the agency, to unit supervisor, then to services coordinator. She had a touch for administration, the perseverance to doggedly finish the detail work, and the personal skills to allow and encourage others to do their best work.

But lately, Barbara's boss observed, things did not seem to be going well with her. She had a shouting match with one of the unit supervisors and made such abusive remarks that he threatened to quit. Some of Barbara's reports were coming in a day or two late, and were sometimes vague and careless, which had never happened before.

Her boss had no idea what the problem was. She asked Barbara into her office to talk over the situation. Barbara wasted no time in explaining what was interfering with her work lately:

"All the changes around here have left me behind. For years I knew exactly how everything was done; I knew the history of things. But since you've started this "planning system," as you call it, everything is different. We're not supposed to do the same things now as last year, and you're working right now to make it even more different next year. It makes me feel like I can't do my job, like I'm not even interested in doing my job anymore."

A. Is Barbara covering something? Or could the new planning system really create feelings like these?

B. If the planning system is the cause, how did it happen?

C. What should the boss have done in the past? What should she do now?

CASE 3: ENOUGH IS ENOUGH

"Virginia, you can take that stack of forms and . . . get out of here. I've tried to cooperate, but you planning people are driving me crazy. I've got a department to run."

It had been like this almost from the start. Virginia had been hired as a staff planning specialist eight months ago and had run into nothing but resistance. She had a complete planning program set up. It was truly comprehensive and based on thorough data gathering, multiple sources for every important forecast, frequent meetings to keep everyone informed and get their ideas, and cross-checking among departments and managers. The program had everything Virginia could think of to make good plans and get managers involved in them. But the managers were not involved in them. They wouldn't even give her the information she needed.

Virginia had worked hard and used her extensive training to set up the planning program. She had expected a real success, and even thought the program would be a stepping stone in her career. Now she wondered whether her very job might not be in peril. The program was not working.

A. Why isn't the program working?

B. Is there something wrong with Virginia? With the uncooperative managers? With planning?

C. What should Virginia do to improve the situation?

CASE 4: THE MISSING MACHINISTS

When the time came, the company simply could not find the people it needed. The whole growth plan almost collapsed. When it finally was carried out, nearly a year late, costs were higher than expected and profits were lower.

The market for antenna rotators for TV and FM radio had never grown as large as hoped, for a number of reasons. But Elliot Electronics still did a good business making the devices; it had a 37 percent share of the market. Recently, its designers had come up with a patentable redesign of the rotator that would let Elliot sell at a price far lower than its competitors. Jubilation reigned when the market-share projections came in.

The mood was considerably different in a few months, however. The new design was far simpler than the old one, but it required precision machining work that could only be done by expert machinists. Plans had called for hiring new employees to do that part of the work. Elliot Electronics was located in a modern plant out in the country. The setting was beautiful and restful, with the main offices overlooking a big old oak tree and a meadow. But when hiring time came, no machinists were found behind the oak or anywhere else in the county, or even in the neighboring counties. The machinists with the skills Elliot needed were far from any restful meadows; they were in the gray industrial areas of the nearest big city, over 200 miles away. The Elliot managers finally had to bite the bullet; they had to offer premium wages and other incentives to lure the machinists away from the jobs in the city.

A. Is it possible to avoid this kind of situation?
B. What should the managers have done? What alternatives did they have?
C. Is this really a planning problem? Could planning have been expected to handle it?

The Controlling Process

6

After completing Chapter 6, you will be able to do the following:

- Outline a simple control system for a given procedure or activity.
- Judge the adequacy of given standards for use in control, and propose specific actions to correct deviations detected through control.
- Formulate a general control program for a simple organization and identify key areas that need control.
- Analyze a budget variance report and suggest possible actions to take.
- Interpret a flexible budget based on actual production levels.
- Recognize areas of a given organization that need nonbudgetary controls and propose controls to be applied.
- Apply control methods to procedures, judging both employee performance and the procedures themselves.
- Propose key areas and methods for overall control, given the high-level goals of an organization.

The word "control" may bring to mind iron-fisted rulers imposing their will on employees, keeping the workers' noses to the grindstone. Although there is an element of discipline in the process, control in a well-run organization has little to do with regimentation.

A more revealing example of what control is supposed to accomplish is given by the new competency-based tests that so many high schools are beginning to use. The tests start with the belief that the basic goal of a high school is for students to learn certain skills. These would include the ability to read, to do the kind of arithmetic needed for shopping, paying taxes, and so forth, and to write clearly and understandably. Schools set up plans such as course outlines, teaching schedules, and personnel policies to try to reach this goal.

How do the teachers and administrators know if the plans are working, though? More and more, they are using a three-step process:

1. They define exactly what skills they want to teach, trying to work out which skills are most needed.
2. They write and give tests to show whether students really can use the skills they are supposed to have, that is, whether they have "competency."
3. They give extra instruction and training to the students who are found to be lacking in some skills.

This is exactly the same kind of control that is used in running a coffee shop, General Motors, the legal affairs of your hometown, or the entire government of Germany. *Control* is the process of evaluating the progress and results of current operations to find out where plans are not being followed or goals not being met, so that corrective action can be taken where needed.

CONTROLS DISCOVER AND CORRECT DEVIATIONS FROM PLANS

The three-step process of controlling the teaching in a high school applies to any kind of control in any organization. It includes: (1) setting standards, (2) comparing actual results with the standards to find deviations, and (3) taking action to correct the deviations.

A simple control situation exists, for example, in operating a machine that planes wood to a standard thickness. The boards are supposed to be 1 inch thick. The machine is not precise enough to make every board exactly 1 inch thick, so managers have decided to accept a deviation of 1/64 inch over or under the standard. This deviation which is defined in advance as being acceptable is called a *tolerance*.

As the planed boards come out of the machine, the operator checks their thickness. This is a measurement of the actual results of an operation, and is called *feedback*. If the operator finds that many of the boards are too thick or too thin, that they deviate from the standard, the operator will take correcting action by adjusting the machine. This process of measuring, comparing with standards, and making adjustments will be continuous while the machine is operating.

The same process can be applied to any aspect of an organization that can be clearly defined. Suppose that a company's managers find that total costs must be kept below $2 million in order to make a profit. They will keep track of expenses as the year goes by, and cut back if the rate of spending is found to be too high. Take the example of a government office that processes applications for professional licenses. It finds that it must handle an application in an average of 5½ hours to get all of them done with the present staff. Its managers will therefore take action whenever the actual times start running higher.

Standards, feedback, and adjustment apply broadly to scores of organizational goals. The process applies to use and waste of materials, use and maintenance of equipment, quality of produce, personnel attendance and performance, production or service levels, and energy use, to name some of the more common managerial concerns.

Setting Standards   A *standard* is a statement of the way things ought to be: product quality, costs, productivity, morale, management efficiency. Standards are developed in the planning process; they are an important component of the subgoals that support major organization objectives. Most standards are very specific: "Employee turnover will be less than 8 percent annually";

"Every bag will contain 100 pounds with a tolerance of plus or minus 2 ounces"; "90 percent of all orders will be processed within 24 hours"; "100 percent of new clients will receive their first interview within seven days."

All standards should be made as specific as possible if they are to be effective. But some standards may be difficult to define in quantitative terms. Organizations, for instance, are often strongly concerned with morale, with public opinion, with executive decision making, and with other issues that are hard to measure. Standards for such variables tend to be qualitative, to use words rather than numbers. These standards are hard to use in controlling. The current trend is to try to develop objective measures even in these hard-to-define areas. For instance, letters of complaint may be counted to get an idea of public opinion. Turnover and absenteeism figures may be judged as measures of morale. Profits may be used as a gauge of executive decision making effectiveness.

Comparing Actualities With Standards

In exercising control, the key objective is to stay on top of things. This means that the sooner feedback is received and interpreted, the better. Sometimes it is possible to anticipate problems before they become serious. Figure 6-1, for example, shows a graph of measurements made by the operator of the planing machine mentioned earlier. Nearly all of the boards being made are still within tolerances. But there is a clear trend toward producing thicker and thicker boards, even though the operator is repeatedly adjusting the machine. This chart signals that trouble in meeting standards lies ahead. Quick corrective action in servicing the machine may avert the problem altogether.

In most cases, though, problems cannot be identified before they happen. The best that can be achieved is to get measurements of progress and results as early as possible. Then managerial control must attack deviations before they continue for long.

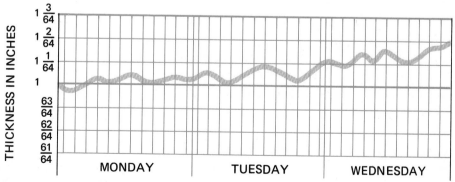

Figure 6-1. Thickness of Sample Outputs From a Planer Machine.

Taking Corrective Action

Once managers have measured actual performance and compared it with standards, a number of possibilities exist. There may be no deviation; in that case, nothing need be done. A deviation may be discovered but be considered so unimportant that the managers decide to take no action. When an important deviation does arise, one that is too great to ignore, there are many possible kinds of action.

The first step, and usually the crucial one, is to find out why the deviation occurred. If costs are over budget, for example, why are they? Are the managers wasting money? If production is low, is it because workers are not making an effort? Is the equipment adequate and in good shape? Are the materials the proper ones? Having looked into the problem to find the causes, one or more of the three kinds of action discussed below will usually be needed.

CHANGE THE PERFORMANCE   If employees are not doing their job, they may need more supervision or better training. Leadership or communication may need strengthening. In cases of incompetence, people may need to be transferred or dismissed. If equipment is a factor, facilities may need improvement. If materials are faulty, closer inspection may be required.

CHANGE THE STANDARD   Often enough, deviations between standards and performance occur because the standard is unrealistic. When this happens, managers must revise the standard and other operating controls that interact with it.

CHANGE PROCEDURES, POLICIES, OR OTHER PLANS   Sometimes, deviations are caused by underlying conceptual errors or conflicts. The whole method of tackling the job may be faulty. The procedure should be revised. Often, even high-level objectives must be changed in light of actual experience in trying to meet them.

Changing performance, standards, or procedures all depend on a basic characteristic of controlling:

> Controlling is effective only when it closely interacts with the other management functions. When the controlling process calls for a manager to take action, the action always uses planning, organizing, staffing or directing.

Deciding What To Control

A manager who tries to maintain complete control information for every minute aspect of the organization will soon be buried in mountains of paper. An avalanche of data will pour in giving hourly or daily results for every machine, every worker, every purchase, and every sale. The answer to this problem is a double-edged approach. Summaries are compiled for some convenient interval, and these concentrate only on certain critical areas that will show how the whole operation is doing. Lower-level managers, like first-line supervisors, will want more frequent summaries of certain information, sometimes even for periods as short as an hour or less. Higher-level managers will prefer summaries from longer periods: monthly, quarterly, or annually. *All* managers need to concentrate on critical areas. Most organizations will need standards to control the main areas shown in Table 6-1.

Managers in Action

"Cost cutting measures had to be taken [at Memorex]. Over a period of time we eliminated over 125 middle management positions and reduced the work force by ten percent. . . . A similar condition existed at Collins Radio. The company was losing cash at the rate of $15 million a quarter. $40 million had to be cut from annual expenses. Arriving at that conclusion was relatively easy; the solution was more difficult. It meant reducing the salaried work force by 30 percent and shutting down several plants. . . . But by the next year Collins had a profit of $13.3 million . . . The real question is: How do you go about doing this without totally destroying company morale? How do you know which people to take off the payroll? . . . It must be done selectively. If you do it with a meat cleaver, you're likely to sever the most vital parts of the business. . . . I spent a great deal of my time getting together with managers and employees alike, whether in groups or alone with individuals, to explain what the situation was and what had to be done about it. People are smart, and I think that they will understand any situation once it is put into perspective. That's why the ability to communicate the facts is so important."

This is Robert C. Wilson speaking. He is president of Memorex Corporation, a computer and business machines company. He is telling of how he rescued two firms, Memorex and Collins Radio, from bankruptcy by taking severe control actions.

Source: "Corporate 'Architect' Helps Troubled Companies Build Stable, Profitable Organizations," *The AMBA Executive,* vol. 7, no. 2, February 1978, pp. 1–18. Copyright © 1978, Association of MBA Executives, Inc.

TABLE 6-1. AREAS WHERE FORMAL CONTROL IS USUALLY NEEDED.

PRODUCT STANDARDS. These maintain quality and usefulness of goods or services provided. They control durability, size, and other specifications of physical products and the success of services.

OPERATIONS OR PRODUCTION STANDARDS. These maintain control of the way things are done, such as time used per unit produced and methods used.

COST STANDARDS. These control expenditures of all kinds, whether directly for producing goods and services or simply for maintaining the organization. They attempt to balance and minimize costs for personnel, equipment, supplies, material, and everything else needed for operations.

REVENUE STANDARDS. These provide current information on income of any kind: sales revenue, contracts, grants, tax revenue, interest on investments. Used for adjusting expenditures to revenues.

CAPITAL STANDARDS. These maintain control of expenditures for capital goods: factories, offices, permanent facilities.

OTHER STANDARDS. These control methods, costs, and results of other activities of the organization; for instance, special projects like the installation of a computer system. They may be relatively intangible, such as in controlling the organization's involvement with the community or the ethical practices of executives.

BUDGETS ARE THE BACKBONE OF CONTROL

One of the most familiar cries heard from controllers is, "You're over your budget; you've got to spend less money." The budget, used as a standard for financial control, is one of the most common of all control methods. Used properly, budgets can be very effective.

Budgets are variously forecasts, plans, and control standards. A manager who makes an expense budget as a *forecast* is saying, "This is how much we will need to spend to meet our goals." With the same budget as a *plan*, the manager says, "This is how much we will spend." Using the budget as a *standard*, the manager says, "This is how much we were supposed to spend; let's compare it with what we are actually spending."

Since there are many kinds of budgets, this same process serves to control many aspects of operations other than spending money. Production budgets control output. Materials budgets control the purchase and use of materials. Personnel budgets control the application and productivity of employees. Capital budgets control costs of equipment and facilities.

Variance Reports   In using budgets for control, the *variance report* is the analytical device that compares the real (actual) with the standard (expected) provided by the budget. Two kinds of budget variance reports are shown in Figures 6-2 and 6-3:

The production budget variance report in Figure 6-2 is similar to ones commonly used in manufacturing companies. The budgeted figures show the quantity of output and productivity needed for the current month and for the entire year so far. The report compares these budget figures with actual output and productivity. This particular report shows that things are not going very well. By the end of August, 200,000 units should have been produced. In fact, however, the company has turned out only 188,000, which is 6 percent fewer than needed. The managers of this operation realized from past variance reports that they were falling behind in output. They have been successful in pushing up production for August by 2,300 units over budget for the month. But this has had a bad effect on productivity. The company is getting fewer units made for each machine and operator-hour worked. This makes the output more expensive and less profitable. It is obvious that more and better corrective action is needed to get operations back in line with plans.

A variance report for an expense budget provides exactly the same kind of information, except that it focuses on operating costs rather than production. The variance report in Figure 6-3 is one prepared for a department in a government agency. The department is responsible for (1) monitoring work on contracts done by outside organizations and (2) assuring compliance with a complex set of performance regulations. Travel and clerical costs are over budget, but several other expenses have been kept under budget to compensate. This shows that the department is in a good position so far in the year. Continued vigilance will be needed. It may not be easy to keep legal and data processing costs as low as they have been so far if the budget figures were realistic to begin with.

VARIANCE REPORT FOR PRODUCTION OUTPUT						
Department: PRODUCTION Account Number: 123 Date: AUGUST 198X						
Units of Measure: Gallons ☐ Pounds ☐ Yards ☐ Pieces ☒						
Production Performance	Current Month			Year-to-Date		
	Actual	Budgeted	Over (Under)* Budget	Actual	Budgeted	Over (Under)* Budget
OUTPUT (UNITS)	26,300	24,000	2,300	188,000	200,000	(12,000)
EQUIPMENT HOURS	759	672	87	5,605	5,556	49
OPERATOR HOURS	1,910.5	1,680	230.5	13,052	13,333	(281)
UNITS-EQUIPMENT HOURS	34.65	35.71	(1.06)	33.54	36.00	(2.46)
UNITS-OPERATOR HOURS	13.77	14.29	(0.52)	14.40	15.00	(0.60)

*Figures in parentheses are under budget. For an output or productivity budget, it is usually desirable to be on or over budget.

Figure 6-2. Production Budget Variance Report.

Figure 6-3. Expense Budget Variance Report.

VARIANCE REPORT FOR EXPENDITURES			

Department: CONTRACT ADMINISTRATION   Date: JUNE 198X

Account Number: 023

Expense Category	Year-to-Date		
	Actual	Budgeted	Over (Under)* Budget
DIRECT SERVICE PERSONNEL	23,850	23,850	0
CLERICAL PERSONNEL	8,000	6,000	2,000
SUPERVISION	5,625	5,625	0
DATA PROCESSING	4,640	5,700	(1,060)
LEGAL COSTS	4,500	6,750	(2,250)
TRAINING AND CONSULTING FEES	2,586	3,200	(614)
TRAVEL, LODGING, AND ASSOCIATED	10,193	9,600	593
SUPPLIES AND POSTAGE	1,497	1,600	(103)
ALLOCATED COSTS (HEAT, RENT, INSURANCE, AND SO ON).	4,718	4,650	68
TOTAL	65,609	66,975	(1,366)

*Figures in parentheses are under budget. For an expense budget, it is best to be on budget or under budget.

Flexible Budgets   The expense budget in Figure 6-3 illustrates a problem with budgets: they are often based on only one output level of operations. This may be all right for an agency, for instance, where a known amount of revenue will be available and the question is how to best spend it. But what about a business that suddenly encounters unexpectedly strong demand for its product? Are its managers to hold to their expense budget, and give up the higher sales revenue they could enjoy if production were stepped up?

Most organizations would emphatically answer no to this question. They wish to be flexible in their spending plans to allow changes in production or service levels to meet the demand that is actually found. Flexible budgets allow this.

A *flexible budget* is one in which the allowed variable costs are automatically adjusted up or down, based on actual production or sales rates. One way to achieve this is to work out separate expense budgets for different output rates. A department manager might have one budget for 20,000 units, another for 25,000, and others for 30,000 and 35,000. The manager would then be expected to follow the budget that most closely matched the actual production level. This permits reasonably close cost control without the inflexibility of a single fixed budget.

When very precise control is needed, it is possible to project costs mathematically for an exact production level. These budgets can be made to vary continuously so as to exactly match output. Figure 6-4 illustrates this concept. Some organizations use a supplementary budget. First, they set up a basic, minimum budget to cover fixed costs and the lowest level of operations anticipated. Then, each month they add a supplementary amount to this minimum to cover the actual level forecast for the coming month. The value of this and other flexible budgets is that they permit logical reactions to changing conditions during a planning period, without giving up the control provided by a detailed expense budget.

Zero-Based Budgeting   Another approach to budgeting looks at the control problem from the bottom up. It challenges the traditional approach, which tends to assume that if a program or operation was given money last year, it should get it again this year. *Zero-based budgeting* requires, instead, that every year each manager justify her or his entire budget request from scratch; from zero. Each budget request is then treated as a separate decision "package" for higher management to examine. This is done by evaluating each package in terms of inputs (or costs) and measurable outputs in the form of benefits. Each package is then assigned a numerical score, or

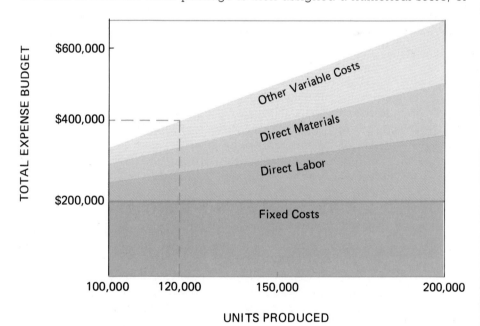

Figure 6-4. A Continuously Flexible Budget. *This kind of budget adjusts allowed expenditures to the exact level of production encountered. It permits a given level of fixed costs, no matter what the output, and adds the variable costs for materials, labor, and other categories associated with the exact output achieved. If, as shown by the broken line, production was 120,000 units, the total expense budget would be $400,000.*

weight. All packages are then ranked in order, with the most "valuable" request at the top and the least "valuable" at the bottom. Based upon how much total money management has to spend, it cuts off those budget packages at the lower end of the scale. While the zero-based budgeting approach began in private business, it has very wide acceptance in government and nonprofit, service-type operations.

THE FULL PICTURE REQUIRES NONBUDGETARY CONTROLS
Budgets and budget variance reports help control everything from the use of a sewing machine in a 10-worker clothing factory to the billions of dollars taken in and spent by the federal government. They do not tell the whole story, though. Many activities and results need control that cannot be easily provided by budgets. Other methods are available.

Controlling Quality   A business that provides goods or services with less than a certain expected quality will not prosper. Shoddy work rarely brings success. Take three common consumer complaints: repair work that does not hold up, client services that do not really help, products that break or that do not fit. All of these are more likely to be the results of unsolved management problems rather than of management's cynicism or contempt for the public. At their root, these problems are control problems.

PRODUCT QUALITY   Every control effort must have a standard. When controlling the quality of goods and services, the standard is the description of the products themselves, their specifications. Standards for physical goods include a physical description of the product (size, shape, weight, material, finish, or any other important characteristics) and requirements for the way the product must perform. A watch, for instance, not only must have the right number and size of gears and other parts; it must also keep time within certain limits of accuracy. A light bulb must create light of prescribed intensity for a certain length of time. It is not enough for it to be just the right shape and made of the right material.

SERVICE QUALITY   Standards for services are harder to define. Since a service often consists simply of the performance of a procedure for someone else, such as in repairing an auto engine, planning a vacation trip, or selling a house, the definition of the procedure is part of the standard. The quality of auto-repair service, for instance, is partly judged by whether the mechanic followed the right troubleshooting steps, used approved parts, and was skillful in applying repair techniques. Again, knowing whether the right procedure was used is not enough. The vital question is, Did it work? Only if the planning process has created measurable goals can providers of services answer that question.

THE QUALITY CONTROL SYSTEM   The key consideration with quality control is to make sure quality does get measured and controlled. Every organization that creates a product of any kind, whether goods or services, should have quality control. It must: (1) identify the important characteristics of the product; (2) measure the actual products in some way; (3) compare these with the specifications developed while planning; and (4) take action if necessary.

Many large manufacturers have developed quality control to a science, using sophisticated measurements, tests, inspections, and statistical analyses to achieve a uniform high quality. Smaller organizations can rarely duplicate these methods. Instead, they must develop appropriate control techniques within the limits of their resources. A retail shoe store, for example, provides a service by making shoes available locally, having them on hand when buyers need them so they do not have to wait for the shoes to be shipped from the factory. The quality of the service is hurt when the store does not have the shoes in stock that customers want. The store manager exerts control by noting out-of-stock conditions, inquiries about shoes the store does not stock, and other indicators that service quality is failing.

Quality control, then, belongs in any organization, large or small, whether a manufacturer or a producer of services. Further, no matter what the type of organization, quality control should be systematic; it should be a planned group of standards and procedures that work together to continuously monitor the final product and its component parts. The manufacturing manager of a foundry, for example, will have final responsibility for a whole range of product goals and inspection and control methods. The patterns from which castings are made will be checked and double-checked for conformity with specifications. Separate quality standards will be set for each critical step of the manufacturing process: the weight, chemical composition, and integrity of the casting itself; the size, position, and alignment of borings; the position, depth, and surface finish of millings; and so on.

Each of these many standards needs a specific performance measure to allow actual results to be compared with desired results. The manufacturing manager will usually delegate the details of setting up physical inspection procedures to others, but will retain responsibility for seeing that the component inspections work together to catch the faults that would cause unacceptable finished products.

Thus, each operator and each machine has standards, measures of performance, and corrective actions when performance is unacceptable. The corrections at this level may involve simple reprimands, additional training, machine repair or adjustment, and similar actions. Higher-level standards and inspections will cover the entire product and may call for corrective actions that affect the entire organization.

Controlling Production and Operations

Quality control looks at the product itself to check for faults. Quality control standards are a description of the desired characteristics of the output. Production and operations control focus on the way the output is produced; these control standards are descriptions of the methods used, the materials used, and the machine operations that go into producing the product.

A fundamental concern of production control is setting and maintaining time standards. The production budget, or quota, is the central tool for this kind of control. But success in keeping output up demands a close look at the way work is being done. When the time comes to count the output, it is often too late to meet production goals.

Correct methods and procedures serve as standards in production control; this means the methods must be clearly defined. For the supervisor of a packing operation to be able to say, "You're not doing that right," for example, he or she must be certain of what is "right." For the manager of a retail sales department to correct the way a clerk fills out a sales slip, he or she must have an exact idea of the right way the slip is to be done. In complicated manufacturing operations where considerable skill and craftsmanship are required, defining methods and giving the training and supervision to be sure they are used can be challenging.

Beyond output levels and work methods, controlling production and operations calls for attention to a number of other factors:

1. *Facilities.* The manager must ensure that the right tools and equipment are being used. Maintenance of facilities becomes a major control area in itself.
2. *Materials.* Production managers must control the inventory of manufacturing materials and supplies. Running out of stock on an essential material can be disastrous to production schedules and costs. The manager must further ascertain that the purchasing and receiving procedures ensure that the materials used are of the necessary quality.
3. *Labor force.* Many individual standards and checks must combine to keep from having too few or too many people at work, to make sure the workers have the right skills and training, to see that general motivational levels are kept up, and to keep absences and tardiness within acceptable limits.
4. *Safety.* Accident prevention is a goal in itself. The safety of workers must be included as an important goal in production control. In general, if proper work methods are used, machinery is kept in good shape, and employees are trained to be safety conscious, accidents will be kept under control.

Other Nonbudgetary Controls

Good managers may choose any of countless other aspects of their organizations to apply specific control efforts. Many use statistical analysis or other special research studies to get at results. A training program, for example, will have goals, usually defined by the kind of performance expected from trainees. It should have follow-up and control (often of a statistical nature) to see if the people trained really can do what they are supposed to be able to do. A public relations campaign will typically have the goal of making a firm better known to the public. This campaign needs follow-up market research studies to see if it has succeeded.

One control method is a great supplement to all other forms and numbers of control: *personal observation*. Effective managers are deeply involved in what is going on inside *and* outside their organizations. They talk to people, watch what they are doing, and ask questions. This clarifies and fills in the gaps in numerical information. Personal observation and involvement is especially useful in controlling such issues as ethical behavior and community relations. Intimate knowledge of people and issues may be the only control "measurement" available to management for these important matters.

PROCEDURES REQUIRE
SPECIAL CONTROL EFFORTS
A *procedure* is a standard way of doing things. The basic production or service activity of an organization may be very simple; the other activities that support it are almost always complex.

What to Control   Martin runs a pharmacy with one employee. What they do is fairly simple from a management point of view. Someone comes in with a prescription; they take the medicine from a shelf, count it or prepare it in some way, give it to the buyer, and take the payment. All the other work that has to be done to allow them to do this, however, can be exceedingly complex, time-consuming, and expensive. Martin must control his inventory to keep from running out of drugs and other stock items; he must place orders and make purchases; he must control expiration dates; he must pay bills; he must handle paperwork from the health department and from public and private insurance companies; he must do the bookkeeping; he must have a payroll setup, even with only one employee; he must compute and pay taxes and insurance. Like managers everywhere, Martin must do countless other things to support and control the main flow of the process.

Procedures determine how managers and employees will carry on the countless activities of an enterprise. A procedure for maintaining standard inventory, for instance, will specify a way to tell the following:

- How much inventory is on hand for each item, and when to order more.
- How to decide from whom to order, and how to follow up on delivery.
- How to verify that the right stock has been received.
- How to check the accuracy of bills received from the supplier.
- How to pay the bill and record the payment.

All of that is needed for just the one operating step of a two-person retail pharmacy. In an organization like the defense department of the federal government, the same kind of inventory-purchasing-bill-paying-accounting process becomes almost unbelievably intricate and costly.

How to Control   Procedures deserve a good deal of attention. They are great users, or wasters, of resources. There are two main areas managers should look at.

MAKE SURE EXISTING PROCEDURES ARE BEING FOLLOWED   Good controls define procedures so that they are as easy as possible to understand and use. A written description helps. If you expect someone to follow a procedure, be sure that you have thoroughly trained that person in how to do so. Check periodically to see that employees really are doing it the right way. It is human nature to come up with a simpler or different way to do things. Employees may not understand all of the ways their procedures interact with others, though, and the new way may cause problems elsewhere.

CONTROL THE PROCEDURES THEMSELVES   Managers must look at the way separate parts of procedures fit together and how different procedures support or conflict with each other. Managers strive to simplify and to eliminate duplication. Good control prevents, especially, the growth of unplanned procedures. When an operating problem arises, it should ideally be handled by existing procedures. If a new procedure really is needed, carefully plan it to be simple and to fit with others. Additionally, managers must be alert to the interactions of procedures. A change in one procedure that represents a great improvement in one area may have a harmful effect elsewhere because it interferes or conflicts with other activities.

VITAL-AREA MEASURES HELP CONTROL THE OVERALL ORGANIZATION
An organization is not successful unless it meets its higher-level goals. A manufacturer may produce 5 million driveshafts, every one perfect, and still fail if no profit accrues. Every budget may be exactly adhered to, yet accomplish nothing, if the organization suddenly is edged out by competitors and loses its market share. Control of the overall organization is the ultimate challenge for managers. It is a task that is typically more difficult and less precise than controlling the dimensions and weight of a glass bottle. This is so because many of its goals deal with intangible, but urgent, issues such as social responsibility and employee devel-

opment. Other goals, such as market share and profitability, are easier to monitor since they provide clear, objective standards with which to compare results. Regardless of specificity, however, top-level managers must keep close watch of progress in areas vital to overall success.

Key-Area Control   This approach to overall control tries to measure results in broad operational areas that correspond to high-level goals. A business typically establishes these main indicators of success: profits, market share, product development, growth, productivity, employee development, and social responsibility. The company managers then try to identify one or more key indicators to show where the company stands in each area.

The problem, as in many other planning and control efforts, is to measure the results. Ingenuity is essential. Employee development is a good example. Most organizations understandably want their employees to improve their skills. To find whether this is really taking place, managers will use interviews, questionnaires, formal observations, and even psychiatrists' and psychologists' evaluations. To judge social responsibility, managers may record decisions made and money spent to protect the environment. They may keep track of donations and public service activities. They may use surveys on the safety and value of products or services, or on unanswered consumer needs. They may formally analyze complaints and other communications from customers or the general public.

In general, the success of key-area control depends on the care given to setting and defining overall goals. If the goals are clear, dedicated managers can find some way to measure progress and achievement in these vital areas.

Profit and Loss   Nearly every business considers profit to be one of the most important indicators of overall success. An income statement shows the actual revenues and expenditures for a period of operations. The company's income and expense budget for the period is the standard with which it is compared. Variances found in particular categories of either revenue or cost will point the way toward what action is needed.

Many managers also compare income statements with another standard, with the income statements of competitors, or with averages for the industry in which they operate. This can be particularly revealing when cost categories are expressed as a percent of total revenue. If company A spends 34 percent of its income on personnel and company B spends only 23 percent, for example, the managers of company A might well begin to wonder if they are using their employees as effectively as possible.

Return on Investment   Another financial measure uses profits to show how efficiently an organization uses its assets. *Return on investment* (ROI) is an arithmetic measure of how much profit[1] is produced from an organization's total investments. It is calculated by the formula shown at the top of page 148.

$$\frac{\text{Total annual sales revenue}}{\text{Total of investments}} \times \frac{\text{Annual profits for the year}}{\text{Total annual sales revenue}}$$

If your division of a corporation had sales of $4,000,000 for the year, earnings (profits) of $500,000 for that year, and a total investment of $8,000,000, your ROI is:

$$\frac{4,000,000}{8,000,000} \times \frac{500,000}{4,000,000} = 0.06, \text{ or 6 percent}$$

If your division could get the same sales and earnings as above using a total investment of only $2,000,000, you would be performing much better. The ROI would be 25 percent.

Managers are obviously interested in the return on investment because it answers the questions, "What are we getting back from your capital? Would we have done better to put the investment somewhere else?" The ROI figure can be hard to interpret, though. Some companies look for an ROI of 20 percent or higher because of the high risk involved in a business enterprise. Other companies have succeeded and prospered with far lower returns. ROI is often helpful in comparing one company with another or one industry with another. Caution is called for in its use, however. A *variety of measures* of overall success must combine to judge progress in meeting high-level goals.

SUMMARY

1. The control process consists of (a) setting standards, (b) comparing actual results with the standards, and (c) taking action to correct any deviations discovered. Control should be applied to critical areas of an organization: products, operations, costs, revenue, capital, and other special programs and goals.

2. Carefully prepared budgets provide a good standard with which to compare costs, production levels, personnel use, and other key control points. Budget variance reports reveal deviations and point to areas where action is needed. Whenever possible, budgets should be flexible to allow for changing conditions and new opportunities.

3. Standards other than budgets provide control of product quality, production, and operations. The key to the use of nonbudgetary control is to clearly define the important characteristics of the product or process being controlled.

4. Procedures consume so much of an organization's resources that they deserve special control. This will focus on: (a) assuring that employees

[1]Typically, ROI is calculated using profit before income taxes are paid. The ROI using profit after taxes is smaller.

understand and follow existing procedures, and (b) simplifying, integrating, and improving the procedures themselves.

5. Control measures should extend to high-level goals. Standards and assessments for such areas as profitability, social responsibility, and employee development will help to indicate the overall functioning of the organization.

REVIEW AND DISCUSSION QUESTIONS

1. What are the three steps of the control process?

2. Give some examples of feedback. Why is it important to the control process?

3. Is it possible to set measurable standards for every area of an organization that needs control? If not, what should managers do to overcome the problem?

4. Is taking action to correct deviations really part of the control process? Explain.

5. When a deviation has been found, what is the first thing to do? What would this mean to someone who is setting up a control program?

6. How would a production budget be used as a control tool? Why is it important?

7. What is a flexible budget? What is its purpose?

8. What is the most important consideration for quality control?

9. Why is it important to have ways to control procedures?

10. What is the major difficulty with key area control? Can it be overcome? If so, how?

Problems and Projects

1. Controlling the quality and usefulness of products is an important aspect of control in most organizations. Quality control becomes difficult when the product is a service. Propose some kinds and examples of standards and methods of assessing actual conditions for use in controlling the quality of the following services. Discuss the suggestions in class.

   a. A messenger service that carries parcels and letters within a single large city.

    b. The social service department of a large hospital. The department helps patients with their home affairs while they are hospitalized and helps them readjust after being released.

    c. A private tutoring service that teaches foreign languages to people who do business overseas.

2. *Performance Situation—Nancy's Hobby:* It all started as a simple hobby, and Nancy still likes to tell people that it's nothing more than that. But with three employees, a small rented building, and sales last year of $52,000, most people don't really believe her. Three years ago all Nancy talked about was working with clay and the unique designs of her vases and flower pots. Now her passion is management. She talks about taxes, return on investment, and systems. She even told one of her customers to let her know about any problems with the vases because she needed his "feedback."

Nancy had never paid much attention to control. She had kept books well enough to make the payroll and to pay taxes. Now she has started setting specific objectives in a number of areas, and she wants to see that her little company is making progress in reaching the objectives.

Making the vases and pots that Nancy sells is a surprisingly complex business. It requires the mixing of several kinds of clays and pigments, hand fabrication on an electric potter's wheel, hand coloring, and firing in a gas kiln that uses a great deal of expensive propane gas. She sells and delivers much of the stock herself and ships the rest by highway freight. She employs two potters and a clerk who handles inventory, materials receiving, and other tasks.

Outline a control network for Nancy. What are the critical areas of this business that she should control? What kinds of standards does she need? For each area, would she use a budget or a nonbudgetary control?

3. A corporation with three divisions uses the return on investment as a partial measure of the overall performance of the divisions. Some of the financial results for the year are:

DIVISION	TOTAL INVESTMENT	TOTAL SALES	PROFITS
A	$88,000,000	$125,000,000	$15,000,000
B	$12,500,000	$ 24,000,000	$ 2,700,000
C	$ 8,000,000	$ 13,000,000	$ 1,300,000

Compute the return on investment for these three divisions. Using this method to judge, which division made the most efficient use of its assets? Which made the least efficient use?

4. Metropolitan Air Services provides one service. In the local market the company serves—one large airport and two small ones—it has become so good at it that there is almost no competition. Metropolitan does everything for private aircraft owned by businesses and individuals, *except* mechanical servicing. The company's employees or contractors do everything from emptying the ashtrays to redecorating the entire interior of a plane.

The managers at Metroplitan have always taken an informal approach, and they feel it has worked well. Recently, though, they did set up a formal control system, complete with checklists, printed forms, and variance reports, to try to measure and improve productivity. Once the control procedures were in effect, the results were very encouraging, with one exception: the performance of the cleaning crews, who do routine work cleaning cabins and cockpits, was far below the standard. The quality of their work was excellent, but they simply were not cleaning as many airplanes in their regular shifts as plans called for.

If this situation were your responsibility, how would you approach it? What would you try to do first? How would you go about it? What general kinds of action would you consider?

5. Budgets are forecasts, plans, and control tools. Make a budget for personal expenses for one week. Record actual amounts you spend and note deviations from your budget. Forecast your expenditures by analyzing the kinds of things you spend money for and by setting a probable amount for each category. Adopt the forecast as a spending plan. Record your actual expenses in each category, and compare them with the budget. Were there any significant deviations? What caused them? Was the standard wrong, or did you spend money you shouldn't have? If you were going to continue the budgeting, what action would you take to correct the deviations?

6. Every undertaking that has objectives is a candidate for control procedures. Using your instructor as a source of information, explore the objectives and controls that apply to the management course you are now taking. Consider the specific nature of the learning that is to take place as well as the nature of nonacademic expectations and goals such as attendance, record-keeping, and the like. Make a list of objectives and of the kinds of control methods used for each. Do these standards and controls follow the areas outlined in Table 6-1 on page 138?

Cases for Analysis and Discussion

CASE 1: TOO MUCH CONTROL

Al Lopez muttered a few choice expressions when he read the memo. The same kind of thing had happened before, and Al had gritted his teeth and let it pass. This case involved a major order, though, as much as $1 million in the long run. If the customers couldn't even find out if the equipment was suitable for the use they had in mind, they were certain not to buy. This time Al was going to do something about it.

MEMO
From: H. Martin, Manager, Product Engineering
To: A. Lopez, Regional Sales Manager

I have received your request for detailed engineering information on the Model 810. It sounds like your customer has an interesting application in mind. Unfortunately, I must inform you that we will be unable to provide the modification data you wanted. Some of the information would have to be summarized from our original design studies, and a few items would have to be newly developed. We estimate that this would take an engineer nearly two days to complete. As I am sure you do also, we pride ourselves on strict adherence to our expense budgets. And our budget, I am sorry to say, does not allow us to expend the time and money needed to give you the information.

A. Was the engineering manager right to answer Al's request as he did?

B. Does this case illustrate a problem with the control procedures in this company?

C. To resolve the problem, who should Al talk to? What should he say? How can he argue his case?

CASE 2: WHY DON'T THEY GET OFF MY BACK?

"If he stops by here one more time, I'm gonna let him have it!" Brenda flourished the heavy wrench with a convincing slash. "What's it to him, as long as I do my job? He wants to see every little step. He must have asked me fifty questions last week about how I was setting up my machine. Then he's got to bring things back from inspection, like that coupler. It was crooked, all right. I forgot to retighten the jig. But he didn't have anything to say about the five hundred that were straight; just the one that was crooked! Sometimes I think it isn't worth working here. Why don't they just let me do my job?"

A. Why did Brenda's supervisor act like that? What was he trying to accomplish?
B. Is Brenda justified in reacting like this? Why does she feel this way?
C. What could the supervisor do, if anything, to make things go more smoothly?

CASE 3: LIKE THERE'S NO TOMORROW

Dwight wasn't really comfortable with his decision, but he said to himself, "I've got to look to my own future; when the chickens come home to roost, somebody else will be here to greet them."

The decision that Dwight was thinking of was a simple one: *to do nothing.* There were a number of distinct signs that the main product of the division which he managed—a line of small electric generators—was gradually becoming obsolete because the generators needed too much fuel to operate. Sales were still good; in fact, the highest they had ever been. Profits were excellent, too. But Dwight had to admit that five years down the road, the picture didn't look too bright. And yet, he had just rejected an extremely well thought-out product development program presented by his engineers. They were convinced that they could design a new generator that would make the same amount of power on 40 percent of the fuel. Why would he reject it?

Dwight knew exactly why. The corporate management was completely sold on return on investment as the only real way to measure overall performance. A high ROI needs high sales and low costs—right now, in the present. The product development program would have been expensive and wouldn't have paid off for at least four years. Starting it would have damaged the ROI at least until that time.

"And besides," thought Dwight, "with this year's performance, I ought to get promoted right away. Maybe whoever gets stuck with this division won't be too likely to blame the problems on a new superior. Anyway, I'll be *very* sympathetic."

A. Did Dwight make the right decision? Why, or why not?
B. What would you have done differently, if anything?
C. What should the corporate managers have done to avoid this kind of situation?

Managers Organize, Staff, and Direct

The Organizing Process

7

After completing Chapter 7, you will be able to do the following:

- Determine the important characteristics of a given role in an actual organization.
- Interpret the relations between the duties and objectives of a given role and the overall objectives of an organization.
- Create an organization chart to illustrate the formal relations in an organization.
- Devise a workable division of a group of duties to allow useful specialization and effective coordination.

- Analyze the activities, decisions, and relations in a simple organization for use in defining job content.
- Write a job description for a position with which you are familiar.
- Judge the suitability of several methods of departmentalization for application to a specific organizing situation.

Mary was a little confused on her first day at work as a programmer analyst. She spent 20 minutes with a clerk in the personnel department filling out forms. The personnel manager then described the pay plan, the policies for vacations, absences, lateness, and what seemed like dozens of other topics. He then introduced Mary to her direct boss, Lennie, the accounting systems analyst. Lennie introduced her to his boss, the data processing manager, and then to two other strangers who seemed to be giving Mary a careful, appraising look. Lennie explained that they were program coders and that Mary would be their direct supervisor.

Lennie explained Mary's job in some detail. He showed clearly what she was responsible for and what she was not responsible for. He gave examples of the kinds of decisions she would be expected to make on her own. Lennie also described the two coders' jobs and outlined the kind of supervision he expected Mary to give them. He told her that she would spend a good deal of her time consulting with other analysts, even though she was directly responsible to him. Finally, he described the work of the program standards committee and told Mary that she would be an active and, he hoped, an important member.

Mary was learning where she would fit in the organization; what her part of the work would be; what her role was. But where did all of the other roles in the organization originate? Who decided that there would be two coders supervised by a programmer-analyst who was supervised by an accounting systems analyst who reported to a data processing manager? How did they decide to divide up the work and authority in that way and to establish those particular relationships? These decisions were made by the company managers. The divisions and relationships were the result of managers carrying out the organizing process.

THE ORGANIZING PROCESS PRESCRIBES HOW PEOPLE WILL WORK TOGETHER

The reason for having companies, bureaus, and agencies is that few important goals in society can be met by a person working alone. Building the World Trade Center in New York City, sailing a cruise ship to the Caribbean, or vaccinating millions of children against polio all require that many people work together in cooperation toward a single goal. When large groups of people attack any problem, the outcome will be nothing but chaos unless each person knows what specific part, what role, he or she is to play. The organizing process establishes these roles and decides how they will work together.

Roles

A *role* in an organization may be thought of as a particular job. It is defined by (1) the specific duties or work a person is to handle, (2) a group of objectives or standards by which the success of the work is judged, (3) an agreed upon degree of authority or personal freedom to act and make decisions to meet the objectives, and (4) a set of relationships to the other people and jobs in the organization.

The head of the inventory department for a wholesaler, for example, might describe his or her role this way:

"My job is to see that the stock is safe and in good order and to record accurately and immediately all inventory that comes in or goes out and pass the information to the purchasing, sales, and accounting departments. I accomplish this partly by supervising the work of three inventory workers. The chief buyer is my immediate boss. We work out plans together for each year, and she judges the quality of my work."

Relations Between Roles

The *first* task of organizing is to decide on what roles are needed to meet overall goals. This determines which roles will exist; for example, to decide that there will be a head for an inventory department, a chief buyer, and other specific roles. The *second* aspect of organizing, which must be handled together with the first, is to decide how the roles can best work together. This second kind of decision determines, for instance, that the head of inventory will be supervised by the chief buyer, instead of by the sales manager or the general manager.

Relationships are not only of the type in which one employee has authority to give instructions to or judge the work of another. *Coordination* of separate efforts is also essential; this establishes the relationships between roles. Different roles at the same level of authority must get their work done in harmony. The output of one department must be ready in time for another department to begin work on it. The accounting department, for example, must be ready to prepare the paperwork when an order is ready to ship. Shipping, purchasing, advertising, and all the rest must synchronize their work. No necessary function should be left undone, but there should be minimum duplication of effort. It is the organizing process that provides the formal structure through which this coordination is achieved.

The Formal Structure

The purpose of organizing, then, is to establish a formal *structure of roles* arranged in a *system of relationships.* What this means for a small business is illustrated by the organization chart in Figure 7-1.

An *organization chart* is a graphic portrait, or picture, of an organization's formal structure. It shows the major managerial roles in an organization and outlines the ways they are formally related. Let's see what the organization chart for the manufacturing company in Figure 7-1 tells us.

The general manager is placed at the top of the chart to show that he is responsible for the success or failure of the entire operation. This company is obviously oriented toward research and new product development, because it calls for a separate role: the assistant general manager is to have special responsibility and authority in those areas. The chart shows how the other roles relate. The finance, manufacturing, and marketing managers have relatively the same degree of authority, since they are placed on the same level. Roles with lesser authority fall below them so that the overall picture the chart portrays is pyramidal in shape. Managers with the greatest responsibility and authority are at the top; those with the least at the bottom.

The lines that connect roles, or positions, on an organization chart show some of the relationships that exist. The manufacturing manager, for instance, is the direct superior of the purchasing manager and will supervise that individual's work. In this company, production and purchasing are seen as different facets of the same general function—manufacturing. They receive special coordination by making the same manager, the manufacturing manager, responsible for both.

The formal structure chosen for a company or agency will depend on the nature of the organization's goals and activities. For example, a bank will need a manager to supervise loan officers, while a clothing manufacturer will have managers who specialize in purchasing cloth, directing the manufacturing of clothing, and selling to the clothing market. Nonetheless, all formal structures are similar in that managers consciously plan to insure that all employees are working in a common effort to meet the organization's goals.

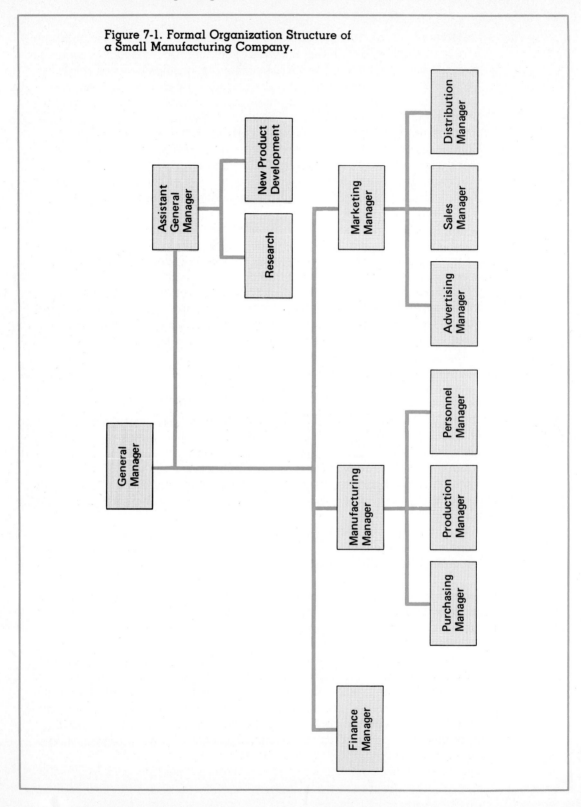

Figure 7-1. Formal Organization Structure of a Small Manufacturing Company.

Managers in Action

"I restructured American Airlines the way I did the *Times-Mirror* subsidiary companies, where I had been president. I reorganized the corporate line—the reporting relationships and assignments to senior officers," says Albert V. Casey, president and chairperson of American Airlines.

"Regardless of the business you're in, I believe that there are only four jobs in any company. There's someone in charge of making the product, someone in charge of selling it, there's a scorekeeper, and there's the boss. I could show you a copy of our chart. It's an absurdly simple thing.

"Our senior vice presidents earn thousands of dollars a year and they get a report card every three months. They all give me ten priority goals each year; the people who report to them must do the same thing. Then I pay people based on their performance. It's very, very competitive.

"I believe in firing people, too. It takes a year to hire the right person, understand him, and to give him an understanding of the goals. Then the person needs some time to show accomplishment. But I never keep people more than two years if they don't perform. If you keep people two years, you've got them for life."

Source: "Competition, Streamlined Management Mark Style of American Airlines Chairman," *The AMBA Executive*, vol. 7, nos. 4 and 5 (April/May 1978), p. 1. Copyright © 1978, Association of MBA Executives, Inc.

The Informal Organization

The planned organization reflects only what its planners would like to have. Many other important relationships exist for one reason or another and *do not* appear on the organization chart. No matter what the chart says, common work groups, friendships, antagonisms, and many other social forces strongly influence the way an organization really works. The distribution manager may think the marketing manager is weak or too involved with playing golf. If a distribution problem comes up, the distribution manager may go directly to the manufacturing manager because they are good friends socially. In many production work groups, the formal supervisor may be less powerful in deciding what goes on than is indicated by the chart. Often, a worker with no formal authority but with a persuasive personality will exert greater influence over other workers. These informal relationships will be explored further in later chapters. The first concern of the manager is to establish an effective formal structure. Later on, he or she must also be vitally concerned with its informal aspects.

ORGANIZING IMPROVES THE DIVISION AND COORDINATION OF LABOR

A basic question is still unanswered: What makes an effective formal structure? What determines whether to have one person handle both advertising and promotion or one person for each function? What decides whether the general manager, the assistant general manager, or someone else should supervise? The answer is that *a structure is successful if it helps individuals to contribute their best toward attaining overall organization goals.* This requires (1) an effective division of labor and (2) the successful coordination of efforts.

The Division of Labor

When you call the accounting firm of Jones and Jones, Inc., a receptionist answers and switches your call to the person you want to speak with. But Jones and Jones *could* have set it up so that when you call, every phone in the place rings. Whoever answers first has the responsibility to make the right connection. Obviously, the latter alternative would create a madhouse of shouting and switching, confusion and wrong connections. Instead, Jones and Jones has established a specialist, a receptionist who carries out a clearly defined segment of the total company work load. This is what managers accomplish when "dividing" up labor. They create specialization.

The advantages of specialization are that individual jobs can be learned faster and performed more easily when they encompass only a small slice of a large, complex activity. In many cases, the division of a large job into smaller ones and the assignment of different workers to each piece creates more output than when each worker carries out all parts of the entire job. This is an expression of the classic economic concept of the division of labor. Dividing up the work into specialties also allows organizations to take advantage of special skills and talents of employees and to partially avoid being hurt by individual weaknesses. Harry may be outstanding at writing reports, but terrible at supervising other people. Alice may be terrific with numbers, but awful with the English language. Both can be put in specialized jobs that will take advantage of their skills.

There is a danger, of course, in too much specialization. If managers create a job role in which an employee does nothing but put nut after nut on bolt after bolt with no freedom for change or initiative, management may soon be faced with morale problems. The same is true in dividing up managerial work. All employees, managers as well as rank and file, usually do better in jobs that have breadth, variety, and richness. Happily, the advantages of division can be realized without building a structure of mind-numbing, routine jobs.

Each instance of dividing up work and responsibilities should meet three tests: (1) Does each segment or job make a necessary contribution to meeting subgoals and overall goals? (2) Is each job and role designed to take advantage of skills? (3) Does it allow each individual to contribute his or her best?

Relating the Roles Dividing up duties and responsibilities does not create an organization. It is also essential that a decision be made as to how the roles created will interact. The prescribed relations between roles provide for three factors:

1. Coordination and control of activities.
2. Assurance that necessary communication takes place.
3. Clearly understood mechanisms for making planning and operating decisions.

It is important to pin down who is responsible for coordinating the activities of every role. Someone must determine which jobs should interact and will thus be mutually dependent. This is a very common requirement. For this reason, organization designers must specify whose job it is to see that the interacting jobs work together in timing, quality, and other activities. Such coordination requires planning and control to make sure that person or department A operates in a way that reinforces the work of person or department B. Other decision-making responsibility must also be specified so as to define role relationships. If Betty discovers that an order is late, for example, is *she* supposed to decide what to do, or should she report it to someone else who will decide? Who judges, for instance, that John's work is unacceptable and then decides what to do about it? Organization control depends upon clear specifications of the kinds of decisions each role should make and the other people (or jobs) on whom the decisions will be binding.

This stage of organizing also creates the levels of management. There are no distinct divisions between the levels, but most organizers think roughly of three categories of management: top, middle, and bottom (or supervisory). *Top management* is responsible for setting the long-term direction of the organization, deciding what markets to compete in, determining financial structure, making major decisions on the overall form of the organization, and supervising middle managers. *Middle management* concentrates on developing the more specific strategies needed to support overall goals, quarterly and annual planning, organizing departments, deploying sales forces and advertising support, designing production methods and facilities, and supervising "front line" managers. *Supervisors* are the first level of managers, the front line. They are responsible for seeing that the daily productive work gets done. They set short-term schedules, make organizational decisions at the work-crew level, and supervise the application of plans and methods set by middle managers.

Another concern in creating the relationships among roles is communication. The organization structure can facilitate the flow of opinion, advice, and information, or it can nearly cut off the flow altogether. When organizing, managers consider who needs to communicate with whom and who needs to know what. The structure then is designed to provide contacts and relationships where communications needs are highest.

THE CREATION OF ROLES SERVES TO DEFINE JOBS

The role a person plays in an organization develops over time. It depends not only on the organization design but also on the individual's personality, knowledge, skills, intelligence, leadership ability, and other characteristics. Many aspects of a role are informal; who likes whom or who fears whom, for example. These are beyond real control by managers. Managers can, however, formally establish the basic organizational attributes of a role. They do this by defining and describing jobs.

Determining Job Content

Each job must fit into the organization's structure along with other jobs. Based upon this analysis, a decision must be made of what duties, activities, and authority (or power) will make up a specific job. As with most managerial tasks, the best way to approach defining jobs is to first look at overall objectives and then work downward. A clear set of goals combined with long, hard thought points to the sort of work that must be performed if the organization is to reach its goals. Such analysis will produce lists of activities to perform, types of decisions to make, and relations to engage in. These three elements make up the components of *job content;* they combine to allow individuals to work toward objectives. Determination of job content, then, is done in three steps.

ANALYZE JOB ACTIVITIES   This is basic to organizing. Managers must decide exactly what work must get done for the organization to achieve its goals. A company's basic process might be, for instance, buying goods at wholesale and selling them at retail. But what are all of the many specific actions that contribute to the process? Receiving goods, checking their quality, counting inventory, writing checks, moving stock from storeroom to sales room, arranging window displays, buying advertising, waiting on customers, and dusting the counters are only a few of the possibly hundreds of activities that combine to buy and resell goods. Nevertheless, no matter how hard such a list might be to make, the proper divisions of labor will require a detailed list of activities.

ANALYZE JOB DECISIONS   Work does not consist only of lifting boxes, driving nails, or typing letters. Decision making is a characteristic of almost any job, no matter how elementary. It is, of course, one of the major parts of most management jobs. For this reason, an organizational design will need a list of types and levels of decisions to be made. For the retail store, such a list might include deciding what specific stock to buy and how much of each item, setting prices, deciding how much and where to advertise, and establishing policies on returns of damaged merchandise. There are dozens of other important ones, too. These decisions should be examined in detail. Who would decide to expand, for instance, or to open the store evenings? Who would decide at which door a truck should park to unload? The list is large, and each decision must be assigned to one job or another.

ANALYZE JOB RELATIONS   The main questions here are those associated with authority, communications, and planning and control for coordination. Who needs supervision, and who will provide it? Whose job is it to see that stockroom personnel and the sales clerks are properly coordinated? Who most needs to talk to and work with whom? Careful job definition will need this basic information.

Activities, decisions, and relations must now be reviewed. Which activities go together? Which ones use the same resources or space? Which ones closely depend on each other? Which decisions immediately affect the performance of work? And so on. Decision making should be moved as close to the affected activity as possible. If goods cannot be moved into stock until their quality has been verified, for example, the quality decision should be in the hands of someone who is on the scene, if possible. Identification of interdependent activities and decisions also points to relations that should be grouped. If fifteen or twenty or more similar activities require close communication and on-the-spot decisions, they make good candidates for a small number of distinct jobs with close formal relations. Consolidation and allocation of specific activities, decision-making authority, and relationships create specific jobs.

Job Descriptions   Once management has parceled the job contents into batches small enough for one person to carry them out, it is possible to convert these roles into real jobs. This is typically done in the form of job descriptions. A *job description* is a written account of the major function of a position, its duties and responsibilities, the extent of its decision-making authority, and its formal relations with other jobs. Since organizing is an ever-changing process, job descriptions must not be absolutely fixed. Goals shift with changing conditions, and with them the responsibilities of individual managers and workers will also change. Nevertheless, a job description should be as specific as possible, with the understanding that duties and authority are subject to revision.

Table 7-1 is an example of a job description. It is an orderly statement of the major formal components of a position. It includes a summary of the function, an outline of duties, supervision received and given to others, and relationships to other than supervisory personnel. Descriptions of this type are valuable organizing tools. They combine with an organization chart to give an accurate definition of the roles that exist and the ways these roles should interact.

TABLE 7-1. JOB DESCRIPTION FOR A MIDDLE-LEVEL POSITION.

POSITION: Assistant Manager

DEPARTMENT: Personnel

JOB SUMMARY: Assists Manager in planning, controlling, organizing, staffing, and directing the functions of recruiting, selecting, and developing personnel. Has major responsibility for the maintenance of a safe work place. Has major responsibility for maintenance of continuing and temporary programs applying testing to the selection and promotion of employees.

DUTIES PERFORMED:
1. The following represent 60 percent of working time:
   a. Maintain roster of current and anticipated job openings and obtain information on requirements from employing departments.
   b. Establish and maintain a safety program to comply with legal requirements and to provide a safe work place.
   c. Plan and oversee the implementation of all formal testing.
   d. Plan and carry out efforts to verify and improve validity of test use.
2. The following represent 20 percent of working time:
   a. Supervise safety, testing, and clerical employees.
   b. Perform screening interviews of applicants for certain middle-level management positions.
3. The following represent the balance of working time:
   a. Assist and consult with Manager on special projects.
   b. Consult with training department on training evaluation.
   c. Correspond and maintain records.

SUPERVISORY RELATIONSHIPS:
1. Supervised by: Manager, Personnel Department.
2. Supervises: one safety technician, one testing specialist, five or fewer test administrators and scorers.

OTHER RELATIONSHIPS: Frequent communications with all employing department heads, with training unit, and with all operating supervisors; occasional communication with legal department and general management.

Most managers are faced with the need to improve the definitions of existing jobs rather than to create an organization of entirely new jobs. The same process applies, however. Managers must analyze activities, decisions, and relations, group them, and write job descriptions. More often than not, this procedure reveals duplications of effort, neglected activities or decisions, conflicts of authority, missing lines of communication, and other obstacles to a smooth-running organization.

JOBS AND ROLES COMBINE TO MAKE UP DEPARTMENTS
An individual employee fulfilling a specified role and doing a single job is the basic unit of an organization. Whether it is sweeping floors or managing the profitability of a billion-dollar

division, the *job,* or position, with its grouping of duties, tasks, and responsibilities, is the focus of the work. It is the lowest unit of specialization. It is the smallest unit in the division of labor. A job is the basic building block of the formal organizational structure.

To establish a formal means of coordinating the pace, quality, resources used, and other relations among individual jobs, managers create departments. A *department* is a group of closely related individual jobs gathered together under the leadership of (usually) a single manager, and is responsible for carrying out a defined function. A shipping department, for example, might combine the jobs of stock picking, packing in cartons, labeling, and loading trucks under the leadership of a shipping manager. Its function is to ship goods. The New York office of a West Coast law firm may be viewed as a department, too. It combines the clerical, legal, research, and accounting jobs needed to represent the firm's clients on the East Coast.

Departments are formed in much the same way that individual jobs are defined. An analysis of activities, decisions, and relations will reveal groupings of jobs that correspond to segments or aspects of organization goals. Closely related jobs, serving to meet common objectives and requiring close and frequent communication and coordination, will form a natural department.

Forms of Departmentalization

The exact way that managers group jobs into departments depends on the size and type of the organization, on the relative stress placed on specific objectives, and on the philosophies and preferences of the managers. Collecting and shipping goods, for example, is clearly the kind of function for which a department is suitable. But what about a very large manufacturer with different plants separated by thousands of miles? Should all the jobs relating to shipping be grouped under one manager? And what if the company has among its product line huge industrial boilers as well as packets of straight pins? Is shipping products as disparate as these really the same function? Answers to these questions require a managerial judgment, and the answers may differ from manager to manager and from company to company. Fortunately, however, a number of underlying principles for creating departments have evolved. Among the most common are departments based on function, product, geographical area, and customer type, or on some combination of these.

FUNCTIONAL DEPARTMENTS

The most common type of department is one set up to carry out a particular function in the organization. "We need someone to do our finance, bookkeeping, and accounting," an executive frequently observes, "so we'll have an accounting department." The major activities of an organization, of course, will depend on its unique type and specific goals. A manufacturing company might see its highest-level functions as production, marketing, and finance. A wholesaler might define the major functions as operations, sales, and finance. An insurance company might give priority to underwriting, agency relations, claims adjustment, and actuarial. The federal government has formed huge departments for defense, commerce, tax collection, and other functions. A town government might have functional departments for streets, sewer and water, trash collection, and other services.

Each major function usually will be further broken down into yet smaller departments, as illustrated in Figure 7-2. The key to this kind of organization is that jobs are grouped according to the kinds of activities and goals to which they relate. One department in the figure includes every activity directly concerned with making goods for sale. This production department may be made up of thousands of people. Smaller departments within production will center around related specialties: manufacturing, planning and control, and purchasing. Manufacturing might further be divided into the specialties of fabrication and assembly. Within fabrication, departments might be needed which are made up of jobs for the operation of a particular kind of machine.

Departments created on a functional base have the advantage of encouraging specialization and an efficient division of labor. It brings together under a common management the jobs and people who have the greatest need for mutual communication. These are people who are working toward common subgoals. Functional departments have the disadvantage of often causing managers and employees to take too narrow an approach. Each concentrates mainly on her or his own specialty and ignores the welfare of the overall organization. Coordination between departments can be difficult under these conditions. This is especially true when responsibility for coordinating is concentrated in one or two positions near the top of the organization.

PRODUCT DEPARTMENTS Large companies with a number of distinct and specialized products sometimes use these products as the basis for creating departments. Figure 7-3 shows this kind of arrangement. This kind of departmentalization groups together all jobs and functions that contribute directly to the design, production, and sale of a particular product line. A product manager heads an entire organization devoted to a particular product or type of product.

One of the main advantages of organizing this way is that it makes coordination easier and tends to encourage devotion to higher-level goals. A manager might be less inclined to say, "My first loyalty is to the accounting department," and more likely to think, "My first loyalty is to contribute to the success of our product." This organization also moves the responsibility for coordination, and for profitability in the business, further down in the structure. However, it is often less efficient than other kinds of departmentalization because it requires duplicate sales, production planning, and accounting staffs. Overhead may also be high in the central office, because the top executives will need full staff assistance in addition to that already distributed among the product divisions.

Figure 7-2. Functional Organization of a Manufacturing Company.

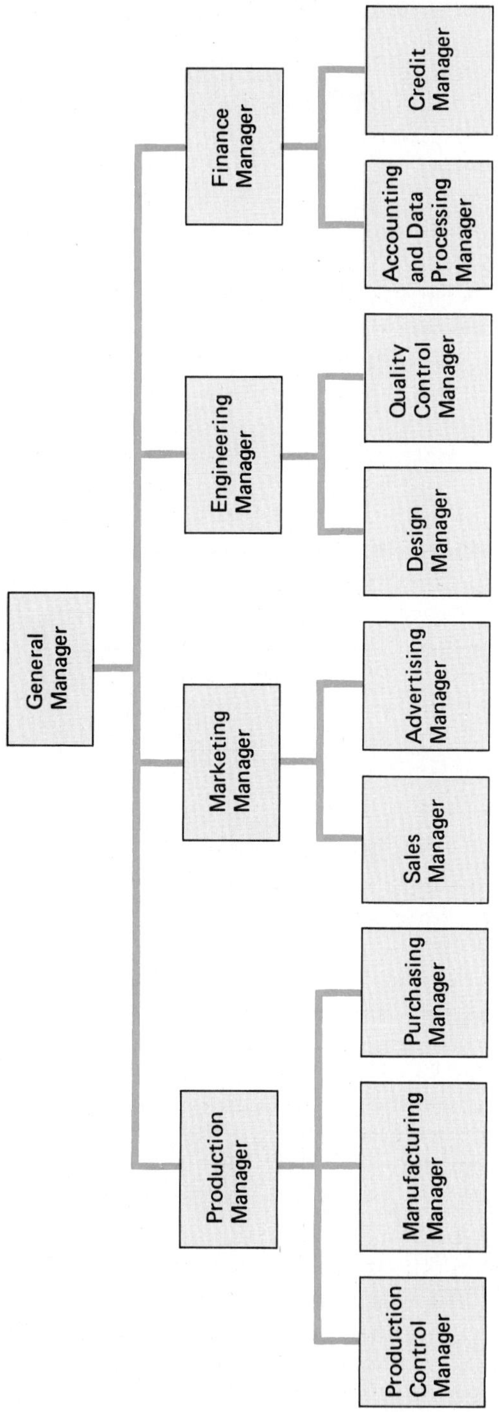

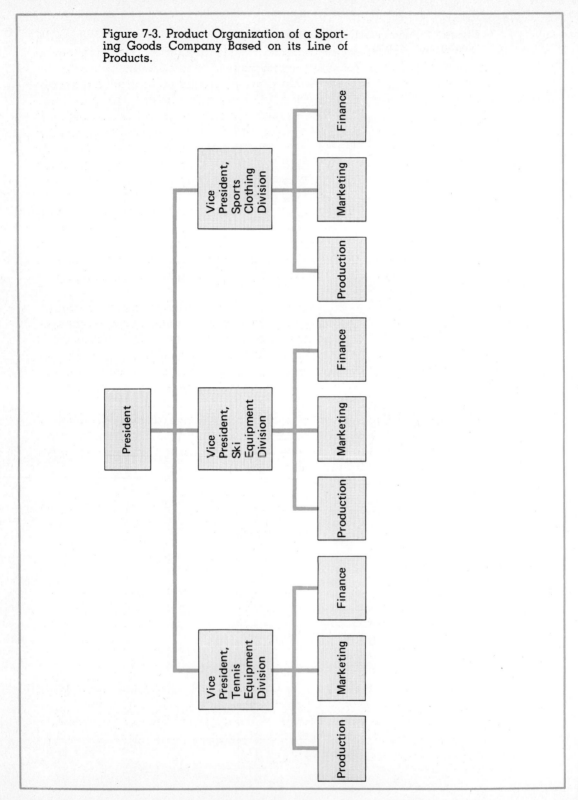

Figure 7-3. Product Organization of a Sporting Goods Company Based on its Line of Products.

GEOGRAPHICAL DEPARTMENTS   The organization shown in Figure 7-4 serves well in many government and business enterprises. Jobs are grouped simply by the geographical area they serve. A manufacturing company, for instance, might divide the country into five regions and appoint a manager to run all of the operations—manufacturing, sales, advertising, personnel, engineering, and accounting—for the region. Sometimes this distribution of responsibility to local areas can be an advantage. There are differences in the way people do business in different parts of the country, and there are regional economic and market trends. A local manager can recognize and take advantage of these regional peculiarities. It has the advantages of moving responsibility for coordination closer to the actual work being done and provides more general management experience for lower-level managers.

The disadvantages of geographical departmentalization are similar to those of product departments. Staffs are duplicated. Central control is hard to maintain. Regional differences may be more apparent than real.

CUSTOMER DEPARTMENTS   The goals and activities of some organizations call for dealing with very diverse kinds of customers. When management creates separate departments to deal with each group of customers, it allows services, products, and sales methods to be tailored to its particular demands. An engineering firm could have one division to specialize in services for local governments and another in services for private industry. A manufacturer might form a consumer division, a government contract division, industrial sales division, and an international division. Creation of departments based on the customers they serve makes sense in many cases. A plastic food container for sale to the Army, for example, might need quite

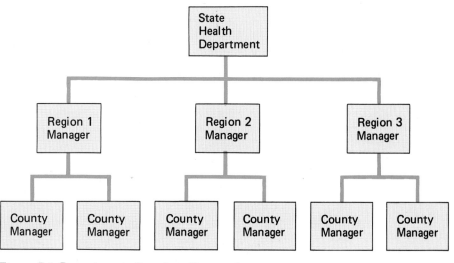

Figure 7-4. Departments Based on Geographical Areas.

different characteristics from those of a similar product for use by the general public. Certainly the sales methods would be different. For instance, TV advertising and distribution through retail stores would not sell many containers to the Army, but would be common in consumer marketing.

Customer departments have a disadvantage in that it is often difficult for them to share facilities and resources in an efficient way. Even though products for two different markets might vary somewhat, it would often be most economical to use the same manufacturing line to produce both. For this reason, customer departments are used most where they matter most, in sales and marketing functions.

Creating Real Departments

Faced with so many possibilities, how do managers decide on the kinds of departments to use in their own organizations? The basic rule is that the form of the structure should match the major factors that determine success in meeting goals. Thus, a company for which success depends on aggressive personal selling in several distinct markets would likely turn to customer departments. If a company wants to make and sell both fertilizer and mattresses, it will likely have to consider a division based on products.

What this means in practice is that most organizations of any size mix the form of their departments. Different goals will prevail at different levels, and this will usually be reflected in the structure chosen. For a large company, the mixed structure illustrated in Figure 7-5 is typical.

When organizing, the manager must consider the size of the organization, the geographical area served, the experience and special skills of its managers, the type and complexity of activities, and the relative importance of different goals, and must try to reflect these in a practical organization structure. This is a tall order, and few structures are ideal. To gain one strength, the manager must often accept weaknesses. In shaping a practical structure, given all these interacting forces, managers often follow these guidelines:

1. Establish clear-cut overall objectives and set up departments to reflect them. If a sharp differentiation of market segments is important, customer departments for some functions should be considered. If specialization is particularly important, it is best to stick with functional departments.
2. Keep plans current. Reorganization is expensive. By keeping an organization flexible and generalized, it can adapt to meet future goals as well as present ones.
3. Make honest assessments of managerial resources. If a company wants a division headed by a super manager with complete responsibility for profits, operations, and growth, does it have a manager who is up to the job? Can the company afford such a manager if it

Figure 7-5. A Mixed Organizational Structure.

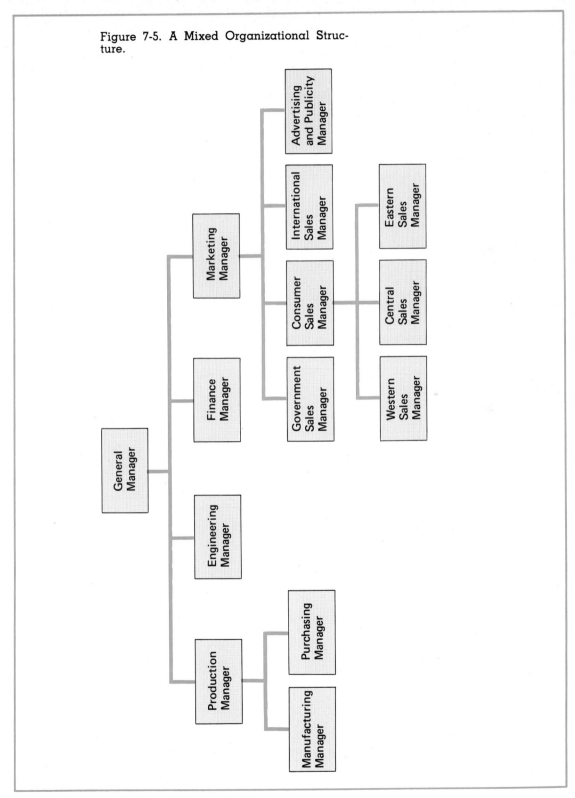

finds one? If product or geographical departmentalization seems logical, can the company afford the separate staffs required?

4. Combine organization structures to uniquely reflect overall goals. Few companies or agencies employ a single organization type. Most use functional organization if it is needed; or product, customer, or other organizations when appropriate. In fact, most product and geographical structures use a functional form at the lower levels.

SUMMARY

1. Organizing is the process of establishing roles and relations between roles to enable people to work together to meet common goals. Roles are defined by the duties, objectives, authority, and relations of a position. Relationships are based on supervision, control, coordination, and communication.

2. An important function of organizing is to allow the effective division of labor without sacrificing control and coordination. It permits specialization to serve major goals.

3. An analysis of activities, needed decisions, and relations shows what the total job contents for the organization must be. A grouping of these three components into a parcel small enough to be performed by one person creates an actual job.

4. The jobs created will themselves form natural groupings based on (a) the similarities of duties or objectives and (b) a special need for coordination and for communication. The groupings create departments based on function, products, geographical area, or the customers or clients served.

REVIEW AND DISCUSSION QUESTIONS

1. Describe the relationships that exist between a job you have held (or are familiar with) and the other jobs in the same organization.

2. What does an organization chart show? What does it not show?

3. What is the main way of judging whether an organization's structure is successful or not?

4. Why should managers be cautious about going too far in dividing up labor into small segments?

5. How can you tell whether jobs are related and should be considered for inclusion in a single department?

6. What are the basic steps in defining the content of jobs?

7. What is the relation between organizing and the other management functions of planning, controlling, staffing, and directing?

8. Given the many possibilities—functional, customer, geographical, and so on, how would a practicing manager decide on the right combination of department forms for his or her particular situation?

Problems and Projects

1. A manager for a corporation is making a rough grouping of activities and decisions. He has developed them from an analysis of a small division that his company is now establishing. As a start to creating an organization .structure, he is sorting the activities and decision types into three categories: top management, middle management, and supervisory management. Top management will probably consist of only one position. Middle management will include jobs on the level of production manager and sales manager. Supervisory management includes the men and women who directly supervise the activities of production workers.

The following is part of the list he is studying:
   a. Decide to significantly change product characteristics.
   b. Decide to discipline a worker for willful damage to a machine.
   c. Plan the plant production schedule for the next three months.
   d. Set up a housekeeping schedule for the shop area.
   e. Design and modify the production process to make it safe.
   f. Assign correspondence to clerks for typing.
   g. Evaluate the performance of a sales representative.
   h. Plan the long-term financial structure of the division.
   i. Decide to divide the marketing department into two separate departments.
   j. Judge the success of production rates, and adjust schedules accordingly.
   k. Decide to send a company representative and display to a trade show.
   l. Tell a worker to stop using an unsafe work method.
   m. Give a pay raise to a supervisor.
   n. Fire the marketing manager.
   o. Plan the day's work for the general labor gang.

Which of these tasks would you assign to top management? To middle management? To supervisors? Does this kind of classification form a basis for creating actual positions? What does it tell about the relations that should be established?

2. *Performance Situation—The Receiving Complex:* A.A.R., Inc., is a small chemical manufacturing firm in the Northwest. It specializes in custom processing of small amounts of exotic compounds. A.A.R. uses a great variety of raw materials, some of which arrive in a single 1-ounce jar, some in cartons, some in 100-pound sacks. Receiving these materials is a job in itself, as the company recognizes. The managers are creating a separate department to handle just this function. The work the department is to do is varied.

Incoming trucks and mail deliveries leave the materials on a loading dock. These materials must be carried inside the receiving room, either by hand or with a hand truck. A record of all receipts expected will be on hand, and this must be compared, item by item, with each receipt; this verifies that the materials ordered were actually received. A typed record of any variances discovered must be prepared. In addition, a number of forms must be filled out; some are for internal use and others are complex and time-consuming chemical receipt and shipping records required by the government. Labels must be carefully checked to make sure none are missing or are unreadable. Then a number of physical measurements must be made to check weight, quantity, and other characteristics. Some of these measurements require the use of instruments and considerable technical skills. All of these results must also be typed in reports. Finally, the materials and all of the reports must be delivered to other departments of the company or be repackaged and labeled to be shipped back to the supplier.

Your assignment is to divide these activities into three jobs. For each job, list the *activities* and a few of the implied *decisions* required. What was your basis for grouping the activities?

3. For the same department described in Problem 2, concentrate on the *relationships* among the jobs you have defined. Assuming that this department supervisor is a direct subordinate of the purchasing manager, draw a simple organization chart with four positions for the department. Complete the "Supervisory Relationships" and the "Other Relationships" section of the supervisor's job description following the format used in Table 7-1.

4. Since the type of structure chosen for an organization reflects its goals, combinations of department types are commonly seen. Figure 7-5 shows a structure that mixes three kinds of departmentalization. What are the three kinds of departments or divisions, and where do they occur in the chart? What does the use of these forms of departments tell about the company? Why would they have chosen to organize this way? What lines of frequent communication would this company need in addition to those shown on the chart?

5. Either by using your instructor as a source or by locating and briefly interviewing department heads, draw an organization chart for your school. If yours is a very large school, limit the chart to a small enough unit to be practical, such as the School of Business Administration. The basic question to ask your sources will be: Who do you supervise, and by whom are you supervised?

Answer these questions yourself: (a) What kind of departmentalization is used? (b) Are there any formal relationships that you find hard to fit on the chart?

6. Find a detailed profile of a manager in a general business magazine like *Forbes, Business Week,* or *Fortune,* or of a government administrator in any general or news magazine. You may have to consider a number of articles before finding one with enough detail. Describe the manager's role in his or her organization, touching on every part of the definition of role given in the text.

Cases for Analysis and Discussion

CASE 1: THE MINI-CONGLOMERATE

There was not a face in the room over 40 years old. In fact, at the age of 37, Glenn Weiss was the "grand old man" at this gathering. It was the monthly meeting of the board of GW Enterprises, Inc., a Chicago data processing services company, begun in the lean year of 1973. It is now a small and sedate local fixture, having endured and grown for what seemed to its founder a very long time.

Weiss and his colleagues were faced with a situation that had been developing for a long time: Rates of profits had declined each of the last 3 years even though sales had grown significantly. For the first time, in the coming year there was the distinct possibility that there would be no profits at all.

The history of the situation was simple. Weiss had started the company with an outstanding computerized general accounting system. He successfully sold it with good profits to many local companies. In 1976, Martha Howell had joined the company with a computer scoring and reporting system designed for public schools. She was given a department to operate and sell that system. In 1978, two other entrepreneurs joined the company with two new products. Each headed another new department with sales and other support staffs. The organization was based entirely on products, with one department (or division) to completely handle each product.

A. Why is GW Enterprises no longer making good profits?
B. How would you improve profits?
C. Can you locate any general management problems in this situation aside from a difficulty with the structure?

CASE 2: THE UNDEFINED JOB

Penny sometimes didn't know where she stood. Her title was administrative assistant, but she often wasn't sure whether that meant clerk-typist or manager of the entire community planning agency. The other day she had had an incident with her boss.

"What's this letter from the Fairfield Town Council? Who told them we'd do the engineering study for the hospital access?" he had said.

"I told them. It's a standard project and there's money in the budget. Frank will be free to do it," Penny answered.

"Who said you're supposed to make commitments like that? Since when are you running this agency? You do your job and I'll do mine!"

What especially bothered Penny was that she had made several decisions just like that in the past, and no one had said a word about it.

Then there was the matter of the reports. Every year, hundreds of pages of information on funding, hiring, dates, deadlines, completions, and other kinds of data had to be sent to the state and to several federal agencies. Who was really supposed to do them? Sometimes her boss got the information together, and she typed them, even though there were plenty of typists available. Other times, she prepared them entirely herself. Still other times, she did nothing on them. But she usually managed to get criticized for doing too much or too little, no matter what she did.

A. Why is Penny having so much trouble? Whose fault is it?
B. Who should solve this problem? How?
C. How does this relate to organizing as a process?

CASE 3: THE LOST DEPARTMENT

"John, I can see how you might think it's a slap in the face. But I assure you there isn't the least bit of dissatisfaction with you or with the engineering department behind this change." David was using his most persuasive and reassuring voice. "There are good reasons for moving product development from your department into the marketing department. In the old days in this company, product development was just a continuous process of fiddling with it to make it constantly better: a stronger knob, clearer numbers, better case reinforcements. We're talking about something completely different now. We've got to start competing much better in consumer products. That means market research, market trials, and completely new products—from scratch. We're losing out, and we've got to do things we've never done before. That's why I'm putting the new product department under the marketing people. That's where it really belongs."

A. Are you convinced by David's argument? Was this a good organization change to make? Why, or why not?
B. How will this affect the engineering department manager?
C. Why is David making such an effort to explain the change? He's the boss, isn't he?

CASE 4: WHO'S IN CHARGE?

"I don't know who to listen to. You tell me to stop work on the PL-510 regulations, but Ms. Burliss just told me yesterday that I should make them my highest priority. And then on top of that, Carlos said that they're not even going to publish PL-510 or 601 now because there are changes coming in."

And so it happened yet again. Clayton's basic work duties couldn't have been clearer. He edited the published regulations enforced by a large agency of the federal government. Given a draft of new regulations, he knew exactly what to do: locate and correct inconsistencies, check references, edit for clarity, and try to reduce the statements to simpler language.

But what was he supposed to do when Gary Mason, his direct supervisor, said to work on PL-601, yet Ms. Burliss—Gary's boss and Clayton's too, since Burliss ran the whole division—said to forget everything else and concentrate on PL-510?

A. What should Clayton do?
B. What kind of problem is this? Is reorganization needed?
C. What should Clayton's supervisor do?

Formal Structure in Organizations

8

After completing Chapter 8, you will be able to do the following:

- Analyze a simple organization by identifying and describing its authority relationships.
- Construct a chain of command to cover the decision levels of a small group of positions.
- Assess the suitability of several types of formal structures to the goals of a specific organization.
- Analyze the characteristics of subordinate positions to set a practical span of control for their superior position.
- Interpret the major goals of an organization as a guide to an appropriate degree of decentralization.
- Apply guidelines in making specific organizing decisions.

A man has a heart attack while riding on the bus. You are seated across the aisle. There happens to be a doctor on the bus, who rushes over and tries to save the man's life. The doctor says to you, "Get me something to put under his legs to elevate them." What would you answer? Would you say, "You don't have the right to order me around?" Probably not. Most people would immediately start looking for something to elevate the victim's legs, without thinking about the legitimacy of the command.

There clearly are situations in which we accept the right of others to command us, to tell us what to do and what not to do. This right is *authority*. In treating the heart attack victim, the doctor's authority stems from a superior knowledge of how to handle what needs to be done and from the emergency nature of the situation. And we typically accept that kind of authority without question.

Authority, basically the right to command others, exists in organizations. Sometimes it derives from superior knowledge, as in the case of the doctor. Usually it is viewed as deriving from the organization itself, as being a characteristic that is assigned to a particular formal position.

AN ORGANIZATION'S STRUCTURE DISTRIBUTES AUTHORITY

When defining jobs, one of the important things to specify is the kinds of decisions the person in a particular job will be allowed and required to make. Some of these decisions are impersonal: whether to spend money on a new machine, whether to change a product or drop a particular service, whether to buy a certain item or not.

Other decisions, though, have to do directly with people. These are the ones that are the most important to authority in the strict view of managing as the process of getting things done through other people. A person in authority has the right to make decisions for other people. A manager can tell his or her subordinates what to do and how to do it. Often the subordinate expects or needs this authority to be exerted. For example, a college student who takes a summer job may come to work the first day having no idea what work he or she will do. The supervisor who decides what the college student will do has organizational authority over him or her.

Right Versus Acceptance

If a woman hires a gardener to cut the grass, prune trees and bushes, and dig weeds, the woman and the gardener have an unspoken contract: The woman will give the gardener money; in return, the gardener will accept the woman's direction and do the work she says to do. If the gardener refuses, or continually ignores her directions, the woman will probably end the agreement by firing the gardener. This is the bald foundation of authority even in a giant, sophisticated organization like the federal government. "You do what I say or you'll lose your livelihood by getting fired." Again, employees tend to understand and accept this kind of *economic authority.*

The operation and function of authority is usually more subtle than these examples, however. There are a number of reasons other than economic why people accept the authority of others above them in an organization. For one thing, it is *traditional* in our society to do so. We are taught by our parents and by observation of other people whom we admire that we ought to accept the authority of people who rightfully hold it. Most people accept authority because, at least to some extent, they accept and *believe in the objectives* of their organization and want to contribute to reaching them. Employees also look for real *rewards* as a result of following orders. They may expect to be promoted or to get a pay raise, or to get recognition and praise. Refusing to accept authority will almost always threaten these rewards. Some people follow the direction of others because they personally *respect* them as individuals and believe they have superior capabilities. Some people accept the decisions of others just because they feel more comfortable when *not having the responsibility* of making decisions themselves.

Note that in a great many instances, authority functions on a two-way street. The person with formal authority has the right to exercise it. Subordinates accept authority under these circumstances and for other reasons such as superior knowledge, economic exchange, tradition, expectation of rewards, loyalty, and respect.

Whatever people's reasons for *accepting* authority, the key is that a person in organizational authority has the *right* to direct others. Contrast this with "influence." Harriet may be able to get Bob and Warren to do things her way because she is a good talker and skilled at persuading, or simply because she really knows what she is doing. But if Bob and Warren are free to choose whether to follow what she says, she can only influence them, not direct them. In strict, formal authority relations, the person who is told to do something does not have the right to refuse.

Delegation and Responsibility

If authority gives you the right to tell people what to do, one thing you can tell them to do is to exercise authority themselves. Passing on to others the authority to make decisions and direct the work of employees is called *delegation*. The woman with the gardener, for instance, may have a large estate requiring the work of six gardeners. She may tell one person, "I want you to be head gardener. Find me five other gardeners. Hire them, give them their work assignments every day, and check on how well they are doing their jobs." She is delegating to the head gardener the authority for getting the gardening done. The head gardener has the authority to do what is necessary to get the work done. He also has a matching obligation, a *responsibility* to see that it is done.

Managers in Action

"The manager of a private country club must be totally involved in all the activities of the club. Sometimes, of course, this involvement is purely a matter of proper delegation. An obvious example is the day-to-day operation of the club dining facilities. The maitre d', hostess, chef, and dining room manager are responsible for the overall success of the food service operation. Periodically, they report to the manager on the problems and successes of their particular departments. The manager's involvement is thus of an indirect nature through designated department heads.

"Other times, the manager's involvement is more direct. This includes regular attendance at board meetings and implementation of the policy decisions into the mainstream of club activities.

"Most people do not expect the club manager to wash dishes, although I am sure that most of us have when circumstances dictate. Too much attention to detail can often produce short-sighted managerial decisions and unnecessary concern with problems that should be handled by others."

This is Norman J. Spitzig, Jr., general manager, Losantiville Country Club, Cincinnati, speaking on the need to become directly involved in some things while delegating some responsibilities to others.

Source: "An Attitude of 'Detached Involvement'," *Club Management*, August 1978, pp. 20–21.

The Chain of Command

If desirable, the head gardener could delegate further: "John, you seem to know what you are doing; I'm going to put you completely in charge of the lawns. You schedule the watering and mowing and decide how much fertilizer and spray to use and when to do it. And make sure that any bad spots get resodded right away. I'll assign Tom to help you full-time." This further delegation creates a chain of command, a vertical system of relationships in which each higher level has authority over all of the levels below it. In this case, the chain extends from the estate owner, who could fire the whole bunch if she chose to, through the head gardener, through John who is in charge of lawns, and down to Tom. A large corporation is similar. The board of directors delegates operating authority, along with related responsibilities, to a president, who delegates to division heads, who delegate to department managers, who delegate to supervisors. Each level has authority and responsibility for all the levels below.

In addition to being a structure of authority and responsibility, the chain of command forms a major system of communication channels. The person at the top receives a great deal of information sifted up through the various levels of the organization. Similarly, information, opinions, and personal reactions also flow downward through the chain to those at lower levels.

DIFFERENT STRUCTURES HANDLE AUTHORITY IN DIFFERENT WAYS

A manager who arranges, or organizes, a formal structure determines how authority will be distributed in the total organization. This structure dictates who has what responsibilities and who has what decision-making and directing authority. The operational needs of an organization are complex, however. As a result, in practice there are shades and types and degrees of authority not reflected in the simplified example of the estate gardeners. These variations in authority relationships are incorporated in certain kinds of internal structures.

Line-and-Staff Structures

To start with, a basic distinction must usually be made between line authority and staff authority.

LINE ORGANIZATIONS

Line authority is the exercise of direct command over subordinates. An organization based entirely on line authority would look like the one in Figure 8-1. The general manager can direct the work of the production manager; the production manager can direct the work of the purchasing manager. This kind of direct command is typically used in the parts of an organization that perform the work basic to the overall purpose of the organization. The role of a sales manager, for instance, is usually defined by line relationships. He or she takes orders from a boss and gives orders to the salespeople. The same is usually true in a manufacturing department. Managers whose authority roles are defined in this way are called *line managers.*

STAFF RELATIONSHIPS   What if the company in Figure 8-1 realizes, however, that it needs someone who is a specialist in personnel matters or needs some people in the house who can advise on the legal aspects of operations? The company managers might then create a structure like the one in Figure 8-2. This is a *line-and-staff organization.* Staff authority is not authority in the pure sense. It is a *specified staff* relationship with clearly defined obligations, but it does not usually include the privilege of ordering others to do something. The people in staff positions advise, persuade, analyze, report, study, give reactions and opinions, recommend, provide services, and generally assist the other people in the organization. They cannot give orders to the people with whom they have a staff relationship. Public relations, legal, and personnel counselors usually have staff relations with line managers, as do executive assistants and other management advisors and aides.

COMPLEX RELATIONSHIPS   Line-and-staff roles are complex, though. A single position often has both line and staff components. A marketing manager might be a line manager in charge of sales, but also have an important advisory capacity to the president and to other department managers without having any direct control over their activities. Even a "pure" staff position, like that of a legal advisor, will have line authority over the assistants and clerks who work in the legal department.

Relations between line people and staff people are a sore point in many organizations. The manager in a line position is directly responsible for what is done. If he or she takes the advice of a staff person and the results are bad, it is the line manager who feels the heat. This makes line managers cautious in following the recommendations of staff people. Also, problems tend to arise concerning conflicts of authority. Staff people often overreach. In so doing, they may try to exercise direct authority over line people or departments even though they do not have the theoretical right to do so. These kinds of problems can be eased by clear job definitions, encouragement of communications, and by letting everyone know what the true relationships are supposed to be.

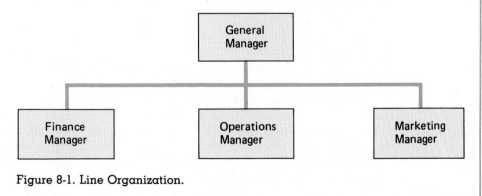

Figure 8-1. Line Organization.

Figure 8-2. Line-and-Staff Organization.

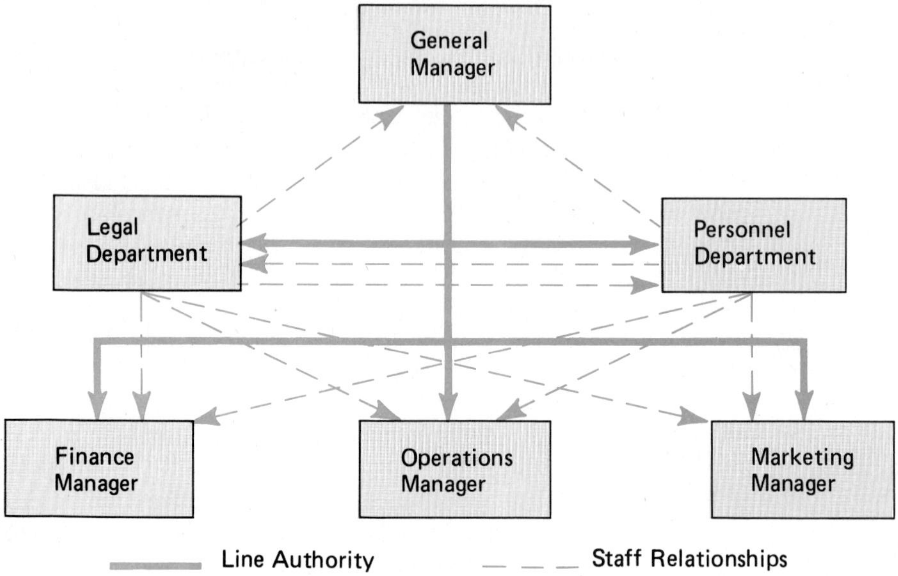

Line Authority — — — Staff Relationships

Functional Authority Sometimes there are good reasons to give people who are normally staff advisors a limited right to direct certain specified aspects of the activities of the departments they advise. A safety expert, for instance, may have the authority to issue actual commands to the managers in the production department or even in the head office if dangerous conditions or practices are found. This right to give limited orders or instructions in departments other than one's own is called *functional authority*. The accounting department, for example, may have a group of specialists in budgeting. The chief executive may decide that their contribution is potentially important enough that it is wise to give the budgeting experts the authority to *require* that operating departments follow their guidelines for budgeting. Their functional authority would not go beyond that limited and distinct area, however. They could not tell the purchasing manager what kind of goods to buy or tell the marketing manager what media to use for advertising.

In public relations, safety, financial control, personnel development, and similar management concerns, functional authority often adds to the strength of the organization. It does so by applying the judgments of experts where it will do the most good. Functional authority can also be dangerous because some managers will feel as if they have two bosses, their regular line boss and the functional expert. The usual problems of serving two masters can occur: conflicting orders, jurisdictional disputes, secretiveness, and lack of coordination. Here again, the answer is to clearly define the proper relations in the beginning and to continually police operations to be sure the relations are being observed. A typical functional relationship is illustrated in Figure 8-3.

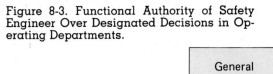

Figure 8-3. Functional Authority of Safety Engineer Over Designated Decisions in Operating Departments.

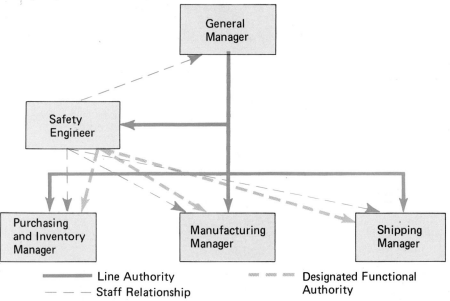

Matrix Organization   Some companies and many government agencies encounter organizational problems because they work on a lot of problems that are temporary in nature and that use different amounts of resources. An engineering firm, for instance, may work for two years on a large construction project that takes fifty employees. When that design is done, the firm may undertake five smaller projects that require ten or fewer employees each. And none of these projects may last more than six months. A matrix organization provides a unique solution in these situations.

In a *matrix organization*, employees are grouped by functional or occupational specialties and placed under a line manager responsible for that specialty, as shown in Figure 8-4. A programming manager will have line authority over the computer programmers; a drafting manager will have line authority over the people who draw plans and blueprints; and so forth with the other specialties of a particular organization. When a project is undertaken, the required number of each needed kind of specialty is loaned temporarily to the project and placed under the indirect authority of a project manager who has responsibility for managing the project. The project manager assigns work, coordinates activities, and handles many other normal management jobs. However, he or she does not have final authority over the people assigned to the temporary project. The line manager retains the right to hire and fire, promote, and make many other management decisions. An employee working under this system might say, for instance, "I work for Tim Brown, the engineering design manager, but right now I'm assigned to Jane Harris for the navigation instrument project."

Figure 8-4. Matrix Organization.

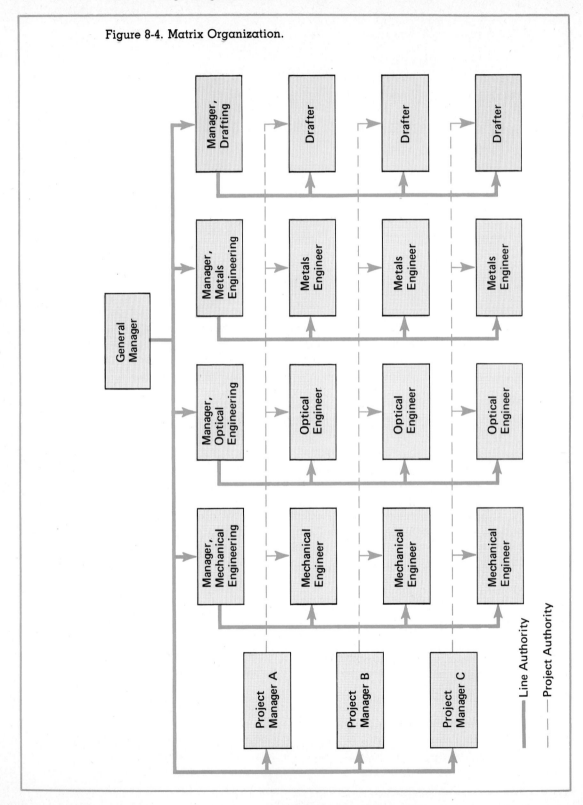

LINE VERSUS PROJECT AUTHORITY   Line authority is vertical and project authority is horizontal, as in the illustration of matrix organization in Figure 8-4. Even though the project manager has some direct authority over the employees assigned to the current project, it often takes a great deal of persuasive ability and personal skill to get the resources and achieve the coordination to get the project completed. Much authority still resides in the line manager.

Matrix organization allows specialists to be assigned where they are needed. People can be assigned temporarily and then moved somewhere else when the need is filled. It focuses attention on the needs of a project, giving it high priority compared with the narrow point of view often found in functional departments. Matrix organization has a disadvantage in that the specialists really do work for two bosses. Conflicts of loyalty and competition between project managers and line managers are frequent. Obviously, the system works best when project managers have the interpersonal skills needed to handle these conflicts.

Committees   A group of people who confer to discuss and deal with some defined matter is a *committee*. A committee may be set up as a component of any other type of organization structure. A line organization may have a committee to resolve certain kinds of hiring or promotion problems. It may have a committee to provide direction for a cost reduction program and still another committee to evaluate safety suggestions from employees. Even a matrix organization may find a committee useful for coordinating separate projects. Committees may have line or staff characteristics or they may combine various types of authority. A staff committee is advisory. It makes recommendations, but it lacks the right to make final decisions or to carry out actions. A line committee, on the other hand, can make decisions and put them into effect. Some committees act just like managers: they hire and fire, give work assignments, coordinate activities, and evaluate results. Some committees meet only once or twice to consider or act on some particular issue or problem. Other committees are long-standing formal components of an organization.

Committees can be very influential at any level:

- Banks often give final authority for making large loans to committees.
- Some organizations have special committees to consider hiring candidates for high-level job openings.
- Many corporations and public agencies have boards (committees) of directors which decide on and enforce the major directions the organization will take.
- Executive committees may be the major force in shaping overall policies and in deciding on long-term plans.

ADVANTAGES   Many organizations use committees because they allow a rapid interplay of ideas and opinions, questions and answers, proposals and rebuttals. Decisions affecting different areas of an organization can often be better decided in this way. Committees can also bring together enough different people with the variety of skills needed to deal with a complex problem. Committees permit the immediate multidirectional communication that contributes to good coordination.

DISADVANTAGES AND CONTROLS   Many committees fail miserably: they waste time; they cannot even decide on what their true purpose is; they make grotesque compromises in an effort to satisfy everyone present. These problems can be diminished, even if they cannot be completely eliminated. The role and relationships of a committee should be defined just as clearly as if it were an important executive position. Committees should be assigned tasks and decisions only if they are appropriate to group action. Policy decisions and long-range goal setting have been successfully handled by groups; day-to-day operating decisions rarely have been. Committees need performance standards and evaluation and control just like any other unit of an organization. The standards can be set if the tasks and relations are defined sharply enough to begin with. Evaluation and control will be successful only if there is someone who is unquestionably given the authority and responsibility to evaluate.

A PROPER SPAN OF CONTROL IMPROVES MANAGEMENT EFFECTIVENESS

How many direct subordinates should a manager have? This is a basic question that must be answered when setting up a formal organization structure. Take the small business in which the owner has always directly supervised each employee individually. Through the years the payroll grows to 20, 30, and then 40 employees, each reporting directly to the owner. Will this work? Can the owner effectively supervise 40 people? The answer is, *it depends*. If the employees all do similar, repetitive, production work, it may be possible to supervise 40 people. If they do complex, frequently-changing tasks that require a lot of supervision, replanning, and coordination, 40 is far too many for one manager. The answer to increasing size and complexity is to create levels of management so as to delegate part of the total supervisory and planning load to each successive level.

Tall Versus Flat Structures

If the owner of the small business decides to create new management levels, there are two general possibilities, as shown in Figure 8-5. If the owner hires two managers and divides the 40 employees between them, each new manager heads a group of 20 subordinates (Part A, Figure 8-5). This is a *flat* structure with few levels; when charted, it is wider than it is tall. Suppose, however, the owner hires four new managers to assist the original two, and eight new managers to assist them in turn. The last eight managers

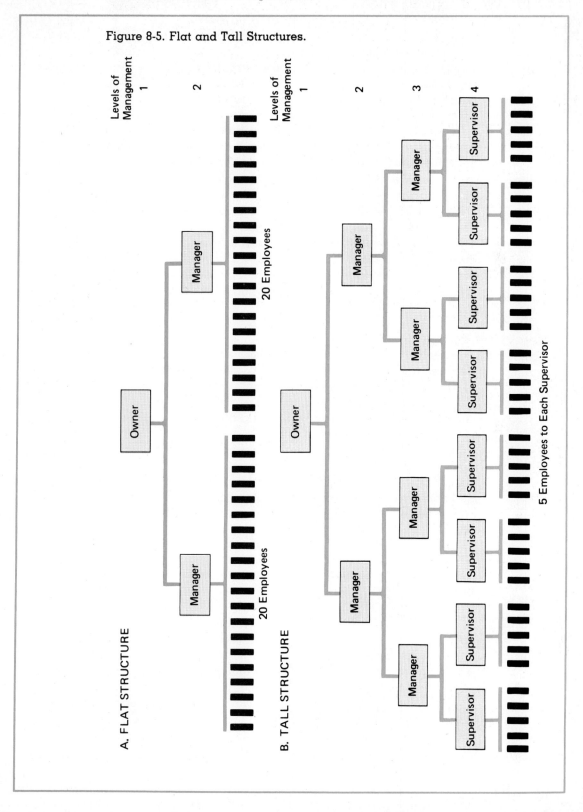

Figure 8-5. Flat and Tall Structures.

each would have only four subordinates. Compared with Part A, Figure 8-5, this is a *tall* structure; when charted, it tends to be taller than it is wide.

Span of control deals with the problem of how many people can be supervised effectively—whether a flat or tall structure is best. The *span of control* is the number of immediate subordinates who report to a single manager.

Tall structures usually have narrow spans of control, say two to five. This has the advantage of allowing managers to be very well informed about the activities directly under their control, and to give quite close supervision. It may also give more time for personal contact, careful planning, and thorough evaluation.

A *flat structure* has a wide span of control, possibly six to twelve or more. This has the advantage of placing decisions closer to daily operations. Also, since there are fewer levels in a flat structure, communication from the top to the bottom and back up is often better and more accurate. Fewer levels means fewer managers, and this means lower costs for salaries, office space, secretaries, and other supporting personnel.

Deciding on the Span

Activities and departments that need very close coordination should be included under as few managers as possible. This argues for a wider span of control even though the wider span may place greater demands on the manager. On the other hand, careful and clear delegation, good training of subordinates, and an orderly planning and control process may make the larger span practical.

In general, the span of control depends on the characteristics of subordinates and of their jobs. If the subordinates (1) need little supervision, (2) have similar activities and responsibilities, and (3) have clear and stable plans and objectives that remain relatively constant over a period of time, the span can be wider. When any or all of these conditions are not found, the span must be narrowed.

AUTHORITY MAY BE CENTRALIZED OR DECENTRALIZED

Since the span of control is always limited to some extent, the levels of an organization, when charted, create a pyramid shape. The manager at the top has only a few direct subordinates; each of those has a few; and so on down the line to a relatively large number of managers or supervisors at the lowest levels. Normally, the amount of authority and the importance of decisions allowed is very high at the top. This decreases fairly rapidly at each lower level. Those on the bottom rung of the management ladder are rather limited in authority and are allowed to make only routine operating decisions.

Major authority does not have to be concentrated at the top, however. The choice is up to management's view of how best to carry out its objectives. Management decides how much authority and freedom to make decisions and set policy will be allowed at lower levels. In some situations, it is desirable to permit considerable autonomy to subunits, the divisions or departments of the overall organization. A business or agency in which a broad range of important decisions can be made by lower-level managers is said to be a *decentralized organization*. In a *centralized organization*, all, or most, major authority and decisions are concentrated at the highest levels of management.

To better understand these distinctions, consider a power company that has several regional divisions. In a centralized organization, all major matters such as capital expenditures, pricing, and types of services would be made by the home office. These plans would just be passed down the line to the district manager to carry out. Consequently, the district manager may do no more than oversee the scheduling of line installations, assign work crews, and handle other routine operating matters. If, on the other hand, the district manager were given freedom to set prices, to decide on locations and types of generating facilities, and to allocate funds to build them, this would be a highly decentralized organization.

Degrees of Decentralization

No organization can be entirely centralized. Otherwise there would be no job for any managers other than the chief executive. Nor can an organization be completely decentralized. To qualify as an organization, there must be some degree of central authority to coordinate the subunits so as to meet overall goals. Every organization, then, falls somewhere between the two extremes. The extent of centralization or decentralization can be judged by the answers to three questions:

1. How many decisions are made at levels below top management? The greater the number of decisions delegated, the more likely the structure is decentralized.

2. How important are the decisions, and with what functions are they concerned? In a decentralized organization, certain crucial decisions, even those involving large amounts of money or affecting the direction of an entire division or department, may be delegated. The authority given may also extend to a great variety of functions such as finance, sales, advertising, production, or operations.

3. How much are lower-level managers required to consult with and inform their superiors before making decisions? In a highly decentralized organization, they may not even have to inform their superiors before making important decisions. In a centralized organization, they may have to get prior approval on nearly every matter.

Choosing the Degree of Decentralization

A greater degree of decentralization may be desirable under these conditions:

1. When fast-changing technology or marked differences in geographical regions make it advantageous to have divisions with considerable autonomy to take advantage of shifting opportunities.
2. When managers capable of handling considerable authority and who have a strong desire for independence are available in the organization. The trust and freedom of decentralization can be strongly motivating.
3. When the overall organization is large enough, with enough levels of management for decentralization to make sense.

On the other hand, centralization has a number of advantages. At least moderate centralization of authority should be maintained whenever separate units must work closely together to achieve overall goals. Close coordination is difficult in a decentralized organization. In general, centralization permits closer control and direction of operations than when authority is moved further down the line. If precise and thorough direction is essential, it will usually be easier to achieve it in a relatively centralized organization.

Many businesses and government agencies have found that a partial decentralization is beneficial. Financial control, policy making, long-range planning, and major marketing and product decisions may be centralized. Other decisions may then be decentralized, the kinds of decisions that contribute most to actually running things: sales, client services, production, and distribution. These and similar functions are moved downward and outward from central management. No matter what the degree of decentralization, success is dependent on good policies for decision makers and on good planning, clear goals, and objective standards. Organization structures are shaped to support these objectives; not the other way around.

CERTAIN PRINCIPLES POINT THE WAY TO SUCCESSFUL STRUCTURES

Like any other management function, organizing depends a good deal on experience and on an intimate knowledge of the needs of a particular enterprise. A few general rules have been found useful in a variety of situations, however. These include the following:

1. *Make the structure reflect objectives.* First, make sure you have objectives; good organizing is impossible without good planning. Then, analyze the specific activities and decisions essential to meeting the objectives. Put the meat of the organization where the fundamental operations and decisions are. If finance is the key to your goals, make

sure important financial decisions will be dealt with near the top. The same is true for any other area where functions are primary.

2. *Balance responsibility and authority in every position and department.* Do not expect a manager to meet a difficult set of objectives unless he or she has the right to control the resources needed and to make the necessary decisions. If a manager obligates others to accomplish something, he or she must give them enough power to operate.

3. *Maintain unity of command unless there are compelling reasons not to.* The principle of *unity of command* calls for each person in an organization to report to one and only one superior. This unity prevents conflicts that arise when one superior says to do one thing and another says to do something else. Providing this unity means caution when giving functional authority and making sure that the ground rules are clearly understood before using a structure like matrix organization.

4. *Clarify and communicate relationships.* When organizing, establish relationships of authority, control, coordination, and communication. Then make sure these formal relationships are practical, realistic, and based on need. If they are, then you must still make every effort to train the real people who fill the roles. These people must be aware of the existence of the ties and of the reasons for the established relationships. This communication should be continual—sharpened and restated from time to time.

5. *Simplify and limit the structure.* Organizing can be interesting work, but it is wise not to carry it too far. The least complex organization is often the one with the clearest relationships. Astute managers simplify the chains of command so that the lowest position lies on a clear line of communication and authority with the highest. They limit the size of management organizations. They strive for a balance between the productive capability of the people who make products and those who provide services. Managers are expensive. As long as vital needs are met, the fewer the better.

SUMMARY

1. Formal structures in organizations are the means by which to distribute authority—the right to make decisions and to direct the work and decisions of others. Authority is delegated to others, and along with it goes the responsibility or obligation to accomplish certain goals with that authority.

2. Different structures divide authority in different ways. Line structures define all direct relationships in terms of giving and accepting commands. Line-and-staff organizations add to this a number of positions which are essentially advisory. Functional relationships may then be added, which consist of direct authority over a small, defined segment of the activities and decisions of another manager. A matrix organization combines line authority with the responsibility given to other managers for overseeing separate projects. Committees may substitute for or supplement nearly any position in an organization.

3. Managers are limited in the number of people they can supervise directly. The number that is best for a given position depends on the characteristics of the jobs being supervised. This limit on the span of control results in the development of levels of management in an organization. When an effective span is exceeded, the positions being supervised must be regrouped and assigned to another level.

4. Organizations may concentrate important authority in a few people (centralization) or may distribute it widely in the organization to managers at lower levels (decentralization). Centralization is good for maintaining tight control and coordination. Decentralization motivates lower-level managers and often allows more specialized and faster responses to rapid changes in conditions or to local problems.

5. The organization structure should reflect objectives. Responsibility and authority should be balanced in every position and department. Unity of command should normally be maintained. Relationships in an organization should be clear and be thoroughly communicated to all concerned. The organization structure should be as simple and limited in size as possible.

REVIEW AND DISCUSSION QUESTIONS

1. Why are people so often willing to accept the authority of those above them in an organization?

2. Do you think it is a good thing for a manager to accept any command without considering its consequences for the organization?

3. What is the function of the chain of command?

4. Describe the difference between staff authority and functional authority.

5. How do you reconcile the use of functional authority with the principle of unity of command?

6. Why would anyone use matrix organization? When might it be too complex to be worth the effort?

7. How does the span of control contribute to the creation of levels of management in an organization?

8. In general terms, what determines a good span of control for a specific position?

9. Should all organizations attempt to decentralize authority?

Problems and Projects

1. The following decisions each relate to one or more of the five principles of organizing given on pages 194 and 195 of the text. On a sheet of paper write the letters *a* through *j* corresponding to the decisions below. Beside each, put the number of the principle to which it relates and indicate with an *A* or a *D* whether the decision agrees or disagrees with the principle.

a. Juan has made Mark completely responsible for getting the trucks loaded on time each day, but won't let Mark decide who will work on each truck or the order of loading.

b. The executive director of a service organization is so dependent on advice and counsel that he has 19 managers and only 11 people doing the direct productive work of the organization.

c. Carla realizes that Larry is getting conflicting orders, so she eliminates the finance director's functional authority in Larry's department and personally explains the change to everyone involved.

d. Harold decides to make the data processing department report to the accounting manager because the main purpose of the department is to help the accountants keep tight financial control.

e. Robert decides to have everyone in his department report directly to him because there are only six people and they need close coordination. This eliminates one level of managers.

f. Ann decides that since Marty has skills in so many different areas, he should not have a direct supervisor and should just generally assist anyone who needs his help.

g. Since Allen now has the responsibility for keeping costs at or below budget, his boss has given him the authority to approve or reject all expenditures.

h. Since government sales will now get highest priority, Henry creates a special department to handle them, with a manager placed high in the hierarchy.

i. Ellen decides to organize her consulting firm into a matrix organization, because efficient allocation of personnel to separate projects has been impossible under the old structure.

j. John decides to take the time to prepare complete written job descriptions for every position in his department because there have been some conflicts of responsibility and authority lately.

2. *Performance Situation—The Burgeoning Bergstrom Business:* Charlie Bergstrom started Bergstrom Forms, Inc., 15 years ago, with the considerable savings he had put aside as a printing sales representative. Bergstrom designed, printed, and sold paper forms for use by business, especially for

keeping financial records: invoices, order forms, statements, and other forms for internal reporting. Bergstrom himself had always kept close to operations, directly supervising each operating department head.

Several years ago, Bergstrom hired a staff financial specialist, Helen Flores. Her central duties, according to the job description, were "to advise the president on sources and uses of funds and to provide internal reports for use in financial control." She soon convinced Bergstrom of the value of computerized reporting, and established a data processing department. Bergstrom noticed that their computer had excess capacity, and he decided to sell part of its financial reporting services to the same customers who bought business forms. Bergstrom then needed consultants and research people to help the financial-services customers make the best use of the computer reporting capacity.

As so often happens, one thing led to another, and soon things got out of control. Two different salespeople from Bergstrom would sometimes call on the same customer in the same day, each trying to sell different products or services. Sometimes the one representative didn't even know the other. The two certainly hadn't coordinated their sales efforts. Billing was incredibly snarled; occasionally, a customer would get three or four different bills from Bergstrom in a month for different products and services. There was a good deal of internal bickering, too, over who was supposed to do what and even over who worked for whom.

Finally, Bergstrom sat down to figure out what was wrong. He knew that the financial services sold to outside customers were a major problem, but he certainly didn't want to drop them. They were doing so well, in fact, that he even planned to give them considerable emphasis in the future. For the first time, Bergstrom drew an organization chart that reflected the real organization that had evolved. See Figure 8-6 on the next page.

Your assignment is to act as a consultant and help this company solve some of its organizing problems. First, analyze these areas.

    a. What is the chain of command between the financial services sales supervisor and the president?

    b. Has Bergstrom clearly delegated authority and responsibility to all units of the organization?

    c. What kind of position is the financial director's? Staff? Line?

    d. Is it desirable to have two billing departments and two sales departments in this case?

    e. Is the data processing manager the logical superior for the manager who is in charge of developing and selling financial services?

3. Consider the span of control in the case of Bergstrom Forms, Inc.

    a. What is the current span for the president?

    b. Is this span too great for this situation, in your opinion?

    c. Are there any other reasons why the span of control for the president might be changed? Should it be changed?

4. Consider the issue of centralization versus decentralization for Bergstrom Forms, Inc.

Figure 8-6.

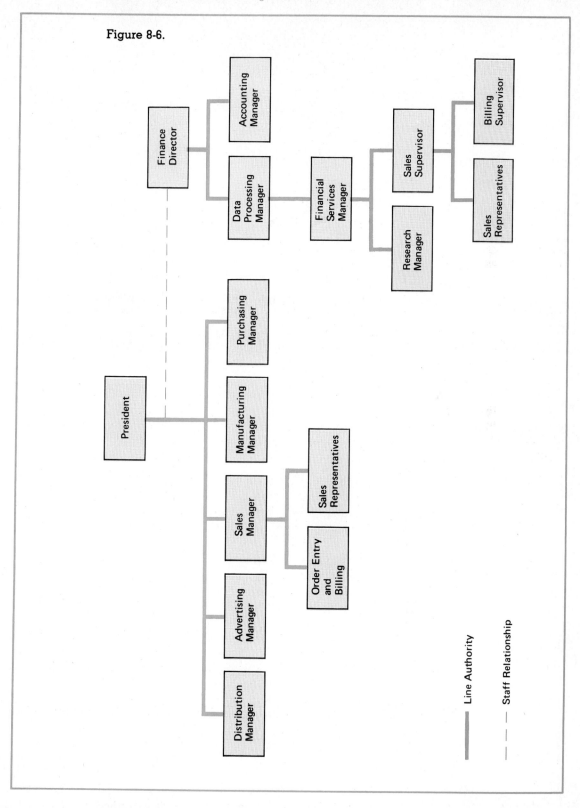

a. Does Bergstrom Forms, Inc., presently have a relatively high or low degree of decentralization, considering the size of the company?

b. Are any of the current problems caused by too much decentralization or too much centralization?

c. What would you recommend? Should the company be more central-ized or more decentralized?

5. Based on your analyses in Problems 2, 3, and 4, draw a new organization chart for Bergstrom Forms, Inc. Try to eliminate any problems you have discovered, and carry out any recommendations you have made. Be pre-pared to discuss and defend your proposed organization.

6. Carry out limited library research on the subject of delegation. Find three references, from business or management magazines, general books, or textbooks, to support or refute this statement: "The reasoned delegation of authority and responsibility is the keystone supporting any and every orga-nization. It is the single indispensable element of effective organizing."

Cases for Analysis and Discussion

CASE 1: THE SALES AND THE (INCIDENTALLY) PRODUCTION DEPARTMENT

Timing was all-important in the small computer business. Orders and cancellations flew. So many new aggressive companies were entering the market that customer loyalties were eroding. If you weren't there on Thursday with your product as promised, you might not need to bother com-ing on Friday.

Louie Ferretti knew this as well as anyone. He should know. He had heard it repeated nearly every working day by Larry Konig, the sales manager. Ferretti was the production manager for Eastern Electronics, and he was not a happy man. Eastern made small, special-purpose computers, mainly for scientific and technical use. Each computer was virtually a custom instru-ment designed and built for the particular use of a particular customer. This meant that the production manager had to be a true wizard at scheduling, allocating personnel and production equipment, and controlling hundreds of complex work steps and quality inspections. Ferretti was the wizard. He was proud of his skills, but wasn't pleased with the way things were going.

Larry Konig was the problem, in Ferretti's opinion. Konig would look at the orders, many of which had been already scheduled, and say: "Move this one to the front of the line; we've got to have it. You've got to get both of these done by the end of August; I don't care how you do it. This is a tough one here, isn't it? But let it go for a while; we can stall them."

After hearing enough of these commands from a manager who was supposed to be his equal, not his boss, Ferretti complained to the general manager. The general manager's answer was: "I think I can understand how you feel. But that's just the way it's got to be. Delivery dates are so important that I told Konig he could set them for you. You don't have the contact with the customers; he does. You'll just have to live with it."

A. What kind of authority does Konig have in the production department? How can you tell?

B. Is this the best way to handle the problem? Suggest a better one.

C. What is Ferretti likely to do? What would improve his morale?

CASE 2: THE MISFIRED DELEGATION

"Sam, these figures don't look too good, do they? What's been going on in your department?" Doris was disappointed and even a little bit shocked. She had delegated complete authority to Sam for running his department, requiring only that he stick to a budget he had made and she had approved. Doris liked Sam and thought he had the makings of a good manager. But now, six months later, it looked as if she was going to have to take over the department again herself. Results were terrible. People were quitting; costs were much higher than they had been; whole blocks of work simply hadn't gotten done.

And Sam knew it. The last six months had been among the darkest of his life. When Doris had told him he was in complete control of the department, he was elated. He had set to work with a will, excited by his new responsibilities. He planned a whole year's operations on paper. He moved staff members around and changed job assignments to what he thought was a better balance. He had never felt better about his job.

In a month, however, he knew he was in trouble. In only four working weeks, the department had fallen eight days behind the schedule he had set up. He had forgotten all about ordering supplies, and they ran out. He had to pay a premium price for replacements that could be delivered the next day. He didn't understand the way the employees were acting. They had suddenly turned very aggressive toward him. He actually avoided talking to some of them because they were so intimidating. The days went by, and the department fell further and further behind. Sam worked even longer hours, trying to deal with all of the problems, wondering what had gone wrong.

A. What did go wrong? How did Sam get in such a spot?

B. What should Doris do now?

C. If Doris is responsible for the problem, what were some of her main mistakes? How can she avoid them in the future?

CASE 3: NOT ENOUGH CHIEFS

"Hennessy, I just can't see you now. It'll have to wait until tomorrow."

Or until next week, or next year, Hennessy thought. But he didn't say anything. He returned to his office with his questions unanswered, as he had done often before.

The old man, Nate Kahn, founder and president of Kahn Enterprises, seemingly had less and less time to do more and more. Everything needed his personal touch, he thought, and everything got it, but only in brief. There were now 11 operating departments and each reported directly to Kahn. Needless to say, the four staff departments also did. In fact, Kahn got upset if the staff people went directly to the operating departments instead of first giving their advice and information to him, for him to deal with as he saw fit.

A. Is this a tall or a flat structure?
B. Is there a problem with delegation in Kahn Enterprises?
C. What would make Nate Kahn or any other manager reluctant to delegate authority and responsibility?
D. Is Nate Kahn right to manage as he does?

CASE 4: THE COMMITTEE OF THE WHOLE

A number of consulting companies have been founded in the last ten years to deal with technical problems arising from a renewed interest in the quality of the physical environment. Art Tanaka founded one such firm, Environmental Services, Inc. Art had grown up in California, studied engineering at Cal Tech, and was well on his way toward designing yet another super highway for a large engineering firm when he decided that it wasn't the life for him. He had spent a lot of time in the mountains as a youth, and he didn't like what he saw in the valleys. He was convinced that humans had gone too far in destroying nature around them.

The company Art Tanaka finally set up was only one of many such environmental consulting firms. Its sole line of work was writing environmental-impact statements for private and government construction projects. As Art and his associates soon discovered, even this work didn't involve much field work. There was little actual investigation of sites, or original research. Art's people mainly sat at their desks and strung together outdated information from whatever source was easily available. That was all most of their clients were interested in and willing to pay for. Even though Art's plans for improving the world were mainly falling to the wayside, he and his employees had come up with some influential conclusions.

The company was unique in one way: it had no management. Tanaka made it clear when anyone came to work with him that there was no chain of command, no central authority, no superiors, and no subordinates. When decisions needed to be made, everyone present acted as a committee and decided democratically what to do. There was strong pressure to reach a consensus, however. After much discussion, it was usually possible to come up with a plan that everyone could live with and support. No one ever told anyone else what to do, although social pressure could be quite strong at times.

A. What do you think of this arrangement?
B. How will such committee decision making affect the long-term success of the company?
C. Would this be a good kind of organization for all companies?
D. Would you suggest that Environmental Services make any changes?

Staffing Organizations

After completing Chapter 9, you will be able to do the following:

- Construct a simple staffing plan to cover the essential needs of a small organization.
- Analyze the major goals of an organization to determine their effect on future staffing needs.
- Employ a systematic approach to selecting among candidates for a specific position.
- Assess the value of the appraisal system in a given organization.

- Formulate an appraisal procedure for a simple organization.
- Determine when training and development are needed in an organization.
- Propose a program for developing a manager to fill a given future position.

They were all dressed in their tuxedos and long gowns—drinking champagne and making complimentary speeches. It was a happy occasion, the retirement of Arnold Rosen, senior vice president, and Iris Downing, marketing manager. Rosen planned to live year-round at Martha's Vineyard and sail every day unless there was a hurricane. Downing already had tickets for the first part of a round-the-world trip. The smile of Joe Coles, president, was a little forced compared with the genuine enthusiasm of the two retirees. Joe's sales manager had retired last year, and before that the vice president for operations had left to become senior vice president of another company. Of the top six executives in Coles' company, four—including the entire marketing department—would be brand new and relatively untried. That meant danger.

The purpose of giving thorough attention to staffing is to avoid such negative situations. Proper staffing enables management to take positive, aggressive action instead. This assures above all that management positions are filled with capable men and women with the ability and the will to meet organization objectives. It is just as necessary, of course, to provide for good staffing all the way down the line. *Staffing* is thus an active, anticipative process of planning future personnel needs. It consists of (1) selecting people from within and without the organization, (2) appraising individual performance to find where improvement is needed, and (3) training and developing personnel to improve performance and to fill future openings.

HUMAN RESOURCES PLANNING UNDERLIES THE STAFFING FUNCTION

Nearly every manufacturing manager pays close attention to the production machinery, providing for thorough maintenance schedules and procedures. Every machine is checked repeatedly to monitor its condition and to help plan for replacements. Capital expense plans for expensive machinery and production equipment may extend 10 years or more into the future. Unfortunately, this kind of care and foresight sometimes is not given to a more complex and essential resource: people. It is all too easy for complacent managers to wait until a job opening occurs and then try to fill it by picking from whoever is available.

A good manager takes staffing far more seriously. Careful planning for the recruitment and development of human resources is essential. Such planning understandably focuses on staffing the managerial positions in the organization.

Assessing the Need for Managers

The first step in acquiring the people an organization needs is to find out what kind of people are required now and will be required in the future when conditions can be expected to change. There are three basic questions to be answered: (1) What jobs need to be filled? (2) How many of each will be open? (3) What knowledge and skills are needed by the persons who will fill the jobs?

PLANS AFFECT NEEDS   In determining the number and type of people needed, organization plans are the main guide. Plans affect personnel staffing needs, especially for managerial positions, in three important ways:

1. Changes in goals or in product or service orientation create new positions and alter the characteristics of existing positions. For example, suppose an electronics company which has spent 20 years selling components to other manufacturers now decides that it wants to sell its products directly to consumers. This is certain to create new requirements in the marketing and sales departments. But it does not necessarily mean that the marketing manager must be replaced with someone who has a strong consumer orientation and experience. The present manager may be trained to fit the new requirements. It does mean, however, that the marketing skills must be acquired somehow, through training if not through hiring.

2. Company expansions create additional and often different positions. When a company grows, more people must be added to handle the increased volume. Different jobs may be needed to carry on the new activities. Plans for expansion should alert the managers involved to begin planning for added positions and new job definitions.

3. Reorganization changes the characteristics of positions. Suppose a service agency, for example, changes from a functional organization to a structure that places a manager in charge of each of several services, somewhat like a product or customer department. The characteristics needed by new managers now will be considerably different from those in the old functional structure. The new, or retrained, managers will need to be general managers, capable of handling all functions associated with a particular service.

NEEDS MUST BE DESCRIBED   The organization chart shows the number of major positions that exist. Job descriptions show the duties each manager must be able to perform. They also imply certain skills, talents, and experiences the managers will need. Existing job definitions must be expanded somewhat before they can serve as a clear guide to selecting and developing people to fill the positions described.

A position description for making staffing decisions must include the following:

1. The position name and department.
2. A job summary specifying the main function.
3. Duties performed, specifying major responsibilities and authority.
4. Supervisory relationships.
5. Other relationships.
6. Specific education, technical, and managerial skills, and experience required.
7. Concrete motivations and rewards to be offered, including salary range and other forms of compensation.

The first five of these items occur in the basic job description previously illustrated in Table 7-1. The final two are specific concerns of the staffing function; they aid in selecting a person to fill the job. The sixth item—education, skills, and experience—stems directly from the duties of the position. It answers the question, What does a person need to know and be able to do to perform this job? The seventh item—salary and other compensation—reflects (1) the rank of the position in the organization and (2) the free-market value of a person having the skills required.

This expansion of job definitions will create a collection of position descriptions that require managers with certain known characteristics. The positions described may be current ones that are already filled or they may be positions anticipated for the future. The next step in staffing is to plan specific actions that will assure that the right kind of people are available now and in the future.

Making Personnel Plans Active

At this stage in staffing, managers integrate three main components:

1. *Positions that are already filled.* Some of these people will need to have their skills improved to perform adequately today; all of them need to be developed to perform better tomorrow. (This situation is discussed later.)
2. *Positions that are open now or will be open in the future,* for which managers or employees need to be located or trained.
3. *Sources* from which to choose people to fill open positions.

FORECASTING THE OPEN POSITIONS   The jobs for which people must be found arise for a number of reasons. Expansion or reorganization creates new positions that did not exist before. People are promoted to more important jobs, leaving their old positions open, or leave to take jobs with other firms. Others retire, become disabled, or die.

The human resources planning (HRP) phase of the staffing process requires periodic forecasting and monitoring of the open positions. A typical HRP forecast begins with a list of existing jobs, with the number of incumbents in each. Added to that list are all the new jobs that will be created to fulfill growth plans. The present work force plus the people who must be added for growth provides a picture of the size and nature of the future work force. An estimate is then made of how many of the present job incumbents will leave for one reason or another and thus create open positions. The total number of open positions predicted for the future will simply be the sum of those needed for growth plus those needed to replace employees who leave. Table 9-1 shows how an electronics firm uses forecasts like these to plan for future personnel needs.

SOURCES OF REPLACEMENTS   There are only two real sources for management personnel: they may be promoted from within, or they may be hired from outside the organization. Rank-and-file employees may be

				FORECAST PERIOD JAN. – DEC.			
COMPONENTS DIVISION	A	B	C	D	E	F	G
Position Categories	Present Staff Jan.	Planned Changes, Growth and Cutbacks	Future Staff Dec.	Attrition*			Net Openings
Managers							
Operations	30	+10	40	+3	+1	+2	+16
Sales	10	0	10	+1	0	+1	+2
Other	20	+5	25	+1	+1	+2	+9
Engineers	20	−5	15	0	+3	+2	0
Technicians	40	+10	50	0	+2	+2	+14
Clerical	80	−10	70	+5	+5	+3	+3
Hourly, skilled	300	+50	350	+20	+13	+13	+96
Hourly, other	500	+90	590	+20	+40	+25	+175
TOTAL	1,000	+150	1,150	+50	+65	+50	+315

TABLE 9-1. HUMAN RESOURCES PLANNING.

*Attrition = Column D (Promotions and Transfers) + Column E (Unplanned Outs) + Column F (Planned Retirements).
Columns A + B = C Future staff size in December.
Columns B + D + E + F = G Net openings to be filled between January and December.

recruited mainly from outside the organization. They are then moved upward into increasingly responsible positions, some ultimately to managerial spots. A major objective of staffing is to draw on internal and external sources to fill open positions with appropriate, effective employees and managers.

Promoting from within is a policy in many organizations, and it has some distinct advantages. People are motivated, sometimes strongly, by the knowledge that good performance is likely to lead to promotion to positions with higher pay, more responsibility, and greater prestige. Someone promoted from within already knows the organization fairly well and does not have to learn about the company from the ground up. Someone already working for the company will always be better known to management than someone outside; it is far easier to judge a present employee's skills and potentials over a period of time than it is to evaluate an outside applicant on the basis of a week or two of interviews and tests.

Promoting from within, however, has one definite disadvantage: it can lead to "inbreeding." Managers in every organization will come to have unique ways of looking at problems. These ways will be passed on to subordinates, and this can cause dangerous "tunnel vision" if no fresh ideas are brought in from outside. New technical methods, a new aggressive management style, a talent for cutting through protocol to get to the heart of matters, all can be supplied by the right outside manager hired at the right time.

SEARCHING INSIDE THE ORGANIZATION   To locate replacement personnel from inside the organization, certain kinds of information must be made available. In carefully planned organizations, a roster of current managers is maintained. This list shows the incumbents' education, technical skills, and experience and also describes the pool of internal managers from which open positions will be filled. To anticipate open positions, a list is kept of expected retirements, of dates when newly created positions will be needed, and of dates of openings to be created by promotions. For every major current and future position in the organization, whether filled or open, two or three candidates are identified. These are people who could at some future time be promoted to the position. Finally, promotion from within requires a management-development plan. Under such a plan, the managers considered for promotion receive the appropriate training and experience so that they are ready when needed.

This orderly process of filling positions from current managers is called *succession planning*. It minimizes problems that can occur when three or four key positions suddenly become open at the same time. It helps to assure that persons are available with the right skills to fill the positions. In a smaller organization, some of the information needed for succession planning might be kept in a file of cards like the one shown in Figure 9-1. Larger firms or government agencies often make such data available to management in the form of computer-based reports. An excerpt of such a report is shown in Figure 9-2.

Figure 9-1. Succession Planning File. *Small companies might maintain succession planning cards like the one illustrated below.*

Position: National Sales Manager

Current Manager: Roberta L. Rothstein

Expected Retirement Date: June 198X

Possible Successors:

1. Name: Elisa Morris   Current Position: Western Sales Manager

Strengths: College degree in marketing. Familiar with competition. Nine years of supervisory experience.

Weaknesses: Has worked only in western region. Has been with firm only four years.

2. Name: Carlos Santana   Current Position: Assistant to National Sales Manager

Strengths: Outstanding academic preparation. Has personal contacts with most sales people. Directed sales in western and northeastern regions. Was sales manager in central region.

Weaknesses: Supervisory experience limited to less than three years. Hard to replace in current position.

3. Name: _____   Current Position: _____

Strengths: _____

Weaknesses: _____

Figure 9-2. Succession Planning Data. *Large companies and government agencies often provide management with succession planning information through computer-based reports such as those shown below.*

REPORT A	PAGE 1	REPORTING RELATIONSHIPS - ECHELON CODING	
DEPARTMENT NUMBER	ECHELON CODE	POSITION TITLE	EMPLOYEE NAME
010	B	SENIOR V.P.	KLEIN
010	C	VICE PRESIDENT, FINANCE	GRUBER
010	D	TREASURER	MCWIT
010	D	CONTROLLER	

What does the organization actually look like?

REPORT F	PAGE 1	PROJECTED RETIREMENTS FOR THE NEXT THREE YEARS			
EMPLOYEE LAST NAME	LOCATION NAME	JOB TITLE	BIRTH MO.-DY.-YR.	YEARS OF SERVICE	ANNUAL EQUIV.
CHEEVERS	CORPORATE FINANCE	CONSOLIDATION ACCOUNTANT	12-04-X8	22	12,500
CARLUCCI	CORPORATE TREAS. OFFICE	SENIOR ACCOUNTANT	08-16-X8	10	11,700
BILLMEYER	DIVISIONAL HEADQUARTERS	STAFF CONSULTANT	06-04-X8	30	18,000
GOMEZ	HOUSTON SALES OFFICE	STENOGRAPHER	03-29-X8	5	7,500
BURROWMEISTERN	INTERNATIONAL SALES	CORRESPONDENT	09-17-X8	16	15,200

Who is retiring in the next three years?

REPORT B	PAGE 1	POSITION PROMOTION REGISTER		
TITLE	INCUMBENT	PROMOTION NOMINEE 1	PROMOTION NOMINEE 2	PROMOTION NOMINEE 3
V.P. ADMINISTRATION	SANTANA	DIAZ	DUPREE	SANCHEZ
V.P. DATA PROCESSING	KINGSTON	DONNELLY	REYNOLDS	CARSON
V.P. MARKETING	JONES	JACKSON	CROSS	WATKINS
V.P. OPERATIONS	KRONSKI	SINGH	GRAY	COHEN
V.P. FINANCE	EDWARDS	DAVIS	O'BRIEN	NASH

What key positions are backed up?

REPORT C	PAGE 1	EXECUTIVE TIME IN POSITION		
DEPARTMENT	NAME	TITLE	POS. YR.	DEPT. YRS.
010	ABACROMBIE	VICE PRESIDENT	5	5
010	CHRISTIANSEN	CONTROLLER	8	15
010	ZAMBINE	SENIOR VICE PRESIDENT	4	10

Are executives being kept too long in one position?

REPORT D	PAGE 1	MANPOWER PLANNING TALENT LIST		
DEPARTMENT	TITLE	NAME	EXPERIENCE SPECIALTY	NUMBER OF YEARS	YEAR LAST USED
001	DIRECTOR, ADMIN. SERVICES	CHON	BENEFITS ADMIN.	2	71
001	ASSISTANT VICE PRESIDENT	HOLLISTER	BENEFITS ADMIN.	4	72
001	ASSISTANT VICE PRESIDENT	BRAUN	BENEFITS ADMIN.	8	69

Can we staff a new department with in-house talent?

Adapted with permission from: John E. McMahon and Joseph C. Yeager, "Manpower and Career Planning," *Training and Development Handbook,* McGraw-Hill Book Company, New York, 1976, p. 11–9.

SEARCHING OUTSIDE THE ORGANIZATION　Positions sometimes cannot be filled with candidates from within the organization. No one appropriate may be available; "new blood" may be desired; or it may be easier to hire from outside than to make a difficult choice among closely matched internal candidates. To the greatest extent possible, however, the decision to hire someone from outside should be made with the idea of meeting some specific goal, such as getting new ideas and innovative approaches for an organization that has become ingrown. It should not be a desperate attempt to fill an unexpectedly open position for which planning has failed to provide a successor.

RECRUITMENT AND SELECTION FILLS OPEN POSITIONS

Planning to meet personnel needs will obviously not do the whole job. Faced with a knowledge that jobs will open up, management must also answer these questions:

1. Will you choose potential successors for positions from inside or outside the organization?
2. When a job is to be filled from outside, where will the candidates come from?
3. If there are many to choose from, how will you tell if one candidate or another is more likely to be successful in the open position?

The best answers come from following an orderly approach. Good management uses whatever methods are available and remains flexible in recognizing mistakes so they can be corrected.

Recruitment

Over a long period of operations, it is not possible to fill all positions from within. If everyone were eventually promoted, no one would be left at the lower levels. Realistically, situations do arise in which the best solution is to seek job candidates from outside even when there are candidates already in the organization. In choosing the replacement for an important manager, for example, it helps to have a variety of people to evaluate. When there are only one or two employees who have the qualifications for the job, it makes sense to look outside as well; this extends the pool of people considered.

Active efforts to find candidates from outside an organization are called employee *recruiting.* The most common approach to recruiting is to make it widely known that a job opening exists or will exist and to invite people to apply who believe they are qualified. The ways of making the opening known are fairly standard. Newspapers carry sections of classified advertising specifically for this purpose. Many trade and professional organizations have similar sections in their publications for advertising position openings. Employment agencies, in return for a commission paid either by the employer or the applicant, will serve as go-betweens. Federal and state employment offices provide similar services free. A company's employment office routinely gets spontaneous applications from people who believe they would be qualified for work there. A company's current employees are often able to recommend qualified candidates.

COLLEGE RECRUITING   For lower-level management positions, it may be possible to hire people with no experience, if they have suitable education. College recruiting has become popular with large organizations seeking to fill such positions. Companies and government agencies advertise in college newspapers and send representatives to campuses to make personal contacts with students. Many colleges and universities have special offices to facilitate this kind of recruiting. An important point about recruiting in general is especially apparent in college recruiting efforts: candidates should be found who have future potential, not just the qualifications to fill a short-term need.

Personal contact is always an important adjunct to recruiting. Most managers keep their eyes and ears open for potential job candidates when they are dealing with people outside their organization. Many successful marketing and operations managers have been recruited after being seen in action in a related job with another firm.

ASSESSING THE LABOR MARKET   Positions to be filled may be of great importance, as most management jobs are, or they may be seemingly routine jobs at the bottom of the organizational ladder. Regardless of the nature of the open positions, sophisticated employers make regular assessments of labor markets. This helps them to determine where new people will be found and how difficult it may be to find them. In the tight labor market of a decade ago, International Business Machines Corporation had to recruit 42,000 technicians over a 6-year period. (See Figure 9-3.) In looking back, IBM found that 5 percent came directly from college and 30 percent from technical schools; these people were qualified by their education. Some 15 percent were recruited directly from high schools, and had to be trained from scratch. The remaining 50 percent of the technicians were recruited from returning military veterans, from college dropouts, and from other firms. Many in this group, especially those from other firms and those who had partially completed a science or engineering curriculum, needed far less training than those hired directly from high school. IBM was able to draw up valuable recruiting plans for the future based upon this experience.

Selection   Managers who are successful in locating many applicants for a job opening create another problem: how to choose the single best person for the job. If a job is advertised, many who respond can be eliminated immediately. Their education or experience may not match the requirements of the position. In the same way, many people who already work for an organization

Figure 9-3. Hiring for 42,000 Technicians Over a Six-Year Period.

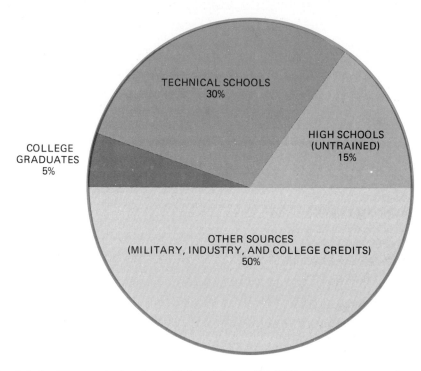

Reprinted with permission from: Nelson Heyer, "Fulfilling Requirements for Specialized Manpower," *Manpower and Planning*, Industrial Relations Monograph 31, 1970, pp. 103–117.

will not be considered because their abilities or preparation are clearly unrelated. This first elimination of candidates is based on a careful comparison of the position's requirements with the applicants' backgrounds.

GATHERING BACKGROUND DATA   The job requirements will already be known from the expanded job description. Backgrounds of internal candidates are shown in their work records. Backgrounds of outside candidates, which are less certain, are determined by résumés and data on application forms.

Selection among internal candidates is aided by employment records that are suitable for this purpose. These records should show what training and special skills each individual has and what jobs he or she has held in the past, inside and outside the organization.

Résumés and job applications from outside candidates provide background information in three main areas: personal, education, and experience. Application forms typically request personal information for identification purposes. When personal information is strongly related to ability to perform a job, additional details may be requested. Information on education and work experience is requested in as much detail as is practical. It concentrates on specific acquired skills, responsibilities, and successes of past jobs. Increasingly, equal employment opportunity legislation restricts the kind of information that can be requested on application forms. The intent of these regulations is outlined in Chapter 16.

Selection among internal candidates is also aided by the availability of work appraisals and personal observation. Testing and interviewing will often supplement this information. For outside candidates, these two approaches may be the most reliable selection tools available.

Testing   A *test* is some kind of behavior which a candidate is asked to perform as an indication of likely success in a particular job. Employment or psychological tests may range from marking personal interests or preferences on a checklist through actually carrying out some of the activities of a given job, such as typing or making supervisory decisions in hypothetical situations. The underlying purpose of using tests for personnel selection is to predict success. The tester wants to be able to say that a person who receives a certain score on one or more tests will perform in a certain way if put on the job. Different kinds of tests may be used for personnel selection.

1. *Intelligence tests* measure some type of mental capacity, which may be defined differently in different tests. Many tests involve the ability to recognize relations and the ability to reach conclusions from given information.
2. *Aptitude tests* attempt to measure the ability to learn a particular kind of skill. A candidate who has never worked on a complex assembly line might be asked to take a mechanical aptitude test to indicate mechanical dexterity.
3. *Knowledge tests* measure whether a candidate knows certain facts. A manager in a production department, for instance, might be expected to know certain machine specifications. Someone in the personnel department might be tested on knowledge of equal-employment-opportunity laws.
4. *Proficiency tests* measure the ability to perform a skilled operation. A typing test is an example.
5. *Personality* tests are meant to discover whether a candidate has personality characteristics that are thought to be important for a given job, such as aggressiveness for a salesperson or sensitivity for a personnel counselor.
6. *Vocational tests* measure interests, knowledge, skills, and other factors in an effort to discover the particular occupations for which a candidate is suitable.

Organizations are required by law today to show that their personnel tests do not unfairly discriminate against racial minorities or other identified groups. This is increasingly difficult to demonstrate. Whether employment tests do, in fact, predict performance on the job is difficult to prove. Testing of all kinds is currently under fire from many sources ranging from minority groups to the Equal Employment Opportunity Commission of the United States. For these and other reasons, it is essential that plans and decisions about tests be made by management only after consultation with a trained and qualified specialist.

Interviews   A face-to-face interview may yield useful information if it is relatively systematic and has clear goals. A skilled interviewer can learn, for example, a good deal about an applicant's career plans and motivation that would be hard to specify in a written form. A danger with interviews is the possibility of putting too much stress on a general impression of the candidate: how likable or attractive he or she is. This can be overcome somewhat by following a checklist of points to be covered during the interview. The information sought during employment interviews is also greatly restricted by law. For example, no questions may be asked of minority-group or female applicants that are not routinely asked of white male applicants.

ON-THE-JOB PERFORMANCE REQUIRES REGULAR MEASUREMENT

The staffing function also includes finding out how well people are doing once they are on the job. This process of measuring management performance is called performance *appraisal*. Appraisal may be thought of as a control step related specifically to the people in an organization. It is a measurement of actual results obtained, compared with a job standard. Its most important purpose is to encourage improvement. Often, simply telling a person about deficiencies found leads him or her to overcome these failings.

Appraisals also provide the main guide for choosing training and development programs for employees and managers. The appraisals point out areas in which training is needed. They also are essential to choosing people with the potential for promotion. They serve in making decisions about the rewards, including pay raises, given to individuals. Appraisals also serve as a motivating force. Everyone likes to know where he or she stands. Knowledge of satisfactory results is rewarding and becomes an incentive to more good performance. Constructive criticism from a superior is a sign of his or her interest and an indication that the position is considered important.

Appraisals are clearly useful. But they are very difficult to conduct. In the first place, it is hard to state a precise performance standard. No simple, objective definition of "good" management, for example, has been found. Management in particular is largely a mental activity, one that includes making decisions, planning, and discussing. Such behavior is hard to measure, but a number of appraisal methods have developed that try to overcome the problems.

Managers in Action

Proper staffing depends upon a wide range of selection and placement and evaluation techniques. That's the view of Marion S. Kellogg, vice president for corporate consulting services of General Electric Company. She directs a large internal staff that advises other managers about anything from manufacturing to marketing. Miss Kellogg began work as an industrial psychologist. "The field was growing," she says, "and I was able to grow along with it." In her earlier years at GE, Kellogg ran the engineering department's placement testing program for supervisors. Later she organized a management and professional development section for its aircraft turbine division. And as manager of employee relations for the flight propulsion lab, she devised and installed a performance appraisal system that became the model for the entire corporation.

As GE's headquarters manager of individual development, Kellogg taught pioneering management-by-objectives methods that integrated psychological techniques into the planning process. This involved, for example, a sales manager's "negotiating," rather than imposing, sales quotas on salespeople.

Since 1968, Kellogg has concentrated on developing GE's marketing managers and in providing consultant services all over the world. In so doing, her travels are legendary as she introduced GE's methods to Kuba Co. in Germany, Bull Co. in France, Olivetti and Pirelli in Italy, Barclays Bank in South Africa, and Volvo in Sweden.

"I'm a workaholic," says Kellogg, but she smiles as she says so.

Source: "Up the Ladder, Finally," *Business Week*, November 24, 1975, pp. 58–68.

Results Measurements

Every manager will have objectives. If the objectives themselves are measurable, as they should be, they will provide an appraisal method. This is done by comparing the results achieved with the specified and measurable objectives. The appraiser writes down the objectives that have been agreed upon, including the ways they will be measured. At the end of an operating period, the appraising manager sees whether objectives have been met. If the appraised individual had agreed to try to reduce employee turnover to 4 percent, for example, and actual turnover has risen to 8 percent, performance has been less than adequate on that objective. If profits of $2 million have been achieved, and the objective of the division officer had been to reach $1.5 million, performance has been outstanding for that objective. This kind of appraisal is useful for every organization. It is especially applicable for management jobs, as is discussed in Chapter 10. One limitation is that factors other than management failures—an economic slump, for instance—can cause objectives to be missed. Another limitation is that when objectives are long-term, appraisals can be delayed for too long.

Activities Measurements

Activities Measurements   Many appraisals of managers try to measure their activities and functions. These usually are based on a rating of performance made by the manager's immediate superior. Ratings may be made on general characteristics such as those shown in Figure 9-4. Even when the factors being rated are well-defined, however, this method tends to be impressionistic and subjective.

Ratings can be made somewhat more specific and pertinent by judging the extent to which the person being appraised does or does not carry out defined managerial functions. Does she or he, for example, set goals that are measurable and use consistent standards in controlling operations? Such a list of every important performance standard, or criterion, can be lengthy and complicated. If properly designed, however, the list will serve as a guide for more objective appraisals.

MANAGEMENT APPRAISAL FORM					
Department: Production				Date: March 5, 198X	
Name of Manager: Mark Komanski					
Position: Production Supervisor					
Trait	Outstanding	Above Average	Average	Unsatisfactory	
Initiative: Able to assume responsibility for completion of projects. Originates improvements in activities. Uses creativity in solving problems.			X		
Quality of Work: Maintains control of duties and activities. Completes projects on time and up to specifications. Does not neglect essential functions.			X		
Leadership: Exercises authority and influence in reaching objectives. Inspires cooperation, loyalty, and effective performance. Uses control information and communication to improve performance of subordinates.			X		

Figure 9-4. Management Appraisal Form for Rating of General Traits and Characteristics.

Critical Incident
Method

Another appraisal method is based on *critical incidents*. These are the specific behaviors or events that have been found to be most closely associated with success or failure in a particular job. For managers who oversee a number of supervisors, for instance, being able to help supervisors set their objectives may be critical to success.

In an appraisal by this method, a number of critical incidents will be noted and recorded, along with observations about the effective and ineffective ways they were handled. In the example of helping subordinates set goals, the appraiser may note that an incident was handled effectively because the manager being appraised allowed subordinates to contribute to objectives, made department and company goals clear, and expressed the objectives measurably. This critical incident serves as a basis for appraisal. For the appraised individual, it serves as an example of what the superior judges to be good performance.

Whatever appraisal method or combination of methods is employed, one thing is essential: the appraising manager must do something about the appraisal after it is made. The manager must communicate the judgments to the person who was appraised. The occasion may be used to reward and praise good performance or to make plans for improving poor performance. The appraisal can be used to set up training and development exercises if appropriate. And the guiding principle is to encourage improvement rather than place blame.

TRAINING AND
DEVELOPMENT IMPROVE
PERFORMANCE

Three situations commonly arise in well-managed organizations. Each calls for executive-level actions to provide training and development, especially for the managers.

1. The appraisal system will identify managerial weaknesses that can be strengthened through training. In examining critical incidents, for instance, Margaret may be found to have trouble communicating effectively, or Tom may lack a thorough knowledge of the work procedures in his department.

2. Changing conditions may make some technical and managerial skills obsolete. Orientation toward a new market will demand knowledge about the new field. An affirmative-action plan may call for new management attitudes. Automation may require significant changes in the work force skills.

3. People about to be promoted will not have all of the skills and experience needed to be totally capable to handle higher-level jobs.

When management plans a training and development effort, all of these needs should be met. Appraisals should be designed and continually reviewed to reveal weaknesses that formal training can shore up. Changes to be made in the organization should be scrutinized. Most likely to occur are the reshaping of major goals, altering of the internal structure, or adoption of a major new procedure. When any of these are anticipated, plans should not be considered complete until a decision has been made as to whether staff development will be needed to make the change a success. Succession planning is especially helpful in these instances. It provides a guide to career planning for the managers being considered for promotion. If a company plans to promote John to replace the retiring vice president in five years, what is it going to do to make sure John has the needed abilities when the time comes? A basic program to meet these three needs usually combines formal instruction with other, more flexible, management-development approaches.

Formal Training   Many needs for specific knowledge and abilities can be met with formal training programs. These formal approaches include (1) classroom instruction, whether given by the organization itself or taken at a college or university, (2) self-instruction with special materials, and (3) guided reading programs and other teaching methods.

Formal training is especially helpful in providing technical information and skills. The new marketing manager can get technical instruction about choosing advertising media; a production manager may take a course in applications of automatic machine and process control.

Formal training is not limited to technical knowledge, however. The study of cases or situations that have occurred in business and government is an effective way of improving managerial insights. Such study provides managers with practice in identifying the important elements in a situation and in drawing conclusions from conflicting and incomplete data. This tends to improve decision-making skills. Special role-playing techniques, in which participants act out defined roles and become involved in extensive human interaction, are popular and contribute to leadership and communication abilities.

The key to the effective use of formal training is, first, to make sure that a need for specific skills and knowledge has been identified, and second, to carefully evaluate whether a particular training course does contribute to meeting the goals set for it. Training in itself accomplishes little unless it gives participants something that helps them to perform better back on the job.

Development Approaches   Formal instruction meets many specific needs. In many other cases, especially in preparing someone for promotion, it is not enough. A thorough program will combine formal training with other approaches. If a department store chain wishes to develop a general manager for a new division in five years, it cannot just pick the top three candidates for the position and send all of them to the Harvard Business School to learn to be general managers. Typically, each candidate will be strong in certain areas and weak in others. The training coordinator must discover these areas and provide whatever else is needed by each candidate to become a well-rounded executive. Three developmental approaches are commonly used.

COACHING   This is the single most important development tool. *Coaching* is the provision of guidance, counseling, and advice to subordinates; it is on-the-job training for managers by other managers. The department head, for example, explains to a subordinate why he or she made a decision in a particular way. Or the vice president may describe the background to a situation and invite the subordinate to respond; the vice president then points out the good and bad points of the subordinate's analysis.

JOB ROTATION   This technique moves managers to different areas of responsibility—from finance to production to marketing, for example. Its purpose is to give individuals broad management experience and firsthand knowledge of the overall organization. It is an excellent way to develop general managers, but it takes time. The rotated manager must truly assume responsibility in each of the training areas, not merely pass through as an observer.

SPECIAL PROJECTS ASSIGNMENTS   This is similar to job rotation except that here the manager being developed is given responsibility only for a temporary, one-time undertaking. Such project assignments can give important experience in organizing and decision making, and in the use of leadership and initiative. Service on a new-product committee, for instance, provides involvement in decisions about pricing, materials purchasing, production, facilities, marketing, finance, and nearly every other function of a manufacturing firm. As another example, a government agency might place a developing manager in charge of extending services into a new region. This would give the manager contact with all aspects of the service without having the greater responsibility of a top-level position.

SUMMARY

1. Staffing is a process of planning current and future personnel needs, selecting people from inside and outside the organization to meet these needs, appraising the performance of employees and managers, and training and developing personnel to improve performance and fill future position openings.

2. New positions and new specifications for existing positions are created by changing objectives, expansion, reorganization, retirements, promotions, dismissals, resignations, disability, and death. A personnel plan identifies and specifies development activities for internal candidates for all current and future management positions in an organization. It may also be extended to include critical positions of any kind.

3. Most organizations must recruit some personnel from outside, through advertising or personal contact. Selection of the potential outside candidates for an open position is based on application forms, tests, and interviews. Work appraisals and personal observation may be used as well in the selection of candidates from inside the organization.

4. The appraisal of management performance gives managers feedback to improve their performance, guides training and development plans, helps in choosing managers for promotion, gives a basis for pay raises, and serves as an important motivator. Appraisals can be based on a comparison of performance with measurable objectives, on a rating of general traits or specific functional performance, or on the identification, observation, and rating of critical incidents. Appraisals for all employees, managerial or otherwise, is a valued technique in most successful organizations.

5. Training and development improve performance in current positions and prepare employees and managers to handle higher-level positions. A broad effort combines formal training with developmental approaches such as job rotation, coaching, and assignment to special projects. The key to successful training and development is to clearly identify needs, plan to meet the needs over a period of time, and evaluate the results to judge success.

REVIEW AND DISCUSSION QUESTIONS

1. How is staffing related to the other management functions of planning, controlling, organizing, and directing?

2. How do overall organization goals affect specific staffing needs?

3. Why do basic position descriptions have to be expanded to help in picking the people who will fill them?

4. What is succession planning? How is it related to career planning for the people in an organization?

5. Compare the candidate-selection process as applied to people who are already in the organization with the kind of selection that must be used for outside people.

6. How can a manager make a face-to-face interview a more effective selection technique?

7. What are two limitations to basing appraisals entirely on whether measurable objectives have been met?

8. Why do organizations bother with training and development? Why don't they simply hire people who are already trained?

9. What is the purpose of job rotation? Isn't it a waste of good managers to always have them on jobs that they don't know very well?

Problems and Projects

1. The National Association of Municipal Accountants (NAMA) is a professional association. It had always had the reputation of having a good deal of influence in certain important state legislatures. When the association changed its membership rules to allow anyone to join who was even remotely connected with finance in local government, NAMA suddenly grew into a very substantial organization. Now, four years later, its managers are still struggling with some of the results of the growth. The organization structure is composed of three levels of management and nearly 300 nonmanagerial employees. At the top are the executive director and a director of development with a staff relationship to the executive director. On the next lower level are six functional managers: of member services, certification, publications, research, legislative information, and systems and data processing. Below these managers is a complex level of regional and state managers. Some handle local applications of all six functional departments; others deal with only one or two. Despite the complexity of this structure, NAMA is satisfied with its operation, and plans no changes.

   This organization is large and is likely to grow in the future. It needs a systematic and thorough approach to staffing. Act as the executive director, and outline the steps of a staffing system. Leave the details (for instance, the specific items to be used on an appraisal questionnaire) to other specialists, but be sure to outline a plan that will cover all the essential phases of staffing. Discuss the results in class.

2. The position of controller in a medium-sized corporation is being defined for staffing purposes. The general function of the position has been described as follows:

> Maintains accurate and complete financial records; designs and supervises preparation of financial reports for managers; advises on cost control in all departments; maintains records of quantity and value of inventories; assists external auditors.

The controller reports to the director of finance and supervises the data processing manager and numerous analysts and clerks in the controller's office.

   A. What are the characteristics needed of a person to fill this position? Specify education, experience, and special skills.

   B. What kind of training might be likely to improve current performance?

3. Glyck's department store has been a fixture in San Antonio for over a hundred years. It has shown sound management and conservative growth through the decades. Maria Pizek started 22 years ago as a clerk in the jewelry department. Through the years, her skill and determination moved her upward, and now she manages the entire store. Maria is making plans for the next year. She has just started by making informal notes of some things the store should try to accomplish during the year:

- Increase revenue by 3 percent after discounting inflation.
- Create public awareness of store as *price competitive;* quality image no problem; reduce margins in some areas; place stress on advertising and publicity.
- Stress *services* much more: upholstery, photo, travel, interior decorating, automotive?
- *Reduce* decorating and display costs on main floor; *increase* in clothing and housewares.
- Move budgeting from finance to merchandising department.

Maria knows from hard experience that before adopting major goals she must consider their implication for every function of running the store, including staffing.

A. List the major steps Maria must take to plan her staffing for the coming year.
B. For your list, or as separate answers, consider the following questions: What should Maria deduce from these potential goals and actions about staffing during the year? What should she do now to help her plan the staffing? What specific staffing actions might she be likely to take if she adopts the goals and plans she has sketched out?

4. *Performance Situation—The Ineffective Training Program:* Gene Minas was a natural manager. He kept in touch with everything. He was well-informed and courageous in making decisions. He inspired cooperation, loyalty, and hard work. But he had his weak spots. Having studied business and management in college, Gene knew that he should have a good manager-appraisal system and should plan succession, but he just couldn't take it seriously. He had an appraisal form, which he and the 16 managers under him dutifully filled out for all subordinates. It looked like Table 9-2.

After the forms were filled out, they were placed in the appropriate personnel files and forgotten about. Gene had used formal training programs quite a bit, but it seemed that they never had quite the effects on performance he had hoped for. In fact, it seemed they never had *any* effect. The same was true of some of his other efforts, such as counseling, to improve performance.

TABLE 9-2			
	OUTSTANDING	AVERAGE	UNSATISFACTORY
Initiative			
Loyalty			
Leadership			
Technical performance			
Quality of work			
Judgment			

Comments: _____
_____
_____
_____
_____

    A. You have been temporarily assigned as a consultant to Gene's department to help improve his appraisal system. List five steps he should take to make it work better.

    B. How would you sell these actions to Gene?

5. Consider the succession chart in Figure 9-5 shown on page 226.

Charts such as these (also called management replacement charts) are often used to keep track of the promotion potential of managers and to give an advance look at positions that may soon be open. The letter in the box to the left of each name is a current rating of promotability; the numbers to the right are a manager's age and number of years in the current position.

    A. After looking at a chart like this, what kinds of action might a top manager plan to take?

    B. What positions are likely to become open in the next few years?

    C. Does a chart like this give any guidance for training and development plans? How?

6. From whatever sources you believe will be best (the library, local companies and agencies, your school administration, instructors' files), obtain several examples of formal appraisal forms (sometimes called "merit rating forms"). Analyze these forms with the main purpose of discovering how they work and evaluating them for their usefulness in a staffing system. What will be your criteria for evaluation?

Figure 9-5.

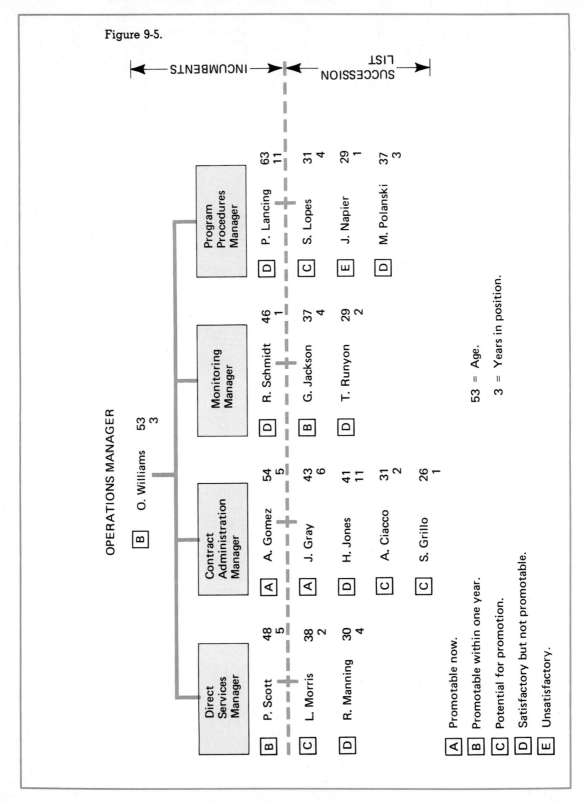

OPERATIONS MANAGER

[B] O. Williams 53
3

| INCUMBENTS | SUCCESSION LIST |

Direct Services Manager

[B] P. Scott 48
5

[C] L. Morris 38
2

[D] R. Manning 30
4

Contract Administration Manager

[A] A. Gomez 54
5

[A] J. Gray 43
6

[D] H. Jones 41
11

[C] A. Ciacco 31
2

[C] S. Grillo 26
1

Monitoring Manager

[D] R. Schmidt 46
1

[B] G. Jackson 37
4

[D] T. Runyon 29
2

Program Procedures Manager

[D] P. Lancing 63
11

[C] S. Lopes 31
4

[E] J. Napier 29
1

[D] M. Polanski 37
3

53 = Age.

3 = Years in position.

[A] Promotable now.

[B] Promotable within one year.

[C] Potential for promotion.

[D] Satisfactory but not promotable.

[E] Unsatisfactory.

Cases for Analysis and Discussion

CASE 1: NO ONE IN THE PIPELINE

"Hello, Jerry? This is Ross Bradley. I've got a problem. Carol Pilevsky just quit. That's right, the budget and cost manager. She claims she got a better job with someone else. Yes. Effective *immediately*. What do you expect? I threw her out. If that's all the loyalty she shows . . . . But, anyway, that's not the question. I need a replacement fast. The first phase of the budget cycle comes up in six weeks. I've got to have someone broken in by then. . . . What? I don't have any idea. You're the personnel manager. You're supposed to handle these things. . . . Sure, I've got a few good people but they're all doing a good job where they are. I never thought of any of them as budget and cost manager. I don't know whether they've got any background in that area or not. What does a personnel manager do if you don't handle personnel matters? It's up to you. But find me someone—in a hurry!"

A. What do you think of Ross Bradley's attitude toward staffing?
B. Is it the personnel manager's job to handle personnel matters like this one?
C. Make some proposals for improvements in Bradley's department.

CASE 2: THE PASSED-OVER MANAGER

Mary Wein normally had a rather cool and calculating approach toward her job and toward her professional relations with her colleagues and superiors at Keystone Manufacturing Corporation. She wouldn't have gotten where she was without such an attitude. Today, though, she was stewing. Paul Carson had just breezed into her office with the news that he had been promoted to vice president for marketing, a position that Mary had wanted and believed she was qualified for. Mary had the education, the experience, and the proven performance—more than Paul did, in her opinion.

Mary confronted her boss later that day. "John, I'd like to talk with you about the promotion of Paul to vice president. I think I'm better qualified for the position than he is. I'd like to know your reasons for passing me over."

"Well, Mary, I don't know exactly what to tell you. We just felt that Paul was better suited to the position. He . . . ah, seems to get along better with the top brass."

"In the first place, I don't think it's true that he gets along better than I do," said Mary. "In the second place, if he's not really qualified for the job, as I suspect, he won't continue to get along when they see his performance start to slip."

"Mary, it's not your job to judge whether we pick qualified people for promotions or not. It is our decision."

"I realize that, but I don't think you can deny that I have the background for the job. In our marketing, sales performance is the biggest item. Since I've been sales manager we've had an average 8 percent increase every year. That's better than ever before. And you know I have a degree in marketing. And since I've been studying at the university at night, I've practically got another entire degree in market research for the new projects you want to get going. And you know I started in advertising over at Ammon Industries. I was running the whole department before I went into sales here."

"I know all that, Mary. You're an excellent manager. But, you weren't the one for the vice president's job."

"But why not? Just tell me why not!"

A. Has Mary's boss handled this situation well?
B. At what aspect of staffing has her boss apparently failed?
C. What should he do now?
D. What should Mary do?

CASE 3: A FAIR APPRAISAL

Malcomb Bunch prided himself on the thoroughness and objectivity with which he kept track of the performance and development of his subordinates. He was now talking with Marty Nimitz about the last year's results. He began with a general review of the objectives he and Marty had agreed upon a year ago. Malcomb was glad to say that production levels, costs, turnover, and other key factors were right in line with goals. Cost control had been outstanding, in fact, and he told Marty so with considerable praise.

"Look at this, though, Marty," Bunch said. "The quality control reports for your department don't look as good as they should. You averaged a 5 percent rejection, with not much more than half of those being good enough to rework. If you hadn't had so many rejections and reworks, your cost figures would be even better. In fact, they would have been the best in the plant."

Marty said, "I don't know what to do about it. We can't spend a fortune keeping the machines aligned, and the workers are sure to make some mistakes."

Malcomb answered, "Let me give you an idea of what I think is happening. Two of the critical incidents I look for are related to this problem. Realigning the entire bench is expensive, as you say. But it's possible to use the unit cost figures from your daily rejection rates to figure out the point at which putting off realignment is costing you more than it's saving. You didn't do that. The second thing is the communication of quality control reports to your workers. I've observed that you do tell them, and you often say that you want to cut down on rejections and want better quality, and so on, but you don't get specific. The rejection reports give summaries of faults. Now, you know the process inside and out. I'll bet you can spot the exact cause of every fault. You've got to spend some time with the fault summaries, get to the specific causes of the problems. Show that to your workers and they'll be more likely to listen."

    A. What do you think of this session? How well has Malcomb Bunch handled it so far?

    B. Is this kind of thing worth the effort it takes?

    C. How is this session related to the entire staffing process?

CASE 4: THE THWARTED ASCENSION

Blair Johnson was a good, sound manager. His capacity for hard work was exceeded only by his ambition to move up in the organization by whatever legal means were available to him. Blair had a young man working in his department who from the first month on the job showed exceptional promise as a manager. He was quick to grasp the essentials of a situation. He had the courage to make decisions and the sense not to make them when they lay outside his authority. He was intelligent and thorough in his analyses; he didn't jump to conclusions.

Unfortunately, Blair's response to all this talent was to view the young man as a threat. Blair was not good at delegating. He felt confident that he himself could keep things from going too far wrong. And when things went right, he didn't want to have to share the praise. As a result, the promising young man took his place in the ranks of the other middle- and lower-level managers in the department. He went to meetings and wrote reports, but he never gained any real responsibility and never developed the skills needed to handle greater responsibility.

Then, one day, Blair learned that he had missed out on the promotion he had been sure he would get. One of the main reasons his boss gave was that Blair hadn't developed anyone in his department to take his place if he were promoted.

    A. Do you think situations like this really occur in organizations?

    B. Are there any formal steps that can help prevent this kind of problem?

    C. Would the possibilities demonstrated by this case be sufficient reason for a manager to devote effort to developing subordinates?

Directing

10

After completing Chapter 10, you will be able to do the following:

- Interpret the role of different kinds of authority and influence in a specific management situation.
- Orient employees and issue instructions in a manner that suits the requirements of the organization as well as the personal characteristics of subordinates.
- Predict some difficulties that are likely to arise with delegation, and propose steps for avoiding them.

- Apply management by objectives (MBO) to integrate directing and influencing with the other management functions.
- Identify personal and social factors that influence directing, and interpret their contribution to the responsibilities of the management job.

A squad of soldiers pinned down by enemy fire may huddle in the mud with only the desire to be somewhere else. But with the right training and the right discipline, the squad leader can say "OK, Let's go," and the soldiers will advance into a rain of bullets to escape their containment, or even advance farther against odds and attempt to capture a new position.

The "OK, Let's go," of the squad leader is the essence of direction. Directing and influencing include a complex group of managerial actions that (1) orient the people in the organization toward their tasks and goals, (2) instruct them in what they are to do, and (3) inspire, motivate, and influence them to do their work to the best of their ability. Business managers or civilian government administrators do not have to send their subordinates into battle. But after all the planning, setting of structures, and analyses of jobs and relationships are carried out, they will still have to say "Go to it" before anything further gets done.

MANAGERS ACTIVATE ORGANIZATIONS BY DIRECTING AND INFLUENCING

A distinction should be made between directing and influencing. *Directing* involves the exercise of formal authority; it uses orders and instructions backed up by the strength of the organization. *Influencing* includes all of the ways of getting people to behave in desired ways without the use of formal authority. These means include, especially, persuasion and motivation.

The definition of authority is important when organizing because needed authority relationships will affect the structure set up for an organization.

Authority combined with other sources of influence also affect the way people deal with each other when the organization is functioning.

Formal authority is the right to command others, to order them to do certain things in a certain way. Formal authority is impersonal; it does not depend on the individual who fills a position, but is formally assigned to the position itself. Suppose the position of executive vice president has been delegated the authority to open and close the manufacturing plants of a corporation. Whoever has been placed in that position has the right to close the Omaha plant, for example, regardless of her or his personal characteristics. Formal authority stems from the organization.

Functional influence derives mainly from the recognizably superior skills or knowledge of an individual. The batting coach for a baseball team, for example, will have very little influence on the players unless it is clear that the coach knows more about batting than the players do. We seek and follow the advice of doctors and lawyers and accountants because they know more about their specialties than we do. In an organization, functional relationships may be formally set up as in a staff position for personnel administrators. They will mean nothing, however, unless the persons in the functional roles can convince others that they have special abilities in the field. Functional influence is of course sanctioned by organizations; it is the essence of the staff concept. Organizations seek needed experts and encourage or require certain members to become authorities in essential areas.

Personal influence derives almost entirely from the individual characteristics of a person. Any number of charismatic leaders come to mind: Winston Churchill, Joan of Arc, General Patton. Every organization has people who can exert great personal power. Organizations recognize and encourage personal influence, but they cannot provide it; their individual managers must possess or develop the abilities to persuade, motivate, lead, and communicate. The exercise of personal influence is unique. It requires the ability to get others to do things, without relying on orders backed up by the power of the organization.

Table 10-1 summarizes the characteristics of managerial authority and influence. The most effective managers make use of all three kinds of authority and influence when the occasion demands. Unless a manager can acquire or develop at least one kind, he or she will be crippled as a manager. The job of getting things done through other people demands these abilities to direct and influence.

Standards for Directing and Influencing

How can an observer tell if a manager is doing a good job of directing? Again, the answer lies in the extent to which organization goals are being met.

Effective directing allows subordinates to contribute their best to meeting objectives. A good manager recognizes the potentials and current skills of employees. Through direction (combined, of course, with training, develop-

TABLE 10-1. AUTHORITY AND INFLUENCE.		
FORMAL AUTHORITY	**FUNCTIONAL INFLUENCE**	**PERSONAL INFLUENCE**
• Derives from organizational position.	• Derives from knowledge and special skills and experience.	• Derives from personal characteristics such as forcefulness and sensitivity.
• Includes the right to give and enforce orders.	• May have force nearly equal to direct orders in areas such as law and accounting standards.	• Is distinct from giving orders or instructions.
• Can be gained by occupying a position.	• Can be gained through expertise and experience.	• Can be gained by improving leadership, communication, and motivation skills.
• Is formally established in the organization structure.	• May or may not be recognized in formal organization structure.	• Is not normally recognized in formal organization structure.

ment, good organization, and the other management functions) good managers draw out and build upon the talents of personnel.

Effective directing is perceptive and flexible. It helps subordinates to harmonize their own goals with those of the organization. This is to everyone's benefit. Subordinates are motivated when they can accomplish their personal goals; the organization profits from the increased motivation and effort.

DIRECTING ACCOMPLISHES
SPECIFIC TASKS
Issuing instructions and orders has traditionally been seen as the main task of exercising formal authority, and it remains an important one today. However, a manager must also communicate information associated with the formal structure and with formal authority.

Orientation   The most familiar application of orientation is the introduction of new employees to their work and surroundings. When new people join a unit of the organization, it is extremely important that they have an accurate picture of the essentials of the work and of the environment. To become properly oriented, new employees should learn about many things. The important information to communicate includes: pay practices; work hours; holidays and vacations; sick leave and other absences; facilities for the use of employees, such as rest rooms and dining rooms; training and promotion opportunities; safety rules; and the locations of various departments and facilities of the organization.

Every employee, on a continuing basis, must also be given other information vital to organizational effectiveness. Employees, including managers, need information about organization plans, objectives, policies, and work procedures; otherwise they cannot proceed intelligently in an assigned position. The purpose of this orientation, the process of giving the information needed to play a formal role in an organization, is twofold:

1. To provide an understanding of what the whole organization, and the unit or department of which an individual is a part, is trying to accomplish.
2. To give a working knowledge of the current structures, relationships, and policies through which objectives will be met. Much of the continuing job of clarifying staff relations to avoid conflict with line authority, for example, would fall under the general head of orientation.

Orientation is not a one-time activity; it must be carried out on a continuing basis. It is easy for managers to neglect the task of providing new information to the people who need it. Slight organization changes or shifts in department goals may affect many people. Unclear or conflicting role definitions or relationships may go unrecognized for a long time. Proper orientation requires vigilance and continued effort to stay on top of such needs and developments.

Issuing Instructions   In the context of formal authority, an *instruction* is about the same as an order: it tells a subordinate what to do and how to do it. Even in modern organizations where motivation and influence are given more stress than power and discipline, giving orders is still an important function of managers. In the most common situation, instructions may be given only to line subordinates. They are enforceable by the authority of the organization.

ACCEPTABLE INSTRUCTIONS   To be enforceable, instructions must be clearly related to the accomplishment of some organizational goal. A manager could not get away with ordering everyone in the department to dye their hair red simply because the manager favored red hair. Orders are given, and followed, specifying company dress and grooming codes in considerable detail. But it must be shown that this is necessary to project an image that is important to the organization's success. The issue of what is an acceptable order has never been finally decided. What is acceptable and expected in one decade may seem outrageous twenty years later.

EFFECT OF DECENTRALIZATION   The extent of decentralization in an organization must be carefully considered in developing an approach to issuing instructions. Suppose managers have a good deal of autonomy, as may happen when they are physically separated from top management in a distant office. In that case, it may be necessary to make orders rather general so as to give freedom to deal with local problems and opportunities. If a good deal of freedom is granted, however, it is often wise to make the orders that *are* given relatively formal, in written form. Control is a common problem in decentralized organizations; the clarity of orders and the ability to refer back to them later on is helpful.

EFFECT OF ORGANIZATION SIZE   The size of an organization affects the issuing of instructions. Many large, complex firms or agencies find a structure of written, formal orders essential in avoiding conflicts and achieving coordination. Orders in written form make it easier for the person responsible for coordination to find out who has been told to do what.

Managers in Action

"Anyone who screams or shouts or uses profanity—that person is handling the situation wrong and going against company policy," says Bill Meadows, owner-manager of a garden shop and nursery in Sterling, Virginia. His firm employs 70 people and grosses $3 million a year.

Meadows' philosophy of management is "guidance, not yelling. . . . The lowest person on the totem pole should be treated with as much respect as if he were the vice president," he says.

Meadows holds two "problem-solving" meetings a year for each of the company's two departments—retailing and landscaping. Two weeks before the meeting, all employees are asked to submit a list of problems they have found on their jobs. A typical list contains nearly 200 problems and these are put into a mimeographed program to form the agenda for the meeting. Problems range from "better communications between the pullers, checkers, and loaders" to "too much mud in the yard."

One recurring complaint was about the way some of the supervisors had been "short" or "curt" on the two-way radios connecting shop and yard. "We have to be more courteous," says Meadows. "Sometimes our office staff forgets that, including me."

Source: Megan Rosenfeld, "Farmer Meadows' Nursery: The Style is Unusual," *Washington Post*, December 19, 1977, p. C-1.

EFFECT OF RELATIONSHIPS   Two of the important influences on the style for giving instructions are (1) the personality of a subordinate and (2) the quality of the relationship he or she has with a superior. Giving orders is, after all, a human interaction and a very personal one. An employee who performs best when given the security of close supervision might prefer an instruction like, "Check this with last month's production figures and show me the comparison before you go ahead." An employee who prefers to use personal initiative might prefer to hear, "Let me just mention that last month's production figures might have an effect on what you decide." If there is mutual respect between employees and their superiors, considerable freedom in expressing instructions is possible. If the trust and personal knowledge are lacking, formal written orders may be best.

EFFECT OF ANTICIPATED RESULTS   The clarity with which the possible outcomes of results can be anticipated will make a difference in giving instructions. If an executive wants someone to put together a list of sales figures, a specific, detailed request is called for. If, however, an executive wants a manager to start up a new division to manufacture and market a new product, so many unknowns may be involved that it will be impossible to specify every action the manager is to take. In that case, it is best to find a manager who can be trusted. The executive can then provide good general instructions backed up with clear goals and all of the information available. Although the instructions will be loose, the expected outputs will be more concrete.

The most important rule for giving orders is to suit the technique to the specific situation and to the person involved. No standard procedure will fit every situation.

MANAGERIAL DIRECTING IS THE PRACTICE OF DELEGATION

The decision to delegate is normally seen as part of the organizing function; it is undertaken in the relaxed atmosphere of rational advance planning. The "how-to-do-it" of dealing with employees to whom responsibility and authority have been delegated is a vital aspect of directing. This function is carried out under the pressure of day-to-day operations. Less time is available for reflection. Advance thought and preparation for how to do it is called for.

For managers at any level above the front-line supervisor, dealing with employees who themselves have authority is the crux of the directing function. Delegating a simple task such as to "Rent an office in Toledo at a monthly rent no higher than $600" is relatively easy to do. It is fairly clear what is to be done, especially if matters like location, facilities, size, and other specifications have been discussed beforehand. However, when a manager wants to delegate the handling of a specific area of responsibility on a continuing basis, far more skill is needed. Take, for example, the routine delegation of the authority to manage the purchasing function for a company. It brings up continuing questions about what decisions the manager is authorized to make, how he or she is to work with other related managers, and exactly what results the manager is expected to produce. These problems can be anticipated, and a prescribed agreement can be reached as to how they should be handled.

Problems With Delegation

Delegation is essential to an organization because the amount of productive work one person can oversee is limited. The only way to go beyond this limit is to give responsibility to others. Logical as this reasoning may be, many managers simply do not delegate effectively.

FEAR   Many managers, unfortunately, are afraid to delegate. They are unsure of their ability to direct and influence others, and prefer to try to do the bulk of the work themselves. When they do delegate, such managers often define the limits of responsibility so narrowly that the employee is left with no real discretion.

LACK OF CLARITY   It is genuinely difficult to clarify the exact extent of responsibility and authority being delegated to others. A good written description of a position gives some definition of its authority, but it may still leave some questions unanswered. Suppose, for example, the position of contract administrator calls for "negotiating cost and time extensions for operating contracts." Does the administrator have the authority to approve a cost increase of 100 percent? A related problem involves the attempt to separate from others the authority for single areas in the organization. Overlaps always seem to crop up. For example, both the product manager and the sales manager may think they have the authority to change prices; or both the budget manager and an operative unit manager may think they can change budgeting procedures.

NO ONE AVAILABLE   Of course, delegating is only possible when there is a person ready and able to take the delegated assignment. The acceptance of responsibility requires skill, experience, and maturity. In spite of an organization's development efforts, the responsibilities that need to be delegated may exceed the qualifications of people available.

The Art of Delegation

Delegation may well be viewed as a model of all kinds of directing, including orientation and the issuing of direct instructions. The goal of delegation is to get the work done and, at the same time, to develop the organization and its individuals to be able to perform better in the future. Delegation *will* work. When controls are appropriate and are actively used, major errors by employees can usually be avoided. Open communication between them and their superiors will prevent those nasty surprises.

MUTUAL TRUST   The basic rule of formal direction is to combine the training, coaching, and development of employees with the daily activities and decisions of keeping operations moving ahead. Mutual trust is possible if appraisal and selection methods are thorough and convincing. In an atmosphere of trust, it is possible to allow small errors to occur and to view them as occasions for learning. How did the employee decide the issue? What went wrong? What will prevent a reoccurrence of the same problem? When these matters are discussed patiently, performance will get better and better as time goes on.

DELEGATION GUIDELINES   Beyond the basic approach discussed above, practical guides such as the following have been found useful by managers who are successful at the art of delegation:

1. Make a conscious decision to delegate, and explicitly communicate it to all involved.
2. Match responsibilities to the individuals who hold them. If a manager has not been able to bring employees along to the point where they are ready to accept major responsibility, they should not be swamped by a flood of delegated tasks.
3. Be available to help when a problem arises. Obviously, the point of delegation is to encourage others to deal with problems themselves unless exceptional situations arise. They should take the responsibility, but the superior's experience and knowledge should always be there as a backup.
4. Base controls on the especially important aspects of the function, and make sure that the controls are used. The controls should not be so rigid that they take away the discretion of employees. At the same time, the superior cannot assume that everything is going well, but must remain well-informed about significant measures of progress.

MANAGEMENT BY OBJECTIVES INTEGRATES DIRECTING WITH OTHER FUNCTIONS

Assume that a manager knows *how* to direct, is able to suit the style of instructions to the situation, and can handle the problems that arise from delegation. How does this manager know *what* to direct? Much of the ability to know what instructions to give to others comes from a technical knowledge of the specialty in which the manager works. A sales manager, for instance, should know from experience what kinds of efforts are likely to sell particular products to particular markets. The manager can direct that these activities be carried on. Many other specific instructions are generated by the need to put the organizational structure and its plans and controls into action as illustrated in these examples:

- Structure ("Get a credit check from accounting before processing the order.")
- Plans ("Put on a second shift beginning in February.")
- Controls ("Compare the rejection data before starting the new run.")

There is a good approach that helps tie the specifics of direction together with the other management functions. It is appropriately called management by objectives (MBO).

MBO and Results   *Management by objectives* is a management system in which activities are planned and evaluated and resources are allocated according to their contribution to desired results. And then another factor is added: a commitment from each manager to operate within this framework to meet the agreed-upon objectives.

It may seem that all management would follow this approach, but this is not the case. Instead, there is a tendency to put greater emphasis on contributing factors (such as a good equipment-maintenance program) than on results. To better understand this concept, think of an operating organization as consisting of three major components:

1. *Inputs* consist of the money, materials, equipment, labor, energy, and other resources upon which the organization operates. An undue emphasis on inputs management leads to an obsession with conserving resources, even when it is damaging to the organization.
2. *Activities* are the actual work and procedures of the organization. It is easy to give too much emphasis to the work at hand ("I'm supposed to write this report") instead of giving prime attention to what the work is meant to accomplish.
3. *Outputs* are the results of operations. They may be finished products, services rendered, needs satisfied, public response, profits, or anything that is created, purposely or accidentally, from operations. In nearly every case, the main reason an organization exists is to accomplish desired results. Activities engaged in and resources used are incidental except when they contribute to meeting those goals.

Management by objectives forces attention on the third component—results—because it has been shown that people who focus hard on objectives, and keep them constantly in mind, are more likely to meet the goals than people who are distracted by too much emphasis on inputs or activities. George Odiorne, who perfected the MBO concept, has observed that too many managers get caught up with the middle component—what he calls "the activity trap."

The Process of MBO   The basic application of management by objectives is fairly simple. At the beginning of every planning period, which may be any convenient length of time, a manager gets together with, for example, a supervisor to discuss the past and the future. They set objectives for the coming period and decide on how success will be measured. That is, they agree upon how they will tell whether the goals have been met. Setting the objectives is a process of negotiation. Both the manager and the supervisor will come into the meeting with an idea of what the supervisor can and should accomplish in the coming period. The ideas of the two will usually differ somewhat. Through discussion and mutual persuasion, they must compromise to set objectives for the supervisor that they can both agree on. It is essential that the objectives be realistic and achievable, not some far-out notion of what would be nice to accomplish.

In the same meeting or in a separate one, the managers and supervisor will also review the past. They will compare actual results with the objectives that had been set for the previous period. They will seek causes of deviations and try to find solutions. This is, of course, a form of performance appraisal.

With objectives set and agreed upon, it is the major responsibility of the supervisor to reach them, using whatever skills and resources he or she has. The role of the manager during the period of actual operations is to facilitate the success of the supervisor. The manager must provide advice or analysis when needed and be sure to provide plenty of information and encouragement.

At the end of the prescribed period, the process continues, with a new appraisal of the results achieved and another negotiating session to set objectives for the next period.

As another example, the boss might call a production manager into a meeting to discuss goals. The production manager might consider ten or twenty or more different measurable objectives. The boss might note that manufacturing quality was poorer than it should have been, and give considerable emphasis to a quality-control objective such as "Cut the quality-control inspection-rejection rate from its current 6 percent to 1 percent." If the production manager feels this objective is unattainable, he or she must negotiate for a change. Part of the cause of the high rejection rate might be faulty equipment that is not scheduled for replacement for a year or two. The boss might then respond with figures showing that the equipment is only part of the problem.

Using this technique and applying as much hard evidence as is available, the two can usually reach a compromise, an objective that is mutually agreeable. In this case, if the faulty equipment really does contribute to the high rejection rate and cannot be remedied during the operating period, the boss and the production manager may agree on a lesser goal, such as reducing the rejection rate only to 3 percent.

In any situation, hundreds of specific objectives are possible, depending on what is important to success. Sales, finance, safety, profits, materials use, or anything else can be the subject of an MBO objective. The important thing is that the stated planning objectives are clear, measurable, and attainable.

ADVANTAGES OF MBO   The entire process of management by objectives is a form of directing: it puts managers into action. MBO's great value is that it closely integrates this action with all of the management functions. Directing is closely wedded to planning, control, appraisal, development, and the other phases of the management job. The directing associated with MBO is applied not in an authoritarian, commanding manner, but in a way that encourages initiative and acceptance of responsibility. That, in turn, increases motivation. MBO has the further advantage that the direction given is systematic and orderly. The person being directed is not faced with a series of seemingly unrelated orders. To the contrary, he or she has the opportunity to understand the context of every goal and instruction.

Management by objectives forces attention to results and helps overcome the tendency to overemphasize activities. MBO helps clarify the role of each person involved and can reduce the amount of overlap and conflict of positions. In the process of setting objectives, it is possible to integrate the objectives of all managers. This harmonizes subgoals so as to contribute to overall goals.

MBO improves individual managerial performance in many cases, because managers can focus on the clearly defined and important goals. MBO is also an excellent basis for the development of managers. It provides at least one form of specific appraisal that can show areas of weakness, and it gives lower-level managers a logical framework for gaining experience and accepting more responsibility.

DISADVANTAGES OF MBO   One distinct drawback of management by objectives is that it is often hard to find agreement upon objectives or to quantify them so that they can be measured. Also, the process tends to focus on short-range goals of a year or less. This can leave the future untended. A division manager, for example, may meet a series of annual profit goals, but at the expense of long-term investment in research for new products. MBO objectives are also rather inflexible, and the motivation to attain them can be so strong that a manager will shortchange necessary attention to inputs and activities. Finally, the MBO process is time-consuming and depends upon the willingness of all who are involved to commit themselves in advance.

DIRECTING TAKES PLACE IN A COMPLEX HUMAN ENVIRONMENT

The traditional view of directing, commonly held in the nineteenth and early twentieth centuries, concentrated on giving direct orders to immediate line subordinates. It was founded on formal authority. Workers and lower-level managers were typically seen as much like production machines, individual units of labor purchased by wages and salaries. There was a tendency in this approach to treat workers as interchangeable and dispensable objects, like a wrench or a machine tool. The foundation for the approach was the view that compliance with orders is a moral requirement. It implied that the economic power and social status of top managers was adequate to force submission upon lower-level managers and employees within an organization.

This purely authoritative approach to directing worked fairly well in its day, especially when viewed from the top. It worked because its philosophical basis was widely accepted by employees as well as by management. It was also supported by the rapid industrialization and economic expansion of the period.

A Shift in Values   As the discussion of management by objectives illustrates, directing is not that simple today. MBO increases motivation by giving responsibility and encouraging initiative. None of these matters were given much consideration by the traditional authoritarians. Today, these factors are becoming widely recognized as contributions to long-term success, productivity, and efficiency of organizations. Operations of private and public enterprise alike require an understanding and management of complex human factors.

This shift in values has arisen from a number of sources. For one thing, social scientists have become interested in the world of work. They have persuaded managers that it is in their best interests to recognize the human and social forces in their organizations. For another, there has been a trend toward a greater concern with human values in society at large. This trend is reflected in businesses and other formal organizations. Furthermore, employees have come to seek more and varied rewards from their work. It was common at one time to view work as predominantly a means of generating income. Today, employees tend to stress the inherently satisfying nature of their work or the lack of such satisfaction. While they still expect good pay for their work, employees place great stress on the pleasure and stimulation of social interaction and on their personal development on the job.

Work As a Human Activity   The complex attitudes and motivations of humans at work are only slowly coming to be known. This knowledge has come about through a long and often painful process of trial and error. Much of what we know is based upon finding out what works and what does not work in a variety of specific situations.

INDIVIDUALS   A whole person comes to work. Each manager and worker has personal concerns and interests that seemingly have little to do with work: family, travel, religion, aesthetics, or whatever else is important to an individual. People look for different things in work. At any given time, most people will be only partly motivated by the interests of the organization. They will be far more interested in trying to satisfy their own desires *through* the organization. Therefore, a manager who creates a climate in which individual needs and desires are in harmony with the needs and goals of the organization, will help that organization be more effective and productive.

GROUPS Each complex individual also becomes a part of a social group while at work. These groups influence behavior and attitudes in largely unpredictable ways. A manager has to deal not only with individuals but also with them as a group. Experience has shown that a group will have characteristics different from any of its individual members. Management must direct, influence, motivate, and encourage groups as such. It must do so, however, in a way that puts forward the interests and needs of the overall organization without trammeling individual employees or violating their rights and expectations. A manager's relationship with human groups and individuals is illustrated in Figure 10–1.

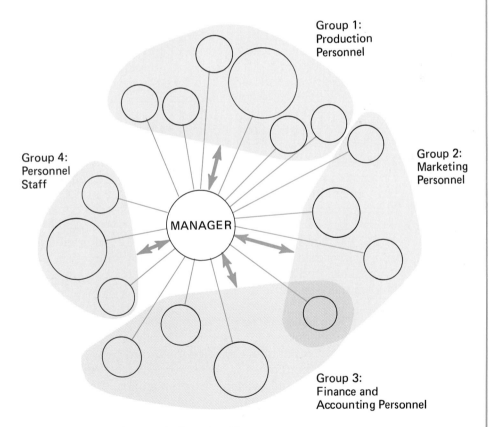

Group 1:
Production
Personnel

Group 2:
Marketing
Personnel

Group 3:
Finance and
Accounting Personnel

Group 4:
Personnel
Staff

MANAGER

Figure 10-1. The Manager's Complex Human Environment. *Managers constantly interact (1) with individuals who vary in influence, personal characteristics, skills, attitudes, and aspirations and (2) with groups that vary in size, influence, and cohesiveness.*

A Contemporary Approach

For the reasons developed above, it has become the responsibility of contemporary managers to do the following:

1. Make every effort to understand the aspirations and motivations of the people supervised and to recognize social groups and deal with them effectively.
2. Adjust modes of communication so as to be effective with individuals and work groups.
3. Use an understanding of employees' motivations to *induce* good performance without relying exclusively on organizational authority.
4. Develop and apply leadership abilities based on the complex nature of the human and social situation of the organization.

SUMMARY

1. Directing and influencing make up the management function that puts the organization into action. Formal authority, functional influence, and personal influence combine to (a) orient employees toward their tasks and goals, (b) communicate what is to be done, and (c) motivate employees to give good performance. Directing and influencing are effective when each employee can make his or her best contribution to meeting organization goals and can harmonize personal objectives with those of the organization.

2. Directing accomplishes the tasks of orientation and issuing instructions. Orientation provides the information needed to do a job. Issuing instructions is a continuing process of telling others what to do and how to do it. The style of giving instructions must be adjusted to the specific situation and individual.

3. For the higher-level manager directing other managers, the day-to-day operation of delegation will be the major form of directing. Delegating, clarifying roles, and developing managers is a major responsibility of higher-level managers.

4. Management by objectives (MBO) is a system of management that places primary emphasis on results to integrate the functions of managers. It employs negotiation of verifiable objectives, continual facilitation, and appraisal in a continuing cycle. It permits direction to be given in a way that encourages subordinates to accept responsibility and use initiative.

5. Directing and influencing involve complex human and social interactions which place certain responsibilities on managers. These include (a) making an effort to discover the motivations and aspirations of employees, (b) developing communication methods that work for particular individuals and groups, (c) using knowledge of motivations to induce desired behavior, and (d) developing leadership abilities appropriate to human concerns in the organization.

REVIEW AND DISCUSSION QUESTIONS

1. From the point of view of a manager, what is the difference between an employee's resistance to being directed and resistance to being influenced?

2. Can a line manager have functional influence in the sense used in this chapter? What is the role of functional influence in gaining performance from employees?

3. Name two main standards for the quality of directing. How can a manager apply the standards in practice?

4. What are some of the things that a manager should try to communicate to a new employee during orientation?

5. Can you provide a standard technique for giving instructions that will be suitable for all occasions? If so, what is it? If not, why not?

6. In what sense is delegation related to directing?

7. Name three difficulties you can expect to encounter when delegating authority and responsibility.

8. Why does the text say that management by objectives (MBO) is a form of directing and influencing?

9. What difference might you expect to see between an organization that uses management by objectives (MBO) and one that does not?

10. Contrast the practical effects of the traditional view of directing with the effects of a newer approach that recognizes complex personal and social influences.

Problems and Projects

1. Each of the following sentences illustrates one type of authority that might be found in formally managed organizations. On a separate piece of paper, write the letters *a* through *l* and identify each statement by marking the number of the type of authority shown as follows: 1 if formal authority, 2 if functional influence, and 3 if personal influence.

    a. You don't have to take on this job, but let me tell you why I think you are the best person to do it.

    b. Visit these three clients today and make the presentation of the new stacking shelves.

    c. I'm going to let you handle it your way, but I want you to keep these facts in mind.

d. I'll do what you suggest because I know you've tried every way there is and must know the best way by now.

e. You sure learned all the tricks when you attended that tax institute training. It was well worth the money and time.

f. Stop cutting prices on your own authority. That's my decision to make.

g. If you would be willing to take more responsibility for making a profit, you'd have a much better chance of getting the promotion.

h. If you accept the transfer even though it means moving, it will make you a more capable and better-rounded manager.

i. Cut out all expenditures for new equipment until the first of the year.

j. Design a new turret that will weigh 13 ounces less.

k. I'm going to use your budgeting system. It's obvious you've given it a lot of thought and really know what you're talking about.

l. I'll tell you what I think about it, and I hope you'll take all of this into account.

2. *Performance Situation: The Four Personalities.* You are one of the top managers of an electronic components firm, and the following four managers work under you.

a. Joel Miller runs your West Coast office, which was set up specifically to deal with the high-technology companies around Los Angeles. You see Joel only every two or three weeks. He has a long history with the company and has been quite trustworthy. However, there have been a few control problems with the West Coast office.

b. Susan Malnic heads the research department. She has great initiative and good sense and is very competent technically. She has successfully shouldered a lot of responsibility up to this point, but does not like to take direct orders. In a company like yours, research is especially important because constant product changes are needed to keep up with customer demands.

c. Grace Sanchez has headed the order-entry department for 11 years. She is resistant to change, and turned down a promotion offered to her two years ago. Productivity has been quite good in her department, but turnover has been higher than it should be, and you suspect there may be some morale problems.

d. Leroy Washington was brought in recently from outside to run a subsidiary set up to market your company's only consumer item, an electronic depth-finder for pleasure boats. He was formerly the general manager for a large marine wholesale firm. He is a mature manager, used to taking charge. You don't know each other well, though, because he only accepted his position three months ago.

It is your job to direct and influence these people. What approach would you take to each? How specific or general, how formal or informal, would your instructions be? What considerations would be especially important with each manager? What would be the main thing to accomplish with each? Write a brief paragraph answering these questions for each of the four: Miller, Malnic, Sanchez, and Washington.

3. The town manager of a very small town in the Northwest has decided to create a new managerial position to handle sewer and water service. He had been taking care of these crews himself, but now, with the new water plant, it has gotten to be too much. In thinking about the new position, he recalls hearing about the trouble that others have had with delegating in similar situations. He is determined to avoid their mistakes.

The town manager has decided to promote one of the current crew chiefs, if possible. Beyond this, he has decided little except in regard to the general duties of the position.

List five steps or processes the town manager should follow to help avoid some of the major pitfalls of delegating. Be as specific as possible about what he should do to get the new position established and in operation. Don't worry too much about selecting the proper candidate for the job. Concentrate on issues related to delegation and directing.

4. A flowchart is a graphic method for showing the order and relationship of activities, inputs, outputs, and decisions in an operating system. For example, Figure 10-2 is an extremely simple flowchart for the repetitious job of putting letters into addressed envelopes. An activity is shown in a square box; the arrows show the order in which the activities are carried out. After placing one sealed envelope in the postage meter box, for instance, the clerk goes back to folding the next letter.

Draw a chart of this type to illustrate the general process of management by objectives. Show three main elements of the process. Is it repetitious like the filling and sealing of envelopes?

5. Assume that a new student is going to join your class. The student has been studying independently and has mastered all of the material up to this time, so that will not be a problem. Outline a specific orientation procedure you would give this new student to help him or her fit in as soon as possible and begin to do well in class.

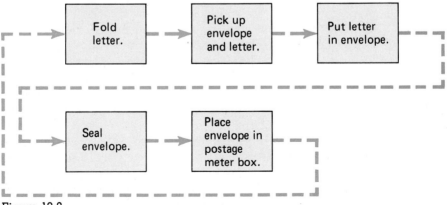

Figure 10-2.

A. What would be your main goals in orientation?
B. What specific points would you cover?
C. Might any of the things you have included be of value to a student who has been in class all along, repeated or made more explicit?

6. From your own experience, list three examples of having been given direct orders or instructions in a way that you consider inappropriate. What made them inappropriate? Was the person wrong in giving the instructions, or were they phrased in a way that was unsuitable to you? What do these experiences tell you about how you would function as an employee in an organization? What do they tell you about how you would function as a manager in an organization, directing others? Discuss in class.

Cases for Analysis and Discussion

CASE 1: THE DELAYED PROJECT

Mark Geddes was flabbergasted. Surely it was impossible: the specifications for the Central Tool Company contract were not finished on time this week and wouldn't even be done next week—probably not even next month!

Mark had told Carl Taxis exactly what was to be done, where to get the information, and even what format it was supposed to be in. Mark had gone so far as to draw little diagrams to illustrate the way he wanted the modifications of the switch controls to be shown in the contract backup documents. But there weren't any finished diagrams. There weren't even any switch modifications yet. Mark had allowed two months for the entire job. But now, after the two months had passed, he had learned from Carl that there were still probably six weeks to go on the project.

As he confronted Carl in his office, Mark was still too amazed to be angry. "Carl, I just read your memo on the schedule for the Central Tool specs. How can you possibly need six more weeks? I know the work could have been done in two months. I've done as much many times. Was there any problem that I didn't hear about?"

Carl was a little evasive: "No, there weren't any particular problems. We just got behind. We didn't get it done."

"You don't get that far behind unless you just don't work on it," Mark answered, "You simply ignored what I told you to do, didn't you? What have you been doing for two months?"

"I've been working."

"Why didn't you follow my instructions? Ignoring my assignment completely—that's nothing but insubordination!"

Carl sat up very straight in his chair, his face reddening. "Now look, Mark. What do you expect? Do you think I'm going to keep on forever doing your dirty work? You treat me like some kind of slave, anyway. You didn't tell me what the work was for. You certainly didn't tell me it had any importance. You act like nothing matters around here except what you do personally. Anything that the rest of us do, you work out so exactly before you give it to us that you take all the credit for it anyway. You're going to find that I'm not the only one who stops listening to what you say to do. You're responsible for this stuff. Do it yourself!"

A. Is Mark responsible for the work? Should he do it himself?

B. Why didn't Carl get his assignment done on time? Is Carl's behavior good for himself? For the organization?

C. What should Mark have done differently to avoid what happened?

CASE 2: UNMANAGEABLE MANAGEMENT BY OBJECTIVES

"Betty, I don't care if this so-called system does have 'management' in its name. It has my department so fouled up that I'm not doing any management, and nobody else is doing any work. We're spending all of our time *talking* about getting the work done, and hardly any time actually *getting* the work done!"

"But what's the problem, Mort? MBO should let you get more work done, not less."

"I don't see how we're supposed to get *anything* done. Do you know how hard it is to come up with objectives that you can measure with numbers? I've spent hours talking with the people who work for me, and we still haven't gotten anywhere. The same thing happened last quarter and last year. We come up with something eventually, but it sure isn't working the way you said it would. We're going to have to hire someone else to work full-time on MBO, at this rate. It's a stupid idea that interferes with our getting the real work done.

A. What has happened in this case? Does Mort have a point?

B. What caused the problem? Is it an unavoidable difficulty with MBO?

C. What should be done now?

CASE 3: THE HEAVY WORK LOAD

"Bob, I'm very displeased with the way you have been handling the shipping department," said Bob's boss, "I think it's pretty clear that the whole operation is your baby. I don't believe you can say I have interfered or set any limits that would keep you from doing a good job. But the whole thing is fouled up. We've always had a few problems, but this is getting out of hand. You've got to take control of the situation."

"You can be sure I don't feel any better about it than you do," said Bob. "In fact, I'm sure I feel worse. I worry about it all the time. It keeps me awake at night. I work as hard as I can. I'm afraid the problem is that I just don't know how to do the job."

"I suspected that might be the problem," replied the boss, "but why haven't you said something about it before now?"

"You made such a point of how the responsibility was entirely mine," said Bob, "and that I should handle everything and make all the decisions. So I just didn't feel like you wanted me to bother you with my problems."

"Hmm. Well, I can see how you got that impression, I guess. I just wanted to make it clear that you had the freedom you needed and that I wanted you to accept responsibility."

"Well, it's more than I can handle right now," said Bob.

"Maybe not, though," said his boss, "I want you to try the job for a little longer, but this time I'll work with you more closely. I think I've spotted a couple of your problems, and I've got some ideas on what you can do about them. I also think you might profit from a little formal training in supervision. The community college has a short course; I'll see about getting you registered. Above all, though, I want to clear up the idea that I'm not available when a problem comes up. Come to me whenever you need to. I think you'll find that it happens less and less as you get more experience."

A. How did Bob's boss handle this situation? Do you have any suggestions to improve it?

B. What does this case show about delegation? Has Bob's boss done a consistently good job in the past?

C. What does this case reveal about the human side of organizations?

CASE 4: THAT OLD GANG OF MINE

Barbara was one of the most competent people in the quality control department. Greg was sure of that; that's why he had promoted her to handle the production output section. Barbara had started as a line inspector, making routine physical measurements. She was an excellent worker and extremely careful with her work. She soon gained the attention of her supervisors, who were especially impressed with how well she got along with the other workers; she could laugh and joke with them even while pointing out defects in their work. She had even talked some of the other inspectors into taking some night courses with her that might make them all better candidates for promotion. If anything, in fact, she got along too well; too much talking and socializing threatened to interfere with her work. But she was efficient enough to make up for the lost time.

Because of her promise and her education in technical courses, Barbara moved up a step and continued to do well both as a worker and as an in-plant socialite. She found her new companions especially congenial and obviously enjoyed their long conversations on any subject under the sun. Her work became even better despite the cocktail-hour atmosphere she seemed to create. That was when Greg decided to promote her again.

The promotion, however, was starting to look like a bad idea. Her promotion had created a good deal of distance in her social relations, and had made her a boss to many of her former comrades. She complained to Greg about feeling isolated in her new position, and seemed to be missing the friendlier times she had enjoyed before the promotion.

A. How does this situation relate to directing and influencing?
B. Why is Barbara unsatisfied with her new position?
C. What can Greg do now? Should he put Barbara back in her old job where she was happier and more productive?

Managers Function Within Human Organizations

4

Persons, Groups, and Organizations

11

After completing Chapter 11, you will be able to do the following:

- Identify the kinds of rewards people seek at work, and relate these to individuals' performance and choices in specific situations.
- Analyze the viewpoints or approaches of Michael Maccomby and Douglas McGregor regarding the way employees and managers, either as individuals or in groups, cope with real or perceived situations within an organization.
- Assess the probable roles of formal and informal organization in given interactions.
- Describe some of the advantages and disadvantages of informal organization and identify these advantages or disadvantages in specific cases.
- Predict the influences of group cohesion, group norms, and informal leaders on individual behavior, given key facts about the group.
- Use an understanding of human and social influences to initiate change in an organization.
- Recognize the existence of conflict, and propose approaches to its resolution in specific cases.

Why do you go to school? If you are like most people, some reason will immediately come to mind; preparation for a future career or advancement on your job, for instance. But, if you think about it longer, you will probably discover a more complex group of personal aspirations, interests, expectations, and satisfactions. A college degree increases social status. College can be fun, in spite of the hard work, because of the social contacts. The work itself is often interesting and rewarding for its own sake. In many families, it is simply expected that everyone will go to college. These and many other factors cause people to go to college in the first place, and shape their experience of college once they are there.

A similarly complex human outlook propels and guides people in the world of work. People have many different reasons for working, and look for many different things once they are at work. Their individual attitudes and backgrounds cause them to behave differently and to react to and deal with situations differently. In addition, people at work become members of formal and informal groups. Group membership modifies individual behavior, and the groups themselves become important forces in the function of the overall organization.

Managers must recognize these human and social forces if they are to be effective. Getting people in a department to pull together to get something accomplished requires far more of a manager than drawing little boxes on an organization chart. It takes the ability to function in and to shape a complex, constantly changing social structure.

The starting point for more effective functioning in this regard is the acquisition by a manager of knowledge concerning the role of individuals and of groups and their interaction within the social structure of an organization.

THE PERSON IS
THE FUNDAMENTAL UNIT
OF AN ORGANIZATION

An interviewer thinking of hiring a bright young individual might well wonder what he or she is like behind that shining, eager face. What are the conflicts, the pains, the strong likes and dislikes, hopes, and interests that make up the person sitting there? Everyone who joins an organization brings a unique personality. People differ markedly in their desire to work, in their ability to deal with others, in intelligence, and in the things that give them pleasure and satisfaction. They differ in countless other traits that affect the way they relate to work. Human relations in organizations are strongly influenced by what managers *expect* people to be like as well as by what they really are like.

What People Look for in Work

When asked "Why do you work?" most people give a fairly simple answer such as "Because I have to make money to live on." This answer is probably true, but is greatly oversimplified. Admittedly, many people would not work if they did not need the money. And yet, most rich people *do* work, and work as hard as or harder than you and me. The Rockefeller, Kennedy, and Ford families attest to this. So there must be rewards other than financial ones that lead people to work. These same rewards must also influence the way individuals act while they are at work. It will be instructive to examine these rewards of work.

ECONOMIC REWARDS   Salaries and wages are probably as powerful as they have ever been, even though other rewards tend to be discussed more today. People who work in organizations usually depend on the work for their livelihood, their food, shelter, clothes, entertainment, and the other things they need and want.

SOCIAL REWARDS   Most people get some pleasure from being with others at work. For some, this reward can be predominant: "I work because it gets me out of the house." Besides the pleasure of other people's company, employees may look for specific social rewards. Some enjoy a feeling of power in the office; some find the intrigues of office politics rewarding; others use their work as a way of gaining social status and respect.

CRAFTSMANSHIP REWARDS   There is pleasure in contemplating a job well done. The knowledge that one has used skills, patience, and hard work to accomplish something worthwhile is a strong reward in itself. The job provides a good place to get such rewards.

DEVELOPMENTAL REWARDS   Nearly everyone has a picture of what he or she would want to be like; the picture is usually of a better, more capable, more fulfilled person. Work can provide an environment for self-development, for learning, for gaining new technical and personal skills. To successfully move upward on a chosen career path is rewarding in itself to most people.

OTHER REWARDS   Work can satisfy other interests and needs. Some people work, and select a particular kind of work, because they want to help others, want to further religious beliefs, or want to make the world a better place. Other people work because they have nothing else to do. Still others may work for distraction from personal problems.

THE INTERACTION OF REWARDS   Most workers will look for many or even all of these rewards from work. The relative importance of each reward will differ for different people, and even for the same person at different times. A man who has just run into financial problems may start to emphasize economic rewards, even though craftsmanship was his main concern beforehand. A woman who has been working just for extra income may now see opportunities opening up and become more concerned with work as a path to personal development.

The predominant rewards being sought from work affect the way an employee acts. Take the man who was mainly interested in craftsmanship. In the past he might have been willing to take great risks with his job to make sure that he turned out the best work possible even if it meant stepping on other people's toes. With his new concern for money, he may become more cautious. He may act mainly to protect his job security, even if the work suffers. The woman who becomes more interested in career development might become willing to sacrifice financial advancement temporarily to get greater education and experience. The manager has a responsibility in all this. She or he (1) must know the people in the organization well enough to judge the rewards each individual considers important and (2) must use this knowledge for the benefit of the individual *and* the organization.

Coping With the Organization

Everyone who joins a large organization must sometimes have the feeling, "It's them against me!" The organization is large and powerful. It has many ways of enforcing its wishes. People adopt different ways of coping with this real or perceived situation. The individual must use whatever skills are available to meet his or her own needs. Michael Maccoby, in *The Gamesman*, has described some of these approaches.[1]

1. The *craftsman* is mainly interested in the process of doing the work well, in gaining knowledge, and in creating. This person judges coworkers and superiors by the extent to which they help or hinder the work process. Such an approach to the organization stresses the work

[1]Michael Maccoby, *The Gamesman*, Simon & Schuster, New York, 1976, pp. 46–48.

itself. It tends to withdraw from the larger question: how to influence and interact with the social system of the organization.

2. The *jungle fighter* strives for power in a system that is seen as being like a jungle, says Maccoby. It is eat or be eaten; the winners destroy the losers. This person often judges others simply as enemies or accomplices. Such a view is mainly defensive; the power of the organization is seen as a threat.

3. The *company man or woman* readily identifies personal well-being and interests with the needs and goals of the organization. The organization is seen as protective and fostering, almost like a parent. Coworkers, subordinates, and superiors are judged by their contribution to organization goals as much as by their personal characteristics.

4. The *gamesman* focuses mainly on the competitive challenge of the organization. It is a complex and exciting environment in which cleverness and skill can make him or her a winner. This person views the power of the organization not as a threat, but as a game with interesting rules. She or he sees other people as competitive players who use their own tactics and strategies for advancement and winning the contest.

These four approaches, while overdrawn for emphasis, illustrate some of the ways of integrating the self with the organization. Managers need to recognize these approaches in themselves and in others. To repeat, the manager's goal is to channel the styles of individuals to meet their own needs and those of the organization.

The Manager's View of People Who Work

Employees are affected by what their managers *think* they are like. Douglas McGregor, in *The Human Side of Enterprise*, identified two contrasting managerial views, or groups of assumptions, about subordinates.[2] He contended that managerial behavior and the performance of employees was strongly influenced by the extent to which a manager held one or the other view. McGregor called the two groups of assumptions "Theory X" and "Theory Y."

THEORY X   According to McGregor's definition, the Theory X type of manager believes the following:

1. The average person dislikes work and will avoid it if he or she can.
2. Because of this dislike, people must be threatened and forced to make the effort needed to meet goals.

[2]Douglas McGregor, *The Human Side of Enterprise*, McGraw-Hill, New York, 1960, Chapters 3 and 4.

3. Most people are basically passive; they prefer to be directed by others and to avoid responsibility. The average employee is mainly interested in security.

THEORY Y   McGregor observed that the Theory Y type of manager believes the following:

1. Physical and mental work are as natural as play and rest, and are not avoided.
2. Self-motivation will be strong when employees are committed to organization goals; force is not the only way to get people to work.
3. The necessary commitment needed from employees comes as a result of the rewards received and felt from successfully meeting objectives.
4. Given the chance, the average person learns to accept and to actively seek responsibility.
5. The capacity to use creativity and innovation to solve organization problems exists in many people, not only a few.
6. In modern organizations, the true intellectual potential of employees is only partially being used.

Every individual is unique, of course, and there truly is no such thing as a "typical" employee. There is growing agreement, however, that the Theory Y view is closer to the reality of the modern work world. It deserves attention from every manager, no matter what his or her natural inclination might be. The best manager will try to judge the attitudes and capabilities of each employee singly and adapt the management approach on a one-on-one basis accordingly.

AN ORGANIZATION IS A SOCIAL SYSTEM

A *social system* is (1) a collection of fairly stable roles, (2) continuing human interactions, and (3) expectations as to what behavior is and is not proper. A company, charity, or government agency can be seen to fit this definition in two ways: in its formal structure and in its informal structure.

The Formal Organization

The formal organization is usually neat and orderly, as in the top half of Figure 11-1. It looks like this because it is rationally planned out by managers during the organizing process. As discussed in Chapters 7 and 8, the formal organization consists of roles defined by job duties, authority, and responsibility, set into a planned network of communications and interaction.

Figure 11-1. Designed Formal Structure and
Superimposed Informal Structure.

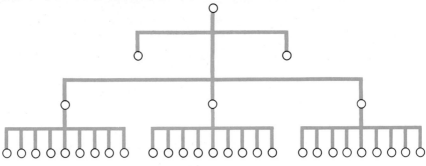

FORMAL ORGANIZATION

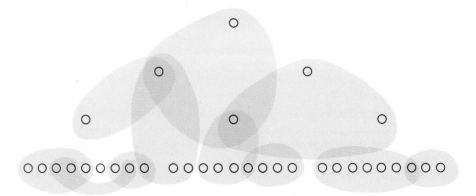

INFORMAL ORGANIZATION

In the strict formal organization, relationships between people are impersonal and utilitarian; they are meant to achieve economic or procedural
goals rather than to provide pleasure or personal satisfaction. The formal
organization, through its planned procedures and policies, specifies the
way things are to be done. Job descriptions and written procedures may, for
instance, state that only the engineering department has the authority to
design or modify production work methods. In this formal organization, for
anyone else to do methods design would be "against the rules."

The Informal
Organization

In functioning businesses and agencies, the formal organization is
only part of the picture. The informal organization, a whole other structure
with its own roles and relationships, will greatly shape the way things really
are done. Someone may have the formal role of manufacturing manager,
under the vice president for production and on the same organizational level

as the purchasing manager and the advertising manager. That same person will have many informal roles. He or she may be a friend of the vice president for sales because they both work on the same charities outside of work hours. The manager may share particularly close personal ties with the people in the department where he or she started, or may dislike the purchasing manager for personal or political reasons. These informal roles and relationships—friend, advisor, confidant, enemy, competitor, and many others—always arise when there are groups of people doing things. In many cases, they carry more weight than the formal relationships and channels set up in the organization. The manufacturing manager, for instance, might be likely to go directly to the vice president for sales, when seeking to slip a delivery date to deal with a production delay, than to follow the chain of command.

These relationships are seen everywhere. David may spend much of his time talking with Ned, even though their formal roles do not call for it. Claire may be better than Margaret at getting things done in the accounting department, because of her contacts and personal influence, even though Margaret outranks her formally. Carlos may do his own drafting work at night, even though there are people employed at the plant to do it for him. Whenever people work together, they will settle on their own ways of relating and performing. They will modify and extend the formal organization according to their own attitudes and personalities, producing an unplanned organization such as the one represented in the lower part of Figure 11-1.

People at work create *informal organizations*. These informal patterns of work, friendships, and unofficial personal influence arise naturally and affect nearly everything that goes on. People subtly adjust their job descriptions and their activities. They do so by emphasizing one part of the work or by taking on activities that have not been assigned to them. They alter their interactions. They like to spend time with their friends; they tend to avoid people who they do not like. They talk about sports, movies, and TV, and they talk about work in unofficial ways. They influence the way others do work. They experience and react to feelings, a factor that never appears in an organization chart.

As in any system, the main elements of the social system at work—the activities, interactions, and feelings—mutually influence each other. If Clayton changes his activities by beginning to work many hours of overtime, for example, the change may affect the way his coworkers feel about him and interact with him. This in turn may then change his activities again.

ADVANTAGES AND DISADVANTAGES OF THE INFORMAL ORGANIZATION   Early management theoreticians tended to view the informal organization as an enemy of good management; they commonly assumed that the goals of the informal organization nearly always conflicted with the well-being of the formal organization. This view is changing rapidly as more managers become aware of some of the benefits to be gained from the informal organization.

The informal organization provides employees with an important reward from working: social satisfaction and pleasure from working with others. It can provide stability and solidarity as employees come to share goals on a personal, emotional level as well as in the formal structure. It can provide an effective means of communication if managers are able to supply accurate information and if they can stay well-informed enough to head off rumors. It can sometimes be a training ground for leaders, since effective leadership depends heavily on the exercise of personal influence.

The early opponents of the informal organization did have some cause for their objections. Informal groups sometimes restrict output levels by mutual agreement, to make the work easier. Malcontents may become influential and cause an epidemic of dissatisfaction among other workers. Informal groups may enforce such a high level of conformity that creativity and innovation are lost. Personal status and influence may come to be more important than achieving the organization's formal goals. The interests and attitudes of informal leaders may conflict sharply with the policies of management, causing continued skirmishes and lowered efficiency.

SMALL WORK GROUPS DOMINATE THE INFORMAL ORGANIZATION

The informal relationships in which people spontaneously engage cause groups to form. The most common group is the formally prescribed work group. When people work together, in the typing pool or in the board room, they automatically become a group because they deal with each other continually. They get to know each other, they form mutual likes and dislikes, and they begin to agree on what is desirable and undesirable behavior.

The members of informal groups need not be the same ones as those in a formal work group. They may be people who get together socially after work. They may be people who seek each other out at work, even though they are in different departments, because they share common interests.

These small, formal or informal work groups are important to managers because groups have a life of their own. They function apart from the characteristics of individual members. They can be quite potent in determining how people will act; in many cases, they are even more potent than management efforts.

The Formation and Strength of Groups

Coworkers are more likely to form an informal group if they are relatively isolated from the rest of the organization. The coal stokers on the old steamships, for example, were famous for forming close-knit, separate groups. People with similar social status who work together tend to form groups or cliques. People who use the same technology, such as computer programmers, or those who have the same occupational or professional interests are likely to form groups. This is especially likely if they are in a position to communicate with each other easily.

Similar factors influence the *cohesiveness* of a group—its tendency to be unified and strong. Loose groups, based mainly on casual contacts and scattered conversations, have little cohesiveness. Groups made up of people who are relatively similar in ethnic, educational, or environmental backgrounds tend to be more cohesive, as do groups whose members are similar in age, status, and outside interests. One of the greatest forces that increases cohesion among members of a group is pressure or a threat from outside. A very authoritarian manager who makes life difficult for workers will likely find them uniting into a strong group for self-protection. Figure 11-2 illustrates groups that differ in cohesiveness.

Group Norms   Groups develop standards, or expectations, about the way people in the group should act. These *group norms* are ideas or beliefs held by the people in a group about the right way to do things. A norm might concern the way people dress, how hard they work, or what they think about their supervisors.

A work group, for instance, may have developed the norm that people in the group should view the supervisor as a hard-nosed and incompetent manager. The group's view is that its members should try to get around the supervisor's orders in getting the work out. A new member who joins the

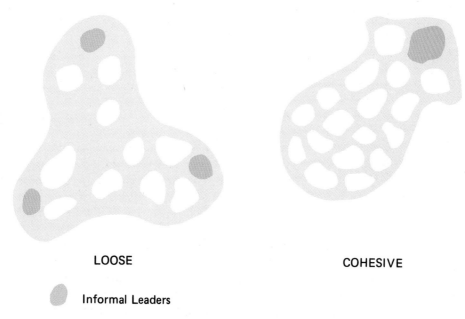

LOOSE   COHESIVE

Informal Leaders

Figure 11-2. Types of Small Work Groups.

group must learn to share this belief and behavior. Otherwise, he or she will have to do without the support of the group. The new employee who comes in and insists that the supervisor is one of the most agreeable and competent managers there ever was will meet heavy opposition.

Groups communicate norms in two main ways. Members pick up norms indirectly, by listening to and imitating the behavior of other group members, usually that of one or more members who are especially respected and influential. Groups also put direct pressure on people who deviate from norms. They may ridicule them, threaten them, refuse to offer help when needed, and deprive them of companionship.

Informal Leaders   The people who are especially respected in groups may have so much personal influence that they function as important leaders in the organization, even without having been given any formal authority. These leaders are often well-informed and are willing to communicate their knowledge to other group members. Their influence may depend upon friendships with other influential people in the organization. Informal leaders understand the group and are able to express what it stands for. They know how to get things done, often without following formal channels. Such people are extremely important in shaping the formal organization and in determining what it is able to accomplish.

Most experienced managers have found that the existence and influence of informal leaders is more of a benefit than a liability. Informal leaders have been invaluable in many instances when a formal manager wishes to introduce changes to the organization. For example, if an operating supervisor wants to make substantial revisions of work methods, these changes are likely to be seen as a threat to security by the workers. A leader among the work group can play an important role in gaining acceptance of the changes if he or she can be convinced that the new methods will benefit the workers and, particularly, that they will not threaten the group as a whole.

Working With Groups   Social groups are important in organizations. A good manager must learn to work with them effectively. The manager should recognize the existence and influence of informal groups and leaders, and should communicate with and influence them without interfering with their basic function.

A good manager can often be successful at opening up communications with informal groups and their leaders. If their confidence can be won, they will be a great source of support for management policies and will provide an added way of communicating with employees. If their confidence cannot be won, and if the group is uncooperative, it is difficult and often dangerous to try to change the situation by management action. However, there are certain approaches to solving this sort of problem practically and reasonably, and these will be discussed in a later section of this chapter.

Group Morale   When group members enthusiastically join together to work to meet worthwhile goals, they are said to have developed *group morale*. High morale is almost universally considered to be desirable. There can be

Managers in Action

How does an individual manager deal with committees? Often the hard way, if the experience of Doris V. Alexis is any example. She is the director of the California Department of Motor Vehicles. When she appeared for confirmation of her appointment before the state's Transportation Committee, Mrs. Alexis wasn't worried, she said, "Legislators treat new appointees gently for the first six months. It will be like a honeymoon." But the hearing turned out to be a trial by fire when Alexis expressed her opposition to an increase in the state driver's license fee. "You are dancing a minuet of political expediency," the chairman charged. Quipped Alexis, "If this is the honeymoon, then I fear for this marriage."

Mrs. Alexis went on from there to show that she knew how to bring together opposing factions and people with differing points of view. She would have to in her job of heading an agency of 8,500 employees with a budget of over $150 million. One of her first efforts was to seek to render better service to the public through error reduction and cost accounting. She sought to reduce the long and often confused line of people swirled around licensing stations. To do so, she instituted year-round registration, set up information booths staffed by bilingual personnel in field offices, and switched recordkeeping from an error-prone manual system to a computer-linked teletype system.

Mrs. Alexis emphasizes her "management skills of scheduling, controlling, and planning." But her subordinates make more of the fact that "she is a terrific lady," as one put it. She instinctively sets a good example by not imposing her privileges on others. For instance, she travels all over the state, and when she makes an early start, say at 4:30 A.M., she travels alone. "I don't think it's fair," she says, "to ask someone else to get up at that hour."

Source: "Boss of California's Freeways," *Ebony*, June 1978, pp. 147–152.

little doubt that it reduces conflicts, cuts turnover and probably absenteeism, and increases individual job satisfaction. It has not yet been clearly demonstrated, however, that high morale necessarily brings about high productivity.

Morale stems from the cohesiveness of the group, the job satisfaction and enthusiasm of individual members, and the extent to which they can agree on mutual goals. It also depends on other specific factors. If the group has experienced past successes working together, for instance, and feels that it will probably succeed this time, morale will be high. A supervisory style that encourages individual freedom, creativity, and responsibility and that does not overburden group members with minute controls also tends to improve morale.

Managers can improve morale by (1) setting reasonable goals and communicating the reasons for selecting them, (2) encouraging individual and group initiative, (3) selecting and developing employees so they will be capable and satisfied in their work, (4) allowing the informal organization to function without undue interference, and (5) providing rewards for goals that have been accomplished.

ORGANIZATIONAL CHANGE DEPENDS ON HUMAN AND SOCIAL ELEMENTS
The human and social aspects of the organization are intricately woven into everything a manager does. Nearly all decisions or actions are influenced by these factors. In some areas, their impact is especially clear and critical. One such instance occurs when managers want to make significant changes in the internal structure of the organization or in the social system itself. This is discussed below. Another instance is found when managers wish to facilitate operations and growth by identifying and resolving personal conflicts. This is discussed in the final section of this chapter.

Changing the Structure
The formal organizing process follows its own rules for setting up the kind of structure most desirable in a given case. Of course, there is more to organizing and reorganizing than simply working out the best theoretical structure. There are human beings behind the structure, and the social relations they have developed spontaneously are critical to the success of organizational change. Management rarely attempts to change the organization structure merely for the sake of change. Changes are nearly always made with the intention of improving the performance of the organization; creating more profits, reducing costs, or providing better service. Human welfare and development must be kept in the forefront, though, and it must be *related* to performance rather than subordinated to it.

RESISTANCE TO CHANGE People do not resist change simply because they are stubborn. Instead, most people concentrate on *continuing* present patterns that are rewarding to them. The results of a planned change are unknown; the rewards of the current situation are known. There are several aspects of change that employees may fear and resist.

1. Change of status may result from restructuring. People will not be happy when moved from a position of influence, authority, and respect to a lower-status position.
2. Career opportunities may be lost. If a company eliminates departments and trims staffs, for example, some people may suddenly feel that they have no place to be promoted to, no way to grow.
3. When work groups and social groups are broken up by reorganization, loss of social satisfaction may occur. This can cause the loss of important rewards for employees.
4. A change in objectives may leave employees confused and uncertain. They may worry about how their performance will be judged or how it will contribute to organization goals. This can lower job satisfaction and morale.

FACILITATING CHANGE OF STRUCTURE There is a proper management response to handling the threats posed by changes of structure. It centers on dealing with employees as important members of the organization. Five approaches in particular are helpful to managers.

1. Become aware of the specific causes of resistance. If some employee is dead set against being transferred, find out what it is the person feels he or she will be losing.
2. Invite comments and reactions. Involve the people who will be affected by the change. If they feel they have played a part in bringing about changes, they will feel more comfortable after the changes are made effective.
3. As much as possible, adjust changes to the people in the organization. They are the ones who get the work done. If they cannot accept changes, the changes will not be successful. Often management must compromise, if possible, to bring about acceptance.
4. Communicate the purpose of the changes and the objectives they will serve. This must be a continual process.
5. Accept the inevitable: some dissatisfaction will result from major changes. Try to develop rewards and provide information that will lessen the objections, even if they cannot be eliminated entirely.

Changing Norms

Suppose the enterprise wants to start a new program, institute a new safety rule, reduce absenteeism, or improve the productivity of a department. What happens when a manager suspects that the work group affected has a strong norm supporting the way things are now? The manager knows that the group norm will be stronger than any memo or poster management is likely to prepare. Obviously, changing the norms under these circumstances is difficult. The social group has resources and influences that management does not have. The group can provide important rewards and punishment. Realistically, management cannot match these. Nevertheless, even in the face of rigid, hindering group norms, managers must try to change them.

STEPS IN CHANGING NORMS   A three-step approach will help toward changing the norms.

1. Educate people in the organization as to the existence and influence of norms. If people in the work group are made to recognize clearly that there are *group* norms that influence their behavior, they may become more open to change.
2. Identify the norms that currently exist. Managers typically use a formal procedure for this. They make a list of behaviors related to the change desired or to the overall performance of the group. If, for instance, the proposed change involves the introduction of a new training program, the behaviors might include volunteering for training, applying the specific learning on the job, or refusing to make development efforts. The people affected are then asked to rate each behavior according to whether they approve and would encourage it, disapprove and would discourage it, or would not care one way or another. Together, their responses will show the patterns of what the group supports and what the group discourages.
3. Make efforts to change the norms that interfere with the desired performance, and strengthen the norms that support it. Possible actions include training, coaching, rewarding desired behavior, persuading group leaders, and simply setting a good example for others to imitate. Above all, managers wishing to change norms must communicate what they want to do and why they want to do it. The focus here is on the norms, not on particular people. This is not a blame-placing process. The efforts at change should stress group growth and development.

RESOLVING CONFLICTS AIDS ORGANIZATIONAL DEVELOPMENT
Conflicts are natural in human affairs. People have likes and dislikes, they make thoughtless remarks, they compete for limited resources, and they disagree on goals. Every imaginable personal conflict may be seen within an organization. In addition, the organization itself often contributes to conflicts. Departmental goals may set one group working against another: for example, the engineering department wants to try out

new production methods, while the production department resists because the experiments interfere with current productivity. Line and staff managers are often in conflict. There is trouble, for instance, when the line manager believes the staff person does not understand the real facts of operations, and the staff person thinks the line manager is unwilling to accept any advice. Managers typically try to protect their "territory," their realm of authority and power. Conflicts arise when other managers appear to exert authority where they are not supposed to. Almost anything can lead to conflict: occupational and status differences, differences in education and amount of experience, or even the way people dress.

Ways of Resolving Conflicts

Faced with a conflict, either between individuals or departments, there are a number of approaches a manager may take.

ARBITRATION   At some point in the upward chain of command, the people or departments in conflict should have a common superior. This person may be called upon to investigate the conflict, judge the merits of both sides, and determine a course of action that both sides will be required to follow.

BARGAINING   The conflicting parties may sit down, air their differences, and try to reach a compromise. One problem, of course, is that a solution may not be reached. Another difficulty is that the situation may be seen by its protagonists as a direct contest in which someone will be a clear loser.

DOMINANCE   A manager who sees a conflict developing may simply do nothing and allow the parties to fight it out. If one contestant is stronger than the other, a resolution will eventually be brought about by strength of force. The drawback of this approach is that there will often be resentment or damaged morale among those who lose.

STRUCTURAL CHANGE   Many conflicts result not from personal characteristics but from a defect in the formal structure. An employee may have two bosses. Areas of responsibility may overlap. Authority may not be clear. In such instances, the organization must be restructured to remove the source of conflict.

In a famous study, persistent conflict between waitresses and kitchen help in a restaurant was resolved simply by removing the need for contact between them. Instead of delivering their orders directly to the chefs, waitresses were directed to place their written orders on a spindle located at the kitchen entrance. Completed orders were passed by the chefs through an opening in the wall to the dining room area, where the waitresses could pick them up without verbal exchange.

PROBLEM SOLVING   This approach involves negotiation between the conflicting parties, but the negotiations are firmly guided to follow two principles: first, focus on the issue and not on personalities; second, find a solution in which both parties can win. The conflict is taken seriously as a problem to be solved. Someone, often the manager of the people in conflict, plays an active role in the discussion. He or she controls the process but not the outcome. The disputants are continually encouraged to communicate clearly and fully, to focus on the real issues, and to look for creative solutions that will benefit both parties. Emphasis is taken away from any compromise solution in which both parties would be forced to give up something.

Choosing a specific approach when a conflict exists depends on several factors, such as the severity of the conflict, its cause, and its implications for other parts of the organization. In seeking to resolve conflicts, the goal must be to minimize disruptions to the orderly progress toward important objectives. However, managers must be resigned to the fact that resolving conflicts is going to take time and effort.

Problem-solving or bargaining approaches are usually tried before other approaches because these have the best chance of eliminating the conflict to the satisfaction of everyone and at a minimum cost. One exception is in the case of minor conflicts with few likely effects on the organization; many managers settle these immediately with arbitration or simply by letting the conflict run its course. Structural change can be expected to be the most expensive response to conflict. But when the conflict is caused by competition for scarce resources or by the genuine conflict of authority and responsibility, structural change may be the only effective solution.

SUMMARY

1. People who work desire a number of rewards: economic, social, developmental, and others. The interplay of these desires affects the way people behave at work. This behavior is also influenced by the overall approach people develop toward their organization and by how their managers view them.

2. The individuals in an organization communicate and interact to form both a formal and informal social system. The formal system is based on roles and patterns established by management. The informal system results from spontaneous activities, relations, and feelings.

3. Small work groups have a powerful effect on member behavior by enforcing norms and providing informal leadership. High morale in groups is largely based on enthusiastic mutual commitment to goals and is partly controllable by management.

4. Making important changes in an organization is difficult because people prefer to hold on to roles and relationships that provide known rewards and satisfactions. Change is facilitated by involving in the planning those who will be affected, by encouraging two-way communication, by demonstrating a high-level commitment to change, and by identifying and dealing with sources of resistance and group norms.

5. Conflicts are normal in human affairs and are certain to arise in organizations. Approaches to resolving conflicts include arbitration, bargaining, dominance, changing the organization, and problem solving.

REVIEW AND DISCUSSION QUESTIONS

1. Give an example of the way an employee's behavior might be affected by the predominant reward that was being sought at the time. How can you tell what rewards employees are seeking?

2. Of the four general approaches that Maccoby suggests managers may take to an organization, which approach or combination of approaches do you think might be most beneficial to the development of the individual and to meeting organization goals?

3. What kind of relationship with subordinates would a Theory X manager be likely to develop? A Theory Y manager?

4. Would an organization be a social system even if it did not have an informal organization? Why or why not?

5. The informal organization both influences and is a result of activities, relations, and feelings. How do these three interact?

6. Outline some factors that would increase the cohesiveness of a small work group.

7. How do groups get individual members to accept and adhere to group norms?

8. What can a manager do to improve morale in a work group? Is it worth doing? In your experience, has good morale increased productivity?

9. As a manager, if you planned to make an important change in the structure of your organization, what would you do to make the change more likely to be accepted?

10. Why do conflicts arise in organizations?

Problems and Projects

1. The behaviors and statements of people who work in organizations can reveal the kinds of rewards they consider important to their work. A recognition of the rewards being sought by employees is useful to a manager in motivating and developing the employees. The following statements and situations illustrate some of the types of rewards people may be looking for. Characterize the kind of reward predominantly being sought in each of the situations. The choices are: economic reward; social reward; craftsmanship reward; developmental reward; or other reward.

    a. "I don't care if you fire me; I'm going to do it the right way or not at all."

b. Harriet was willing to give up a scheduled raise in her current position in order to be transferred to another position at the same level and to broaden her managerial experience.

c. Lionel became dissatisfied and uncooperative when he was promoted to a staff position in the distribution department because he didn't have direct authority over the people in the shipping department any more.

d. "I like this job much better than my last one. Over there, there wasn't even anyone to talk to."

e. "I know you're right, Jerry, but I'm still not going to do it. I'm afraid if they find out it might endanger my raise."

f. Even though her current job doesn't demand it, Rita has been making a real sacrifice by going to college at night to get a degree in management.

g. "Oh, I think it's fun to work. When I stayed home all day it was so *lonely.*"

h. Father Johnson spent twenty-three years of his life in New Guinea, out of touch with everyone he knew and living in genuine poverty so he could teach religion to the tribespeople.

i. Dave went to his boss demanding a raise, but when offered a chance to join a new training program for upper-level marketing managers, he happily agreed and forgot all about the raise.

j. Marion takes unusual pains with her work, sometimes falling behind in her output quantities but turning out work of exceptionally high quality.

2. You have just been transferred into the fibers division of a large corporation and appointed as production manager for one of the company's polyester fiber plants in the South. Your boss tells you that things are generally going quite well in the plant and that a normal management approach will be all that is expected. She makes it pretty clear, though, that she and other top managers fear that there might be a morale problem in your new plant. She doesn't stress the point, but you clearly get the message that if there's trouble brewing and you can't head it off, the resulting bad performance will be in your lap—and on your record.

After getting yourself established for a week or two and learning your way around, you decide you had better get started looking into the morale question. First, review the components of good morale: a group feeling, the sharing of goals that are seen as worthwhile, an enthusiasm for what is being accomplished, and a feeling that success will be likely.

List some of the actions you would take to assess the morale of those under you in the organization. If you were to use a questionnaire or a structured interview, what specific questions would you ask? What information, other than that gained from contact with the employees, would you use? What direct observations might be useful? Remember that you will also want to find out what specific things you can do to improve morale.

3. *Performance Situation—The Restructured Claims Department:* Productivity isn't what it should be in the claims adjustment department, and Al

Maggio thought he knew why: they were violating the prime rule of organizing—make the structure fit the goals. Ever since Ohio Insurance had started phasing down consumer insurance and stressing industrial policies, there had been trouble handling claims. The complex industrial claims, with multiple responsibilities, conflicting legal suits, and tedious technical investigations, were simply not getting the formal attention they deserved. Not with the way the department was set up now.

Naturally, Al's first thought was to reorganize. He had the authority and he knew what he wanted. Ken Morris had been running the whole show up to this time. He was a consumer specialist and had shown little interest in learning the new skills needed to handle the industrial claims. Al planned to divide up Ken's authority and place him at the head of a small department to handle consumer claims. Al would then bring up another manager to develop into an industrial specialist to head a larger department to be created in that area. Ken's staff would be divided, too. The hard-core consumer people would stay with Ken, and the others would go full-time to the industrial claims department. This meant breaking up some work groups that were really good units, but Al thought it was necessary. It also looked like someone would have to be brought in from outside to head the industrial department, at least until the training programs Al was setting up had a chance to do some good. The new person would then be available to succeed Al after an internal candidate had been developed to head the new department.

Assuming that this new structure will better reflect organization goals as they now exist, should Al go ahead with it? Al is likely to run into some human and social problems with this reorganization. List some of the likely problems and resistances to the new structure that he might find. Outline a brief plan for introducing and facilitating the reorganization. Be as specific as possible.

4. *Performance Situation—The Hawthorne Groups:* A group of experiments done at the Hawthorne Works of the Western Electric Company in the 1920s and 1930s have for years provided some of the raw material from which an understanding of social influences at work has been derived. One experiment involved observation of the bank wiring room. Nine wirers, three solderers, and two inspectors assembled complex telephone exchanges, performing repetitious and tedious work.

An informal organization flowered in this department. Interpersonal relations extended far beyond that required simply to do the job. Some of the behavior found included the following:

- Playing games—baseball pools, shooting craps, sharing candy.
- "Binging"—a special kind of game in which one worker hit another on the arm as hard as he could. The worker hit was free to hit back. This practice was viewed as a game, but was actually used as a form of punishment for people who produced above the group norm.
- Arguing over working conditions, such as whether to have the outside windows open or not.

■ Trading jobs and helping one another. Some workers requested help; others did not. Some were refused help even if they did ask. Job trading was against company rules.

The company standard for this group was to complete 7,312 connections a day, a rate based on careful studies by engineers. The actual rate produced was only 6,000 to 6,600 connections a day. It was discovered that the lower production rate was enforced by the group. Individual members admitted that they could easily get more done if they chose to.

How could the group enforce this lower production? What would happen to a worker who overproduced?

The group of 14 men and women was found to be subdivided into two cliques as shown in Figure 11-3. Clique A consisted of four wirers, a solderer, and an inspector. Clique B consisted of three wirers and a solderer, with the partial membership of a fourth wirer who was not fully accepted because he tried to dominate the group.

Of the 14 people, 3 were in neither of the cliques. How might this have affected their behavior and performance? What might the experimenters have observed that led them to believe that these people were not in a clique?

Both of the cliques had considerable cohesiveness. What are the implications of the existence and strength of these sorts of groups for a manager? How might they affect his or her decisions?

The informal organization in this department influenced relations among the workers and between workers and supervisors. What do you suppose the goals of the informal organization might have been? Namely, why did it exist and what did it try to accomplish?

CLIQUE A   **CLIQUE B**

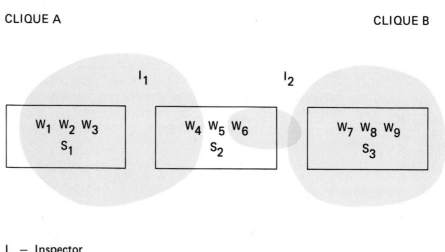

I — Inspector
W — Wirer
S — Solderer
Figure 11-3.

5. The informal organization in Problem 4 was found to enforce the following norms:

    a. You should not turn out too much work. If you do, you are a "rate-buster."

    b. You should not turn out too little work. If you do, you are a "chisler."

    c. You should not tell a superior anything that will cause a reaction detrimental to an associate. If you do, you are a "squealer."

    d. You should not attempt to maintain social distance or act officious. If you are an inspector, for example, you should not act like one.

    e. You should not be noisy, self-assertive, or anxious for leadership.

Some of these norms interfere with organization objectives. The production rate in the bank wiring room is not being met, for instance. Outline a way of progressing to change the norms so that behavior will be more productive. What is the likelihood of success for the program you have developed?

6. The following statements by Douglas M. McGregor describe two contrasting views of the role of managers in dealing with the people in organizations:

> "Without . . . active intervention by management, people would be passive—even resistant—to organizational needs. They must therefore be persuaded, rewarded, punished, controlled—their activities must be directed. This is management's task."

> "The essential task of management is to arrange organizational conditions and methods of operation so that people can achieve their own goals *best* by directing *their* own efforts toward organizational objectives."[3]

With which of these statements do you agree and why? Use examples from your own experience, from research studies found in the library, from material in the text, and from whatever other resources and arguments are available to defend your position. Discuss and debate your position with others in your class.

[3]Douglas M. McGregor, "The Human Side of Enterprise," *Management Review*, November 1957.

Cases for Analysis and Discussion

CASE 1: A QUESTION OF LOYALTIES

Everyone agreed that Jack was a good guy. He was a First Class Operator at a water filtration plant near San Francisco. He liked his work and was good at it. He also liked the people he worked with. Most of the people at the plant had known each other for a long time. Many of the people Jack worked with had been his classmates at technical school, and quite a few had even come from his old neighborhood in the city. They had the same interests and the same ways of looking at things, and they went together to see the Raiders and the A's play.

There was nearly universal agreement among them that big business and big government were parasites feeding off working men and women. They covered for each other at work; no one worked too much or too little. They didn't dislike the supervisors and managers, but they certainly didn't consider them part of their group. Jack was a solid member of this group; not its leader, but one whom the others leaned on and considered a spokesman and representative.

Ed Martinez was the superintendent, and all of the people in Jack's group worked for him. He was a competent and forward-looking manager. He saw something in Jack that convinced him that Jack was a good candidate for advancement to supervisor and probably a lot further than that.

Ed talked to Jack one day. "There's going to be an opening for supervisor in a few months, and I'm thinking of recommending you to fill the spot. You'd have to take some training downtown and we'd want to talk about it a good deal, but I think you're the one for the job. What would you think about it? Would you be interested?"

Jack wasn't sure what to say. He had often thought that he might someday have a better job, and he was pretty sure that he could handle it. But he was afraid of what his friends in the plant would think about it. It was pretty clear that they didn't care for people who were too aggressive about getting ahead. There had been nothing but laughter in the group about training in anything other than the strict technical aspects of their jobs. "I hadn't expected this, Ed," he answered. "I'd like a little time to think about it, if that's all right."

"Sure, you can think about it. But let me know something next week. I've got to make a recommendation soon."

Jack went back to his job feeling puzzled about what to do. Later that day, he talked with George Kassel, who was widely respected in the work group as one who knew the ins and outs of the whole plant. He told George about the talk with Martinez.

George burst out laughing. "So they picked you out for a big shot, did they? You're certainly not going to take it, are you?"

"I don't know," Jack answered. "That's why I wanted to talk with you."

"Why would you do it? There's not that much difference in the money. You want to go downtown and study with all those desk creeps? What are you thinking about anyway? There's nothing better about that job than working here with your friends."

A. What do you think Jack will decide? What support is there for Ed's point of view? For George's point of view?

B. What is there about this group that would give you an idea of the strength of its cohesiveness?

C. If Ed decides to try to deal with the group's influence on Jack, what approach might he take?

CASE 2: AT LOGGERHEADS

"Carol, I'm not going to put up with it any longer! No one, but no one, should make any public statements about Briscoe's trial except me. When the reporters come around, *you* in particular had better button your lip."

"Michael, my job is to deal with reporters. I've done it for twenty years— longer than you've even been in politics. And besides that, I know more about the case than anyone here. If anyone should keep his mouth shut, it should be you!"

One expects disputes in a political party, and there had been many heated arguments among the staff at this state office of the party. This particular dispute, though, was of long standing. It had begun months ago when one of the party's candidates had been charged with selling influence. Now it was beginning to become destructive. Other staff members were beginning to side either with Carol or with Michael, and it looked like there might be a major split coming. The state chairman, Tom Porter, had called this meeting to try to avoid that.

"All right, you two," said Tom, "I think you've made it clear how you can disagree. It's time we looked for some areas where you can agree. Would you agree, for instance, that this fight between you is not more important than the future of the party in this state?"

Both agreed strongly.

"Would you agree that it's about time to get this settled and get back to the work we're here to do?"

They agreed with that too.

"All right, here are the ground rules. First, we *will* reach an agreement. Second, I will control the way a decision is reached, but not what the decision will be. That's up to you. Third, both of you are trying to accomplish something in this fight. We must discover what it is. If it's not destructive to either of you or to the organization, you should find a way to solve this so that both of you get what you want."

A. What is taking place here? What technique is Tom Porter using?
B. What are a couple of things that Carol and Michael might be trying to accomplish in this dispute? Can they accomplish them in a solution to the conflict?
C. Was it good management for Tom Porter to have allowed this dispute to continue so long? Should he have done anything differently? What do you think of the way he is handling it now?

CASE 3: WORK? OH, YES, I REMEMBER THAT NOW

Frank Curzen was the envy of all his friends. Lean and tan, with a drive as potent and controlled as a howitzer, he was the scourge of the golf courses. He was a demon in a chess match, with an end game as precise and inevitable as a guillotine. In conversation he was affable and rambling, finding the wit in small things, picking out the one thing on which his listener prided himself—or more often, herself—but had really never been complimented on before.

What Frank's friends didn't know was that he was in trouble at work. He was a research assistant for a brokerage firm, and had been so for more than four years—an unheard-of length of time for a rising young broker. But Frank wasn't rising; in fact, he was about to fall. When Frank had missed another day of work last week, the higher-ups had considered firing him. They hadn't taken any action yet because they wanted to talk first with Frank's immediate boss, Andy Quiroz.

When Andy Quiroz heard that Frank might be fired, he took it almost like a personal failure. Andy firmly believed that it was his job to motivate his employees and to develop them to be better contributors to the firm. Frank obviously had the talent, but he just wasn't interested. He went through the motions, but his mind was somewhere else. And his attendance record was atrocious.

Andy tried to decide what to do. Should he just go ahead and fire Frank? Or could he think of some way to get him more involved with his work?

A. Why do you think Frank is not very involved with his work?
B. What does this case illustrate about the influence of personal attitudes and interests on performance in the work world?
C. Should Frank be fired? Or do you think there might be some way to get him to focus more on his work?

CASE 4: THE TROLL IN THE PURCHASING DEPARTMENT

"I tell you, the woman is a menace. It's just like in the fairy tale where the guy wants to cross the bridge and there's this *thing* underneath that wants his pound of flesh in return. I got her to change the specs on the plastic sheets on the Wilson job, right? She said, sweet-as-pie, 'Well, Harry, the contract's already written and in the mail. But if you really have to make a change, I'll get a modification written and off to them right away.' But *then*, without a peep to me, she tells my boss that I'm running up costs and making the job miss its deadline because I keep changing the specifications. 'Harry can't make up his mind.' That's what she said. 'Harry can't make up his mind.' "

A. Harry is complaining about an agent in the purchasing department. What approach, of those identified by Maccoby, do you think she takes toward the organization?
B. What can Harry do about this situation?
C. Is the purchasing agent's approach helpful or harmful to the organization? What can management do about it, either way?

Communication

12

After completing Chapter 12, you will be able to do the following:

- Identify the information and communication needs of managers as they perform each of the specific functions of the management process.
- Evaluate the likelihood of success of a given communication approach and describe an orderly process for managerial communications.
- Identify the sources and analyze the effects of obstacles to communications in given interactions.
- Appraise managerial communications practices and apply guidelines to improve them.
- Analyze the communications needs of a small organization and construct a formal network to satisfy these needs.

"Hello, Paris? Buy! Buy! Hello, Rome? Sell! Sell!" Thus Hollywood presents the film image of the financial tycoon. There he sits, closeted in a penthouse in an American city, talking on the telephone with far-flung agents, exchanging terse comments with underlings who glide into and out of the room. Although the glamour of this scene may be missing from most managers' offices, there is a definite element of truth in the portrayal of the executive as a central figure, interacting with a surrounding network of other people, making decisions, and interacting again. Communication may in fact be the core activity of the manager's job. Most managers will spend 70 percent or more of their time exchanging ideas and information with other people, singly and in groups. A manager who cannot communicate effectively simply cannot manage.

For the purposes of a manager, *information* may be viewed as knowledge of particular facts, circumstances, or conditions. An awareness that the building is on fire is information. *Communication* is the act of giving and receiving information to and from other people. We may inform others that the building is on fire by setting off the fire alarm or shouting "Fire!"

The failure rather than the effectiveness of communication is most often noted. So many factors interfere with good communication that many managers are surprised that they achieve as good a degree of understanding as they do. If the person who spotted the fire, for instance, had shouted "fire!" often as a joke, people would not believe him this time; credibility is a factor here. Other times, the method of communication itself may be inappropriate. If the person sighting the fire had decided to dictate an interoffice memo to be typed up and distributed through the interoffice mail, the communication would have been ineffective indeed. These and dozens of other barriers to good communication must be recognized and overcome if an organization is to be successfully managed.

COMMUNICATION SERVES
ALL OF THE MANAGEMENT
FUNCTIONS

You have read in this text any number of statements like, "The best solution to the problem is clear, effective communication." This is so true that it has borne much repeating. Nearly everything a manager does depends to some extent on an ability to communicate successfully. Every one of the management functions below employs communication.

Planning

The essence of planning is to gain knowledge of the facts and conditions important to the organization and to use this information to guide decisions about future actions. The acquisition of information requires communication from others. A prime rule of good planning is to encourage the ideas and suggestions of those affected by the plans. This requires communication. Another rule of good planning is to make sure that the people who will carry out plans understand them thoroughly. This also calls for communication.

Controlling

The knowledge of operational results must be reported back to the manager who controls the operation. In turn, the manager must communicate to others the adjustments to be made to bring operations back in line with standards.

Organizing and Staffing

Nearly every aspect of organizing depends on communication. Job analysis uses information; identifying activities and relationships, learning about conflicts, and spotting organizational problems are impossible without communication. Making sure that people understand roles and relationships involves a continual exchange of information.

Directing

Communication is the essence of directing. Orders and instructions could not be transmitted without it. Letting people know what they are to do and how they are to do it requires the sending and receiving of information. Success in directing depends on a keen ability to pick up personal signals from others and to project clear signals to others.

PERSON-TO-PERSON
EXCHANGE IS BASIC

Modern organizations use many methods for communicating information, from wall posters to the satellite transmission of computer data. The fundamental unit of communication, however, is talk—personal, face-to-face exchange. These exchanges range from two colleagues discussing a mutual problem, to a boss talking with an employee, to a group of workers talking informally about what they have been instructed to do. The possibilities are endless.

Personal intervention determines the long-term success of communications, no matter what other additional means may be used. Personal communication is so commonplace that the difficulties involved are often underestimated. It depends on (1) transmitting information in an effective way and (2) insuring that it has been accurately received.

The Communication Process

If you speak at a club meeting or at a public hearing to change a local ordinance, you engage in purposeful communication. You want to get a message across, to get people to understand your point of view, or to persuade them to do something as a result of what you have said. In speaking, you transmit information. But communication will not take place unless your listeners understand, or accurately receive, what you transmit.

Exactly the same is true whether you are a supervisor in a stockyard overseeing the work of the stock handlers or the President of the United States working out a foreign relations problem with your advisors. To be effective, the communications process must involve more than simply an attempt to convey information. Four essential elements are listed below and illustrated in Figure 12-1 on page 284.

STEP 1: GETTING ATTENTION   No information will be transmitted unless the person you are trying to communicate with—the receiver—has given his or her attention. The communicator must be aware of distractions and preoccupations and take some kind of action to overcome them. It cannot be assumed that the listener is attentive. The communicator must require some kind of response, visual or verbal, to insure involvement.

STEP 2: INSURING UNDERSTANDING   The communicator, or sender, must know what he or she wants to say and then say it directly and clearly. Here again, the sender must make sure the listener has understood by asking him or her to restate the message that was actually received. This restatement is called *feedback.* Simply asking, "Do you understand?," is not sufficient because social pressure tends to force the answer, "Yes."

STEP 3: ENCOURAGING ACCEPTANCE   Individual feelings, prejudices, and attitudes shape a person's understanding of what you say. They also affect the individual's willingness to comply. Managers must recognize this and then be especially clear in expressing parts of messages a particular person may be predisposed to reject.

STEP 4: CHECKING RESULTS   Even with this amount of care, a manager cannot assume that communication has occurred. The sender must be constantly alert to see whether the communication is having the intended results in practice. If not, the message must be restated or the individual must be given more information.

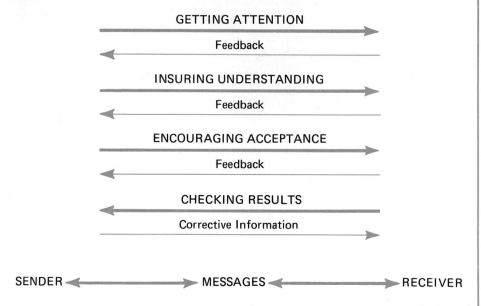

Figure 12-1. Managerial Communication Process.

GETTING ATTENTION

Feedback

INSURING UNDERSTANDING

Feedback

ENCOURAGING ACCEPTANCE

Feedback

CHECKING RESULTS

Corrective Information

SENDER ⟷ MESSAGES ⟷ RECEIVER

Importance of Interpersonal Relationships

The third step of the communications process—encouraging acceptance—reveals something important about achieving a real exchange of information: people who know each other well and are sensitive to each other's feelings and backgrounds can communicate better than people who are isolated strangers. For one thing, much of the information exchanged contains elements of feeling. When Maria tells Carl that she thinks one of their employees should be fired, she may really be as interested in communicating her feelings of dislike for the employee as in getting the individual fired. For another thing, people are more attentive and more open with people they understand and are comfortable with.

Managers improve their communications by making a conscious effort to learn about the people they work with and to help them in turn learn about the managers. Basic things to learn include where the people live, whether they are married, whether they have children, and what their education and experience are. Beyond this, it is equally important over a period of time to learn more sensitive information such as their feelings about their marriages, their children, and the places they live, their preferences in food and entertainment, their prejudices, political beliefs, outside activities, and recreational interests. These are the kinds of information you would need to know about someone before you could say that you know them well. All of these factors shape the way listeners perceive what is said to them. When a manager knows others well, that manager can shape messages to suit the receivers.

HUMAN BARRIERS TEND TO
MUDDLE COMMUNICATION

The urge to communicate is natural. Speech is a spontaneous form of expression. We like to talk to others, to let our feelings be known to them and hear what they have to say. Yet, there are as many obstacles to communication as there are reasons to communicate (see Figure 12-2). Most of the barriers stem from two sources: (1) the personal or social characteristics of the people involved and (2) features of formal organizations. Seven personal or social barriers are described below.

Communications specialists use the general term *noise* to describe any factor that interferes with the accurate exchange of information from one person to another, whether by distraction, by drowning out the important points with irrelevencies, by losing information, or by any other means. (The word noise, used in this sense, originally applied to electronic circuits and described the static, fade outs, and so on that make it hard to hear.) All of the following barriers are sources of noise in organizational communications.

Perception

If a group of people look at a lake in the mountains, each will interpret what they see differently. One may notice the beauty of the scene and pay little attention to anything else. Another may see the lake as a potential site for a housing development and note especially the lay of the land, its suitability for roads and foundations. Another may see the lake only as a potential water supply. Another might notice only the geologic features that caused the lake to form. Each of these people has a different *perception* of the lake, a different awareness of what the object is, what its important

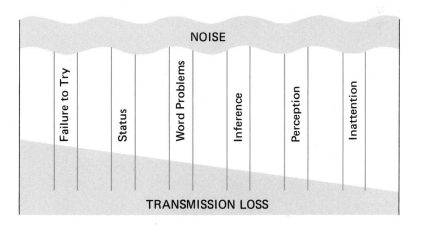

Figure 12-2. Barriers Betweeen People Interfere With Communication.

characteristics are, and what it means. If you were to tell each of these people to "find me an interesting lake," each one would interpret your message quite differently.

Inference   A different problem arises from the impossibility of expressing every single detail of a message. If a mother tells her child, "Go wash your hands," she will have a number of things in mind: to get the hands clean, not to ruin the bathroom in the process, to use soap, to do it immediately or within a certain time period. It would not be humanly possible to express every one of these intentions every time. Therefore, messages are left partially incomplete. Listeners must fill in the missing parts based on the information that is given. This process of filling in, called *inference,* can result in the listener understanding something far different from what the speaker intended.

Word Problems   *Semantics,* the study of meaning, tells us that words often mean different things to different people. We use and interpret words according to our education, experience, and background, or culture. A "bonnet," for example, is a type of hat in the United States, but is the hood of an automobile in England. To be "fast" may mean "quick" in some usages, "attached firmly" in other usages. To a baseball pitcher, "quick" may mean 90 miles an hour; to a purchasing agent, it may mean delivery of an order in less than five days. To assure effective communication, words must be chosen not only to suit the message but also to fit the ears and mind of the listener. Communicators should guard especially against the following: abstract words ("agricultural product" for "hay"); professional jargon (police usage of "apprehend," which also means "to learn") for "arrest"; and slang, which is quickly outdated.

Status   It appears to be a fact of the human condition that people with high status are viewed as more believable than those with low status. Yet, it is as essential for low-status people to communicate with high-status people as for the reverse to happen. Unfortunately, upward communications tend to be seen as less authoritative and often do not receive appropriate weight. At the same time, even casual, uninformed remarks by people of very high status often receive far more attention than they deserve.

Loss in Transmission   In an old parlor game called "Rumor," one person makes up a message about someone whom everyone present knows. He or she whispers the message to another person, who passes it on to another, and so on to everyone there. Once the message has been passed orally through eight or ten people it becomes so distorted that a comparison with the original message is ludicrous enough to make everyone laugh. This same distortion process is not laughable at work. If the information meant to be transmitted is an important machine adjustment needed to protect the safety of workers, distortion can be tragic. Experts say that every time a message is passed from one person to another, up to 30 percent of its accuracy and content may be lost. Long chains of oral message transmission simply do not work in an organization.

Inattention The human mind is complex, and the environment in which it operates is complex, varied, and distracting. People at work are often concentrating on something else when an important communication comes along; they are not prepared to "attend" to the message. With oral communications, feedback checks for attention and comprehension are possible. With written communications, however, such checks are difficult, and if the person receiving the message never reads it, there will of course be no communication.

Failure to Communicate One of the greatest obstacles to communication is the simple failure even to attempt it. Employees may fail to transmit information upward because they misjudge its importance. Or they may fear to communicate, thinking there will be unhappy consequences if information is clearly passed up the line. On the other hand, a superior sometimes purposely keeps employees in the dark, thinking that his or her position may be challenged by well-informed employees. Colleagues who are competing to get ahead in the organization may try to keep information secret from the others. In every case there is especially a tendency to cover up bad news. Furthermore, many avoid communication because it is hard work. Communication takes attention and time, not only to judge what must be transmitted, but also to make sure it *is* communicated and understood. It often seems easier just to let the communication job slip regardless of the consequences.

COMMUNICATION SKILLS CAN IMPROVE INFORMATION EXCHANGES
Despite the psychological and sociological obstacles, communication must take place. Managers will achieve better communications by trying to follow the seven basic guidelines below.

1. *Know What You Want to Say.* Managers must first understand the goal they want the message to convey before they try to transmit the message. Information must be checked for consistency and technical accuracy. Instructions should be postponed, for instance, when their impact is only vaguely understood.

2. *Choose Understandable, Slightly Repetitive Language.* If technical language is necessary to a communication, this guideline is critical. Simple language is always the best choice. Strange and complicated words may gain a manager a reputation for having a large vocabulary, but that will be small comfort when the manager is consistently misunderstood. It is a good device to repeat the key parts of a message in different words. Repetition in any form is the surest aid to helping others remember what was said.

3. *Develop Good Listening Habits.* Listening well is of course an aid to receiving information. It is sound practice not to evaluate what the speaker is saying until the whole picture is understood; given judgments from prejudices must be kept out of the way. Good listeners try to make out what is really being said, not what they think should be said. Listening is also invaluable in sending information. It is difficult to tell whether a message has been understood unless the sender pays close attention to the receivers' reactions and comments.

4. *Communicate Through Actions.* It is surprisingly common for a manager to say one thing and then demonstrate through actions that the statement really is not true. A manager, for instance, may tell employees that cutting costs must have the highest priority for the coming year. But if the manager then goes ahead and spends freely in cost decisions, the verbal communication will be rejected; others are unlikely to be very cost conscious if the manager is not; employees will more likely imitate what is done than follow what has been said.

5. *Recognize Informal Channels.* An important part of the communications flow in most organizations is through the grapevine. The *grapevine* is a network of informal communications carried on without the intervention of management. Much of what is conveyed in the grapevine may seem to be idle gossip, but other news may concern matters that are vital to the operation of an organization. If someone is about to be promoted or transferred or fired, for instance, chances are good that many others will have heard about it before it is officially announced. Anticipated changes in work procedures tend to leak out before they are put into effect. Unfortunately, distortion caused by long chains of oral communication is typical of the grapevine. Often the facts are twisted so much that employees are dead set against the changes before they have even tried them.

   Managers are quite unlikely to succeed at abolishing the grapevine. It is important, however, to recognize its existence and to try to learn what is being informally communicated. A well-informed manager can often head off trouble by volunteering accurate information or by correcting errors in the information flowing in the grapevine.

6. *Develop Sensitivity.* The quality of interpersonal relationships has a strong influence on the ease with which communication takes place. Accordingly, it makes sense to do everything possible to improve the quality of these relationships. As we already know, learning about the people you work with and allowing them to learn about you is a good

Managers in Action

"We tell [employees that] they are not making zippers, but suitcases, and Jeep tops, and trousers and everything else zippers go into," says Yoshida Kitano, president of the world's largest zippermaker (YKK), which has an ultra-modern plant in Macon, Georgia. His point is, of course, that people work best when they know where the end-result of their efforts will go.

Kitano communicates more with self-drawn charts and pictograms than with the English language. But he adheres to no national style of management, blending everything into a highly personal method.

While Kitano does not use the Japanese *ringi* under which potential decisions are circulated among employees to get their opinions before final action, he does do much more than many American-born executives.

When Kitano talks with workers, he tries to create the impression that he cares about them. He and his aides meet regularly with employees to measure and discuss their productivity. This is often done with the help of gigantic charts mounted to the walls of the factory. "We find that [workers] enjoy the challenge of breaking the previous score," observes one of Kitano's colleagues.

YKK grew rapidly from a small, family-owned business to one with $2 billion annual sales each year. Only recently did it begin to develop formalized managerial responsibilities. But for the growth ahead, Kitano says, "We will use what we have always used: *joshiki, joshiki* [common sense]."

Source: Lawrence Minard and Ayako Doi, "Will Success Spoil YKK?," *Forbes*, October 16, 1978, p. 109.

way to do this. Too great an intimacy may be undesirable; there is work to be done, after all. But trust and mutual understanding is essential. Managers must always remember that the thoughts and feelings of others will always affect the way they understand and respond to communications.

7. *Create a Communications System.* Planning can improve communications. Although it will not solve every communications problem, the issuance of formal, specific instructions about what information should be given to whom is a great aid. Managers must analyze the activities and decisions of the organization and then pinpoint the kinds of information needed for each. Based upon this analysis, they must set up specific means by which this information can flow and they must check regularly to be sure that it is in fact flowing.

AN ORGANIZATION PRESCRIBES ITS FORMAL COMMUNICATIONS SYSTEM

An organization regulates itself through its communications system. An action by one person or department affects others; the effect is not felt until communication has taken place. If the finance department learns that a major loan will not be available after all, many different people in the organization will have to reshape their plans and strategies. They cannot do so until they learn the details of the new conditions. As a consequence, management must underlie its organizational structure with a communications network, or system. Its goal should be to make sure (1) that information is there when needed and (2) that an unnecessary deluge of irrelevant information is avoided.

Communications Networks

Groups of people or departments which pass information among each other may be called *networks*. The lines of communication which connect the people or departments are *channels*. Channels may be arranged differently to achieve different kinds of control over the information flow by creating networks with different characteristics.

Part A of Figure 12-3 shows a *wheel network*, which results in a relatively restricted information flow. The manager assumes a position at the center of the network, and all communications are routed through him or her. The manager has channels with everyone in the network, but the others do not have channels among themselves; in fact, they are actively discouraged from communicating directly with each other. The wheel network has the advantage that the manager can control the information that everyone receives and can maintain privacy and personal contact. It has the disadvantage that the manager may spend all his or her time acting as a message exchange. In addition, the wheel network is slow at problem solving, and there is a tendency for important information to get lost simply because the manager may forget to refer it to the people who needed it. Despite these liabilities, the wheel network may be chosen when very tight control of information is desired.

The *web network*, shown in Part B of Figure 12-3 is quite open; everyone is encouraged to communicate directly with everyone else in the network. Every person has a channel with every other person. The web network distributes complex information rapidly and frees the manager of the burden of message exchange. Information is far less likely to be hidden, purposely or accidentally, from others who need to use it. The web network has the disadvantage of possible loss of control. Since the manager is not aware of all information exchanges, it is not always possible to verify their accuracy. Nor can the manager be sure of getting essential feedback from operations. The partial loss of control may be compensated for by the tendency of the web network to encourage initiative and to foster group approaches to solving problems and meeting goals.

Figure 12-3. Two Approaches to Organizational Communication.

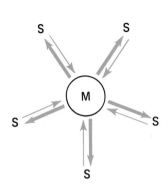

Part A: Wheel Network

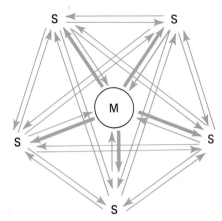

Part B: Web Network

M = Manager

S = Subordinate

Communications Channels

In addition to considering whether the system should be open or restricted, a manager must analyze where communication channels are needed between the specific units of the organization. There are many points where information originates; there are equally numerous points where it is used. Managers must decide specifically what direct and formal communication links are needed to make the organization work. The four main areas in which to seek needed channels are discussed below.

UPWARD CHANNELS Managers need to know what is going on below them in the organization. Employees must have channels with their superiors for transmitting this information. These channels usually follow the chain of command. Information for control purposes is the most obvious kind of message transmitted on these channels. Nevertheless, upward communication should never be restricted to numerical results of operations; qualitative and emotional information should flow as well. The channels from employees to superiors are among the most critical ones for learning the human and social influences operating in an organization.

DOWNWARD CHANNELS These usually are similar to the upward channels. They also follow the chain of command, but the information flows in the other direction. Downward channels are needed to give employees work instructions and to provide the information needed for exercising delegated authority. The downward channel is closely associated with the managerial function of "directing." Much of the decision making of lower-level managers, for example, depends on the downward flow of policies, plans, and goals.

LATERAL CHANNELS   It is possible, of course, for one department to learn what another is doing by having the information flow upward in the chain of command and then down again. However, efficiency often calls for direct communication among people and departments on the same level in the organization. The sales department and the distribution department, for example, have large areas of common interest. It is often useful to establish a formal channel between such departments to coordinate shipping priorities and to handle other issues, such as out-of-stock products.

DIAGONAL CHANNELS   A line-and-staff organization typically finds it necessary for staff people to communicate directly with operating departments. This may be called a diagonal (or cross-over) channel because the organization chart line connecting a staff person with a line manager will usually be diagonal. Such channels are necessary. It is generally impractical for top executives to serve as an information clearinghouse for communications among staff managers and line managers.

Communications
Media and Their Use
Media are the means for transmitting information. The chief communications media available to managers are oral communication, written communication, and certain others such as digital readout devices and television.

ORAL COMMUNICATION   Information that is presented by speaking is *oral communication*. It may be face-to-face, on the telephone, tape recorded, or recorded on film or television. Face-to-face communication is the fundamental unit. It allows immediate feedback and encourages the development of understanding and trust. It is also much faster than written communication. Its chief drawback is that long chains and complex webs of oral communication are notorious for introducing gross distortions.

WRITTEN COMMUNICATION   Anything expressed in words on paper or even on the wall of the locker room is a *written communication*. These include memorandums, policy manuals, reports, training materials, computer printouts, filled-in forms, and many others. Written communications are useful when many people must be informed of some matter. They provide a permanent record of the information that was presented, and can be referred to when needed. Technical information that needs extended study is suitable for written presentation.

Writing has a number of failings. Feedback is long delayed and may be nonexistent. It is impossible to tell right away whether someone understands what has been written unless the manager has a face-to-face oral communication. It is also easier to ignore written communications than oral ones. Writing things down is time consuming and requires great precision. Unintentional errors may creep in and may be hard to detect and correct.

OTHER MEDIA   For certain purposes, combinations of oral and written communication are effective. Posters that combine words and graphics can convey information in an attention-getting way if they are well designed and frequently changed. Television is a good way to get a message to many people at one time. Films, tapes, photographs, and TV cassettes are useful for teaching work methods and for communicating policies and procedures. Group meetings are a form of face-to-face oral communication. They provide the added dimension of a variety of viewpoints and skills. Even the bells and horns that signal the start and end of work in many factories are useful communications media for that restricted purpose. Increasingly, the demand for very fast communications is satisfied by direct-reading digital devices and cathode-ray tubes (CRT).

Creating the System   The fundamental tasks for creating the formal communication system are (1) to identify the necessary channels, (2) to choose the proper medium for each message on the channels, and (3) to check the success of communications and make improvements when needed.

The first step depends on an analysis of the creators and users of information, to determine who needs to know what in order to do their job. Operating information for two departments, for instance, must be available regularly to the manager who is responsible for coordinating the departments. Data on results of operations must always be given to the person responsible for deciding on actions to correct deviations. For example, a two-way channel for cost and purchasing information must be available to anyone responsible for profits. There are scores of other essential connections to suit any specific operation.

The second step is to choose the media. This, too, should be based on the requirements of the senders and receivers of the information. Control information, for instance, is continuing and formal; it needs frequent analysis and checking. Communications should be written. Information used in planning will be partly numerical and partly based on mutual discussion and analysis; part of this communication should be written, and part oral. The plans themselves should always be written because they must be constantly referred to. General work procedures are better if written down. Detailed instruction and performance improvement, however, usually need the immediate feedback of face-to-face contact. Regular information about decisions made and overall results obtained may well be presented in required written reports. These reports often will need backup from personal contact to be sure they have succeeded in communicating important points.

The third step is the provision for control. Management may have devised an ideal system of regular forms, scheduled meetings, required periodic reports, policy and procedure manuals, training materials, personal contacts, and regular consultations among all of the people who need to exchange information. Unfortunately, the system may still not work unless management keeps informed about how successful the information flow is in reality. Management may find that channels are missing; it may find media misused; it may find personal communications neglected. In short, if managers are to keep their communications working effectively, they have a continuing need for information about information flow.

What this means in practice is that every manager must look at the organization surrounding him or her, must analyze the information flows that are needed, and must decide on the best ways to facilitate the transmissions. The manager of a small machine shop, for example, might need to develop a fairly comprehensive system, even for a small business. Policies, job descriptions, and production and sales plans would probably be communicated downward to supervisors in writing. Staff meetings, phone calls, brief special-purpose conferences, and so on would make up an important segment of the manager's work load. Lower-level managers would use a range of written work orders, schedules and procedures, descriptions of methods, and so on to formally communicate with workers. Face-to-face contacts and meetings also would be called for at this level. Posters, handbooks, and a range of training media such as video cassettes would almost certainly be needed.

Another complex network moves information upward. Production tallies, written maintenance requests and reports, out-of-stock reports, cost records, and scores of other items will be recorded and used. Staff meetings and informal discussions give employees opportunities to express their feelings and ideas to superiors.

Fortunately, this complex system grows slowly as the company grows. A large communications network usually does not have to be created from scratch in a large company. Improvements after analysis at each stage of growth can save money by eliminating waste and make money by making the organization more effective and efficient.

SUMMARY

1. Communication is the process of sending and receiving information. It is essential to every management function because the knowledge of what needs to be done and the distribution and use of resources to get it done depend on exchanges of information about the organization and its environment.

2. Understandable personal communications are the first requirement in an organization. The communication process consists of getting attention, insuring understanding, encouraging acceptance, and checking results. Since communication is a human interaction, the quality of communication will improve when mutual trust and understanding can be developed.

3. Many barriers stand in the way of effective communications: misperceptions, false inferences, distortions caused by status differences, losses of content or accuracy during transmission, inattention, and the simple failure to attempt to communicate.

4. Managers may improve their communications by (a) knowing what they want to say, (b) using understandable, slightly repetitive language, (c) developing good listening habits, (d) backing up their words with actions, (e) recognizing informal communications, (f) developing sensitivity, and (g) creating a formal communications system.

5. A communications system establishes channels between people and departments in an organization to create a network. Channels may be upward, downward, lateral, or diagonal. Networks may be open or restricted. Establishing an effective network requires (a) the identification of necessary channels, (b) the selection of the proper medium for each message on the channels, and (c) the continual checking of the results of communication, and making needed changes in the network.

REVIEW AND DISCUSSION QUESTIONS

1. What are some of the communications needs of a manager who is performing the planning function?

2. The manager of a successful retail clothing store says, "I don't direct; I only communicate." Is that possible? How?

3. What are the four steps in the process of personal communication?

4. A consultant tells the executive director of a large foundation that her main problem with communicating is that she has not learned to develop sensitivity. Why would that be a problem? How can she solve it?

5. Can managers shape their communications in such a way that receivers are not required to use inference? What does your answer imply about effective communication?

6. What are some reasons for a person in an organization not even to try to communicate?

7. John has just been commended by his boss for having good listening habits. How would these habits be useful to John both in receiving and sending information?

8. What attitude should a manager take toward the grapevine? Can the grapevine have any positive effects?

9. Contrast a wheel network with a web network.

10. Identify four kinds of communications channels in an organization.

Problems and Projects

1. The following statements and situations illustrate common barriers to communication in organizations. On a sheet of paper, write the letters *a* through *k*, corresponding with the items. Identify the specific obstacles found in each statement by marking each with one or more of the following communications problems: perception, inference, status, loss in transmission, lack of attention, word problems, and failure to communicate. Some statements may illustrate more than one barrier.

   a. "Sure, you solved the problem, but how could you possibly think we could afford an entire new machine! Surely you knew I didn't want you to do that."

   b. Mr. Banyon, who has never been able to get ahead in the organization, has an outstanding idea for cutting costs but can't get anyone to listen.

   c. "I'm not going to tell *him* anything I don't have to; I don't trust him."

   d. Harold thinks the cost overrun was caused by his bad decisions and he is trying to cover up the increased costs as long as he can.

   e. Barbara was working on an especially complex circuit board. She heard her supervisor's suggestions about making the board easier to handle, but didn't hear his important remark about using the spotting machine safely.

   f. "I didn't know you wanted it to look like that. What difference does it make whether it's clean or not?"

   g. "Get Mary to make sure Mark has John tell all of his printers that the new tolerance on registration is 0.0025 inches."

   h. The president of the company caused a serious problem in engineering when he told them to give up the internal standards and start to use ANSI standards. The engineers knew the president was wrong, but said nothing about it.

   i. "Of course I threw it away. Why would you want me to save it? It's not worth anything, is it?"

   j. The chief executive of an organization told her finance director to delay payment of interest on a debt, to provide money for an immediately profitable venture. A week later, Martin, on the assembly line, hears that the company might go out of business because it can't pay its debts.

   k. In a leather goods shop, an employee was told to "fix" a purse handle. The employee could find nothing that needed repairing. What the boss had really meant was to "glue" the handle to the purse.

2. This exercise is similar to Problem 1, except that here you should concen-

trate on ways to *improve* communications, rather than on identifying the obstacle to effective communication. Each statement and situation illustrates an instance of poor communication. Suggest ways of improving each situation by matching one or more of the seven guidelines for better communication, given in the text on pages 287 to 289, with each item. Write the letters *a* through *j* and put the number of the guideline that applies next to each letter.

a. "How can I manage when I don't know what's going on around here? I never hear anything about quality control; the entire production schedule was changed last week, and I didn't hear a word."

b. Marion didn't notice, even though she was standing nearby, that Carl got it all wrong when he tried to repeat her instructions to his workers.

c. "Mr. Painter told me to be sure to have the platen aligned before laying on the paper, but I don't know what he's talking about. These new machines don't even have a platen."

d. "It must be true what Cheryl heard about the layoff. I asked Mrs. Rouse about it, and all she said was 'You people ought to work more and gossip less.' "

e. Bob has told all of the lathe operators to use safety face masks, but when he was training the new employee he didn't wear one himself.

f. Kelly was forced to leave college and go to work as an oiler when his father died. He's embarrassed by his lowered status, but does his best to do a good job. Every time his supervisor has something to tell Kelly, he says, 'Hey, Greaseboy, come here'."

g. "I told you about it a month ago when we were talking about next year's funding. If you had corrected the reports then, we might have gotten a better rating."

h. Harriet has tried very hard to keep the news about closing the department a secret, but she finds that the employees are suddenly uncooperative, that absenteeism is way up, and that they always seem to stop talking when she is in the room.

i. Mr. Lake has a strict policy that all employees must be at work on the dot of 8:30, but he himself likes to play squash before work and often doesn't get in until 9:30 or later.

j. "There's no way in the world that we can ship these orders according to the priorities set by the salespeople if we never learn what those priorities are!"

3. *Performance Situation—Monitoring the Contract:* Nathan studied public administration in college, and it was beginning to be clear that he would need everything he had learned and more. After a few years' experience, Nathan has become the manager of the contract monitoring department for a public works authority in one of the mountain states. In theory, the process of which Nathan's work is a part is simple. Money comes in from the federal government, from the state and from local governments. Public works projects such as water plants, certain local highways, access areas, and

drainage conduits are planned by the authority's board and specified in very detailed contracts. Local construction companies bid on the contracts, and the winning bidder goes to work.

That's where Nathan's department comes in. Its job is to inspect the work while it is in progress and make sure that the contractor is really doing what the contract calls for. People in the department measure pipe, check grades, investigate the quality of materials and workmanship, and generally determine the quality of work while it is being done. They also check compliance with federal hiring and nondiscrimination laws and deal with a maze of safety regulations. It is complicated work.

Nathan oversees five monitors, one secretary, and two clerks. He reports directly to the projects superintendent. One thing that makes his job difficult is that if he finds something wrong in the work of a contractor, he himself does not have the authority to do anything about it. If, for instance, it turns out that the pipe specified in the contract is not flexible enough for its intended use, the pipe will have to be changed. This may increase costs and cause a delay. The only people who can authorize the new costs and the delay are the ones in the contract administration department. Nathan discovers problems; the contract administrators solve them.

Nathan needs and uses a great deal of information. In general, the information may be divided into three classes: (a) data on the progress of contracts, (b) information about the people in his department, and (c) information about the organization that surrounds the department.

As an exercise, list some of the specific kinds of information that Nathan must have to run a good department. As a guide, remember that he will have to plan, control, organize, staff, and direct the department in addition to accomplishing the department's assigned activities. This kind of analysis of information needs is commonly the first step in establishing or revising a comprehensive communications system. Do not attempt to be exhaustive; real analyses of this kind may take weeks or even months. Give representative examples only.

4. For the department described in Problem 3, draw a simple diagram showing the information channels needed to connect the department to its surrounding organization and to the contractors. Show specific staff people in the department. The two clerks are supervised by the secretary. The monitors report directly to Nathan, as does the secretary.

What kind of network have you created with the channels you provided? Is it a web or a wheel? How does it relate to the chain-of-command?

5. Nathan has compiled a list of information exchanges essential to the management and operation of the department described in Problem 3. Five items from the list are given below.

Describe the specific means (or media) that should be used to transmit each type of information. What medium should be used? Should the exchanges be regularly scheduled? Who should be involved in the exchanges? Consult pages 292 to 294.

   a. Notice that a contract specification is unworkable in practice and a contract modification will be needed.

    b. Revisions in federal regulations on contractors' hiring practices.

    c. Control information on how well monitors really are achieving compliance with contract specifications.

    d. Appraisal of individual employee performance and communication of the appraisals to the employees.

    e. Training of new employees in inspection techniques and in the meanings of specific contract requirements.

6. The public relations campaign your firm has been conducting for one of your clients has begun to backfire. The public recognizes the name of the client company far better than before, but the only association they have with its name is a scandal over political bribery that the company was involved in several years ago.

You want your assistant to investigate whether this public reaction really is occurring, and if it is, to propose solutions to the problem.

Write a dialogue showing your approach to communicating this message to your assistant. Show what you would say and give the responses you would expect from the assistant. Remember the communication process and the guidelines for improving communication.

Cases for Analysis and Discussion

CASE 1: KNOWING THE BUSINESS ISN'T ENOUGH

Paul had a real knack for the real estate business. By the time he was 23 he had already made profits of $150,000. He had done so by buying old unrented buildings, making minimal repairs, renting the buildings to tenants, and reselling the buildings to investors. Now, at the age of 34, Paul really knew the business; he could play all the angles. He was the head of his own company, with 16 employees; he had a nice office; people knew who he was.

Still, things didn't seem to be going as well as they should. Paul had the gnawing feeling that, through the years, as he had added employees, the amount of work done and the success achieved had not increased proportionately. Regardless of who he hired, they never seemed to grasp what this business was all about. Paul ended up carrying the ball, even though he would have liked to delegate all the details. At a bar one night, Paul was shocked to hear one of his friends confirm this feeling. "You've really been successful, Paul," the friend said, "but I think the fire has gone out. What have you done *lately?*"

At work the next day, Paul was too busy and preoccupied to think of these things. He felt as if he were carrying the whole company. Craig Banes, the industrial properties manager came in.

"Paul, I want to talk a little about that factory building in Windsor."

"What about it?"

"Uh, I don't think it's a good idea to buy it."

"Why not?"

"I think the price is too high for us to find a lessee to cover the interest."

"Get it for less, then."

"I don't think they'll come down."

"They'll come down if you handle it right. You worry too much and get tough too little."

A. In general, why do you think Paul is not doing as well now as when he first started out?

B. Does poor communication play a part in Paul's problems? How?

C. What is the way out of this situation? Is there anything Paul can do? What about his subordinates? Can they be expected to contribute?

CASE 2: THE SIGN OF THE FOUR

Their business card was large enough to command attention—and undoubtedly to get thrown away, because it wouldn't fit the little compartment in desk organizers meant to hold business cards. The card showed only the afterparts of a flamingo rushing off to the left—in beautiful color, naturally—and the words "The Sign of the Four: Graphic Design"; this was followed by the address and phone number. Carl Gross, one of the four designers, explained the flamingo: "Beauty in service to commerce."

"The flamingo wasn't frightened away, as some think; it's only busy," added Jean Carras, another one of the designers.

Carl and Jean, with Allen Bass and Sal Tocci were the four designers referred to in their firm's name. They were the best of friends; in fact, three of them had studied together. Although they came from far-separated backgrounds, they shared the same outlook: creativity and fun take precedence; if people will pay for it, that's all the better.

In fact, people did pay for it, very handsomely. After receiving payment for a major "corporate image" campaign, the four had literally rolled in money, loose stacks of $1 bills strewn on the floor expressly for that purpose.

Each of the designers felt, with reason, that he and she knew everything to know about the others. They were all involved with each other's work. If they had a problem, they talked about it at great length and with considerable candor. Each knew something about the clients of the others and could contribute ideas. Discussion of common undertakings was not constant, but it was very frequent and prolonged.

A. What kind of communications network exists here? Does this firm have a communications system?

B. What would be the chances of establishing this kind of working environment in a department of a large organization and having it succeed? If it could be done, should it be done?

C. Is the kind of communication shown here desirable for an organization? What does it imply about the future of the firm?

CASE 3: THE SECRET
CONFLICT

Phil was dissatisfied. His boss, Marion, was also dissatisfied.

Phil had been in the client information department of the Landover Insurance Company for 13 years. He had always performed fairly well, although it could never be said that he went out of his way to look for work. Marion had joined the department only last year. She had considerable supervisory experience. Being made head of the information department was a logical first step into middle management for her.

The problem as Phil saw it was this: Marion didn't seem to like the quality of Phil's work, but he could never tell why. Phil came to feel that he didn't even know for sure what his job was. Everything he did seemed to be the wrong thing. He eventually came to believe that Marion just didn't like him and that the problem didn't have anything to do with his work at all.

The problem as Marion saw it was this: Phil lacked initiative and was slow to adopt the new procedures that Marion was starting to introduce. Marion saw Phil as a mask of pouting resistance, determined to do things his own way and to do nothing if possible. What Phil did was barely adequate, and he didn't show any interest in improving. The only answer to this, Marion felt, was to fire Phil.

A. Why is this conflict "secret?"

B. If Phil and Marion really do not get along very well, is there any answer other than firing Phil?

C. How does this situation relate to the management function? Which functions are involved? Is Marion failing to perform any of the functions? What should she be doing?

CASE 4: LOST IN
THE MAZE

Once again George was in the dark. The customer on the telephone was chewing his ear off because a promised rush shipment had not been received. George honestly knew little about it. He knew the order for the shipment had come in, because he had taken it himself. From there on, though, the order might as well have flown out the window and right now be perched on an electric wire overhead.

The order-processing routine was tortuous. An order moved from sales to the order entry department, to the accounting department, to the shipping department. Information about what had been shipped went back to the accounting department for inventory control and eventually made its ponderous way back to the sales department, usually a week later. The salespeople were strictly instructed not to communicate directly with the shipping department but to stick to the chain-of-command. This rule was made because of some angry conflicts between the sales and distribution departments several years ago.

A. What kind of network is illustrated in this case? Why do you think the network was chosen?
B. Would you add any channels to improve communications in this company? What would you add? Are there any other solutions?
C. Is this kind of communications block likely to have any effect on informal communications in the company? What might the effect be?

Motivation

13

After completing Chapter 13, you will be able to do the following:

- Prepare a list of needs people may try to satisfy at work and judge the extent to which each is likely to influence behavior in a given situation.
- Propose a practical application of each of several theories of motivation.
- Identify and evaluate the implications of expectancy theory for the design of a motivation program in a given organization.
- Compare the strengths of a number of specific motivators commonly used in organizations.
- Outline and use an orderly approach for developing a consistent motivational program for an organization.

To the gray-uniformed men swinging their sledge hammers in the penal quarries of the past, there was an implicit message: "Keep in line and break up those rocks, or you'll be shot." The watchful guards armed with powerful rifles provided the main reason for the prisoners to work hard.

Although some managers today might feel that this is a pretty good system, there is a general realization that much more than the fear of punishment is needed to make people perform well in an organization. Informed managers want to take advantage of the motivations that already exist in their employees and to guide and direct, rather than force, the efforts of workers toward organization goals. In fact, there is a growing belief that a basic practice of management should be to *allow* people to perform well, to create an atmosphere in which employees harmonize their own goals with those of the organization and work to meet both at once.

What does it mean to say someone is motivated? We cannot see motivation directly, only its effects. *Motivation* is an internal psychological state of humans and other animals that causes them to behave in certain ways. When we are thirsty, we are motivated to drink; at other times, even if offered a glass of water, we would be likely to refuse. The actual motivation—the thirstiness—is invisible; we can only judge its presence by the behavior we observe.

Managers are most interested in a certain subcategory of motivation: the characteristics that make people want to work hard and perform well in an organization. This motivation, too, is invisible. If people are working enthusiastically and well, we judge that they are highly motivated. If they stand around doing nothing or refuse to work, we assume that they are not motivated, or are motivated to resist or to interfere with work.

Managers are also interested in "motivate" as an action verb. Managers, perhaps more than all others, realize that people do not automatically give their best to an organization. Managers must actively provide the atmosphere and incentives that create motivation in employees. Managers must motivate as a conscious function. They do so in two ways: through formal programs such as financial incentive plans and through personal interactions, based on an understanding of what their employees are looking for in their work.

PEOPLE WHO GO TO WORK BRING NEEDS WITH THEM

Why did the chicken cross the road? We cannot be sure, of course, but probably there was something over there she wanted and she went across to get it. That, at least, is the general interpretation that psychologists make of motivated behavior. Motivated behavior begins with *needs*, lacks of physical things or activities—such as food, drink, or recreation—that are required by humans to maintain a physiological, psychological, and social balance. We feel a lack, as when we are hungry, and are motivated to fill it. The motivation results in *goal-directed behavior:* activities that we believe, from experience or from reasoning or from guesswork, will result in the satisfaction of the needs we feel. If the goal-directed behavior is successful, the need will be satisfied. In theory, at least, if the behavior is not successful, the need will continue unsatisfied indefinitely.

The needs of humans are extremely complex. The behaviors that result from such needs are equally complex. To make an exact connection between a single, clear need and a single, explicit action has proved difficult in research. Much disagreement has arisen about what the important human needs are beyond the obvious ones of food, shelter, protection from the elements, and others on that survival level.

What is clear is that people who come to work bring a varied collection of needs with them; many of these needs may be unrelated to the process of working and functioning in the organization. These needs, nevertheless, affect behavior and must be recognized by managers, even though the managers may be mainly interested in behavior that relates directly to the effective performance of a job.

The question of what human needs are important to work performance will be dealt with again in the next section of this chapter. As an example of this type of need, the three categories identified by David C. McClelland are appropriate. McClelland proposed three kinds of higher-level needs that would affect the quantity and quality of complex, goal-directed behavior of humans:

1. *The Need for Power.* This is demonstrated by the seeking of control and influence over others. People with strong power needs may be authoritarian and demanding. Their forceful and positive approach may make them good leaders if their behavior is reasonable and balanced.

2. *The Need for Affiliation.* This can be seen in desires for love, approval, and friendly human interaction. People with strong affiliation needs

may take great pains to avoid rejection. They will usually stress warm friendships and enjoy consoling and helping others and being consoled and helped themselves.

3. *The Need for Achievement.* This is expressed as a strong drive toward success and a strong avoidance of failure. People with strong achievement needs tend to be moderate risk-takers: they set goals that are difficult to reach but that probably can be achieved. They are realistic about their capabilities and try not to put themselves in situations that will overpower their abilities. They like responsibility and like to know immediately whether their efforts are successful or not. Since they are so strongly oriented toward reaching goals, and since they tend to be realistic in their assessment of themselves, they are often quite successful in accomplishing what they set out to do.

None of these needs can be seen directly. They have been hypothesized to explain observed behavior. The same is true of other needs that may be important to the way people perform in organizations. The practical point for a manager is that it is worthwhile paying close attention to the people he or she works with. That way the manager can try to judge what kind of motivating needs are operating in each individual. Avenues for the satisfaction of human needs must then be provided. A person with high achievement needs, for instance, will not long be satisfied if denied the opportunity to assume responsibility and if kept in the dark about the quality of his or her work. Sensitivity to human needs helps to avoid frustrated employees and to provide positive factors that motivate people to give their enthusiastic best.

MOTIVATIONAL THEORIES TRY TO EXPLAIN WHY PEOPLE DO WHAT THEY DO

It is a reasonable assumption that all behavior is motivated by something. A truly comprehensive theory of motivation would have to explain the most thoughtless scratching of an itch as well as the extremely complex behavior required to build the pyramids or to send a man to the moon. Such comprehensiveness usually is not sought by managers when looking at motivation theories. Managers judge theories of motivation by their relation to management goals: Can the theory contribute to an understanding of how people behave at work and to the creation of conditions that will make or allow them to perform better? A number of theoretical approaches have been found to partially satisfy this criterion.

Maslow's Hierarchy of Needs

Goal-directed behavior stops when the goal has been reached; that is, when the need has been satisfied. Humans, though, have so many needs and such varied needs that when one need has been satisfied, other needs are waiting in the wings to initiate *their* goal-directed behavior. This was the starting point of a theory of motivation proposed by Abraham H. Maslow. He placed human needs into five categories (or levels) arranged in priority order. The kinds of needs thus create a hierarchy like the one shown in Figure 13-1. The lowest level needs—physiological ones—have highest priority. They must be satisfied first before attention can be given to other needs. The needs of one level do not have to be completely satisfied before the next level becomes important, but they must be acceptably satisfied.

Once a level of needs is substantially satisfied, it no longer serves to motivate behavior. The next level then assumes the major motivating role. Thus, when physiological needs are satisfied, safety or security needs will become uppermost. When those needs are satisfied, the person will begin to concentrate on fulfilling social needs.

No needs are permanently satisfied. People are continually shifting up and down the hierarchy as their circumstances and conditions change. A theoretical physicist who has reached the highest levels of personal development may still become highly motivated by physiological needs if he or she becomes hungry enough. Thoughts of further development will take a back seat until food is found.

Maslow described five specific levels of needs in the hierarchy.

PHYSIOLOGICAL NEEDS   These are needs for the necessities of staying alive. They include food, drink, and protection from the elements in the forms of clothing and shelter.

SAFETY NEEDS   These are needs for protection from damage from the environment. Physical protection from accidents and pain is an obvious example, but the needs include financial security and the desire for an orderly, predictable environment.

SOCIAL NEEDS   These include human desires for contact with, and acceptance by, other humans. The range of contacts includes friendly conversation, game playing, intimate talk, love, and marriage.

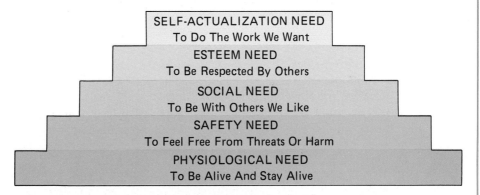

Figure 13-1. Maslow's Hierarchy of Needs.

ESTEEM NEEDS   These include the natural desire to be important and to receive recognition and praise for that importance.

SELF-ACTUALIZATION NEEDS   These may well be the most uniquely human needs identified by Maslow. They include a desire to fulfill our individual destiny, based on our background, natural abilities, personal goals, and interests. They create a drive to become the best and most able person that we can be.

Herzberg's Two-Factor Theory

When Maslow's theory is applied to people at work, it is apparent that most people in the United States who have secure jobs have gone a long way toward meeting the needs of the first two levels in the hierarchy. Someone with a regular paycheck who lives in an orderly society usually has satisfied survival and security needs. According to Maslow, then, these "lower level" needs would not normally be important motivators for people working in organizations. This has been borne out by research and by a theoretical approach proposed by Frederick Herzberg and others.

Herzberg and his associates proposed two factors to explain the motivational level of people at work. The first factor is called hygiene elements and the second factor is called motivators.

HYGIENE ELEMENTS   Many things that people get from work have the power to make them unhappy if they are denied. But they do not serve as positive motivators when they are provided. These factors are similar to physical hygiene. Staying clean and eating a good diet will not make you healthier than you were before (unless you were sick to begin with), but neglecting hygiene will make you sick if you were healthy to begin with. Herzberg identified a number of elements in the work environment that operate in the same way: money, quality and type of supervision, job security, status, working conditions, relations with other people, and general administration. Note that these are all elements of the environment in which work takes place. These hygiene factors, according to Herzberg, will make people unhappy if they are inadequate but will not really motivate people when they are adequate. A threat to job security, for example, will harm morale and lower work quality. However, providing good job security will be no guarantee of high quality performance.

Herzberg also calls these hygiene factors *"dissatisfiers"* because in their absence employees may become dissatisfied with their working arrangements. They are required, he insists, just to provide maintenance of the status quo. For this reason hygiene elements are sometimes called *maintenance* factors.

MOTIVATORS   Other elements of the work situation do provide positive motivation, Herzberg says. These are largely related to the characteristics of the work itself: the type and inherent interest of the work activities, personal development and learning, recognition and advancement resulting from good performance, general exercise of responsibility, and personal rewards of achievement. Herzberg found that, in practice, most people will not really work harder to get more pay. Of course, to people desperately in need of money, this probably would not be true. They will, however, improve their performance to achieve advancement and self-development. People will work hard on a task that is interesting and challenging to them. If interesting work and the other motivators are lacking, all of the money, good supervision, and job security in the world may not produce top performance.

Herzberg also calls these motivation factors *satisfiers* because only these truly provide satisfaction for the need to do more than survive and be a social human being.

McGregor's Theory X and Theory Y

The descriptions given by Douglas McGregor, discussed in an earlier chapter, of the ways managers view their employees have been influential in determining ways to motivate people in organizations. A manager who leans toward the Theory X view of employees is almost certain to stress money and the force of authority as motivating factors. A Theory Y manager can be expected to put more faith in motivators, such as responsibility and personal development, that Herzberg identified as satisfiers.

McClelland's Needs Analysis

The theory of human needs put forward by David McClelland has also been influential in motivation programs in organizations. Channels for satisfying each of the three needs—power, affiliation, and achievement—are available in the work world. Opportunities for satisfying these needs, combined with the extent to which each need predominates in an individual, may be important in explaining how much job satisfaction a person feels. The need for achievement apparently can be taught; motivational training has exploited this. The training emphasizes the rewards of prestige. It also stresses the effective analytic and decision-making techniques typically used by people with high achievement needs. Such programs have increased the apparent achievement needs of trainees in experimental settings.

Expectancy Theory

There clearly are times when people have needs but do not take any action to try to satisfy them. This situation can be seen at work when, for example, a salesperson desperately needs money but still does not put out the extra effort to earn higher commissions.

Instances like this are hard to explain within a strict needs theory of motivation. They have led many researchers to believe that motivation is considerably more complex than indicated by approaches like Maslow's hierarchy. A number of modern theories have begun to shed some light on this complexity. The motivation theory of Victor Vroom is an important example of recent efforts to explain the motivations of individuals.

According to Vroom and others working along similar lines, there are two basic necessities for a person to be motivated to behave in a certain way, for instance, to work hard. The person (1) must have a desire or preference for the outcome of the behavior and (2) must believe that his or her efforts are, in fact, likely to lead to the outcome.

The preference for outcomes of actions is not based on random likes and dislikes. Vroom says that first-level outcomes and second-level outcomes must be considered. The "first-level outcome" is the immediate result of the behavior. Getting up earlier and not wasting any time in the morning will produce the first-level outcome of getting to work on time, for example. A person's desire for this first-level outcome must depend on something more, though. Getting to work on time is not usually satisfying in itself. For a first-level outcome to be motivating, it must be seen as leading further to a "second-level outcome" desired by the person. Getting to work on time may greatly increase the chance of getting a raise, which is something the person is really interested in. The relationship between first- and second-level outcomes is called *instrumentality;* one outcome is instrumental in producing the other.

Instrumentalities are learned through experience and observation. They can be taught. Higher productivity is likely to bring promotions, lower absenteeism will bring praise, or more aggressive selling efforts will bring higher commissions.

A person's perceptions of the instrumentalities between first- and second-level outcomes will produce certain preferences for and feelings about the first-level outcomes. The strength and direction of each of these preferences is called its *valence,* which may be positive, negative, or zero. Following the example of getting to work on time, a person who really wants a raise and who sees clearly that getting in early will be important to getting the raise will have a positive valence for the first-level outcome of arriving on time. If the person thinks there is no relationship between punctuality and the raise or other desired goals, the valence would be zero because punctuality is seen to be unrelated to important rewards. Valence can actually be negative if the first-level outcome is seen as leading to an unfavorable second-level outcome. This could happen, for instance, if the person's work group had a group norm of defying work rules; in that case the person might want to arrive late to avoid ridicule and expulsion from the informal society of the work group. The roles of instrumentality and valence in human motivation are shown in Table 13-1.

Even when desired second-level outcomes are seen as resulting from certain first-level outcomes, a person may not be motivated to try to produce the first-level outcomes. The reason is that he or she does not think personal efforts will be successful in achieving the outcome. For example, a salesperson who needs money but still does not try harder to sell may understand perfectly well that more sales will produce more income. But he or she may not fully believe that working harder to sell will really produce more sales.

	THE VALENCES OF FIRST-LEVEL OUTCOMES		THEIR INSTRUMEN-TALITIES IN PRODUCING SECOND-LEVEL OUTCOMES		THE DESIRABILITY OF SECOND-LEVEL OUTCOMES
The Motiva-tion to Work Faster and Achieve Higher Produc-tivity Equals the Sum of:	1. Exceeding production quota: Valence $= +1$	Which Depend on	1. High	and	1. Praise from supervisor: desirable.
	2. Exceeding production quota: Valence $= +0.5$		2. Moderate		2. Increase in pay: desirable
	3. Exceeding production quota: Valence $= -1$		3. High		3. Pressure from work group to work slower: undesirable.
	4. Having less time to talk: Valence $= -1$		4. High		4. Loss of social satisfaction: undesirable.

TABLE 13-1. AN EXAMPLE OF THE EXPECTANCY THEORY OF MOTIVATION.

In this case, expectancy is assumed to be high: The worker knows that by working faster, he or she can easily exceed the production quota but that there will be less time for socializing. This worker would not be motivated to work faster because the sum of the valences shown is nega-tive. Increasing the instrumentality between meeting the quota and receiving higher pay—by instituting a formal bonus system, for example—would not in itself be likely to provide motiva-tion; combining that change with some other second-level reward, like the chance to use spare time for socializing as long as the quota is met, might be sufficient.

The perceived likelihood that one's efforts will actually produce a certain first-level outcome is called its *expectancy*. A relatively high expectancy is needed for motivated behavior to result. If we are convinced that our best efforts will not produce the desired outcome, we will not even try very hard. The *belief* that efforts will succeed is the key, whatever the likelihood of success in reality. It is easy to find examples of people who have labored away mightily on some pet project for years when their real chances of success were slight.

In summary, Vroom's theory holds that for a person to be motivated, he or she must believe that personal efforts will produce a first-level outcome that is instrumental in achieving a second-level outcome that is truly desired.

Although theories such as Vroom's are well advanced and give managers insight into the behavior of employees, it is accurate to say that the exact dynamics of employee motivation have not yet been worked out in detail. One conclusion is certain, no matter what model of motivated behavior is accepted. Different employees will be motivated by different things and each employee will find different rewards more strongly motivating at dif-ferent times. The practical conclusion is that effective managers need sensitivity and good communications to keep in touch with individual employees. Many people are quite clear about what motivates them and are more than happy to reveal the information to their managers. The managers should listen, evaluate, and act.

Patton's Motivators of Executives

Theory aside, commonsense observation has yielded some understanding of what people are really looking for in work. Arch Patton, an expert in executive motivation, has identified some of the rewards and goals that seem most motivating to higher-level managers.

1. The challenge and rewards of doing the work itself.
2. The respect and self-esteem that come from elevated status.
3. The opportunity to exercise leadership.
4. The satisfaction of succeeding in competition.
5. The fear of failure.
6. Money and other forms of compensation.

Similarly, the wise manager complements knowledge of theory with commonsense observations to understand the factors that motivate people at all levels of the organization.

MANAGERS CAN MOTIVATE OTHERS TO PERFORM BETTER

Much of the emphasis in studying motivation has been on discovering principles of what motivates people to behave as they do. A manager approaches the question from a different angle: "What can *I* do to motivate people to work to meet both the organization's and their own goals?" In the early days of the modern industrial organization, even in non-manufacturing concerns, managers stressed physical facilities—plants, machines, and office buildings. Organizations and their managers have come through the years to realize that the heart of a company or agency is the people who work there.

Financial measures of corporate success, such as the balance sheet, place value on physical resources like inventory and equipment. They show little of the value of the people in an organization. Rensis Likert, in his book *The Human Organization*, challenged this view as being unrealistic in the modern world. As a remedy to the undue emphasis placed on physical facilities, he proposed the addition of a technique now called *human resources accounting*. This is a method of placing financial values on the human resources of an organization to reflect their contribution to the value and success of the enterprise. Intelligence and training, leadership skills developed through years of experience, decision-making ability, the capacity to achieve teamwork, and other contributions of human skills receive their due emphasis in this approach. Human resources accounting clarifies the role of motivation: Costly resources are being wasted unless managers find ways to motivate people to give their best efforts.

Specific Efforts to Motivate

Earliest efforts to motivate people to be more productive centered on money. The '"piece rates" and financial incentives of the scientific managers are examples. Money is still important but today a range of motivation techniques are believed to be needed.

AUTHORITY   The use of formal authority is still a motivating factor. Simple respect for a manager may lead an employee to try to perform well in response to his or her instructions. Authority also includes a threat that may be quite motivating. Fear of being fired because of inadequate performance is a spur to hard work if the job is essential to the employee's well-being.

FINANCIAL REWARDS   Money still provides an important reason for working, and the possibility of getting a pay raise sometimes will make people work harder. Piece-rate pay schemes (wages directly related to individual output) have largely been found ineffective as motivators. The social system of the work room tends to restrict output in spite of the financial incentives. Pay increases may serve as incentives partially because of the status that is associated with higher pay and partially because they are an overt expression of praise for work quality.

PRAISE   Praise for work well done has been found to be motivating in a wide range of situations. Praise is rewarding. We all like to hear that we have done a good job. In some experiments, a consistent pattern of praising a particular kind of desired behavior, or even an approximation of the behavior being sought, has been effective in shaping performance in the desired direction.

PARTICIPATION   Recognition as an important part of the operation and direction of an organization seems to increase the energy levels of employees. It makes them more active in improving their own performance and that of others. Participation in planning, decision making, and shaping the environment in which work takes place thus serves as a motivator. Many of the approaches of modern management, such as management by objectives and the development of two-way communications systems, serve to increase participation.

JOB ENRICHMENT   Nearly every view of human motivation agrees that the challenge and achievement associated with the work itself can be an important motivator. Unfortunately, many jobs are not by their nature challenging, nor do they offer much feeling of achievement. Placing washers and nuts on bolts all day is not an interesting and absorbing activity. Sometimes it is possible to modify or enrich jobs by building in more capacity for decision making or varying the pace of the work, for instance, to increase the interest of boring, repetitive jobs. The effort is more likely to be successful if the employees themselves contribute to the changes that are introduced.

Designing the Program

Motivation of employees deserves management effort. People in organizations usually give a minimum level of effort even with no motivation specifically provided. This minimum level, however, is costly for the organization because more people will be needed to do a given amount of work. It is also often unsatisfying to the employees because they will miss the rewards of real involvement with the organization and of personal accomplishment. Planned organizational efforts to provide motivation might be broken down into four categories or steps:

1. *Making sure that hygiene factors are adequate.* Although motivation may be more complex than predicted by Herzberg's model, there can be little doubt that the hygiene elements he identified really can cause dissatisfaction and impaired performance. Managers must continually check the fairness of salaries and wages, the quality and justice of supervision, and the clarity and reasonableness of administration and policies, and must avoid interfering too much with the informal social rewards of employees. Programs for supervisory training and improvement of personnel policies help insure adequate hygiene.

2. *Creating a climate for motivation.* In general, people are more motivated when they feel their contributions are essential to the success of the organization. Encouragement of and reward for participation in the function and growth of the organization fosters high motivation. The observations of Rensis Likert are again revealing. He identified four styles of management which he labeled as four systems, numbered 1 through 4. *System 1* he described as "exploitive-authoritative" because its managers were highly autocratic, had little trust in their subordinates, and allowed little participation in decision making. *System 2* he called "benevolent-authoritative" because even though the managers are interested in the well-being of employees, they still do not allow them an important role in shaping the operations of the organization. *System 3* was called "consultative" because it allows considerable communication of the interests and desires of employees and welcomes their advice and suggestions. Final decision making still rests with managers and trust in subordinates is not complete. *System 4* is based on managers' complete trust in subordinates and is called "participative-group" because employees play a major, direct role in making the decisions needed to operate and to select future directions. Systems 3 and 4 encourage initiative on the part of employees, and when the systems are put into practice they are likely to have a motivating effect on employees.

Managers in Action

"I was sent to manage a milk plant in Orland, California. It had the highest operating costs of any in the Pet milk company. The man I succeeded said: 'I don't think much can be done with this bunch of guys. They're pretty independent.' And they were. Each worker had a little farm, an orange grove, or a few acres of almond trees. They weren't totally dependent on the plant for their livelihood. But we sent costs down for 16 straight quarters, even though the unions were getting the men regular increases."

"There are a lot of ways to motivate people to cut costs in a plant like that. You motivate people to be cost conscious. You get them to use a lift fork properly instead of jabbing it through a case of expensive cartons. You get more production on the line and more cars loaded with the same number of people. You make sure that your equipment is running smoothly; your maintenance people have a lot to do with that."

"But basically, I think people feel good about their work who are more productive. If you feel useful and needed, and if you believe that what you do is important, you'll be more productive. It is management's job to create that kind of atmosphere."

This is Boyd F. Schenk, president and chief executive officer of Pet, Inc., speaking about the experiences that make him one of America's leading executives.

Source: "The Route to Personal Success in Busines," *Nation's Business*, November 1977, pp. 59–64.

3. *Communicating freely with employees.* Motivation techniques that succeed depend upon an intimate awareness of each employee's needs hierarchy. This knowledge comes from a sensitivity to their behavior which is heightened by regular give-and-take exchanges between manager and worker. By talking and listening freely and alertly, sensitive managers can gain an insight into the individual's aspirations and self-judgment about his or her skills and capabilities. This kind of awareness allows the manager to shape motivational efforts along expectancy lines. Thus, managers can predict what outcomes would be preferred by an employee—based on his or her unsatisfied needs—and to estimate their expectancy: the employee's own judgment of how likely individual efforts are to satisfy personal desires.

4. *Based on awareness of employees' needs, using specific motivators.* If properly used, training can be an important motivator. If an employ-

ee's expectancies are low because of the lack of skills, training in these skills will raise the expectancies. Clearly communicating the consequences of both desired and undesired behavior helps. Bonuses, praise, job enrichment, and the judicious use of formal authority also contribute positively to overall motivation improvement.

The key, as in most other aspects of human relations in organizations, lies in two seemingly simple elements: understanding the people involved and providing motivators specifically suited to them. Motivation should be approached as part of contingency management; the best approach to use will depend on the needs of specific employees in specific situations.

SUMMARY

1. Motivation is a psychological condition of humans that leads them to engage in goal-directed behavior to meet their needs. The needs of humans are quite complex and varied. They range from the simple need to eat fairly regularly up through the spiritual and aesthetic concerns that provide uniquely human self-fulfillment.

2. A number of theories have tried to explain human motivation in a systematic way. The theories point in common to the necessity of satisfying higher-level human needs in an organization rather than relying entirely on low-level rewards like money and working conditions. At least two of the theories indicate that motivation depends partly on learning and experience and possibly can be taught.

3. It is the responsibility of managers to use the resources of the organization to meet goals. Human resources deserve at least equal consideration with material resources. For this reason, it is part of the management job to motivate employees for top performance. Specific efforts to motivate others may use formal authority, financial benefits, praise, participation, and job enrichment. Motivation efforts should be integrated into an overall approach that insures hygiene, creates a climate for motivation, communicates to learn employees' aspirations and self-judgments, and applies training and other motivators based on specific knowledge of individuals in the organization.

REVIEW AND DISCUSSION QUESTIONS

1. How can you tell if someone is motivated or not? Why can motivation not be measured directly?

2. Joe always says about his employees, "All they want out of this job is the paycheck." Do you think this is likely to be true? Why or why not?

3. What would you do, as a manager, to make work satisfying for a subordinate who had a very high need for achievement?

4. Briefly describe the relation between Maslow's hierarchy of needs and Herzberg's two-factor theory.

5. A consultant calls the manager of a dry goods wholesaler "a real Theory X woman." What kind of motivators would she be expected to rely on?

6. Carl wants the status and respect that would come from being promoted to manager of the design department, but he rarely puts out much effort, in spite of his real talent. Use expectancy theory to give a possible explanation for this.

7. Compare authority and participation as motivators for better performance in an organization.

8. What four steps should the manager of an advertising agency follow to design a motivation program for the company?

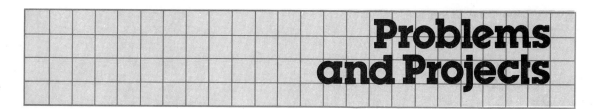

Problems and Projects

1. In each of the situations described below, a person is revealing, directly or indirectly, a need that is important to motivating him or her at that time. For each situation, describe the need that is operating. Use either your own words or the terms used in the theories presented in the text.

    a. Carlos is unwilling to take over the management of a new division in spite of the high salary and status offered because he is convinced there is only an extremely slight possibility of making the operation a success.

    b. Joan's husband has become seriously ill, creating high doctor's bills, and she has become obsessed with a fear of losing her job. She is working so hard that her boss fears for *her* health.

    c. Maynard is a little-known poet who has always managed to get by on very little income. His cabin burns and he has no place to live. In desperation, he takes the first salaried job of his life to pay for rent until he can build another cabin.

    d. Marty always works much harder in the blocking room than in his other assignments because he enjoys the contact with other people there and hopes to be assigned there more often.

    e. Clair works especially hard on gaining technical knowledge about her job because she thinks that is the most likely way to gain the respect of the people she works with.

    f. John spends so much of his time scheming about how to manipulate the other people in the division that his management work suffers in other areas.

g. Norman's work improved substantially when he was transferred to a job in which he had to learn many new technical and management skills.

h. Even though the conversation is sometimes distracting, Alice always gets more work done when she is assigned to a work crew with her friends.

i. Peter drove himself mercilessly for years to get to the top of his organization so he could shape its direction toward providing more of the social benefits that he thought could be his best contribution to the world.

j. Frank was looked up to by the other people in the office and did everything he could to continue to deserve their respect.

2. Listed below are a number of theories of motivation or systematic observations of management style that relate to ways of motivating employees. For each item in the list, provide one or two practical actions or decisions a manager might make to improve motivation in his or her organization, based on the understanding provided by the theory. Be sure to make the actions specific; that is, things a manager could really do.

a. Maslow's Hierarchy of Needs.

b. Herzberg's Two-Factor Theory.

c. McGregor's Theory X and Theory Y.

d. McClelland's Analysis of Needs.

e. Vroom's Expectancy Theory.

f. Likert's Systems of Management.

3. *Performance Situation—Potts' Old-Fashioned Department Store:* "It doesn't matter what you do around here. They might eventually fire you for doing a bad job, but you sure don't get anything out of doing a good job." So thought Karen Gold. But it was a thought shared by nearly everyone in the merchandising department. Potts' Department Store was an institution in the city. It had been founded in the nineteenth century when Nathanial Potts realized that he wasn't going to find a vein of silver after all, so instead he invested his remaining money in a supply of dry goods. The store was still profitable, but it had lost the lead in local retailing. Its management, to an outsider, appeared old and tired. The approach of the managers might be called System 2. Top managers were paternalistic and benevolent, but they really didn't think much of the skills of these newcomers who had only been with the store for ten or fifteen years.

Pay raises and promotions were based almost entirely on seniority. Even then, most people in the merchandising department thought that favoritism had been a big factor in picking the last assistant manager. He was the nephew of a close friend of the general manager. Karen Gold, who thought she was best qualified for the position, wasn't even considered, or if she was she never heard about it.

Even Karen wasn't sure she really was qualified, though. She had the buying contacts from her years of experience, but the store had no training or development programs. Thus, she was not sure that she had the technical skill in merchandise control and budgeting that the job called for. Neither did she feel completely comfortable in her current job. From her frequent conversations with others in the department, Karen had become convinced that they felt the same.

Analyze this situation using an approach suggested by expectancy theory. What first-level and second-level outcomes are mentioned in the description? What is the degree of instrumentality? What is the apparent expectancy of Karen and her co-workers? Based on expectancy theory, what would you predict to be the level of motivation for high performance in the merchandising department?

4. Your analysis of the situation in Problem 3 probably led you to conclude that things were not as they should be. Design a program to improve the motivation in the merchandising department. Continue to use interpretations based on expectancy theory. What would you have to provide to meet the requirements for high motivation? What concrete actions would be likely to provide the essentials?

5. Doing what is needed to keep motivation high in an organization requires frequent, repeated attention. It is not something that is done once and then forgotten. One way to insure the repeated attention is to use a checklist to refer to at regular intervals. Based upon everything you have learned about what motivates people to perform well on the job, from experience as well as what you have read in the text, create a checklist for your personal use. List at least ten actions that you should take to keep motivation high. Make them specific enough to judge with certainty whether you have done them or not.

6. Frederick Herzberg and his associates derived the two-factor theory of motivation at work by interviewing 200 engineers and accountants from a number of companies in the Pittsburgh area. Perform a greatly simplified version of this research in your own area. Do one of the following: (a) Identify at least 20 students who work part- or full-time, (b) Contact at least 20 employees—professional and non-professional—at your college, or (c) Get permission from a local industry or government agency or other formal organization to interview at least 20 employees at some time that is convenient both to the organization and to the employees.

Design a very simple interview format. Ask each subject to name three things that make him or her happy with work and then to name three others that make him or her unhappy with work. Ask the subjects to be specific in their answers. Perform a basic analysis of the results by tallying the number of times each factor is mentioned. Place the responses for factors that make people happy and factors that make people unhappy in order according to the number of times each was mentioned.

Discuss the results in class. Do your results agree with Herzberg's? Are the items on the "unhappy" list largely hygiene factors? Are the items on the "happy" list similar to the motivators he identified? How can you explain the differences that you find?

Cases for Analysis and Discussion

CASE 1: THE SQUARE PEG IN THE ROUND HOLE

"I must be getting old," Barry thought to himself. "I never used to sit at my desk dreaming about the good old days."

In fact, Barry wasn't getting old at all. But he was showing some disturbing signs that the old vigor was waning. He sat at his desk daydreaming, remembering the winning run for a touchdown in his last high school football game or his first job where he had gotten two promotions in sixteen months. Barry wasn't worried that he had failed in life, but he felt pretty sure that he wasn't really reaching his potential either. He just couldn't seem to get involved in his work the way he used to. He felt bored, even when the work piled up and he got behind. He felt frustrated, as if he were in a jacket that was just too tight to let him get that one deep breath that would let him plunge ahead.

Ironically, Barry's feeling that he wasn't getting ahead anymore began with a promotion. Barry had sold furniture for a major manufacturer in the South. He began as an order taker for some small stores. He had been so successful that in only a few years he had sole responsibility for most of the biggest accounts his company had. Barry set his own goals, and even though they were challenging, they were reasonable and he almost always achieved them. He was in such close contact with his clients that he always knew where he stood immediately. He felt almost as if he were his own boss—without the grave risks of being in business for himself.

Then he was promoted. Since major accounts were so important to his company, it had seemed reasonable to Barry's superiors to make him assistant marketing manager. Barry had been proud of the promotion, but when the time came, he wasn't proud of the job. Tied to a desk in the home office, he felt he no longer had responsibility for his own performance and success. He certainly didn't have any opportunity to set his own goals. Divorced from the reassuring yardsticks of success of direct customer contact and quarterly sales volume, Barry felt that he was operating in a vague, bureaucratic wasteland.

A. What has happened to Barry? Why does he feel he is achieving less even though he is now in a higher-level job?

B. What kind of needs does Barry have that are unsatisfied in his new position? What theory of motivation might be most obvious to explain this situation?

C. Is Barry doomed to frustration for the rest of his life? Could his company do anything that might improve his motivation and make him happier with his job?

CASE 2: IS IT MOTIVATION?

Emery Air Freight Corp. competes in a tough market in which to make a profit. It has to move large numbers of small packages for long distances in a hurry. To cut costs and handling time, Emery's managers decided to presort many small packages into large containers before shipment. This reduced the number of times each individual package had to be handled.

It was a good idea and everyone assumed it was working. Both managers and dock workers thought that containers were being used 90 percent of the time when possible. But then someone became suspicious and started to measure how much the containers really were being used. The results were far from 90 percent; they were closer to 45 percent. Education was not the answer. The managers were sure that everyone knew how and when they were supposed to use the containers.

What was the answer? Emery tried an experiment. They combined three main elements: Every dock worker kept a written record of when he or she used containers and thus got immediate feedback about results each day. Workers were shown how profits would increase if they used the containers. Supervisors and regional managers were told to be very free with praise for the proper use of containers.

The results? For eight out of ten offices, container use increased from 45 percent to 95 percent in a single day, saving Emery over $500,000 a year.

A. Was the problem here that the workers were not motivated to use the containers? If they were not, why not?

B. What general conclusions about the relation of goals to motivation could you draw from this case?

C. Relate this case to what you have learned about motivation theory.

CASE 3: YOU DON'T HAVE TO BE CRAZY TO WORK HERE— BUT IT HELPS

Byron McFarland was a tyrant. His wife thought he was a tyrant, everyone who worked for him thought he was a tyrant, and even his own mother thought he was a tyrant. McFarland published *This Week in Washington,* a small weekly newspaper that gave in-depth coverage of legislative and regulatory developments in the federal government. Tyrant or not, McFarland ran one of the most successful publications in America.

The wages he paid were terrible. One of his senior editors had been with the paper for 13 years and still hadn't reached a salary of $13,000 a year. McFarland himself was a disagreeable man—arrogant, condescending, and personally abusive. The office was a dump, stifling hot in summer and cold and drafty in the winter. The typewriters hadn't been cleaned or adjusted in years. The one tape recorder that McFarland provided the editorial staff of six literally gasped and wheezed.

Yet, the six reporters and writers for *This Week in Washington* were among the most productive and respected in the city. They worked long hours. They doggedly chased through the tangles of red tape to find the real events and what the events meant to their readers. Their enthusiasm was obvious to everyone. Not a single one of the men and women who wrote for the newspaper had failed to win at least one important award in the last three years.

A. It would appear from this case that salary, working conditions, and supervision have little effect on the performance of these employees. Do you think this would always be true?

B. How could you explain the high productivity of these people, given the unpleasant circumstances of their workday?

C. What could this case tell you about motivating people in your own management position?

CASE 4: THE PARTICIPATION BLUES

"What was wrong with the way things used to be? All of this new stuff is baloney. I just can't stand it!"

Marcia had been with Banker's Equity Financial for a long time. Her performance had always been adequate, although never spectacular. She was a satisfied lifer, casting her eye more and more on her pension. She had begun now, however, to start to wonder how she was going to stick it out for the nearly seven years she had left until retirement. Some recent changes had made Marcia acutely uncomfortable.

It all started when Marcia's old boss was replaced by Todd Graham, a youngish business school graduate filled with what seemed to Marcia to be radical new ideas. Marcia's old boss had been seen by everyone as a kindly old duffer who told everyone exactly what to do and saw to it that they did it. If everything was done exactly his way, he was generous to a fault with holidays, pay raises, and praise. Todd, though, was different. He redefined a lot of jobs and gave them more responsibility. He had regular group meetings to talk over the direction of the department with employees. He actually asked Marcia for guidance in many matters. On quite a few occasions, he simply told her that an important decision was her job—and she should go ahead and do what she thought was best.

But Marcia didn't like it. She was convinced that she didn't *know* what was best. She told her friends, "It's not part of my job to make all of those decisions. All it does is make me worry. What if something goes wrong and everyone finds out it was my fault? Why doesn't Mr. Graham take responsibility for the way things are done like he ought to?"

A. There has been a change here from one kind of management system described by Likert to another system. What was the old system? What is the new?

B. Encouraging participation was mentioned in the text as an important motivator. What does this case tell you about its use?

C. How could Graham have handled the transition better? What should he do now, if anything?

Leadership

14

After completing Chapter 14, you will be able to do the following:

- Describe instances of leadership behavior as examples of the factors and dimensions of leadership theory.
- Compare and contrast a number of different models of leadership behavior.
- Apply Fiedler's contingency view to predict the success of particular instances of leadership behavior in given situations.

- Assess the contribution of different models of leadership to accomplishing the functions of an organization.
- Identify the factors in a given management situation that influence the choice of a leadership style and judge the direction of their influence.

A group of naturalists wandering lost in the threatening jungles of the Amazon Basin would have genuine and pressing reasons to fear for their lives. Not knowing where they were, they could easily starve to death before reaching a source of familiar food. Being relatively unfamiliar with the territory, they would be easy prey for potentially dangerous insects and animals. If they were to come upon a child who was thoroughly familiar with the area and its perils, the naturalists, college professors and community leaders in their own familiar environment, would willingly follow and adhere to the child's every instruction.

This situation, although different in many ways from the kind of leadership seen in formal organizations, is similar in one important way: people will willingly follow someone who they believe will be able to help them achieve their own goals. The wandering naturalists are highly motivated to find their way back to civilization; the attractiveness of a leader depends on the naturalists' perception of that person's ability to help them find the way.

Leadership will thus depend to an important extent on the ability to understand motivation and to provide motivators. Leadership will also require skill at helping people to harmonize their personal goals with the goals of the organization. It is the goals of the organization that a manager will wish to lead toward, but it is personal goals that will be most motivating to the people he or she is leading.

Leadership is the ability to influence people to work toward achieving group goals. This is a much broader and more important skill than it may appear at first glance. The other managerial functions and skills, such as planning, controlling, motivating, and communicating, accomplish much in keeping the organization moving. By and large, people in the organization do try to do their jobs and, if the jobs are properly designed and related, employees' work will contribute to overall goals.

Good leadership can considerably expand on the contributions employees make, by creating the conditions in which they feel truly dedicated to group goals and accept them as important elements of personal goals. Nearly every production manager, for example, will be faced with the organizational goal of keeping costs down. If the manager feels strongly that costs must be controlled also because it is personally important to make that contribution to the welfare of a group of people whom the manager respects and identifies with, the manager's efforts will be that much more intense and effective. A good leader can instill that feeling of mutual striving, of "one for all and all for one."

Further, the quality of performance of an individual can vary greatly in different situations, even if the person is trying hard at all times. For example, a person selling electronic equipment to industrial customers may make an effort but still give a lackluster performance, forgetting important points, showing little energy, not being able to think of good answers to customers' objections. At another time, the same person may be filled with energy, flowing over with good ideas, capable of intense concentration on the problems at hand. A good leader can also increase the frequency of good performance, arousing people, spurring them to use their creativity, drawing out their energy and ability, relieving their personal obstacles to top performance.

Leadership can draw forth that extra bit of effort, that one good idea, that one persuasive argument that can make the difference between success and failure. Leadership is the ultimate expression of the manager's human skills in an organization. It is the end point toward which motivation, personal communication, and social interaction aim. Leadership is ultimately what makes the organization go.

DIFFERENT MANAGERS APPROACH LEADERSHIP DIFFERENTLY

As is true with motivation, leadership has been subjected to a great deal of theoretical analysis. Much of this analysis has centered on what managers themselves are like, on how they view the people they wish to lead, and on the styles of management and leadership they adopt.

Trait Descriptions of Leaders

The early formal views of leadership held that good leaders had certain necessary qualities that inspired others to follow them. Different authors named a great variety of personal traits that were supposed to be found in all successful leaders. Many of the traits were vague and poorly defined, such as "courage," "moral force," or "mental energy." Others, such as "intelligence," "maturity," or "social ability" could be defined measurably, but failed to contribute much to an understanding of the process of leading. Trait descriptions were not much help in guiding someone who wanted to become a leader.

The trait approach to leadership is rarely used today. More modern theories concentrate on the way leaders behave—on what they do—rather than on some set of "internal" characteristics they may share.

The Leadership Continuum

One approach to analyzing the behavior of leaders is to observe the extent to which they either demand complete obedience or encourage democratic participation in decisions. Managers are seen as falling somewhere between the two extremes. Authoritarian managers, on the left in Figure 14-1, make decisions and impose them on subordinates. Democratic managers, on the right in the figure, encourage freedom and responsibility in subordinates.

Authoritarian managers like to have everything under their personal control. They make the plans and decide how they will be carried out. They issue orders to others, giving specific procedures. They limit communication to the minimum needed to get the job done. At the other extreme, *democratic managers* encourage or require participation by employees in decision making. They delegate responsibilities more often and permit a considerable degree of freedom to employees. They encourage communication from others and tend to communicate more themselves.

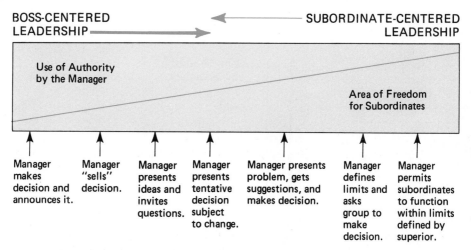

Figure 14-1. Continuum of Leadership Behavior.

Reprinted with permission from: Robert Tannenbaum and Warren H. Schmidt, "How to Choose a Leadership Pattern," *Harvard Business Review*, May-June 1973, p. 164.

Leadership Quadrants

The continuum, or range, from authoritarian to democratic is useful in describing the general view managers have of leadership, but to many it has seemed too narrow. Observing that a manager falls two-thirds of the way toward democratic along the continuum, for instance, says something about the manager, but not enough. One response to this weakness is the combination of two factors to describe management behavior. This expansion of the continuum concept significantly deepens the descriptive powers of the model.

Researchers at Ohio State University proposed such a two-factor approach. They said that leaders could be described by their position on two dimensions: (1) initiating structure and (2) consideration. "Initiating structure" refers to such managerial activities as creating formal relationships and clearly defining procedures and communications channels; it also means the creation of a rigid, formal structure. "Consideration" is a measure of warmth, friendliness, and mutual respect and trust in human relations.

Managers vary on either of these two dimensions, as shown in Figure 14-2. Thus, it is possible for one manager to have a very tight structure with rigid procedures and numerous formal controls, but still show a great deal of warmth and consideration in personal contacts. Another manager might delegate much responsibility and have little formal structure, but still not have the kind of communications and personal contact that might be expected in a highly participative and democratic environment.

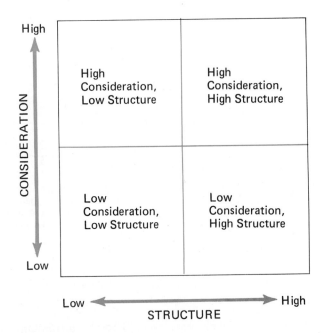

Figure 14-2. Ohio State Leadership Quadrants.

The Managerial Grid®   Robert R. Blake and Jane S. Mouton also used two factors to describe leadership behavior, but identified the important factors as (1) concern for production and (2) concern for people. The two factors might almost be seen as expressions of the early scientific management school and the human relations school of management. "Concern for production" expresses a strong orientation toward getting the work done efficiently; human elements are judged by whether they contribute to this. "Concern for people" stresses the encouragement and enjoyment of warm human relationships and the development of individual potential. On the grid, these two variables are shown in nine different degrees, as in Figure 14-3.

Although a particular manager may fall anywhere on the grid, five positions in particular may be taken as benchmarks to represent typical managers. Someone who is low in both concern for people and concern for

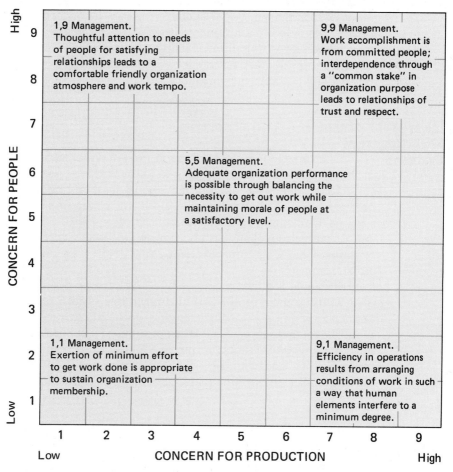

Figure 14-3. Managerial Grid.
Reprinted with permission from: Robert R. Blake and Jane S. Mouton, *The New Managerial Grid*, Gulf Publishing Company, Houston, Texas, 1978, p. 11.

production—someone who scores 1 on both scales—is not very involved with the organization at all. If things function well, they do so with little help from this kind of "cream puff" manager. A 1,9 manager—one who scores 1 on the first variable, concern for production, and 9 on concern for people—mainly concentrates on human and social contacts and has little orientation toward the work to be done—a "country club" manager. A 9,1 manager is the opposite: very concerned with the tasks of the organization and little bothered about the social system or social contacts of the job—literally a "task master." A 5,5 manager is in the "middle of the road," equally concerned with both people and production but not wholly involved in the job or the goals of the organization. A 9,9 manager has maximum concern for both people and production—truly a "professional."

The Managerial Grid is useful for describing the behavior of specific managers and is useful as a guide for managers who wish to change their behavior to make it more productive. The developers of the grid believe that the 9,9 style of leadership behavior is the most effective. They have worked out a procedure to help managers (1) to analyze their own leadership styles and the goals and needs of their organizations and (2) to work toward matching leadership to the organization.

Likert's Analysis of Management Systems

Rensis Likert's four systems of management were described in Chapter 13 as they related to creating a climate for motivation. As might be expected, considering the close relation between motivation and leadership, Likert's analysis has also been influential in the understanding of leaders. The four systems are closely related to the authoritarian-democratic continuum. System 1, with its exploitive-authoritarian approach corresponds to the left extreme of the continuum. Systems 2 and 3 fall in the middle sections of the continuum.

Likert has found that a single style—System 4—does seem to be associated with the most productive and profitable organizations. The System 4 point of view emphasizes the following: great trust in subordinates; the use of higher-level motivators such as opportunities for self-development; free and full communication; friendly human contacts based on mutual understanding and trust; and wide participation by everyone concerned in decision making and in setting the course the organization will follow.

MANAGERS MATCH LEADERSHIP STYLES TO THE SITUATION

According to Henry Ford, the auto maker, "The question, 'Who ought to be boss?' is like asking 'Who ought to be tenor in the quartet?' Obviously, the man who can sing tenor." Ford is expressing his belief that there is one person right for the job of leadership and that that person would be a leader no matter what the circumstances; this is a trait view of leadership.

Experience has shown, though, that there is not a single set of characteristics that are best for leaders in all situations. This realization has led to a focus on the question, What is it about the people in a given group that controls the kind of leadership behavior that will work best with that group? Early thinking on these lines stressed the power of the situation to create leaders. Later work has focused on ways to match leadership styles to the requirements of different situations.

The Situational Approach to Leadership

It has been observed many times that in a crisis—a flood or epidemic disease, for instance—"natural" leaders emerge to show people how to deal with the threat. Often these unrecognized leaders are ones who would have been thought least likely to succeed in leading others. These observations led to early thinking about the influence of the situation on shaping the behavior of leaders. The conclusion of the early situational view was that certain kinds of events or conditions, particularly a chaotic state of affairs or a physical or economic crisis, could force men or women to become leaders even though they would not normally have done so.

To extend this conclusion, researchers started looking at the specific characteristics of the situation that produced leaders. They found, in fact, that leaders are everywhere. The styles of some are more suited to particular situations than other styles; the person with a style appropriate to a given situation emerges as the leader in that instance. The characteristics of the situation that determines the most suitable leadership style have been identified as: (1) the personal and social characteristics of the people in the group, (2) the kind of activity the group needed to accomplish, and (3) the physical, social, and economic forces that surround the group. These factors, when more clearly defined, appear to determine the best leadership style for a given situation.

Fiedler's Contingency View

It is obvious that the harsh, sometimes savage, approach of an army squad leader pulling soldiers into battle would not be appropriate for leading a group discussion of peonies at the garden club. Many other cases are not so obvious, however, and a good deal of attention has been paid to the question of which style works best in which situation.

Fred E. Fiedler has been a leader in this research. He has developed a widely accepted contingency view, or model, of the effectiveness of leadership. In general, the view states that the style of leadership used should be contingent on the characteristics of the specific situation.

Fiedler identified three ways in which a leadership situation can vary:

1. *Position Power of the Leader*—the formal authority given to the leadership position by the overall organization.
2. *Task Structure*—the clarity with which people's specific jobs are defined and controlled rather than being free-form and variable.
3. *Leader-Member Personal Relations*—the extent of warmth and mutual intimacy and trust that exists between group members and the leader.

Thus a situation can have strong or weak position power, can be structured or unstructured, and can have good or poor relations between the leader and group members.

Fiedler also described two kinds of leaders who might try to function in any of these situations. The first is a *task-oriented leader* who concentrates on getting the work done, even at the risk of damaging human relations. This manager is also described as a "directive" leader, and corresponds to the 9,1 manager of Blake and Mouton's Grid. The second is a *relationship-oriented leader* who stresses human contact and mutual consideration. These leaders are described as typically permissive; they correspond fairly well with 1,9 managers.

How do all of these variables interact? Considering the number of variations possible, Fiedler found surprisingly clear relationships. Task-oriented leaders performed best in extreme situations, ones that are very good or very poor. For situations with good relations, structured work, and strong position power or with poor relations, unstructured work, and weak position power, call on a task-oriented leader. In mixed situations, ones that are neither markedly good or bad, a relationship-oriented leader performs best. The mixed situation is probably the one most commonly found in organizations, although extremes certainly do arise.

The real lesson of Fiedler's view is that managers should learn to adapt their behavior to fit the situation in which they are functioning. Fiedler distinguishes between behavior and style. A manager's style reflects the needs he or she is trying to satisfy. It may be difficult to change style, but behavior can be adapted as needed if managers analyze the situation they are in.

Leadership Adjusted to the Life Cycle

The maturity of the employee being directed also influences the leadership style chosen. Just as a parent's relationship with a child varies through the life cycle, a manager's relation with an employee may vary according to the maturity of the employee. Toward an infant, parents are basically task-oriented; they feed, clothe, clean, and generally concentrate on getting things done for the child. With an older, more mature child, a warmer, more trusting relationship develops, but much of the need for getting tasks done continues. This corresponds to a high task and high relationship orientation of the professional manager. A still older child will have learned to do most of the tasks without help, but will maintain very close emotional ties with his or her parents. This is largely a relationship orientation for the parents. As the child matures and begins to make his or her way in the world, the task and relationship orientations of the parents will decrease, leaving the child a free, independent person.

The same kinds of relationships exist between a manager and an employee. The maturity of employees, their ability and desire to accept responsibility and to motivate themselves, varies considerably. A directive, task-oriented approach is needed to guide the work of an immature person. Somewhat greater maturity will allow the development of closer human ties, but will not free the manager from considerable responsibility to see that work is still done. An even more mature employee will be likely to respond well to a supportive, warm relationship, with relatively little attention paid to specific tasks. A quite mature subordinate will function well with minimum leadership; both task and relationship orientations on the part of the manager are likely to diminish.

This life-cycle approach reexpresses the main thrust of modern investigations of leadership; the best way to lead depends on the people involved and on the varying characteristics of the situation in which leadership is exercised.

MANAGERS INTEGRATE LEADERSHIP WITH OTHER FUNCTIONS

Clearly, leadership has been given a variety of interpretations. The fundamental question that these descriptions and theoretical approaches try to answer is, What is a good leader? How can this question be answered in light of the leadership studies?

Any management position requires someone who can influence and induce others to give their best efforts on the job to meet organization goals. The analyses of leadership performance and style each have something to say about what kind of behavior will best accomplish this purpose.

The leadership continuum of Figure 14-1 sounds the keynote for leadership analyses. Its insight that the behavior of leaders may vary anywhere from the extremely autocratic to the extremely democratic underlies other studies. The extreme positions in the Ohio State quadrants, for example, correspond fairly well in actual behavior with the end points of the leadership continuum. Take the manager who is strongly concerned with structure and order and relatively little concerned with warmth and consideration for others. That manager tends to act pretty much like an autocratic leader. The same could be said of a manager described in other corresponding terms— a 9,1 manager, a System 1 manager, or a strongly task-oriented manager.

The different views of leadership contribute to a general understanding of what is involved in leading and of what makes a good leader. All the leadership studies agree that the behavior can vary in a number of ways. Specific definitions of the dimensions involved differ, but a synthesis might be possible. All the studies suggest the following:

1. Leaders differ in the extent to which they try to control other people and specify and define the structure in which work takes place.
2. Leaders differ in the extent to which they are willing to sacrifice warm human relations in order to get tasks done as efficiently as possible.
3. Leaders differ in the extent to which they are involved with their organizations; some are quite aggressively active and have many contacts with other people, while others use more of a "hands-off" approach.

None of these particular approaches to leading is necessarily good or bad. If there is any agreement on exactly what constitutes a good leader, it is on the fact that "It depends." Rather than learning to emulate General Patton or the Buddha, modern leaders are told that they must be flexible and adapt their behavior to the requirements of the particular people they are dealing with and the particular environment of their organization.

Fitting Leadership to the Situation

Successful managers are able to integrate leadership behavior with the requirements of their organizations. This requires adapting their behavior to specific needs. How can they know, though, what adaptations are needed?

Robert Tannenbaum and Warren H. Schmidt have considered this question in the context of modern leadership theory.[1] They found that three factors operate to determine the most effective kind of leadership behavior:

- Forces in the manager
- Forces in the subordinates
- Forces in the situation

To be able to fit leadership behavior to a particular case, a manager must be aware of each of these influences.

FORCES IN THE MANAGER   It is easy to identify the leader with his or her position; people sometimes see the President of the United States as a decision-making executive, forgetting sometimes that the real person in the office has needs, feelings, prejudices, and personal weaknesses. No leader can for long succeed at ignoring his or her own attitudes and needs. The personal values and inclinations of the leader strongly influence leadership style. Someone who feels very strongly that it is an ethical requirement for the individual manager to shoulder the burden of responsibility and decision making will have difficulty in establishing a group-oriented relationship. Furthermore, many managers feel little confidence in employees. The feeling may be justified by the employees' lack of skill or it may be a figment

[1]Robert Tannenbaum and Warren H. Schmidt, "How to Choose a Leadership Pattern," *Harvard Business Review* (May-June 1973), pp. 162–164, 168, 170, 173, 175, 178–180.

Managers in Action

Most manager-leaders today are gamesmen, people who flow with the organization, adapting their style to the ever-changing needs of the groups in which they serve or lead. That is the view of social analyst Christopher Lasch and psychoanalyst-author Michael Maccoby. Lasch contends that this is bad for society since the modern system rewards the self-seeking, egotistical manager. Maccoby disagrees. He believes that the system fosters careerism, which is good for all. To be self-seeking is natural in the self-sufficient person, Maccoby observes. It helps to identify gifted leaders in all kinds of organizations, and that is what is badly needed today.

Such a "narcissistic" manager may lack, or have not developed, human understanding, generosity, compassion, and courage. These are traits that have long been admired in our leaders; but the trait approach to identifying good leaders hasn't worked in practice. It is far better, reasons Maccoby, to select leaders for business and government "who are intellectually qualified to cope with their work, who have a sense of fairness, and a willingness to experiment." This type of manager will test new ways of leading others and is more likely to learn from mistakes.

It is true that the manager whose approach to leadership is intellectual and flexible may be more inclined to manipulate others, Maccoby agrees. But, at its root, perhaps that is what the modern organization—with its ever-changing complexity and makeup—needs in the way of leadership.

Source: Michael Maccoby, "Corporate Character Types: The Gamesman Vs. Narcissus," *Psychology Today*, October 1978, p. 60. Reprinted with permission from *Psychology Today,*Copyright © 1978, Ziff-Davis Publishing Company

of the manager's prejudice or imagination. Nevertheless, lack of confidence makes democratic management difficult if not impossible. The manager's desire for security will also influence the choice of style. Someone who is extremely upset by vague and unpredictable situations will have a difficult time with highly democratic, group-oriented management systems. In such situations, outcomes are less predictable and are to some extent beyond the control of the manager.

FORCES IN THE SUBORDINATE   The characteristics of the people who follow leaders influence the style and nature of leadership. Different employees expect different things from a manager; these expectations must be taken into account. Specifically, a leader must be aware of the extent to which the employee exhibits the following characteristics:

1. Has a high need for independence.
2. Is ready to assume responsibility for decision making.
3. Is able to tolerate an ambiguous situation.
4. Gets satisfaction from dealing with a particular problem, and considers it interesting.
5. Understands and accepts the goals of the organization.
6. Has the necessary knowledge and experience.
7. Expects to share in decision making.

Employees who have a positive orientation to these factors will react favorably to participative leadership. Those who do not desire to share in decision making, who like to have things spelled out in clear detail, and who are made tense and nervous by undefined, ambiguous situations will not make much of a contribution to a participative decision-making atmosphere.

FORCES IN THE SITUATION   Influences outside the manager and the employees must also be considered. The type of organization affects the type of leadership that will be expected. Compare the Los Angeles Police Department with a farming commune in Tennessee. Each organization has different needs for discipline and control; leadership must provide the right kind of discipline and control if the organization is to succeed. The strength and effectiveness of the work group affects leadership. A group approach to decision making will not work if the group is not able to work together.

The nature of the specific problem being dealt with will partly determine the best leadership approach. It would not be a good idea, for example, to call a committee meeting to decide to open a relief valve when the boiler is about to explode. In many other instances there is only one person who has the range of experience and knowledge needed to deal with a problem. It is often more convenient for that person to handle it alone than take the time to educate others on all of the details. Intense time pressures may also argue for a more directive approach.

Organization Development

Of the many factors that influence the choice of a leadership approach, some can be changed over a period of time. A manager may conclude that in the long run a more participative style would be good for the organization. The fact may be, however, that the organization or the employees are simply unprepared for it at the time. In a case like this, *organizational development* (OD) may be undertaken. This is a broad-based process. It involves a range of individual and group training and development activities aimed at reshaping an entire organization. When successfully carried out, OD can make the organization more creative, more active, and more responsive to the needs of the organization and the people in it.

Many of the changes brought about may lead to an atmosphere better suited to a System 4 management style. The effectiveness of groups may be increased, for instance. Individuals may be given training to bring their technical skills up to that required by their job assignments. Managers and employees may be trained in more effective ways of dealing with ambiguous and changing situations. Such a program takes a long time, however. The underlying point is that managers cannot assume that an organization is ready for a democratic leadership style simply because they wish it to be. Leadership must meet the needs of the organization as it exists now, as well as the needs it may have in the near future.

SUMMARY

1. The leadership behavior of a manager at a given time can be described in a number of ways. It can be located on a continuum from authoritarian to democratic. It can be placed in quadrants describing different levels of structure and human consideration. It can be located in a grid showing different strengths of concern for production and concern for people. It can be described as an example of one of Likert's four systems of management.
2. The modern view of leadership holds that there is no single style that is most effective in every situation. Fiedler found that leaders who were very task oriented performed best in situations that were extremely favorable or unfavorable. Leaders oriented toward human relationships succeed best in the in-between situations. Another view holds that leadership style should be adapted to the level of maturity of the people being led.
3. Managers look for common features in the studies of leadership and try to integrate these features with the everyday responsibilities of management. In choosing a leadership pattern suited to a given problem or condition, the manager must understand and allow for three factors: forces in the manager, forces in the subordinate, and forces in the situation.

REVIEW AND DISCUSSION QUESTIONS

1. The managers of a woolen mill need to decide how to replace their aging facilities. Contrast the way a very authoritarian manager would handle the problem with the approach that would be taken by a very democratic manager.
2. Describe the ways the Ohio State leadership quadrants and the Managerial Grid are similar and the ways they are different.
3. The Managerial Grid shows a 1,1 manager to be relatively detached from the organization. According to the life-cycle theory, is there ever a situation when this might be a successful management style?
4. Paul runs a large print shop and is accurately described as a benevolent autocrat, a System 2 manager. Where might Paul's style appear on the Managerial Grid? If the work is loose and unstructured, if Paul's position is only vaguely regarded as the top spot, and if Paul has relatively poor relationships with his employees, is he likely to be an effective leader or not?
5. What kinds of situations seem to allow success for a task-oriented leader,

according to the contingency view? Can you give an example from your own experience of a case that called for a very task-oriented leader?

6. In what way are Likert's management systems comparable to the concept of a leadership continuum?

7. Martha uses fairly distinct approaches to leadership according to the maturity levels of her employees. Based on the life-cycle theory, which approach is best suited to the least mature? Which to the most mature?

8. Using *all* of the descriptions of leadership behavior, name three ways in which leadership behavior can vary.

9. What are some of the forces in the manager that will influence the choice of a leadership style? Can these forces be changed?

Problems and Projects

1. Most of the models of leadership behavior discussed in the text correspond fairly well with each other, even though specific terms and definitions may differ. Draw a diagram showing how the following models relate to each other: the leadership continuum, the Ohio State quadrants, the Managerial Grid, Likert's four systems, and Fiedler's types of leaders. Place the continuum at the top of the diagram and arrange the descriptors used by the other models in their proper correspondence beneath it. The two-factor models present the two variables as being independent, but do not try to show this in your diagram.

2. Look at Figure 14-1 again. It gives examples of management behavior at seven points along the leadership continuum. Number these points from left to right from 1 through 7. Select the number that represents your first inclination of the way you would naturally tend to handle a management situation. If you would give employees complete freedom to solve a problem, choose a 7; if your inclination would be to make a decision and then sell the idea to employees pick a 2. In class, add up the numbers chosen by all class members and divide by the number of people in class. This average will give an indication of the class position on the continuum.

Discuss the results. Why did each class member choose the number he or she did? Was it simply a response dictated by personality, or were there other reasons? Are there important personal values supporting the choice? What does this say about the recent emphasis on varying leadership styles to suit individual situations? Would it be easy for the people in the class to vary their leadership styles? Could they change their values if they wanted to?

3. *Performance Situation—Leading the Leaders:* After years of experience and study in the field, John Stegler has become a successful consultant specializing in helping others improve their leadership effectiveness. The foundation of his popularity as a consultant has been his skill in inducing others to identify the important elements in operating situations and to adjust their leadership styles and behavior accordingly. Stegler currently has contracts in which he is advising the managers responsible for the five departments or organizations briefly described below in paragraphs *a* through *e*.

Take Stegler's role and act as a consultant in each of the five situations. First, analyze each of the cases and identify factors that might influence the kind of leadership that would be most effective in each. Then, for each case, describe the *kind of behavior* you think would be best for a leader. Give reasons and, when appropriate, mention a leadership model to back up your choice or advice.

- **a.** The pattern-making department consists of seven persons who are absolute experts in their work. Most patterns are completely handled by one man or woman; since most are quite complex, a single pattern may take weeks or even months to complete. Everyone in the department has been with the firm at least eight years.

- **b.** A television station on the West Coast has attracted a lot of misfits and neurotics to its staff, for reasons unknown to management. The general manager is further plagued by the station owner, who allows him little real authority. Many of the staff members are self-centered and cannot get along with each other. They certainly have no high regard for the general manager. Since the stations' selling point is its very extended coverage of local news, work loads and assignments continually change to suit the news events.

- **c.** The bookkeeping department of a paper box manufacturer has been a plodding little group for years. The employees have made it clear that they like things the way they are. They avoid responsibility, concentrate on their jobs, and stick together to frustrate any changes the manager tries to make.

- **d.** A work gang for the state forestry service is made up entirely of convicted juvenile lawbreakers sent there by the court for experience at working. The young men and women are resentful of authority; they are insecure; they have no work skills; their social skills are limited to the devious cleverness needed to survive on the street.

- **e.** Everyone in the tax assessor's office knows pretty well what jobs have to be done. Years of good administration have created a tight structure, with policies covering nearly every possible event and activity. The elected assessor has complete authority over the department. No one even asks how things are going. The only problem is that the people in the department simply do not like the new assessor. Relations started out bad and have gotten steadily worse.

4. Chris Argyris in *Personality and Organization* (New York: Harper & Row, 1957, pp. 50–51) described a continuum from immaturity to maturity. Figure 14-4 on page 340, based on his analysis, will serve as a basis for an exercise with the life-cycle approach to leadership.

First, identify the kind of leadership you prefer *in people who are leading you.* Would you rather follow someone who is highly task-oriented and puts little stress on human relations? Would you prefer someone who is separated and does not get involved deeply either in relationships or tasks?

Next, make a self-rating of your maturity as defined by Argyris, using the seven scales in Figure 14-4 shown below. Pick the number that you believe accurately describes yourself on each item. If, for instance, you have a very subordinate position, pick a 1 on that scale; if you have a moderate position, pick a 3; if you have a very superordinate position in which you have great influence over others, pick a 5. Guard against choosing all 3s; be as honest as possible. Add up your selections and divide by 7 for an average for all the scales.

Does your choice of style in a leader agree with the prediction of the life-cycle theory? If not, why not? Is the leader you prefer really the best leader for you, the one who would be able to influence you to perform best? Do you think your ratings on the scales accurately reflect your maturity? Is there anything an organization could do to increase the maturity of the employees?

5. Choose one of the following options to investigate the characteristics of a real person who is a successful leader.

   a. Recall someone from your own experience who you believe was effective as a leader. You may have encountered the person in school, at work, socially, or in other ways. Write a description of his or her behavior as a leader. Concentrate on what the person actually did to be a good leader. Briefly relate the behavior and the situation in which it occurred to the models discussed in the text.

   b. Select some historical person who was noted for leadership ability. Read a biography of the person and write the same kind of description called for in option a.

IMMATURITY	1	2	3	4	5	MATURITY
Passivity						Activity
Dependence						Independence
Capable of behaving in few ways						Capable of behaving in many ways
Shallow interests						Deep interests
Short-term perspective						Long-term perspective
Subordinate position						Superordinate position
Lack of self-awareness						Self-awareness and control

Figure 14-4.

6. Consider the following statements:

a. "Participative, democratic leadership is the best approach because it frees employees to be creative and active and to contribute their best."

b. "Managers must keep tight control and use an authoritarian approach because otherwise employees will simply not get anything done."

With which of these two statements do you agree, and why? Be prepared to defend your choice in writing or in a class debate.

Cases for Analysis and Discussion

CASE 1: THE RELUCTANT LEADER

Suddenly it dawned on Allen just how many important marketing decisions had still not been made. This dismayed him since the new easy-open, "child-proof" medicine bottle was to go on the market in six weeks—in theory at least! Even if everything were settled that day, there was no possible way advertising and distribution arrangements could be made in time.

Allen thought the problem was the fault of his boss, Jane Woltz, and didn't hesitate to tell her so. "The work's just not getting done," he told her. "The marketing department has been sitting on the problems with the new cap, and we're really in trouble now. I think you should have leaned on them before now. They're not going to do anything unless you see that it's done."

Jane Woltz was used to hearing talk like this. "Allen, an organization won't work if the managers can't do anything but 'lean on' people, as you put it. This is a democratic group; people know their jobs and can do them. I'm not going to run through the ranks like Ghengis Khan hitting people over the head. Others have got to take some responsibility for getting things to work right."

A. What leadership style has Jane Woltz adopted? Is it working?
B. Who do you think is right in this confrontation? On what do you base your answer?
C. What should Jane Woltz do? Is there any way she could improve her organization?

CASE 2: ONE BIG HAPPY FAMILY

Marty was a file clerk, and he really never expected to be anything other than a file clerk. He worked with 30 others in a large office with no partitions. His boss told him exactly what to do and how to do it. The boss had strict procedures and insisted on solving any difficult questions himself. It was a rare day when Marty or any of the other clerks had to make a decision of any greater difficulty than where to eat lunch.

Marty's boss spent a good deal of time with each of the clerks, clearing up problems, talking about their work and how they were doing, or just passing the time of day in casual conversation. If there was a problem with payroll, or if overtime didn't get credited right, or if someone had trouble collecting on health insurance, the boss always stood up for his clerks and knew how to get things ironed out. One or another of the clerks was often seen in the boss's office seeking his advice even on personal problems.

A. Could this be a real situation? Are there departments run this way?

B. What term from one of the leadership models describes the boss's behavior? Is he task oriented or relationship oriented?

C. Would the boss's approach to management work in the long run? Does it satisfy the needs of the employees?

CASE 3: THE STAB IN THE BACK

Cable Engineering was undoubtedly the leader in its field. Admittedly, the application of high-energy physics to industrial processes was in its infancy, but whoever had an application sooner or later ended up working with Cable.

Most of the people who worked for Cable were pretty "high-energy" themselves; there were far more aggressive, young Ph.D.s than there were typists. Two of the top scientists were Grace Hite and Dale Shell. Cable had a fairly free-form style of organization, and it was clear that the group of people near the top was far more important in making decisions than was any one individual. Grace and Dale were of roughly equal status; if there were a hierarchy, they would both be one step from the top.

Dale was talking to the field supervisor, who said, "You know we're going to run into real trouble with the power supply over at Tate Electronics. The one they delivered was the one that was specified, but I had it tested and it's not nearly going to do the job."

Dale said, "That's one of Grace's projects. Does she know about this?"

The supervisor replied, "I don't know. I didn't say anything; that's the account manager's job."

Later Dale was talking with Grace. He fished to find out whether she had heard anything about the power supply. It became clear that she hadn't. All Dale said was, "I don't guess you have any problems then, do you?" Grace looked at him sharply. "I don't know. Do I have any?" Dale answered, "No. None that I know of."

The next day Dale had his regular meeting with John Cable, the president. After going over some routine matters, Dale changed the subject: "By the way, I've hesitated to mention it, thinking that she would find a way to work it out, but everybody knows that Grace is in real trouble with the Tate Electronics installation. The power supply's a turkey. I didn't know whether you had heard about it."

A. What kind of management atmosphere seems to exist at Cable?
B. What does this case have to do with leadership? Has this situation been created by a failure of leadership?
C. What should John Cable do? Does he need to change his entire management approach to deal with this kind of problem?

CASE 4: LONELY AT THE TOP

Jerry Cole, if the truth were known, was a little scared. Jerry's company was small enough that the stockholders were real people to him, not shadowy figures in Peoria cackling and clipping bond coupons. He knew the people personally who were backing the company and he was afraid of losing their money.

Jerry had been convinced—largely from what the professors had told him in his masters program with a specialty in management—that a democratic style of managing made a productive company. So he had made an effort through the years to create that kind of atmosphere. He delegated without being too restrictive about how things were to be done. He always listened to what others had to say about a problem. He gave people free rein whenever he could.

But it wasn't easy. Jerry came from a straight-laced, authoritarian family, and he could not get rid of a nagging feeling that the only way to get people to work was to use an iron hand.

And there were real concerns, not just feelings. Some of the solutions to problems that his staff came up with looked awfully strange to Jerry, but he had to admit that they seemed to work. Still, they made him uncomfortable. At times, no one seemed to be sure who was supposed to do what, but they always worked it out. Jerry stayed a little tense, wondering whether this time the crisis might develop that would put them out of business.

A. How did Jerry decide to use a free-form, democratic leadership style? Was that the right way to decide?
B. Should Jerry continue with the leadership approach he is using? What things should he consider before deciding?
C. Why does Jerry feel afraid and tense? Is that all part of the management job?

Managers Function Within a Social, Physical, and Legal Environment

Social Concerns and Management Decisions

15

After completing Chapter 15, you will be able to do the following:

- Analyze the effect of different sources of social concern in management decision making.
- Evaluate the influence of formal organizations in causing, preventing, and repairing damage to the physical environment.
- Propose steps that a manager might use to promote fair employment opportunity in an organization.

- Describe and evaluate the common responses of businesses to consumerism.
- Identify the needs and rights a manager must balance in creating a socially responsible organization, and judge the extent to which they are balanced in a given situation.

Company A is run by a manager who has no interest in anything but making the most money for the company and for himself as quickly as possible. The company processes chemicals to make a potent cleaning material. There is a flaw in the process, and a very toxic chemical continually escapes into the air around the plant. The manager discovers this flaw, but decides to do nothing about it. He keeps it a secret because he judges, accurately, that to fix it would ruin the company's profits for years to come. The manager lives in a beautiful house overlooking the plant. His grass dies, his cat dies, his dog dies. Eventually, the manager himself dies, killed by the fumes of his own making.

Company B is run by a manager with an acute awareness of the needs of others. When he joined the company it was fairly successful, with moderate profits. Even though sales were only $5 million a year, the manager soon had spent $25 million on pollution-control devices and on expensive changes to improve the safety of the company's products. He engaged in and committed the company's resources to major community-improvement activities: building better housing for the poor, opening a free health-care clinic, contributing generously to charity after charity. In three years, the company was bankrupt. It was so heavily in debt that even some of its creditors were financially ruined.

The stories of these two companies are fictitious, but they represent extremes of real situations that must be faced by many managers. The activities of managers and the decisions they make largely concern the organization internally, working with the people of the organization to get useful work done. Many of the influences on and accomplishments of an organization are, however, external. A business, an agency, a college, a charity, or any other organization affects the society that surrounds it, favorably or adversely. Managers must be aware of these effects and try to control them. Furthermore, society at large affects an organization's operations and outcomes. Managers must also recognize and deal with these influences.

SOCIAL CONCERN ARISES
FROM DIFFERENT SOURCES

Social concern is the awareness of the impact of an individual or organization on the welfare of others, combined with an effort to make the effects favorable—or at least to avoid injurious effects. The manager of Company A at the beginning of this chapter showed such a lack of social concern that it damaged life. The manager of Company B showed such extreme concern that it damaged the organization.

Why would managers care about society at all? In a business, especially, the main reason for the organization's existence is to create products that can be sold to make a private profit. That is why the manager is hired to manage in the first place. Even in a government agency or other nonbusiness organization, there are usually some defined tasks or activities to be accomplished that have nothing directly to do with general social good.

Yet, the influence of an organization on society at large is a significant issue to its managers. It shapes many of the major decisions about how the organization will operate. There are a number of reasons for this concern. Many managers feel it is good business to show social consciousness. Society often forces organizations to assume responsibility. Finally, many managers behave responsibly because they believe it is right to do so and wrong not to (see Figure 15-1).

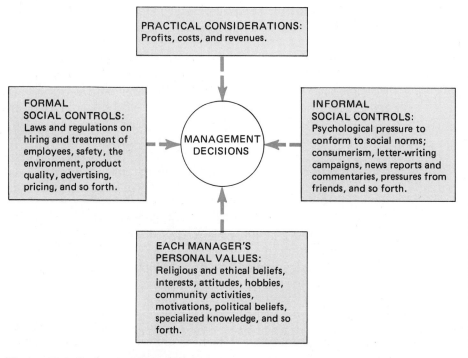

Figure 15-1. Sources of Social Concern.

The Practical Basis
of Responsibility

In the days of workhorses, some farmers and draymen treated their animals like royalty, even if they personally did not like horses. The idea was that a well-treated animal would be able and willing to work harder. Somewhat the same thinking lies behind certain management behavior that appears to be socially responsible. The reason some managers, for instance, provide good working conditions, safe equipment, decent wages, and considerate treatment may not be that they believe the employees deserve them. Rather, they treat their workers well because they believe that is the best way to get them to produce. If these managers thought they could get good work without this consideration, they might decide to withdraw it, thereby saving money and increasing profits. This is an example of managers showing social "concern" because it is good for business to do so.

The same motive may appear in many other areas. The design of safer products, for example, may be influenced by the consideration that unsafe or unusable products are harder to sell, and especially to resell, in the long run. A chain saw manufacturer might be able to shave $20 off the cost of a saw by substituting a cheaper chain clutch. The lower-cost clutch might be known to be subject to failure. The lower product price might give the manufacturer a temporary competitive edge. If the clutch were to fail and cause injuries, however, this would soon become known to buyers, and they would begin to avoid the saw as unsafe. Thus the long-range effect of the poorer design would be to lower profits for the company. A well-informed manager would realize this and avoid an unsafe product no matter what his or her view of social responsibility.

Unethical, deceitful, or illegal activities also affect the general reputation of an organization. A company that uses false advertising or bribery or engages in price-fixing, for example, will usually suffer in the long run because consumers begin to avoid that company when the practices become known. Even if the effect of the impaired reputation is not strongly felt, it tends to make peak success impossible.

These practical considerations do not completely control irresponsible and unethical behavior, of course. It is always possible for managers to think, "We can get away with it; no one need ever know." Furthermore, practical supports for responsible behavior tend to lead people to try to maintain the *appearance* of social concern without any substance. If people think a product is safe, they may continue to buy it even if it is potentially lethal. Keeping up appearances has always been a problem with morals in society. In the world of formal organizations, the effort has been institutionalized to a degree by advertising and other methods.

The Social Enforcement
of Responsibility

Society does not simply leave it up to individuals to decide whether they will act responsibly or not. Although individual freedom is considerable, society as a whole exerts influence and control over individual behavior.

The most obvious social control over managers is the force of law. Civil and criminal law make many possible management actions illegal. The promise of punishment is a strong deterrent against many of these acts. In addition to the normal legal constraints that affect all of us, managers must adhere to a body of law specifically designed to control some of the ways organizations are run. These regulations affect businesses, agencies, and many other kinds of organizations and play a significant role in the decisions managers make. Legal regulations will be discussed in Chapter 16.

Legal control is a formal means of control. Society also applies informal controls that affect managers. Societies have norms, just as small work groups do. A *norm* is a belief that is generally accepted by the members of a group about the right way to behave in given situations. Particularly in the case of a norm of a large society, while most members accept the belief, some members of the group or society may not. It is a norm in Western society, for instance, to cover most of our bodies with clothes when at work or at school. It is also a norm to permit much scantier dress at a swimming pool or beach. Nearly everyone conforms to these norms, but some people may think the first norm is silly and other people may think the second is scandalous. Societies and their members also have values. A social *value* is a belief or feeling about what is truly worthwhile, important, and worth sacrificing for. Home ownership is a value in the United States; many people are willing to work and sacrifice to buy their own house even when other alternatives are available.

Social norms and values apply to managers. Outright lies about the qualities of products or services, for instance, are not generally accepted. The use of physical threats in labor or supplier negotiations is rare. Extreme deceit is proscribed. But the clever omission of a point or two of information is widely accepted. Especially among higher-level managers, devotion to the organization is an important value. Managers will sometimes make considerable sacrifices of time, health, or family life to work for the benefit of the company or agency.

These general social norms are enforced the same way as the norms of work groups. People who violate them will have trouble getting along with others; they may be ostracized; others will refuse to do business with them; they may be insulted or ridiculed. Society also gives rewards for accepting norms. Financial success, community respect, and the support of other people in the society are usually given most generously to those who follow the prevailing norms closely.

Some of the norms and values that affect managers have to do with social concern and responsibility. Generally, informal influences such as social rebukes will enforce norms to provide a relatively safe work place, for instance. Gross environmental damage is frowned upon, even by managers in other companies which may themselves cause moderate pollution. Extreme violations of individual human rights in the work place are not accepted. Society will use psychological force against managers who violate these and other related norms.

The Personal Values of Managers

Both practical considerations and social force are external reasons for displaying social concern. A great many managers also try to function in a way that is beneficial to society for no other reason than their belief that it is right to do so. Many managers believe it is morally wrong to sell unsafe products or to discriminate against an employee because he or she is from a different ethnic group. These feelings are social values expressed in the personalities of individual managers. The values are learned in the process of an individual's growing up and developing effective ways to function in society. In expressing socially responsible personal values, managers behave in a way that helps others, not because they are being forced to, but because they believe they ought to, that it is wrong to act otherwise.

Ultimately, the existence of strong personal values among managers is the best guarantee that the great strength of business and government organizations will be used for the good of society. Such values come with maturity. One argument that can be made for strong development programs and for the greater use of democratic, participative management is that these cause managers to mature. In this sense, it is possible for a committed organization to teach social concerns to its managers. The viewpoint is that managers will have reason to be motivated to act in a socially responsible way (1) when social responsibility is built into the overall goals of an organization and (2) when the achievement of objectives is used as the measure of management success.

ORGANIZATIONS CAN AND DO ACT TO PROTECT THE ENVIRONMENT

Businesses and other organizations have begun to include a variety of social concerns in their top-level objectives. Three that have received special attention in recent years are (1) the protection and improvement of the physical environment, (2) the promotion of equal rights for employees, and (3) the protection of the interests of customers and clients. It is in these three areas also that the government has been most active legislatively and in regulating business. (The specific laws and regulations that affect managers and organizations in these areas are explored at greater length in the next chapter.)

The protection of the environment was among the earliest of these concerns to gain widespread attention. In the early years of modern industry, the size of the American countryside and the strength of the forces of nature seemed immense. People were generally deluded into thinking that no matter what was done with factories, automobiles, and housing developments, the impact on our surroundings would be unnoticeable. As the decades went by, it became more and more obvious that this belief was unjustified. The huge scale of modern industry, transportation, and housing has threatened in some cases to overwhelm the physical world we live in; in other cases, it often makes it unpleasant and dangerous.

A great part of the destruction and pollution of the environment is not caused by businesses and other large institutions. It is caused by individuals. The manufacturer of a soft drink can does not cause the buyer to throw the can on the side of a road. The makers of automobiles do not cause users to insist on driving to work, one person to a car, instead of taking public transportation. Yet, there has been a growing social belief that large institutions, especially businesses, should solve even the pollution problems that they have not caused. To the extent that this belief is accepted, business managers are expected to be *more* socially responsible than others.

However, some part of environmental damage has been directly caused by industry and government. Many manufacturing processes create by-products and wastes that are difficult to dispose of. These processes have often been carried on for decades without adequate environmental safeguards. Government construction and public works projects such as highways and dams have caused considerable destruction.

The real problem with trying to protect and improve the environment is that the destruction has been cumulative over many years while the effort to find solutions has had to be condensed into only a few recent years. Society is pressing business and government now to spend much of the money that was saved over the last two hundred years by *not* installing pollution-control and conservation devices. The cost is high, and resistance has been considerable. Resistance is based on the adverse effects on business profits and the increased costs of government projects. Social pressure has been so strong, though, that significant progress has already been made.

Air Pollution   One of the hallmarks of the industrial age has been the pollution of the air with chemicals and by-products of combustion. The famous London fogs of the nineteenth century were caused largely by England's immense consumption of coal for industrial use and for home heating. The fallout from the smokestacks was so great that butterflies began to evolve into darker and darker colors so they would remain camouflaged against the soot-blackened trees.

Air pollution remains a by-product of today's industrial society; automobiles and the generation of electric power have been among the major contributors. Thankfully, pollution from these sources has been significantly reduced in recent years. Discharges into the air of by-products from manufacturing processes are substantially smaller than only a decade ago. Legal requirements brought on by a public demand for change have been the main cause of the changes.

The management problems of the automobile industry since 1960 illustrate the strong effect of legal and social pressure on decision making. Almost since their inception, automobiles had been designed with the aesthetic and cultural expectations of the consumers in mind; pollution control was given virtually no consideration. When the United States government mandated a significant reduction in auto pollution, it caused a crisis in the industry. The managers of auto firms had to make important and rapid design changes in their products because of the sudden pressure.

Water Pollution   Industry has also contributed to the pollution of rivers, streams, lakes, and ground water. Efforts and expenses similar to those for cleaning up the air have begun to be successful in most parts of the country. The control of water pollution has strongly affected managers in municipal governments: it is not unusual for a small town with an annual budget of $500,000 to suddenly find itself in need of a $10 million sewage-treatment plant. Federal and state funds are available to help pay for sewage-treatment facilities, but this only lessens the blow. Initiation and administration of such major projects has proved a difficult challenge for many local officials.

ORGANIZATIONS CAN AND DO PROMOTE THE RIGHTS OF INDIVIDUALS

An enduring social problem in the United States and elsewhere has been the lack of opportunity for employment and advancement given to minorities. At the time when social pressure grew to combat environmental destruction, legal pressure also rose for promoting more job opportunities for minority groups that had been traditionally discriminated against in hiring. This pressure paralleled the increasing dissatisfaction with discrimination against women in the work world.

Substantial discrimination did exist in the past, and much continues today. Managers in business and government, however, have increasingly accepted the legal responsibility for giving equal treatment to everyone at hiring and promotion time. Furthermore, many organizations have begun to take positive steps voluntarily or by requirement of law. These firms specifically seek to provide opportunities for minorities and women and to develop individuals so they are able to take advantage of the new opportunities.

The reasons for the changed attitudes show the workings of all four sources of social influence. Many regulations have been established, especially by the federal government, *requiring* an end to discrimination. There is also a practical advantage to providing equal opportunity, because it does expand the labor pool and because efforts in this area can be publicized to improve the organization's reputation. Social values have shifted toward giving equal opportunity. The psychological influence of community leaders and other people outside of organizations now tends to support an end to discrimination. Additionally, many managers have become better educated about the harmful effects of discrimination. They have initiated equal-opportunity efforts because they believe that it is right and that they owe it to the society.

How do managers go about ending discrimination and providing equal opportunity? Sound management practices help to avoid much discrimination. For example, an assessment system, based on actual performance rather than on opinion will help prevent promotions based solely on race or sex. If pay is tied to job descriptions and performance assessments, people who contribute the same amount to the organization should get the same pay. If training and development programs identify and eliminate areas of weak individual performance, all should have a good opportunity to advance. When hiring is based on clearly defined qualifications and abilities, discrimination is less likely.

More aggressive efforts are common today to help make up for the effects of discrimination in the past. Many organizations have programs that actively seek minority and women candidates for open jobs. In some instances, the law requires *affirmative action*—programs designed to promote the hiring and advancement of minorities and women. Many organizations have specific training and development programs to overcome educational deficiencies. Federal and state programs support such activities. Many companies have redrawn their policies so as to specifically encourage the consideration of women and minorities for jobs that bring prestige and higher pay.

Equal opportunity may progress further. But it is not likely that the efforts of organizations that hire people will, by themselves, be able to overcome the effects of a pattern of discrimination that extends to every sector of society. Businesses, governments, and other organizations have led the way in overcoming discrimination. Some believe, therefore, until more extensive social change occurs in other areas of our culture, the aggressive efforts of some employers will only serve as a model for future progress.

ORGANIZATIONS CAN AND DO WORK TO GIVE A FAIR DEAL TO CUSTOMERS AND CLIENTS

The growth of mass-manufacturing techniques has created a large distance between the maker of a product and the ultimate buyer and user. At one time, it was a common practice for everyone to visit a local cobbler to have a pair of boots custom made. If the product was unsatisfactory, the cobbler was there to hear the complaint. The situation is far different when tens of thousands of the same kind of shoe are manufactured at some distant point and then distributed through a chain of middlemen to buyers all over the country. Consumers feel isolated. They believe that they have little influence in the design and quality of the things they buy.

Not many years ago, buyers created a largely informal but potent movement called *consumerism*. This is action by consumers to increase their power and influence in the relationship between sellers and consumers. The main goals of consumerism have been twofold. First, consumers want to influence producers to improve the quality of their products, especially in making them safer. Second, consumers want to increase the flow of information between seller and buyer. Specifically, consumers want sellers to give more complete information about products and to listen more to the desires and needs of consumers.

As with other social forces, different methods of influence have been combined. Considerable new legal protection has been granted consumers. Direct social influence and the expression of changing values have backed up the government regulations. One of the most potent tools of the consumer representatives has been simple publicity of their grievances. The widespread knowledge of a design or production fault in a product can be extremely damaging to the manufacturer. If consumers learn that there is something seriously wrong with one of a company's products, sales are likely to fall for others of their products as well.

Many firms have taken action in response to consumerism. One response has been the relatively negative one of using advertising to offset the claims of consumer groups, rather than making changes in the practices that caused the complaints. Other responses have been more positive. Some complaints arise from misunderstanding by consumers. Manufacturers have generally increased the amount and clarity of information they give to buyers. Some have sponsored clinics and other training programs to educate buyers as to the characteristics and uses of their products. Other companies have created positions and departments with the specific responsibility of communicating with buyers and investigating and resolving their complaints. Still other firms have made it an official policy to incorporate the responses of consumers into the design of future products.

As with the efforts to provide equal opportunity, the resolution of consumer problems has not yet been accomplished. The very nature of the mass-production method tends to isolate buyers and reduce effective communication between makers, sellers, and buyers. This is true even in government agencies. In a welfare department, for instance, whose main business is dealing personally with clients, the tremendous growth of services in recent years has created a distance similar to that found with manufactured goods. Modern managers must investigate such problems as they touch a particular organization, and seek solutions within the organization's capabilities and resources.

MANAGERS BALANCE
A VARIETY OF CONCERNS
This chapter began with two illustrations: one of a socially irresponsible manager who ran into trouble, the other of a socially responsible manager who also ran into trouble. Like any single function or viewpoint of management, social concern must be integrated with the activities and goals of the overall organization. It must be balanced with other considerations, as illustrated in Figure 15-2 on page 356.

The Continued Success
of the Organization
Unless the organization contributes to the good of society, it will not continue to exist. Decisions about committing resources based on social concern must take this into account. The following argument, though,

Figure 15-2. Balance of Concerns

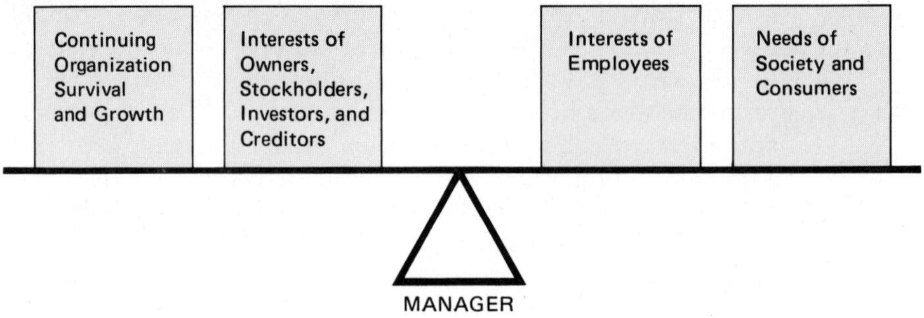

| Continuing Organization Survival and Growth | Interests of Owners, Stockholders, Investors, and Creditors | | Interests of Employees | Needs of Society and Consumers |

MANAGER

has been used to justify unethical practices: "If we hadn't used kickbacks, the company would have gone out of business and all of the employees would have been out of work." It takes maturity in a manager to draw the line between the legitimate deemphasizing of social concern to protect the existence of the organization and out-and-out irresponsible behavior.

Interests of the Owners

In any business, the owners have legitimate interests in protecting the assets of the firm and in having operations run so that they make a profit. Managers have an important responsibility to protect the interests of owners. Management that does not create a profit over the long term is failing, no matter how socially responsible it is. In the same way, government managers must consider the interests of taxpayers. The best social action program may be ill-advised if it creates a disruptive tax burden or strains too much the resources of government that should be used for other legitimate purposes.

Interests of Employees

Just as customers and clients have legitimate interests, so do employees. Reasonable working hours, self-development opportunities, and the chance to make a mistake from time to time need not be sacrificed either to profits or to the needs of consumers. At the same time, a manager's interest in the welfare of workers must not be allowed to cause the production of shoddy or dangerous products.

The Needs of Society

Concerns for the organization itself, its owners, and the people who work there must be integrated with the fourth concern, the needs of a healthy society. Managers must look both ways. They must be concerned with avoiding some of the damaging results of operations—pollution, for instance. They must give attention to the effects of their products on the people who buy and use them; only the managers are in a position to

Managers in Action

"It gives me the license to stick my nose into anything that energy impacts upon," says Robert H. Steder, energy manager for PPG Industries. Steder is one of a new breed of managers whose responsibility it is to find ways for their organizations to cut down on the use of energy. In so doing, they often combine both staff and line responsibility. They may make decisions about certain matters, and only advise on others. Typically, they set conservation goals and approve plans for the company's various divisions. They oversee fuel purchases and seek alternative sources of energy. They must also predict the effect of changing government energy regulations. They may even be called upon to lobby for the company's energy position.

The energy manager may function as an independent department, or as at Kaiser Aluminum and Chemical Co. where three formerly separate departments of planning, purchasing, and conservation have been consolidated into one.

While the duties of energy managers vary widely from company to company, at least two such managers can cite impressive results. Dow Chemical Co. reduced its energy consumption per unit of product output by 40 percent in the 1970s. United Technologies Corp. initiated an ambitious program calculated to save an average of 35 percent of its energy cost. The company will spend $33 million for more efficient equipment, but it expects to realize in return a $6 million savings in energy costs.

Source: Nancy L. Ross, "Enter the Second-Generation Specialist, the Energy Manager," *Washington Post*, October 8, 1978, p. F2.

effectively ensure quality products. They must also try to run their organizations so that they make a positive contribution to society; maturity and social responsibility go hand-in-hand. Self-fulfillment is believed to be the highest motivation of humans. It will always be thwarted in an organization that is destructive of its human and physical environment or that has a cynical disregard for the legitimate needs of customers or clients.

SUMMARY

1. The social concerns of managers are expressed by their recognition of the impact of their organizations on the world outside and by their efforts to make those effects beneficial rather than harmful. Socially responsible behavior may result from practical considerations, from legal force, from psychological pressure from customers, friends, colleagues or people in the community, or from the personal values of managers.

2. Contrary to popular belief, much of the damage to the physical environment has been caused by individual actions rather than by the operations of organizations. Nevertheless, significant pollution comes from industrial processes and from the products of industry, especially the automobile. Legal and social pressures have led government and business to invest heavily in redesigning processes and products to reduce air and water pollution.

3. Discrimination in hiring and promotion of minorities and women has been a serious social problem in the United States. Prudent management and carefully written personnel policies will decrease the extent of discrimination. Many organizations make aggressive efforts—using special recruiting and training activities, for instance—to help overcome the past accumulation of discrimination.

4. Consumerism is a social movement with the goal of increasing the power of buyers in relation to that of manufacturers and sellers. It is partially a symptom of the isolation of the consumer as a result of mass manufacturing and distribution. Consumerism has pursued with some success the objectives of forcing manufacturers to improve the quality and safety of their products and to make more detailed product information accessible to buyers.

5. Managers cannot concentrate all of their attention on any one aspect of the organization, but must balance a number of concerns. The main factors that must be integrated if an organization is to be socially beneficial are the success of the organization, the interests of owners, interests of employees, and the needs of consumers and of society as a whole.

REVIEW AND DISCUSSION QUESTIONS

1. Do you think that the manager of a textile mill, for instance, should be deeply worried about the effect of the organization on the society as a whole? If so, why? If not, why not?

2. Give some examples of the ways practical considerations can cause managers to act socially responsible. Is responsibility from this source just as good as from other sources?

3. Name one norm related to behavior in the classroom. Name a value widely accepted by the class.

4. Mary feels very strongly that the government should spend as little money as possible and she applies this feeling in the management of her office of a federal agency. Where did she get this feeling? Is she right to apply the feeling at work?

5. Why are business and government faced with such immense costs for protecting and improving the physical environment today?

6. In your opinion, is it possible for formal organizations alone to save our physical environment? Why or why not?

7. John wants to make sure his consulting company doesn't unfairly discriminate in hiring or promotions. What are some of the things he might do to accomplish this?

8. Why has the need arisen for a consumer movement in this country? Do you agree that there is a need?

9. What are four kinds of needs a manager must balance to achieve a socially responsible organization? How can this be accomplished?

Problems and Projects

1. In an organization, the first formal expression of social concern is usually in written overall goals. These goals usually reflect the general achievements needed for the organization to fulfill its purpose. Using everything you have learned from the text so far, write five high-level goals reflecting social responsibility for a small manufacturing company in South Carolina. The plant processes chemicals into a finished product that is used by other manufacturers as a final coating on fiberglass products. One of the raw materials is moderately toxic, and the plant uses water for cleaning and rinsing pipes and other equipment. In preparing your objectives, remember the guidelines for writing overall objectives discussed in earlier chapters, and remember to balance the needs of the organization and its people with those of the human and physical environment.

2. *Performance Situation—The Indifferent Fruit Packer:* Gleneagles Packing Company is an old, Washington State fruit cannery with a large regional market in the Western states. Sales and profits have been reasonably good for most of the last 50 years. Gleneagles' management has always been extremely paternalistic: decisions are made only by the very top managers; everyone else is told what to do, when to do it, and how. Most of the managers and employees have been with the company for years. To an outside observer, it would be obvious that they were getting pretty stale. A certain amount of cynicism is developing. A statement by the plant superintendent was typical: "Employees here don't care anything about what I think, so I don't even try to tell them; I just do my job and get out as soon as I can."

Gleneagles has been hearing from the public recently, most notably in the form of a public demonstration in front of the plant by a group of people who live downstream. Certain fruits that the company cans are not mechanically peeled. They are put into a chemical bath to remove the skins. The remains of the chemicals have been simply dumped into the stream that runs past the plant. Further problems have begun to come to light as well. A state consumer-affairs agency has discovered that quite a few of Gleneagles' cans contain less than their labels claim. The problem has become so bad that buyers sometimes even notice the difference. Fruit pits are often found in finished products, and the quality of the fruit itself is often inferior. This is partly because the company's buyers have been choosing the cheapest fresh fruit to reduce costs and partly because of sloppiness in processing.

Use this case to analyze the relationship between management maturity and social responsibility. For a company to be socially responsible, is it only the managers who have to be mature? What are some of the causes and results of immaturity in a business operation? Why, for instance, does the plant superintendent feel the way he does, and what would be some possible results of his feelings? Write a brief analysis and discuss the results in class.

3. Consider the practical difficulties facing a manager in the company in Problem 2. Assume that you have been brought in from outside to turn Gleneagles Packing Company into a socially responsible firm without doing too much damage to sales or profits. What would you do? List 10 specific *management* steps that would help turn the company around. The goal of the proposals should be to create a climate in which employees and managers can develop the desire and ability to establish a better relationship with the company's human and physical environment. They should also know that social concern is an important goal of the organization.

4. *Performance Situation—The Amazon Oil Pipeline Contract:* John Hardin, president of Hardin Pipeline Construction, is facing the hardest series of decisions in his business career. The company has a chance to take a contract to construct an oil pipeline in the far reaches of the Amazon Basin. The contract is written so that the work would be certain to produce a substantial profit for John and for the other investors in the company. The federal government has shown considerable interest in the project. It has even applied some pressure to go through with it because U.S. companies would get a preferential rate on the oil from the line. The pipeline construction has gotten a lot of attention in the newspapers. The new oil supply at the lower rate would be a clear benefit to the economy and thus to society.

At the same time, there would be no possible way to avoid considerable damage to the natural drainage of the Amazon. It would also disrupt the lives of the natives, many of whom live in relatively undisturbed primitive tribes. John has been getting telephone calls and letters expressing every possible view of the issue. In addition, the project would be extremely dangerous and difficult for the workers who would have to put the line through the jungle and over unexplored mountains. A few have said flatly that they wouldn't go.

John Hardin has a strong feel for the importance of the environment. He has been proud of his record in the past because he has been able to avoid doing significant damage in the company's construction projects. That would not be possible this time; severe damage would be certain.

Analyze this situation based on the discussion in the text. List five ways that society is influencing John's decision of whether to take the contract and how to operate it if he does. List five areas of concern that John must balance in making his decisions.

5. Consumerism has had a significant effect on many companies and on local governments and other government agencies. Assume that you are the manager of a town government or of a small manufacturing company and that you sincerely want to comply with the goals of consumerism. Propose a plan of specific actions that would allow your organization to achieve this. Use the text discussion to clarify the goals. Remember to balance social concerns with the needs of the organization and the people in it.

6. Use incidents from your own experience to demonstrate the influences of social pressure, formal or informal, on decisions about behavior. Give examples of times when you or someone you know wished to do something but were prevented by each of the following: practical considerations, legal restraints, current or anticipated social pressure, and personal values.

Cases for Analysis and Discussion

CASE 1: THE CITY'S RESPONSIBILITY

"Mr. Mayor, the situation is simple." Brad Lipz was getting himself in hot water, as he had done so often before. "The houses west of Bay Street are simply uninhabitable. They are unsafe; they are unsanitary. The people there freeze in the winter and are driven out onto the streets by the heat in the summer. And the streets: they're littered; they're full of holes. I tell you the people in that neighborhood are not getting the same city services everyone else in town is."

Lipz had only been city manager for less than two years, and he knew that he had the job only as long as the city council wanted to keep him. He noticed some distinctly disapproving looks from certain council members, but continued anyway. "The area west of Bay deserves some concentrated attention from this government. The people there need better trash collection; they need street cleaning; they need to have sewer and water lines replaced. And, as much as anything, they need our help in repairing and replacing the buildings out there. They can't do it by themselves."

Of the several voices that broke in at this point, that of Councilwoman Brooks won out through sheer volume. "Mr. Lipz! In the first place, it is the job of this council, not of the city manager, to set the major priorities of the city government. I'll ask you to remember that. In the second place, the people you are talking about get more services than they pay for as it is. Tax revenues from that area don't begin to cover what we already spend there. There is no justification for us to spend even more. There is no money for it now, and it is certainly unfair to ask the other taxpayers—who are straining under their tax burden as it is—to pay higher taxes to subsidize an area that is already not paying its way. We need a tax cut, not an increase."

A. What are the issues involved here? Is it a question of conflicting legitimate interests, or is there a clear direction for social responsibility?
B. What is the city manager's proper role in an issue like this? Should he keep his mouth shut if his personal values are being violated?
C. Which side are you on? What should the council do, if anything?

CASE 2: THE CREATIVE MATERNITY LEAVE

One barrier to women getting advancement in an organization has been the maternity leave. Companies and agencies have usually granted these leaves, but when the mother came back to work, she often wasn't even guaranteed a job. Almost always, her seniority was lost. Even a woman who had advanced to better jobs might be told to start all over as a secretary again. Obviously, there was no equal opportunity in such a situation.

Safeguard Insurance Company is one of a number of organizations that have done something about the problem. The first step was simply to give official status to the maternity leave. Women working for Safeguard can now take six months off to have a baby and can then return to the organization with the same status they had when they left.

Safeguard has taken a further step. For some women with the company, it is now possible to pick up writing assignments at the office and work on them at home while they are on leave. Group insurance contract proposals or analyses and reports on real estate deals can be handled this way, for instance. Working on such projects during leave can actually contribute to advancing the woman's career. And, it's good for the company. One of the personnel officers says the plan is "economical, keeps us supplied with women managers, and has legal advantages, too."

A. Is it reasonable for an organization to go to such trouble to help women get ahead? Men do not get maternity leaves; should women?
B. Why have Safeguard and other similarly motivated companies made changes like this? What are the sources of the social concern?
C. Do you think Safeguard is balancing its legitimate interests in this plan? Would they have made the change if it had benefited the women but not the company?

CASE 3: THE CASE OF THE CASES

"Here's the problem right here. It's not going to take much study to find out what's wrong. Although, we will do some stress tests, if you want."

When Ed hired the engineering consultant, he had expected a three- or four-month study with page after page of technical data, and a substantial bill. But now the engineer had spotted the difficulty on her first visit.

The engineer explained, "I don't think there is anything wrong with the material; it seems strong enough. The problem is with this screw that holds the back of the case on. When you tighten these down, it makes an unequal tension on this side here. That puts continual stress on the side. I'll bet if you look at the others, you'll see that all of them broke on the same line, from the screw here straight to the corner."

Ed got someone to check some of the other broken cases, and they had all broken just where the engineer predicted. But that was bad news, not good. It meant that the design of the case was wrong, and the constant breakage wasn't caused by some simple fault in materials or manufacturing. Changing the design meant spending a lot of money on retooling. The radios were a big seller, but the profit margin on each was so slim that the change might wipe out profits altogether.

Still, something had to be done. Thousands of the radios had been returned by angry customers. And nearly all of them were still under warranty when they came back. That was expensive.

Ed considered three alternative solutions to the problem:

1. Reduce the warranty to 30 days and leave the radios as they were. The radios would still work even if the cases were broken.
2. Leave the last screw slightly loose when the cases were assembled. This would take the stress off and prevent breakage, but it would make a shoddy-appearing product.
3. Redesign the case and retool the company's facilities to produce the new one. Studies showed that this would just about eliminate profits for the next three years.

A. Does this company have a practical reason to improve its product?
B. Which of the alternatives given is the best? Why?
C. Are there other alternatives? What would you do?

CASE 4: TOO MUCH BUSINESS

"This just isn't fair! I can't work again tonight! Do you know how long its been since I've spent more than an hour with my husband? Do you have the names of my children in my personnel file? It's been so long since I've seen them I forget who they are."

Mike Accio felt terrible. He hadn't wanted to ask Dotty to work overtime again, and it was more than obvious that she didn't want to work overtime. But what was he supposed to do?

Mike was in the heating business and had been for years. There was always a push in the late fall to clean and recondition furnaces, and this year, for unknown reasons, the demand was out of control. Mike suspected that the problem was a fire that had just killed a mother and several children. The cause of the fire was discovered to be an oil furnace that hadn't been cleaned and adjusted. Apparently everyone had taken the lesson to heart at the same time.

Mike only had four employees. Dotty worked in the shop on motors, blowers, and other furnace parts that were repairable. Three other employees made road calls. The work load had been going on for weeks and it was starting to cause real trouble. Dotty was right. It was unfair. Mike was even more worried about Sam Toller. He had had heart trouble for years. He never had felt comfortable under pressure, and Mike was afraid that the recent pace might be too much for Sam. But Mike kept thinking about the terrible fire. He wondered whether one of the people who had signed up to have their furnace checked might have a similar fire before Mike's people had a chance to get there.

A. What are the groups whose interests are in conflict here?
B. Is Mike justified in being concerned? Is it really his responsibility to worry about what happens in a case like this?
C. What should he do? Is there really any way Mike can balance interests in a conflict like this one?

Government Regulation and Management Decisions

16

After completing Chapter 16, you will be able to do the following:

- Locate, in a given management situation, the responsibility for complying with legal regulations.
- List four areas of federal legislation affecting personnel and staffing decisions, and judge whether given decisions are in accord with the general requirements of the laws.
- Describe the overall goals of federal laws protecting consumers, and use the provisions of three specific acts as a guide in given decision-making situations.
- Describe the general responsibilities of managers for protecting the natural environment.

- Analyze given management decisions for compliance with the goals of federal free-competition regulations.
- Describe three former abuses in the issuance and exchange of securities, and describe the actions now required of managers to protect against such abuses.
- List seven areas of state and local regulation and influence that a manager should be familiar with in operating an organization.

Nearly everyone would assume that this business practice is illegal: A man goes door to door in a suburban neighborhood selling vacuum cleaners. He points a shotgun at prospective customers and tells them he'll kill them if they don't sign a sales agreement.

We can judge that this technique for generating sales is illegal just from living in our society and having an everyday familiarity with its values and laws. This is true of managers also. A manager can be pretty sure of some of the things that should and should not be done and must act in accordance with the values of the society in which he or she lives.

Many situations arise in which this common sense is not a sure guide, however. This is because of the mushrooming growth of detailed government regulations that affect management decisions. The increase in the number and complexity of regulations and guidelines has been especially notable in this century. These government controls extend even to such basic matters as the ownership of property. If a company declares bankruptcy, for instance, its sales of assets in the six months preceding the declaration can be recalled to make the assets available to pay off creditors. Additionally, many prohibited practices are not obvious. A manager today who does not pay close attention to the requirements of law and regulation has a much reduced chance of being successful on the job. That manager also runs the risk of running into legal problems as an individual as well as creating them for the organization in which he or she works.

MANAGERS FUNCTION WITHIN A NETWORK OF REGULATIONS

It is clear that formal organizations have a profound impact on the welfare of everyone and on their quality and style of life. Specific decisions made by business managers may affect who is able to work and who is not, who will be subject to environmentally induced health damage and who will not, who will achieve an adequate standard of living and who will not. The strength and welfare of the entire nation depends on the productivity of formal organizations and on the extent to which their goals agree with the interests of all the people. For these reasons, governments have imposed regulations on business and other organizations throughout history; for example, some of the earliest written records reflect government regulation of commerce.

As the complexity of the industrial society has increased, and in response to changing ethical and social concerns, government regulation has multiplied in the Western world especially. Managers today function within a complex matrix of laws and formal social controls that may become the single critical factor in many important management situations.

Some kind of federal, state, or local regulation will touch nearly every decision a manager must make. Often the regulations interact like a system: adherence to one regulation makes the organization subject to other regulations that would not normally apply. Such interrelationships create complex situations. Suppose, for example, that a charitable organization wants to build a new office building in certain environmentally sensitive areas of the United States. The organization may be required to perform an environmental-impact study before building. The study might then require that construction employ a range of special techniques to be used to minimize damage—special sewage treatment facilities, for example. In the process of providing the special facilities, the organization may, in turn, run into a maze of federal, state, and local codes, laws, ordinances, and agencies, many with different and sometimes conflicting requirements.

A novice manager faced with this situation might be inclined to shrug it off by saying, "It's a legal matter; let the legal department handle it." Complying with regulations can be so important to success or failure, however, that the solution chosen is critical. In the long run, responsibility lies with the line manager, and he or she cannot dispose of it.

In addition to increasing the burden of responsibility, regulation adds a significant administrative chore. In many cases it is necessary not only to comply but also to *prove* that the organization has complied, by filling out lengthy and detailed reports. For the most part, governments operate on information. Providing the information they want costs money and adds significantly to overhead in an organization.

Regulations can also be a source of opportunity. One obvious example of this is the number of private consulting companies that are growing prosperous by helping other organizations to comply with regulation. For most managers, though, the major concern must be the compliance itself, not the chance to prosper from the new regulations. Keeping out of trouble with government agencies while continuing to aggressively pursue the business of the organization is a sizable challenge. Table 16-1 illustrates the extent of federal regulation and the inherent penalties for managers who do not comply.

TABLE 16-1. MANAGEMENT ACTION AND POTENTIAL LEGAL PENALTIES.					
AGENCY	YEAR ENFORCEMENT BEGAN	COMPLAINT MAY NAME INDIVIDUAL	MAXIMUM INDIVIDUAL PENALTY	MAXIMUM CORPORATE PENALTY	PRIVATE SUIT ALLOWED UNDER APPLICABLE STATUTE
Internal Revenue Service	1862	Yes	$5,000, three years, or both	$10,000, 50% assessment, prosecution costs	No
Antitrust Div. (Justice Dept.)	1890	Yes	$100,000, three years, or both	$1 million, injunction, divestiture	Yes
Food & Drug Administration	1907	Yes	$1,000, one year, or both for first offense; $10,000, three years, or both thereafter	$1,000, for first offense; $10,000 thereafter; seizure of condemned products	No
Federal Trade Commission	1914	Yes	Restitution, injunction	Restitution, injunction, divestiture, $10,000 per day for violation of rules, orders	No
Securities & Exchange Commission	1934	Yes	$10,000, two years, or both	$10,000, injunction	Yes
Equal Employment Opportunity Commission	1965	No		Injunction, back pay award, reinstatement	Yes
Office of Federal Contract Compliance	1965	No		Suspension, cancellation of contract	Yes

TABLE 16-1 *(Continued)*.					
AGENCY	YEAR ENFORCE-MENT BEGAN	COMPLAINT MAY NAME INDIVIDUAL	MAXIMUM INDIVIDUAL PENALTY	MAXIMUM CORPORATE PENALTY	PRIVATE SUIT ALLOWED UNDER APPLICABLE STATUTE
Environmental Protection Agency	1970	Yes	$25,000 per day, one year, or both for first offense; $50,000 per day, two years, or both thereafter	$25,000 per day, first offense; $50,000 per day thereafter; injunction	Yes
Occupational Safety & Health Administra-tion	1970	No*	$10,000, six months, or both	$10,000	No
Consumer Product Safety Commission	1972	Yes	$50,000, one year, or both	$500,000	Yes
Office of Employee Benefits Security (Labor Dept.)	1975	Yes	$10,000, one year, or both; barring from future employment with plan; reimburse-ment	$100,000, reimburse-ment	Yes

*Except sole proprietorship.

REGULATIONS INFLUENCE EMPLOYMENT POLICIES AND PRACTICES

An organization cannot function without employees. As a result, every organization is faced with a degree of regulation because many laws and guidelines deal with the way employees are hired and treated. As a minimum, practically every employer has to pay social security taxes and file basic employment reports. In addition, many employers

Managers in Action

"There is more need for me to seek advice from lawyers than ever before," says Raymond F. Good, president of Heinz U.S.A. The manager of an affiliated H. J. Heinz Co. plant in Tracy, California, for example, received a six-month sentence after being cited by California food and drug officials for unsanitary conditions in his plant.

"You have to be alert. You shudder at the risk of innocent violation," says William B. Johnson, chairman of IC Industries, Inc. "For example, we have no interpretation of what the new pension law really means, but we're supposed to be applying it right now."

Increased paper work is a major complaint. Robert J. Brotje, Jr., treasurer of Champion Spark Plug Co. says that the firm files 500 reports to some 15 bureaus and agencies of the federal government and 2,500 other reports to local and state agencies across the country. Mr. Good of Heinz says that he must sign annually 25 copies of an alcohol control document for the U. S. Department of Agriculture "stating that our vinegar is not used for alcoholic purposes."

Company staffs also increase as a result of government regulation. At Deere & Co., a giant manufacturer of farm equipment, for example, Charles W. Toney, director of minority relations, says that his staff has grown from two in 1972 to eight today. And it spends more than $1 million annually on EEOC (Equal Employment Opportunity Commission) compliance matters.

Moreover, even the most conscientious manager can fall in the trap of conflicting rules enforced by different agencies. Good, of Heinz, U.S.A. cites one instance where the company followed an FPC (Federal Power Commission) order to "Turn down the lights, you're using too much power," only to be told by OSHA (Occupational Safety and Health Administration), "Turn up the lights, you are creating a safety hazard."

Source: "The Law Closes in on Managers," *Business Week*, May 10, 1976, pp. 110–116.

must comply with regulations controlling wages and hours, unfair discrimination, unsafe working conditions, and unfair practices in dealings with labor unions.

The Fair Labor Standards Act

This federal law (also known as the Wages and Hours Law) was passed in 1938 to guarantee a minimum compensation for work performed. Its two most important provisions require (1) the payment of minimum wage rates, and (2) the payment of overtime rates. The minimum wage started out at 25 cents an hour in 1938 and has been repeatedly raised to keep up with inflation since then. Most employers must pay at least the minimum wage or face prosecution. The law also makes it mandatory to pay overtime to non-management and nonprofessional workers if they put in more than 40 hours a week. The established rate is 150 percent of regular wages.

The Equal Employment Opportunity Act

This act was originally part of the Civil Rights Act of 1964. It was revised in 1972 to become more comprehensive. The act prohibits employment discrimination on the basis of race, color, religion, sex, or national origin. It does not specifically apply to all employers, but only to (1) those organizations with 15 or more employees, (2) labor unions with 15 or more members, (3) employment agencies that deal with employers of 15 or more people, and (4) apprenticeship programs.

The intent of the law is to keep organizations from refusing to hire, from firing, and from refusing promotions to people for reasons that have nothing to do with their performance. To take action because of sex or race is illegal, for instance. It is obvious that the best way for an organization to prove compliance with the regulations is to make employee selection and assessments that are clearly based on performance. In any event, this is good management practice.

The equal employment opportunity (EEO) requirements are especially apparent in their influence on selection and hiring procedures. The use of employment tests, for example, is permitted only if the employer can show that the tests really do predict performance on the job. This characteristic of tests—measuring what they are meant to measure—is called *validity* and can be demonstrated statistically and in other ways. The law does not allow use of a test that simply measures some ability, such as knowledge of history or politics, that has nothing to do with the requirements of the job.

The Occupational Safety and Health Act

Originally passed in 1970, this act (OSHA) requires nearly all employers to provide a safe and sanitary work place for their employees. If the operations, materials, or products of a business affect the nation's commerce, it must comply with the act. The act and its accompanying regulations specify many detailed safety standards that an organization must meet. In addition, OSHA makes it an offense to permit the existence of any condition—even if not specifically named—that can be recognized in advance as a safety or health hazard. OSHA also requires employees to follow safety regulations; the burden is not entirely on the employer.

Government inspectors can legally enter offices and factories to check on compliance. Violations, especially when they are repeated or when they cause severe injury to an employee, can be severe, including fines and imprisonment of the managers who are responsible.

Legislation on
Organized Labor

Many employers and managers need give little thought to organized labor legislation because their workers do not belong to unions and have not shown any interest in joining one. For many other employers, though, this area of regulation includes some important restrictions. The National Labor Relations Act of 1935 specifically forbids certain kinds of "unfair labor practices." Under this act (also called the Wagner Act), an employer cannot interfere through force or dominance in the formation of a labor union, cannot discriminate against people who belong to or want to join a union, and cannot refuse to collectively bargain with a legally chosen union.

The Labor-Management Relations Act of 1947 added provisions restricting practices that unions could use. Except in certain cases under this act (also called the Taft-Hartley Law) a union cannot, for example, force a worker to join, refuse to bargain collectively, or require an employer to pay for work that has not been done.

The Labor-Management Reporting Act of 1959 required unions and employers to report much more thoroughly on their relations, especially in financial matters. Its main purpose is to counteract racketeering in labor unions and to prevent employers from using payoffs to get preferential treatment from unions. It also prohibits certain union practices like those specified in the 1947 labor law. For instance, a union cannot picket organizations it is unsuccessfully trying to unionize.

REGULATIONS TRY TO
PROTECT CONSUMERS

To a great extent, the relationship between producers and buyers is still a private matter; responsible management remains the best guarantee of quality products and fair treatment. Certain government agencies, however, take an active part in enforcing a fair deal for consumers. False or grossly misleading advertising, for instance, is prohibited by the Federal Trade Commission under its powers to prevent unfair competition. The philosophy behind this FTC regulation is that false advertising is damaging to other producers trying to sell similar products, and is for that reason anticompetitive; thus the regulation protects consumers as well as businesses from deceptive advertising.

The Food, Drug,
and Cosmetic Act

Among the earliest efforts of the federal government to legislate the quality of privately produced goods was the Pure Food and Drug Act of 1906. That act was considerably expanded in 1938 by the Food, Drug, and Cosmetic Act. Both acts give the Food and Drug Administration (FDA) broad powers to ensure the sanitary preparation, purity of content, and proper labeling of cosmetics and products that are consumed internally. The effectiveness and safety of new drugs must be proved before they are sold to the public. Food and drug labels must show accurate weight, list ingredients, and show additives and colorings used. After a 1962 amendment, the FDA has been required to withdraw approval of drugs that have been generally recognized as safe in the past if new evidence points to their likely harmful effects.

The Truth-In-Lending Act

The extension of credit, both in the form of direct loans from banks and in financing plans from retail stores, has been heavily regulated for some time. The Truth-In-Lending Act (enacted in 1969, and also called the Consumer Credit Protection Act) is a clear reflection of the goals of the consumerism movement. Its thrust is to assure that consumers have complete information about the terms of a lending agreement. The consumer is then free to accept the terms or to reject them. The law requires that lenders clearly inform borrowers of the total amount owed, of the annual interest rate expressed in a percent, and of any other charges that will be made for processing the loan.

The Truth-In-Packaging Act

This act (passed in 1965 and also called the Fair Packaging and Labeling Act) also requires that producers give buyers accurate information about their products. A package label must clearly and accurately identify the contents of the package, accurately and prominently show the amount in weight or volume, and give the net quantity of a serving if the package makes any claims like "serves six."

Other labeling laws apply to specific products. Wool products must show the total fiber content and give some information about how the wool was processed and mixed with other fibers. Fur products must show the correct name of the animal from which the fur came and give further information about the processing that was given the fur. Cloth and other materials used for clothing must accurately be identified. Labels must show what care is needed for clothes.

Product Liability and Warranties

Product liability refers to the responsibility of a manufacturer or seller of a product to compensate a buyer who has been injured by the product. By 1976, companies in the United States had over a million such claims filed against them, for a total of $50 billion in damages. This was largely due to passage of the Consumer Product Safety Act, of 1972, which reversed the concept of "buyer beware" to "seller beware." A *warranty* is a contractual promise, written or implied, made by the seller. The warranty usually is made with regard to a product's performance or durability, together with what the firm commits itself to do in order to repair (or refund) products that do not measure up to the promise. Much of the supporting law for warranties and liability resides in the Uniform Commercial Code, a set of state-approved guidelines for making and ruling on business contracts. Additionally, specific regulations affecting warranties are set forth in the Magnuson-Moss Warranty and Federal Trade Commission Improvement Act.

Legislation Affecting Automobile Manufacturing

Because of the major role the automobile plays in our society, it is not surprising that the process of designing, making, and selling cars has received a good deal of legislative attention. The Automobile Information Disclosure Act, passed in 1958, for instance, requires auto makers to clearly show a breakdown of the costs of options, preparation, and shipping, and the total suggested retail price.

Two other areas have seen heavy regulation: auto safety and air pollution from cars. Regulations have specified in detail certain features to be included in passenger cars. Seat belts are an obvious example; the search is now on for a substitute for the belts so that drivers and passengers will be protected passively even if they make no effort to protect themselves. Since the automobile has been such a major source of air pollution, the government has set strict standards for the reduction of dangerous chemicals from car exhausts. The emission of hydrocarbons, carbon monoxide, and nitrogen oxides has been greatly reduced between 1968 and the present as a result of these direct federal mandates.

With the coming of fuel shortages in the 1970s, government became interested in the fuel economy of automobiles. Again, direct federal intervention, combined with market pressure, has been effective in significantly changing the auto makers' product; fuel efficiency has improved.

REGULATIONS PROTECT THE PHYSICAL ENVIRONMENT

Nearly all of the improvement in the quality of our physical environment has been brought about by direct legislation and regulation by federal, state, and local governments. Since every organization uses facilities of some kind, many managers must be concerned with complying with government requirements affecting air and water quality. In the auto industry, for example, management decisions are deeply influenced by these regulations. Nearly every phase of operations in that industry has been affected, from the basic design decisions, through the operation of production facilities, to the distribution and sales process, and even in the provision of service and repair after the cars are sold. Government directives that require auto makers to recall faulty cars are visible examples.

Most managers will not be so strongly influenced by regulation. But even in the operation and maintenance of a small office or factory building in a rural area, the force of environmental law will be felt to some degree.

The Environmental
Policy Act

Passed in 1969, this act formally commits the federal government to comprehensive efforts (1) to protect the environment from further damage and (2) to help repair the damage that has already been done. The act establishes a council to consider and recommend federal policy on environmental quality. It also establishes the Environmental Protection Agency and gives EPA the assignment of coordinating federal programs and laws for improving the environment and for enforcing a wide range of specific environmental regulations. For example, EPA had the power to ban the use of DDT as a pesticide in the United States, and did so in 1972. The ban was based on evidence that the pesticide did not break down rapidly in the soil, but kept on harming wildlife for years after spraying had been stopped. The agency also has broad authority for enforcing specific air- and water-pollution-control legislation.

The National
Air Quality
Standards Act

This act is probably the strictest and broadest reaction to environmental damage made by the government. Standards for water quality and stream protection evolved over a considerable period of time. Air-pollution controls were more sudden and have received more resistance because of it. The act was passed in 1970 at the height of public awareness of the extent to which the scale of modern industrial life was capable of affecting something as huge in volume as the atmosphere that surrounds the earth.

The major thrust of the legislation and the regulations that followed its passage has been toward lowering pollution from automobiles and manufacturing plants. The reduction of auto emissions, already discussed, was specified in the law. The act also gave individual states the authority to enact laws to enforce the standards. If they failed to do so, the federal government was authorized to set the regulations for the states. The act further specifies that all new factories are required to use the most effective air-pollution-control devices in their manufacturing processes.

The act allows the Environmental Protection Agency to sue violators and permits private citizens to sue both the agency and the polluters if the government does not take effective action. Companies that violate the provisions of the act can be fined heavily for each day of continued violation. Offending managers or owners may even be sent to jail.

Water Quality
Standards

The 1966 Clean Waters Restoration Act was passed to give the federal government authority to stop the discharge of pollutants into streams and waterways. Industrial pollution of water had grown so severe that one river in the Midwest actually caught on fire. Discharges from human-waste-disposal plants, operated mainly by local governments, were introducing so much biological material into rivers that a huge amount of oxygen was being consumed. The oxygen use left the water unfit for the life that normally existed there. Fish and other river-dwellers died. The federal law and much state and local legislation have begun to bring the water-pollution problem under control.

REGULATIONS SEEK TO PROMOTE COMPETITION

Many government regulations apply to any organization, even to the government itself. One group of laws and regulations, however, is aimed only at business: laws to promote free competition and to protect businesses from unfair competitive practices. This has long been an area of great activity for the federal government. Only free competition can protect businesses, buyers, and the economy as a whole by allowing the influences of the marketplace to function. By the beginning of this century, the power of monopolies had become great enough to threaten the extinction of the private enterprise system. Competition was well on its way to being completely stifled in many areas of commerce.

An extensive body of law including The Sherman Antitrust Act (1890), the Clayton Act (1914), the Robinson-Patman Act (1936), and the Wheeler-Lea Act (1938), among others has emerged to promote free competition. The thrust of these laws is to prohibit business practices that give one company an *unfair* advantage over another. The growth of very large companies is seldom seen today as being disadvantageous in itself to competition. Large companies, the law implies, are dangerous only if they use their power with the specific intent of eliminating competitors so they can control an entire market and set prices so high that they are damaging to the economy. It is illegal for a grocery chain, for example, to start business in a new town and charge prices 50 percent lower than the other stores in town; the law implies that the store's intent is to drive the other local stores out of business.

The Federal Trade Commission Act

This act was passed in 1914 as part of the government effort to combat monopolies. It created the Federal Trade Commission to enforce regulations against unfair competitive practices. The powers and range of duties of the commission have grown over the years. Today the FTC is an important force in consumer protection and safety. It has the power, for example, to force companies to retract false advertising or to make adjustments when discriminatory pricing policies have been followed.

REGULATIONS CONTROL THE ISSUANCE AND EXCHANGE OF STOCKS AND BONDS

Legitimate corporations regularly issue stocks and bonds to raise funds for their production facilities and to finance operations. At one time, however, it was common for stocks and bonds to be sold by corporations that were not legitimate; they were established for the primary purpose of selling stock so as to swindle unsuspecting investors. Many companies advertised stocks for sale, falsely describing tremendous profits to be made in gold mines, oil drilling, or in manufacturing some consumer gadget. They then took investors' money and sneaked out of town; investors never heard from them again.

Outright fraud was not the only problem. Even companies that were successfully engaged in continuing operations naturally wanted their stock to seem as attractive as possible to buyers. Such companies often misrepresented their chances for profits or exaggerated their assets to make the firms seem more prosperous than they really were. Stock traders caused trouble, too. For instance, if someone who had inside information about a manufacturing company heard that the company was about to take a big loss, that person could keep the information a secret until he or she had unloaded their stock onto others who did not have "inside" information.

Another problem lay with the investors themselves. A speculative mood has always surrounded dealings in corporate stocks. When anticipating large profits on investments in stocks, many speculators borrowed huge sums of money, often more than they could afford to pay back, to buy more and more stocks. These investors intended to use the future proceeds and profits from the sale of their stocks to repay the loans and interest. Frequently, though, there were no profits, and speculators had to sell for far less than they had paid. If they had no other resources to repay their loans, they were financially ruined. If enough people were ruined at one time, as happened during the stock market crash of 1929, the disruption was serious enough to trigger problems in the entire economy.

The Federal Securities Act

Regulation to prevent some of the abuses connected with the issuance and sale of stock began in 1909. This marked the date when the U.S. Post Office was able to get legislation passed making it a crime to use the mails for defrauding others. The most significant investment regulation, however, came during the great Depression in the early 1930s. In 1933, Congress passed the Federal Securities Act. It required corporations issuing stock to the public to give potential investors all pertinent information about the company so as to truthfully guide the investors in judging the likely profitability of their investment. The law set up two main requirements. A company issuing stock must: (1) file a detailed registration statement describing the company assets, liabilities, and operations and telling how the revenue from the stock issue will be used; and (2) summarize the detailed information of this statement in a *prospectus* and give this prospectus to every potential buyer of the stock. The registration laws applied mainly to businesses; nonprofit organizations were exempt, as were cooperatives. Sales that took place entirely within a single state, or that were made individually to private investors without a public offering, also were not covered by the registration laws.

The Federal Securities
Exchange Act

Congress extended federal control over sales of stocks and bonds in 1934 with the passage of the Federal Securities Exchange Act. The act created the Securities and Exchange Commission (SEC) to enforce regulations in this area. The SEC has the authority to stop the sale of an issue of stocks or bonds for any purpose if it has reason to believe the issue violates federal law. The 1934 act also imposed the following regulations beyond those specified in the 1933 securities law:

1. All companies listed on a major stock exchange must file an annual registration statement, even if they are not in the process of issuing new stocks or bonds.
2. Stock dealers connected with national exchanges are not allowed to use inside information to enrich themselves or to manipulate stock prices.
3. Investors are not allowed to finance more than a stated proportion of stock purchased by borrowing. The allowed proportion is changed depending on economic conditions.

In general, federal regulations of the sales of stocks and bonds follow the directions of consumerism as applied to other kinds of products sold to the general public. They require the seller to provide the buyer with enough information to make an informed buying decision. They outlaw fraud and they limit the exercise of power that accompanies the possession of inside knowledge.

STATE AND LOCAL
GOVERNMENTS
ALSO INFLUENCE
ORGANIZATIONS

Federal laws in general apply only to organizations that are in some way involved in activities that cross state lines. For example, a company that manufactures in one state but buys materials or sells products in other states (or a charity that solicits money nationally) is subject to applicable federal laws. The separate states, townships, counties, or cities also have numerous laws and regulations that managers must take into account. For example, an engineering company located in a town near a large city may have to consider regulations from the town, from its surrounding county, from the nearby city, if it does business there, from regional water and sanitation authorities, from the state, and from numerous federal commissions and agencies.

State agencies usually govern banking, financing, and credit transactions within their jurisdiction. They may limit the amount of interest legally charged or, for the protection of the lender, they may require certain levels of collateral or security on specified loans.

States normally have complex requirements that protect the health and safety of citizens and employees. In addition to meeting federal requirements for air emissions and sewage treatment and disposal, a corporation may also have to deal with state and local regulations. Most states also enforce strict rules on sanitation in the processing and serving of food products.

Many states control discriminatory pricing. They make it illegal to sell at different prices for different customers *unless* the price difference can be justified by the varying quality of the products, by quantity orders, or in some other way.

State and local governments almost always require some kind of licensing for formal organizations, especially for businesses. These licenses are often merely a form of tax, since a fee is charged for them. In the licensing process, the governments may set certain requirements for operations and reporting that the organization must meet. State and local governments may also sell franchises; a cable TV company is one example. If the company wants to establish service within a county, it may have to pay the county a franchise fee for the right to operate there. Along with the franchise often come local regulations that partly determine the ways the company can operate.

Most local governments, on the parish, county, township, town, and city level have zoning and building ordinances that partly limit the freedom of decision making for organizations. For example, zoning may prohibit the construction of an office building or factory in most areas of a town. Some zoning ordinances are even so strict as to prevent changes in an existing facility. Building codes specify certain details of construction to ensure that the final building will be safe for the people who use it. Some of the procedures required by building codes, especially for large buildings such as factories, contribute significantly to costs. Differences in building and zoning requirements can be so important that they sway managers' decisions about the areas in which to locate their facilities.

SUMMARY

1. Nearly every decision a manager will make will be influenced at least to a minor extent by the network of federal, state, and local regulations. Each manager is responsible for knowing and adhering to the laws and regulations that apply to his or her position or area of responsibility.

2. Federal law affects personnel and staffing decisions through requiring minimum wages and the payment of overtime, through the requirements for equal opportunity in hiring and promotion, through the regulations to provide every employee a safe place to work, and through federal involvement with and partial regulation of management-labor relations.

3. Organizations that deal directly with consumers are limited by federal laws requiring sanitary and safe food, drugs, and cosmetics, by requirements for full and accurate disclosure in lending and packaging, and by other regulations that define the liability of certain products, such as automobiles.

4. Nearly every manager will be faced with regulations to protect and improve the quality of the physical environment. These laws center on the prevention of air and water pollution by reducing automobile emissions, decreasing the chemical emissions of manufacturing processing, and requiring thorough treatment of human and chemical liquid and solid waste.

5. Businesses are also regulated to protect the free competition needed for the success of the private enterprise system. The laws forbid unfair competitive practices such as false advertising and temporary underpricing to drive competitors out of business.

6. Corporations that use the public sale of stocks and bonds to provide financing are subject to regulations prohibiting fraud, manipulation, and deceit in securities sales and exchanges.

7. State and local governments further regulate and influence organizations through health and safety requirements, credit and interest laws, pricing regulations, licensing, franchising, and zoning and building ordinances.

REVIEW AND DISCUSSION QUESTIONS

1. According to the text, line managers must accept the responsibility for complying with government regulations. Why must they do so, rather than leaving it up to lawyers or the legal department?

2. Paul, who is a manager in a heavily regulated business, says, "There are two main things wrong with all this regulation." What might the two be, from a manager's point of view?

3. What are the two most important requirements of the Fair Labor Standards Act that a manager would have to be aware of?

4. Carla wants to use a written test to help her select from among the people who have applied for a job opening in her department. What would she have to be able to prove about the test in order to comply with Equal Employment Opportunity regulations?

5. What is the *main* goal of both the Truth-In-Lending Act and the Truth-In-Packaging Act?

6. Differentiate between product liability requirements and a warranty.

7. Why has the federal government passed so many laws and regulations to promote free competition?

8. What is the main purpose of the Federal Trade Commission? Give an example of a business practice it can prohibit.

9. What is a prospectus? Why are corporations that are issuing stocks or bonds required to give one to prospective buyers?

Problems and Projects

1. The statements below represent violations of the goals of the following federal laws affecting organizations:
    a. Environmental Policy Act
    b. Equal Employment Opportunity Act
    c. Fair Labor Standards Act
    d. Federal Securities Act
    e. Federal Trade Commission Act
    f. Food, Drug, and Cosmetic Act
    g. National Air Quality Standards Act
    h. Occupational Safety and Health Act
    i. Truth-In-Lending Act
    j. Truth-In-Packaging Act

On a separate sheet of paper, write the numbers 1 to 10 corresponding to the actions below, and beside each write the letter of the law to which the violation relates.

(1) The Acme Brush Company forced its employees to work 60-hour weeks and paid no overtime.

(2) Huygens Drugs, Inc. sold a new antibiotic to the general public without testing it for safeness or effectiveness.

(3) The management of Tecknicult Co. continued processing in the plant even though it knew that potentially explosive vapors had collected.

(4) It was a policy of the Keystone Lending Company not to reveal the total interest rate on their loans even when borrowers asked.

(5) Grayson Corporation sold its stock through flashy ads in national magazines and did not give a prospectus.

(6) The brand new factory of Black Manufacturing poured huge quantities of sulfer dioxide from its stacks even though effective control devices were available.

(7) The Main Course Macaroni Dinner says on the wrapping that it serves twelve people, but doesn't give a serving size. If you work it out, each serving is less than a tablespoon.

(8) Even though the Environmental Protection Agency said not to, the Bolling Company went ahead with their plans as originally designed.

(9) Faight Wholesalers refused to sell to the stores in one town because Faight wanted to drive them out of business and set up its own retail stores there.

(10) Exton Securities Company used an employment test that had little relation to the skills needed on the job and that clearly discriminated against minorities.

2. *Performance Situation—Regulation Down on the Farm:* Georgia Produce made a lot of money. Taking advantage of a buying trend it had spotted, the company started a marketing plan called "Home-Made Gift-of-the-Month." Now, four years later, the company has stopped selling to wholesalers and does all of its marketing by direct-mail sales through the Gift-of-the-Month club. There had been only one problem along the way. Another company, seeing Georgia Produce's beginning success, had started a similar club. Georgia Produce reacted swiftly, cutting its prices temporarily below the costs of manufacturing, to a level the other club couldn't begin to compete with. When the other club's sales began to flounder, Georgia Produce bought it. GP then raised its own prices considerably higher than they had been to make up the losses resulting from the former deep cuts.

Georgia Produce's products were pickles, jams, jellies, relishes, and similar edible goods. The company's unique selling point is brought out in their ads: "Organically-grown, all natural, homemade delicacies from our country kitchens in the Georgia countryside." The company buys its fruits and vegetables from local farmers and from wholesalers in Atlanta and agents in New York. No check is made on how the produce is grown, since many of the fruits and vegetables come from as far away as Mexico and Oregon.

Georgia Produce uses mass-production techniques for making its products, but control is lax. The managers make no systematic inspections of the quantities in the jars; many have been shipped that were as much as 20 percent underweight. Their "Pure Quince Jelly" actually contains nearly 60 percent apples because the apples are needed to make the jelly set. The label of the blackberry preserves says, "Fresh blackberries simmered to perfection in old-fashioned kettles." The preserves are actually made from frozen berries boiled under pressure in 1,000 gallon vats.

Employee turnover is very high at Georgia Produce. During certain seasons, workers must routinely put in 12 hours a day. Even though the company is very generous with overtime pay, paying double the regular rate for hours over 40 in a week, conditions are so poor that workers often do not stay for a whole week. A particular problem has been the escape of high pressure steam, which has caused several injuries during the last three years. Some employees object to the quality of the product. One vat tender said, "They're organic preserves, all right: flies, mice, straw, dirt." The company continued to use a certain dye in its cherry preserves and tomato relish even after the dye had been banned; they could find no other way to get the color they wanted.

A unique feature of Georgia Produce's Gift-of-the-Month club that makes it so attractive to the company is the way bills are written and collected. The company sends only two bills each year to each customer, each after six months. Not only does this save money on billing and mailing, but it allows an interest charge to be built into the bill. The company is actually extending credit to its customers and adds a 1½ percent interest charge for each month, even though the charge is not identified as interest on the bill. They also add a 10 percent service charge to make up for credit losses caused by the delayed billing.

Analyze the operations of Georgia Produce from the point of view of compliance with government regulations. List all of the violations you can spot. You should find at least six. Identify the violations according to type (false advertising, for example).

3. Think about Georgia Produce, described in Problem 2, from another point of view. Consider each of the management functions in turn—planning, controlling, organizing, staffing, and directing—and evaluate the extent to which each appears to be successfully carried out in the company. If you had to pick two of the functions that particularly needed improvement, which two would they be? What kind of improvements would you propose in the two areas if you became a new manager for this company?

4. The passage and enforcement of the Occupational Safety and Health Act has caused noticeable disruption in the operations of some organizations. The regulations are complex and often require a wide range of minor changes in facilities and operations to bring an organization into compliance. Use what you have learned elsewhere in this text to propose a brief plan for ensuring that an organization that you manage will comply with the regulations of the act. Write the plan as if you actually were about to carry it out. If it were your responsibility, what would you do to see that the organization met the requirements?

5. Four situations having to do with fair and unfair competition are described below. For each of the cases, tell whether it complies with the *goals* of federal regulations prohibiting unfair competition. If the practice described appears to you to be a violation, propose other ways the company might try to achieve its aims of profitability without breaking the law.

   a. Berwyn Garments, Inc. radically changed the design and materials in its line of winter coats so as to be able to sell for $60 a coat that superficially looked like another manufacturer's coat with a $130 price tag.

   b. Hydra Industries systematically bought out all of the ball bearing manufacturers in the country so it could control the market and charge much higher prices.

   c. Margold Candy Company sold its products at a very low markup (the average price per box was $1.10) to any store that carried their candy line exclusively. Stores that carried other competing lines either could not get any service from Margold at all or were charged prices as high as $3.50 per box. Margold products were very popular, and more and more stores began to refuse to carry competing brands.

   d. Silverstone Manufacturing makes outdoor grills. Silverstone raised the prices on its leading unit by 19 percent in an effort to increase profits. The unit was popular enough so that sales fell only slightly, in spite of the increased cost. When other manufacturers saw Silverstone's success, they also raised their prices by exactly the same percentage.

6. Corporations have special regulatory problems because they must deal

with the general public in the process of raising their basic capital. Governments have moved to protect the public from abuses in the issuance of stocks and bonds. Central Data, Inc. is a medium-sized corporation in Indiana. It started as a privately owned company, and had incorporated only when it needed a large investment to increase its market area to embrace the entire Midwest. Central raised the money by selling stock to the public. Its managers knew that computer-service stocks were attractive, and they decided to handle the stock sale like any other marketing campaign. The managers were inexperienced in the process of making a public offering. They sold the stock directly themselves. They had no contact at all with any federal or state regulatory agency. They gave investors little real information about the company. Instead, Central stressed the amount of money investors could expect to make. When Central got a major service contract shortly after they had issued their stock, stock prices were expected to go up rapidly. The president of Central had a friend on the Chicago stock exchange and gave her an advance tip about the important contract. She was the only one who knew about the expected rise and was able to buy many shares at a low price and sell them a month later at a high price.

Have any laws been broken here? If so, name them and describe their provisions that apply to this case.

Cases for Analysis and Discussion

CASE 1: AVOIDANCE
AT ALL COSTS

Charles Morgan was a good manager in most ways. He worked hard; he knew his business; he was fair to his employees. One thing his employees always dreaded, though, was when Charles said—and he said it often—"Here, you take care of this; it's another one of those regulations. They're going to put us out of business."

Dana Wysocki was one of those who heard this statement most often. One day, Charles handed her a thick packet of materials in a folder labeled "Equal Employment Opportunity Regulations and Guidelines for Private Businesses." His only instruction was the usual, "Here, take care of this."

Dana tried. She learned the regulations cold. As a lawyer she was more used to the kind of language of the regulations than many people. Still, they were complex, even to her. After considerable study, she drew up a summary of what the laws call for, and gave it to Charles. He sent the summary back with a note attached: "See that we do the absolute minimum to avoid breaking the law. That's what the legal department's for."

Dana tried again. To avoid breaking the law required quite a few changes. Hiring was a particular problem. Dana sat down with the people in personnel and worked out some sweeping changes. For one thing, they decided to eliminate employment tests altogether, because they felt they couldn't come up with a test that they could prove was effective.

A couple of months later, Charles stormed into Dana's office. "Who are these numbskulls we've got working on the assembly line! Do you know what a jam-up we've got down there? Nothing like this has ever happened before. From now on, you'd better stay out of the personnel department. Out! Who gave you authority over the personnel department, anyway?"

A. Is this incident just one of those things that happens in organizations, or is someone at fault?

B. What is the basic problem here? If you see more than one thing wrong, describe them.

C. How could the people involved have avoided this incident? Is there anything they should do routinely in the future?

CASE 2: BACK TO THE SALT MINES

"I'll bet if I were an Anglo-American I'd be sitting in that corner office now instead of out in the cow pens. There's no way for anyone to get a promotion around here unless they came from Brookline and went to Yale!"

Manuel Ruiz had just lost out on a chance for advancement he had been counting on. In fact, the way things worked out he got what looked to him like a demotion. When Will Steele was promoted to department head, Manuel was transferred to take Will's job. Manuel thought the job he had before was better.

Manuel hadn't finished his complaint. "There was every reason to pick me for department manager. I've been here longer. I've worked in more different jobs in the department. I know better how it works. Who was it that worked out the Interstate mess? Who was it that got the funding for the Greenway project? I'll bet you can't point to any reason at all for picking Steele over me."

Manuel's boss answered. "Not promoting you at this time has nothing to do with your ethnic background. It wasn't realistic for you to expect to be promoted now, anyway. We've talked about this twice a year for several years, every time we have our appraisal session. The reason you're not ready for a spot as department head is that you have no supervisory experience to speak of. You have no training in management. In addition, you've shown time and again that you have trouble getting along with the other people in the department. We've offered you opportunities to improve in every one of these areas. You could have been head of the field inspection crew; you'd have had 20 people to supervise and gotten lots of experience. But you didn't want it because you thought a field job was beneath you. We offered to send you to school at night to get a degree in management, but you didn't want to do that. You've shown interest only in the technical parts of your job. I've offered many times to talk with you about the problems you have with the others in the department, but you never wanted to. You always said you didn't need any help."

A. Manuel is thinking about filing a suit charging his employer with unfair discrimination. Do you think he should?
B. What is your opinion of Manuel's boss's answer? Are the reasons convincing?
C. If Manuel did file a suit, what would his boss need to back up the case that his action was not discriminatory?

CASE 3: THE SAFETY CHECKLIST

"You know, Betty, this consumer business is starting to get dangerous. I think we've always done the best we could for customers, but imagine what would happen if we accidentally let some products slip through that were dangerous! It was a little different fifteen years ago. Today, with the new regulations and with juries giving such big settlements to people who are hurt, it could put us out of business. That's your area. See what you can come up with. We ought to have some kind of procedure or routine to try to make sure we don't get in a spot where someone is hurt by our products and then comes after us."

Although Betty was in the marketing department, she was very closely involved with product design and even with quality control. She was the logical person to ask to study the problem, though she might not have the formal authority to carry out any changes that were needed. She sat down with the assignment off and on for the next two weeks. She talked to other people in her company and made several calls to some of her friends in the management association and in her marketing club. She came up with the following checklist of what should be done.

1. Include a formal step in the product-design process for predicting product failures and results of failures.
2. Begin in-house testing of the quality and composition of raw materials.
3. Set up a continuing procedure for scanning outside research in product performance and safety.
4. Analyze existing products for potential failures, and use independent laboratories to investigate any faults located.
5. Continually analyze customer complaints to locate any indications of unknown dangers from products.
6. Review product information given to customers.
7. Educate salespeople about safety features and about what, if anything, may cause the features to fail.[1]

[1]Information in part from: "Consumerism: The Mood Turns Mean," *Sales Management*, July 15, 1969, p. 40.

A. What do you think of this checklist? What is good about it? What is bad about it?

B. If a company actually made this much effort and still produced a product that was accidentally dangerous, do you think the company should have to pay damages?

C. What can you think of to add to the checklist?

CASE 4: ON THE ONE HAND; ON THE OTHER HAND

The state office of consumer affairs had broad powers given by the legislature to set regulations to protect consumer interests in the state. The actual number of regulations that had been produced by the agency was quite small, however, because of a raging battle between two points of view within the agency itself. One group, which included the agency head, had a background in business. The members of this group tended to look on regulations mainly as a hindrance to business managers. They argued that managers had a right to use private property and to run their privately owned companies as they saw best. Regulations cost money, they said, and if government increases business overhead too much it will be damaging to the economy and to the consumers in turn.

The other group conceded that regulations cost money, but argued that the direct interests of consumers were more important. This group tended to use case histories in its arguments: the woman up North who had burned to death because her electric heater was faulty and set the house on fire; the boy on the coast who poked his eye out on a very unsafe toy. They were vehement that these problems could be solved without damaging the economy significantly. One strong spokesperson was heard to say: "If you've burned to death while asleep, it's not going to make much difference to have a strong economy."

A. What do you think about this dispute? Which side are you on?

B. Is the pro-business group necessarily anti-consumer?

C. Is there any kind of hard evidence that you think might be useful in settling this dispute?

Managers Work
in Specific Fields

6

Executive-Level Management

17

After completing Chapter 17, you will be able to do the following:

- Differentiate between the roles and responsibilities of the top executives of an organization and those of lower-level managers.
- Identify and describe six tasks that must be accomplished by the top-management team in every organization.
- Analyze an organizational situation to determine if provision has been made for performing all top-management tasks.
- Relate operational opportunities to the task of defining the purpose and direction of an organization.
- Judge whether organizational plans include essential top-level strategies.
- Analyze an organization and its environment to determine whether the organization is the right size; name two ways to increase and two ways to decrease organization size.
- Describe an advantage and a disadvantage of diversification.

Look at the organization chart in Figure 17-1 on page 392, showing one internal structure for a manufacturing company. The goods produced could be anything from matchsticks to giant oil tankers. The basic functions are the same in any manufacturing company. Someone has to get materials and perform a manufacturing process on them. Someone has to sell the goods to customers. Someone has to handle the money and protect the assets of the organization.

In the chart, each of these functions is handled by a specific manager. Bob Perlucci, Tony Carbone, and Mac Lendon take care of production; Muriel Albers manages purchasing and Zip Lord handles quality control. May Marshall takes care of advertising and Roger Brown oversees distribution. Al Smith, Agnes Riggo, and Ramon Perez handle direct sales. Peter Busch approves major credit purchases by customers, and Nathan Cohn is responsible for collecting the company's accounts.

But if the managers at the lower levels take care of purchasing, manufacturing, quality control, marketing, accounting and finance, and the like, what do president Louise Bregg and vice presidents Gil Chapman, Harvey Shell, and Claudia Gold do? Could their positions be eliminated, saving the company a lot of money in salaries?

The answer, at least in a well-run organization, is an emphatic no. Even though middle-level managers may in fact accomplish most of the operational work of an organization, much work and responsibility remains for top-level people. Middle managers are essential to, but not sufficient for, organizational success. If middle managers are responsible for the major functions of directly making a product or providing a service and delivering it to customers or clients, what is the contribution of top managers?

Figure 17-1. Organization Chart for Typical Manufacturing Company.

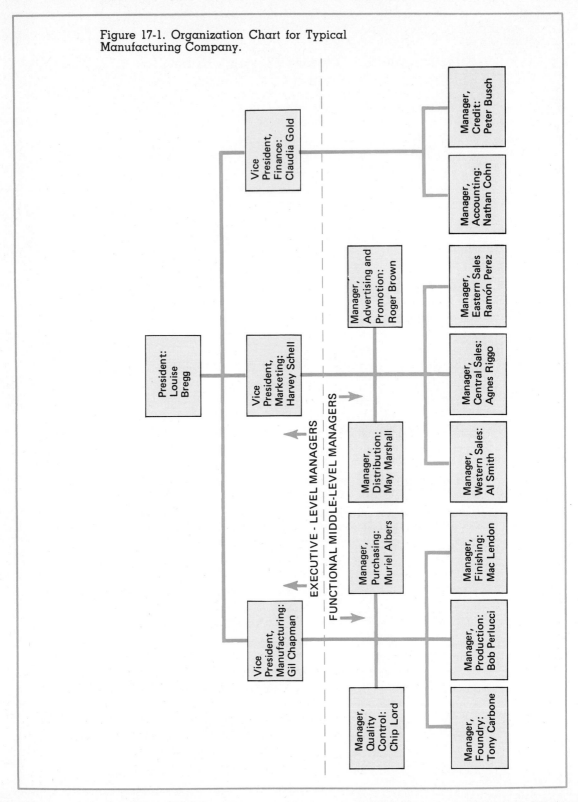

TOP MANAGERS HAVE A DISTINCT JOB

Top managers, or executives, manage: they plan, control, organize, staff, and direct. But they do it from a unique perspective. The span of interest of top managers is extended both in relation to the parts of the organization and in the length of time that is considered centrally important.

An *executive* may be defined as someone who has the authority and responsibility for (1) deciding what a whole organization will aim to accomplish and for (2) finding ways to use the resources of the organization to achieve these aims. As used in this chapter, the term "executive" will refer to managers responsible for the total, overall organization; for example, for General Motors with all its branches and divisions, rather than for the finishing department of one of the company's automobile plants. In common use, the term "executive" is often applied to any manager with substantial responsibility. Throughout the following discussion, however, the word will be restricted to managers on whose shoulders the fate of the entire organization rests. These are the people who fill the special role, often called the "executive function," of finding the right niche for the organization in the world at large and of shaping the organization and its resources to function best within that niche.

It is this need to determine the proper character and soundness of the organization to accord with opportunities in the outside world that produces the scope and challenge of the executive job.

A top manager is concerned with the whole organization and with the interrelation of its parts. This includes not only seeing that the right people and methods are available in the component departments to meet goals, but also making sure that departmental goals are coordinated and mutually supporting so the organization as a whole will accomplish its mission.

A top manager is concerned with a longer time span than middle- or lower-level managers. While a first-line supervisor may use daily and weekly results as control points for meeting quarterly goals, top-level managers typically use quarterly and annual results as signs of movement toward five-year or even ten-year objectives.

Defining the nature of the entire organization and establishing its role in the economy and in society is uniquely the job of executive management. Performing this job requires a range of skills, knowledge, and abilities. The ability to analyze diverse information and draw inferences and conclusions is essential. The ability to influence others and discern their motives and goals is also needed. Key executives must display aggressiveness, force, and the knack for putting themselves and others into purposeful action. They must be able to represent the organization and its interests to people and groups outside the organization.

This diversity of skills needed at the top requires one further characteristic of executive management: the ability and inclination to form part of a team effort. Rarely, if ever, will one man or woman combine all of the skills needed to set and maintain the direction of a major organization. It is doubtful that a single person could perform all the required tasks of top management, even for the smallest enterprise. Thus, top management is usually a team.

EXECUTIVES PERFORM SIX
ESSENTIAL TASKS
Although executive managers fulfill the same basic functions as other managers, there are notable differences in emphasis and in the character of goals. The studies of Peter F. Drucker provide important insights into these differences in the role of executive-level management.

Drucker's Classification of Executive-Level Duties

Drucker has suggested that six tasks are particular to the role of high-level executives:[1]

1. Determining the mission of the organization.
2. Maintaining standards.
3. Building the human organization.
4. Maintaining outside relations.
5. Taking part in "ceremonial" functions.
6. Dealing with crises.

DETERMINING THE MISSION   The *mission* of an organization is its basic purpose or function, broadly defined as its role in society. The mission of a business enterprise is the creation and distribution of goods and services to meet the needs of people in society. The mission of a local government is to preserve order in its jurisdiction and to provide the services requested by its citizens. An organization would not exist without some mission. Top managers have the responsibility of continually redefining the mission, or purpose, as conditions change. The top management of a town government, for instance, must repeatedly examine the expectations of its citizens, the demands of state and federal government, resources, and crises, and must continually reshape the exact role the local government will fulfill.

MAINTAINING STANDARDS   Top managers are uniquely responsible for maintaining ethical standards and for setting examples. This is what Drucker calls the "conscience functions." If an organization is to strive for excellence in its products or services and in its relations with society, top managers must lead the way.

---

[1]Peter F. Drucker, *Management: Tasks, Responsibilities, Practices,* Harper and Row, New York, 1974, pp. 611–612.

BUILDING THE HUMAN ORGANIZATION   Every manager is concerned with the development of human resources, making today's employees more capable and training younger employees to handle responsibility in the future. Top management is especially concerned with key high-level personnel because the managers of the organization are the backbone of future success. Top managers must look to building a better team for using and increasing resources.

MAINTAINING OUTSIDE RELATIONS   Many of the most critical contacts with people and groups outside the organization can only be handled by top management. An important supplier, for instance, may be critical to an organization's success because it provides a scarce raw material that must meet precise specifications required by the manufacturing process. The price of the raw material may be the limiting factor in the prices the manufacturer can ultimately charge for its products. A relationship of this importance will often be handled, at least in part, by top executives. The same situation applies when a few major accounts or customers are essential to success. Top managers often maintain relations with government agencies or with legislators because the health of the whole organization demands it.

TAKING PART IN CEREMONIAL FUNCTIONS   Most organizations must play a role in the lives of the communities in which they operate. The plant manager of a corporation will get many invitations to speak at civic activities, to take part in charity drives, to attend award dinners, and so forth. These activities are time consuming, but necessary in maintaining community relations. Some executive functions inside the organization can best be seen as at least partly ceremonial—dinners for retiring employees, for example, or playing softball at the company picnic. These inside activities, though, usually have at least a secondary goal of motivating and rewarding employees or of maintaining good human relations within the organization.

DEALING WITH CRISES   Crises arise in the operations of every organization. When the basic health or existence of the organization is threatened, such as by bankruptcy, government action, or law suits, people in the enterprise look to top management to take charge. Executives should have the skills and special range of experiences to deal directly with crises and protect employees and the organization from danger.

Fitting Executive Duties to the Needs of the Organization

The specific tasks required of top management will vary with the type of organization. In some public agencies, executives must devote nearly all of their time to outside relations. They deal almost exclusively with sources of funding and with legislative affairs. In some companies, top man-

Managers in Action

PRESIDENT
for real estate insurance company

The candidate will direct a staff that administers an insured-warranty program on new homes through 120 licensed member corporations. Annual business is 25 million and growing. Must have demonstrated administrative and managerial abilities. Experience in insurance and housing field would be helpful but not mandatory. Oral communications with individuals and groups of all kinds a prerequisite.

Vice President of Construction
for major industrial and shopping center developer

Must have extensive field and purchasing experience. Entrepreneurial ability and the capacity to integrate finance and marketing activities is essential. Position requires top notch problem solver.

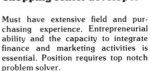

VICE PRESIDENT/ CASHIER
for rapidly growing NATIONAL BANK

Policy level work. Oversees lobby operations, proof and bookkeeping, comptrollership, personnel and security, lending, budgeting, and profit planning. Requires related background and record of sound and seasoned judgment.

Executive Director
for the Preservation Society of Newport, Rhode Island

Accountable for all operations: budget, development, personnel, programs, services, and nine properties including historical buildings and museums.

VICE PRESIDENT/GENERAL MANAGER

for manufacturing company with $25 million in sales

Must be accomplished professional manager. Report to president. Will direct efforts of managers in marketing, manufacturing, industrial relations, finance, engineering, and quality control. If you join us, you must aspire to and have potential to assume a chief executive responsibility.

agers become directly involved in certain functional jobs (advertising or marketing, for instance) if those jobs are absolutely essential to the mission of the organization. In a firm whose health is dependent on continual innovation, top managers may take partial responsibility for new products, and may even serve as idea people. The breadth of experience of executives and their grasp of the needs of the entire organization make them particularly able to function in these areas. The organization needs top managers to accomplish all of the executive tasks, and this underlines the need for a top-management team, with each member handling certain of these responsibilities.

TOP MANAGEMENT SETS DIRECTION AND STRATEGY

The essential role of executives is to define, protect, and energize the entire organization. This is not an abstract process. It is far more specific than merely musing on the function of the enterprise in society. It must focus on a practical approach to creating and maintaining a sound organization. Accordingly, an executive must combine some of the abilities of a visionary with the shrewd reactions of an opportunist.

The president of a company that makes pleasure boats, for example, must first plan—and even dream—of the organization that will exist in five or ten years. Then the president must start making changes in production, marketing, distribution, and finance that will make the dream realizable. At the same time, the executive must keep a calculating eye on actual developments and seize any opportunities that arise. Plans will never anticipate everything. For the boat company, a market may unexpectedly develop for very small, fast, power boats. The top executive is the one who exerts the muscle to reshape operations to exploit the market change.

This dual role of executives—planning and energizing—means they must pay attention to certain key areas of operations. These concerns focus on the purpose and direction of the organization, on its major strategies, on its size and growth, and on the activities and areas of operations that constitute its total function. And as a general rule, the larger and more complex the organization, the greater the time, effort, and attention a chief executive officer must devote to the planning and energizing functions as well as the handling of these key operations and areas of responsibility. *See Figure 17–2* as an illustration of how organizational size and complexity affects the time needed by the chief executive to handle responsibilities.

Purpose and Direction

Defining the mission of the organization is a continuing process. An advertising agency, for example, may be established to operate in a very small niche. It may propose to be expert in the sale of machine tools to industrial customers. The top executive may set up the firm to operate only in that specialty. A year or so later, it may become apparent to the agency executive that there is room to take on other clients selling to the same market. Later, one of the industrial clients may want a campaign designed for a product sold to the consumer market. Later still, the machine-tool-promotion business may wither for one reason or another and be dropped altogether. As a result, the agency may then focus on the consumer market. The firm may change completely through the years as a result of taking advantage of opportunities discovered. At any given time, its management must define the current direction and guide operations to meet current goals.

Major Strategies   A *strategy* is a particular way of combining facilities and resources so they will work together to achieve a major goal. The term originated in military science to describe major deployments of troops and equipment to try to gain important targets in warfare. In management study, strategy refers to the major approaches an organization uses to succeed in a competitive environment. A watch manufacturer, for instance, may adopt the strategy of producing inexpensive copies of other manufacturers' products and selling them at half the price. An employment agency may adopt the strategy of concentrating only on filling job openings that have salaries of $20,000 a year or higher.

Strategies are part of plans. They reflect highest-level goals such as market share, product type and quality, and social responsibility. They are largely the responsibility of top managers, although other managers may make important contributions in specific areas. Strategies may roughly be divided into three classes: operational, organizational, and social.

Operational Strategies   These refer to the productive process of the organization, its products, its methods of creating the products, its choice of and approach to consumers and markets, and its means of obtaining resources.

PRODUCTS STRATEGY   Managers must decide what products will be made or what services will be provided. Generally, the basic product area will be defined in the mission of a business organization. A company president may say, for example, "We're in the oil business." Executive management must turn a general statement like this into one more precise if the company is to find its proper role in the market: "We will use our knowledge of the petroleum industry and our extensive financial resources to provide diversified goods and services to consumers and to other industries." Operational product strategies would break this down further by specifying, for example, the exact petroleum products to be sold, what chemicals will be made, and whether profits will be used for finding more sources of oil or will be devoted to developing other product lines such as coal or nuclear power.

MARKETS STRATEGY   Top managers are usually the ones to decide on the major markets in which an organization will operate. One company may sell almost exclusively to colleges and universities. It would require a top-level decision to begin extensive selling efforts to general consumers. A public agency may serve only the economically disadvantaged. To begin serving anyone who requests help would also take a top-level decision, probably by the legislative body that created the agency.

FINANCE STRATEGY   This strategy is typically set by top management. They must decide where the capital needed for operations will come from and how it will be used. Suppose, for example, that a private company needs more funds and decides to incorporate and sell stock to the public. It is not appropriate for such a decision to be made by a manufacturing manager or a sales manager. Only top executives with an overall view could make such a major change. Executives usually retain control over indebtedness as well, since excess debt can become a serious threat to the organization's health. Also, top executives often become personally involved in seeking major funding from investment or from borrowing.

Organizational Strategies

The essential character of the organization also remains the responsibility of its executives.

INTERNAL STRUCTURE   The top executives must decide whether the organization will have two divisions or ten, whether its structure will be based on products or markets, whether there will be 25 vice presidents or none at all.

PERSONNEL DEVELOPMENT   Top managers must personally ensure that the organization has the key personnel to make it strong now and in the future. They will usually influence directly the selection of higher-level managers such as marketing directors and production managers. They will also take a direct role in developing the people who will be taking their place in the future. Executives themselves can best give younger managers a behind-the-scenes insight into running the whole organization. Developing this kind of skill in successors is an important part of the top-level management job.

Social Strategies

It is clear that the expression of social concern by organizations requires some difficult decisions. The needs of the organization and its people must be balanced with the needs of society. Often, unpleasant compromises must be made. Determining this balance is part of the executive's job. It is the executive who must decide whether to spend money to improve products to benefit consumers. It is the executive who must decide whether installing anti-pollution equipment will bankrupt the company. Top managers set the tone for social responsibility in an organization. They must somehow meld their consciences and their practicality to produce a successful but also beneficial organization.

EXECUTIVES MAKE THE
CRITICAL DECISIONS
An organization's size and structure must fit its mission and its environment. So, too, must the mix of its activities and functions. For many, the temptation to grow is great. For others, the decision to remain small may spell ruin. Accordingly, it falls upon the shoulders of top management to choose the right organizational size and to maintain the optimum functional mix.

Organization Size
Organizations often have a difficult time finding a size that is just right. In some industries, such as auto manufacturing or steel production, a company has to be very large to compete at all. A small company in the steel business is at a real disadvantage. Being small is an advantage in many other commercial areas, such as in producing specialty items or running a flower shop, and certainly in many nonbusiness fields. With small size, overhead is lower and reaction time to new conditions may be faster. Small scale makes personal contact and relations with the outside easier.

Top management must face the facts of its industry and control the size of the organization to make it suit current conditions. To be the wrong size is destructive. If a business is too small, top management must find ways to expand resources so it can compete more effectively. The main ways of growing are by (1) increasing sales, (2) reinvesting profits in the firm, and (3) buying or joining other companies. If a company is already too small to compete, there will be no profits to reinvest or to use to buy other firms.

On the other hand, organizations can also be too large. It is the job of top management to recognize this and do something about it. A local government, for instance, can easily grow beyond an efficient size because of the acquisitive nature of its administrators. Taxes then become burdensome, the production of services becomes inefficient, and the structure becomes more important than the function. The answer is to start paring the organization. Businesses can grow so large that their ability to respond quickly to opportunity is destroyed. A company with a huge share of a single market must be careful about its decisions to grow, because of possible antitrust action; the willingness to accept a smaller share of several different markets might allow the company to compete more aggressively without the risk of antitrust suits. A company that has become a dominant force in its local economy is also limited. It may have to be content to remain as it is or extend its activities into other geographical areas.

The methods of reducing size are often painful. Simply eliminating those functions which contribute least to major goals (cutting out the fat) is the most obvious approach. In many cases, it is the only choice. Such a move takes jobs away from people, and many executives avoid this action even when needed. Another method is *divestment,* selling off part of the functions or products of the company. Where one company may be too big and another may be too small, selling a slice of the big company to the small company may make both companies sounder.

The Makeup of
the Enterprise

Two organizations of the same size may be very different in the mix of activities they pursue. One company with 10,000 employees may produce only a single product, such as an air compressor, to be sold by traditional methods in a single market. Another company with 10,000 employees may make a range of products for different markets, such as fiberglass insulation, bowling balls, and industrial axle bearings. The first company is an example of *concentration*—applying all resources to a strictly limited product and market segment. The second company is an example of *diversification*—competing in a variety of markets with a range of products.

Executives must decide whether their organizational focus will be concentrated or diversified. This is the diversity strategy, and is one of the more difficult decisions they will have to make. Concentration has a disadvantage. If market conditions change so the single product is no longer in demand, the company will have nothing to fall back on. At the same time, diversity has serious drawbacks. Management cannot possibly be as familiar with fifty different products and markets as they could be with one or two. Diversity brings complexity. Different markets require different marketing techniques. Scores of different manufacturing processes may be needed. Processes will require a wide range of starting materials rather than just a few. Storage, transportation, and nearly everything else a company does become more complicated as diversity increases.

One answer to the dilemma appears to be a planned diversity that does not destroy the integrity or manageability of the organization. Executives striving for diversity often still try to move into new fields where facilities, marketing channels, manufacturing processes, and materials overlap with the ones already being used. A company that makes wooden furniture could diversify into the wooden toy market, for instance, applying this strategy. Even though the marketing channels would be different, the expertise already on hand for manufacturing from wood could be directly applied to the new venture. The same company could diversify in another way by manufacturing or purchasing goods for distribution through its existing marketing channels. It could begin the manufacture of plastic or metal decorative items, for instance, for sale through retail furniture stores.

SUMMARY

1. Top managers plan, control, organize, staff, and direct just as other managers do, but they play a distinct role in the organization. Top executives define the entire organization, protect and exploit its resources, and shape its role in the economy and in society.

2. Included in the tasks of top management are (a) determining the mission of the organization, (b) maintaining standards, (c) building the human organization, (d) maintaining outside relations, (e) taking part in ceremonial functions, and (f) dealing with crises. The specific executive tasks for a given organization depend on its size, kinds of services or products, and relationship to markets or environment.

3. Although many operating decisions are best left to middle and lower managers, certain plans and judgments are particularly associated with the role of executives. Top management must continually redefine the purpose and function of the whole organization as conditions change. It must develop major strategies in products, markets, finance, internal structure, personnel development, and in the social role of the organization.

4. Top management must determine the right size for the organization and initiate action to achieve it. It must judge the relative advantages of concentration and diversification and work toward the desired degree of diversification for the particular organization.

REVIEW AND DISCUSSION QUESTIONS

1. If top managers carry on many of the same activities as functional and lower-level managers, what is it that makes their jobs distinct?

2. The success of the chief executive of a major manufacturing firm is considered by her colleagues to be based on a combination of four particular abilities for the job. What could the four be?

3. Why is dealing with and establishing the human organization a key responsibility of executives?

4. The president of a company that makes electronic components from rare and exotic materials insists on maintaining a close personal relationship with the firm's major suppliers. Why?

5. Would the specific tasks of the top management of a company that makes toys for sale to consumers be the same as the tasks of the top managers of a state government? Why or why not?

6. Why does the text say that an executive must combine the abilities of a visionary with the reactions of an opportunist?

7. What is a strategy? How do strategies relate to plans?

8. Why is it that some companies would be more successful if they were bigger, while others would probably be even more successful if they were smaller?

9. A paper manufacturer has decided to diversify into many different areas—food products, franchising auto repair shops, and TV broadcasting, among others. Discuss this decision. What is the major advantage and disadvantage of diversification?

Problems and Projects

1. From the following list of decisions, select the ones that are characteristic of executive management as contrasted with lower-level management. Write the letters of your choices on a separate sheet of paper.
   a. The decision to allow total indebtedness to increase to 40 percent of the value of assets.
   b. Scheduling the use of machinery for production runs.
   c. Deciding to concentrate only on industrial markets.
   d. Organizing a firm on the basis of markets.
   e. Deciding which maintenance engineer to assign to the second shift.
   f. Selecting among candidates for future promotion to division head.
   g. Promoting an outstanding production worker to supervisor.
   h. Testifying before a senate committee on proposed laws affecting the entire industry.
   i. Deciding to sell the industrial tool division because it is too small to compete effectively.
   j. Checking product quality to see that it meets specifications.

2. *Performance Situation—Bob, the Persuader:* Everyone was confident that Bob would come through in an emergency. When federal government auditors had examined Psychological Services, Inc. to look into their use of federal educational funds, serious problems were discovered. The government even threatened to cancel the contract totally. But Bob Miehl, president of Psychological Services, was able to remedy a few performance problems, make some changes in organizational structure and in control procedures, and use his inspired persuasive abilities to get the money continued. His same persuasiveness was invaluable in handling the school board in their continuing relationship. The public schools produced 65 percent of Psychological Services' income, and Bob had them eating out of his hand. If Bob could handle the school board, which was as hard to deal with as Ghengis Khan's mischievous brother, it goes without saying that Bob was a big hit whenever he made one of his frequent appearances at a local civic organization or club. After Bob had given a speech at the Rotary Club one day, a large local company gave Psychological Services a tidy contract with no further investigation or negotiation.

Bob admitted that he enjoyed the limelight. Whenever someone in the organization complained that too many control problems were cropping up or that scheduling of the consultants and counselors was getting hopelessly snarled, Bob answered, "Those are just low-level problems; I keep the contracts coming in. The more contracts the better, no matter what they are. Those other things will get solved."

Peter F. Drucker suggests a partial list of six tasks that every top manager or top-management team must accomplish (page 393). Analyze this case and indicate which of the six tasks are covered by the executives of this organization and which are not. Propose two or three steps the top managers could take to make sure all of the tasks are taken care of.

3. Psychological Services, described in Problem 2, is a business set up to make a profit. It provides psychological consulting to anyone who is willing to pay for it and provides direct counseling for school students, employees, and managers under contracts with the school system and with private companies. Two major developments now face the company. The first is that a new state law has made a good deal of money available for private or public agencies to provide direct therapy for people with mental health problems. This is a totally new area for Psychological Services. If it enters this field it will have to revamp the organization, hire new people, and retrain some of its present employees. The second development concerns size. Bob's practice of taking any contract that is available has resulted in the firm having to cover a very large geographical area. Some of the firm's consultants spend as much time traveling as they do consulting. There simply is not enough business in the local area to support a company as big as Psychological Services. The problem is that these far-flung clients are proving to be unprofitable, in spite of the fact that travel expenses are included in the original contracts.

Analyze this situation as if you were a member of the top-management team of this company. How would you react to these two developments? Would you change any of the company's operational strategies? Why or why not? What would you do about its size? Write a description, in one or two sentences, of the mission of this firm.

4. Size is difficult to manage in an organization. Finding out the right size and taking action to correct errors in size are common problems for top managers. Consider these two situations:

- *Government agency A* is responsible for all state recreational programs, for enforcing fish and game laws, for proposing legislation on preserving the natural environment, and for enforcing existing preservation laws. The agency has 47 employees, of whom 29 are engaged full-time in routine office administration. The director has judged that the agency is almost completely ineffective in accomplishing the tasks required of it by law.

- *Government agency B* is charged with a single task: managing the state's workmen's compensation program. It has 830 employees, or an average of 33 workers for each county in the state. A significant number of the employees devote their time to personnel processing for the other employees; three people work full-time on payroll, for example.

What is wrong with these two organizations? Describe two actions that the managers of each agency might take to improve matters.

5. In the library or in your general reading, locate an article that discusses a business organized as a conglomerate. Business periodicals such as *Busi-*

ness Week, Fortune, and *Forbes* have given considerable attention to conglomerates, especially in the years between 1968 and 1974. What is a conglomerate? What are the product lines of one of those described in the article? Why was the conglomerate formed? What advantages to this form of organization are mentioned? Does the article give any indication of the long-term manageability of this kind of organization?

6. As an individual project (or in conjunction with two or three other classmates) schedule a brief interview with the top management of your school. Concentrate on the issue of size and growth. Does the school want to grow in size? If so, how will it be accomplished? Will growth come about by enlarging present activities or by adding new ones? What are the advantages of the school's current size? What are the disadvantages? How would growth help? Would there be any reason for the school to become *smaller*? Report on and discuss the findings in class.

Cases for Analysis and Discussion

CASE 1: THE FINANCE WIZARD

Judy Beck started her career as an investment analyst for a New York securities dealer. One of the companies she studied in that job was so impressed with her understanding of the finance process that it offered her a job managing the company investments. Judy moved into responsibility for financing the company's expansion when a major new product was added. Slowly but surely she moved up the corporate ladder. Finance was always her specialty; she was a genius at it.

After 13 years with the company, Judy Beck was elected president when, in the midst of a company crisis, the former president unexpectedly resigned. The crisis involved the near impossibility of selling a proposed bond offering at a reasonable price. The income from the bonds was absolutely essential to retooling the firm's one manufacturing plant. The problem was financial, and the board turned to their financial wizard, Judy Beck.

The problem was solved in three months. In a complicated series of moves—combining the bond purchases with stock options, personally promising to be freer with dividends, and selling hard and long—Beck was able to get the bonds placed at a price that was far more favorable than had seemed possible. Some people felt the stock had been diluted, but there were no major complaints. The board beamed.

Now, three years later, some board members were still beaming, some were angry and disillusioned, some were merely confused. The company's stock was more valuable than it had ever been. The organization had a sounder financial structure than any of its competitors, but serious trouble was brewing in the board room. "What's going to happen to earnings next year, and the year after that?" one of the board members demanded. "Where are the new products that were in the works when you took over? Every meeting it's the same: 'Work is progressing,' you say. Well, it had better progress far enough so we get something on the market. Barr Industries has got some new equipment coming out that's going to shoot us out of the water. What are you going to do about it?"

A. Is the board doing its job here? If there is a problem, shouldn't Judy Beck have heard about it before now?

B. Is it wrong for Beck to concentrate on her specialty of finance? Why or why not?

C. What is the answer here? What is Beck doing wrong, if anything?

CASE 2: THE WALNUT-PANELED OFFICE

"Pure solid walnut," thought George, "and it's all mine." George Jenkins was admiring the discreet gleaming of the brand new paneling in his huge office. Admittedly, it had cost a fortune, but it was worth it to George. It wasn't his money, anyway.

George managed Arrow Industries, formerly a provider of optically level equipment-bench installations, now a producer of a little of this and a little of that. George had forced growth. He had acquired companies that no one else would touch. He had used every cent of revenue to finance expansion. He had hired staff members and then allowed them to make up their own jobs. The new personnel always seemed to need more new personnel to help them with the work they found to do.

George glanced back at a letter he had just been reading. It was from a stockholder. Its tone was far from complimentary. A few phrases in particular had stuck in George's mind: "Unmanageably large," "completely unfocused either in markets or products," "no one in the organization anywhere who knows anything about minicomputers, but you are trying to enter the toughest market in the world," "directed by self-interest bordering on megalomania."

"What are they griping about?" thought George. "Don't they own a big company now instead of a small one?"

A. Is it necessarily better to be part owner of a large company rather than of a small one?

B. Why does it appear that George has driven too hard for the company to grow?

C. What does this tell you about top management? How should one's personality enter into managerial decisions?

Marketing, Distribution, and Sales Management

18

After completing Chapter 18, you will be able to do the following:

- Analyze general descriptions of organizations to estimate the extent of their application of the marketing concept.
- Analyze organization descriptions to identify the major markets of the organizations and the type of market segmentation that underlies their choices of products and marketing methods.

- Evaluate organization structures to locate points where failures of coordination and communication are likely to occur within the total marketing effort.
- Evaluate given examples of organization marketing plans to judge their completeness in providing needed strategies.

In 1869 Charles A. Pillsbury looked to one side and saw fields full of ripening wheat and looked to the other side and saw a stream with the potential for producing abundant water power for running milling machinery. In that year, he went into the business of grinding wheat for flour. Today, Pillsbury Foods is still in the business of grinding wheat, but almost all other things about the company have changed. It is a huge, multiproduct corporation with a management philosophy greatly revised from the outlook of its founder.

Robert J. Keith describes the change in outlook as a "revolution" divided into four eras.[1] In the first era, which lasted into the 1930s, emphasis at Pillsbury was almost entirely on production. The primary business of the company was to make flour and other products; only secondarily did the managers look for people to buy the products. The products manufactured were chosen more for their ease of production than for any known suitability for consumers. The second era at Pillsbury stressed sales. Every effort was made to find as many buyers as possible for the company's products; retail outlets and distributors began to get more attention. But Pillsbury still thought of itself as a company that made certain products and then had to find a way to sell them. The third era began when Pillsbury started making serious efforts to develop new consumer products, the first of which were ready-made cake mixes. It became apparent that there was a huge range of products that *could* be made. The question was, How was management to choose which of the products it *should* make? Management's decision in this matter was the revolutionary part of the process: instead of simply picking the ones that were the easiest to make, it decided to let the consumer decide. Pillsbury's management placed the future buyer at the center of the whole design, production, and distribution process. The prime question was what did the *consumer* want to buy, not what does the company want to make.

[1] Robert J. Keith, "The Marketing Revolution," *Journal of Marketing*, January, 1960, pp. 35–38.

The fourth era at Pillsbury persists to the present day and reflects the management outlook found in many other companies today. It extends the influence of consumer demands not only to product selection, as in the third era, but to other management areas: finance, procurement, research, production, and distribution. Nearly every function is organized and operated to allow the company to respond quickly to shifting demands in the marketplace.

MODERN BUSINESSES ADOPT THE MARKETING CONCEPT

The revolution in outlook that has taken place at Pillsbury has been duplicated in nearly every other major industry and company in the country. Management has increasingly adopted a point of view that may be called "the marketing concept." Along with the changed philosophy, the activities and functions of marketing have assumed growing importance in the overall organization.

Marketing is a process of using the resources of an organization—advertising budgets, salespeople, product design specialists, and even production and financial resources—to satisfy certain needs and wants of selected groups of buyers. In a business organization, marketing tries to carry out this process in such a way that the company can make a profit.

Marketing traditionally included such activities as advertising, selling, and shipping goods. Today, the role of marketing is constantly expanding because of the *marketing concept,* which holds that the demands and needs of customers should be the central influence in every area of operations. What the consumer wants should be the prime factor in deciding what to produce, how to produce it, and how to distribute and sell it.

It should be apparent that the marketing concept places marketing functions close to the responsibilities of top management. If the entire direction and mission of a company is to satisfy identified wants and needs of consumers, then top management becomes, effectively, marketing management. In some companies this philosophical position is reflected in organizational structure. The marketing department head is assigned direct authority over more and more of the functions of the organization.

ORGANIZATIONS CHOOSE MARKETS

Marketing managers share other managers' concerns with government regulation, with the community, and with other elements of the environment. But the prime outside orientation of marketing people must be to markets. A *market* consists of all the people or organizations who are current or potential buyers of a particular product or service.

There are three traditional divisions of markets for a company operating in the United States:

1. The *domestic consumer market* consists of all the people in the country who buy goods for their own use. In the United States, virtually every one of the over 200 million population is a potential consumer of some product. Consumer markets are not static: buyers' tastes and needs continually change as their economic, educational, social, and cultural characteristics change.

2. The *domestic industrial and business market* includes all buyers in the country who purchase goods and services (1) for use in further processing or (2) for resale. A man who purchases a car radio to install in his own auto is a consumer. A buyer who purchases car radios to install in cars that are being manufactured for sale is part of the business market. The business market differs from the consumer market in several important ways. Business buyers are usually well informed about the goods and services they buy and have a clear idea of the needed specifications. Business buyers tend to buy in quantity, so a company selling to this market would usually have fewer orders of a larger size. Business buyers are known to be less influenced in their buying by the marketing efforts of the seller; instead, they tend only to buy what they need.

3. *International markets* include any kinds of buyers outside the home country of the producer. International markets have increased in importance as nations move slowly toward a world economy in which foreign trade becomes the norm. Dealing with international markets is especially challenging. It requires an ability to deal with cultural variations, financial and legal complications, and the extreme diversity of individual and organizational income worldwide.

Any market may be further subdivided. This can be done on the basis of an important characteristic that makes it easier (1) to sell to smaller, more homogeneous groups or (2) to design products that they will be interested in. This subdividing process is called market *segmentation*. It might be very difficult, for example, to design a pair of shoes that could be sold easily to every consumer in America. After all, the range includes 3 years old to 103 years old, male and female, rich and poor. It is quite possible, however, to design shoes suitable for a group of buyers, each of whom is an adult, engages in manual work, has a moderate income, works outdoors in a cold climate, and needs strong foot protection from falling objects. By expanding upon the characteristics of buyers, markets can often be precisely defined. This provides guidance in designing products and in choosing methods for their distributing, sale, and advertising.

Executive management usually takes major responsibility for the selection of markets and the choice of product lines because these decisions are so intimately associated with setting the mission of the organization. The chief executive of a company, though, will nearly always work together with others who are specialists in serving markets when making these crucial decisions. These specialists—marketing managers, sales managers, distribution managers, advertising managers, and others—also will have direct responsibility for much of the strategic planning and operating decisions needed to reach the chosen markets. The remainder of this chapter focuses on the particular concerns of these marketing specialists.

MANAGERS MUST ORGANIZE TO ACCOMPLISH THE MARKETING FUNCTIONS

Possibly the prime management problem of marketing managers is coordinating the variety of tasks and goals that make up the marketing effort. Although marketing may have a unified goal, it consists of numerous, more or less discrete processes and activities. If the parts do not work together—in objectives, market orientation, and timing—the whole effort will fail. The need for coordination must be reflected in the organizational structure that marketing managers establish.

Five Primary Functions

A relatively simple marketing operation may have five groups of activities that are seen as distinct: product development and pricing, market research, advertising and promotion, distribution, and sales (see Figure 18-1). Although the tasks are distinct, none of the areas can be independent of the others in a well-run marketing effort. Product development must be closely guided by market research, and market research must be constrained by the realities of producing products for sale. It would be of little practical value today, for example, for an airline to learn that there is a huge market for low-cost trips to the moon. Advertising and sales efforts will also obviously be influenced by the information gained from market research. Advertising must work together with sales and distribution. The work of the sales force is made easier by effective advertising, but the advertising will fail if the sales force does not follow up. Finally, a classic marketing disaster is the launching of an effective advertising and sales campaign that creates real demand but ultimately flops because physical distribution was inadequate and there are no products in the stores for consumers to buy.

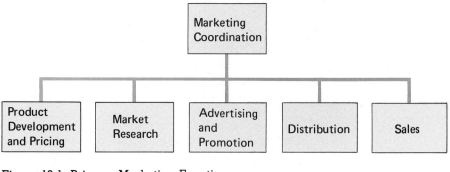

Figure 18-1. Primary Marketing Functions.

Centralized
Coordination

Integration must be of primary concern to marketing managers. It means a concentration on both formal and informal communications, on scheduling and programming, and on coordination early in the planning stages. It also requires that the integration be reflected on the organization chart. A unified marketing effort is extremely difficult to achieve if, for example, the product development people are closeted in the engineering department and the people who ship the products are under the direction of the purchasing department. The activities of the total marketing effort are easier to coordinate if all functions fall under the same umbrella of authority. Typically, these functions will be placed under a vice president of marketing or a distinctly identified marketing manager.

PLANNING IS THE KEY TO
MARKETING SUCCESS

Planning is essential to any management effort, but its contribution is particularly apparent in successful marketing programs. It is in marketing that strategic thinking flowers fullest. Marketing is future oriented in nearly all its aspects; decisions must be made today if a firm is to have the products and promotional and distribution methods needed tomorrow.

Market Research

The central importance of planning in marketing efforts helps explain why marketing managers are so partial to research. Probably more than in any other functional area, marketing people embrace formal research and numerical forecasting for help in planning and decision making. The most familiar type of marketing research is the analysis of market demand. This helps managers to judge the probable sales success of a new product or of an old product in a new market. The demand study, although important, is only the beginning. Marketing managers also do the following:

1. Study the effects of advertising. From such studies, they try to learn what motivates buyers to buy in the first place or to choose one brand over another.
2. Analyze business and economic trends, business cycles, warehouse locations, shipping methods, profit potentials, and diversification opportunities.
3. Test products to seek possible improvements.
4. Analyze the characteristics of competing products.
5. Study the effectiveness of packages and even of shipping crates.
6. Perform sales analyses, market share studies, and general tests of market characteristics and demands even in areas unrelated to their current products.

Much of this research has paid off. It is true that numerical indicators can never take the place of sound business sense and experience. Nevertheless, the research orientation of marketing managers has made the development of strategies better understood in this field than in most others. In general, a marketing program requires five types of strategies: (1) an overall, or basic, marketing strategy combined with specific plans for (2) new product development, (3) distribution, (4) advertising, and (5) sales. These are examined below.

Basic Marketing Strategy

Generally, a basic marketing strategy concentrates on market selection, product differentiation and mix, pricing, and the marketing mix.

MARKET SELECTION   The number of possible, finely segmented markets is virtually uncountable. A market can be as specific as "first-generation immigrant men from a Spanish-speaking country, living in the metropolitan New York City area and wishing to improve their English-speaking ability for employment purposes through a low-cost teaching method that does not require them to travel far from their homes." Or it can be as broad as "every household in the United States." It is clear that a key part of plans is a statement of the markets the company will compete in.

The chief characteristic of a market that makes it attractive is that it contains enough unsatisfied demand to allow a company to sell a product at such a price and in sufficient quantities to make a profit. *An existing company* will already be operating in some market. Its task is twofold. Its managers must use their experience and research to maintain and improve the company's position and to locate new markets with unsatisfied demands for expansion or diversification. *A new company* is faced with the often overwhelming task of locating a profitable but unfilled niche in the vast welter of potential markets.

PRODUCT DIFFERENTIATION AND MIX   A marketing manager is faced with a dilemma: whether to try to sell the same product to an entire market or to develop a range of products with each one specifically targeted to a segment of the total market. The manager may decide to use an *undifferentiated strategy,* in which the product and marketing strategy concentrates on mass appeal. This has production advantages because many units of a single product are cheaper to produce than a few units of each of a range of products. On the other hand, a *differentiated strategy,* in which products are tailored to segments of the market, has the advantage of meeting demand better and often of increasing total sales. Close analysis of costs and potential sales is necessary for choosing between the alternatives. The problem is compounded when a company operates in several different major markets and has to choose a degree of differentiation in each. The goal then becomes to create a *product mix,* a combination of offerings to segments of different markets, that will be profitable to the company.

PRICING   In theory, market demand controls the prices of products: if consumers will not buy at a given price, producers will lower their price until buying starts again. In practice, though, there are many more controls on pricing decisions than this. Goods cost a certain amount to produce; the need to sell them at a profit will almost always set a lower limit on the price charged consumers. Producers may have to sell a certain quantity of a product in order to recover their investment in development and facilities. This usually sets an upper limit on price since very high-cost goods will not sell in large quantities. Within this range, prices may be adjusted to market demand, as determined by actual sales and by market research. Prices are further adjusted to maintain a competitive position. Buyers consider many elements in deciding on the specific product to buy, but a slight advantage in price may be sufficient to give one company a significant edge over competitors.

MARKETING MIX   The price of a product will partly determine the quantity that can be sold. There is little question that a quality automobile priced at $1,000 would be a hit on the market no matter how many people are looking for more than low-cost transportation. Products and price are far from the only determinants of sales, however. Sales, advertising, and distribution efforts also affect the quantity that can be sold. The quantity sold of a product with a design and quality that suits it to some market will be a function of its price and the amount of money spent on advertising and distribution. As price is reduced and advertising and distribution expenditures increase, sales can be expected to go up.

The trick is to find the right combination of price and promotion costs—called the *marketing mix*—that will produce maximum profits. Managers seeking higher sales have a choice: they can spend more on promotion, or they can accept reduced revenues per unit resulting from lower prices. Cost-benefit analysis and other mathematical techniques, combined with good research on market demand, help solve this slippery problem.

New Product Strategies

Successful products often have life cycles (see Figure 18-2); they are introduced, become popular, and then decline in the market. This, combined with the desire to grow and to achieve planned diversity, means that companies must create new products. Marketing managers usually play a major role in the process of selecting potential products and refining their design features to fit the desires of future customers.

The process of creating new products is a long one. The road is made harder by the knowledge, shared by all marketing managers, that of all the new ideas proposed, few will make it to the market and that of all the new products that do make it to production, few will succeed. A typical process for creating new products includes the following:

1. Generating new ideas from knowledge of market demand, from technological developments, from customers' stated needs, or from people in the organization.
2. Screening the ideas for the few that look most promising.
3. Carrying out a business analysis to estimate costs and revenues so as to guess at the product's likely profitability.
4. Completing engineering and design work on the few ideas that survive the business analysis.
5. Testing both the product's performance and its actual sales potential.
6. Introducing the product and selling it in the market.

Distribution Strategies

If thousands of customers want the products of a company and have been convinced by advertising and selling efforts to buy them, how do the customers get the actual products? This is a decision for marketing managers, and it is critical to success. The question is one of choosing channels and physical distribution methods.

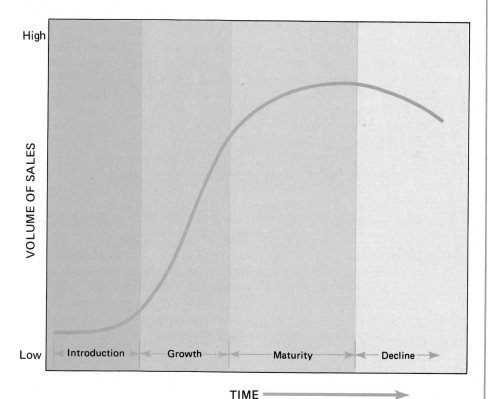

Figure 18-2. Product-Life Cycle.

A *channel* is the combination of people, organizations, and methods that make up the chain that moves products and services from manufacturers to ultimate consumers. One company may sell all of its woodworking tools through direct-mail advertising; it invites customers to order by telephone or mail direct from the factory. Another tool manufacturer may sell to a national distributor who resells to regional wholesalers who resell to local retail stores who then sell to consumers. These channels differ considerably in their characteristics. Scores of other types of channels with their own unique properties are also available to producers.

Physical distribution is the process of transporting goods to the locations where they will be bought and used. It requires managers to make a wide range of plans and decisions about how goods will be stored and shipped in their complicated movements among factories, warehouses, wholesalers, retailers, and consumers.

Channels and physical distribution methods must be integrated with all other marketing decisions. If a manager decides to distribute through wholesalers, for instance, many factors such as price, packaging, warehouse location, and product features must be adjusted in advance to make the product suitable for this marketing method.

Advertising Strategies

The role of advertising is to inform potential buyers of the availability of products and to persuade them that the products have unique characteristics that justify purchase. This process is a highly creative one. It combines an understanding of consumer motivation and desires with technical presentation skills. In advertising, however, the guidelines must remain the same as in any other managerial function: a decision is a good one if it promotes the achievement of organization goals. In the typical situation, this means that advertising is good if it generates more revenue than the cost of the advertising. Specific strategies such as where to advertise, how much to advertise, or what the content of the advertising will be must finally be judged by this criterion.

Sales Strategies

The administration of the sales force is probably the area of marketing in which the broadest range of managerial skills is needed. *Planning* must allocate territories, set quotas, determine the specific selling strategy, and integrate the sales force effectively with the distribution channel. *Control* of sales is one of the most critical areas for a profit-making company, since revenues are the first requirement for continued operation. Structuring and *organizing* the sales force is a complex process. It requires the balancing of factors such as travel time, cost of salespeople, regional differences in markets, and potential conflicts in diverse product lines and market segments. *Staffing* and *directing* may be difficult because a wide range of selling skills—from simply delivering orders to applying high-level technical knowledge and creativity at spotting customers' needs—are often needed within a single sales force. Further, field representatives often work with a minimum of direct supervision. This presents special motivational and communication problems.

MARKETING HAS BROAD APPLICATION

In its early years, the marketing concept focused on manufactured products. Today the concept is applied broadly to the marketing of services of all kinds—transportation, communications, food and lodging, insurance, banking, and entertainment, to name some. Indeed, the marketing concept has been extended to include nonprofit institutions and all manner of government services.

In the service industry, for example, radio stations and magazines have become masters at applying shrewd marketing management to grasp revenue from an environment characterized by shifting consumer interests, high costs, and strong competition. Radio stations, for instance, attempt precise market segmentation, defining their target audience in terms of age, income, type of neighborhood, buying habits, and other factors. They back up this market definition with market research and use the results of the research both to shape their product—the on-the-air programming—and to generate revenue through the sale of advertising time. The product, in some major urban markets, may be almost minutely differentiated: popular music stations sometimes must try to distinguish themselves from competitors through slight differences in music selection, through contests, and through the intangible personalities of their on-the-air personnel. The buying characteristics of the audience, the price of advertising for customers, the zeal and experience of the sales force, and even advertisements placed by the radio station in other media, all must combine to produce a successful operation.

Modern charitable and nonprofit organizations are often as skillful at marketing as their commercial brethren. The marketing environment for these institutions can be extremely complex. A large metropolitan art museum, for example, must satisfy a number of different markets; museum directors today are usually sharply aware of the demands and characteristics of these markets. Museums use market research to discover and define the segment of the population likely to use the museum. They maintain up-to-date lists of potential contributors and use sophisticated mail and direct-selling efforts to bring in the contributions. They use subtle lobbying, public relations, and promotion techniques to seek government financial support. And, true to the marketing concept, they shape their product—the displays and services of the museum—to appeal to the demands identified in each of these markets.

The same general approaches are found in nearly any organization today that exploits management ability to achieve success. Hospitals, federal programs, and charitable organizations like the American Cancer Society and the Red Cross have all begun to apply the techniques of modern marketing to improve their effectiveness in fulfilling their missions.

Managers in Action

DIRECTOR OF CONSUMER MARKETING & SALES

for decorative consumer hardgoods corporation located in midwest

Must provide innovative leadership in a highly visible corporate environment. Must be able to develop creative marketing plans, manage sales including merchandising through catalog groups, department stores, distributors, and premium outlets. Strong administrative skills required.

SALES PROMOTION MANAGER

for national pharmaceutical company

Responsibilities include:

- Planning, coordination, and general supervision of the development and execution of aggressive and imaginative sales promotion policies and programs.
- Creative development, direction, and dissemination of promotional materials, merchandising, point-of-purchase displays, and sales aids.
- Advertising sales promotion and cooperative advertising planning.

REGIONAL SALES MANAGER for

manufacturer of electrical housewares

Responsibility for total sales volume of Southern region and development of aggressive sales goals and plans. Controls distribution of all promotional funds for sales within territory. Ability to communicate with and motivate varied types of individuals. Articulate, hard working individual who is results-oriented. Must have staying power.

ADVERTISING DIRECTOR

for real estate development company

Conceive of and implement comprehensive advertising program, including budgets, agency relationships, and media selection. Works closely with sales department. Supervises small group of professional and clerical people.

SUMMARY

1. The marketing concept holds that the needs and demands of consumers should be the central influence on planning and decision making in every area of operations of an organization. This views the traditional marketing functions—product development, market research, advertising, distribution, and sales—as methods of satisfying demands rather than simply as a way to distribute goods that have already been produced.

2. The major divisions of markets are (a) domestic consumer, (b) domestic industrial and business, and (c) international, both consumer and business. Any market may be further subdivided on one or more characteristics—age, income, geographical region, and many others—that affect needs for products and buying habits. This division is called segmentation.

3. The greatest organizing problem for marketing managers is providing the very close coordination and communication needed among the elements of the total marketing effort. Every marketing function must be integrated with every other function; in a marketing-oriented company, this usually calls for centralized marketing management.

4. Marketing success is highly dependent on planning. This partly accounts for the strong emphasis on research and forecasting found today. Plans must specify major, or basic, marketing strategies: market selection, product differentiation and mix, pricing, and marketing mix. In addition, careful planning is required for developing new-product strategies, distribution strategies, and advertising and sales strategies.

REVIEW AND DISCUSSION QUESTIONS

1. How could you tell whether or not a company has accepted the marketing concept? What objective differences might you find between the company that has and one that has not?

2. In an organization that stresses the marketing concept, how would the marketing managers be related to the top managers?

3. Heater Products, Inc. has always sold exclusively to consumers. Now it is entering the domestic industrial market. What changes might it make in its marketing efforts, based on the differences between these markets?

4. Suggest at least five examples of buyer characteristics that might be used to segment the domestic consumer market.

5. Bert van Dyne has taken over as chief executive of a large consumer products company. He has set as his first major task the total reorganization of the marketing functions. What is the single most likely problem he will encounter with the current organization? Why?

6. Why is research stressed so much in marketing? Give two reasons.

7. Harriet Bako is starting from scratch, looking for a new market for her company. What is the major characteristic she will look for?

8. Describe briefly the difference between a differentiated product strategy and an undifferentiated product strategy.

9. What three elements would be involved in the marketing mix for a paint manufacturer? How would the managers judge whether the mix was correct?

10. Many types of organization other than businesses have begun to apply the marketing concept in recent decades. Why do you think this has happened? Give an example of a nonprofit or government organization that can be operated more effectively through the use of marketing techniques.

Problems and Projects

1. Four decision-making situations are given below. For each, tell what decision a production-oriented company would make and what decision a company that accepted the marketing concept would make. Give your reasons for each case.

   a. The sales of a regional distributor of fresh food products are falling sharply because of competition of highly processed "convenience" foods. Two solutions are being considered. One is to expand to cover a larger area so as to regain sales volume. The other is to shift into the processed-food business.

   b. Because of plummeting sales of its product in traditional local jewelry stores, a maker of old-fashioned pocket watches has almost been forced out of business. The choice is to try to find a new channel for selling its products or to reorient the whole company.

   c. An American maker of high-quality kitchen knives has been quite successful selling knives similar to the respected imported knives at a slightly lower price. Rising production costs are now forcing the domestic manufacturer to raise its prices even higher than the prices of the imports. The question is whether to put the price increases into effect or to try another approach.

   d. A major chain of auto repair franchises has been hurt by the increase in the number of people doing their own repairs at home. The chain must decide whether to try to increase business by cutting prices and advertising more or to make a shift in company philosophy.

2. The ten products listed below were designed to be sold to specific markets, in some cases to highly segmented markets. Indicate the market for which each seems aimed. First, write the letters a through j, corresponding to the products. Beside each letter, write a 1 if the product is best suited to the domestic consumer market, a 2 if the product was created for sale to the domestic business and industrial market, or a 3 if the product is aimed at the international market. (Indicate the international market only if the product

was specifically designed to fulfill a demand that exists overseas but not domestically.) Then for each product add a few words describing the basis—age, income, or geographical region, for instance—upon which the market has been segmented.

a. An inexpensive term life insurance policy that, if either husband or wife dies, pays an annuity for child-raising costs.
b. A very plain, sterling silver caviar-serving spoon.
c. A machine for taking bark off of large logs. It is small enough to handle economically only a few dozen logs per day.
d. A sleeve to allow French and German manufacturers to use American-sized bearings on metric products.
e. A synthetic tire for use on heavy earth-moving equipment.
f. Instant grits in 10-pound bags.
g. A low-cost glue with a small but very eye-catching package.
h. An inexpensive imitation of a famous doll, which says "Mama."
i. A $400 rosary with the Ave Maria engraved in Latin on the back of the crucifix.
j. An aluminum shovel for scooping manure from a barn.

3. The short cases given below illustrate management situations that occur in companies' marketing efforts. Some represent successful management decisions. Others illustrate problems that might be encountered. For each case, tell whether it is an example of good practice, what the problem is if you see one, and what a possible solution would be.

a. Sloan Manufacturing Company spent $300,000 advertising its new electric can opener. All of the advertisements said "Available at your local discount appliance or housewares stores," but when customers went to make purchases, there were none of the products there.
b. Muhammed Golin ran the market research department for an industrial electronics firm. He maintained an up-to-date information file on all current and potential customers. He concentrated special research efforts on sales potential for products that could be produced with today's technology.
c. The managers of a company that makes inexpensive furniture determined that one of their plastic TV tables was nearing the end of its life cycle as a profitable product. They decided to give it one more push so as to try to create a final volume sale before discontinuing it. They set up a national advertising program that presented the product at a price 10 percent lower than normal. The company's salespeople, though, were still showing the table to stores at the old wholesale price.
d. The managers at Cole Financial Services have a marketing planning checklist. They use it at the beginning of every planning cycle to be sure that every marketing function is covered for every project.
e. Marketing research at Sevesi Industries is on a calendar year cycle running from January to December. For internal accounting reasons, however, all revenue allocations, including those for advertising campaigns and especially for major campaigns, must be made on a fiscal

year basis running from July to June. This has the effect of causing advertising plans to be made before current research results are available.

4. *Performance Situation—The Flaming Firewood Market:* Toby Grasso is a graduate student in marketing at a university near a large Eastern city. Toby and his girl friend were reading the paper one day when he exclaimed, "Look at this. Eighty dollars for one cord of firewood!" Toby knew something about firewood because his family had used wood stoves for heat when he was growing up. His family still owned their farm 40 miles from the city, and it still had 160 acres of good timber on it.

Toby, his girl friend, and three of their friends decided to try a part-time firewood business. Their aim was both to make a little extra money and to try out some of the marketing principles they were learning in school.

Here are some of the facts they examined. There are two basic uses for firewood in a city: making a fire that is cheery and pretty to look at and making a fire that produces heat. Some wood makes a colorful flame but burns quickly and produces less heat for the same-sized stick. Other wood burns more slowly and makes more heat. Some wood is light in weight; some is heavy. Wood that has been cut and dried for six months or more burns better than wood that has just been cut. Drying takes time and requires a large storage area; therefore, dry wood is more expensive.

(1) Based on this information, list four potential market segments for Toby's firewood business. What are the bases of segmentation you have used? How could Toby decide whether to use a differentiated product strategy or an undifferentiated one?

(2) Toby learned that prevailing prices for wood in the city ranged from $20 a cord (a cord is a stack 4 feet wide by 8 feet long by 4 feet high) for uncured pine to $85 a cord for well-seasoned black locust and other desirable types. As a marketing planner, what should Toby consider in setting prices? What information other than competitors' prices would he want to have?

(3) Toby and his friends believe that distribution would be their biggest problem, and possibly their biggest competitive opportunity. Firewood is bulky, heavy, and inconvenient to handle. Just stacking the amount on a pickup truck takes a good deal of time. From the point of view of a typical customer, what would be the best distribution system the young entrepreneurs could adopt, ignoring its cost? From the point of view of the customer, what would be the least convenient distribution system?

(4) Advertising also seems to present an opportunity. The advertising and promotion of the competitors was unimaginative and not at all persuasive. Most of the other suppliers used simple notices in the classified sections of the newspapers. Does advertising represent an opportunity in a case like this? Why or why not? What should Toby and his friends consider in deciding on the method and extent of advertising?

5. Outline a marketing strategy for the business described in Problem 4. Write a sentence or two giving an approach that you think might be successful for each of these areas: (a) product differentiation and mix, (b) market segmentation, (c) pricing, (d) marketing mix, (e) distribution, and (f) advertising. Remember that your overall goal will be to give the business a competitive advantage over other suppliers of firewood.

6. Select any product and create a marketing plan for it that you think would be superior to the way the product is currently being marketed. You may propose different channels, a different advertising approach, new packaging, different marketing segmentation, or any other marketing change that you think would be successful. Take the point of view of a marketing manager in making your plans. How would your proposed changes affect your organization? How would the external changes you plan be reflected internally in personnel, structure, and other management concerns?

Cases for Analysis and Discussion

CASE 1: A DIVERSITY OF FUNCTIONS

A large, leather belt manufacturer sells both to the general public and to the federal government for supplying the armed forces. A small section of the firm's organization chart, as shown in Figure 18-3 on page 424, illustrates the structure of some of the marketing functions. The company's distribution people are assigned to a different department that reports directly to the production manager.

This internal structure has been used effectively for some time. Now, though, an internal struggle has developed. Driven partly by personal ambition and partly by some well thought-out views of what would be good for the company, Marty Springer, the consumer sales manager, has started calling for a more unified marketing structure. Joe Bullis, the government contracts manager, is not so keen for the idea. Even though government contracts account for 65 percent of the company's volume, Joe fears that the change may make Marty his boss rather than his equal. Because of the nature of the market, Marty has far more subordinates than Joe, even though Marty's sales volume is smaller.

A. Under the present arrangement, who would be responsible for coordinating marketing activities?
B. What are some of the reasons Marty might give when arguing for a unified structure?
C. What type of organization is this? What is the basis of the structure?
D. Should the structure be changed? Why or why not?

Figure 18-3.

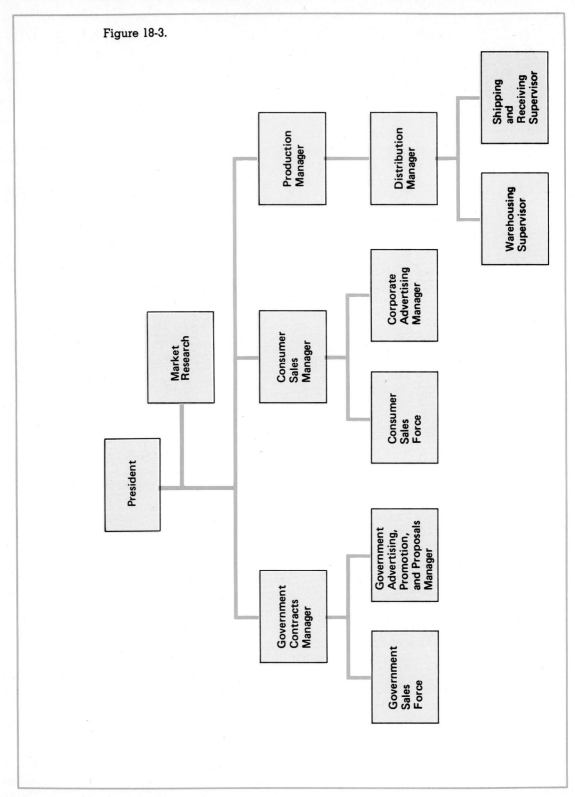

CASE 2: CONTROLLING THE PROCESS OR PROCESSING THE CONTROLS?

"Sharon, I called you in here today to tell you that you're doing a good job. I still intend to do that, but while I was thinking of what I was going to say to you, something came to me. How do I really know you're doing a good job?"

Sharon Carson, the marketing director for Myrdahl Fabrics, was a little taken aback by this introduction. She must have appeared offended, because her boss quickly reassured her.

"No, no. Don't take that the wrong way; I don't mean the least reflection on you. Let me explain. We have probably the best sales information system in the business. If I cared to look, I could find out that we had sold 5,000 bolts to the Chicago region yesterday and only so-many thousand bolts to that region on the same day last year. I know exactly what our sales are because we really process the life out of that information. Now, I'm not a marketing specialist, as you know, but what I was wondering is how could I tell that our marketing really works. How can I tell that the way we are doing it is better than some other way that we might do it? How can you control something like that? Production control I understand very well, but until now I never gave much thought to marketing control."

A. Should there be such a thing as marketing control at this company? Why hasn't the boss thought of this sooner?

B. Is the sales information useful? Is it control information?

C. How would you answer the questions of Sharon Carson's boss? What could you use to control marketing?

Production and Operations Management

19

After completing Chapter 19, you will be able to do the following:

- Describe the essential concerns of three levels of production plans and controls.
- Judge whether a given organizational structure provides for all of the needed functions in an operation.
- Estimate the consequences of given technical decisions on the general production strategies of a firm.
- Evaluate the possible success of given production strategies in supporting overall competitive and marketing strategies.

Exxon Corporation has assets of well over $20 billion. Its refineries, chemical extraction plants, mining and drilling operations, and massive storage facilities are spread all over the world. In contrast, a small leather-working shop in a rural town may have assets of only a few hundred dollars. These may consist only of a rack of hand tools, pieces of unworked material, and a small inventory of finished goods. Yet, these two companies, different as they are, share a common problem: procuring materials and performing a manufacturing process on them to make a saleable product.

Production management describes the management functions applied to solve this complex and critical problem. Production managers are directly charged with (1) buying the materials needed for making finished products; (2) designing the manufacturing process, specifying, and acquiring the equipment needed to carry it out; (3) maintaining the productivity of the facilities and of the people who work there; and (4) continually refining and improving the manufacturing process, or changing it to meet changing conditions. All of these efforts must combine to meet overall goals of the company: production quantities, product quality, cost targets, customer satisfaction, and related social responsibility.

Operations management faces many of the same requirements except that it is concerned with the process of providing a *service* rather than a physical product. (See Table 19-1.) Operations managers must allocate and organize combinations of human resources and mechanical equipment to accomplish (1) saleable activities (or services) in a business, or (2) economical public services in a nonbusiness organization.

Production and operations management makes unique technical demands. These include design of machine applications, layout and operation of complex schemes for moving many different kinds of materials within the plant or office, and scheduling scores of interacting activities to produce finished products or services when needed. In the past, the technical aspects of this kind of management may have been overemphasized. Today, emphasis is placed on the management functions—planning and controlling, organizing and finding the right people to do the work, and

TABLE 19-1. PRODUCTION VERSUS OPERATIONS.	
PRODUCTION-ORIENTATION	**SERVICE-ORIENTATION**
Industries that provide *products* through "production" processes: • Manufacturing. • Construction. • Mining. • Farming.	Industries that provide *services* through "operations" processes: • Banking and Insurance. • Transportation and Communications. • Government Services: fire, police, and so on. • Education and Health Care.
Industries that provide both *products and services* through "production/operations" processes: • Public Utilities (electricity, gas, and water). • Wholesaling and Retailing. • Restaurants.	In-company departments that provide *services* through "operations" processes: • Accounting and Finance. • Data and Word Processing. • Purchasing and Personnel. • Maintenance and Engineering.

putting them into action. These are the fundamental tasks needed for success in production and operations management, as in any other functional area.

For convenience, the term "production management" will be used in this chapter to refer to both production and operations. The traditional emphasis will be given to manufacturing, with examples illustrating the extension of principles and issues to service operations.

PRODUCTION MANAGERS PLAN AND CONTROL WHAT IS MADE

Production planning and control takes place in a constantly repeating cycle. First, managers decide what and how much to make; they make it; they check the results; they then use that information to decide what to make in the next period as the cycle begins again. Production plans fall into three fairly distinct categories: long range, intermediate, and short term.

Long-range plans concern the types of products that will be produced and the major facilities that will be used to produce them. Typical questions answered at this stage include: Shall we make four different kinds of air conditioner or concentrate on only one? Shall we build three small factories or one large factory? Shall we install automated equipment or stick with manual control? Shall we electrify our urban lines and replace our diesel locomotives? Shall we operate many small branch banks or concentrate our services in a few areas? These plans look ahead for several years. Plans at this level *must* be integrated with high-level marketing strategies and with overall company goal setting.

Intermediate plans concern product types, quantities, and costs for a shorter period, typically a quarter or a year. These plans answer questions like: How many units of product *A* will we manufacture next year? How many of product *B?* Given expected materials and labor costs, what will the product cost per unit be? Will minor design modifications (either in the product or in the manufacturing process) be introduced during the period? What will the quarterly client load be? How many courses and sections must be taught this semester?

Short-term plans control the day-to-day, week-by-week operation of the facilities. These plans concern questions like: Will we use the big milling machine on the Able job or on the Baker job? Who will move the cartons of jars from the storage room to the input conveyer? Shall we work the entire shift two hours overtime to get this big order out by the deadline? Which crew will we assign to repair the outage in Section 7?

Terms of the Trade   Production planning and control uses special terms for the activities that make up short-term planning and operation. For example, deciding what specific manufacturing steps will be carried out, at what work station or with what machine, and by whom the steps will be performed is called *routing.* On the other hand, *scheduling* decides when each step will be begun and completed. Taken together, routing and scheduling have the goal of using facilities economically: (1) keeping workers and machines occupied in doing productive work; (2) keeping a minimum of people or equipment sitting idle; and (3) minimizing the backlog of work waiting to be done because there are no available facilities or service personnel for it.

The process of putting the planned activities into action is called *dispatching;* it sends the work orders to the people involved. After the work is completed, or at a number of stages in between, managers must provide follow-up to check results and adjust operations when undesirable deviations from plans are found. *Follow-up* is simply another term for control; it involves measuring results and making corrections.

**Purchasing
Management and
Inventory Control**   Production planning and control extends beyond the basic processing operations. Two further areas for attention are purchasing management and inventory planning and control. Both manufacturing and service organizations use components, materials, and supplies that are crucial to output.

For both purchasing and inventory, an important question presents itself: *How little can we afford to keep on hand?* Purchasing managers answer this question for raw materials and supplies; inventory managers answer it for the stock of finished goods. Its importance lies in the financial effects on the business. Both raw materials and finished goods represent money that has been spent. If a yarn manufacturer buys huge stocks of raw cotton, the cotton has to be paid for; that money is then unavailable for use elsewhere. As a consequence, the company needs a greater investment to produce the same output than if a small stock of raw materials were maintained. The same applies to finished goods. If the company keeps a warehouse full of unsold yarn, that yarn represents money spent that is not producing an income.

The inventory problem does not yield an easy solution because efficient production requires that an adequate reserve of materials and products be on hand. If the company keeps no store of cotton, production stops if an incoming shipment is delayed. If the company keeps no supply of finished goods, every order must wait to be filled until the needed products have been manufactured. Production managers continually juggle these two factors. They try to keep money invested in inventory at a minimum while still maintaining an adequate store of materials and products so as to keep production and sales going smoothly.

Integration of Planning and Control

The great problem of production planning and control lies in tying together all the parts. A major concern of long-term planning, for instance, is to provide the total production capacity needed for expected future sales of products. If short-term scheduling and routing are poorly done, however, the long-term plans will be distorted; they will provide more capacity than needed and thus spend more money on facilities than needed. Poor utilization of current facilities wastes production capacity. If the wasteful processes are used as the standard for planning new facilities, this extends the waste far into the future and makes inefficiency the normal condition.

Similarly, a change in plans or operations in one area has definite, but sometimes unpredictable, effects on other parts of operations. Suppose, for example, an efficient manufacturing process gradually becomes wasteful. It does so because of a series of bad management decisions, and its effects on planning the inventory of finished goods are not immediately recognized. In such a case, the inventory control manager may keep levels low, expecting a continual replenishment at an orderly rate. If production output becomes erratic, however, the old inventory reserve will be too small, causing disruption in shipments to customers. For this reason constant communication among persons performing manufacturing, quality control, purchasing, inventory control, and sales activities is essential.

THE PRODUCTION ORGANIZATION MATCHES STRUCTURE WITH PROCESS

Organizing for production is often more complicated than in other functional areas. Technical considerations abound. For example, the decision on whether to have a number of small factories or one large, integrated factory cannot be made simply on the basis of what is easiest to manage. Scores of influences must be weighed. These include such factors as labor markets and prevailing wage rates, transportation costs for finished goods and for raw materials, land costs, building costs, and the applicability of automation to the company's products. The guiding consideration, however, is how well each factor supports the production process or the provision of services.

Typical Organization Structures

In a manufacturing company, an overall production manager, at or near the level of vice president, usually has responsibility and authority for the production process. Service companies or nonprofit organizations that provide services will have an operations manager at that same level, although the specific title given the position varies widely among different organizations. These managers have the prime responsibility for seeing that resources are applied to get goods made or services provided.

A MANUFACTURING ORGANIZATION   As reflected in the typical organization chart in Figure 19-1, the main production functions are obtaining materials (purchasing), applying a conversion process (manufacturing), controlling the process (production control), and assuring that the end prod-

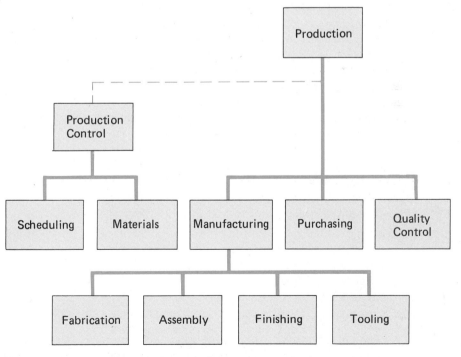

Figure 19-1. The Structure of the Production Department of a Manufacturing Company.

uct meets standards (quality control). In Figure 19-1, production control, which includes preparing detailed manufacturing schedules and overseeing the internal storage and movement of materials, is shown as a staff function of the production department. In many organizations, it may just as well be made a line function and organized as a separate department with direct authority over schedules and materials.

The specific departmental subdivisions under the manufacturing manager may take hundreds of different forms, depending on the nature of the manufacturing process. Typical general subdivisions are the ones shown in Figure 19-1: fabricating, assembling, finishing, and tooling. Even these general categories may not apply in every case. A bakery, for example, will have a fabricating step consisting of mixing and baking, but usually will have no assembly step. Many electronics companies apply a process consisting only of assembly and finishing; all component parts are bought from outside suppliers.

A SERVICE COMPANY   A structure that might be found in a service company is shown in Figure 19-2. The company in the figure is an airline, providing the service of moving people and freight by air. In a sense, only one of the 14 managers shown is directly charged with providing this service: the manager of the flying department, under the flight operations department. All of the other departments were created and structured to provide the organizational environment for this operation.

A key point to be drawn from Figure 19-2 is that, as with manufacturing, service companies must create a structure that serves operational goals. A bank, for instance, clearly will have no flying department, but will probably have a consumer loans department. Most distinctions are subtler than this obvious example. To an outsider, Bank A and Bank B may appear pretty much the same. If an examination of their organization charts shows that Bank A has a trust department with 11 subordinate managers and Bank B has no trust department at all, the service goals of the two organizations must be quite different.

Designing the Structure

The job of dividing up production work is challenging. This is especially true when a production process includes hundreds or thousands of individual steps, as in the manufacture of an automobile. Even simple processes take thought. The buckle on a hiker's backpack, for instance, can be made in three steps: stamping the frame, forming the tongue, and attaching the two parts. These steps can be done separately, or they can all be performed on a single-purpose machine. In the first case, the company would employ stamping machine operators and wire formers, and assemblers; in the second case, it would employ only buckle machine operators. (See Figure 19-3.) The difference is an organizational one. It depends on many factors, such as cost of machinery, skill levels required of operators, time for moving materials, and flexibility for changing the process.

Figure 19-2. The Structure of the Operations Department of a Service Company: A Commercial Airline.

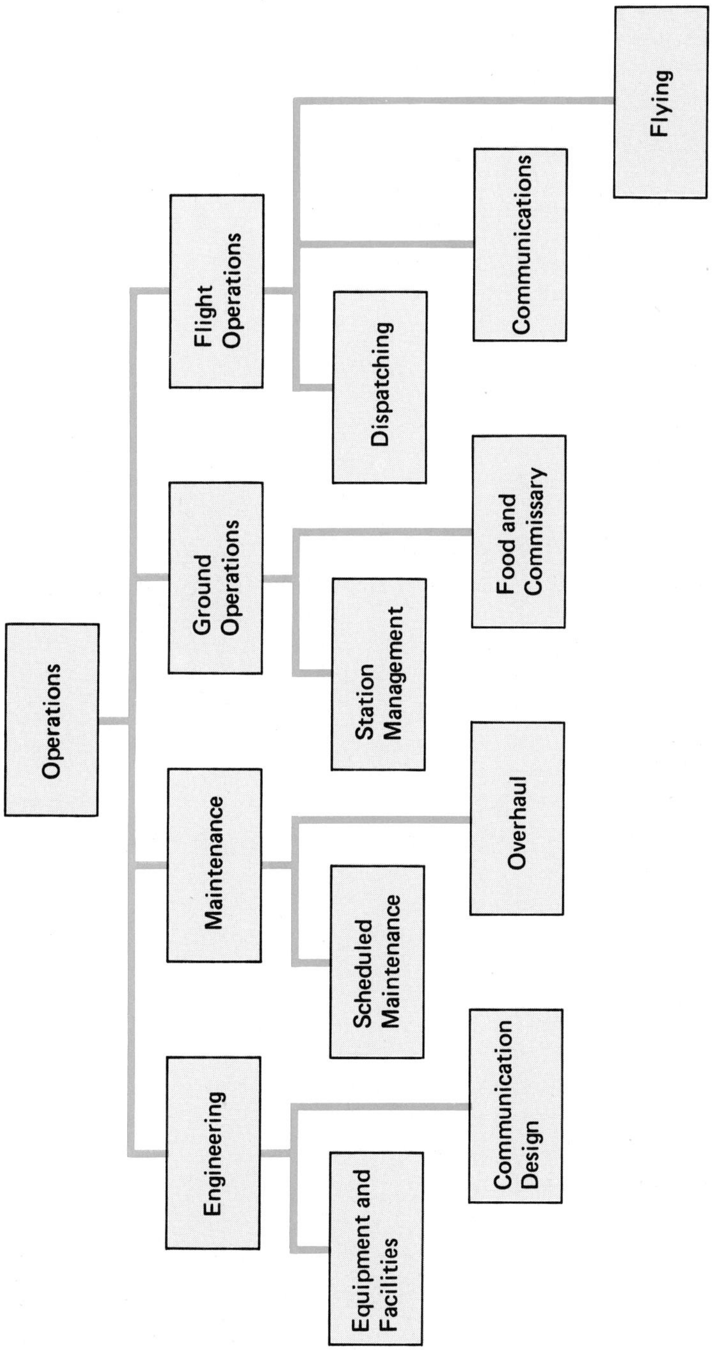

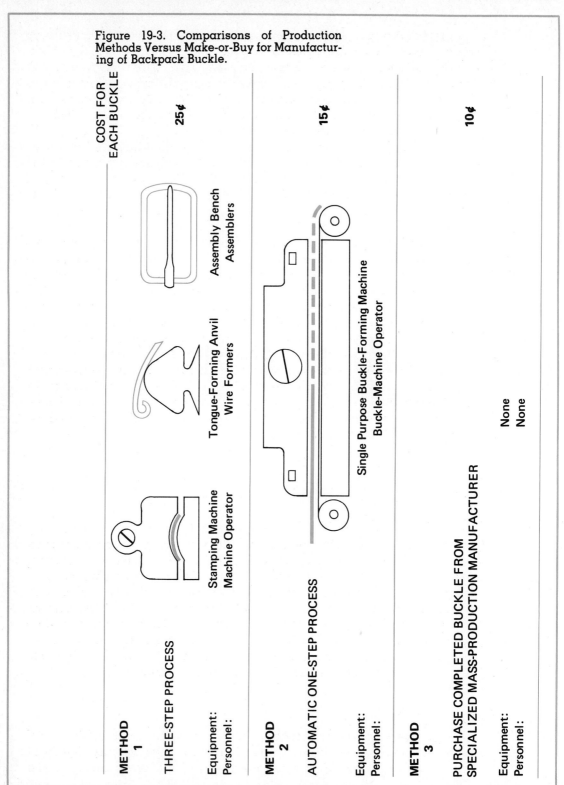

Figure 19-3. Comparisons of Production Methods Versus Make-or-Buy for Manufacturing of Backpack Buckle.

COST FOR EACH BUCKLE

METHOD 1

THREE-STEP PROCESS

Stamping Machine
Machine Operator

Tongue-Forming Anvil
Wire Formers

Assembly Bench
Assemblers

25¢

Equipment:
Personnel:

METHOD 2

AUTOMATIC ONE-STEP PROCESS

Single Purpose Buckle-Forming Machine
Buckle-Machine Operator

15¢

Equipment:
Personnel:

METHOD 3

PURCHASE COMPLETED BUCKLE FROM
SPECIALIZED MASS-PRODUCTION MANUFACTURER

10¢

Equipment: None
Personnel: None

Production managers have a nearly unique situation when organizing production work: they, in consultation with other managers, can decide not to perform certain steps of the process in their own factories. The backpack manufacturer, for example, might decide not to produce any buckles, but to buy them ready-made from another producer who specializes in buckles. This *make-or-buy decision* affects organizational structure, and its resolution depends on a complex set of influences.

Managers in service companies and nonprofit organizations have their own equivalent of the make-or-buy decision. Many of the activities and tasks that combine to produce a service can be subcontracted to other companies or agencies outside the organization. Public school systems, for example, very frequently subcontract the operation of school buses to private companies and they go to outside agencies or consultants to provide psychological testing and counseling or even to provide direct training in certain areas. An auto rental company may perform its own auto maintenance in large metropolitan areas where a garage staff is justified by the size of the fleet, but subcontract maintenance in rural areas where fleets are small.

The physical layout of operations also influences certain organization decisions. Rarely would a marketing manager, for example, assign an employee to a certain department just because the employee's desk was physically located next to other members of that department. Such a decision occurs often in manufacturing processes, however. It does so because work stations may be spread over a large area. Any other kind of organization structure would cause geographical problems of supervision. A specialized employee's station may simply be too far away from the person who might otherwise logically be the supervisor.

PRODUCTION MANAGERS ARE PREOCCUPIED WITH TECHNICAL PROBLEMS

In many areas of operation, technical considerations exert a major influence on the performance of the production management functions. Production planning involves complex interactions, often requiring mathematical solutions. Control adds precise physical measurements of performance and product quality to the essential human aspects of operations. Organizing may be influenced by the labor market in Peoria, Illinois, and by the availability of private trucking companies in Montana. Staffing and personnel decisions must deal with a great range of skills and qualifications and often with huge numbers of workers. Some specific decisions and tasks require special attention from managers.

Plant and Location Factors

Few companies today make a single product with no variations. More commonly, companies produce a range of products, each varying slightly or greatly from the others. As a consequence, many managers are faced with the question of whether to establish a single, flexible production facility or to build several specialized factories. This question can be resolved only by strict analysis of dozens of factors such as economies of scale, the potential wastefulness of flexible equipment and processes, the restrictions on product development in the future, and shipping costs to markets and from raw material suppliers. The choice of a production location presents a similar problem. Centralization offers an advantage in that it makes management easier and minimizes duplication of facilities. On the other hand, the dispersal of operations to be near local markets or materials sources may present advantages that outweigh those of centralization.

Buildings and Equipment

A substantial part of the capital investment of many firms goes to the factory buildings and equipment used to produce goods. Management decisions must be shaped by the need to fully utilize and protect these investments. Production managers in particular must apply considerable skill and knowledge in real estate, construction, design, and renovation to obtain economical facilities in the first place. Then the selection and design of equipment must be fully integrated with decisions that affect routing, employee skills, departmentalization, and product design.

Maintenance and Plant Engineering

The protection of capital investment is a major goal of the production maintenance program. Well-maintained equipment contributes much to product quality, employee safety, uninterrupted production, and the elimination of waste. In a company with dozens of factories and a huge inventory of equipment, the task is enormous. Different machines require different maintenance schedules; many repair jobs cannot be anticipated. As a result, job assignment and control is a constant problem. Plant engineering departments must design operating controls that not only ensure product quality and quantity but also point to places where failures are occurring in the equipment or steps in the process. An effective maintenance program aims to prevent misadjustments and failures in the first place, but the early discovery of failures is absolutely essential.

Personnel Factors

Production departments typically employ large numbers of employees; there are tens of thousands in companies such as General Motors, Du Pont, and General Electric. This imposes a severe burden of personnel recordkeeping, job assignment, appraisal, training, and staffing.

1. A formal approach to personnel records with standard reports required regularly is almost always needed.
2. The degree of job specialization can be intense, especially in mass production plants. It requires a close coordination with the selection and training of people to undertake each class of work.

3. Supervision of first-line workers is a skill in itself. It requires a unique combination of management skills, and production know-how. Finding and developing men and women who manage well at that level is an important job of production management.

Product Factors Production managers contribute their special skills in shaping the firm's products to make them manufacturable by practical methods and with economical materials. In today's world, product design characteristics are basically a marketing decision. It is essential, however, that production managers communicate with the marketing specialists during the design program. Even in a heavily market-oriented company, a product design that cannot be produced economically and without flaws is of no practical value.

For this reason, the responsibility for product inspection and quality control, for making sure manufacturing or service standards are met, is usually placed within the production function. The responsibility for quality assurance, however, may be placed at a level above, and independent of, both production and marketing management. *Quality assurance* represents the total organizational effort to produce a product or service that measures up to its design specifications or promises made to customers in the form of warranties or other commitments.

PRODUCTION AND MARKETING STRATEGIES ARE INTERDEPENDENT

Chapter 18 presented the view that marketing managers have assumed a major role in developing overall organization strategy, replacing finance and manufacturing managers in this regard. Although this may be a sound reaction to today's market and economic conditions, the possibility exists for going too far in de-emphasizing manufacturing and production. Earlier in the century many companies manufactured a given line of products and, in effect, told the salespeople, "Oh, incidentally, you'll have to sell these." Suppose that today a marketing department devised and designed products it would like to sell and then told the production department, "Oh, incidentally, you'll have to manufacture these." Neither of these situations appears to be desirable.

Marketing management and production management can work together; in a successful company, they *must* work together. Any major change in competitive or marketing strategy is likely to require an equally major change in production strategy. The two groups of strategies must be worked out together.

Consider, for instance, a musical instrument company that wishes to enter the highly competitive piano market. Two alternative strategies are being considered:

Managers in Action

MANUFACTURING MANAGER

for a leading manufacturer of data communications products

Requirements: must be systems oriented, have five years manufacturing management experience, and have an engineering degree.

Responsibilities: all phases of production, budget control, costing and cost reduction, liaison work with engineering design.

Materials Administrator

with high technology division of Fortune 500 company

Key role in assuring company compliance with diverse, complex government regulations affecting a high volume, high value material function. Responsibility for developing appropriate procurement methods and practices, interacting frequently with company buyers and contract administrators.

Construction Superintendent

for well established construction company

Opportunity for highly motivated person with knowledge of all residential trades. Supervising personnel and subcontractors with full responsibility and authority. For someone who wants a career with security and pride of accomplishment.

PLANNING and SCHEDULING DIRECTOR

for metal working production job shop

To direct activities of 10 or more people in carrying out production scheduling and control and inventory management functions. Three to five years experience in a computerized environment preferred.

PLANT MANAGER

for inorganic chemical company

Responsibility for productivity improvement, budgeting, supervisory development, process management, and equipment maintenance.

PRODUCTION MANAGER

for medium-sized brass foundry

Position entails scheduling of operations, supervising production and assembly forepersons, and inventory and quality control.

■ Produce an instrument of acceptable quality to be sold at a rock-bottom price to the widest possible national market.

■ Produce the highest-quality, high-cost instrument for the specialized top of the market, even resorting to custom construction in some cases.

Choosing one or the other of these competitive strategies places very different requirements on the production department. The first strategy would require concentrated manufacturing facilities. These would be set up to process the longest possible manufacturing runs at the lowest possible costs. Production operations would be standardized and require the least skills possible to keep labor costs low. The second strategy would require highly skilled workers, an extremely flexible and nonstandard production process, a wide variety of materials on hand, extremely strict quality control systems, and a precise routing and scheduling department to handle the many product and process variations that result from custom work. These different requirements, and their costs, must be considered from the beginning. Production strategy and marketing strategy must *combine* to create a product that attains success in the marketplace. Neither is adequate alone.

SUMMARY

1. Production and operations management apply all five management functions to carry out the process that produces goods or services. Planning and control are integrated to (a) determine the exact characteristics of products and provide the facilities for creating them, (b) manage product quantities, quality, and costs, and (c) make day-to-day allocations of workers, materials, and equipment to get the production work done.

2. Organizing production and operations may require more detailed analysis than organizing other functions. The reason for this is that complex, technical decisions about work methods and equipment affect the internal structure. The organization must reflect the physical layout of operations, decisions about manufacturing parts internally or buying components from suppliers, and the specific methods and equipment used for manufacturing.

3. Production management deals with an unusual range of technical concerns: plant locations, buildings and equipment, maintenance, the difficulties of handling large numbers of workers, and the engineering and design characteristics of the products themselves. Technical analysis and judgment must contribute to the performance of the management functions, however, rather than substitute for it.

4. Production strategies do not just call for efficient manufacturing; they support and make possible the overall competitive and marketing strategies. A market strategy that calls for selling huge quantities of a standard product at the lowest possible price cannot succeed, for example, if production facilities are designed to handle only small batches of variable jobs.

REVIEW AND DISCUSSION QUESTIONS

1. Explain the difference between production management and operations management.

2. Give some examples of issues that might be treated in long-range production plans.

3. John Stone is looking for methods and standards to use in controlling the long-range plans of his paint manufacturing company. Propose some approaches he might use.

4. Briefly describe the four steps in short-range production planning and control.

5. Gold Electronics is considering closing its six regional plants and centralizing manufacturing in one large, automated plant. Describe at least three things the company should investigate in trying to predict the consequences of this move.

6. Why do you think the text refers to first-line supervisors as the key element in an effective production organization? Do you agree that they are?

7. The president of a large machine-tool company says that the production manager's maintenance program is so bad that it might put the company out of business. What are some of the ways a poor maintenance plan might harm a company?

8. Why do some personnel decisions that production managers must make involve more technical considerations than similar personnel decisions made by many other managers?

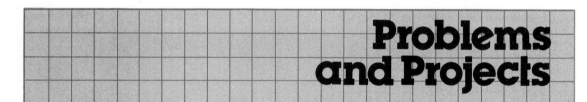

Problems and Projects

1. Operations management applies the management functions to perform the activities of providing a service: banking, wholesaling and retailing, advertising, radio and TV, food service and hundreds of others. Specific techniques differ from those in manufacturing—the recording of bank deposits as contrasted with assembling electronic equipment, for instance. Operations and production management are similar in their most important feature, however. Both require the kind of strategic thinking that will make the methods and processes of putting out a product serve the overall competitive and marketing aims of the organization.

An airline is a service company. It engages in many activities such as taking reservations, buying airplanes, training pilots and flight crews, maintaining and repairing planes, and buying and preparing food. These activities combine to provide the service of transporting passengers over long distances in as much comfort as possible. You can practice the application of strategic operations management by considering the planning needs of an airline. Briefly describe three issues that must be resolved in each of three types of plans: short range, intermediate, and long range. Do the plans serve the same purpose for a service as for a manufacturing company? Do the three types of plans interact in the same way for a service company? Explain.

2. *Performance Situation—Structuring the Truss Company:* Jacksonville Floor and Roof Company makes wood and metal trusses for the local construction industry. It provides standard-sized roof trusses and makes many custom substructures to the exacting specifications of builders and architects. The company uses four main types of materials: fir and pine lumber, and aluminum and steel channels, bars, rods, ells, and tubes. It also needs a variety of fastening materials and supplies. On some critical jobs, the stress resistance of materials must be tested to ensure the overall strength of the finished trusses. Since so much custom work is done, routing and scheduling is an everyday job. To remain competitive, the managers change some of the basic manufacturing and assembling steps with some regularity. It happens that Jacksonville's designers have not built excess strength into its products; this means that if an individual truss is found to have a fault of any significance, it is unsaleable. Stores of lumber and metal take up a lot of space. For this reason, Jacksonville has a large warehouse near its factory and another smaller warehouse out near the interstate highway. An individual truss represents a considerable investment, and the company keeps a close watch on inventories to make sure money is not wasted in stock that lies around for long periods waiting to be sold.

Design a simple organizational structure for the production function of this company. Include only *four* people above the first-line-supervisor level. Draw an organization chart for the structure you choose and list some of the responsibilities for each position you create. You need not define the positions of supervisors, but show them on your chart.

3. The technical decisions that production managers make must support high-level strategies if they are to be effective. For each of the situations and decisions described below, suggest one effect on overall organization strategies that could be expected. As an example, a change to automatic manufacturing equipment that reduces the unit cost of products by 15 percent might lead top managers to design a marketing strategy based on price competition.

   a. The managers of a business forms company decide to locate their factory near Chicago because that is their major market for their printed forms, but this means they will have to pay high shipping costs for raw materials.

   b. A plastics fabricator replaces the company's obsolete equipment with new machines that require very highly skilled operators.

   c. A printer increases the routine maintenance schedule for a large four-station press from once a week to once a day.

d. A large bank decides to eliminate all of its local branches because operating costs there are too high.

e. A department store decides to narrow the specialties of its sales clerks and give them training in the detailed characteristics of the goods they sell.

4. Globe Foods is a small chain of retail food stores in a very large American city. One of Globe's long-term goals is to grow considerably in size during the next 10 years. The company's hope for growth is based on a marketing judgment: the specialized food tastes of the city's many ethnic neighborhoods represent an opportunity for modern mass distributorship. The managers' idea is to use volume buying to provide Spanish, Chinese, Eastern-European, and other specialty foods in neighborhood stores in a number of large cities. The volume buying, they hope, will allow them to be very price competitive with the predominantly small shops currently in the market.

Briefly outline an operations strategy for this company. Concentrate on long-range issues such as purchasing policies, supplier type and location, distribution requirements, warehousing, and outlet locations. Remember that the main goal of operations plans is to support overall competitive strategies.

5. Consider propositions *a* and *b* below. With which proposition do you agree and why?

a. "The primary function of a business organization is production."

b. "The primary function of a business organization is marketing."

Be prepared to defend and debate your position in class.

6. Consider the operations strategy of your school. What are some of the issues that must be resolved in short-, intermediate-, and long-range operations plans? How are the decisions made? What kinds of forecasts or other information would be needed in the decision-making process? Use your own knowledge of the school's operations, information from your instructor, and interviews with school administrators, if desired.

Cases for Analysis and Discussion

CASE 1: THE CONFUSED MANUFACTURER

"How is it possible for things to get so incredibly messed up?" A person of lesser fortitude than Belle Giles might well have asked that question long ago. Belle was made of tough stuff, though, and it took a monumental foul-up to make her despair. The situation at Nordata, Inc. was a match for the strongest spine.

Nordata manufactured small computers for special-purpose use in industry. Some of its computers controlled huge machinery; others collected research and control data; others operated the heat, lights, and cooling in big office buildings. Nordata computers were popular. They were designed to be flexible enough for a huge variety of applications. The quality of construction was top-notch. And the price was not only competitive; it was absolutely a bargain considering the capabilities of the machines.

The problem that Belle Giles was facing was what happened after the computers were sold. The phone had been ringing all day, as it had rung so often in the past, with more demands for customers than Belle was equipped to handle. Twenty-nine repair calls had come in since 8 A.M. Many of the calls, Belle knew, were genuine machine problems. Anything as complex as a computer was bound to go haywire once in a while. Many others of the calls were caused by the customers who simply did not know how to use the machines. Others were caused by a few problems that were known to exist in the operating programs that were supplied with the computers.

A. What is the basic problem here? Why is Nordata's computer so good but still the source of so many difficulties?

B. Is this a production problem or a top-level problem? Who do you think should be responsible for solving it?

C. What *general* solution do you think is required? Strategic? Personnel? Mechanical? Explain.

CASE 2: THE SCIENTIFIC MANAGER

John was proud of his scientific mind; it had gotten him where he was today. He had been with Grossman Industries for almost fifteen years and his work history was a succession of ever more complex assignments in making technical redesigns and process adjustments in the company's nuclear products division. Finally, the proud day came when John moved into the empty office of the just-retired production manager.

The new job went well for the first months. John quickly learned the administrative ropes of his new position. Complexity didn't faze him at all. He was a little surprised at the extent to which the floor supervisors still expected him to be closely involved with day-to-day work. That was their job, he thought. His job was productivity. And he set about it with a will. He began a program of job analysis and strict work measurement. He had time-and-motion studies made on nearly every physical movement involved in the operations. Even the smallest improvement in methods or procedures was of burning interest to him.

One day, something unusual happened. One of the shop supervisors made a formal appointment to talk to John, who assumed it had something to do with a complaint about salary or with some other kind of grievance. The supervisor's interests were more related to the good of the company than that, though.

"Things aren't going so well in the plant," the supervisor said. "I guess maybe it's none of my business, but I thought maybe you'd like to know. A lot of the people who work there aren't too happy with so many work changes and all of the studies. They think they're doing a good day's work and that the company ought to be satisfied with that. A lot of them think that all the company cares about is getting more out of them. Some are getting pretty dissatisfied."

A. What is scientific about John's approach?
B. Is he doing a good job as production manager, judging from the information given here? Why or why not?
C. Do you think the supervisor is probably right in her judgment of the mood among the workers? Why would they feel that way?
D. Is there evidence here to make you think that John is ignoring at least one of the management functions? Which one?

Financial Management

20

After completing Chapter 20, you will be able to do the following:

- Identify the most important tasks and functions of financial management.
- Classify financial management activities into direct and indirect work.
- Evaluate the success of the financial management in a given organization in integrating overall planning and control.

- Distinguish between capital-expense planning and working-capital planning and give an example of each.
- Compare the benefits and disadvantages of equity and debt financing in a given situation.

To the rank and file employee—the assembly-line worker, file clerk, or shipping-room packer—the job of the financial manager often seems remote and alien. In the employees' eyes, financial management is something that takes place in a cold and lofty world of bankers and stockbrokers. At worst, the financial manager is seen as the tight-fisted moneylender who refuses credit when you need it and who unforgivingly collects payments when due. Or, closer at hand, the finance manager is viewed as a Scrooge who sits behind the cashier's cage dealing out paychecks from which outrageous deductions have been made. As a result, employees are hard put to think of the financial manager as having a healthy effect on their organizations, as a person who helps to make their business world run smoothly.

Yet, of all the management specialties, financial management is the only one that production workers and office clerks normally carry out in their personal lives. Every worker has certain sources of earned income (a regular paycheck and interest on a savings account, for instance) and sources of borrowed money (credit accounts with stores, bank loans, loans from friends). He or she uses this money to buy the goods and services needed to keep the household running. With the exception of planning to make a profit—a necessity in a business organization—this is precisely the role of the financial manager.

Financial management applies the management functions to provide an organization with the monetary resources it needs to fulfill its mission. It regulates the use of these funds in buying facilities, materials, supplies, labor, and other essential resources. The *sources of funds* for a business are equity and debt. *Equity* is money invested by owners, including profits generated from sales revenues and other income. *Debt* is money borrowed from banks, private investors, and other sources. The *uses of funds* are twofold: (1) for the provision of long-lasting facilities and other acquisitions, called *capital investments,* and (2) for purchases and payments needed for day-to-day operations, called *working capital.*

Accounting is the process or system used by an organization for the collection, analysis, and presentation of information (especially in monetary terms) about a firm, institution, or agency. Because of the monetary emphasis, the accounting function is inseparably associated with financial management.

FINANCIAL MANAGERS PERFORM A VARIETY OF FUNCTIONS

Although the basic task to which all financial managers contribute is the regulation of sources and uses of funds, in practice their activities are varied. As many as five other general functions are commonly assigned to finance departments.

1. *Financial planning.* This includes the responsibility for finding out and helping to decide what funds will be used in both long- and short-term plans and for anticipating the sources for the needed money. In performing this function, financial managers help establish the following policies and strategies:
   a. How much debt will be allowed.
   b. How much of profits should be reinvested.
   c. How much working capital will be provided.
   d. What sources of investment will be used.
   e. Other matters that determine the financial structure of the firm.
2. *Financial control.* This is a classic control process applied to the flow of funds in a company. It includes the establishment of income and expenditure standards, usually in the form of operating and capital budgets, and the measurement of actual revenues and costs to locate any deviations from plans. Financial managers also devote considerable effort to *replanning*, adjusting future plans based on information provided by financial controls.
3. *Coordination.* This is an important concern of financial managers because many of the lines of communication that tie the organization together are part of its financial control or accounting system. The coordinating function is also expressed in the establishment of an internal structure for carrying out financial activities and in influencing the organizing of the rest of the company to satisfy financial requirements.
4. *Credit management* involves direct contacts with the company's customers. It requires that policies on the extension of credit and on the collection of outstanding payments be set up and followed. In some organizations, credit management is handled by the marketing or sales department rather than by finance managers.
5. *Inventory management.* This function, too, may be assigned to the finance department because the purchase of materials and the stock-

ing of unsold finished products represents an investment of capital. In other cases, inventory control may be the responsibility of production managers.

Additional functions also may fall to the finance department. Data processing systems and procedures for the whole company often are worked out and supervised by specialists in financial control. It follows that in many firms the operation of computer centers is also the responsibility of the finance department. It is not uncommon, either, to assign general office administration to this department.

FINANCE ACTIVITIES HAVE UNIQUE ORGANIZATIONAL REQUIREMENTS

Financial management has distinct functions and activities, but these often are not used as the basis for organizing the finance department. Instead, a more general organizing principle has been found to be successful. Finance tasks can be divided into two categories: direct and indirect. These roughly correspond to line and staff duties. *Direct activities* include credit management, the collection and payment of bills, the leasing and purchasing of property, negotiating loans, and other tasks that directly carry on the work of the company. *Indirect activities* support the organization and provide internal financial services. These include accounting, budget assistance, the preparation of cost and income reports, data processing, and other tasks. (See Figure 20-1.)

These two types of financial work traditionally have been functionally separated. The first group of activities, the direct ones, are usually the responsibility of the *treasurer*. The *controller* is assigned the second group of activities. Both of these managers may be coordinated by a chief financial officer (CFO), or they sometimes report directly to the firm's top executive. The treasurer in a large organization may establish a number of subordinate departments: cash management, banking, capital expenditures, real estate, taxes, and others. Departments supervised by the controller include accounting systems and records, internal auditing, general and cost accounting, and budgeting.

Financial activities are often more influenced by the board of directors than are the other management specialties. It has traditionally been true that people selected for boards tend to be stronger in financial experience than in other areas. As a result, the finance committee of the board may become an active force in making internal financial decisions.

FINANCE MANAGERS HELP UNIFY INTERNAL CONTROLS

Financial managers have special control responsibilities. They deal with the fundamental resource of an organization—capital—and their recordkeeping activities make them a good target for the delegation of responsibility for report preparation.

Figure 20-1. Organization of Financial Management Functions.

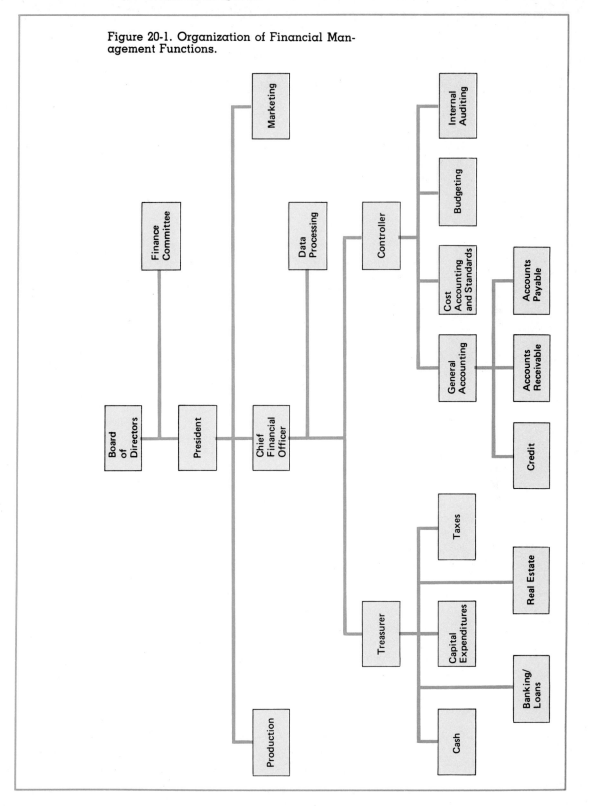

Integration of Standards and Controls

The role of finance managers in controlling the organization starts at the top. While each department or activity handles specific controls, such as product quality, the efficiency of sales routings, or the productivity of research, someone must see that these controls are tied together. This is usually the job of the finance department. It requires several steps.

1. Finance managers begin by assisting other departments in establishing standards. They apply, and help others to apply, special techniques to determine what it *ought* to cost to produce a single manufactured product, or what it *ought* to cost to provide a certain kind of service to a customer.
2. Through routine accounting systems, finance departments measure the flow and outcome of operations. They determine exact costs for manufacturing and sales. They count inventory and add up all of the expenses that were encountered in producing goods or services. For a manufacturing company, they tally production amounts, product rejects, and materials spoilage. For an airline, they record the number of passenger miles, the number of empty seats, and the hours that equipment is out of service for overhaul or repair.
3. Finance departments prepare comprehensive summary reports of the information gathered during operations. These reports bring together data from all of the operating departments to inform top managers on success in meeting standards. Reports also go to individual management specialists—production, sales, marketing, and distribution, for example. This helps them in adjusting their operations and helps to give an idea where they stand in total company progress.
4. Finance managers have a special responsibility for integrating a firm's overall financial plans and budgets. The separate operating departments usually know their needs and potential resources. It is the finance department, however, that makes sure that all of the separate proposals do not add up to a total resource demand greater than the organization can provide.

Specific Control Areas

Any operating activity may be subject to financial control. The extent of this control depends upon the cost of measurement and reporting and is related to the importance of the activity. Certain activity areas are generally believed to be critical to operational success. These have justifiably received major attention when financial managers design internal control procedures.

1. *Manufacturing or operations expenses and efficiency.* Accounting measurements of production include both production quantities and costs. Measurements are typically broken down by department, by

Managers in Action

FINANCIAL MANAGER

for mid-sized manufacturing company

Broad range of responsibilities:

Manage financial planning, supervise preparation of operating and capital budgets, assist in converting manual systems to computerized systems, analyze operating results, advise on tax minimization opportunities. Evaluate new business opportunities. Guide a competent, but young, accounting staff. Interface with a hard-driving, but friendly, informal management team.

PAYROLL SUPERVISOR

for western engineering firm

Take charge of payroll function for firm with 500 employees. Must supervise small section in payroll procedures including processing through automated system and preparation of payroll taxes and return. Good oral and written communication skills are essential.

ACCOUNTS RECEIVABLE MANAGER

for retail hardware chain

Responsibilities include routine accounting and bookkeeping procedures and collections. Must design and implement an effective credit system and work effectively with sales department in evaluating risks and making collections.

ACCOUNTING CONTROLLER

for environmental energy and health service company

Controller will supervise cost accounting activities and assist chief executive officer in budgeting and business planning.

ACCOUNTING MANAGER

for regional warehousing organization

Responsibilities include supervision of staff of five accountants and internal audit department. Must be able to install effective systems and procedures. Good report writing is essential. Will report to financial vice president.

job step, by time periods, and often according to individual workers and machines. Special assistance is given in distinguishing between "direct costs" such as labor and material and "overhead or indirect" costs such as plant maintenance and insurance.

2. *Sales revenues, costs, and effectiveness.* These controls include expense budgets, sales quotas, income, and sales volume reports for territories, product types, customer types, individual salespeople, or sales departments. Special reports and analyses may also be provided on incentive plans, salaries, and commissions.

3. *Distribution costs and effectiveness.* These include tallies of warehouse and shipping expenses, delivery costs, transportation between storage points, and charges for agents' services.

4. *Administrative and financial expenses.* These costs include interest, bad debts, taxes, losses from excess facilities, office expenses, contributions, legal fees, and others. They are often thought of as overhead and as nothing but a drag on profits. Viewed another way, though, they are a source of gain: a $1,000 savings in office expense is $1,000 that can be contributed directly to profits.

INVESTMENT DECISIONS DETERMINE HOW FUNDS WILL BE USED

Financial planning at the top level includes two main aspects; investment decisions and financing decisions. The first determine what funds are needed for. The second decide where the money will come from.

Investment decisions are complex and risky. It is widely recognized that personal investments, such as stocks, bonds, real estate, or livestock, have the potential for creating losses as often as they may provide gains. The same is true for the financial management of a company. When managers decide to replace a machine, to lease new warehouse space, or to buy advertising time on television, they are investing money. Such investments can make money or lose money. The trick is to make the investments profitable. This is a challenging task, indeed.

Some of the possible applications of an organization's money are listed in Table 20-1. For purposes of discussion, these can be roughly categorized into two kinds of uses: (1) capital expenses for long-lasting facilities and (2) working capital for supporting day-to-day operations.

Capital-Expense Planning and Budgeting

All plans should contribute to overall objectives. Nowhere is this guide more essential than in planning capital investments. The long-lasting facilities of an organization are called *fixed assets;* they cannot easily be turned into cash. They usually represent large investments of money, especially when measured as a proportion of total capital available. A serious flaw in capital-investment plans can quickly prove fatal to the organization.

TABLE 20-1. USES OF FUNDS.

- Addition to fixed assets:
  Property.
  Buildings.
  Equipment.

- Repurchase of company's stock.

- Reduction of long-term debt.

- Decrease in current liabilities:
  Payment of short-term loans.
  Payment of creditors' bills.

- Increase in current assets:
  Addition to cash account.
  Addition to accounts receivables.
  Addition to inventories.

- Payment of dividends to stockholders.

- Net increases in working capital.

The basic problem in the planning of fixed-assets acquisition is evaluating the desirability of alternative ways of using money. The manager must ask, "Should I buy that abrasives company for $15 million, or should I spend $20 million to build our own abrasives plant with the most modern equipment?" The decision will affect profits and losses for years to come.

Finance managers look at a number of factors in making such decisions. A natural question is, "How long will it take to get our money back if we invest it this way?" The time it takes to earn back the investment is its *pay-back period*. Everything else being equal, a short pay-back is usually more attractive than a long pay-back. Managers also ask about the expected profits expressed as a percentage of the investment. A 10 percent return obviously looks better than a 2 percent return. A complicating factor in any method of evaluating capital investments is the cost of the money invested. Borrowed money requires the payment of interest; money invested by stockholders requires the future payment of dividends. Even cash held on hand is costly. If it were invested in a project or kept in a savings account, it might earn an income. Further risk is introduced because revenue and cost estimates, upon which profit projections are based, are just that, estimates of the future. They may be, and often are, wildly inaccurate.

For all its difficulty, capital-expense planning and budgeting is essential. Capital-expense budgets are the financial reflections of an organization's long-range goals. Suppose a firm wants to diversify into the cardboard-packaging business in seven years. To do so, it must have plans on the board far ahead of time for generating and using capital needed to acquire the necessary manufacturing and storage facilities. Otherwise, the diversification will not be achieved.

Working-Capital Management

Money is not invested only in fixed assets. Firms also buy goods that are relatively easy to convert into cash—in theory, at least. These are called *current assets*. They include raw materials, supplies, goods in process, finished products, money owed (accounts receivable) from customers, and cash itself. Organizations are also concerned with the extent of their current liabilities. These are their short-term loans plus their unpaid bills. In order to keep operating without interruption, a firm needs to have a larger sum of current assets than current liabilities. The difference between these two amounts is called working capital, and its management is one of the most critical that finance managers face. It should be neither too large nor too small.

A company that continuously has hundreds of thousands of dollars invested in working capital, but produces sales of only $1 million a year is not doing well with that investment. In general, the less working capital—up to a point—that can be used to generate a given sales level, the better. One practical approach to this problem concentrates on holding operating expenses to a minimum. Techniques include keeping the smallest inventory possible without disrupting sales, and maintaining the smallest store of raw materials possible without interrupting production or having to pay premiums for small quantities. Another approach focuses on collecting customers' bills as quickly as possible, while deferring the payment of the firm's bills as long as is practical.

The financial question of how much working capital is enough is difficult to answer in practice. As the amount of working capital provided for a given sales level decreases, for example, the firm's risk increases—but so does the potential profit. Every organization must work out for itself the proper balance point at which the risk does not outweigh the profit potential.

FINANCING DECISIONS DETERMINE THE SOURCES OF FUNDS

The expenditure of funds raises another question: Where does an organization get the money that it invests in facilities and operations? The fundamental source of this money is always the owners. The owners of a company put up money for its use in the expectation of sharing in the profits created by operations. This equity capital is the basis of the entire business structure. Organizations also borrow money both for capital investment and for operations. Debt financing is attractive in many cases because, even though interest must be paid on it, it increases the productive capability far beyond that provided by owners' investments. See Table 20-2.

An important responsibility of financial managers, and of executives and the board of directors, is determining the proportion of funds that will derive from equity financing and the proportion from debt financing. The situation is similar to that with working capital, since it cuts two ways. The more money a company borrows, the greater its capacity for producing profits, but the greater its risk of being unable to meet interest payments or to repay the loans.

Equity Financing   This presents less expense and risk than debt financing, since owners do not usually require fixed repayments of their investment. They often expect never to withdraw the original investment; they plan, instead,

TABLE 20-2. SOURCES OF FUNDS.	
FROM EQUITY	**FROM DEBT**

• Additional investment by owner.
• Issuance and sale of stock to investors.
• Profit derived from operations.
• Interest or dividends from marketable securities owned.
• Sale of assets.
• Depreciation expenses deductible from income taxes.
	• Long-term borrowing (over a year):
	   Mortgages.
	   Bonds.
	• Short-term borrowing (less than a year).
	• Credit from suppliers of materials and equipment.

to share in its earnings for long periods. For financial managers of ongoing operations, equity financing requires decisions related to two main questions:

1. Do we need to increase equity investment by finding new investors? This would involve the sale of additional stock for a corporation, or finding new partners in a privately owned business.
2. How much of this year's earnings will be distributed to investors, and how much will be retained to buy assets for the company? This is a critical decision because, on the one hand, distributing profits to stockholders attracts investors, but on the other hand, retaining large shares of earnings is a sound way of financing growth. In a private company with limited credit opportunities, reinvesting earnings may be the only good way to grow.

Debt Financing   This comes from many sources, such as the sale of bonds, short- or long-term loans from banks and other financial institutions, and credit purchases of materials and equipment. As with other financial decisions, a genuine problem is determining the real cost or real value of the borrowed funds. Interest rates, loan processing costs, length of repayment periods, and other sources of expense and benefit can vary considerably.

Government Funding   The source of money for most government-operated institutions and agencies is, of course, funds appropriated by legislative bodies from tax sources. The financial manager's role, however, differs only slightly from that in private business. Planning and control objectives are similar as are reporting needs and procedures. A government financial officer, however, may expect to meet even more complex legal regulations of the use of funds.

SUMMARY

1. Financial management applies the management functions to regulate the sources and uses of funds for an organization. Its main tasks are financial planning, internal control, coordination (especially by means of the accounting system), and often credit and inventory management.

2. Organizing for financial management usually divides work into direct and indirect activities, reflected in the positions of treasurer and controller. Subordinate departments may be established to handle banking, cash management, real estate, and other financial or accounting-related concerns.

3. Finance departments usually integrate controls for the entire organization. They help set standards, gather financial and certain nonfinancial information, make comprehensive summaries combining data from different departments, and help integrate plans and budgets. They apply financial controls to manufacturing and purchasing, sales, distribution, and administrative and financial functions.

4. A major responsibility for financial managers is evaluating the effectiveness of current and proposed investments of funds. The two main areas of investment for an organization are in fixed assets and in working capital. In both cases, managers must balance risk, costs of funds, and profit potential.

5. The two major sources of funds for an organization are equity and debt. Debt financing has the advantage of expanding the productive capacity of the firm, but it introduces fixed expenses for interest and repayment and it increases risk. Equity financing is safer, but may be harder to obtain. Its main sources are original investments by owners, sale of stock, and profits that have been reinvested.

REVIEW AND DISCUSSION QUESTIONS

1. How do you think financial planning should relate to top-level planning and to marketing and production planning in an organization?

2. The text lists coordination as a major function of financial management. What are some of the things financial managers coordinate? Why isn't this the job of top management?

3. A major carpet manufacturer formerly had assigned credit management to the marketing department and inventory control to the production department, but moved both these functions to the finance department. What could be its justification for the reorganization?

4. What is the difference between a treasurer and a controller?

5. What is the role of finance managers in integrating the budgets of different units of the organization? What do finance managers try to accomplish?

6. What are four activities of financial managers that help to integrate plans and controls?

7. Briefly describe two factors a finance manager might consider when deciding whether to invest in fixed assets.

8. The conservative president of a hosiery manufacturing company refuses to use any debt financing at all. What might his justification be for this policy?

Problems and Projects

1. The planning done by financial managers is like other planning in that it varies in the length of time covered in a planning period. Financial plans may be short term, intermediate, or long range. Financial managers must usually make plans for each of the five functions listed below. For each function, propose one long-range strategy or goal and one strategy or goal suitable for a one-year intermediate plan. Use your proposals to illustrate the planning concerns of financial managers.

   a. Investment and finance
   b. Financial control
   c. Coordination
   d. Credit management
   e. Inventory management

2. *Performance Situation—The Big Real Estate Broker:* Northern Properties, Inc., is a prosperous real estate company specializing in commercial and industrial property. The firm has several good-sized offices and a staff that includes specialists in every relevant area, from engineering to law. Since the company not only acts as agent for other buyers and sellers of offices, factories, stores and undeveloped land, but also buys and sells on its own, managers must be organized to handle complex financial situations. Ten of these tasks are:

   a. General accounting for the firm.
   b. Negotiating loans.
   c. Collecting money owed to the firm.
   d. Distributing earnings to owners of the company.
   e. Preparing internal financial reports.
   f. Keeping records of expenses for supplies.
   g. Payment of bills owed by the company.
   h. Helping prepare project budgets.
   i. Cost accounting and reporting.
   j. Data processing.

Provide a simple financial organization for this company, using two financial managers. Name the two positions and distribute these 10 tasks between the two. Describe the basis upon which you made the distribution.

3. The controller of a company that provides classroom training, consulting, and educational materials to industrial customers is working on a comprehensive reporting system. Although the existing accounting system already provides a variety of regular reports, the company managers have complained that they do not get the specific information they need when they need it. As a result, the controller has decided to start from scratch. She will try to identify exactly what information is needed by top managers to judge the success of operations and decide on needed adjustments. The controller has put three headings on a large sheet of paper: marketing, operations, and administration-finance. List five specific kinds of information for which reports will be needed for each of these three areas. Propose at least one way the separate types of information could be put together to be useful for top-level decision making.

4. Since financial management makes decisions about how an organization's capital will be invested, finance decisions must be thoroughly integrated with planning and strategy building in other areas, principally marketing and production. Consider a new company that is getting started in the market for high-priced, hand-built sports cars. It would have to consider manufacturing, marketing, and finance more as different aspects of an overall top-level plan than as separate management activities. The company's managers hope to build and sell 75 cars in the first three years of operation, with each car having a retail price of around $30,000.

For each of the three areas listed below, propose two strategies that would work together to give this company entry into their market. Remember that each strategy must aim toward an organization goal and that all strategies must be mutually supporting.

   a. Marketing
   b. Production
   c. Finance

5. Choose an enterprise, agency, or group with which you are familiar or about which you can easily get information: a club, a civic group, a town government, a local business, or your school. Analyze the organization you have selected to answer the following questions:

   a. How are its financial functions organized? How many people engage in financial activities, and what structure and positions have been established? Draw an organization chart for the finance department, if appropriate.

   b. What kind of financial planning does the organization carry out? What are its major sources of funds? Its major uses of funds?

   c. What kind of financial controls does the organization use? Who is responsible for gathering internal financial data? Who is responsible for interpreting it and making decisions based on it?

Discuss in class the similarities and differences among the organizations analyzed by each student.

6. Prepare a personal financial plan for yourself for the coming year. Consider the major issues important to financial planners for an organization. What income or revenue will be available and from what sources will it come? How will you spend the money? Will you buy any fixed assets such as a car or furniture? What portion will be used for day-to-day "operations" or living expenses? What proportion of your capital will be from current earnings or savings or from debt? How will you maintain control of income and expenses? How will you be sure that bills are paid when due? How will you maintain records?

Cases for Analysis and Discussion

CASE 1: THE MISSING CAPITAL

Martin was dearly hoping that a soft answer would "turneth away wrath," but it didn't seem to be working that way. In response to the boss's tirade about the year's poor financial results, Martin answered quietly, "Yes, we planned. Of course we planned. But it isn't possible to anticipate everything. We obviously missed something."

The boss answered, "You sure did miss something. And we're all going to be missing a lot more if we don't come up with that money. What happened to the profits anyway?"

What happened was this: Central Bank, Martin's employer, had planned to reinvest $1 million of its profits for the year (60 percent of the anticipated total profits of $1.67 million) in new computerized tellers' stations and other service equipment. Top management considered the new equipment absolutely essential if the bank were to remain competitive with the other banks in town. When the year ended, though, the profit was found to be only $1 million altogether, rather than the $1.67 million expected.

Martin knew where the missing profits were, but he hesitated to say so because it was his boss who made the decisions that had caused the drop in profits. In further efforts to stay competitive in a tough market, the boss had started an expensive—and unbudgeted—advertising campaign halfway through the year. The boss had also made a quick decision to open a branch in a shopping center location that had unexpectedly become available.

A. What is behind this problem? Was there a failure in financial management? If so, what kind of failure?

B. What alternatives does the bank have now? What possible actions could they take concerning the new equipment and their profits distribution?

C. Is there anything management could have done to prevent this situation from occurring, or at least from coming as a surprise at the end of the year? What does this say about the relation of financial controls and financial plans?

CASE 2: YOU RUN YOUR DEPARTMENT; I'LL RUN MINE

"The expenses just don't work out for that location, Harry. Look at these taxes; they'll eat us up. And what about insurance in that neighborhood? Vandalism, arson—the rates are terrible." That's Betty Jarvis, the financial manager, speaking.

"I tell you, Betty, it's the best place for the plant. Look. We need really top people to work in this factory. Machinists. Do you know how tight the market is for machinists? I've got to have people with years of experience in industrial testing. Even the people who do the drafting—just drawing plans—have to have special qualifications. Those people are only found in a city. If we put the plant out in some meadow where the taxes are low and you only need insurance against damage by cows, there's not going to be anyone to work in the factory. That spot we picked out has got everything we need: the transportation is perfect, the building is already there, and it's cheap for that much space, and the workers we need are there." That's Harry Carr, the manufacturing manager, speaking.

A. Is this a legitimate disagreement, or is either Betty or Harry being unreasonable?

B. Harry eventually ends up telling Betty to run her own department and to let him make the manufacturing decisions. Is he justified in this? Who really should make a decision like this?

C. In what way could the organization be changed to prevent this kind of disagreement? How could it be changed to make it easier to resolve such disagreements?

Personnel and Labor Relations Management

21

After completing Chapter 21, you will be able to do the following:

● Analyze the major objectives of a personnel department to judge whether all essential functions are included.

● Propose a simple structure for organizing the personnel functions, bearing in mind their staff relationship with the overall organization. Draw an organization chart of your proposed structure for the personnel functions.

● Describe the purpose of organization development and propose steps a personnel manager might take to evaluate and improve a given organization.

● Name three criteria for the success of wage and salary administration and apply them to specific decisions to be made by personnel managers.

● Identify and describe three responsibilities of personnel managers when dealing with labor-management relations for their organization.

Industrial managers are fond of giving visiting dignitaries a tour of the plant. They stride down the long walkways pointing out the smooth-running automatic conveyors, the gleaming machinery, the efficiently humming power plant. In the office they display the word processing equipment, the colorful new modular furniture, and the impressive computer sitting behind its thick glass screen, silently running through thousands of operations a second. Yet, if those same managers had to come to the factory or office and there were no skilled people working there, the conveyors would be still, the power plant silent, the machinery dead and useless. All of their shining equipment would take on a different aspect; it would be only a burden, unproductive and impossible to pay for.

The job of personnel management is to make plants and offices lively and productive by filling them with willing men and women who use their skill, dedication, and imagination to get the organization's work done. It has often been said that people are the most important resource an organization has, and there is justification for this view. Given the right managers and workers, the other resources, even capital, can be obtained. Without the right managers and workers, all the capital in the world will produce little or nothing useful.

Every manager must be concerned with human resources: staffing, developing the skills of others, motivating, communicating, and deciding on promotions, pay levels, and other kinds of rewards. A typical line manager, understandably, is most interested in staffing as it applies to his or her department. A personnel manager, however, must take a comprehensive view of the human resources of the organization. A personnel manager must be concerned with staffing from top management to the direct production worker, and in every functional area.

PERSONNEL MANAGEMENT FOCUSES ON FIVE KEY AREAS

Personnel management applies the management functions in order to supply people who are willing and able to carry on the activities needed to accomplish the organization's mission. Generally, managers whose responsibility is personnel administration accomplish their main task by performing in the five areas outlined below: employment, planning and development, wage and salary administration, employee services, and labor-management relations. See Figure 21-1 on page 465.

An important overall concern and responsibility surrounds these five specific functions. To an increasing extent, personnel managers directly reflect the social responsibility of the organization toward its employees. They are charged with eliminating unfair discrimination in hiring and promotion, with protecting employees from injury and job-related illness, with promoting the development of interesting and satisfying jobs, and with finding ways to balance the legitimate interests of employees with the need to achieve the goals of the organization.

As discussed in Chapter 16, many of the interests of employees are protected by law, and it becomes a common duty of personnel managers to ensure compliance with legal and regulatory requirements in personnel matters. Complex programs and policies may be called for by government safety rules. Equal-employment-opportunity regulations call for constant attention to hiring and promotion practices; many organizations have affirmative-action plans, making a commitment to take positive action to increase the job opportunities of women and minorities. Personnel specialists usually design and oversee the operation of these plans. Many of the detailed activities of the personnel department, such as administering wages and hours, also come under government regulation.

Employment This function recruits and selects people to do the work of the organization. It includes: job analysis to determine the qualifications needed for each distinct segment of the total work; advertising and using other means to locate potential candidates for open positions; selecting from among the candidates; orienting new employees to the work place; advising on promotions and transfers; dealing with dismissals, retirements, and resignations; and recordkeeping for all of these activities. For management-level positions, the main role of personnel specialists is to aid and advise in these activities. For production-level employees, personnel managers often carry out directly the employment function.

Human-Resources Planning and Development Successful organizations are future oriented. If future plans for production or marketing are to be fulfilled, for instance, the human resources of the organization must be planned and marshaled so as to be ready when needed. The organization structure must be decided upon in advance. The people must be prepared to fill the positions created by future needs. Nearly every manager joins in this activity, but personnel managers play a particularly important role in guiding and unifying the shape of the internal structure. Additionally, the personnel department is usually responsible for designing and/or providing the training needed to bring employees' skills up to meet future needs.

Wage and Salary Administration

Despite popular emphasis on nonfinancial motivation for performance, the fact remains that people are paid for their work. Accordingly, the rational administration of wages and salaries is essential. This job includes: deciding on the difficulty and contribution of different kinds of work; setting pay scales for specific jobs; working out the specific forms of payment (such as incentive plans, fringe benefits, profit sharing, and other kinds of compensation); assisting with performance appraisals; and dealing with overtime, work shifts, and other scheduling matters that affect wages.

Employee Services

Many of the detailed activities of personnel managers result from the need to assure employees of a safe environment and to provide the kinds of services needed wherever groups of people gather. The personnel department may be charged, for example, with providing food service, administering the safety program, overseeing plant security and employee protection, providing first aid and medical services, and maintaining employee facilities such as lounges and recreation areas.

Labor-Management Relations

Traditionally, the responsibility for collective bargaining with employee representatives, for administering labor union contracts, and for dealing on a daily basis with labor-management relations is assigned to the personnel department.

PERSONNEL ADMINISTRATION FUNCTIONS AS BOTH LINE AND STAFF

The organization of personnel activities is complicated by a distinguishing characteristic similar to but more marked than that of finance management: personnel administration is a staff function, but in many organizations the department has duties that are at least partially line responsibilities. When a management position becomes open, for instance, it is normal that the line manager who supervises the position has both the responsibility and the authority to fill it. The personnel manager is purely advisory

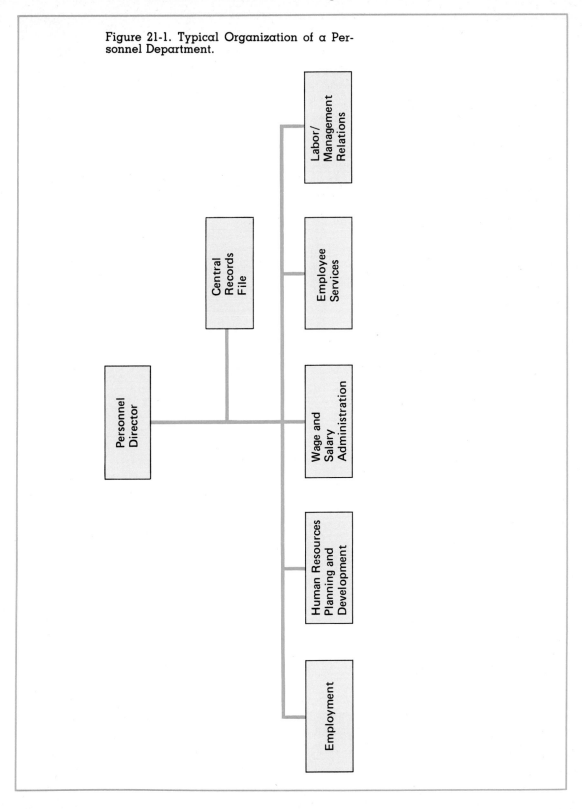

Figure 21-1. Typical Organization of a Personnel Department.

Managers in Action

MANAGER OF PERSONNEL

for leading bank in southwest

Position is responsible for recruiting, salary administration, affirmative action, and employee counseling. Good oral and written skills plus the ability to deal with all levels of management is essential.

COMPENSATION MANAGER

for Florida health care center

This person will be expected to:

- Develop uniform merit salary administration guidelines based on employee performance.
- Formulate performance standards.
- Develop and implement the critical steps required for success of program.

PERSONNEL ADMINISTRATOR

for liberal arts college in northeast

Manages recruitment and employment functions, oversees promotion and transfer policies, provides professional consultation on employee/employer relations, supervises recordkeeping program, assures that all employment matters conform to EEO and Affirmative Action policies and practices.

TRAINING AND DEVELOPMENT SUPERVISOR

for a multi-unit retail corporation

Individual to supervise in-house training programs. Primary responsibility includes planning, development, and training of store personnel and management. Essentials are a vigorous, imaginative, and bold approach to achieve results; willingness to work in an "energetic" style, and ability to get things accomplished in a large chain organization.

in this case. But when direct production or operation jobs must be filled, there is a subtle shift in emphasis: the personnel manager is often charged with all of the employment activities of recruiting and selecting; the responsible line manager usually has the role of concurring with the selections or vetoing them. Handling this shifting nature of advisory and active roles is a challenge to those who serve in the field of personnel administration. See Figure 21-2.

Bearing in mind this special consideration, the task of organizing the personnel function requires the same considerations as organizing any other function. The basic step is the analysis of the work to be done and its division into units. The five key personnel functions described in the previous section often provide the framework for the division. Variation of structure may take place based upon similarity of work and emphasis given to specific organizational goals. For example, salary administration may stand alone, or it may be joined with the employment function since it is closely related to job analysis and promotion decisions. In other instances, employee training and development, which is part of the planning and development function, may be placed alongside employee services. Some companies combine functions on the basis of the extent of recordkeeping involved and thus link salary administration to employment or to planning and development in order to centralize records.

DEVELOPMENT GUIDES THE ORGANIZATION INTO THE FUTURE

A great deal of the work associated with the personnel function is routine, especially that of keeping a central data file of all employees and positions, including wage, salary, and overtime records. These tasks are essential, but they are basically maintenance duties. They keep track of historical information. Legally, at least, no organization can function without this data. Personnel managers, however, must perform another central role: helping to create a strong organization made up of capable, innovative people, today and in the future.

LINE APPROACH:

Employment of Production and Clerical Workers.

STAFF APPROACH:

Employment of Management Personnel.

Figure 21-2. Dual Nature of Personnel Role.

Organization (or human resources) planning and development is the personnel activity concerned with this goal. This role may be seen as having two aspects: (1) providing formal and direct development activities and (2) acting as a consultant for organizational change.

Formal Development   The formal organization planning and development carried on by personnel managers is similar to that part of the staffing function required of all managers. It differs in that personnel managers must consider needs for *all* employees, and that the personnel department plays a unique coordinating role in integrating the personnel planning of different departments and divisions of the organization.

ANALYSIS OF CURRENT CONDITIONS   The first step is to analyze the existing structure and its positions and labor requirements. Planning should provide for correcting faults in the current organization and for reshaping the organization to meet future needs. Identification of present problems can be guided by such questions as the following:

- Have positions been created to suit the abilities of specific persons, and should these be changed when the persons leave or retire?
- Are there jobs that are no longer as productive or as necessary as they used to be because of changes in operations?
- Are there activities that have grown large enough so as to be separated from their parent department?
- Are there conflicts in coordination that could be reduced by combining activities?

PROJECTION OF FUTURE CONDITIONS   Looking to future needs must first provide replacements for normal turnover, retirements, transfers, and dismissals. More important, though, the planning of personnel managers must create a human reflection of the organization's future strategies. If, for example, a small-appliance maker plans to become more marketing oriented in five years, it must plan now to have people with marketing strength when the time comes. If a manufacturing company, for another example, expects to swing toward the provision of services, it must now start building the kind of team of workers and managers that can run and sell a service operation.

PROGRAMS TO FILL THE GAP   Such analysis and planning will provide a fairly specific idea of the number of people, along with their defined skills and experience, the organization will need in the future. The task then becomes one of helping to find and/or develop these people. (See Figure 21-3.) Personnel managers advise managers on the development of subordinate managers. They may help design the appraisal system; they may help set performance standards; they may provide special appraisal and

Figure 21-3. Task of Human Resources Planning and Development.

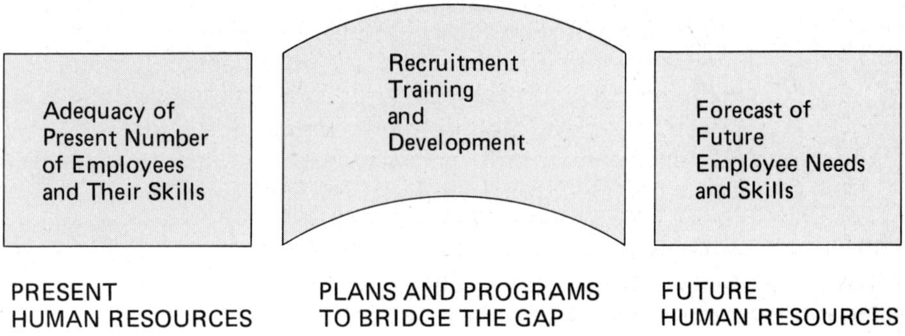

Adequacy of Present Number of Employees and Their Skills	Recruitment Training and Development	Forecast of Future Employee Needs and Skills
PRESENT HUMAN RESOURCES	**PLANS AND PROGRAMS TO BRIDGE THE GAP**	**FUTURE HUMAN RESOURCES**

development services. They will almost certainly be in charge of providing formal training programs to provide specific skills and knowledge needed by both workers and managers.

Consulting for Change

Some of the changes that are desirable in an organization cannot be brought about by teaching workers how to operate a new lathe or by teaching managers a new way to calculate return on investment. Technical training will not work to overcome some of the conditions that hinder organization performance. For example, what about the manager who has such an autocratic personality that he or she destroys morale in the department? Or the work group that limits production to what is very easy for its least competent member? Or the clerks who stash half of their work in a file drawer to purposely get behind schedule so they will have to work overtime and be paid more wages?

It is clear that problems like these result from the personal and social makeup of the organization. It is equally clear that someone with special personal and technical skills is needed to initiate change in such subtle and complex human situations. That person often is a personnel manager.

Acting as consultants, personnel specialists can sometimes help other managers change their leadership and motivating styles. They can sometimes help work groups examine their individual expectations and group norms. They can help managers and workers to know each other better and to harmonize their goals to create a true team. Such results require great skill in personal relations and a greater degree of patience. Changes on the human level are slow, sometimes painful, and often quite difficult to maintain.

Additionally, personnel specialists often serve as the "change agents" in formal organizational-development (OD) programs. These programs have been briefly described in Chapter 14 as formal, broad-based efforts to improve the abilities and attitudes of the people and groups in an organization to make them better able to work together to meet shared goals. To be effective, the people undertaking organizational development need sophisticated skills in understanding and analyzing where the problems lie in the human organization; for example, where communication is poor, where group norms are depressing productivity, where a leadership style is unsuited to the situation, or where technical skills are lacking. Further skills are then needed to make changes to improve functioning in the organization and its people, through training, development activities, counseling, introducing new management techniques, and other approaches. Personnel managers often have special training and experience in these techniques and play an important role in bringing about the needed changes.

PERSONNEL MANAGERS HELP REGULATE EMPLOYEE COMPENSATION

Salaries and wages are important to an organization because they are an important source of costs, they partly determine employee satisfaction, and they effect the quality of workers and managers an organization can attract.

Criteria for Wage and Salary Administration

Reflecting the ways that wages and salaries are important to the smooth functioning of an organization, many managers apply three criteria in judging the success of wage and salary administration:

1. Wages and salaries should be fair and equitable. The basic expression of this standard is "equal pay for equal work." Fairness demands that people doing work of the same difficulty and making the same contribution to meeting goals receive the same pay, making rational adjustments for such factors as length of service. When the rate of pay is based on individual performance, fairness also calls for raises to be given most often to the best performers and least often to those whose work quality is poor or who do not apply themselves to their work.

2. Wage and salary costs should be minimized, to the extent that this can be done without conflicting with other goals. Efficiency and productivity demand that the least resources possible be used to produce a given level of output. This means that wages—which must be paid from the financial resources of the organization—should not be artificially inflated. They should be high enough to be fair, to help motivate and satisfy workers, and to keep the organization able to hire good employees, but no higher.

3. Wages and salaries should attract capable employees and provide some incentive to good performance on the job. This requires that

wages and salaries paid be high enough to keep the organization competitive in the labor market and to make most employees feel that they are being fairly paid for the contribution they are making to meeting organization goals.

Rational planning will help satisfy these criteria, but only if wage and salary policies and decisions are well coordinated with other personnel functions. In making wages fair, for instance, managers typically try to give equal pay for equal performance within each type and level of skill and responsibility. To do this, however, requires several things. Managers must know the skill and work each job demands; this requires that jobs be analyzed. Managers must know how well each individual performs his or her job; this requires an effective appraisal system. Managers must know how much each type of work contributes to the operations of the organization; this means there must be some kind of ranking of jobs. Each of these activities—job analysis, performance appraisal, and job ranking—are needed for reasons other than pay decisions, but they contribute to those decisions.

Forms of Compensation

Anything given to employees in return for their work may be called *compensation*. Monetary compensation includes wages and salaries. *Wages* are hourly rates paid only for hours actually worked. *Salaries* are periodic time payments made for filling a given position, and are not based directly on the number of hours worked. Compensation may come in other forms. These include rates paid for each unit of a product produced (a piece-rate incentive), commissions based on quantity of goods sold by salespeople, and bonuses based on some measured performance that exceeds a standard output.

Increasingly, fringe benefits are assuming nearly the same importance to employees as basic compensation. *Fringe benefits* are compensations given to employees in a form other than direct cash pay for work performed. The range of these benefits is tremendous: paid vacations and holidays; sick leave; hospitalization; medical, dental, and disability insurance; life insurance; paid day care for children; retirement and pension plans; and many others. Careful planning and management of these employee benefits is important. The proper selection of a benefit package can increase the motivation and satisfaction of employees with varying needs and interests. At the same time, careful attention to the costs of benefits is critical; they can add one-third or more to direct personnel costs and become a significant item in overall operation costs.

Compensation Policies

The principle job of wage and salary administration is threefold: to decide (1) the form of compensation for each job in the organization, (2) the amount to be paid, and (3) when and if pay increases will be given, and if so, how much. The personnel manager's role in these decisions is mainly advisory. It is the line manager's task to decide such issues, but personnel managers provide expert guidance on the factors that underlie pay decisions.

EXECUTIVE COMPENSATION   The compensation of executives and high-level managers is influenced by the size of their organization, the type of organization it is, and the amount of responsibility they carry. Where the chief executive of a business is responsible for the profitability of the whole organization, total compensation may be very high. In larger corporations, this salary sometimes runs into hundreds of thousands of dollars. Managers below the chief executive receive salaries that are often set in relationship to that of the top manager's. One company could decide, for example, that managers at the level immediately below the top should receive around 70 percent of the compensation of the chief executive; managers at the third level down might then be scheduled to receive about 50 percent of the top salary. This ranking of executives' salaries—regardless of the exact proportions used—helps maintain consistency and fairness within the organization. The absolute, or dollar, amount of compensation will normally be affected by the prevailing pay rates in the industry or type of organization. If the typical executive director of large charitable organizations, for example, makes over $100,000, a charity that does not match or better that figure will not be able to compete for the best talent.

EMPLOYEE COMPENSATION   Wage and salary levels for production and clerical workers are also determined by the need for fairness and by the competitive situation in the labor market. Low-paying companies have trouble hiring employees except in times of high unemployment or in geographical areas where few jobs are available. The need for fairness, however, can create problems with wage earners who expect periodic raises. If pay raises are granted each year to an unskilled worker who stays with an organization for many years, that person will eventually earn more than a highly skilled worker who is just beginning work for the company. Organizations have two responses to this. Some firms limit the maximum wage that can be paid for a given job category; the only way to exceed the maximum is to learn the skills needed for promotion and then be promoted to a higher-level job. Other employers simply let the pay differential continue. They reason that a very loyal unskilled worker who has been with the company for years is worth more than a skilled worker who is just starting out.

LABOR-MANAGEMENT RELATIONS ARE A PERSONNEL SPECIALTY
Personnel managers deal mainly with employees. In any organization they are supposed to ease and facilitate relations among the people who work there, from a sweeper in the warehouse to the chief executive. One characteristic of workers is that they sometimes form labor, or trade, unions. In organizations where employees belong to

labor unions, dealing with union matters is usually a specialized responsibility of the personnel manager. In some companies, the personnel department serves only in an advisory capacity; in other cases, specialists in personnel may be appointed as representatives of management to carry out contract negotiations and other relations with unions.

Handling relations with labor unions includes a number of different responsibilities: among the most important are collective bargaining, contract administration, and grievance handling.

Collective Bargaining

Collective bargaining is the process in which representatives of the workers meet with representatives of management and negotiate the terms of employment for the workers. Typical issues to be negotiated include wages, hours of work, and working conditions. Working conditions include production quotas, the protection of employee's health and safety, and the handling of complaints and grievances. The bargaining process can be long and grueling, with each side seizing the slightest opportunity to advance its own interests.

Contract Administration

This is often the key to the success of the whole process of maintaining good labor relations. Even the most detailed labor contract must state many issues as principles, in general rather than specific terms. The application of these general provisions to actual operations on the shop floor is the job of first-line supervisors. They do so, however, with the assistance of personnel specialists. A good job of administering the contract—one in which decisions are fair and consistent—will usually bring harmony. A poor job in this area will result in nothing but trouble.

Grievance Procedures

The handling of grievances is usually a formal process with progressive steps defined by the labor contract. (Such procedures are also followed in many non-union companies.) A *grievance* is a complaint about pay, hours, working conditions, supervisory treatment, or any other matter for which an employee tries to get redress. If an employee thinks he or she has been unfairly transferred to a lower-paying job, that is a "complaint." If he or she tries to get the company to do something about it, such as restoring his or her former wages, the complaint becomes a "grievance."

Handling grievances is usually easier if a step-by-step process, a *grievance procedure*, is agreed upon by management and labor in advance. The first step might include a conference between the employee and his or her direct supervisor. The goal is to come to a mutually satisfactory resolution. If the first effort fails, the grievance then may be carried to higher and higher levels of the organization. At the same time, the procedure involves progressively higher-level union representatives until the dispute is finally resolved.

SUMMARY

1. The five main tasks handled by personnel managers are (a) employment—defining positions and recruiting and selecting candidates to fill them; (b) human resources planning and development—analyzing the organization and proposing changes and methods to meet future needs; (c) wage and salary administration—regulating compensation to make it both fair and competitive; (d) employee services—providing a safe and satisfying work environment; and (e) labor-management relations—negotiating and administering labor contracts.

2. Personnel management and administration is a staff function with certain line responsibilities. Its organization must reflect the need to maintain relationships with other managers, ranging from purely advisory to directly functional.

3. Personnel managers play a key role in the development of the organization to improve current deficiencies and provide the structure, relationships, positions, and people needed for the future. The development process combines (a) formal approaches, such as assisting with job analysis, performance appraisals, and work-standards development, with (b) consultant activities to facilitate changes in less-clearly defined areas such as leadership style and employee morale.

4. Personnel managers administer wages and salaries to control personnel costs and to enable the organization to compete in the labor market for the skilled and imaginative employees it needs. The major decisions involved are the forms of compensation to be given for each job, the amount of pay, and when pay raises will be given and in what amount.

5. Relations with labor unions are usually at least partly the responsibility of personnel managers. The duties may include collective bargaining, administering labor contracts, and dealing with grievances.

REVIEW AND DISCUSSION QUESTIONS

1. How is the *employment* function of personnel managers related to their responsibility for *human resources planning and development?*

2. How is the *employment* function related to *wage and salary administration?*

3. How does the personnel department fit into the structure of the overall organization? Is this a problem for personnel managers?

4. Griswald Equipment Co. has decided to begin a regional chain of company-owned, consumer, auto parts stores. How would the personnel department play a role in the preparation for this major new venture?

5. The text says that personnel specialists act as consultants in bringing about changes in factors such as leadership style and employee morale. Give two reasons why you think the personnel managers might be able to do this better than the responsible line managers.

6. The compensation planning for a small printing company has failed because emphasis was given solely to keeping costs to an absolute minimum. What are two other factors the personnel managers should have considered?

7. Name four specific decisions that must be made in determining the compensation for a particular job at a particular time.

8. What is collective bargaining? Do all personnel managers have to take part in it?

Problems and Projects

1. A medium-sized government agency has five staff personnel specialists who report to a director of personnel. Each of the specialists has particular responsibility for one of the following functions:
   a. Employment
   b. Planning and development
   c. Wage and salary administration
   d. Employee services
   e. Labor relations

A separate manager handles routine administration, correspondence, maintaining files, keeping records, and similar duties.

The list below includes decisions, activities, and tasks with which the personnel department is confronted. Assign each item on the list to one of the personnel specialists who will be given primary responsibility for it. A number of the items may typically require close coordination among more than one specialist. Identify these and indicate which managers would have to work together on each. Assume that recordkeeping details will be handled by the manager of routine administration.

   (1) Employee turnover and absenteeism have become excessive in the licensing department. It is suspected that the problem is caused by low morale.
   (2) One employee feels she was unfairly deprived of overtime pay, and hasn't been able to work out the dispute with her supervisor.
   (3) A new law passed by the legislature requires the agency to begin field inspections of certain classes of licensees. This is an entirely new activity.
   (4) The commissioner, who has ultimate authority over the agency, has requested a report justifying the ranking of positions and the compensation assigned to each.
   (5) The data processing manager has resigned, and a replacement must be found.

(6) A new law requires all agencies to have a formal program for the prevention of alcoholism and a procedure for referring alcoholics to treatment and rehabilitation.

(7) The new insurance policy covering the agency requires hard hats to be worn in the stock room.

(8) Currently, only the low-level clerical workers are unionized, but there is a move to extend the union membership to all employees except those who are legally managers.

(9) One of the department managers wants to change some important work procedures. The changes would alter the relations among different jobs and might require new skills for some of the employees.

(10) Another department manager wants to promote someone from within the department to fill an opening, but is not sure of the best way to decide who to promote.

2. *Performance Situation—The Dispirited Chain Store:* Marvellous Foods needs organization development badly. The company operates the largest local chain of retail food stores in a Western state. After years of solid profitability, the company has begun to decline. A new president has been brought in to try to pull the firm out of its recent nosedive. The president finds problems in marketing, purchasing, merchandising, and many other areas. There are also problems with the organization itself and with many of the people who work there. Some specific problems are:

a. Labor costs are out of control because many employees simply do not put in full days; they come in late, take long lunches, and often disappear during the middle of the afternoon.

b. In two new stores that have been opened, the president can't locate a single person who thoroughly knows how to do the job that he or she was assigned to.

c. The manager of the company's largest store, for unknown reasons, has become more and more a tyrant. Shouting matches are common. People are quitting left and right.

d. In spite of the stores being a "chain," they have never really been linked together. Even purchasing isn't really centralized. This move has not been made because the store managers are jealous of their independence.

e. Few people in the organization seem really committed to company goals. They appear dispirited and seem just to go through the motions of doing their jobs. This is even true at relatively high management levels.

Using everything you have learned so far, and particularly your knowledge of the role and responsibility of personnel managers, outline a proposal to bring about improvements in this organization. Place yourself in the position of a personnel director who has been presented with the problems by the president and told to propose a plan of action to overcome them. Suggest a step-by-step approach that you think would succeed.

3. The five short case examples given below refer to wage and salary administration. Analyze each to answer two questions:
  a. Which of the three criteria for successful wage and salary administration are satisfied in the case and which are unsatisfied?
  b. What action could a manager take to increase the extent to which the criteria are satisfied?
  (1) Faced with an inability to hire the skilled workers it needed, management of a machine shop increased the wages it was offering. Unfortunately, labor costs went so high that profits were nearly wiped out.
  (2) A newly negotiated union contract has raised the pay of unskilled production workers above that of salaried computer programmers and technicians with special training and responsibility.
  (3) When it was discovered that morale was poor among its foundry workers and that performance was suffering, company managers decided to give an across-the-board pay increase (same raise for everyone regardless of position) to improve morale.
  (4) Girardi Millwork Co. pays the lowest wages in the area, by far. On the other hand, it has a very careful job-ranking scheme and is able to provide every employee with satisfying and creative work.
  (5) One company pays a very low wage for beginning workers, but it increases this wage substantially to an attractive amount for workers who stay with the company over a year. Working conditions are so poor, though, that few employees ever stay long enough to get the higher wage.
4. A typical grievance procedure might have four steps:
  a. Formal or informal discussion of the complaint by the person with the grievance, the immediate supervisor, and the first-level union representative (the shop steward).
  b. If not resolved, a further discussion among the plant or office manager, the union grievance committee, and company personnel specialists.
  c. If still not resolved, a further negotiation among high-level union officials and the employer's top management.
  d. If still not resolved, assistance or judgment by an outside agent (called an arbitrator), chosen when the procedure was set up.
  What do you think the personnel manager's role should be in this procedure, other than attending the discussion in Step *b*?
  How is a procedure like this related to the process of collective bargaining and of negotiating a contract?
  How is a grievance procedure related to contract administration? What should be the goal of managers who have to administer grievance procedures?
5. Explore the process of negotiating labor contracts by dividing the class into two groups to hammer out a "student-management contract." After preparing in advance, have one group (or selected representatives of the group, if the class is large) represent the interests and desires of the students;

have the other group represent the instructor and school administrators. Negotiate a contract specifying some of the conditions and policies of the students' attendance and performance at school. Some possible issues for negotiation are listed below. The equivalent issue for a labor contract is shown in parentheses for each.

    a. Who may attend class? (membership requirements)

    b. Grading methods and requirements for getting credit. (wage rates and performance appraisal methods)

    c. Instructor's and school administration's rights to discipline, expel, etc. (management rights)

    d. Will absenteeism and tardiness be permitted? (same issues, plus vacation and holidays)

    e. Grievance procedure. (same)

    f. How long shall the contract be in effect? (same)

6. Explore the activities of personnel specialists in the real world of management by contacting personnel managers with local firms, agencies, or other organizations. Divide the class into five groups. If the groups are very large, have each choose three or four representatives. Have each group locate one personnel manager and interview him or her about the specific duties or activities associated with one of the main areas of personnel management: employment, planning and development, wage and salary administration, employee services, or labor-management relations. Choose a manager with a unionized company for the last topic. Prepare in advance a brief description of the function each group will investigate, and ask specific questions to learn of the actual activities the manager performs to carry out the function.

Cases for Analysis and Discussion

CASE 1: EVERYTHING IS SO DIFFERENT THIS WAY

Belle thought, "I just can't stand having him look over my shoulder while I'm working."

She was silent, and so were the other sewing machine operators at Mohawk Garment Co. If everyone had spoken up, her thought would have been echoed. Few of Mohawk's workers were contented. These were typical of their inner thoughts:

"All of these people around; they're so distracting, I just can't concentrate on working."

"I get tired and make mistakes if I can't start and stop when I want to."

"I worry about the kids all the time; I wonder if they got home from school all right."

The noble experiment had failed. Now the effort to pick up the pieces wasn't going too well either.

Mohawk Garment Co. is in the business of hand-sewing women's clothes that have been designed and cut by a large company in New York. Mohawk is located in a rural area, and the managers thought they had the perfect answer to their labor problems: they would arrange with local women to work in their own homes on equipment provided by the company and receive payment on a piece rate. This would allow the women to work without paying a babysitter, and they could work as much or as little as suited their own needs.

The company managers saw only the good points: the plan would help the workers, many of whom desperately needed extra income; it would save the company the money needed for a factory building; it would give the workers the pride of doing their own work in their own way.

Problems arose from the first. Communication was difficult and expensive. Delivering materials and picking up finished products turned out to be far more expensive and time consuming than had been anticipated. Although the operators were skilled, almost from the very beginning the lack of supervision caused the quality of work to be too inconsistent to satisfy the New York contractor. Worst of all, production was only about 45 percent of what was needed.

Mohawk then decided to change over to a conventional factory operation. It moved the machines to a centrally located building and hired the former home workers to work in this plant. This solved the supervision problem. Difficulties with moving materials and finished goods were relieved. Communications costs were reduced nearly to zero. Production output, however, continues to be far lower than the managers know the workers are capable of turning out. It is certainly too low to satisfy Mohawk's contracts and to make a profit for Mohawk.

A. Why do you think production is still so low?
B. What personnel functions are needed here? What specifically could a personnel manager do to improve things?
C. What form of payment should Mohawk use now? Should they continue with the piece rates they were paying?

CASE 2: THE UNION VERSUS THE UNION

The Amalgamated Manual Workers of America had, in the brief period of 40 years, become one of the important labor unions in America. Proud of the union's record of honesty in forwarding the interests of its nearly

200,000 members, the AMWA managers sat in their conference room in Washington, overlooking the Potomac. Their pride was not apparent now, though; their faces showed little of the placid smoothness of the waters that flowed by in the river below. The reason for their agitation could be seen on the wide walkway between their building and the river: pickets, carrying signs reading, "AMWA IS UNFAIR." The AMWA managers were faced with a problem they had often relished when they were on the other side: their office workers were on strike.

Two years ago the clerical employees of the union—the people hired by the union to handle its huge correspondence and recordkeeping load—decided that they needed the power of collective bargaining to improve their wages and working conditions. Against the protests of the AMWA, the workers elected to have a large office-workers' union represent them in dealings with their management.

After heated wrangling that lasted for months, a 3-year contract was finally signed. It was clear now, though, that for all their negotiating, one issue hadn't been adequately resolved. The contract called for time-and-a-half pay for all overtime work; the amount was acceptable to both sides. Nevertheless, a dispute arose within two months of the signing of the labor agreement. A number of clerks claimed that their supervisors were quickening the pace of regular work so the clerks would never get any overtime pay. The supervisors claimed that the clerks were delaying their work so they would fall behind and have to work overtime just to get the extra pay. Several grievances were filed, but the clerks with the complaints never were convinced that they were handled fairly. The dispute flared up again and again, with never a firm settlement. Finally, the clerks had walked off the job. By their interpretation of the labor contract, they were staging a legal strike justified by unfair treatment. To the AMWA managers, it seemed that the clerks had simply walked out and were engaging in an illegal strike.

A. What would cause a problem like this to escalate to a work stoppage when there was so much advance warning that a problem existed? Who should have headed it off?

B. What does this case tell you about the personnel manager's job in handling labor-management relations?

C. What should the union managers in their conference room do now? What is the first question they should ask themselves? What action can they take?

Supervisory Management

22

After completing Chapter 22, you will be able to do the following:

● Propose specific objectives appropriate for supervisory management in a given situation.

● Analyze the planning and controlling tasks and responsibilities of a supervisor, given a description of objectives and authority.

● Name five areas of special concern for a supervisor when dealing with the work force and, in a given situation, judge whether criteria for handling each have been met.

● Propose improvements in work methods in given situations, using job enrichment and work simplification to increase motivation and improve efficiency.

It is 7:30 A.M. The keypunch operators in the accounting department load cards into their machines, test the controls and feeds, and pick up their sheaves of data to be punched. Three of them work on different sections of the weekly payroll; one is verifying quality control reports; the rest are doing billing records.

In the main shop, 13 different components are already loaded on the final assembly line. More materials await loading within the yellow-striped temporary storage area. Assemblers move to their work stations, and the line starts to roll.

A forklift truck hums through the central bay carrying a bin of castings toward the abrasive machining department. There, the machinists are setting up their equipment, referring to work orders on each bench.

In the customer service department, order takers are already on the phone to Yakima and Mishawake, Ho-Ho-Kus, and Tuscaloosa. They are reporting order statuses to customers and recording new orders on thick yellow pads.

A machine maintenance worker walks slowly to the far truck bay, burdened by his tool box. In his mind, he is wording his complaint to the shipping supervisor. The worker is disturbed because the supervisor didn't give enough detail on the maintenance work order for him to know what parts to bring with him.

Amid all this activity there is one quiet spot. In the central office, the lights haven't even been turned on yet. The president, the production manager, the marketing manager, and the rest, are not even scheduled to come to work for another hour and a half. How, then, did all the activity get started? How did the keypunch operators know to begin on the payroll, and how did the materials handlers know what parts to put at the assembly stations? Who decided what the machinists would work on for this day?

The answer, of course, is that all this work gets started and carried on through the initiative of the workers themselves and the guidance provided by their supervisors. For the purposes of this chapter, *supervisory management* refers to the use of the management tools—planning, controlling, organizing, staffing, and directing—to get work done at the first level in an organization. This is the level at which the actual "hands-on" production or service work is accomplished. Every manager who has subordinates must supervise. The real burden of overseeing the hard, useful work of an organization, however, falls on these front-line managers.

THE MEASURE OF SUCCESS IS
THE WORK ACCOMPLISHED
The job of a supervisor is to make short-term detailed allocations of the organization's resources in order to perform useful work. The useful work varies. In the most obvious cases, supervisors make use of the men and women, the equipment, the materials and supplies, the electricity and fuel of the organization to produce useful products, goods, or services. The nature of this productive work varies widely. It may be the detailed recordkeeping of the accounting department, preparation of plans and drawings by the drafting unit, or typing and mailing of correspondence in the typing pool. It may be direct personal selling by the floor clerks in a department store or by traveling sales representatives. Whatever the type of work involved, though, the subordinates of first-line supervisors perform the directly productive work; the subordinates are not managers, they are production workers.

Supervisors are known by many designations: foremen or forepersons; unit, section, or department managers; assistant managers (in fast food chains, for example); and section or craft chiefs to name but a few.

Supervisors in the Management Scheme
No matter how many management levels an organization has, direct supervisors are always at the first level. This position has a number of implications for the way supervisors have to do their job.

DIFFERENT SUCCESS CRITERIA
Supervisors may be judged as successful or unsuccessful by using different criteria from those that apply to higher-level managers. In a business, for instance, the top executive may reasonably be judged by whether the company is profitable or not. Even the best-run production department, however, cannot by itself create a profit; so that measure is inappropriate. Middle-level managers can be judged by broader measures. For example, a marketing manager may be judged by whether a whole marketing effort keeps the company competitive. A production manager may be judged on the basis of whether a whole line of

products is well made and economically produced. On the other hand, supervisors usually have control over such a small slice of an entire process that they cannot, by themselves, be accountable for such measures. The result is that supervisors are usually appraised according to their effectiveness in doing the job itself. The usual criteria for supervisory success focuses on efficiency and economy at using facilities, materials, utilities, money, and the work force to get a large volume of high-quality work done.

A NEARNESS TO WORKERS   The supervisory position on the first rung of management also can make it difficult for a supervisor to define his or her role. It is easy for a supervisor to feel uncertain as to whether he or she is a member of the work force or a member of management. This is because supervisors have a special involvement with the workers. Supervisors must possess and transmit considerable technical knowledge while also maintaining the kind of close personal contact that creates motivation and job satisfaction. In spite of this deep involvement with workers, the answer is clear: *supervisors are managers.* Their main responsibility is to facilitate the work of others, not to do the work themselves. To accomplish this, they apply the usual management approaches.

SHORTER-RANGE CONCERNS   The closeness of supervisors to the day-to-day productive work of the organization requires them to concentrate on short-range and detailed management concerns. A top executive spends a lot of time and energy devising long-range strategies for the entire organization. To only a slightly lesser degree, middle managers have the same concern for their specific functional areas. The supervisor, however, is charged with managing to *carry out* long-range strategies today and tomorrow. This requires supervisors to concentrate on what people are going to do now and next week, not three years from now.

Objectives for Supervisors

In keeping with the emphasis on the work itself that is typical of supervisory positions, supervisors' objectives universally center on three goals: (1) the quantity of work produced and the productivity of facilities and workers, (2) the quality of work, and (3) cost control. (See Table 22-1.)

OUTPUT AND PRODUCTIVITY   Every supervisor has as an important objective the performance of a specified amount of work using the resources that are available. The amount of work accomplished is the *production level.* For a physical product, output may be directly counted or measured: 40,000 toy trains, 10,000 barrels of maple syrup, 1,250 tons of concrete. For services measures, similar units can usually be devised: 130 breakdowns repaired, 1,300 bank deposits entered, 3,000 hotel room rentals handled.

Productivity is a measure of the output achieved from a given amount or value of resources, especially labor. Suppose 10 assemblers normally put together 100 units an hour; later on they become able to assemble 200 units

TABLE 22-1. EXAMPLES OF SUPERVISORY PERFORMANCE OBJECTIVES.		
	PRODUCT-ORIENTED OBJECTIVES	SERVICE-ORIENTED OBJECTIVES
OUTPUT OBJECTIVES	Number of items or units processed or produced:* Castings poured, axles machined, chemicals blended, bread baked, shirt seams stitched, frames welded, cabinets painted, autos assembled, boxes of cereal packaged, miles of highway constructed, and tons of coal mined.	Number of items or units processed or serviced: Orders billed, letters typed, records filed, entries key punched, inquiries answered, complaints handled, passengers ticketed, meals served, bank deposits accepted, claims processed, and telephone calls logged.
	*Per employee. Per hour, day, week, month, and so on. Per machine. Per square foot of floor space, and so forth.	
QUALITY OBJECTIVES	Number or percent of: Occurrences of faulty workmanship, defects, flaws, rejects, scrap, waste, discards, and items needing rework in shop or field.	Number or percent of: Customer complaints, service callbacks, typing errors, misfiled documents, and incorrect bookings or billings.
COST OBJECTIVES	1. Targeted or budgeted total expenses per time period (labor, materials, supplies, power, and so on). Especially the extent to which actual expenses will be over or under planned levels as measured either by dollar or percentage variances. 2. Targeted or budgeted unit costs. Total costs or expenses for the period compared with actual number of units produced or serviced; i.e., $20,000 total expenses for the month divided by 5,000 items or units processed, or $4 per item or unit.	

an hour. This means that productivity has increased, because a higher production level has been met without increasing the resources. Productivity also increases when the same production level can be maintained while resources are reduced. Five workers, for example, might produce 100 units an hour.

To be able to maintain a high level of productivity, a supervisor must be a good manager. He or she must be able to motivate employees, to schedule and organize individual tasks and steps to avoid waste time and effort, to improve work methods to make them more efficient, to improve workers' skills, and to keep a constant watch for wasted materials, time, and money.

QUALITY OF PRODUCT OR SERVICE   The second main group of objectives for supervisors concerns the quality of the results of work. When a supervisor is responsible for producing a product—whether a physical product or a service—the measure is simply how good is the product. *Physical goods* can be measured and tested for comparison with the standard specifications for the product, such as dimensions, weight, and performance characteristics. *Services*, too, can usually be measured in some way, such as by number of customer complaints, number of call-backs on repair jobs, or number of entry errors at a bank. The supervisor's role in creating quality is to build quality into the product or service in the first place. Inspections and quality-control tests may be able to identify off-standard products and keep them from reaching the customer, but they do nothing directly to improve product quality. The supervisor, together with the workers who create the product, must be responsible for its quality.

COST EFFICIENCIES   Another major objective of supervisors is to control costs. There are usually two aspects to this goal. Simple good management, already applied to improve productivity, will minimize costs through eliminating waste labor, materials, and money. In addition, though, supervisors must make active efforts to reduce expenses. These efforts may take many directions. Supervisors may choose to do without nonessentials, postpone purchases as long as possible, reanalyze procedures to look for wasted motion, or make an extra push for higher production. The usual target for success in controlling costs is to meet or better an expense budget provided at the beginning of an operating period.

SUPERVISORS DEVISE AND CARRY OUT DETAILED PLANS AND CONTROLS
The situation faced by the supervisor in a manufacturing department is this: A company's production plans will call for the manufacture of a given number of a specified product, 5,000 wooden lazy Susans, for example. This manufacturing order is given to the supervisor. The supervisor has available certain resources: 20 employees with varying experience and skills; 9 machines, including lathes, sanders, saws, work benches with jigs; truckloads of materials such as raw wood and bins full of supplies such as glue and wiping rags; plus the power to operate the equipment and a working space in which to get the job done. The supervisor's job then narrows down to the specific details. He or she must plan exactly which machines will be used, who will operate them, when and in what quantity material must be available. A supervisor then puts these plans into action.

Schedules for Resource Utilization
The fundamental activity of this part of the supervisor's job is short-term scheduling. The supervisor holds the basic responsibility for productivity. Accordingly, the supervisor must work out schedules for equipment and

workers that will produce the required output with the least expenditure of time and money.

A similar process occurs when a service is the required output. Bank tellers must be assigned to stations and to specialty services. Hotel custodial workers must be assigned to rooms and public areas depending on shifting use patterns. Real estate salespersons and investment counselors expect their supervisors to lay out their portion of the total work load in a systematic and effective way.

Scheduling techniques vary. In complex manufacturing processes, for example, sophisticated mathematical methods may be used. However, the basic supervisory planning steps remain the same as those described for general production and operations management (pages 428 to 430). *Routing* decides what work steps and operations will be performed and in what order. *Scheduling* sets a beginning and ending time for each step or operation. *Dispatching* assigns specific operators to each task and gives them instructions for the job at hand. *Follow-up* requires continual surveillance of the actual operations to spot and remedy wasted time, materials, supplies, energy, or facilities.

Information for
Control Purposes
Typically, the scheduling and controlling process involves detailed paperwork. In fact, the supervisor's job in general includes considerable attention to record preparation and reporting; this is the administrative side of the supervisory management job. Most of the operating information needed by all managers originates at the level of supervisors and workers. Supervisors are expected to complete or contribute such diverse information as equipment use and downtime reports, maintenance records, shipping and receiving reports, stock control tickets, material-yield reports, utility-control reports, cash controls, employee absence and lateness reports, accident records, and productivity and labor-use reports.

SUPERVISORS MANAGE THE
HANDS-ON WORK FORCE
All managers, of course, work with people. Supervisors, however, manage at the spot where the organization's useful output is created. They manage the people who literally put their hands on the work. Their success or failure in administering and motivating the work force is immediately evident according to whether the work is accomplished or not. In the first place, supervisors deal with relatively large numbers of workers. Most organizations have relatively few chiefs and many indians. It is a time-consuming job for supervisors just to keep track of the workers, their assignments, their qualifications, their pay scales and raises, and their development goals.

Managers in Action

PRODUCTION SUPERVISOR

for company that designs and manufactures modern solid-state devices for the telecommunications industry

Successful candidate should have two years college in business management and/or electronics background, with a minimum of 3 years first-line supervision experience, preferably in assembly board or wiring operation. Candidates should be of extremely high personal characteristics and possess the ability to lead and motivate a large number of employees.

INSPECTION SUPERVISOR

for a leading manufacturer of medical and diagnostic equipment and pharmaceuticals

If you have experience in the many phases of pharmaceutical inspection such as sampling, packaging, components, labeling, and filling lines, this is a unique new position. You will have overall responsibility for all areas of inspection in our completed facility.

SUPERVISOR SANITARY LANDFILL

for public works department of county's bureau of environmental services

Responsible for directing of landfill personnel, planning daily operations, maintaining on-site records, personnel training, and developing and implementing safety procedures.

OFFICE SUPERVISOR

for a growing insurance company

Supervision of records and bookkeeping section. Must be able to develop and train file clerks, typists, record entry, and bookkeeping personnel.

EMERGENCY ROOM FINANCIAL COUNSELING SUPERVISOR

for a major community hospital

Person selected will be responsible for developing a financial counseling section in our very busy emergency room and administering the hospital's financial policies and procedures for patients. Must be able to deal effectively with all types of people.

A Heavy
Administrative Load

Work force administration adds to the complexity of the supervisor's job. This is the part that is concerned with detailed personnel or human-resources matters. It includes the turning of general production goals into detailed estimates of how many employees will be needed and what skills and qualifications they must have. It includes decisions regarding the transfer of employees, their promotion to higher-level jobs as their skills increase, the hiring of new employees when openings occur, and the dismissal of employees who prove unsatisfactory. From the supervisor's point of view, these administrative efforts may be a mixed blessing. On the one hand, such decisions are an important tool for building an effective work force. On the other hand, every personnel change of any kind is usually accompanied by forms to be filled out and records to be changed.

A Unique
Motivational Task

Detailed administration work sketches only the bare framework of a supervisor's relations with the men and women of the organization. Supervisors have a special responsibility for leadership and motivation. Compare this responsibility with that of a high-level manager or a marketing manager, for instance. At upper management levels, the relationship between work and important goals is obvious. The work is usually varied and demanding. Rewards are more frequent as manager and subordinate manager see the continuous fruits of their efforts and decisions. Furthermore, people who rise to high-level positions bring a considerable amount of self-motivation and self-discipline with them. Motivating such people in higher-level positions is not a tremendous challenge.

The situation is different at the first level of management. Think of an assembly woman who spends day after day lifting bottom plates for motor cases from a bin and bolting them onto cases. Like many production-level workers, she will find little motivation or reward in the work itself. The work may be boring, repetitive, and seemingly endless. Workers are often isolated and cut off from social contact. Many jobs have little responsibility or challenge; they use only a limited range of skills. It is typical for work at the production level to be divided into many small steps. The individual has trouble understanding how his or her job relates to the entire process. As a result, such jobs often appear unimportant. Finally, production-level jobs often are dead-end. They offer little opportunity for advancement or pay increases.

Supervisors must learn to lead and motivate in this atmosphere. It's important for them to suit their leadership styles to the individual worker, probably to a greater extent than is necessary for higher-level managers. It requires two essential qualities:

1. *The ability to humanize the work place*—to identify the parts of the work and of the surroundings that are potentially satisfying to workers and to enhance these when possible.

2. *An ability to communicate*—to help workers understand their role in the organization and appreciate the importance of each individual's contribution.

A Responsibility for Personnel Development

First-level supervision also presents special demands for training employees. Even in an organization with formal training programs, it is the supervisor's responsibility to ensure that workers know how to do their jobs. This requires special skills. Supervisors should work out a systematic approach to teaching new employees and to orienting old employees to new techniques. Breaking the job down into individual steps simplifies the learning process, which ideally follows a sequence of demonstration, repetition, and follow-up. Many supervisors succeed with a four-step training approach called *job instruction training* (JIT). It includes the following:

1. Preparing the employee to learn. This is done by showing how the training is important and is related both to the employee's job and to the organization.
2. Demonstrating how the job is done. This is accomplished by taking each step in turn, telling and showing the right way to do it.
3. Letting the employee try the job. This allows the individual to concentrate on each step while the instructor is present to provide help when needed.
4. Putting the employee to work on his or her own, but checking back frequently to see that proper work methods really are understood.

The First Ear on Vital Matters

Supervisors are also the first line of action in many other matters relating to work force performance and satisfaction. Take employee grievances, for example. A supervisor is almost always the first to hear about them. A capable supervisor can encourage a full discussion of complaints and create a constructive problem-solving atmosphere when grievances arise. This way, the supervisor saves everyone involved serious headaches later on. Safety is another prime concern of supervisors. It matters little how well a safety specialist in the personnel or engineering department has designed work methods or prescribed other aspects of a safety program. The work place will not be safe unless the supervisor recognizes and enforces safe work methods.

SUPERVISORS MAY IMPROVE WORK METHODS

Many organizations have formal programs for studying and making improvements in work procedures. These may be carried out by specialists trained in job analysis, time-and-motion study, or other analytic methods. Supervisors, however, often make a unique contribution to such improvements, even without special training. Supervisors are on the job every day, watching the work being done. This provides them with insights not readily apparent to the occasional observer. This familiarity enables supervisors to suggest ways to make work methods more effective.

Although methods and procedures can be improved in many ways and for a number of purposes, two approaches to methods improvement are of particular interest. First, jobs may be improved by restructuring them to make them more interesting and satisfying to the people who do them. This increased satisfaction can be expected to improve motivation. Job enrichment is one technique for accomplishing this. Second, jobs can be altered to make the technology of the work process more productive and efficient. This increases output without increasing resources used. An example of this kind of change is work simplification.

Job Enrichment　This can be any effort to make work more satisfying and motivating by making changes in the work itself. The changes may include extending the range of the job by including the preceding and following steps. This "enlargement" gives each worker a greater feeling of producing a finished product. Increasing the range of skills needed may also help provide additional satisfaction. This can be done, for example, by having a worker keep records, inspect materials, make adjustments for poor fits, and file remaining burrs from cast parts. This is far more interesting than concentrating all day entirely on driving bolts. Another change in the work itself that often increases job satisfaction is to give the individual worker more responsibility. It is also fruitful for supervisors to encourage workers to search for better ways of doing the work and to seek their own solutions to problems that arise. The challenge of assuming responsibility appears to be rewarding in itself to many, although not all, employees.

Work Simplification　This can be any change in the work process that removes bottlenecks, reduces wasted effort and duplication, or makes the work easier to do. Work simplification breaks a procedure or process into a number of short, simple steps. Next, it identifies those steps that take the most time, effort, or resources. It then looks for possible ways to change the separate tasks so as to increase their efficiency. Changes made usually are of one or more of four types: (1) eliminating steps that are unnecessary, (2) combining steps to save transportation, setup, or positioning time, (3) changing the sequence of operations to eliminate waiting time or to facilitate the combining of steps, and (4) simplifying or improving the individual movements or operations in each step or in the entire process.

One of the best sources of ideas for simplifying work methods is the people who perform the work. This is true even in cases where an engineering approach is used for work simplification—basing changes on detailed studies of physical motions, materials movement, and similar factors. Workers themselves are often an important part of the process. Without their cooperation, interest, contribution, and support, methods-improvement efforts are likely to fail.

SUMMARY

1. A supervisor's main job is to make detailed, short-term plans for allocation and control of the resources needed to accomplish a variety of useful work. First-line supervisors are a true part of management, with special responsibilities for applying the management functions to the everyday productive work of an organization. The major objectives for supervisors include (a) attainment of adequate quantities of output and productivity, (b) maintenance of the quality of the work or of products and services created, and (c) control of costs.

2. Supervisors carry out planning and controlling to make effective use of personnel, machinery and equipment, materials and supplies, energy, cash, and other resources. The expression of the plans and controls is in successful scheduling—routing, scheduling, dispatching, and follow-up. This process, and other parts of the supervisor's job, requires considerable attention to recordkeeping and report preparation.

3. Supervisors have a special opportunity to improve the success of their organizations because of their close and direct contact with the work force. Specific responsibilities include (a) personnel administration, including estimates of work force requirements and decisions on hiring, transfer, and dismissals; (b) leadership and motivation in an atmosphere where the work itself may be boring, repetitious, and isolated; (c) training and retraining; (d) dealing with grievances; and (e) providing a safe work place and enforcing safe methods.

4. Supervisors can improve worker satisfaction and productivity through methods-improvement efforts. Job enrichment makes various changes in the work itself to improve motivation. Work simplification analyzes and alters work procedures to eliminate waste and inefficiency.

REVIEW AND DISCUSSION QUESTIONS

1. Contrast the chief measure of success for supervisors with the main criteria of success used for middle managers and top executives.

2. The manager of a manufacturing department wants to give her supervisors numerical objectives for the coming 6-month period. Using what you have learned in earlier chapters, describe at least three ways she might present these objectives.

3. Describe some ways that quality of work might be measured for the supervisor of a typing pool, for a machine repair and maintenance department, and for the kitchen workers in a restaurant.

4. A supervisor in a small printing shop wants to design four paper forms to

help him with the job of planning and control. What would the forms probably be and what kind of information would be on each?

5. Why do supervisors have to be responsible for so much paperwork? Is
this desirable or undesirable?

6. Give some reasons why supervisors need to be especially skillful at leadership and motivation. How is supervising the production labor different
from supervising by the vice president for finance?

7. Describe the four steps of job-instruction training.

8. What are two ways that job enrichment differs from work simplification?
In what way are they similar?

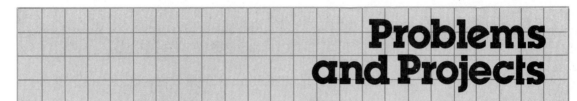

Problems and Projects

1. The production manager of a Midwest manufacturer of industrial belts
(for transmitting power in many kinds of machines) likes to have everything
under control. Specifically at this time, he is interested in performance standards for the supervisors in the manufacturing departments. His goal is to
design a monthly report that will give a good idea of how each supervisor is
doing overall in three areas: quantity, quality, and costs.

Name five measures that might be used as a standard of performance in
each of these areas. From among these possibilities, choose three to five that
you think would be the best overall indicators. Design a simple report form
for the production manager, to show comparisons between standard (budgeted) performance and actual performance for an operating period. (Show
only the column heads for the report, without any actual entries.)

2. Three maintenance workers are available to install a large automatic
ventilation blower in the main shop. The old, faulty blower has already been
removed, but the main duct lines to the distribution boxes have to be
replaced because the new blower requires a larger size than the old one.
There are eight distinct steps in the installation:

    a. Lift from pallet, align and bolt in place (requires three people for ½
       hour).

    b. Replace ducting, restrap and tape (one person for 2½ hours).

    c. Remove shipping blocks and complete mechanical installation (two
       people for ½ hour).

    d. Mechanically install motor and fan (one person for 1 hour).

    e. Install and test controller (one person for 1 hour).

    f. Complete electrical hookup (one person for ½ hour).

    g. Test and adjust (three people for ½ hour).

    h. Clean up (one person for ½ hour).

Assume that each member of the team is equally able to perform any of these jobs. Also assume that the jobs can be done concurrently, with the exception of step *g*, which must wait until installation is complete. Since the cleanup step consists mainly of carrying away the old ducting, it can be done before final testing.

Utilizing Figure 22-1 as a model, on a separate piece of paper, carry out the routing and scheduling functions of a supervisor's planning task. Assign each task to one or more workers by entering the letter of the task in the appropriate space on the chart. How long will the entire job take? Is there anything you might be able to do to reduce the total time needed?

FIGURE 22-1.		
EMPLOYEE BARNES	**EMPLOYEE SUAREZ**	**EMPLOYEE ROCCO**
8:00		
8:30		
9:00		
9:30		
10:00		
10:30		
11:00		
11:30		
12:00		

3. The text discusses five main areas with which a supervisor must be concerned in dealing with the work force: administration, leadership and motivation, training, handling grievances, and safety. Supervisors can take specific actions in each of these areas to improve their performance. Prepare a checklist of concrete actions a supervisor could take to make improvements in each of the five areas. Use ideas from this chapter and from what you have learned in previous chapters. Remember that the goal is to improve overall performance, not just meet minimum requirements. Propose two actions for each area. To get you started, an example for each area is given below.

   a. *Administration:*
      Set up personal employee files and note critical incidents of performance illustrating their weak or strong points.
   b. *Leadership and Motivation:*
      Analyze current job setup to find if more responsibility could be built into employees' assignments.
   c. *Training:*
      Observe one worker each day to assess his or her current skill level.

d. *Handling Grievances:*
Analyze grievances from past six months to discover if there is a pattern to causes of complaints.

e. *Safety:*
Set an example by using proper safety equipment when training new employees.

4. *Performance Situation—The Bored Laboratory Technicians:* The work of one commercial medical laboratory has consisted almost entirely of performing culture analyses of biological specimens received by mail. In this particular lab, division of labor has reigned supreme. One person receives and opens the mail; another does nothing but clean and sterilize culture dishes and other glassware; another does nothing but inject culture medium; and another person adds the specimen. The mail clerk sorts the specimens and orders into groups, based on the type of test called for. A routing clerk then combines all similar orders and writes work orders for the technicians. The person responsible for preparing dishes with culture medium, for example, might receive an order that says only, "2,000 petri; medium A22." The actual analysis of results is performed by a specialist. She writes the results on the original order and reroutes the order back to the mail room for return to the customer.

This system has been efficient except for one thing: the workers are bored to distraction. As the repetitions of each simple step grow into the thousands, eyes glaze, concentration fails, coffee breaks grow longer and longer. Some people find that the repetition and sameness of work cause anxiety; these people sometimes do not come to work in the morning.

Your task is to propose some changes in this operation, based on what you know about job satisfaction and job enrichment. Your objective is to make the work more interesting and motivating. How could these jobs be redesigned to make them more rewarding to the people who perform them? Remember that your changes must not destroy efficiency, although a certain loss of speed will be accepted if it is accompanied by increased motivation, better attendance, and less wasted time on the job.

5. The text says that because of the variability of workers and the nature of the work they do, supervisors have special responsibilities for motivation. Using what you have learned in this chapter and elsewhere, propose five general or specific principles, actions, or guidelines for discharging this responsibility. Answer the question, "If a supervisor is supposed to motivate subordinates, how is he or she to do it?"

6. Examine the question, "What are the respective roles of supervisors, middle-, and high-level managers in providing overall direction of an organization?" Supporting questions are: Who sets policy? Does the supervisor have a role? Is a supervisor a manager in the same sense that a top executive is? What are the differences between their responsibilities, if any? What are the similarities? How does a supervisor tell if he or she is doing a good job? How does a top manager tell?

Explore the question by carrying out one of the following projects:

a. Interview at least one first-level supervisor to discover his or her management role. Collect information on activities, authority, objectives, and performance appraisal. Relate the data to the general question and report on the results in class.

b. Use library research to answer the same question. Compare the descriptions of the activities and responsibilities of supervisors (as described in books and articles on supervisory management) with the duties and objectives of higher-level managers. Make a written report of the results.

Cases for Analysis and Discussion

CASE 1: MOUTHPIECE OR MANAGER?

"If it bothers you so much, why don't you talk to Joe about it? He's the supervisor."

"What good is it going to do to talk to that bag of wind? You know *he's* not going to be able to do anything about it. McGinnis is the one that calls the shots. All Joe ever does is just pass on the word. He could be replaced by a tape recorder."

And so it went, another day at Hilltown Dye Works. Marty Golsen thought he should have been bumped up a notch in the hourly pay scale because he had finished another year with the company and because his output had been consistently high. The rate increase hadn't shown up and Marty was mad enough to quit. But there was no one to complain to.

Joe Mason, Marty's supervisor, never even heard about the complaint. He was sorry several weeks later, when Marty left, but he remained in the dark about the reason. Anyway, to Joe, Marty was just one more of a large number of people who had left in the last few years. There were quite a few jokes about the need for a revolving door at the plant entrance—so the people who had quit wouldn't be held up by the new people coming in. Turnover was always high. Some of the work was dirty and smelly, and Joe thought that must be the reason.

It was true, as Marty said, that McGinnis called the shots. When he hired Joe, he told him, "I'm the manufacturing manager, and this place isn't so big that I can't really manage. Your job is to be there and see that the people really are working. I'll make the decisions and you pass them on. And tell me everything that's happening in the shop. I don't have time to be there myself, so I'll be relying on you."

Joe had faithfully done what he was told. Every day, he had handed out the work assignments, written up the preceding afternoon by McGinnis. Every day without fail, he had reported back what work had been accomplished and what had taken place during the shift. McGinnis decided on pay rates, scheduling, routing, methods, and, in general, everything.

A. Why is the turnover so high in this plant?
B. What kind of supervisor is Joe? Is he really a manager?
C. What changes would you propose here? Give the reasons for your suggestions.
D. What kind of manager is McGinnis? How good do you think he is at the job of manufacturing manager?

CASE 2: WHERE'S THE OUTPUT?

Sharon Weiss was a sweetheart of a supervisor. The packing room, since her assignment there, had become the most sought assignment in the whole company, at least for people who had never worked there before. Had she been asked, Sharon might willingly have marched through the department carrying the standard, "Human Relations."

She knew every worker closely. She asked questions about their families, calling their spouses and children by name. She tried hard to learn the aspirations of all her subordinates—their *real* aspirations, what would fulfill them as human beings. She encouraged each one to work out his or her own work methods. In fact, she forced them to, because she refused to do it herself. Her supervisory management was participatory indeed. The work consisted of hand-wrapping and hand-packing glass and metal household utensils. Her instructions included only the items to be wrapped. It was up to the packers to decide who would do what. If someone asked her what the output quota was, she always replied, "What do you think is a reasonable number to get done?"

Sharon was astonished one day when she overheard two of the workers talking. One said, "Don't knock it; it's a lot better than having a super breathe down your neck all the time, isn't it? What difference does it make to you? You're getting paid, aren't you?"

The answer was, "Sure, I'm getting paid, but how are we supposed to get anything done? You can never tell what's going on around here. All Sharon ever says is 'That's up to you.' Did you see the confusion when we were trying to get started on that new job yesterday? We could have gotten the thing done, but as it was, we hardly got started."

A. In your opinion, is Sharon a good supervisor?
B. What do you think Sharon's superiors think about her supervisory performance?
C. How can Sharon improve? Propose at least one change in her management style or methods that could help her do a better job.

Management of Public Agencies and Nonprofit Organizations

23

After completing Chapter 23, you will be able to do the following:

- Define a nonprofit organization and evaluate the role of nonprofit organizations in modern society.
- Discuss the similarities and differences between nonprofit organizations and profit-making enterprises and how these impact on the problems faced by managers of both.
- Propose measures of effectiveness and of management

success for given nonprofit organizations.
- Assess the effects of environment and objectives on the decisions managers make in five types of nonprofit organizations.
- Analyze given organizational situations in the nonprofit context, and propose applications of special management techniques to improve the rate of success.

The story originally broke as simply a humorous sidelight on the way people carry on their business in the bureaucracy. Several Washington offices in the federal government were installing massive oak doors at a cost of thousands of dollars of tax funds. There was no indication that the new doors were in any way superior in function to the ones they replaced. As the story unfolded, it became less humorous to readers. In fact, it became a minor scandal. What had happened was simple. The funding year was nearing an end, and the managers in this department had not spent all of the money in their budget. They knew well that if any money was left over at the end of the year, it would appear that they did not need the money they had asked for, and they would receive less the next year. To the managers involved, this would be bad for two reasons. First, the reduced budget might interfere with the success of their continuing programs. In addition, a budget cut is in itself widely seen as a sign of management failure. The oak doors were part of the efforts of these managers to bring their spending up to the budget and qualify for the same amount next year.

Although there tends to be a spending spree in government agencies and in certain other nonprofit organizations as funding years draw to a close, the oak-door incidents are, fortunately, the exception. Such efforts demonstrate, however, an important fact about nonprofit organizations of all kinds: the lack of a profit motive in an organization poses difficult management problems. Businesses and nonprofit organizations share many features. They both have the fundamental purpose of using resources to provide something that society needs. They both require some kind of structure, plans, and controls to allow people to work jointly to accomplish goals. Both operate in a complex environment in which different groups of people make conflicting demands on their use of resources. In spite of these similarities, though, nonprofit organizations are unique and require a different orientation of the people who manage them.

PUBLIC ORGANIZATIONS SERVE A WIDE RANGE OF SOCIETY'S NEEDS

Public organizations are far more than businessses that do not try to make a profit. A *nonprofit organization* is a formal structure of capital, people, and other resources. It is created to provide a function or service needed by society, rather than to earn private profits. Some services cannot reasonably be sold to consumers on an individual basis. National defense, for example, must be provided equally to everyone if it is to be provided at all. Society has created an institution—a national government—to provide the service; the profit motive is not involved. Other functions are defined so that the making of a profit is considered unethical, at least in our society. Churches and charitable organizations are examples of ones that provide this kind of service. Yet other services may be either profit-making or nonprofit. A school, for instance, provides an essential social service—education. It may be defined, however, either as a general social requirement, as in the case of a public school system, or as a specific consumer service, as in a profit-making school that teaches data processing.

Satisfaction of Social Needs

Nonprofit organizations have been created to satisfy a great variety of major and minor social needs. Generally, though, the organizations fall into five broad categories.

1. *Government.* The federal government receives revenue from a great many sources, including the sale of goods and services to private buyers. Its central concern, however, is providing needed social functions, and it is ultimately nonprofit. Local and state governments likewise may sell electric power, transportation, or other products, but their reason for existing is to stabilize social relations and to provide services.

2. *Education.* Much of our culture is passed on to succeeding generations through formal education. In a mass society, there is no alternative. The function is essential and is provided, by and large, by nonprofit organizations, either government agencies or private ones.

3. *Health.* Primary health care given by a doctor is usually a consumer service sold on a profit-making basis. The huge facilities for major health care—hospitals and research centers, for instance—usually concentrate on their social function and are nonprofit.

4. *Charitable and religious.* Many needs are not met by business or government. The handicapped, victims of disease and misfortune, or the indigent may receive inadequate aid from the government. These needs, and a huge variety of others, are partially met by charitable organizations. Individual spiritual needs may not be dependent on money and material resources, but churches are. They make up an important group of nonprofit organizations.

5. *Associations and other organizations.* Engineers, doctors, lawyers, manufacturers, workers, and hundreds of other groups have organi-

zations to protect their interests, to provide information, and to exert some limited private regulation. These trade and professional organizations are legitimately nonprofit. Groups of lobbyists, organizations promoting social change, trade unions, and many other kinds of associations may also fall into this category.

A Growing Necessity in Our Society

Two things are striking about nonprofit organizations in a technological society like ours: they are essential, and they are growing in importance. Many features of our high standard of living are derived as much from nonprofit organizations as from commerce and industry. Education and health care, for instance, have done as much to transform us into the leisure society as have the availability of frozen orange juice and disposable razor blades. There is a limit to the extent to which the basic needs of food, shelter, and clothing can be "better" satisfied. At a certain level of development, higher needs and interests—those often met by nonprofit organizations—begin to get more emphasis. Safety and freedom from crime come to be expected; education for its own sake becomes a common value; health takes on the meaning not only of survival but of beauty and vigor. These changes are reflected in the United States today by the remarkable growth of nonprofit organizations. Governments, alone, in the United States have come to use about 30 percent of the national product. This is a tremendous change from the nineteenth century when emphasis was almost totally on the construction and operation of facilities for producing physical goods and for providing basic services like transportation. Every indication points to a continued growth of the service sector and of the nonprofit organizations that are so important in providing services.

NONPROFIT ORGANIZATIONS HAVE UNIQUE MANAGEMENT REQUIREMENTS

Making the primary goal of an organization the performance of a function or the provision of services, rather than the creation of profits, has a number of implications for managing the organization.

Inappropriateness of Business Standards

When the primary mission of an organization is to fulfill a social function, managers must deal with two main issues which normally need not concern the managers of profit-making business organizations.

A SUBSTITUTE FOR PROFIT Many, and probably most, of the plans and activities of a business concentrate on the actual making and distributing of products. Yet, there is always a guiding principle, a standard, that helps in judging the success of plans: "Will this all add up to produce a profit?" Nonprofit organizations lack this concrete standard. The manager of a government agency that regulates water use or of a cancer research clinic cannot say, "I know I did a good job this year; we made a 12 percent profit." In place of profit, the measure of success for a nonprofit organization might be called *effectiveness*. This is the extent to which the organization actually fulfilled the function assigned to it. Such a concept is not always easy to measure.

LACK OF COMPETITION AND CUSTOMER SELECTION   A second unique feature of a nonprofit organization is its relationship with the public it serves. A business is in a clear position: if it does not have products the public wants, it will have no customers. Customers are free to choose whether to patronize a particular business or not; if they do patronize it, that is a sign of success for the business. The situation is often different for a nonprofit organization. The Rockingham, Virginia, county government, for example, is the only Rockingham, Virginia, county government there is. If one lives within its jurisdiction, one has no choice but to pay taxes to support it and to accept some of its services. The managers of that government cannot judge their success by how many "customers" choose to patronize it. They must find other measures of effectiveness.

A reason for the loss of the customer standard of success is that nonprofit organizations so often operate in a noncompetitive environment. In providing water service to a town, for instance, the local government is not *forced* to be efficient and cost effective by the threat of a competitor taking over the water service by offering a lower price. Take, for instance, a national foundation to raise funds for research on a particular disease. It cannot be sure that its efforts are effective and efficient by comparing them with other foundations. There often will be no other foundations operating in the same service area.

Emphasis on Effectiveness   These two features add up to a conclusion for managers of nonprofit organizations: objectives and standards of success must receive special attention. The automatic standards of profitability, ability to attract customers, and success against competitors will often not be available. The obvious substitute is a judgment of performance—the effectiveness at doing what the organization is supposed to do through putting resources to efficient use. To use this standard, though, requires from nonprofit managers an effort and considerable dedication. They must be able to (1) define the true function for which their organization was created and (2) turn this definition into concrete objectives that are as measurable as possible.

MISDIRECTED BUDGETS   The need to concentrate on effectiveness makes another common measure of overall success—adherence to the budget—inappropriate for that purpose. In the absence of profit, many nonprofit organizations have stressed cost control as measured by adherence to expense budgets. But the budget as an overall control tool has many weaknesses. In order to build a cushion into their budgets, managers may purposely estimate that costs will be higher than really expected. This can cause a permanently inflated resource level for results achieved. Furthermore, too much emphasis on the budget causes managers to concentrate on pleasing the people who allocate money rather than on serving the real organization goals. In theory, an organization could grow and prosper without ever accomplishing anything. It could do so as long as its managers were able to convince their sources of funding that their intentions for the coming period were good. In addition, most organizations want to grow. If the budget is the measure of success, managers can be expected to seek a larger and larger budget every year. They are impelled toward higher spending rather than toward saving money and resources.

PRIMACY OF PERFORMANCE   The measure of success should be performance; budgets should always be subsidiary. A college, for instance, is better judged by whether a chemistry major graduate can correctly perform an analysis than by how many buildings the school has or how much money it spends on faculty salaries. A state employment service must be measured by the number of people who were placed on jobs as a prime measure rather than the amount of money it spends. A professional association must measure the number of information inquiries handled successfully or the degree of legislative influence achieved. Every nonprofit organization needs such concrete measures of performance.

OBJECTIVES AND ENVIRONMENTS VARY ACCORDING TO SERVICE AREA

Nonprofit organizations share many problems and activities. Each type, however, operates within an environment that presents unique limitations and opportunities. Each individual organization, of course, will have certain characteristics not shared by others. Nevertheless, generalizations are possible about the activities and goals of each type.

Government Organizations

The basic process of governments is to collect tax revenue and use it to provide certain needs for the public good. Organizations that carry on this process can be placed into three groups: local, state, and federal government.

LOCAL GOVERNMENTS   These receive revenue from a variety of sources. A large portion of income is derived from taxes on real estate ownership and transfers and on local business licenses. For some local governments, sales taxes and local income taxes also generate significant income. Further revenue may be generated by special taxes for the operation of schools, from the sale of franchises, and from payroll and special business taxes. Services provided by local governments include public education, water distribution and sewage disposal, police and fire protection, street lighting, snow removal, maintenance of local public streets and roads, and any number of other services and facilities beneficial to residents. Local governments are typically organized in a smaller reflection of the federal government. A governing body—a town or city council or a board of supervisors—makes major policy decisions and establishes ordinances. An executive and staff is then responsible for carrying out the actual work of putting the policies into effect and providing services.

STATE GOVERNMENTS   These rely heavily on sales taxes and personal and business income taxes for revenue. Additional income may come from licensing, business formation taxes, inheritance and property-transfer taxes, and a variety of other sources. Services include industrial and commercial development, resource protection, provision of a legal system and of police protection, and many other activities associated with health, welfare, employment, public safety, and business and commercial regulation. The structure of state governments normally includes a chief executive, the governor, a large line-and-staff organization, a legislative and policy-making body, and a judicial system.

THE FEDERAL GOVERNMENT   In general, the federal government has the same structure as that of the states. Its revenue derives from a wide range of taxes, leases of public lands, interest earned, and from many other sources including the direct sale of goods and services. The major roles of the federal government are usually defined as national defense and the promotion of the public good through effective domestic and foreign policies. This general goal has been tremendously elaborated to include uncountable activities in every facet of the economic and social life of the country.

Educational Organizations

Colleges and universities may be part of a state government or may be self-supporting private institutions. In either case, they share certain features. Revenue comes from many sources, including interest from endowments, tuition payments by students, research and development contracts and grants, direct donations, and government funds in the case of publicly supported institutions. Services concentrate mainly on educating students and carrying on research. The organization of a college or university usually includes a board of directors (called trustees, governors, or other titles), a president, an administrative staff, and an academic staff. The board may be a major policy-making body, or it may concentrate on finding and hiring the president who then assumes the policy-making role. A special difficulty for educational organizations is measuring the outcomes of their efforts. The major result sought is successful education and research, but there are difficulties in, for instance, defining what an "educated person" is.

The recent trend has been to define the outcomes of education in concrete, measurable objectives, but considerable work remains to be done in the area.

Health Organizations   The major organizations in this category are hospitals, clinics, medical research centers, and public education centers. Funds are obtained from charges for patient care, from government and private subsidies, grants and contracts, and from charitable donations. Management of hospitals is similar to that of educational institutions. Typically, there is an appointed board, an administrative staff, and a professional staff of doctors and nurses. Activities vary from providing medical care directly to patients to public education in health-related matters. Basic research in sciences, such as in genetics, physiology, and epidemiology, contribute to future health care.

Health care institutions have a problem much like that of colleges and universities: it is difficult to measure results. But the source of the difficulty is different. In a hospital, for instance, it would be desirable to restore every patient to perfect health. This is clearly impossible; as a result, objective standards have concentrated on the quality of care rather than on the results of the care. It has been easier to measure the reasonableness and thoroughness of the treatment than to determine a standard for an optimum level or state of health for a given type of patient.

Religious and Charitable Organizations   The main source of funds for these organizations is direct contributions from individuals and businesses. The goal for their managers is usually to pass as much of the revenue as possible through the organization to accomplish its objectives. For a *charity*, this requires that the structure and facilities be minimized, consistent with continued fund raising, and efficiency becomes a major goal in itself. A *church* often will maintain a higher level of facilities for use in the direct provision of services. Even a church needs good, clear objectives to survive and succeed. It is almost impossible to objectively measure spiritual benefits. It is possible, however, to measure the number of people who hear the church's message and to measure the extent to which social benefits, such as hospital visits, are provided. These prosaic measures often help in assessing management's attainment of organizational goals.

Professional, Trade, and Other Types of Associations   These include professional and trade associations, industry groups, trade unions, lobbying organizations, and other special-interest groups. Their main source of revenue normally is membership fees paid by members. Many also gain income from fees for the provision of information, from

Managers in Action

HOUSING PROGRAM MANAGER

moderate price dwelling units program

To implement and manage program. Must be able to supervise housing construction, development, pricing, and marketing. Experience needed in cost estimating and development approval procedures.

HEALTH MANAGER

for state health board

Responsible for fiscal management, contract negotiations, consultant and office support. Experience required in U.S. government contracting regulations procedures either as contracting officer with government agency or as agent for U.S. government contractor.

SUBCONTRACT ADMINISTRATORS

for Argonne National Laboratories

Candidates must be able to participate in evaluation of potential subcontractors by visiting plants, preparing requests for proposals, and analyzing them for final selection. Responsibilities also include review of progress milestones and deliverable items so as to insure compliance with work statement and specifications.

DIRECTOR OF CODE COMPLIANCE

for Wishbone County, Idaho

Requires experienced individual gifted in organizing and managing a variety of complex regulatory activities. Responsible for administration, direction, and coordination of inspection services and enforcement of building construction codes, zoning, subdivision, wetlands, and animal control ordinances. Must be perceptive, positive, innovative, tactful. Ability to analyze problems and recommend action for their solution is essential.

TRAFFIC CONTROL SUPERINTENDENT

for city of Alexandria, Virginia

Plans and supervises activities of a traffic sign and signal shop, including installation, maintenance, and repair of traffic signals. Requires comprehensive knowledge of and familiarity with the principles and practices of traffic control devices. Ability to plan and supervise the work of others.

member training sessions, from a publishing program, or even from consulting fees. Activities usually include collecting and distributing information useful to members, representing the interests of members to the public and to government agencies and legislatures, providing an adjudication service for ethical questions of members, providing limited regulation, and serving as a central source for membership training.

SPECIAL TECHNIQUES HELP TO MANAGE FOR PERFORMANCE

In the absence of profits as a standard for judging management success, a number of techniques have become popular for providing alternative formal standards. Especially notable today are program budgeting, zero-based budgeting, cost-benefit analysis, and formal planning.

Programming, Planning, Budgeting System (PPBS)

When trying to run an organization to produce results, the key question always arises, "What are we trying to accomplish and what will it cost to accomplish it?" Simply stating the problem in this form is a worthwhile step because it focuses attention on results. PPBS gives a formal expression to this focus by requiring that an output goal be set first before the needed inputs are specified and gathered. This places a far different emphasis from the traditional approach. Previously, each agency or department simply planned for its own continuation and then tried to find goals suitable to the existing resources. (See Figure 23-1 on page 508.)

PPBS has several advantages. It forces attention to what is meant to be achieved, since no budgets or resources are allocated until this has been defined in some concrete way. It helps achieve coordination, since it does not assume a division into existing agencies or departments. Instead, it looks at the desired output and then brings together the needed resources. Using this approach, the efforts of many different departments may be combined to achieve one goal.

A disadvantage, or at least a difficulty, of applying PPBS is the complexity of defining the goals of service-oriented organizations as concrete goals rather than as a list of activities. A police department, for instance, will usually have the goal of reducing crime. The incidence of crime, though, is very hard to measure except as reflected in arrest records. The question is, What would a police administrator want the arrest records to show? If arrests go up, that might mean that crime is increasing instead of decreasing. Or, it might mean that the level of crime is steady and that it is being more effectively handled than before. These problems of measurement require serious attention.

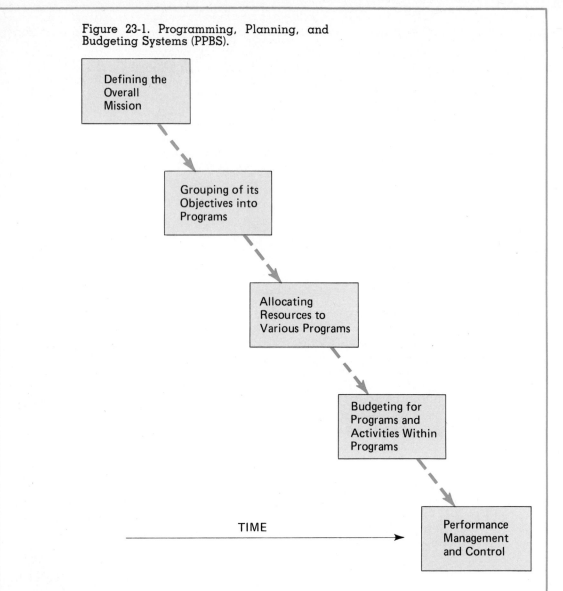

Figure 23-1. Programming, Planning, and Budgeting Systems (PPBS).

Zero-Based Budgeting (ZBB)   As defined in Chapter 6, zero-based budgeting is clearly a potentially useful approach to forcing concentration on getting things done rather than on spending money. ZBB is a resource-allocation system in which all current activities, agencies, departments, and programs are periodically reviewed. This review is unique in that it begins with the question, What would be lost if the activity were reduced to nothing, to zero? This approach requires that every program be re-proposed periodically, with clear, fresh data on goals and costs. All proposed programs can then be ranked in order of importance of their goals and cost effectiveness. The available funds can then be distributed as far down the rankings as it will reach. Highest-ranking programs are funded; lower-ranking programs may fall below the budget cutoff point. (See Figure 23-2 on page 510.)

Zero-based budgeting has the clear advantage of making it harder to continue existing programs just because "that's the way we've always done it." At the same time, it has a serious problem. The proposal and justification process is itself very expensive. It often uses funds that might better be devoted to direct services. Furthermore, ZBB does not *solve* the problem of setting measurable objectives for government and nonprofit organizations.

Cost-Benefit Analysis

Both PPBS and ZBB require comparisons among proposed programs based on their objectives and costs. The goal of cost-benefit analysis for a nonprofit organization is the same as for a business: to set a monetary value on the benefits expected to be derived from an activity and to choose programs that produce the greatest benefits at the lowest costs. The difficulties of accomplishing this in areas such as public education, recreation programs, or military preparedness, for example, are obvious. Many private nonprofit organizations have the same problems. Some, like charitable organizations, are fortunately able to measure strictly financial benefits fairly easily. Nevertheless, the effort to place concrete values on outputs and to choose programs that will produce the greatest expected values does force managers to ask, "What will we really be getting if we accept this goal?"

Formal Planning

Although these budgeting and administrative techniques are sometimes viewed as solutions to the problem of managing for performance, in fact they really only underline the problem. The key to managing nonprofit organizations is finding a concrete substitute for profits as a performance standard. The use of some kind of formal planning that focuses on this issue is more important than the particular budgeting procedure chosen. The final need, no matter what system is used to fill it, is to create definitions of goals that are specific and concrete enough (1) to tell what resources are required and (2) to tell when objectives have been reached.

A public transportation authority for a major city, for example, must guard against the kind of thinking that says, "Our goal is to run a subway and to operate bus service on the following routes." These may be legitimate objectives at a lower level, but they cannot in themselves serve as a standard of organizational success. The real question for such an organization, the one that is of the same importance as profits for a business, is, "Why does society—the people of this city and surrounding areas—need a public transportation system?" The systems managers must search for the answer. They must investigate why people need to travel, and evaluate alternative ways

Figure 23-2. Zero-Based Budgeting Work-
sheet.

RANKING OF PROPOSED ACTIVITIES OR SERVICES

Activity Identification Number	ZBB Ranking	Activity Cost	Cumulative Costs
OP22	1	50,000	
			50,000
MA18	2	100,000	
			150,000
MA17	3	75,000	
			225,000
OP12	4	25,000	250,000
NX02	5	10,000	260,000
MA03	6	80,000	
			340,000
OP24	7	20,000	360,000
OP02	8	40,000	400,000

← CUT-OFF POINT

MA24	9	80,000
NX12	10	30,000
MA09	11	50,000
OP06	12	40,000
NX02	13	30,000
MA15	14	50,000
OP11	15	20,000

Activities 9 – 15
Not Approved

CRITERIA USED FOR RANKING

- Perceived importance of service.
- Potential consequences of not providing the service.
- Legal or contractual agreements.
- Political implications.

TOTAL FUNDS AVAILABLE
$400,000

☐ Approved Activities or Services.

▨ Activities or Services not Approved.

of getting around. As a result, the managers should be able to identify the true social need and function of their organization. That is the real equivalent of profits.

SUMMARY

1. A nonprofit organization manages and uses resources for the primary purpose of meeting a social need rather than earning profits. Nonprofit organizations play a major role in maintaining the standard of living in modern society and promise to become even more important in the future.

2. In the absence of the profit motive, the overall success of a nonprofit organization must be judged by effectiveness, the extent to which it fulfills its social function. As a result, managers of nonprofit organizations must devote special attention to clearly defining this function and to deriving concrete, nonbudgetary objectives and standards from it.

3. There are five main categories of nonprofit organization: governments, educational organizations, health organizations, religious and charitable organizations, and professional associations and other similar groups. For each of these, the nature of the environment, sources of funds, objectives, and activities present unique demands for managers.

4. A number of techniques have been developed to help managers focus on results rather than on ever-expanding budgets. Programming, planning, budgeting systems (PPBS), zero-based budgeting, and cost-benefit analysis are all helpful in judging the true benefits of the activities of nonprofit organizations. No matter what particular techniques are used, the final requirements for success are (a) formal planning to maintain direction toward goals and (b) management commitment to produce results.

REVIEW AND DISCUSSION QUESTIONS

1. What are some of the ways in which nonprofit organizations are like businesses?

2. Since many services (education and health care, for instance) can be provided either by a profit-making or a nonprofit organization, there must be some basis for the organizers to choose between the two forms. What do you think this basis is?

3. Why are there so many nonprofit organizations in technological societies? How do you account for their continuing growth?

4. If the overall success of a nonprofit organization cannot be measured by the amount of profits earned, how can it be measured?

5. Briefly describe two characteristics of nonprofit organizations that shape the general approach needed by management.

6. Why is the adherence to budgets not a good standard for the success of nonprofit organizations?

7. Contrast a local government's relationship with "customers" and that of a nonprofit hospital.

8. What is the basic reason for using zero-based budgeting? Would it be useful for a profit-making organization? Why has it become so popular in nonprofit organizations?

Problems and Projects

1. The managers of four nonprofit organizations described their overall goals as shown in the statements below. Examination of the statements will show that these managers are focusing on *activities* rather than on *effectiveness* or on the kind of goals that will assure that the social function is being fulfilled. Rewrite the statements to make them more useful for judging the overall success of the organization. Concentrate on the function of the organization in society, on the benefits derived from operations, and on measurability. Managers using the goals you write should be able to tell whether their organization has been effective or not.

   a. "Our institute is a nonprofit organization that carries on research on human blindness and its consequences, both for the blind and for society. We use funds from governments, foundations, and private donors to support our clinical and social work."

   b. "Our department maintains the public streets of the town of Oakmont."

   c. "Our agency decides on how federal funds for the unemployed will be used locally and then writes and administers contracts to carry out the planned activities."

   d. "The main job of our association is to select articles from the journals that would be useful to our members and to publish abstracts that we send to members. That way, members don't have to subscribe to all of the journals themselves."

2. *Performance Situation—Nonprofit but Unique:* Rose Hill School is a privately owned, nonprofit school for gifted students of high school age. It stresses rigorous training in science and humanities and maintains the highest standards for both its faculty and students. The school has a substantial endowment, but since it has to pay high salaries to attract the best teachers and also provides excellent facilities, it has to charge substantial tuition to

meet its operating expenses. The school receives only negligible government funding for a few minor activities.

The department of licenses and inspections for a medium-sized city is also a nonprofit organization. It was created by an ordinance passed by the city council and is funded entirely from the annual general revenue budget of the city. Every year the department manager projects costs for the coming period and requests a budget amount from the council. The amount requested is never approved by the council. Every year the council reduces the budget to about 10 percent less than the requested funding. The function of the department is to enforce the city's building codes and to collect a construction tax through the issuance of building permits.

These organizations share the designation "nonprofit," but they are very different in their objectives and in their relationship with their environments. Analyze these differences by discussing the following questions:

    a. How would the source of revenue for each organization affect management goals?

    b. What relationship does each organization have with its clients or "customers"? How would this affect decision making for the managers?

    c. How could each organization measure its success? How can each tell whether it has fulfilled its function or not?

    d. Why do these two organizations exist? Do they fulfill a genuine social need?

3. The International Association of Solar Heating Manufacturers is a newly formed trade association established to work for the mutual interest of its members, companies that produce solar heating equipment. It is a nonprofit organization and its main source of revenue is the substantial membership fees paid by the manufacturers. The executive director of IASHM has decided to establish a publishing program that will find, edit, print, and distribute books of interest and use to the organization's members. The director has written the following general guidelines for the project:

    a. Overall: Publish useful books with hard-to-find information, even if they are expensive to produce.

    b. Marketing: Attempt to sell books to members at a price that will make the program self-supporting, but if necessary subsidize publications up to 20 percent from general income.

    c. Finance: Provide start-up capital 40 percent from surplus revenue on hand and 60 percent from medium-term borrowing.

    d. Production: Use outside suppliers on a cash basis.

Rewrite these guidelines so they would be suitable for a profit-making organization. Compare the two sets of statements. What is similar about the goals and development process of the nonprofit and the profit-making organization? What is different?

4. The executive branch of the government of a large city has among its many departments the following:

a. *The Relocation Bureau.* This office has a staff of 25 people who help citizens find new housing when they have been evicted or left homeless because their old residences have been destroyed by fire or will be torn down for redevelopment or by private owners.

b. *The Neighborhood Planning Board.* This consists of a council of architects, planners, and others who assist neighborhood groups trying to improve housing on their own. The NPB has a staff of 13 people who handle the actual day-to-day contact with neighborhoods.

c. *The Redevelopment Authority.* This large agency with hundreds of employees has the goal of using public money to clear slum areas of substandard housing and replace it with public housing.

d. *The Building Code Enforcement Division.* This office, with 130 inspectors, is charged with periodically reviewing the condition of housing in the city to make sure it continues to meet minimum standards. The division is empowered to condemn dwellings. It offers no assistance to owners who must make improvements, but it does check improvements for compliance.

e. *The Tax Relief Hearings Board.* This board, with its staff of 65, hears complaints about real estate tax assessments and claims under the city's tax relief ordinances for the elderly and other groups. It recommends changes in local tax laws to accomplish certain goals established by the city council.

As currently managed, each of these agencies is independent. Each approaches city council annually to request funds for (1) continuing its current operations for another year or (2) adding new activities that individual administrators consider desirable.

Apply the principles of programming, planning, budgeting systems (PPBS) to this management situation. How would the chief executive or the town council go about deciding how to handle housing activities for coming periods? Propose an *outline* of a program that might result from the use of PPBS, using a few sentences to describe it.

5. Make a list of the services or goods that you personally receive from nonprofit organizations. Think of all your activities and decide how many of them depend on organizations of this type. After making the list, discuss with the class how different life would be without the nonprofit groups. Which of them would likely be replaced by businesses? Which would be very difficult to provide on a profit-making basis?

6. The argument has been voiced that nonprofit organizations can provide goods and services at a lower cost than businesses because they do not have to set prices unreasonably high in order to assure that a profit will be made. Rewrite this statement into a questionnaire form and ask students outside your class whether they (a) agree strongly, (b) agree somewhat, (c) are undecided, (d) disagree somewhat, or (e) disagree strongly. In class, add up how many of those questioned chose each answer and discuss the results.

Based on the information in the text, do you think it is necessarily true that nonprofit organizations produce goods or services less expensively than businesses? Do you think it would be theoretically possible for them to do so? What would be required for nonprofit organizations to succeed at this?

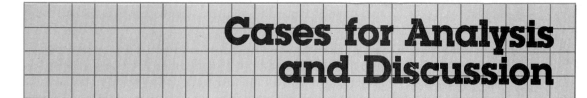

Cases for Analysis and Discussion

CASE 1: MANAGEMENT BY BUDGET

The sign read, "Fairleigh Mental Health Services—Diagnostic Center—Enter." And people did enter, again and again, some of them. The problem was what happened after they had entered. What happened was of little value, in the opinion of many.

Barbara Hallis, the assistant director at Fairleigh, was one who held that opinion. "The whole thing should be dumped; it's a joke," was the way she put it. To Larry Stein, the executive director, these words were not welcome, although they were familiar by now. "We can't just drop it," he said, "It's almost half of our budget. It's an important service."

"Important to whom? To you? To the people who work there? Our job is to help the people in the community who have mental health problems. Right? We have the clinic that works fine if anyone ever gets there. We have the school programs. We have the visiting psychiatrist. But the *diagnostic center* . . .," she said the phrase as if naming some particularly disagreeable substance. "The diagnostic center has never helped a single person, as far as we can tell. All that happens is that they go in and take 20 different tests; the results are added up and put in a folder. The people at the clinic can learn more in five minutes than all of those tests show in a whole day."

Larry answered, "If you are proposing again that we close the diagnostic center, I will only tell you again that it simply is not possible, even if it were desirable."

Barbara went on, growing more animated, "What we need is an education program. We can improve mental health just by showing people about themselves on television or on the radio or in the newspapers. That would really do some good. And it wouldn't cost 50 percent of what we spend on the diagnostic center."

"Let me repeat some facts," he said. "Forty percent of our revenue comes in to support the center. *Fifty* percent of our staff works there. If we close it, we'll be practically wiped out. Anyway, you know that we've been able to build an excess into the center's budget that we siphon off to support some of our other work. And what if we did close it. Can you imagine Dorsey or Whitman or some of those birds on the city council? They'd say, 'What do you mean it didn't work? Are you telling us that we've spent all of that money over the years on a *failure?*' "

A. Do you think Larry Stein really believes the diagnostic center is successful and is an important service? If not, could it really happen that a manager would fight to continue a useless activity?

B. Review Stein's reasons for keeping the center open. How are the reasons related to the characteristics of management by budget?

C. How would you resolve this situation? Is there any way Fairleigh Mental Health Services can concentrate on results and still get the resources it needs?

CASE 2: FROM THE DIRECTOR'S DESK

It had taken four strong men to bring it into the room. Gleaming rosewood with every edge worked in genuine boxwood, the huge desk stood magnificently in the center of the sprawling office. A computer terminal stood to its left, seldom used except when important visitors came. The oriental rugs were genuine, hand-knotted. The oil paintings were somber and rare, and very expensive. This was the sanctum of the executive director of International Medical Charities. It was duplicated on a lesser scale many times in the organization's new office building. Hundreds of busy clerks, computer programmers, direct mail specialists, accountants, and managers filled the five floors of offices.

It had been far different 13 years ago. The man who was now the head of this lavish organization had knelt in a clearing in the jungle in Central America, treating the infected ankle of a native. Supported by a private benefactor and by a $10,000 donation from an American church, he had worked in that jungle for three years, giving medical care to some of the people who needed it most. Then he had been "discovered." There followed television interviews, newspaper and magazine articles, even a book, all praising the work of "the jungle doctor." He had started modestly to raise funds to support other medical workers in developing nations. Then he had used some money from a private foundation to make his first mass mailing, asking for donations. The mailing succeeded, and it was only a tiny step to keeping a permanent staff to make other mailings. From there it took only a series of other small steps to lead to this $3 million building, this desk, and these oil paintings.

Doctors were still working in the jungle, it is true. But even they were regularly recalled to the United States for public appearances to raise even more money. The money was now used, as much as for any other purpose, to hire more fund-raisers.

A. Has this organization moved in a desirable direction? What is good about the way it has developed? What is bad about it?

B. Can you identify any *management* problems here? Could management techniques have been useful for International Charities, or does its direction depend entirely on the personality and character of its director?

C. Is there any way in which this case is pertinent to profit-making organizations as well as to nonprofit ones?

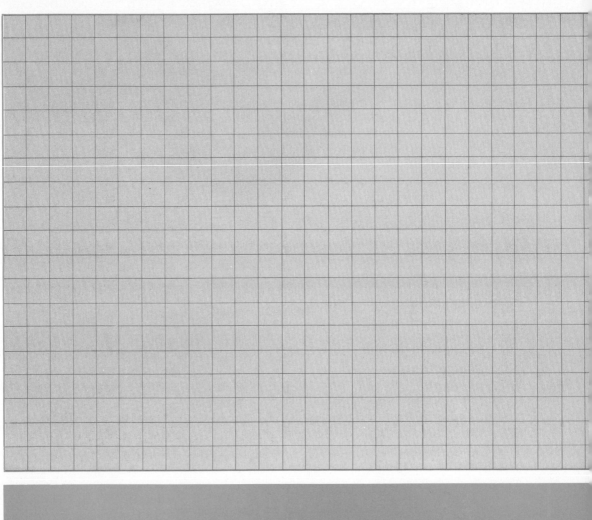

Quantitative Methods and New Approaches to Management and Organization

7

Information Systems and Management

24

After completing Chapter 24, you will be able to do the following:

- Identify information uses, data sources, transmission channels, and processing centers in an actual organization.

- Apply a method of information-systems analysis in simple organizational settings.

- Give an example of the kind of processing a computer can perform and name two characteristics of computer systems that make them useful in integrated information systems.

- Describe and apply two factors important to the decision of whether or not to install a new information system.

In the very smallest organization, the information used by a manager may appear quite simple. If there are only 25 orders received every day, manager Helen Blake can look at each individually. She can see who the orders are from and what was ordered. She can add up the day's sales on a desk calculator, or even by hand. If there is a question about the quantity of inventory on hand, Helen could walk into the stock room and in a few minutes count the entire stock of a single item. Control and knowledge of cash expenditures could be maintained by the simple policy of personally approving or writing all of the checks. In a situation like Helen's, nearly every transaction in marketing, purchasing, finance, inventory, and other operations could be expected to cross the manager's desk at one time or another.

In a large business or government agency, management information does not have even the appearance of simplicity. Millions of transactions—buying, selling, manufacturing, transferring materials and stock, borrowing, repaying—may take place in scores of locations scattered all over the world. Keeping track of what has been sold and for how much during a month or year can require a monumental information-gathering, recording, and distribution organization within the overall organization. This process is extremely expensive.

Futhermore, whether the organization is small or large, there are pressing needs for information from outside the organization. Part of the fundamental doctrine of planning is that the planner needs detailed information on what is happening in the environment that surrounds the organization. This outside information can be as voluminous and hard to handle as the countless transactions that make up internal organizational information. How can a manager keep informed and still keep from being overwhelmed? Not surprisingly, the solution is the same as for many other management problems: there has to be a system to the job.

INFORMATION SYSTEMS UNITE SOURCES, PROCESSORS, AND USERS

For the purposes of a manager, *information* is a fact or group of facts that can be put to use in making decisions and carrying out the management functions. Looked at in this way, *data* is simply a collection of facts, figures, measurements, judgments, and estimates. When the data is arranged, added, compared, and summarized to put it in a useful, practical form for accomplishing something, it becomes information.

Information of this sort always has three characteristics: (1) it comes from somewhere—its *source;* (2) it is *processed* in some way; and (3) it is gathered and processed with some fairly definite end or *use* in mind. To create an information system, many sources, processing techniques, and end uses must be integrated.

Information Sources and Uses

The sources of information that are tapped by managers are those already discussed in the separate sections on planning, controlling, organizing, staffing, and directing. Any attempt at a complete list would be cumbersome, but a few may serve as examples. Managers typically need to know such internally generated facts as the following: How much cash is on hand? How many orders have been received but not yet filled? How much inventory of both materials and completed goods remains? How are departmental costs comparing with budgeted costs? How far has the design of new products progressed? What purchase orders have been issued for which goods that have not yet been received? What is the credit history of present and new customers? What are future personnel requirements likely to be? What is the projected financial condition of the organization? How well are current shipping routes and schedules meeting physical distribution goals?

These few examples of kinds of information used by managers suggest a tremendous number of sources; and these represent only internal information. Add the numerous external sources such as government, market research, and trade organizations, and the sheer volume of detail needed for good management becomes apparent. Nearly everything anyone does, inside or outside the organization, becomes a potential source of useful information—from improperly tightening a nut on the assembly line to passing a new corporate tax bill on Capitol Hill.

Uses of Information

The uses of information also correspond roughly to the management functions:

■ *Planning* requires forecasts of conditions and performance in key

Managers in Action

Pressure from taxpayers to make local governments more efficient spurred Georgia's Cobb County manager of administrative services, William J. Hogg, to install an information system. The system helped uncover dozens of loose ends and uncoordinated decisions made by the county's various officials. One major outcome: an outdated manual property-deed recording procedure was replaced by a fully integrated computer-microfilming-copying system that reduced recording time from three weeks to one day.

Mr. Hogg began his career with Cobb County as a junior programmer trainee. But by dint of taking a broader view of data processing, his job evolved to an overall responsibility for records management, archives, micrographics, word processing, and facsimile systems. These are the instruments and devices needed to create an integrated management information system. "I acquired all these responsibilities," says Mr. Hogg, "not because I'm so smart or knowledgeable in this field, but because nobody else was assigned to anything vaguely resembling administrative services. I did take the initiative, however. And I had the good fortune of having open-minded people around, and they even let me develop my own job description. Its always been my nature to become involved."

He observed at once that "decisions were being made by each section head with little regard to the big picture. Some obsolete systems were in place and both our employees and our customers (tax payers) were becoming increasingly frustrated with the delays in several areas."

Change was not easy, however. In spite of the obvious need for establishing a central information system, it took 13 months to gain some semblance of control. "We ran into the typical objections," Hogg says. He especially identified the "low-bid philosophy," which presumed that low-cost equipment was the best buy for the country, when higher first costs might mean lower operating costs over a period of time. "In areas like copying, we weren't even aware of how much was being spent or how many machines were in place." For years, the individual departments had each gone their separate ways. By centralizing this information processing function, the county was able to go from dealing with nine different copier vendors to a sole source of supply and a quick-copy center that dramatically improved services and lowered costs.

Source: Loren S. Kennedy, "Reform at the County Level," *Administrative Management,* January 1978, p. 36. Excerpted from *Administrative Management,* Geyer-McAllister Publications, Inc., New York, 1978.

areas of sales, revenues, production, operations, market shifts, product failure, equipment and facilities, and many others.

- ■ *Controlling* depends directly on measurements of operational and financial performance to compare with standards, budgets, and plans.
- ■ *Organizing* uses systematic analyses of essential tasks and performances to shape the internal structure.
- ■ *Staffing* requires continuing performance appraisals and analyses of position requirements to meet future personnel needs.
- ■ *Directing* demands a constant knowledge of organization resources and their current and projected conditions.

An information system must not only take these uses into account, but must also tailor the information so provided to the specific operating segments of the organization structure. Although the marketing director handles all of the management functions involved in marketing, the information needed by that department is often different from the information for the finance department.

VARIATION WITH LEVEL OF MANAGEMENT   Information uses—the type and presentation form—also vary with the level in the organization of the manager putting the information to use. A supervisory manager, for example, will devote much time to control and relatively less to planning. The supervisor needs current operating information—output, productivity, inventory, and the like—for continual ready reference. A top-level executive, on the other hand, cannot spend too much time trying to work out details such as why machine number 4 in the Springfield plant is less productive than machines 1, 2, 3, and 5. At the upper-management levels, concerns are with highly summarized information: total production, overall productivity, year-to-year sales trends, company-wide product development, and balance sheets and income statements that may be projected years into the future. Middle-level managers need yet another kind of information: the partially summarized reports that allow them to make the medium-range decisions about uses of assets, overall department performance, personnel planning, and other issues.

The Processing of Information

Data can be manipulated in many ways to turn it into useful information. Any of these manipulations may be called *processing*. Four kinds of processing may occur:

1. *Recording.* In any information system, the first, and possibly most crucial, step is to record data so that it will be protected from unintentional destruction and so it can be found again. This is no simple task, considering the number of transactions that take place in purchasing,

order processing, billing, production, and the other functions of even a small organization.

2. *Transmission.* This processing involves the transfer of data from the point at which it originates (the order entry department, for instance) to another department or person who needs the information (the sales manager or general manager, for instance). An orderly and continual flow of information from sources to users is essential. It may be accomplished in a variety of ways: by a carefully designed system of handwritten reports, by computer-prepared reports, by memos, by telephone calls, and by personal meetings.

3. *Summarizing.* A busy warehouse, for example, will commonly make thousands of transactions a day as it receives, ships, and transfers stock. The manager charged with controlling the warehouse's inventory could not possibly work with each of these individual transactions. Instead, what the manager needs is totals and subtotals for each class of transaction so as to get an overall idea of the changes that have occurred during the day, week, or month. How many units were received for each stock type? How many were shipped? What is the total inventory on hand for each stock item? These questions can only be answered by grouping, classifying, comparing, adding, and subtracting.

4. *Mathematical Analysis.* This applies mathematic analysis and manipulation to basic data to make it more useful for decision making. One example of this process is the use of historical data on sales, costs, or other factors together with trend analysis to create forecasts of future conditions. Other techniques use probability theory, modeling, and other statistical approaches to make the real meaning of figures more apparent. A few of these methods are described in Chapter 25.

Creating an Information System

The key word is "system"—an organized group of parts in which the actions of each interact in fairly predictable ways with the other parts. The parts of an information system are the information sources, the transmission channels, the processing centers, and the end users. The trick is to correctly identify the necessary parts, assign appropriate tasks and goals to each, and tie them together so that they work and interact to meet the goal of giving everyone the information they need and no more. An overview of an information system and its elements is illustrated in Figure 24-1 on page 526.

Simple? No, not even in conception, much less in execution. The usual way of approaching this problem is to start at both ends and work toward the middle. If both the sources and uses of information are clearly defined and understood, it is possible to create a network of transmission and processing to interconnect them. The next section outlines the main features of this process.

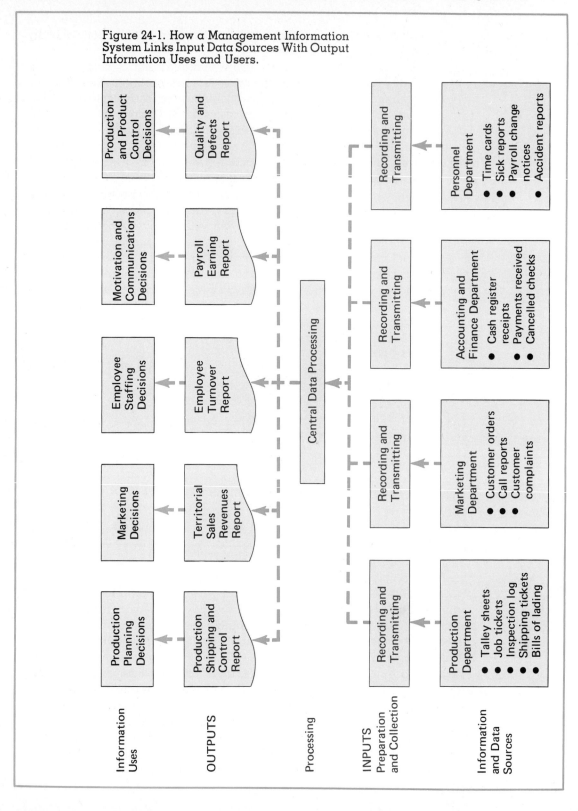

Figure 24-1. How a Management Information System Links Input Data Sources With Output Information Uses and Users.

MANAGERS CAN SYSTEMATICALLY CREATE AN INFORMATION SYSTEM

A broad academic and professional field has been built around the process of studying and developing systems that will accomplish useful work or provide useful information. *Systems analysis* is this process of (1) investigating the operational and informational needs of an organization or its parts and then (2) creating or improving the system to meet these needs. When directed toward the development of an information system (the activities of gathering, processing, and distributing information), systems analysis consists of a range of techniques for identifying information sources and needs, designing information networks, and putting them into operation. Although many systems analysts specialize in the application of computers to solve information problems, a computer is not an essential part of an effective information system. In brief outline, the general approach of systems analysis to organizing an information system requires managers to decide what the system needs to accomplish, identify information sources and needs, and design and put in operation the procedures and other system components required to satisfy the needs.

Setting Objectives

The general goal is usually clear: to create an integrated set of routinely performed activities that will provide every manager with the information he or she needs to effectively carry out the management job. These activities and the information they provide are commonly called a *management information system (MIS)*. Further objectives must flesh out the overall definition. The central one usually concerns costs. The objectives that are finally settled on must balance two considerations: the desirable and the practical. Information in exactly the right form is useful, but it can be expensive. Sometimes it is necessary to settle for less than the absolutely finest system in order to be able to pay for the system that is actually installed. Additional MIS objectives usually concern the efficient use of existing facilities, proper training and use of personnel, and meeting of time limits.

Analyzing Data Sources

It makes good sense to approach the information problem by saying, "Let's decide exactly what we need to know and then set out to gather that data." In practice, though, this sensible approach is not always possible. Any kind of operation automatically generates a good deal of data simply through its routine performance of tasks. Every time a production worker punches in for work in the morning, for instance, a piece of data is created: the worker's identifying number and the time work was begun. This particular piece of data may have little relevance for important management decisions at the upper level, but a good manager will see to it that all data of this sort is handled in a systematic, orderly way.

The basic procedure consists of first making a thorough analysis of what data are currently being created as a principal product or by-product of operations. Examples will be found in the billing department, in production, personnel, inventory control, and everywhere else. A simple list enumerating and briefly describing all of this data is an important first step to getting it under control. Once the data is identified, some basic questions must be answered about each type and item. What may be discarded and what must be recorded? How should it be recorded? How long should it be retained? These and related questions can best be answered in conjunction with an analysis of how information is used in the organization.

Analyzing Information Needs

A common approach to finding out what kind of information each manager needs to perform the functions of the position is to use a formal interview or questionnaire. This systematically reviews each task of every manager's job. Such an interview may be structured in a number of different ways. Specific areas of the organization may serve as a starting point; for example, "Do you use or need information about production? Do you make any decisions that are based on sales levels?" The management functions also can provide a general framework; for example, "In your planning, what kind of information do you need to evaluate courses of action? What kind of decisions do you make about staffing?"

Detailed questioning along these lines helps managers to pin down the exact kinds of information that will really be useful in making decisions. It is also helpful at this point to begin the design of the specific form in which information will be most useful. Thinking can be guided into very specific channels by trying to decide, for example, what the column headings on a report will be, what totals and subtotals are needed, and whether production data should be presented in dollars as well as units of output such as pounds, tons, or gallons. A design made at this point will be subject to considerable revision, but it helps get the analysis down to brass tacks.

One question that must be resolved in the analysis of information uses is the frequency with which information is needed. For some strategic decisions, quarterly summaries may carry more meaning than a detailed day-to-day reporting of operations. For some other applications—in product quality control, for instance—information may be needed as frequently as every hour.

For most managers, it will be useful to make a distinction between information that is needed routinely and regularly and other kinds of information that may be called for only in special circumstances. Every organization will want a regular stream of financial and operations reports. These should be carefully planned for in the system. In addition, however, situations are certain to arise in which extraordinary information is needed. A marketing manager may suddenly need the complete sales history of a single product. The purchasing manager may need the price-increase history for a particular material over the last five years. Such needs are unpredictable and cannot thoroughly be planned for. It is possible, though, through the interviewing technique, to get some idea of needs of this type that have arisen in the past, and to try to make some provision for them in the future. This means that recorded information must be extremely well organized and easily accessible.

Connecting Sources and Uses

Ultimately, the information system must interconnect data sources and information uses. The major questions in providing the interconnections are the following:

1. Through what routes will information be transmitted? How, for instance, will a customer's order just received in the sales order department be communicated to all of the people who need to know about it—the accounting office, the production shop, the shipping department, and so on?

2. How frequently will information be transmitted? Orders may be transmitted to the shipping department daily or immediately as received. The information may be stored up for a separate transmission to the production control manager only once a week or once a month.

3. What processing must be given data to make it useful? What mathematical analysis will be applied? What summaries and comparisons will be prepared?

4. Who will do the processing, and how will they do it? Some of the work may be assigned to people who serve as information sources. A billing clerk, for instance, may be told to look up customer numbers in a register or to prepare single-order totals when orders are received. Other processing may be assigned to analytical clerks or to departments especially set up for that purpose. Some processing may be left for the end users to do themselves. Much of the processing work will go to the computer center or data processing department when one is available.

5. How will transmission physically take place? Will computer-printed reports be hand-carried to the people who need them? Will a data source simply telephone a user periodically? Will the information be electronically transmitted to video screens?

6. How will the network be installed? What equipment is best? What paper forms and methods will be used? How will people be trained to use the new system? A fully developed information system represents a major change in most organizations. This presents important technical problems in installing processing and transmitting equipment and procedures. It requires significant human adjustment to make sure the new ways of doing things actually take place.

COMPUTERS INCREASE THE NUMBER OF DECISION OPPORTUNITIES

Computer applications have had an overwhelming impact on organizational information systems in recent years. Too often, they have been equally overwhelming to the managers responsible for them. The reason for the emergence of computers in this area is simple: they were designed and developed specifically to process and transmit information. They help collect data. They perform all of the standard processing methods. They produce output reports of information for use in decision making and other management activities. The problem with all of this is that a computer has no decision-making capabilities except in the simplest and most clearly defined situations. It cannot handle exceptions unless it has been told in painstaking detail in advance how to handle them. The simplest error in data preparation or in writing instructions for computer processing can cause serious errors in the results obtained. When computers are assigned major jobs such as recording and summarizing millions of bank transactions, the human support activities may become so vast and complex that they are hard to organize and control.

In spite of their shortcomings, computers have made many tasks far easier and quicker to do than they were by hand. Because of their huge information capacity and speed, computers have made management information available that was simply unobtainable in the past.

What a Computer Does

To give a better idea of their capabilities, let us take an example of a typical computer application. This will be more revealing than a detailed analysis of electronic and mechanical operations.

DATA COLLECTION In a large shipping room, 20 clerks each take a shipping order from a stack, pick the required merchandise from inventory, pack it, attach a typed address label, mark the package for postage or freight costs, and stack it near the loading dock. For each separate package, they then fill out a slip like the one shown in Figure 24-2. (This example has been designed for simplicity rather than to exactly duplicate methods and forms that would be used in a real shipping room.) The package shipment form shows the identity of the packer, the contents of the package, and the total shipping costs, and gives a code that indicates the method of shipping. (In Figures 24-2 and 24-3, PP stands for parcel post and AF for air freight.)

DATA PREPARATION These filled-in forms are collected twice a day and sent to the data processing department where they are prepared to be read by a computer. In most cases, computers are unable to read human handwriting or ordinary typewriting. Of a number of kinds of "writing" they can read, the punch card is a familiar example. A keypunch operator takes the forms from the shipping department, and using a machine with a typewriter

Figure 24-2. Typical Form Used at Data Source.

PACKAGE SHIPMENT FORM

Date _12/10/81_

Packer _19_

Contents

Quantity	Stock Number
4	A2398
10	C8136
1	M8190

Shipping Costs $ _8.25_

Shipping Method _PP_

keyboard, punches the information from the forms onto punch cards. If the data on the punched cards were printed out before the computer read it, it would look like that in Figure 24-3. Each item from the forms has been transferred to a single string of figures. On each line, the first six numbers show

121081170006B2503:002250AF

121081190004A23980010C81360001M8190:000825PP

121081220001C4399:000095PP

121081190019A23980001C4112:001125AF

121081180026A23620008B2593:000965PP

121081180012A23980001C4112:000431PP

Figure 24-3. Package Shipment Form Coded for Computer Entry.

the date, the next two show the packer, and the next groups of nine numbers each show the contents of the package, giving first the quantity and then the stock number. The colon (:) is an arbitrary symbol indicating that there are no more items in the package and that the numbers following will be the shipping cost and the shipping method code. When coded on punch cards in this way, the computer can read the data that originally appeared on the shipping forms.

DATA SUMMARIZING   Once the computer has read the numbers, what can it do with them? The goal of processing is to put the raw data in a form that is easily understood by the people who use it to make decisions. The simplest kind of processing consists of summarizing all of the individual transactions and collecting them together into categories that mean something. Figure 24-4 shows this kind of report. The separate shipping transactions have been added together to show how many of each stock number were shipped during the day. The computer has also used some information from a separate file that it maintains to make the report have more meaning. It keeps a running record of the inventory for each stock item. It subtracts from the total when shipping forms show that some have been shipped out and it adds to the total when stock-receipt forms show that some have been added to inventory.

DATA INTEGRATING   Another report that uses the data from the package shipment forms is shown in Figure 24-5. In this report, most of the information comes from other sources—accounting records and the computer's files—and the shipping forms contribute to only one line. The computer first added together all of the shipping charges for the 3-month period ending December 31, 198X. It then automatically looked up in a file the amount that was budgeted for shipping costs during that period. Next, it subtracted the budgeted amount from the actual amount and printed all three figures on the report line Freight and Shipping. From information like this, a manager is able to make judgments about the financial performance of the department, and take control action if needed.

This example of part of a computerized information system is on the simplest level. It demonstrates a straightforward approach to the collection and

STOCK ITEMS SHIPPED FROM INVENTORY, DECEMBER 10, 198X		
STOCK NUMBER	NUMBER SHIPPED	QUANTITY REMAINING
A 2398	329	9,436
A 2406	11	2,412
.	.	.
.	.	.

Figure 24-4. Summary Report for Management.

Figure 24-5. Summary Report for Management.

```
BUDGET VARIANCE - SHIPPING DEPARTMENT    QUARTER ENDED 12/31/8X
```

	BUDGETED	ACTUAL	VARIANCE
PAYROLL	81,000	83,982	+2,982
FREIGHT AND SHIPPING	57,600	63,290	+5,690
. . . .	.	.	.
. . . .	.	.	.

processing of data to create useful information. This simple process is duplicated in other departments and combined with other activities and kinds of reports and processing. The result is a truly powerful tool for management involvement with the essential operations of an organization. The essence of such a system is *integration*—making all the necessary connections between data sources and users. A computer can make this integration easier because of its two unique abilities: it can handle and combine huge amounts of data from diverse sources; it has a capacity to maintain central files of data that can contribute to a wide variety of user needs.

COSTS AND BENEFITS DETERMINE COMPUTER USAGE

A computer consists of a number of electromechanical devices to handle input, processing, and output. *Input* consists of the raw data to be processed. Input devices may read electronic codes on magnetic tape or disks, punch codes on cards or paper tape, special typewriting or handwriting on paper sheets, or a number of other forms of recording data. *Output* is the results of the computer processing after it has been somehow transmitted back to the world outside the computer. It may be produced by devices that write codes on magnetic tapes or disks, cards, or paper tape, or print readable reports on printed paper forms, video screens, or some other medium. The processing within the computer includes the operations—adding, subtracting, temporarily recording, comparing, and so on—that turn the data into usable information.

Computer Costs Computer devices are precise, complex, and expensive. Buying or leasing a computer large enough to do the needed job of information handling is an important cost factor for most organizations. A very small company or agency has smaller information-processing needs than a giant organization, and it is also less able to pay. A large organization has greater financial resources, and far greater processing needs.

Technological development is rapidly making computers more accessible to the medium and small companies that could benefit from automated processing but have been unable to afford it in the past. Increasing miniaturization and mass production of computer systems has reduced prices. Additionally, more computer makers are producing the scaled-down equipment and providing the kind of easy-to-operate designs that are more suitable for a wide range of smaller organizations.

HARDWARE   A computer suitable for the basic accounting and reporting functions for a small organization may be purchased outright for only a few thousand dollars. A computer system able to meet the requirements of the largest companies and agencies may rent for hundreds of thousands of dollars a month. These costs are only for the basic costs of computer *hardware* such as card and tape readers, processing units, printers, and video consoles. The costs for the human analysis and effort needed to make the machinery productive are also substantial.

PROGRAMMING AND OPERATING   Computers must be instructed in what to do at a very detailed level. The process of providing these detailed instructions is called *programming*. It is an exacting skill that consumes a great deal of personnel time and money. Together with these programs used to make the computer work, there is a need for many detailed procedures telling operators, clerks, and others in the department how to handle the data, how to distribute the reports, how to operate the machinery, and so on. These procedures almost always include numerous detailed forms to be filled out, and often call for lengthy standards, definitions, and descriptions. All of these items that support the hardware operation—the programs, procedures, and accompanying documentation—are commonly called *software*. Additionally, someone has to analyze thoroughly the data sources and information needs and specify exactly how the two will be connected. Added to this are all of the people needed to operate the computer, prepare data in computer-readable form, design input and output forms, and keep records for the entire operation. It is clear that a major effort is needed.

Computer Benefits

Decisions about computers and information systems are like other management decisions: they must be based on economic factors and on an appreciation of interactions with other functions of the organization.

A first question when evaluating the installation or improvement of an information system, whether to include a computer or not, is whether the benefits of the system will be greater than the cost of installing and operating it. This can usually be estimated with some accuracy. First, the analyst adds up the financial benefits—personnel savings, capability to handle additional business, improved collections of accounts receivable, and others. Then these benefits must be compared with projections of all the costs of acquiring, installing, and operating the system.

A second consideration is how well the proposed system will fit with all of the other functions and tasks of the organization. After all, the real work of a sheet-metal factory, a national charity, or a government agency that funds and evaluates energy research is *not* to gather information about its own operations; this activity merely supports the real work and helps to make it more efficient and effective. The ultimate question when deciding whether to spend money and time on an integrated information system is, "Will it help us do a better job of achieving our objectives?"

SUMMARY

1. An information system consists of data sources and information users tied together in a network of communications channels. The network collects and processes data and transmits it to those who need it. The system actually creates information because it turns raw data into a useful decision-making tool by processing it in some way.

2. The process of creating an information system requires systems analysis. This involves systematically investigating existing and projected sources of data and existing and projected users of information, and establishing effective links between them. Many of the links require processing as well as simple transmission.

3. Many information systems use computers for both processing and transmission. The speed and capacity of computers makes them capable of integrating large information systems. They can readily process and combine many diverse data sources and can maintain huge central files that can be rapidly accessed to contribute information to diverse reports.

4. As with other management decisions, economic and organizational factors must influence decisions about computers and information systems. The key questions are (a) Will the benefits of investments in information systems outweigh the costs? (b) Will the information system really aid the units of the organization in meeting their objectives.

REVIEW AND DISCUSSION QUESTIONS

1. To a manager, what is information? Is it any different from data? If so, how?

2. What are some sources of information generated in the corner gas station? Name at least three kinds of decisions the station manager might make based on this information.

3. Briefly describe four kinds of data processing that you might find in a management information system. Do these kinds of processing apply equally to all kinds of management information systems?

4. If you were asked to go into a local brick manufacturing company and describe its information system, how would you go about it? How could you tell if the information flow really made up a system or not? Is there any way it could not be a system?

5. What is the goal of systems analysis?

6. Give an example of a report that the manager of an electric motor assembly department would probably want to see routinely and regularly. Give another example of a report the same manager might want on a special, nonroutine occasion.

7. Very large computer systems have created some challenging problems for the people who manage the human support activities surrounding the computer. Why are these support people needed and why is it important that they perform well?

8. Economically, how could you judge whether or not a proposal for creating a new computerized information system was a good idea or not?

Problems and Projects

1. *Performance Situation—Information for the Publications Department:* Jan Foss runs the publications department for the home office of the International Brotherhood of Metalworkers. Although the union is not a profit-making organization, Jan's department is set up just like a little business. She and her colleagues publish *Metalworker* magazine every two weeks and put out a wide variety of books, booklets, and pamphlets used for informing and training local officers, for organizing, and for generally keeping in touch with, and even entertaining, members. Jan's department was specifically instructed to set prices and services to cover operating costs and make a slight profit. Since, by-and-large, local offices and members were not required to buy from the publications department, Jan has to be a business manager with a marketing operation to bring in the needed customers and revenue.

The people in Jan's department use direct mail as their main advertising and selling method. They handle their own orders, contract for their own printing and production, and keep track of their own inventory, even though it is physically stored at the warehouses of the firms that handle their printing. The department has a budget, but it is not just a giveaway from the parent organization. It is always firmly based on past revenues generated by the publications and on prospects for the coming year.

Like any manager, Jan is responsible for planning, controlling, organizing, staffing, and directing. Also like any other manager, she has a great need for the right kind of information. Using what you have learned elsewhere in the text, briefly describe five information needs Jan has. What are five kinds of information and reports she would use regularly in running her department?

2. Choose any one of the information uses you have identified in Problem 1 and design a report form that will present the necessary information in a convenient, clear way. Examples of such report forms may be found in Figures 6-2, 6-3, 9-2, 24-4, and 24-5, in the text. Show identifications for columns, ways information should be categorized and compared, and anything else that you think is necessary to make the data useful for practical decision making. Keep in mind (a) how the report will be used, (b) whether a feasible amount of processing can produce the report, and (c) whether the basic data needed for the report will be available somewhere in the organization.

3. For each of the information uses you named in Problem 1, name the essential data source or sources from which the information can be produced.

4. Continuing with the information uses given in Problem 1 and with the data sources identified in Problem 3, for each information use, give a brief description of the processing needed to turn the basic data into the usable management report.

5. In Problems 1 through 4 you have described the elements of a portion of a management information system: data sources, processing requirements, and information uses and reports. Draw a diagram—similar to the one in Figure 24-1—showing the system as a network interconnecting all of these parts. Show all data sources, processing centers, and information uses. Assume that some processing will be done at each data source (in the publications department, for instance, where orders are opened, recorded, and transmitted) and that the remainder of the processing will be done in a central data processing department.

6. In the preceding problems you have done the basic analytical work of creating a portion of an information system. What is this system good for? The five types of information asked for in Problem 1 were described as information needs or uses. How would they be used? For each of the five, briefly describe one decision that would be influenced by that kind of information.

Cases for Analysis and Discussion

CASE 1: A MACHINE WILL STRAIGHTEN OUT THIS MESS

"That does it! Call that computer sales representative and say we're ready to buy. We've got to get this mess straightened out."

Martin Barth didn't get to be the head of the state bureau of commerce by making impulsive decisions, but this time he had boiled over. For weeks he had been trying to get a report of new business starts, needed for an upcoming presentation he had to make before a committee of the state legislature. He thought he had noticed suspiciously vague reasons for the report not being finished when he asked for it. There had been so many information delays, however, since his agency had doubled in size in recent years that he thought no more about it. But today he had gone to the business analysis department and demanded action. The color had drained from his face when he learned the truth: the department hadn't simply been going slow on writing the report, as he had suspected. They couldn't write the report; they might never be able to write the report. What they had been keeping from Barth was the terrible news that they didn't even have the raw data on business starts they were supposed to be collecting. In a reorganization last year, that activity had simply gotten "lost." No one had sent out a single questionnaire form. No one even knew where the forms were.

A. Will the installation of a computer be the answer to the problems in the Bureau? Why or why not?

B. Describe an approach that Barth might take to providing a long-term improvement in the information handling in the Bureau.

C. Who failed in their responsibility here? Whose job do you think it was to have managed well enough to prevent this kind of situation from arising in the first place?

CASE 2: PENNY-WISE, POUND-FOOLISH

In the final report from the computer service center, the introduction highlighted this statement: "In accordance with the original objectives given in writing by Ms. Clarkson of Purcell Manufacturing, our system design efforts have adhered to the *primary* objective of absolutely lowest operating costs when installed and operating."

Adelle Clarkson, a staff aide in the production department at Purcell, was pleased when she read this sentence. Lowest operating cost had been the objective she had stressed. She did so because she knew her superiors would never approve the computerized information system if monthly costs were sizeable. The people from the computer center came, installed the equipment, and taught people to use it. A number of clerks and analysts were eliminated. This saved money immediately. When the computer center technicians left, the system started turning out its periodic reports just as they had promised.

Operating costs were, in fact, amazingly low. The six full-time people devoted to operating the system, plus the equipment rental and other costs, were significantly lower than the hand methods they had replaced. For weeks, everyone was beaming on the new system.

It wasn't long, though, before Adelle began to notice little things that made her feel uneasy. It began to appear that her boss was spending a great deal of time poring over the computer printouts and making dozens of hand calculations. She learned from one of her friends that some of the production and quality-control supervisors weren't using the reports at all.

Instead, they were going directly to the data sources and keeping their own handwritten records. She even got a formal request from the purchasing department for a programmable calculator with a small disk storage capacity to handle their supplier-history records.

A. Think about the information needs of managers at different levels in this organization and try to analyze what is happening in this case. What is there about the computer reports that is causing trouble?

B. Was the objective of absolute minimum operating expense a reasonable one? Why or why not?

C. What can Adelle do now? Does she have any good options?

CASE 3: ARE THE OLD WAYS THE BEST WAYS?

Bill had always taken pride in looking out over the office at desk after desk of diligent clerical workers. His pride was justified. There was scarcely a man or woman who worked for Bill who was not a real expert at the job, enjoyed the work, and gave his or her best efforts. Bill's department handled all of the basic administrative recordkeeping for his company except those for purely accounting records, and he supplied the basic information for most of them. Bill's department handled order entry, shipping, inventory, and most of the other administrative procedures that keep a company running. For the most part, the department handled its work well. There were sometimes delays, and at certain times of the year there was quite a bit of overtime. But things were working just the way they were.

Bill had some doubts about the current operation, though. It was clear to him and to anyone else who happened to walk by that there really were quite a few clerks sitting there. It cost a lot of money in salaries to pay them and in overhead to support them in other ways. It was also clear that individual operations were not as fast as they could be. In spite of Bill's analysis of procedures over the years, there was still a lot of walking around, hand delivery, and telephone consultation.

Should he get a computer and set up his operations in the modern way, like most of his competitors? He called in some high-powered consultants who proposed an entirely new system. "Eliminate nearly all of the clerks," they said, "our methods will work faster and less expensively." At the center of the system, of course, was a brand new computer humming in mysterious ways that Bill was convinced he would never understand.

A. Based on the text, what are the first things Bill should look into in deciding whether to adopt the new system? How will he get the information he will need to decide?

B. What is a second factor Bill must consider?

C. What about all of the clerks who will be without jobs if the new system is adopted? What do you think should be done about them? Is there any strictly rational way to make this decision?

CASE 4: TELL ME
ALL YOUR NEEDS

Systems Analyst: "Hello, Mr. Pareto. Thank you for setting aside some time for me. I know that as a production manager you're busy."

Production Manager: "That's all right. I'm hoping that what you're working on will do us some good in the long run."

Systems Analyst: "I hope so, too. I guess you know already that what we're trying to do is set up a new management information system that will really give people the information they need to do a good job of managing. We want to find out where information comes from and who uses it, and then work out an efficient way to put the sources and the users together."

Production Manager: "And what can I do?"

Systems Analyst: "The basic question is, What do you need to know to do your job?"

Production Manager: "Well, I supervise the managers of three departments—purchasing, manufacturing, and quality control. I need to know what kinds of results the departments are getting. I need to have good sales projections for production planning. I need good financial information about inventories. I need costs, productivity, that kind of thing."

Systems Analyst: "Could you be a little more specific?"

Production Manager: "I thought that was your job. What kind of information can you give me? The more I know, the better."

Systems Analyst: "I realize you haven't made a detailed study of your information needs. That's what we want to do now. But, if you can't give me an idea to start with of what you use in running your division, we don't have anything to work with."

A. How is this interview going so far? Where do you think it will lead, given this beginning?

B. How is the systems analyst doing? Is he well prepared? What should he be doing differently, if anything?

C. What does this part of an investigative interview tell you about the technical skills required of someone who designs information systems? What about the human skills required?

Quantitative Methods for Management Decisions

25

After completing Chapter 25, you will be able to do the following:

- Recognize situations in which a limited range of quantitative methods may be useful, and identify a technique applicable to each.

- Analyze decision-making situations to reveal which aspects may be assisted by quantitative techniques and which may not.

- Describe a manager's role in putting quantitative methods into action in specific management situations.

- Apply a decision tree to a decision, given appropriate numerical information.

- Interpret a simple game-theory matrix.

- Propose possible applications of linear programming to management problems.

- Describe the goals of queuing theory.

- Apply the formula for Economic Order Quantity, given appropriate information.

In businesslike black type, the label read "Automated Decision-Making Machine." Inside the small wooden case was a 25-cent coin accompanied by long-winded, straight-faced instructions for tossing a coin. Obviously, the device was a poke of fun at managers. Rarely would a business manager be willing to make an important decision using this so-called machine: "Heads we put the $25 million in a new processing plant; tails we put the money into new product research." Nevertheless, there has been and remains a great deal of guesswork in making even decisions as important as choosing among alternative investment strategies for $25 million. From the time of Frederick W. Taylor, many analysts have tried to reduce the guesswork associated with management decision making by devising rational guidelines. This tradition has gained considerable influence in handling certain management concerns, such as inventory control. It is rapidly spreading to other areas, including the development of top-level organization strategies. Systematic, quantitative approaches are available for a far wider range of decisions than even thirty years ago. Undoubtedly, more and better methods lie in the future.

Quantitative methods are systematic, analytic approaches that use numerical measurements or estimates of important factors. Their application to decision making depends on information. One of the advantages of a modern, integrated information system is that it can provide some of the raw data needed for such formal decision-making aids. In most instances, however, all of the information needed for a decision will not be obtainable. Areas of ignorance, risk, and uncertainty will always remain. An important point about quantitative methods is that they do not eliminate uncertainty; they merely impose order on it and help reveal its magnitude.

DECISIONS PRECEDE
EFFECTIVE ACTION
Everything a manager does is, in the long run, aimed at moving the organization into action toward its goals. Before anyone can take effective action, someone must first decide which actions are best from among the many possibilities. Thus, *decision making* might be described as choosing from among alternative courses of action. In brief review, the process of making decisions includes:

1. Remaining informed of conditions inside and outside of the organization in order to be aware of what decisions are needed.
2. Creatively devising alternative courses of action that may solve the problem or exploit the opportunity, developing new information in the process, if necessary.
3. Evaluating the potential effectiveness, costs, and consequences of each alternative action.
4. Choosing from among the alternatives to determine the best action or combination of actions to take.

In this process, quantitative methods are most helpful in steps 3 and 4. Knowing when decisions are to be made and developing alternative courses of action depend on the skill, experience, and creativity of managers. Evaluating and choosing from among the alternatives also are aided by the intuitive skills of an experienced manager. Fortunately, they are sometimes responsive to an analytic approach for which numerical methods are useful.

Problem Solving
Versus Opportunity
Exploitation
It is sometimes helpful to make a distinction between decision making that is meant to solve problems and decision making for the purpose of exploiting opportunities. The same basic process is needed for both situations, but a different emphasis is sometimes appropriate. A *problem* exists when something interferes with achieving goals that would otherwise be attainable. The basic goal of problem solving is to identify the obstacles and eliminate them. A manager might state a problem in a simple way: "Production in the plant is not as high as it should be, given the equipment and employees we have." The simplicity stops there, though, because the process of finding the causes of the overall problem can be challenging indeed. Dozens of interacting factors, such as motivation, scheduling, purchasing, and equipment maintenance will usually be found to add up to the general problem. The emphasis in problem solving must usually be on finding all of these contributing factors.

In locating and exploiting *opportunities*, emphasis is placed on the creative development of alternative actions. For problems, the solution is often relatively easy to devise once the true source of trouble is identified. For opportunities, the best actions often are far less clear. Managers also must make an active effort to search for opportunities. Problems often make themselves known without looking for them.

Again, quantitative methods may fail to be applicable to the toughest parts of either problem solving or exploiting opportunities. For problems, finding the true sources of trouble is the greatest difficulty. Numerical methods are most useful in working out a solution once the sources are known. For opportunities, locating the opportunity and devising alternative ways to exploit it is the key. Numerical methods are most useful for choosing among alternatives once they have been developed.

MANAGERS NEED NOT BE EXPERT MATHEMATICIANS

Many of the modern quantitative methods used in management depend on highly sophisticated mathematical analysis. The whole field is often called *management science* or *operations research* (OR) and is defined as "the application of the tools of natural science to management concerns and problems." Yet, managers are managers; they are not scientists. What is the role, for instance, of the marketing manager for a fuel oil distributor or the personnel director of a cotton manufacturer in taking advantage of these new techniques? Can a nonscientist really direct the use of scientific methods?

A nonscientist manager's ability to use sophisticated quantitative analyses depends on two factors:

1. Much of the work of applying these methods is nontechnical and is, in fact, closely related to traditional management tasks.
2. A grasp of the specific techniques used in the strictly mathematical analysis is not essential, in most cases, to an understanding of the results.

Nontechnical Aspects   Most mathematical applications in management can only be used at certain points of the process of investigation and decision making. The use of probability estimates, as described in Chapter 5, is an example. A manager can derive a numerical estimate of the relative value of alternative actions by multiplying (1) the expected benefits of each alternative by (2) an estimate of the probability of achieving the benefits. This is a systematic, quantitative method. Yet, the majority of the work of applying it, and the real basis of its success, is not mathematical at all. Calculating and estimating the monetary benefits and making an estimate of the probability of gaining the benefits are the critical steps. These usually can be done by managers able to apply their experience and "feel" for the situation. The quantitative aspect of the method does not reduce the manager's need for management skill.

Specialists' Involvement   Many managers in recent years have become mathematical experts specifically so that they would be able to use sophisticated numerical techniques in management. The fact remains, however, that most managers are not mathematicians. Fortunately, quantitative methods can still be meaningful without fully grasping the theoretical or computational background to the results. It is likely that subtleties of interpretation are easier with this full understanding, but the results can be useful without it. In practice, the job of the line manager is threefold: to realize that numerical methods are available for certain problems, to know what the problems are, and to be able to work with a specialist who is an expert in the actual application of the numerical techniques. It is far more important for the manager to recognize when decisions are needed and to be able to carry out the decisions than to be able to make the actual calculations needed for a quantitative decision-making tool.

NUMERICAL METHODS CAN
HELP FORM STRATEGIES

Many of the most precise applications of operations research have developed in support of lower-level management functions like scheduling, as described in the next section. Quantitative methods can be useful, though, for analyzing planning and decision making at the highest level. There is a difference, of course. A computational approach to a complex scheduling problem may yield a single best answer that can be applied with a high degree of confidence. On the other hand, a computational approach to an important strategic decision, such as an investment question, may serve only as a formal guide to thinking. In deciding whether to introduce a proposed new product, for example, many important factors such as price and market are unknown. In such cases, it is not practical simply to plug a series of numbers into a formula and accept the result as a certainty. This is not to say that the numerical analyses are not useful. They are, but they supplement and guide the experience and skill of top managers rather than replace it.

From among a number of techniques useful for analyzing strategic decisions, two are especially illustrative: decision trees and game theory.

Decision Trees   A *decision tree* is fundamentally a graphic representation of the use of probability estimates in making decisions. It helps managers analyze the consequences of decisions in light of what might happen in the future. Figure 25-1 shows a tree for the single decision of adopting part of a marketing strategy for a new product.

ESTIMATES OF REVENUE   The decision for which the tree has been constructed considers two alternates: (A) to introduce the new product with an expensive splash of national advertising or (B) to limit advertising to very restricted uses and rely on the normal selling push of the distribution channel. Strategy A would invest $1.5 million in advertising; Strategy B would allocate a modest $75,000. The decision between these strategies is under the control of the managers. The actual success (the sales volume) of the product is not controlled by the managers; it is greatly affected by chance. Sales may be high, moderate, or low, no matter what the managers decide. The high

Figure 25-1. Decision Tree for a Marketing Strategy Decision.

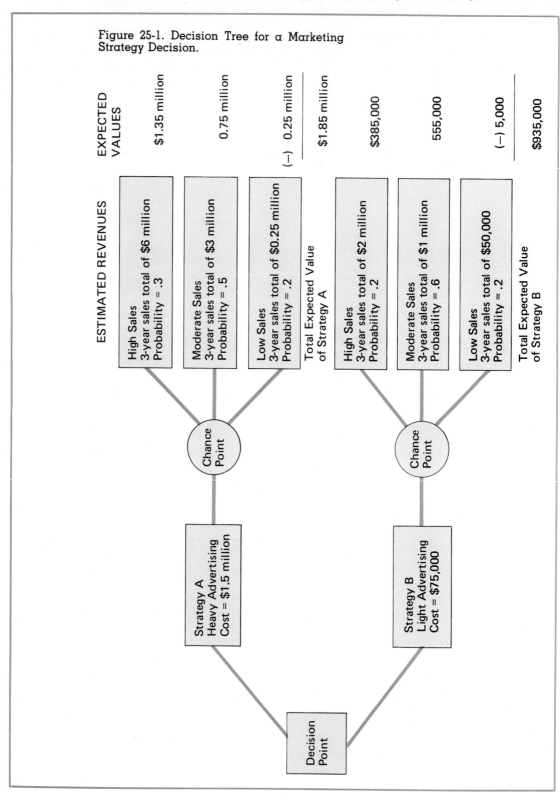

	ESTIMATED REVENUES	EXPECTED VALUES
	High Sales 3-year sales total of $6 million Probability = .3	$1.35 million
	Moderate Sales 3-year sales total of $3 million Probability = .5	0.75 million
	Low Sales 3-year sales total of $0.25 million Probability = .2	(−) 0.25 million
Total Expected Value of Strategy A		$1.85 million
	High Sales 3-year sales total of $2 million Probability = .2	$385,000
	Moderate Sales 3-year sales total of $1 million Probability = .6	555,000
	Low Sales 3-year sales total of $50,000 Probability = .2	(−) 5,000
Total Expected Value of Strategy B		$935,000

Chance Point

Chance Point

Strategy A
Heavy Advertising
Cost = $1.5 million

Strategy B
Light Advertising
Cost = $75,000

Decision Point

advertising budget (A) can be expected to increase sales under any conditions. The managers predict that it will create 3-year sales of $6 million, $3 million, and $.25 million under high, moderate, and low success. A low advertising decision (B) would almost certainly produce smaller sales revenue, but it is considered because of the relatively low risk of investing only $75,000 rather than the $1.5 million needed for major advertising.

PROBABILITIES OF SUCCESS   How to decide? The managers estimate the *probability* of achieving high, moderate, or low sales with each of the two choices. They multiply (a) these probabilities by (b) the revenue created by each success level minus the cost of advertising for that strategy. Thus, moderate sales success for the high advertising strategy would create $3 million in revenue and cost $1.5 million. The difference is a gain of $1.5 million, which, multiplied by its probability of occurring of .5, yields an expected value of $.75 million. Each strategy can be evaluated as a whole by adding up its expected values for each chance condition—high, moderate, and low success—to find a total expected value for the alternative. Strategy A can be seen to have a significantly higher total value ($1,850,000) than Strategy B ($935,000).

VALUES FOR JUDGMENT   The higher expected value for Strategy A means that the choice of high advertising is more likely to produce high revenues than is the choice of low advertising. The best decision to make, however, still depends on the goals and judgment of the managers. If the guiding objective is to accept carefully assessed risks in order to maximize revenue and profit, Strategy A is best. If the guiding objective is to minimize risk while creating some moderate amount of revenue—a very conservative approach—Strategy B might appear more attractive. Strategy A presents a small but genuine possibility of losing over $1 million if sales are low. Strategy B is much safer; its worst loss could be no larger than $50,000 minus $75,000, or $25,000.

The point and the value of the method is that it clarifies the options. By describing the likely consequences of decisions in an orderly, measured way, it guides decision making. It does not turn decisions into an automatic process.

Game Theory   A complex analytic method, virtually an entire field of study, has sometimes been used to guide decisions in managing competitive organizations like businesses. *Game theory* applies logical and mathematical analysis to the selection of strategies in situations in which the interests of one organization or person conflict with those of another organization or person. In this competitive situation, each organization tries to take into account what the other organization is likely to do. With this in mind, each adopts strategies that are seen to give a competitive advantage. Game theory provides an orderly way of looking at the benefits of different courses of action for the combating organization. It helps managers to choose a strategy that will give the greatest benefits (or the least losses) in a particular situation.

PAYOFF MATRIX The methods by which the strategies are analyzed and evaluated are too complex to be meaningful without a lengthy and specialized treatment that would be out of place here. An example may give an idea of the fundamental approach of game theory. Table 25-1 shows the financial gains or losses under different strategic conditions for a company that is in close competition with another company. For the sake of simplicity, the number of alternative strategies has been kept to a minimum. Company A is considering only two strategies: A1, in which it would increase the price of its product to make higher profits, and A2, under which it would launch a major advertising campaign to increase sales. It is considering only two strategies that might be adopted by the competitor: B1, in which the competitor would reduce the price of its product, and B2, in which the competitor would make no response but would simply continue under current strategies.

If Company A raises its prices (A1), it will receive a moderate benefit if Company B does nothing (B2). It will be at a great disadvantage, however, and lose $2 million, if Company B decides to lower its prices (B1). If Company A adopts the advertising campaign (A2), it stands to gain either $500,000 or $2 million, depending on what Company B does. Thus, strategy A2 appears to be the best for Company A.

This kind of situation can be greatly elaborated in computer-aided game-theory analysis. The matrix may add more competitors, more alternative strategies (including situations in which everyone can gain something or lose something), and incorporate probability estimates for competitors' actions and results. The value of game theory for managers lies in its ability to logically and mathematically analyze the selection of strategies in competitive situations. In many cases, it contributes to an orderly decision-making and planning process.

TABLE 25-1. GAINS OR LOSSES (PAYOFF MATRIX) FOR COMPANY A UNDER DIFFERENT STRATEGIC CONDITIONS.			
		COMPANY B STRATEGIES	
		B1	B2
COMPANY A STRATEGIES	A1	−$2 million	+$1 million
	A2	+$500,000	+$2 million

Strategies:
A1   Increase product price.
A2   Launch advertising campaign.
B1   Lower product price.
B2   Do nothing new.

FORMAL METHODS AID IN MAKING OPERATING
DECISIONS
The use of quantitative methods in making strategic decisions is in its infancy in the management of civilian organizations, although it is more developed in the defense establishment. Decision trees are fairly commonly used by business managers, but game theory and the other mathematical and logical approaches to high-level decision making have not yet gained wide acceptance. The situation is considerably different for decisions on the operating level. Statistical methods are widely accepted and are especially common in the areas of production scheduling, distribution planning, and other everyday management concerns. Of the many techniques available, three are representative: linear programming, queuing theory, and the calculation of economic order quantities.

Linear Programming   A mathematical technique called *linear programming*, has been developed to analyze the best way to achieve a specific, concrete goal by carefully allocating resources that can be used in alternating amounts and ways. It is useful in situations where workers, money, time, machinery, shipping facilities, distribution channels, or other resources can be used in a number of different ways and where there is a clear numerical goal that is sought, such as minimum costs or maximum production. As was true with game theory, a detailed discussion of linear programming is inappropriate, but an example may clarify its basic nature.

SCHEDULING WORK CREWS   Take a company that manufactures and sells industrial heating units. It may know, for example, that the units are unreliable unless they are installed in the field by trained crews working for the manufacturer. Suppose the company has two such installation crews covering three geographic regions. It might profit from linear programming if the technique helped to meet the goal of minimum installation costs by assigning the crews to the regions in the most efficient way.

For the coming 3-month period, these orders must be installed: 50 in Region 1; 150 in Region 2; 200 in Region 3. Crew A is larger, better trained, and better equipped than Crew B. It is therefore able to make 250 installations in a 3-month period. Crew B can install only 150 orders in the same time. Because of its location, Crew A can make an installation in Regions 1 or 2 for an average cost of $500 for transporting personnel and products; the same costs for an installation in Region 3 are $1,000 for this crew. Crew B has transportation and shipping costs per installation of $200 for Region 1, $1,500 for Region 2, and $500 for Region 3. All of this information is summarized in Table 25-2 on page 550.

WHICH CREW WHERE?   The question is, which crew should make installations in which regions? It is an important question, since it plays a major role in determining total installation costs. If, for instance, Crew A divides its total capacity of 250 installations by making 150 in Region 2 and 100 in

Region 3, while Crew B installs the 50 orders in Region 1 and the remaining 100 orders in Region 3, total costs are $235,000. This is derived by multiplying costs for each region for each crew by the number of installations made in the region, and adding the results: $(150 \times \$500) + (100 \times \$1,000) + (50 \times \$200) + (100 \times \$500) = \$235,000$. If, on the other hand, the assignments are made so that Crew A installs 50 in Region 1 and 200 in Region 3 while Crew B installs 150 in Region 2, the total cost is $450,000: $(50 \times \$500) + (200 \times \$1,000) + (150 \times \$1,500) = \$450,000$. That is $215,000 more than the cost with the first set of assignments.

THOUSANDS OF POSSIBILITIES   In operating situations like this, tens of thousands of different combinations are common. To work these out by hand is nearly always impossible. Linear programming uses mathematical analysis to make these individual calculations unnecessary. Managers merely make a formal statement of the demands and limitations of an actual operating problem. Statisticians, aided by computer programs, calculate the specific allocation of resources that will best satisfy these requirements. The resources and constraints included in the calculations may be of nearly any sort, including personnel, skills, machines, space for operations, travel time, budgets, distances, and delivery schedules.

Queuing Theory
Queue is another word for a waiting line. Whenever there is more demand for a service than there are facilities for providing it, a waiting line will occur. *Queuing theory*, also called waiting-line theory, is an analytic method for deciding what facilities should economically be provided to meet expected demand.

MINIMIZES COSTLY WAITING LINES   The whole issue of waiting lines would be irrelevant if demand for service were constant. If 30 people approach an airline ticket counter every minute during an 8-hour shift and each transaction takes exactly 30 seconds, the airline clearly needs exactly

	TABLE 25-2. REQUIREMENTS AND LIMITATIONS FOR SCHEDULING A FIELD INSTALLATION CREW.			
	TRANSPORTATION AND SHIPPING COSTS PER CREW BY REGION			NUMBER OF POSSIBLE INSTALLATIONS PER CREW DURING PERIOD
	REGION 1	REGION 2	REGION 3	
Crew A	$500	$500	$1000	250
Crew B	$200	$1500	$500	150
Total Installations Scheduled per Region	50	150	200	

15 clerks on duty at all times. Demands rarely operate this way in real life, however. Most demands are irregular. Consider a bank, for instance. In a small branch, the number of customers requiring service each minute may easily vary from less than one in a very slack period up to two dozen or more a minute during and just after lunchtime on a busy Friday. The question to be answered is, How many tellers are to be assigned to this branch? The goal, of course, is to have as few tellers as possible, to reduce personnel costs, while having enough so that lines will not be unacceptably long at peak-demand periods.

A PROBLEM WITH MANY VARIATIONS   In a branch bank, this problem is often worked out by trial and error and by transferring employees from other types of work to handle teller windows during peak periods. This kind of solution breaks down, however, when facilities and resources are very complex or cannot easily be varied to meet irregular demand. An electric company, for example, has the same situation as the bank. The utility has widely varying demands for electricity, which it must meet with fixed facilities costing often billions of dollars. Other typical problems concern the following:

- Auto traffic flow, which varies widely on main and cross streets, but must be controlled by fixed traffic signals.
- Sales and customer orders, which vary irregularly for manufacturers, but must be filled by production from relatively fixed manufacturing facilities and machinery.
- Incoming truck deliveries, which are irregular and largely unpredictable; it is not possible to add new loading docks if many trucks arrive at nearly the same time.

Waiting-line theory provides a powerful tool for dealing with these and similar situations. The technique makes it possible to analyze the probable duration and extent of waiting caused by varying levels of facilities under irregular demand conditions. Given the results of the mathematical equations, managers can then be guided by company policies on how much waiting is acceptable to determine the optimum level of facilities.

Inventory Control
A primary goal in controlling the level of most inventories is never to run out of stock. Common sense points to the basic method for achieving this. If it takes 60 days from the date of order to receive an item of stock and 100 of the items are used each month, the order must be placed before the remaining inventory falls below 200 (two months' supply). Many companies have worked out elaborate tagging procedures and inventory-counting methods to allow them to meet this basic requirement. Unfortunately, there is more to the question of inventory maintenance than that.

COSTS OF ORDERING AND CARRYING   An important consideration is how many of the items to order when the purchase is made. If very large quantities are ordered, the frequency of purchases will be lower and the costs of preparing orders, shipping, inspecting receipts, paying bills, and other associated activities will be reduced. These purchasing activities may be called "administrative costs"; they make an important contribution to overall costs, and it is worth some effort to reduce them. At the same time, there are considerable expenses associated with maintaining a large inventory. These are called "carrying costs," and they increase as the order size goes up. They include warehouse space costs, inventory taxes, insurance, and the interest costs of the basic investment required to buy the large inventory.

As with a number of quantitative methods, a reasonable goal in this situation is to seek an optimum point: the order size and frequency that will bring the total of administrative costs and carrying costs to a minimum. When frequent, small orders are placed, carrying costs are low, but administrative costs are high. When infrequent, large orders are placed, administrative costs are low, but carrying costs are high. What is the ideal frequency for placing orders?

HOW MUCH TO ORDER AT ONE TIME　For an example, assume that it costs $500 to place an order for preassembled gearboxes because a number of complicated specifications must first be drawn up. If a company uses these components at a constant rate, the average inventory on hand at a given time equals the total inventory carried divided by 2. (This can be verified by assuming that only one order was placed in a year. For the first half year, the inventory on hand would be greater than the amount purchased divided by 2, and for the last half of the year, the inventory on hand would be equally smaller than the amount purchased divided by 2.) Company managers would know the value of each gearbox, $100 in this case, and would know the costs of keeping the inventory in storage—taxes, insurance, cost of storage space, and so on. (20 percent, for example—a modest figure). Further, they would know that a certain number of units—5,000 in the example—were expected to be used during the year.

HAND CALCULATION METHOD　With this information, it is possible to construct a number of calculations like those in Table 25-3. Total carrying costs equal: (total inventory ÷ 2) × (cost of each item) × (rate of storage costs). If only one order is placed in a year, administrative costs for placing the order are only $500, but carrying costs are quite high, at $50,000, because so much money is tied up in a large inventory. If the purchasing people order gearboxes 20 times during the year, ordering 250 units approximately every 2½ weeks, carrying costs are quite low because so few are on hand, but administrative costs for placing so many separate orders balloon to $10,000. The most economical number of orders to place for the cases worked out in the table is 10, since that is the point at which the total of administrative and carrying costs is a minimum. The only way to determine by hand calculation exactly the most economical number of orders to place is to work out each individual number, figuring total costs for each, and then selecting the lowest *total* inventory cost figure.

TABLE 25-3. ANNUAL ADMINISTRATIVE AND CARRYING COST FOR FIVE ORDER SIZES.

NUMBER OF ORDERS PLACED EACH YEAR	QUANTITY PURCHASED ON EACH ORDER	ADMINIS-TRATIVE COSTS AT $500 AN ORDER	CARRYING COSTS (VALUE OF INVENTORY ITEM × TOTAL INVENTORY ÷ 2 × RATE OF STORAGE COSTS)*	TOTAL INVENTORY COSTS FOR EACH YEAR
1	5,000	$ 500	$50,000	$50,500
5	1,000	2,500	10,000	12,500
10	500	5,000	5,000	10,000
15	334	7,500	3,340	10,840
20	250	10,000	2,500	12,500

*Value of each inventory item = $100
Interest rate for storage costs = 0.20

EOQ FORMULA METHOD   As with many cases like the above, there is a formula that makes these repeated calculations unnecessary. It gives directly the *economic order quantity* (EOQ), the size of order that will result in an order frequency and inventory size that will minimize the sum of administrative and carrying costs. The formula is

$$Q = \sqrt{\frac{2UA}{cs}}$$

where:

Q = economic order quantity
U = number of items used per year
A = administrative costs of placing an order
c = the cost or value of a single item of inventory
s = storage costs such as taxes, insurance, and warehouse space (expressed as a percentage of inventory value).

Applying this formula to the case of the gear assemblies just described yields:

$$Q = \sqrt{\frac{2 \times 5,000 \times \$500}{\$100 \times 0.20}} = \sqrt{250,000}$$

$$Q = 500$$

This means that the most economical quantity to purchase on each separate order is 500. Since 5,000 are used each year, 10 orders (5,000 ÷ 500) is the optimum number to place per year. The company might approximate this optimum by ordering 500 gearboxes every 5 weeks.

Managers in Action

"Many of [our] materials are often ordered in bulk only once a year or once a quarter. The fixed cost of processing a release for a truck or rail car is normally $10–20 per release. The order quantity in [our] formula often must be adjusted to allow for full carloads or trucks. This is especially true for bulk chemicals which have low value per pound and relatively high freight cost per pound. The problem can generally be handled by comparing the sum of annual ordering, holding, and freight costs at the traditional Economic Order Quantity with the freight break-even points for multiple car/truck loads."

That observation made by Matthew J. Liberatore, a staff manager for the industrial chemicals group of FMC corporation illustrates the kinds of compromises that must be made when applying statistical techniques. Mr. Liberatore went on to show how he adjusts for other statistical problems. For instance, when planning for the amount of safety stock to hold in a raw material inventory, he relates the plant's experience with purchasing lead times with expectations of material usage by means of a Monte Carlo simulation. From this, the manager in charge of inventory control and production scheduling can find the probability of a stock-out that might shut down a production process.

One positive result of such statistical techniques was cited by FMC's Modesto, California, plant controller, who watches over expenditures. He noted that the penalty paid by the plant for holding unloaded carloads (demurrage) of a vital chemical in readiness for usage cost was $11,940 in 1976; application of the Monte Carlo technique in 1977 cut the demurrage bill to $7,420, for a savings of $4,520.

Similarly, use of the modified Economic Order Quantity technique at the Modesto plant reduced the average inventory of another critical raw material from $292,000 to $256,000. If the typical 25 percent estimate for the annual cost of holding inventory were applied, this would indicate a savings of ($292,000 − $256,000) × .25 = $9,000.

Source: Matthew J. Liberatore, "Using MRP and EOQ/Safety Stock for Raw Materials Inventory Control: Discussion and Case Study," *Interfaces*, Vol. 9, No. 2, Pt. 1, The Institute of Management Sciences, February 1979, p. 1, used with permission.

Judgment Is Still Needed   It should be noted that even though the formula for Q is a useful guide, good management cannot be derived from mathematical formulas. There are often other considerations. The supplier may give a lower price if larger quantities are purchased on each order. The money needed to keep order frequencies low may be desperately needed in other areas of the company on a temporary basis. Carrying costs are not, in fact, directly related to inventory size. Warehouses are not expandable and contractible. They stay the same size, and generally cost the same, no matter how much is stored in them. As a result, storage costs for small inventories may be higher per unit than the storage costs of a large inventory, unless the organization has very flexible storage arrangements.

Considerations such as these demonstrate a general conclusion about the use of quantitative methods in management. They are extremely useful in situations to which they properly apply. In many complex cases, they provide the only orderly and rational approach to decision making. They cannot, however, replace the detailed information, the thoughtful analysis, and the personal judgment of an experienced manager. It is a rare case indeed in which a manager can look at the computer printout from a mathematical analysis and say with confidence, "OK. That's exactly what we'll do."

SUMMARY

1. The process of decision making includes identifying needed decisions, creating alternative actions, evaluating the alternatives, and choosing the best action or combination of actions to pursue. Quantitative methods use formal, numerical or statistical analyses of alternatives and their consequences and are of special value in the last two steps of this process.

2. Managers are not normally specialists in the use of quantitative methods. The informed manager should, however, be able to handle the nontechnical aspects of these techniques, to recognize when the techniques are applicable, and to interpret the results as one factor in the group of forces that shape decisions.

3. Quantitative methods are applicable to the formation of major strategies if some key information can be expressed concretely and numerically. Decision trees help evaluate the potential payoff of alternative strategies in situations where both chance and decisions operate. Game theory provides a rational approach to the situation in which two or more people or organizations are competing for advantage over limited resources.

4. A number of quantitative methods have been developed that help make operating decisions. Linear programming helps allocate resources to best achieve specified objectives. Queuing theory helps indicate the best level of facilities for providing service when faced with irregular demand. Inventory-control computations make it easier to maintain adequate stocks of materials and products while minimizing administrative and carrying costs for warehousing that inventory.

REVIEW AND DISCUSSION QUESTIONS

1. What are quantitative aids to decision making? Are they really any different from any other kind of decision making?

2. At what point or points in the decision-making process are quantitative methods usually most useful? Why is this so?

3. How is the emphasis different in problem solving and in exploiting opportunities?

4. Summarize the role of managers in applying quantitative methods. What is their responsibility?

5. In what kind of situation is a decision tree useful? Why does it help?

6. What would the managers of a major breakfast food company need to know about their company's competitors in order to use game theory effectively? Would they be likely to have the needed information?

7. Give an example in which linear programming might be helpful to the managers of a specific manufacturing company. Why would it help in the case you have chosen?

8. Would a grocery store need to use queuing theory for staffing the checkout counters if exactly the same number of people checked out each hour? Why or why not?

9. Why would the manager of an auto parts store be likely to use the formula for economic order quantities? What is its goal?

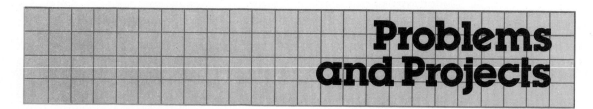

Problems and Projects

1. The first necessity for successfully applying quantitative methods is to recognize when a numerical technique might be useful and to know which specific method is applicable to a particular problem. The techniques described in the text are listed directly below, followed by 10 brief descriptions of situations with which a manager might be faced. On a sheet of paper, write the numbers 1 through 10, corresponding to the 10 situations. Next to each number, write the letter of the technique that would be *most directly applicable* to that situation. If none of the techniques listed is directly applicable, write the letter "f."

    a. Decision tree.
    b. Game theory.
    c. Linear programming.
    d. Queuing theory.

e. Economic order quantity.

f. None of the quantitative methods is directly applicable.

(1) Deciding how much of an inventory item a retail store should include on a single purchase order.

(2) Choosing between an increase in the advertising budget and a price cut, when chance events, rather than a competitor's strategy, play a major role in the outcome.

(3) Assigning a limited number of sales representatives to cover scheduled calls in a large geographical area.

(4) Choosing major courses of action when a good deal is known about competitors' strategies and their likely consequences.

(5) Deciding whether to establish a centralized or decentralized management structure in a multiproduct manufacturing company.

(6) Deciding whether to increase production to lower unit costs when it is fairly certain that a major competitor will either lower prices or increase advertising.

(7) Choosing between two management styles to increase worker motivation.

(8) Deciding how many loading docks to put in a new warehouse when the arrival of trucks to be loaded and unloaded is irregular.

(9) Assigning production quotas to two factories that must keep four geographically separated warehouses supplied with a product.

(10) Developing possible responses that might be made when a competitor introduces a popular new product.

2. *Performance Situation—Battle of the Banks.* Susan J. Winston manages the First National Bank Corporation in a Midwest city. The bank has been prosperous for decades, but in recent years has been threatened by aggressive competition of another city bank. The damage has been especially felt in First National's commercial banking for business and industry.

Winston sees their competitor doing one of two things in the future: (a) concentrating on a real takeover of commercial banking where they've already made such successful inroads, or (b) using the same kind of consumer marketing they are known for to steal a bigger share of the credit, checking, and savings business of private, non-commercial customers.

Winston decides in response to these two possibilities to become much more aggressive in the consumer banking efforts of her own company and to open new branches in formerly untried neighborhoods. The idea is to get the jump on the competition.

Winston considers the costs and probable benefits of two plans: (a) opening a single new branch to try out the waters, and then expanding if success is found, or (b) opening several new branches at once in a real blitz. Considering a number of factors, including the original motivation for opening new branches, she chooses the latter alternative. She selects four new locations for branch banks to serve a large portion of the city that her company formerly had not touched. She has the buildings designed and decides on the type of services and number of employees that will be assigned to each.

She establishes a new management organization to handle the expansion and sets up strict financial and profit controls for the new operations.

Winston has gone through the entire decision-making process from beginning to end. Answer the following questions about her actions.

A. Which parts of this process are *not* likely to be aided by quantitative methods? Why?

B. Which quantitative methods might she have used? To which parts of the process could each apply?

C. Do you think the quantitative methods by themselves are a sufficient basis for making final decisions in the situations where they could be used? Give an example to support your answer.

3. A city housing agency has not had notable success in the past with renovating and leasing or selling housing to low-income residents. The agency's managers are considering a new basic strategy for their approach to the problem. One possibility is to buy the properties, renovate them, and handle the sales and rentals. This option would cost $10 million. The managers estimate that when chance events are taken into account, there is a 0.6 probability of achieving a high success with benefits of $20 million and a 0.4 probability of achieving a low success with benefits of $2 million. The other alternative is to establish an incentive plan for private developers, at a basic cost of $4 million. (There would be other costs, but these have been subtracted from expected benefits and need not be considered further.) With this plan, they expect a 0.3 probability of high success, creating $20 million in benefits, and a 0.7 probability of low success, creating benefits of only $1 million.

Draw a decision tree for this decision situation. Calculate the expected values for the alternatives, as in Figure 25-1. Choose the most attractive alternative based on the results of the tree. Is this necessarily the choice the managers would make?

4. Table 25-4 is the payoff matrix for Company A, which is in a competitive position with Company B. Interpret the table by answering the questions below.

A. What is the meaning of the top-left cell? Of the bottom-left cell?

TABLE 25-4.			
		COMPANY B STRATEGIES	
		B1	B2
COMPANY A STRATEGIES	A1	+ $10 million	+ $6 million
	A2	− $6 million	+ $8 million

B. Which strategy should Company A choose, based only on the information in the matrix?

C. Given the payoffs shown here for Company B, what strategy should Company B choose? Explain your answer.

5. A large manufacturing company has two factories that make components, and three assembly plants. Both of the component factories make a part that is needed in all three assembly plants. Because the component factories have different kinds of equipment, and because they have different shipping costs to each of the assembly plants, their costs vary when their components are used by different assembly plants. The specific costs, total monthly outputs for each component factory, and total components required monthly by each assembly plant are shown in Table 25-5.

The outputs of the two component factories can be distributed among the assembly plants in many different ways. Compare the total monthly costs for these two distributions:

■ Factory A ships 50,000 parts to Plant 2 and 50,000 parts to Plant 3. Factory B ships 25,000 parts to Plant 1 and 25,000 parts to Plant 2.

■ Factory A ships 25,000 parts to Plant 1 and 75,000 parts to Plant 2. Factory B ships 50,000 parts to Plant 3.

What is the total monthly cost for each of these distributions? Which one is cheaper? How much is saved by using the cheaper distribution? What quantitative method would be used for this kind of problem?

6. A mail-order electronics dealer does a thriving business selling equipment and parts to the do-it-yourself electronics repair market. Carrying literally thousands of different parts in stock is an expensive business, and the company's management uses very careful inventory-control measures. One popular item, for example, sells 1 million units every year, without fail. The

TABLE 25-5.				
	COSTS (PER COMPONENT) FOR SUPPLYING COMPONENTS TO ASSEMBLY PLANTS			TOTAL COMPONENT OUTPUT PER FACTORY PER MONTH
	ASSEMBLY PLANT 1	ASSEMBLY PLANT 2	ASSEMBLY PLANT 3	
Component Factory A	$20	$10	$40	100,000
Component Factory B	$50	$30	$15	50,000
Total Components Required per Assembly Plant per Month	25,000	75,000	50,000	

value of the part itself is $5 and it costs 25 percent of the value to pay for warehousing, taxes, interest, and other related inventory expenses. At the same time, it costs the company $250 just to place a single order for the part.

Use the formula for deriving the economic order quantity to determine how many of this part the mail-order house should purchase on each individual order. How many times a year should they place an order?

Cases for Analysis and Discussion

CASE 1: NUMBERS DON'T LIE?

"I tell you, we're in the business of making money. It's perfectly clear what we ought to do. We've got to go for the new tooling. Look, these numbers don't lie," Julius Born had scratched for twenty years to get to be the head of his division, and he didn't always take it gracefully when someone disagreed with him, even, as in this case, his boss.

W. L. Grady was president of New London Manufacturing Co. He was a tough old bird and didn't flinch a bit in the face of his adamant subordinate. He knew Julius worked hard at being a good manager and that he really thought his decision was right.

Grady's approach was reasonable and calm: "Julius, I don't say the numbers are lying; they're just committing a sin of omission. There's more to this situation than what you've got on that paper there. You know that in five years the heating equipment division—your division—is going to have to make a major expansion, with completely new products. You know, too, that if you don't make that expansion, you're not going to be able to keep up. You also must realize that if you don't reduce your indebtedness, you're not going to be able to get financing to pay for the expansion. *That's* the critical issue."

"But look at this again. I still don't think I've made my point clear," Julius answered. "If we put $8 million into retooling for our current products we can reduce their price substantially. That means more sales; that means more profits. It's got a payoff of nearly $5 million on the decision tree. The alternative of putting the money we have into "this-and-that" projects has an expected value of less than $3 million. Spending the money is clearly better."

Grady was still patient. "But if you do that, you'll win the battle and lose the war. You might not even win the battle. If you put out the $8 million, you've got a fair chance of making a good gain. But you'd have to go $4 million deeper in debt. That means you'd also have a fair chance of losing a big chunk of money. With the conservative alternative, you don't have to borrow. You get a reasonable return, and you're not likely to lose your shirt. *And,* it'll leave you in shape to make the big shift when the time comes."

A. Why has this disagreement arisen in the first place? What's at the bottom of it?

B. Who's right, in your opinion? Why?

C. Is there any way to make sure the right decision is made in cases like this? If so, what is it?

CASE 2: THE UNSPECIALIZED SPECIALIST

The job description said her job was "operations research," and she was, in her own mind, an operations researcher. Six years of college, two years with a small computer company, and here she was in the planning department of a large manufacturing company. Her head was crammed with sophisticated formulas and techniques, and she knew better than most how to use them and what they meant.

Yet, Catherine Larken couldn't really say that she felt like a success in her job. Her feeling was not surprising, considering that in the last week alone she had heard from her boss, "What good is this stuff? What do we pay *you* for? Why don't you try to do something useful sometime?"

What had happened was simply a replay of a common course of events. The boss had called her into his office and told her about a serious production problem. Some changes in the standard schedule for an assembled product had destroyed the coordination with the departments that supplied component parts for the final assembly. Some departments were suddenly turning out more parts than were needed, while others were falling behind. The original schedule change had been made because total output was considerably lower than it theoretically should have been. His instructions to her were, "Find out what's wrong and fix it."

Catherine was in the dark, but she did her best. After three weeks of floundering, she had found what she thought were motivation problems and a breakdown in communications among the operating departments. She also observed what she perceived as a secret desire among the employees and supervisors to break the new scheduling because no one in operations had been consulted about the changes. The only concrete thing she had in hand was an analysis of the fluctuating daily demand for each component part, as the first step in applying queuing theory to part of the problem. She was so sure that that wouldn't solve anything, however, that she didn't even finish it. It was after her presentation of her efforts that she heard the boss's choice evaluations of her performance.

A. Why was Catherine unable to find the solution to this problem?

B. What do you think of her boss's performance in this situation? Is he doing a good job of working with her?

C. What should Catherine do? Is there any way she might be able to improve her situation?

CASE 3: OUT OF STOCK, OUT OF LUCK

Dalby Merchandise is a medium-sized wholesale distributor of housewares. Things had run smoothly for a number of years: a thousand tea strainers here, a hundred gross of egg beaters there; standard items moving in standard channels to standard customers. A change was developing, though, and Kenneth Dalby soon began to realize that it was causing some problems for his company.

The market was becoming more volatile. Manufacturers had gone much more heavily into national advertising and had begun making frequent product changes. Now they introduced a new product every two weeks rather than every two decades as in the past. It was the marketing concept in practice, and it meant big profits for the manufacturers. What it meant for Dalby was headaches. Wholesalers live and die by their inventory. Controlling the inventory in such a market was a thorny problem. Dalby started seeing more and more yellow "out-of-stock" slips and watched costs steadily creep up as the orderly purchasing system began to disintegrate, overburdened by special orders and other irregularities.

Dalby decided to approach the problem by looking closely at a single item. A particular set of porcelain cookware had been a steady, but slow, seller for over five years. Its slow sales were almost certainly caused by its high price. Dalby had to pay $50 for the set. When it was passed on to the retail stores, its price put it out of the range of someone just looking for something to cook in.

Then came the microwave oven. By chance, the cookware, because of its shape and size, was ideal for microwaves. It was even recommended by a number of oven manufacturers. Where Dalby had handled 2,000 sets a year in the past, he was now trying to keep up with a demand for 8,000 sets a year. Even that demand was clearly still growing. Dalby first revised his order frequency. He figured the administrative costs of placing an order at $100. It cost 20 percent of the stock item's value to cover warehousing, taxes, and insurance. After performing a few calculations, Dalby decided that using the new order quantity and frequency shown by the formula would protect his company from running out of stock in the future. He gave instructions for making the change, and took no other action.

A. What was the economic order quantity and order frequency when demand was 2,000 a year? What are they now that demand is 8,000 a year?

B. Do you agree that Dalby is safe and well protected from out-of-stock conditions if he adopts the new order sizes and frequencies? Why or why not?

C. What does this case tell you about using quantitative methods like the economic order quantity? What does a manager have to keep in mind when using these techniques?

CASE 4: HOW MANY MACHINES?

The toxicology laboratory was entirely supported by the federal government. It had two major divisions. The first handled a contract from the government for carrying out substance analysis for the public health service. Many of these analyses were done in an emergency atmosphere, with the aim of discovering whether outbreaks of disease were caused by toxic substances. The goal was to identify the toxin, if present, and protect people from it immediately. The other division handled sophisticated research into the nature of toxic illness. Its goal was to improve basic understanding of the way environmental substances cause disease in humans.

When the laboratories were set up, Dr. Gomez, the director, looked at budget requests from the two heads of the divisions. She questioned, among many other items, the requests by each division for $750,000 for 10 each of automatic analyzers that determine the chemical composition of samples. She questioned whether each division needed 10 of these expensive machines, and requested the division heads to go back, analyze their use demands, and use queuing theory to substantiate their needs. The division heads did so, and returned in several days with the results. After looking carefully at their calculations, Dr. Gomez allowed the emergency-investigation division 12 machines, rather than the 10 they had requested. She allowed the basic toxicology division only two machines, even though this might cause waits for results of up to two days.

A. What was Dr. Gomez thinking? Why did she allow so many more machines for the one department than for the other?

B. Is this a legitimate use of a quantitative method? Why or why not?

C. Is Dr. Gomez doing a good job? How do you think the division heads will react to her decision?

Appendix
Pursuing a Management Career

Managerial positions are more appealing than ever. The work is challenging, status is high, and salaries are good. Perhaps you, too, will be among the millions who seek to join and advance in the ranks of management.

THE OUTLOOK FOR
MANAGERIAL POSITIONS

More than one in every ten persons employed in the United States today holds a managerial position. That is more than 10 million managers, and the future is even more promising. The U.S. Department of Labor projects that the total number of management positions will grow from 10.1 million to 12.2 million during the 1980s. In addition to the 2.1 million new management jobs created by this expansion, over 5 million management positions will become open because of projected attrition in the work force.

In general, the greatest number of new management jobs will be available in industries in which total employment growth (including nonmanagerial workers) is greatest. For the 1980s that means more jobs in the service industries and relatively slower growth in manufacturing positions. Here is how the general picture for the 1980s shapes up.[1]

Trends in Service Industries

Employment in the service-producing industries is expected to increase 26 percent between 1976 to 1985, from 56.1 million workers to 71.0 million workers.

- *Wholesale and Retail Trade.* This is the largest of the service industries. It is expected to grow by about 20 percent between 1976 and 1985, from 17.7 million to 21.3 million workers.

[1]Excerpted from the *Occupational Handbook,* 1978–1979, U.S. Department of Labor, Bureau of Labor Statistics, bul. 1,955, pp. 19–27

- *Direct Service.* This industry includes services, such as health care, maintenance and repair, advertising, and commercial cleaning. This is the fastest growing segment of the service industries. Employment is projected to increase from 14.6 million workers in 1976 to 20.6 million in 1985, a 40 percent growth rate.
- *Government.* This is the second fastest growing service industry. Growth has been the greatest in agencies providing education, health, sanitation, welfare, and police and fire protection. Between 1976 and 1985, employment in government is expected to rise 22 percent, from 14.9 million to 18.3 million workers.
- *Transportation and Public Utilities.* Between 1976 and 1985, employment in transportation and public utilities industries is expected to rise from 4.5 million to 5.2 million workers, an increase of 16 percent.
- *Finance, Insurance, and Real Estate.* These industries will grow faster than services as a whole. Employment is expected to increase from 4.3 million to 5.6 million workers between 1976 and 1985, an increase of 30 percent. Within this group, the two fastest growing industries have been banking and credit agencies.

Trends in Goods-Producing Industries

Employment in the goods-producing industries—agriculture, mining, construction, and manufacturing—has changed very little since 1960. Significant gains in productivity resulting from automated production, improved machinery, and other technological breakthroughs have permitted large increases in output without additional workers. Between 1976 and 1985, employment in goods-producing industries is expected to increase by about 17 percent, from 26.6 million to 31.1 million workers.

- *Mining.* Once declining in employment, mining increased abruptly between 1970 and 1976. The industry experienced a 26 percent growth rate during this period, matching that of the fastest growing industry group, services. Much of this growth is a direct result of our need for additional energy. Employment in the oil and gas extraction industry rose 33 percent between 1970 and 1976, and it is expected to rise another 70 percent by 1985.
- *Manufacturing.* Although employment in this industry was adversely affected by the economic conditions of the early 1970s, it is expected to grow from 18.9 million to 22.8 million between 1976 and 1985, an increase of 20 percent. Manufacturing is divided into two broad categories, durable-goods manufacturing and nondurable-goods manufacturing. Employment in durable-goods manufacturing is expected to increase by about 25 percent, from 11 million to 13.8 million workers, while employment in nondurable-goods manufacturing is expected to increase by only 13 percent, from 7.9 million to 9.0 million workers.

Progress for Minorities   To date, equal employment opportunity legislation has enabled minorities and women to make only small inroads into traditional managerial positions. In 1977, for example, 5,993,000 of all salaried managers and administrators were white, while only 363,000 were black. Women made up only 27 percent of the white managers and 29 percent of the black managers. In each instance, these percentages were far lower than the proportional numbers of blacks or women workers in the United States labor force. Furthermore, most observers agree that the great majority of managerial positions held by both blacks and women are at the lower levels of their organizations. In the 1980s, however, with continuing awareness on the part of employers and increased pressure from society and government, the outlook is for managerial opportunities for minorities and women to grow at a faster rate than for whites or men taken as a whole.

CHOOSING A MANAGERIAL
CAREER PATH
Many authorities say that the most important decisions individuals ever make are their choice of specialty, industry they enter, and company with which they begin their careers. Certain specialties may be essential to an industry and provide great job security, but may not be accepted as a basis for advancement in that industry. In magazine publishing, for example, statisticians are valued as market researchers, but are rarely given consideration for general management positions. Instead, salespeople are usually chosen for these positions.

There is an expression that says, "If you want to get ahead, you must pay your dues." In the steel industry, for example, paying your dues means that regardless of your talent, you must serve time on the floor of the mill. In the construction industry, you may pay your dues by working at the job site, even though your academic skills would make you more valuable at headquarters in a design or estimating department. Any career strategy, however, should be accompanied by the setting down of specific short- and long-term job goals to be attained—goals that satisfy your personal ambitions. Above all, you must examine your career path with an eye to what it will demand of you, so that you are prepared to make the necessary sacrifices along the way.

Analyzing Organizational Cultures   If you were to visit a foreign country, you would make the most of your experience there by finding out how the native population lives, their political attitudes and spiritual values, and their indigenous customs. You should take the same view of the profession, company, and industry in which you will pursue a career. In this regard, there are four important considerations:

1. *Your Expectations and Theirs.* Understandably, you may wish to advance as quickly as possible, remaining in each position only long enough to prove your competency. Unfortunately, many organizations take the view that after having trained you to perform in a particular position, you should return their investment in you by carrying out the work in that position expertly for several more years. If this is the case, it is a wise idea to be patient and to extend your exposure in the organization by volunteering for special assignments and serving on broadly-based committees. Obviously, it is an even better idea to determine these attitudes before accepting employment and hunt for a company whose expectations best match your ambitions.

   Managerial approaches, especially concerning leadership, differ from company to company. If you are employed by an organization where autocratic leadership prevails, for example, your use of participative approaches may be looked upon as a sign of weakness or indecision. Accordingly, you will have to choose your style with discretion and avoid making it the subject of contention.

2. *Political Sensitivity.* Regardless of the objectives, all organizations are, at their core, social or political in nature. A company's employees, especially its managers, are acutely aware of power centers. Many decisions and commitments are based on a sense of what is desired "upstairs" or what will be acceptable in the ranks, rather than on logic and justice. Just as in politics, tradeoffs are expected—the production department moves up a sales order for an important customer with the expectation that the sales department will return the favor by overlooking a late delivery another time. The person who bucks the political system, or who is even unaware of its existence, will progress very slowly, if at all.

3. *Loyalty.* As it applies to organizations, loyalty is a very ambiguous term. Many dedicated, hardworking managers have been taken by surprise when accused by their bosses for lack of loyalty. What does loyalty mean? It can mean several things.

   a. *Outright Obedience:* "I expect you to do what you are told without questioning its appropriateness."

   b. *Personal Protection:* "Make your own decisions if you wish, but don't get me or the department in trouble. Remember, it's us against them."

   c. *Unstinting Effort:* "You can show your loyalty to me by going all-out, all the time; by coming in early and going home late."

   d. *Exceptional Performance:* "Don't let me down by turning in work that is anything but the best."

   e. *Honest Information:* "Don't hide your mistakes from me. Keep me fully informed of what's going on out there. I don't want to be put on the spot upstairs by something that happens in my department that I don't know anything about."

Just as in politics, the astute manager determines what his or her superior expects in the way of loyalty and tries to conform to that standard.

4. *Lines of Managerial Progression.* Your career path will be affected directly by two principal factors: (a) the traditional career paths in your specialty, company, or industry, especially as they are limited by your company's organization structure and current staffing and (b) your personal capabilities and goals.

A company's organization chart portrays its division, or delegation, of managerial responsibilities into an orderly chain of command. The most influential positions are at the top, and the least influential are at the bottom. If you study the organization chart for the company of your choice from the point of view of your entry position, it provides a map of the career path that you must follow. If you fully understand the organizational structure, you will know which jobs, even at the same level, are considered more influential than others. You will also know (1) which jobs are traditionally the best springboards to advancement, (2) which jobs are likely to be dead ends, and (3) which departments are repositories for managers who have "plateaued out" and have been shelved awaiting retirement. You will want to plot a career path on the organizational map which provides you with the most useful experience in positions that are most favorable to your advancement. You will also want to choose a specific target position as your long-range goal (greater than five years). Finally, you will want to block out the possibility of sidetracking assignments, especially those that head you toward dead ends.

Getting Started   It is only natural for you to ask how one gets started in a managerial career. Unfortunately, the answers are not definitive, and they vary according to where you are right now in terms of present employment, your community, and your personal potential. Typically, however, you may pursue any of the following options:

1. You can start your own business, or purchase a franchise, and manage your own firm. This is a difficult, and often, costly route. The great majority of people simply have neither the personal nor financial resources to pursue this option.

2. You can start at the bottom of a local firm. You may be expected by many companies to begin as a clerical, production, or sales employee. This way, you make an immediate contribution to the firm. Meanwhile, you can learn about that particular business and the industry in which it operates. If you demonstrate above-average performance, initiative, and the capability of carrying out objectives successfully, you may be offered a chance to cross the bridge between employee and manager.

3. You can seek employment as a managerial trainee, intern, or assis-

tant. Large organizations routinely provide such starting points. Smaller firms do so only informally. Your college placement bureau is a good source of information and advice. It can also help you with interview opportunities.

4. You can enter government employment. Entry procedures and lines of progression into management are carefully spelled out in government. Entry and advancement is highly competitive, however, and considerable emphasis is placed on academic and intellectual achievement.

5. You can search outside your local community. This requires a high degree of mobility for you and your family. In many communities, managerial opportunities are limited, especially ones leading to significant advancement. Even if you find employment in the branch plant or office of a national firm, you may be expected to relocate elsewhere in order to advance.

6. You must be patient. Even for very talented managers, advancement comes slowly. In one landmark study of managerial progression, it was found that top-notch performers stayed at least two or three years at the first-level of management, while more middle-of-the-road performers spent an average of eight years there. Almost all managers, regardless of capabilities and performance, spent ten or more years in the middle ranks. Most managers advance no further.[2]

EVALUATING YOUR MANAGERIAL POTENTIAL

The dimensions, or requirements, of management, particularly as one climbs higher up the organizational ladder, are based on a number of studies and experiences conducted by major companies, most notably AT&T. A brief definition of each follows:

1. *Managerial Process Skills*—those required to carry out the managerial process or cycle—include the following:
   a. *Planning:* The ability to analyze external and internal conditions, set goals, and establish policies and procedures.
   b. *Problem Solving:* The ability to identify problems and their causes and find ways to remove or minimize these causes.
   c. *Decision Making:* The ability to evaluate various alternatives and choose the most effective course of action.
   d. *Organizing:* The ability to delegate operational responsibilities and tasks in such a way as to create the most effective structure of relationships.
   e. *Staff Development:* The ability to recruit and select the best possible people for your organization and then develop their skills.

[2]E. E. Jennings, *The Mobile Manager,* Graduate School of Business Administration, University of Michigan, 1967.

      f. *Communications:* The ability to activate an organization by creating and utilizing appropriate communications channels.

      g. *Leadership:* The ability to provide the kind of personal leadership needed to give your organization direction and motivation.

      h. *Interpersonal Skills:* The ability to establish supportive relationships, anticipate and resolve conflicts, and develop cooperation.

      i. *Creativity:* The ability to conceive of and initiate change when it is needed and suggest and follow new directions for your organization.

      j. *Control:* The ability to coordinate, evaluate, and control the processes and people under your direction to meet specified standards and objectives.

2. *Valuable Managerial Skills*—those methods and techniques that give certain managers an edge over others, that help these managers to make the most of their managerial-process skills—include the following:

      a. *Analytical Skill:* The ability to be rational and apply systematic logic to problems, decisions, and interpersonal relationships.

      b. *Quantitative Skill:* The ability to understand and apply mathematical and statistical methods to managerial problems.

      c. *Informational Skill:* The ability to develop personal and organizational information systems that best utilize information sources in making organizational decisions.

      d. *Writing Skill:* The ability to convey information clearly and succinctly in written memos and reports.

      e. *Oral Communication Skill:* The ability to speak publicly and be effective in face-to-face communications.

      f. *Listening Skill:* The ability to hear and understand what others are saying.

      g. *Counseling Skill:* The ability to establish rapport with troubled individuals and help them redirect their energies in a productive fashion.

      h. *Negotiating Skill:* The ability to participate in give-and-take effectively in your employer's behalf with vendors, customers, and government agencies. The ability to exercise diplomacy and compromise when prudent.

      i. *Appraisal Skill:* The ability to evaluate performance objectively and convey this information to employees in such a way as to motivate them toward improvement.

      j. *Conference-Leadership Skill:* The ability to conduct small and large, formal and informal meetings effectively.

      k. *Time-Management Skill:* The ability to maximize the use of your own time and that of your subordinates.

3. *Personal Characteristics*—those traits that have come to be associated with successful managers, characteristics that can often be improved

by self-observation, education, and training—include the following:

   a. *Energy:* The capacity for working long hours to meet a variety of pressing problems without fatigue.

   b. *Breadth:* The extent of your knowledge and interests, curiosity, and versatility.

   c. *Tenacity:* The ability to persevere under unfavorable circumstances—to persist, achieve "closure," and get the job completed.

   d. *Adaptability:* The capacity for adjusting to a variety of circumstances. Flexibility. Acceptance of change.

   e. *Stress Tolerance:* The ability to hold up under the pressure associated with job demands, deadlines, and uncertainty. Resilience.

   f. *Impact:* The ability to project yourself, make a good first impression, and command attention and respect. Self-confidence.

   g. *Decisiveness:* The ability to recognize the need for action and take it. The ability to take risks when required by the situation.

   h. *Ambition:* Motivation—the desire to succeed, not only as an individual, but particularly in organizational situations.

   i. *Social Awareness:* A sensitivity to organizational nuances, political situations, and cultural differences.

   j. *Independence:* The ability to strike out on your own and take a position or recommend an action based on your own convictions rather than following the pack.

GUIDELINES FOR GROWTH IN MANAGEMENT

A number of researchers have studied organizations and executives to discover clues as to what makes some managers progress to the top faster than others. No one is quite sure of what it really takes, but here are several conclusions that are agreed upon by a number of authorities:

1. *Find out what criteria are used to judge your performance,* and then strive to excel in those areas.

2. *Remember that you will be judged first, and most often, by your immediate superior.* Try to please that person, not by becoming a sycophant, but by doing well the things that he or she believes are important.

3. *Seek out high-visibility assignments.* These are the ones in which your success or failure will be exposed, of course, since they are usually high-risk tasks. You need not be completely successful at them if, in trying, you demonstrate an ability to accept challenge and to come to grips with difficult situations. Many an aggressive prob-

lem solver "fails" his or her way to the top. Very few people get there who shun the limelight.

4. *Stick closely to achieving managers.* If you can, develop a relationship with an upwardly mobile executive who finds that your spectrum of skills nicely complements his or her own. That executive may take you along as he or she progresses.

5. *Accept advice from organizationally-astute individuals.* If you can, find a mentor, or coach, who has reliable insights into organizational relationships and political situations. Seek and accept his or her advice, but do not allow yourself to become deeply identified with that person if he or she is outside the central core of power.

6. *Stay near the influence core of the organization.* Find your friendships, and spend your time with people in the organization who are on the move. Take your coffee breaks and lunch hours with them rather than with those who are outside the power circle.

7. *Learn your job quickly and do it well.* The latter is usually a prerequisite for advancement, even if the results are not always forthcoming. More importantly, the faster you show proficiency, the faster the organization may consider you ready for the next move.

8. *Don't take a promotion solely for the sake of a pay increase.* First of all, evaluate its requirements and your capabilities to fulfill them. If you believe the assignment is over your head, you are better off passing it up. Second, be sure that the assignment truly represents an advancement that will pay off in terms of your career goals.

9. *Try to broaden your job responsibilities.* Your job ought to keep you so fully occupied that it challenges your skills. Most organizations recognize and reward people who reach out from their job descriptions to seek additional, meaningful assignments.

10. *Actively pursue new assignments.* Make your advancement interests known. Too much modesty does not pay off, especially in an organization large enough to lose track of its younger personnel.

11. *Be ready to compromise.* Organizations are political, and tradeoffs are part of the expected social exchange. If by taking too inflexible a stance or by being too critical of conflicting points of view you deeply offend others in the organization, you may have difficulty in finding influential people who will support your position in the future.

12. *Align your goals with those of the organization.* You need not be a chameleon, but your attitudes and behavior should find an acceptable harmony in the company in which you work. If your views are always at odds with the organization's main thrust, your influence, and career, will inevitably diminish.[3]

[3]Adapted from E. E. Jennings, *Routes to the Executive Suite*, McGraw-Hill Book Company, New York, 1971.

Index